THE UNIVERSITY OF WINCHESTER

Lord of the Three in One

Lord of the Three in One

THE SPREAD OF A CULT
IN SOUTHEAST CHINA

• *KENNETH DEAN* •

PRINCETON UNIVERSITY PRESS

PRINCETON, NEW JERSEY

Library of Congress Cataloging-in-Publication Data

Dean, Kenneth.
Lord of the three in one : the spread of a cult in Southeast China
/ by Kenneth Dean.
p.   cm.
Includes bibliographical references and index.
ISBN 0-691-02881-8 (alk. paper)
1. Cults—Fukien Province—China—History.   2. China Religious
life and customs.   3. Confucianism—China—Rituals.   4. Buddhism—
China—Rituals.   5. Taoism—China—Rituals.   6. Lin, Chao-en,
1517–1598.   I. Title.
BL1802.D43   1998   299′.51—dc21   97-46181   cip

This book has been composed in Galliard

Princeton University Press books are printed
on acid-free paper and meet the guidelines
for permanence and durability of the Committee
on Production Guidelines for Book Longevity
of the Council on Library Resources

http://pup.princeton.edu

Printed in the United States of America

1   3   5   7   9   10   8   6   4   2

· C O N T E N T S ·

LIST OF
· *ILLUSTRATIONS* ·
AND TABLES

MAP

PLATES

CHARTS

TABLES

THIS BOOK is based on fieldwork conducted from 1986 to 1995 in Putian and Xianyou, Fujian. This volume would not have been possible without the support and encouragement offered by many members of the Three in One movement. Many people generously provided access to historical records and their personal copies of scriptures and liturgical texts and answered questions about their ritual traditions and the interaction between the Three in One and the surrounding community. I would like to thank Professor Zheng Zhenman of the Institute of Historical Studies, Xiamen University, for his friendship, assistance with fieldwork over a decade's time, and inexhaustible supply of historical knowledge and analytic insight. I thank Brian Massumi for his continued input into the discussion of the central issues in this book. I am grateful to Professor Lin Guoping of Fujian Teacher's Normal University, who shared his extensive knowledge of the Three in One with me. Dean Judith Berling of the Graduate Theological Seminary, Berkeley, California, generously shared materials and made valuable suggestions for research. Mr. Huang Qingyi of the Fupuxian Huiguan in Klang, Malaysia, provided helpful information on the Three in One in Malaysia and Overseas Chinese links with the Xinghua region.

Professor Michel Strickmann first encouraged me to pursue this topic and then made several valuable suggestions as the research progressed. I deeply regret that he will not see this volume, for I am sure he would have pointed out its shortcomings and provided a wealth of information and insight, and in the process make me laugh at my own mistakes.

Much of the research for this volume was conducted under the auspices of the Xinghua Popular Culture Research Centre in Putian, Fujian. The centre is jointly operated by the Department of East Asian Studies of McGill University and the Putian branch of the Chinese Academy of Social Sciences. Funding was provided by the Social Science and Humanities Research Council, the FCAR, and the Chiang Ching-kuo Foundation. The American Council of Learned Societies and the U.C. Berkeley Chinese Popular Culture Project provided a year of postdoctoral research in 1988–89, where some of the material in this book first took shape. I am grateful to all these institutions for their support. My thanks as well to Michael Szonyi, David Ownby, and the reviewers for Princeton University Press for their many useful suggestions.

Some of the material presented in this book has been published in the following articles. I thank the conference organizers and the editors and publishers of the journals and books concerned for permission to draw from these publications:

"Irrigation and Individuation: Cults of Water Deities along the Putian Plains," *Proceedings of the Conference on Chinese Ritual and Ritual Theater, Min-su ch'u-yi (Folklore and Theater)*.

"The Development of the Three-In-One Religion in Southeast China," *Proceedings of the International Conference on Temple Fairs and Chinese Culture* (Taipei: Taiwan: Center for Chinese Studies).

"Comic Inversion and Cosmic Renewal in the Ritual Theater of Putian: The God of Theater in Southeast China," in Wang Ch'iu-kui, ed., *Proceedings of the International Conference on Popular Beliefs and Chinese Culture* (Taipei: Center for Chinese Studies, 1994).

I especially thank my family, who spent several years with me in China: Catherine, for her many insights, enthusiasm, and lasting interest in Xinghua culture; and my children, Cora and David, who endured the heat and the pressures, and who chased chickens and stepped over pigs in countless villages on the way to yet another temple.

Lord of the Three in One

Plate 1. Image of Lin Longjiang distributed to pilgrims at the
Dongshan Zongkongtang

SCENE 1

By the light of the full moon of the first lunar month, men and women quietly leave their houses built of packed earth and walk silently in small groups to the top of a nearby hill. China is in the midst of the Great People's Proletarian Cultural Revolution, but these people are quietly and quickly setting out offerings on the tomb of Lin Zhao'en (1517–1598), founder of the Three in One. When they finish the rushed ceremony they hurry home, anxious not to be observed by neighbors. They would talk of the ceremony to no one.

SCENE 2

A woman begins to half cry, half sing in a high, eerie voice. Then she stands up from the table and begins hopping toward the altar. She dances in front of the altar, waving her arms, with her fingers forming a sword mudra. She is possessed by one of the great female warriors of the Yangjiajiang family.[1] Soon she stops and then bows and visibly relaxes. She smiles. She takes a talisman from the newly painted altar and passes it three times over the fumes of the burning incense. She hands it to a grateful patient who holds it carefully in his hands. She directs him to a large desk set against the wall across the spacious temple hall. There a team of pharmacists will provide him with an herbal remedy. There is, however, no doubt in his mind that the talisman is the essential ingredient in the medical recipe. The temple he stands in has been built with the donations of grateful patients such as himself. Over $150,000 had been spent since 1985 toward the construction of one of the largest Three in One temples in Xianyou.

---

[1] This family, and the literature that developed around it, are discussed in Hsia (1974). The saga begins with the story of Yang Ye (Yang Jiye) recounted in the *Song Shi* (j. 272). The tale of this general and his famous progeny reached completion in the Jiajing (1522–1566) *Bei Song zhijuan tongsu yanyi* (Romance of Northern Song history) and the Wanli (1573–1619) *Yangjiafu shidai zhongyong tongsu yanyi* (Romance of the loyal and valiant Yang family warriors throughout the ages) and circulates in various simplified versions with titles such as *Yangjiajiang* (The Yang family warriors). Yang Ye gave his life defending the Song throne against the Liao and was succeeded in these efforts by his six sons, led by Yang Yanzhao. The fifth son, Yang Yande, became a monk on Mt. Wutai but came down from time to time to assist in battle. He later became an important deity in the Xinghua region (Yang Taishi). In the novels, after Yan Yanzhao's death, the (Xixia?) Dada kingdom attacked the Song, and Yang Congbao and twelve Yang family widows drove them back. In other versions, the twelve widows later intervened to save Yang Wenguang from imprisonment. The female Yang warrior tradition begins with Yang Ye's widow, She (Yu) Taijun, also known as Yang Lingpo, and the three wives of Yang Yanzhao. In the Ti Qing story saga (as recounted in *Wuhu pingnan*), the Yang widows led by Yang Jinhua free Ti Qing from Nong Zhigao's imprisonment. The best known of the Yang women warriors is Mu Guiying, who first imprisons and then marries Yang Congpao and subsequently fights valiantly against the Heavenly Gate maze magic warfare configuration. These figures have been the subject of many plays, including many in Puxian regional theater.

SCENE 3

The chairman of the Political Consultative Congress, a man of wealth and influence, leans heavily over the podium and lays down the law. "There will be no feudal superstitious behavior at this conference!" After the political speeches, and after many distinguished professors from Beijing and Fuzhou have spoken, an elderly man with a long, wispy, white beard is allowed to speak. His lecture is unlike that of the academics, yet it is profoundly scholarly. He is explicating a passage from the *Four Books,* from the *Analects* of Confucius. He is elucidating the commentary given to a particular phrase by Master Lin Longjiang, founder of the Three in One. His discussion moves fluently from the philological to the philosophical, and soon he is discussing the virtues of self-cultivation and the heart method of inner alchemy. The other adherents of the Three in One, and there are many in the room, lean forward, listening carefully, deeply interested in his discussion of the stages of the heart method. The chairman of the Political Consultative Congress is nowhere to be seen, for he had another engagement and left the room soon after delivering his warning to the first International Academic Conference on the Thought of Lin Longjiang. (July 1986, Putian, Fujian)

Modern Chinese history has often been interpreted in terms of the interrelated themes of modernity and revolution. Without denying the importance of these themes, this study of the cult of the Lord of the Three in One (Sanyijiao) takes its point of departure to lesser-known developments in post-Mao China: the explosive resurgence of popular religion, and indeed of local culture in general, that began in Southeast China, particularly in Fujian, in 1979. By the end of the 1980s, Buddhist and Daoist liturgy, Confucian lineage ritual, and, in some areas, sectarian rites and popular Christianity were again playing a central organizing role in the rites and festivals of rural Chinese popular culture (Dean, 1993). Although the Chinese government responded with shows of force, determined to keep a lid on these developments, it was confronted with the reemergence of locally based networks that mobilized tremendous social and cultural forces. The massive investment of human labor and capital in these ritual performances and the restoration or reinvention of "traditional" Chinese cultural forms poses a challenge not only to Communist ideological control but also to theories of the secularizing, rationalizing effects of modernization.[2]

---

[2] In an analysis of the reassemblage of fragments of "traditional" ritual elements in religious activity in Guangdong in the 1980s, Helen Siu (1990) pointed out the reinvented and contingent quality of this "revival" and its relationship to contemporary economic transformations. Anne Agnacost (1987; 1994) has shown that these reinvented traditions based on older cultural practices are continually challenging the symbolic order of the state in an effort to reappropriate specific sites. My fieldwork in Fujian has traced the increasing complexity and intensity of this ritual activity over the past fifteen years (Dean, 1986; 1988a; 1988b; 1993; Dean and Zheng, 1993; 1995). For research on other areas of China, see Tanaka Issei (1981; 1983; 1993) and Wang Chiu-kui, ed., *Min-su ch'u-i ts'ung-shu* (Studies in Chinese ritual, folklore, and drama series) (Taipei: Shih Ho-cheng Min-su ch'u-i chi-chin-hui, 1992–), 60 vols. covering recent developments in fifteen provinces of China. In general, urban areas (particularly political administrative centers) continue to restrict or outlaw religious practices beyond those confined to authorized

The current Chinese cultural renaissance demands careful documentation and analysis. An abundance of hitherto unstudied historical materials has been brought to light through these developments, including stone inscriptions, Buddhist, Daoist, and sectarian liturgical manuscripts, lineage genealogies, and local historical archives.[3] Beyond their documentary value, these materials also provide an excellent opportunity to rethink not only post-Mao developments, but a much broader set of key issues across the entire stretch of modern Chinese history. Earlier research in the field of Chinese history had suggested that the relationship between the imperial center and the peripheral, localized cultures of China was largely one of ideological or orthopractic control (Hsiao, 1960; Watson, 1985). A Confucian, ritualized, homological model of state, region, family, and self was said to explain Chinese popular culture, with variations accounted for by differences in education and access to power (Johnson, 1985). My research into the resilient, co-optive, and sometimes rebellious nature of distinct Chinese local cultures in different parts of Fujian suggests a far more dialectical or *agonistic* relationship between the center and the locale. This book seeks to develop a model of the repertoire of transforming cultural resources that was drawn upon by the Three in One over the process of its development, and to examine the processes of selection and

---

Buddhist monasteries and Daoist temples or officially recognized popular cult temples. The degree to which religious activities are tolerated in the different regions, counties, townships, and villages of China is highly variable (see Dean, 1993). There is a serious lack of attention to rural or urban religious activities and organizations in the literature on contemporary China (with the exception of studies of Chinese Christianity, Muslim groups, and Tibetan and minority peoples). For a study of the reestablishment of an urban, city ward temple system in Quanzhou, Fujian, see Wang Mingming (1992; 1995).

[3] These materials raise fundamental questions about the nature of the archive. They are unclassified and potentially unclassifiable, since the very parameters of the body of documentation are still unknown. No adequate historical model has yet been developed to trace the interrelations among the many kinds of locally circulated documents and manuscripts. Anthropological studies of China have so far failed to adequately address theoretical problems rising from the multiple levels of the circulation and employment of literary sources. Sources for the study of the Three in One are listed in the bibliography under "Primary Sources," and in the appendices under the categories of "Editions of Lin Zhao'en's Writings" and "Liturgical Manuscripts." In addition to the collected writings of Lin Zhao'en and one or two scriptures and writings of disciples previously studied by Mano Senryu and Berling (1980), many of these sources either are discussed here for the first time or have just begun to be studied (see Lin, 1992; Ma and Han, 1992). Many sources for this book were gathered in the course of fieldwork on several research trips to the Xinghua region over the 1985–1995 period. We now have available, in addition to 130 works by Lin Zhao'en, three sacred biographies, several works by early adherents of the Three in One, several alchemical works, over a dozen stone inscriptions, several collections of spirit writing, over 250 liturgical and scriptural texts, a novel, and many miscellaneous documents. In addition, we have the surveys conducted by the Three in One of its temples and their participants, fieldwork notes, and several new studies of the tradition. Sources for the study of the Chinese cultural renaissance elsewhere in China are voluminous. For a start, see the sixty volumes of field reports, bibliographic studies, collected essays, and documentary materials (liturgies and scripts of ritual operas) from fifteen provinces of China in the *Min-su ch'u-i ts'ung-shu* (Studies in Chinese ritual, folklore, and drama series), ed. Wang Ch'iu-kui (Taipei: Shih Ho-cheng Min-su ch'u-i chi-chin-hui, 1992–).

local differentiation through which the Three in One entered into local cultural organization.

The Sanyijiao was developed by Lin Zhao'en (1517–98), the scion of a gentry family from Putian, Fujian. Lin renounced the official examination system and set out to popularize Confucianism by combining Confucian studies with Daoist inner alchemical techniques and Buddhist Chan philosophy into something he called the Three in One Teachings. Lin Zhao'en's life and thought have been carefully studied by Judith Berling (1980). His biography, writings, teaching activities, travels, and temple founding have been examined by Mano Senryu (1952; 1962; 1979). His healing method and the influence of his ideas on subsequent religious sects have been touched on by Sakai Tadao (1960). Recently Lin Zhao'en and the Three in One have been studied by Lin Guoping (1985; 1986; 1991; 1992), Zheng Zhiming (1988; 1988), and Ma Xisha and Han Bingfang (1992). However, so far little work has been done on the evolution of the Three in One, especially after Lin's death, with the exception of Berling's study of the *Romance of the Three Teachings* (Berling, 1985), Wolfgang Franke's articles on the Three in One in Southeast Asia (Franke, 1972; 1973), and Zheng Zhiming's (1988) brief treatment of the Taipei Three in One groups.[4] Berling (1980, p. 235) concluded her study with the following questions:

> What is the curriculum of study? Has there been a direct line of transmission unbroken since the sixteenth century? Is the priesthood of Masters now hereditary, or how is it chosen? Do all believers practice the meditative regimen of the nine stages? Has the healing method survived? Is there still an attempt to include adherents of all Three Teaching? What festivals are observed? Is the teaching still predominantly Confucian? Are the petitions to heaven still offered by believers, or by the Masters of the cult? What distinctions in practice and study are there between lay followers and those who aspire to become Masters? Is it exclusively a Hsing-hua dialect association, or are people who do not speak the dialect welcomed into the cult on some basis?

[4] Lin Guoping and I coauthored a paper on the "historical remains" of the Three in One (Ding Hesheng and Lin Guoping, 1987, reprinted in 1991), which details some of the major temples and materials we had located at that time. Lin (1992) provides a brief historical summary of the Three in One, but his editors did not allow him to provide further details on the contemporary situation of the Three in One. Lin presented a paper entitled "Sanyijiao xianzhuang gaikuang" (The current situation of the Three in One Religion) at a conference on Secret Societies held in Nanjing in 1991, which provides further information and was subsequently published in translation in Japan (Lin, 1994). In most of his work, however, his emphasis is primarily on the intellectual history of the tradition; thus the development of the religious organization is treated as a decline from an earlier philosophic project. Similarly, Zheng Zhiming's 1988 study makes an important contribution to an understanding of the philosophic views of Lin Zhao'en. However, his contention that Lin received limited support from *shidafu* sectors while failing to spread his message to the "common people" is open to question on the basis of the material presented in this volume. Wolfgang Franke plans to publish an account of his visits to Three in One sites in his forthcoming *Reiseberichte* (personal communication, Nov. 1995).

This volume sets out to answer these and other questions concerning the transmission and current status of the Three in One. Whether Lin knew what shape the organization he founded would eventually take is unlikely. Today the Three in One has over a thousand temples— one in virtually every village in the populated plains of the Xinghua area of Fujian Province, made up of Putian and Xianyou districts. Most of these temples have been restored or rebuilt since 1979. There are now tens of thousands of initiates into the Three in One, and many more who come to worship (see map and table 3).[5] Probably more than half a million people are now regularly involved in worship or ritual activity within the Three in One. The Three in One has spread beyond Xinghua to Taiwan and Southeast Asia. The temples are open to anyone, people are free to participate and eventually to undergo initiation into the Three in One. Artists, lawyers, farmers, tradesmen, and even some retired cadres are involved in this tradition. Advocates of the Three in One express confidence that the teachings of Lin Zhao'en will soon spread around the world.

[5] According to the 1993 update of the *Fujiansheng dituce* (Handbook of maps of Fujian Province), the population of Putian and Xianyou at that time was 2,579,600, with over 300,000 Overseas Chinese. Administratively, the Xinghua region is divided between the Putian City government (which governs the city of Putian and three nearby townships and the Hanjiang urban area) and the county governments of Putian and Xianyou counties. The Xinghua region covers 3,792 square kilometers and has 3 cities, 30 towns (zhen), 14 townships (xiang), and over 908 administrative villages. Per capita income in 1986 was estimated by the *Fujian diqu jingji* (Fujian Regional Economy, Fuzhou, 1986) at 817 yuan for workers and 264 yuan for farmers. Major economic changes have transformed the area over the past ten years, leading to the rise of light industry, especially the manufacture of shoes, and the rapid commercialization of villages along the Fuzhou–Xiamen highway, and per capita income has more than tripled in some areas, with the economy growing at 20 to 30 percent each year for over a decade. (See table 3 for estimates of the number of adherents in the Three in One, and the map showing the number of Three in One temples in Putian and Xianyou.) These figures were gathered by the leadership of the Three in One Dongmen temple as part of an ongoing effort to secure official governmental recognition. While the figure for the number of temples is fairly reliable, the estimated number of adherents is based on widely varying standards—from a strict count of initiates, on the one hand, to wild estimates of the numbers of people who come in to burn incense anytime in a year, on the other. Verification would involve extensive survey work in the area. An initial report compiled in September 1986 listed 55,106 people in 757 temples, with 33,000 adherents in 425 temples in Putian and 21,557 in 229 temples in Xianyou. There are in addition 22 temples in northern Hui'an and 38 in Fuqing and Fuzhou. A second report in July 1989 listed 513,432 adherents worshipping in 1,044 temples in the Xinghua area. The first list may give a closer sense of the number of initiates, while the second perhaps reflects the wider impact of the Three in One in the area. Over a dozen temples are active in Singapore and Malaysia (Franke, 1972; 1981). There are also five temples active in Taiwan (Zheng, 1990). The major Three in One temples in Taiwan are listed in Ch'iu (1981). The Longshan temple has recently been restored; a stele in the temple traces its origins back to northern Hui'an. The adherents perform funerals and commemorative rituals wearing the same blue gowns and conical white hats with blue tassels worn by adherents of the Mingxia branch in western Xianyou and the Malaysian adherents who brought copies of Lin Zhao'en's *Xiawunijing* and other writings to Taiwan a decade ago. In both Taiwan and Malaysia, Hokkien is increasingly used in Three in One rituals in place of the Puxian dialect.

Distribution of Three in One temples in Putian and Xianyou Counties, by township

DEFINITION OF TERMS

In this book I generally use the term "Three Teachings" or the "Three in One" to translate "Sanjiao," also referred to as "Sanyijiao." From one point of view the Three in One may be considered a religion, for it has a (loose) organizational structure, scriptures, doctrines, rules of conduct, initiations, differentiated functions for ritual specialists, and a range of rituals parallel to those provided by Buddhist monks and Daoist priests. From another point of view (that of the Imperial, Republican, and Communist governments), the Sanyijiao is best seen as a sectarian religious movement. Many of the features just listed can be used to define a sect, although in Chinese sectarianism there is usually stronger emphasis on organization, esoteric teachings, mantras, meditations, and millenarianism. Some scholars have seen elements of these features in the Three in One as well. After all, Lin Zhao'en identified himself with the Buddha and composed a Maitreya scripture. As will be seen below, many villagers offer the deified form of Lin Zhao'en a cult similar to that offered to other popular deities. Thus from the point of view of many people in the Xinghua region, the term "popular cult" would also be appropriate. The Three in One defies easy definition, in part because it has transformed itself in reaction to many different milieus and changing social and cultural forces.

Several terms in this discussion require further qualification. Talal Asad (1993) has recently pointed out some of the problems with the Western, post-Reformation definition of religion, with its emphasis on belief, as well as with its successor, the cultural anthropological definition of religion as a symbolic system. Asad notes that the definitions of religion as a symbolic system and ritual as a means of making symbols meaningful are direct descendants of Enlightenment theories of "natural religion" and Kantian "transcendental subjectivity." He argues that religion should not be separated from other realms of activity as a sphere of timeless values, but instead viewed in particular historical contexts as a product of specific discourses, disciplinary regimes, and modes of authorization. Asad goes on to question the analysis of ritual as a representational text, arguing instead for an analysis within a wider institutional context as forms of disciplinary practice central to the production of knowledge and the creation of particular potentialities—individual, social, and cultural.[6] In this study I examine ritual-events as practices that enable different levels of power formation. Ritual-events are machines that gather individual and social forces into specific configurations, activating distinct ways of perceiving, sensing, and knowing.

Since the Chinese imperial center maintained a copyright on *li* (rites, propriety, ritual form, the model of modeling), the issue of emergent ritual forms at the periphery implies a challenge, or a new balance of power. Rather than simple opposition expressing an essentialized local community or a totalistic counterhegemony, these changing localized forms must be explored in context, as the temporary consolidations of a host of transverse flows, many arriving from the outside, well beyond the reach of the imperium. At the same time, these localized, dynamic ritual forms themselves open out onto a cosmic level, drawing upon the forces of the earth, the heavens, the void, and beyond in order to impose a new unification of self-cultivation with a harnessing of the powers of nature and cosmos.

Fritz Staal (1983; 1985; 1986), in the context of Vedic ritual studies, has also criticized the post-Reformation Christian emphasis on belief as opposed to the practice of ritual in most Asian religions, and he has argued that this emphasis distorts the understanding of these traditions. He suggests instead a formal analysis of the syntax of ritual, arguing that in and of itself ritual is meaningless and therefore open to endless interpretation. However, Staal's

[6] Asad's studies of judicial torture and Christian self-mortification elsewhere in his 1993 volume build upon Michel Foucault's studies of disciplinary regimes and technologies of the self in medieval Christianity.

effort to develop a transformative structural syntax of ritual restores a linguistic model. In this book I explore the channeling of social and cosmic forces enabling formations of power through formal features of group ritual and self-cultivation, such as pattern, movement, music, gesture, visualization, and dance. These features refuse national or linguistic boundaries and disrupt the cultural essentialism of much Western ritual theory.[7]

The problem of the conceptualization of religion and ritual is particularly complicated in mainland China, where a rigid Western-derived Marxist-Leninist definition of religion has been applied to what C. K. Yang has characterized as a "diffused religious structure" (Yang, 1960; MacKinnis, 1972; 1989; Dean, 1993: 173–176).[8] Yang argues that Chinese religion is deeply embedded in all aspects of Chinese society but only takes distinct institutional form in certain religious traditions and under certain circumstances. Demands that popular cults produce their religious doctrines (*jiaoyi*), their religious rules of conduct (*jiaogui*), and a statement on their organizational structure for evaluation by the Bureau of Religious Affairs frequently lead to a frustrating impasse. In this case, groups like the Three in One or other "sectarian"

[7] Thomas LaMarre's (1994; 1998) challenging analyses of Heian poetics expose the ideological urges underlying the common modern critical insistence on the links between national, linguistic, and cultural boundaries. While struggling to preserve a meaningful role for what she describes as strategies of ritualization, Catherine Bell (1992) demonstrates the circular logic within the Western study of ritual as a separate category.

[8] Hardacre (1989: chapter 3) discusses the rise of a Western conception of "religion" in Meiji Japan in the debate over constitutional protection of "freedom of religion" in the 1870s and 1880s, which was largely forced upon the Japanese government by Western powers insisting on the protection of Christian groups. Another issue that was debated at that time was the desirability of a separation of church and state, or, alternatively, the possibility of institutionalizing a form of State Shinto: "The cultic life of shrines . . . constituted the major part of Japanese religious life in the era immediately preceding the creation of State Shinto. The center of shrine life lay in the observance of rites and such communal observances as festivals and pilgrimage. Thus the character of pre-Meiji Shinto was liturgical and closely integrated with social life. In pre-Meiji Japan there existed no concept of religion as a general phenomenon, of which there would be variants like Christianity, Buddhism, and Shinto. People spoke of having faith (*shinko*) in particular kami and Buddhas, but no word existed to designate a separate sphere of life that could be called "religious" as opposed to the rest of one's existence. This may indicate that religious themes and concerns were deeply integrated in popular consciousness and social life in a way fundamentally at odds with modern Christocentric notions of religion as a private matter of an individual's relation to a deity." (p. 18) "Early in the Meiji period . . . both the terms religion *shukyo* (*zongjiao*) and Shinto were new to vernacular speech, and intellectuals wrote a great deal about religion and its role in a modern nation." (p. 22) The term *zongjiao* (lit. "ancestral teachings") in this Western sense entered China from Japan. The conception of religion in postliberation China was later elaborated on the basis of Soviet Marxist doctrine (Luo, 1993). Religion was treated with particular contempt as an ideological support of feudalistic remnants during the Cultural Revolution, but the 1979 constitution provided for "freedom of religion" and authorized religious organizations. Religious expression has now been distinguished from both private superstitions (foolish but harmless individual beliefs) and feudal superstitions (which require payment to a specialist for supernatural services and thus materially harm the masses). Anagnost (1994) has noted the necessity for the Chinese state to maintain the negative role of the residual category of religion/superstition to legitimate (by contrast) the positive role of the vanguard party in leading China to modernity.

groups are in fact better off than local god cults or even Daoist ritual practitioners. The former may be better able to articulate their beliefs due to their efforts to establish a consciously syncretic tradition.

As regards "popular religion," Bernard Faure (1991: 79–95) quotes Peter Brown (1981) in exposing the pejorative derivation of the term. Faure warns against adopting a "dualistic model" of elite versus popular, or a model of fusion between official and popular religions (see also Bell, 1989). Numerous alternative formulations have been proposed, including the notion of a "common religion," particularly for the Warring States period (Harper, 1995). Many scholars, however, have insisted on the validity of distinguishing a sphere of religious activity separate from that of Confucian ritualists, Buddhist monks, and Daoist priests, beginning at least with the Han dynasty. Teiser notes that "some time around the Song dynasty all of the components that we associate with popular religion in the modern period had 'come together to reformulate popular religion as a tradition in its own right' (Overmyer, 1987: 281; cf. Seidel, 1989–90: 284–285; Ebrey and Gregory, 1993). The next major benchmark in the history of this tradition occurs in the early Ming, which saw a relatively stable synthesis of ideas and practices to which historians refer unproblematically as the popular religion of 'late imperial China'" (Teiser, 1995: 380). Many scholars have worked on the long process of interaction and mutual influence among what Ebrey and Gregory (1993: 12) refer to as the "four unequal traditions" (see also Stein, 1963; 1979; Zurcher, 1983; Schipper, 1985a). In addition to ethnographic studies of particular communities, a number of anthropological studies have been devoted to the structure, function, and logic of practice of contemporary Chinese popular religion (Ahern, 1981; Sangren, 1986; Feuchtwang, 1992). As will be seen, the Three in One spans the entire range of Chinese religious expression, from Confucian classics and commentary to spirit writing and mediumism.

The sociological usage of the term *sect* derives from Max Weber's discussion of Christian organizations in *The Protestant Ethic and the Spirit of Capitalism,* where he referred to the "believers' church . . . a community of personal believers of the reborn. . . . In other words, not as a Church but as a sect" (Weber, 1958: 145).[9] He noted that membership was restricted to "adults who have personally gained their own faith." Other characteristics of sects were a belief in exclusive salvation and a possible response of separation from the world. Weber further underlined the importance of the personal charisma of the founder and noted the likelihood of routinization over time into a more institutionalized religious organization (i.e., a denomination). He also stressed that sects were autonomous, voluntaristic organizations, featuring a relatively extended probational period for new initiates and, frequently, strict moral discipline for members.

The sociological literature on sects and cults evolved through an analysis of Christian religious denominationalism, with a key concern being the rou-

[9] This discussion of the literature on sects is based in part on Hall (1987).

tinization of the charisma of the religious founder and the extremist nature of cult behavior. Such issues have limited relevance for China. Weber's distinction of (Christian) church and sect was elaborated by Ernst Troeltsch. Troeltsch (1981) argued that sects were comparatively small collectivities that renounced the world and sought direct personal fellowship. He distinguished a third category, which he called "mysticism," symptomatic of the rise of individualism, and with little emphasis on fellowship and thus a fluid organizational form. Rudolf Niebhur and Howard Becker examined the conflict between the religious and social sources of sectarianism in the North American context and the unintended consequences of sectarian austerity, which often led to a compromise of values and institutionalization.

Becker used the term *cult* for Troeltsch's category of individualistic mysticism, and defined such groups as loosely knit, unstructured, and unconcerned with protecting their organization. Instead they sought "purely personal ecstatic experience, salvational comfort, and mental or physical healing" (Becker, 1932: 627, quoted in Hall, 1987). J. M. Yinger (1957: 154–155) noted the category of the "established sect" that lasted over several generations without compromise of values or institutionalization. He attempted to distinguish cults from sects by their small size, localization, dependence on a leader with magnetic personality, and beliefs and rites that deviate widely from the norms of society. He argued that cults are short-lived and focus on individual needs, rather than attempting to transform the social order.

Yinger and Bryan Wilson went on to develop a typology of sects, including formulations such as Yinger's acceptance sects, aggressive sects, and avoidance sects and Wilson's conversionist sects, revolutionist sects, introversionist, pietist sects, and gnostic sects; to which he later added manipulationist and thaumaturgical sects, reformist sects, and utopian sects. Elwood (1973: 28–31) provides a list of fifteen characteristic of cults. Wallis (1975; 1976) noted that certain cults, such as Scientology, could transform over time into soteriologically defined sects. Wilson (1990: 266–288) takes the terminology full circle by suggesting that groups like Scientology have transformed from a sect into a religion. Much recent analysis of the cult phenomenon, new age religion, and new religions in North America and Japan has conflated the term sect with cult, or turned the latter term into a four-letter word.

In much of the scholarship on Chinese religion we find an oddly similar bias against sectarian religious expression, which is often linked with rebellion. One early exception was the work of J. J. M. DeGroot on sectarianism and persecution in China, which focused on the Chinese state's role in driving sectarian groups into acts of violence. The scholarship linking sectarianism with millenarianism and rebellion has gradually given way to an understanding of sectarian groups as usually peaceable partners and a potential alternative channel for individualistic religious expression in contrast to institutional religions or village religion (Overmyer, 1976; 1985; Jordan and Overmyer, 1986; Naquin, 1985; Ter Haar, 1992).[10] Overmyer (1976: chapters 3, 4, and 9) in-

---

[10] Ter Haar (1992) discusses the relevant Japanese scholarship.

troduced comparative perspectives on sectarianism as a religio-sociological phenomenon specifically to emphasize the generally nonrebellious, nonsecretive nature of Chinese sects. Ter Haar (1992: 11–15) has suggested replacing Western sociological terms with terms such as "religious group," "movement," "tradition," and "teachings." The greater flexibility this approach allows is demonstrated in the increased depth of understanding his study provides. In general, I use a similar approach in this book. I use the term "Three in One" when discussing Lin Zhao'en's religious movement as a whole, and "branch" for discrete groupings within the Three in One that have developed semi-independent organizations or ritual traditions.

Cohen (1988) emphasizes the individualistic aspects of Chinese sectarian worship, arguing that the primary focus is on the salvation of the soul. He has suggested that the term "cult" may be misleading in the Chinese context, where an individual was often simultaneously a member of several different associations, many if not all of which were organized around the worship of a god (e.g., patron saint of a guild or native-place association, territorial god). Jordan and Overmyer (1986: 7) define a sect as "a group of believers and its organization. A cult is its system of ideology and religious practice." They thus distinguish between organizational form, on the one hand, and practices and beliefs, on the other. They contrast sectarian religion with "village religion," claiming that the former is individualistic, providing an avenue for individual participation in a self-fulfilling process of merit making as opposed to obligatory participation in village ritual. While this insight holds true for much of Three in One activity, we will see cases where the categories of individualistic and village religion break down.[11]

I have nonetheless preserved the use of the term "cult" in the title of this book. Recall that the term has three basic meanings, all of which relate to certain aspects of the Three in One. A cult is defined as (1) worship: reverential homage rendered to a divine being or beings; (2) a particular form or system of religious worship, especially in reference to its eternal rites and ceremonies; and (3) devotion or homage to a particular person or thing, now especially as paid by a body of professed adherents or admirers (*Oxford English Dictionary,* 1989).[12] I choose to use the term in a broad sense, encompassing all three of these definitions. This is because rather than comparing the Three in One with contemporary cult phenomena in North America or Japan, it is more useful to compare Chinese cults of local gods with the cult of the saints of medieval

[11] Among anthropological studies of Chinese religion, Seaman's (1978) detailed case study of a medium cult that took control over social and religious life in a Taiwanese village remains a unique application of Weberian approaches to Chinese religion and social organization. Sangren (1984) has pointed out that certain associations (including cults of female deities) transcend patriarchal formations such as family, lineage, and orthodox, state-sanctioned cults and provide mechanisms for diverse social interaction.

[12] *The Oxford English Dictionary* (Oxford: Clarendon Press, 1989), vol. 4, p. 119, notes that the term "cult" derives from the Latin *cultus,* worship (from *colere,* to attend to, cultivate, respect, etc.), and its French adaptation *culte* (1611), used in the seventeenth century (? from Latin) and then rarely till the middle of the nineteenth, when often spelled culte as in French.

Europe (Delehaye, 1961; Geary, 1978; Brown, 1981; 1988; Wilson, 1984; Bynum, 1991; Van Dam, 1993). Issues such as the nature and forms of popular worship, differing views of the efficacy of the saints, varieties of saints (local, [inter]national, or transnational; popular victims of violent death; elitist; ascetic; orthodox, etc.), competition between cults, official canonization, control of cult expression through the editing of hagiography, expanded opportunities for participation by women, children, and lower social classes, and religious experience and regimentation of the body all open interesting angles on the study of Chinese local god cults (see Naquin and Yu [1992: *Introduction*] for a call for comparative approaches to pilgrimage). Chinese cults are open-ended, and the Three in One is a good example. Although initiation and secrecy have been important elements of the Three in One (particularly when under Qing government suspicion), the Three in One openly proclaims its doctrines and rituals, welcomes worshippers at any level whenever possible, and is not exclusive. Through all the different phases and manifestations of the Three in One, the cult rendered to Lin Zhao'en as the God Xiawuni is the unifying thread.[13]

PURPOSES OF THE BOOK

There are three major issues to be addressed in this book. The first concerns the transmission of the Three in One from its founding, the schisms between the first set of disciples, and the establishment of an organizational matrix that would enable it to expand and respond to new, changing social possibilities throughout the late Ming and Qing period. This issue will be dealt with by examining the early disciples of the Three in One and the evolution of the principal ritual traditions. Here we are interested as well in the vision of unity of religion, society, and culture that a new sector of the scholar-literati class was attempting to bring into a new realm of activity, namely, the villages. This section will also discuss the rituals of division of incense within the different branches of the Three in One.

The second issue to be explored is the process of reception of the Three in One by local society. There can be no doubt about the successful growth of the Three in One over time. However, as it penetrated into village life and became a matrix of social organization in many villages, the structure and needs of village organization led to the selective development of various aspects of the Three in One. Thus, paradoxically, the Three in One led to the indepen-

[13] The term *xia* is generally understood to mean great or vast. The title Xiawuni is based on the identification of similar elements in the titles for the founders or principal deities of Confucianism (Kong-zhong-ni or Confucius), Buddhism (Shi-[jia]-mo-ni or Śākyamuni Buddha), Daoism (Dao-qing-ni or Laozi), and thus for the Three in One (Xia-wu-ni). By a curious mathematics, $1 + 1 + 1 = 1$, that is, all Three are One, just as the original substance is one. But it is also true that $1 + 1 + 1 = 4$, since Lin Zhao'en, apotheosized as Xia-wu-ni, completes the series and is worshipped alongside the other three as the realization of the Three in One.

dence of local culture, rather than to the grand unification that the founders had envisioned. This issue will be addressed by examining a range of village social structures in which the Three in One plays a significant role. These two aspects of the development of the Three in One must be seen in the context of the many concurrent social and cultural changes in this region from the late Ming through to the present day. This process involved efforts on the part of the elite to bring a particular vision of a unified cultural order and a new organizational rubric to the populace. At the same time we can begin to grasp the various ways in which elements of this vision and the organizational potentials were absorbed, co-opted, and reinterpreted by the intended recipients, transforming the development of the Three in One into a particularly intriguing example of the process of the transformation of local culture and local identities.

The third issue concerns the nature of participation in a new ritual tradition. The Three in One, while new in comparison to Confucian, Daoist, and Buddhist ritual traditions, began little more than a half century after Martin Luther's (1483–1546) Reformation and already has a history of over four hundred years.[14] What social, moral, or religious objectives could be attained by taking part in the Three in One in the late Ming and Qing dynasties? What desires are currently being fulfilled or channeled by the Three in One? What effect does personal involvement, through initiation, training in inner alchemy, and sustained liturgical practice, have on individual officiants or on participating worshippers and onlookers? How does ritual experience impact upon the formation of identity or the process of subjectification?

These three issues—the organization and transmission of a cultural vision, the differentiated social reception of this vision, and the construction of subjectivity within a ritual tradition—will be examined in each phase of the transformations of the Three in One.[15] These issues will also be examined in relation to several key elements of the Three in One movement—inner alchemy, scripture, iconography, ritual practice, and spirit mediumism. These elements and issues are examined in order to bring out the underlying problematics of the Three in One, its basic contradictions, and the underlying desires that drove it forward. This book seeks not only to document the spread of the cult but also to demonstrate the potential for social and individual transformation a ritual tradition such as the Three in One provided both in late imperial China and today. This book presents the Three in One in its various actualizations as a vector of structured and structuring change, a vehicle for group formation and individual participation that responded to surrounding changes in

---

[14] Adherents of the Three in One frequently mention a prophecy by Lin Zhao'en to the effect that the Three Teachings will have spread throughout the world by the five hundredth anniversary of his attainment of the Dao.

[15] The notion of subjectivity used in this book is based on the provisional definition given in Guattari (1995: 8–9): "The ensemble of conditions which render possible the emergence of individual and/or collective instances as self-referential existential Territories, adjacent, or in a delimiting relation, to an alterity that is itself subjective."

social structure and power relations among the government, gentry, lineages, Buddhist monasteries, popular temples, and other autonomous associational forms within local Chinese society.

Naquin (1985: 289), discussing the transmission of White Lotus sectarianism, hypothesizes that "not only did the sects provide, as Daniel Overmyer has suggested, an alternative to popular religion, they may also have tried to provide the same services. Thus where religious professionals (such as monks, priests, and spirit mediums) were unavailable, experienced sectarians performed their functions." In Xinghua the situation was more complicated. Powerful Buddhist monastic organizations, well-known hereditary Daoist families of ritual specialists, elaborate local god cults, and a high level of culture and Confucian education would seem to have provided a wealth of traditional ritual forms and specialists. Nevertheless, by emphasizing pragmatic, orthodox Confucian values and incorporating Buddhist and Daoist ritual and inner alchemical methods, the Three in One was able to gain acceptance as an alternative ritual tradition. The degree to which the various branches of the Three in One have achieved this viability is an index of their overall integration with the community. Unlike certain secret societies or "secret religions," the Three in One in general did not aspire to political change or eschatological rebellion. With the apotheosis of Lin Zhao'en as the god Xia Wuni, who combines and completes the triad of Confucius, Laozi, and Buddha, the Three in One moved into a postapocalyptic mode, no longer political at the level of the state, but more intimately involved in the politics and structure of everyday village life.

The Three in One developed differently in different areas, creating a niche for itself in the religious life of particular communities. For example, around Putian City and to the north toward Hanjiang along the developed coastal plain, the adherents of the Three in One are a distinct minority group, and the traditions of monastic Buddhism and hereditary Daoism are strong. But in the inland mountainous areas of Xianyou District, the Three in One has in some cases overwhelmed the opposition and become the principal matrix of the religious life of the community. Along the rough southern Putian coast bordering Xianyou, complex social changes have created centrifugal forces that bring all the local deities of the community into an alliance with the Three in One under one temple roof. The survival of the Three in One in Fujian thus provides the possibility of examining the variety of responses of Chinese society and local culture to a religious movement.

BRIEF HISTORICAL OVERVIEW OF THE THREE IN ONE

The Three in One is now primarily based in the Xinghua region, comprising Putian and Xianyou counties beneath Fuzhou and above the Minnan cities of Quanzhou and Xiamen on the Fujian coast. The people of this region speak a dialect of Northern Min, Minbeihua, called Puxianhua. This subdialect is largely unintelligible to their neighbors to the north, south, and west.[16] Nevertheless, the Three in One has spread into the districts of Min-qing, Anhui, Fuzhou, and Taiwan, not to mention Southeast Asia. In several areas the Three in One has transcended linguistic barriers: in Fuzhou, recitation of scriptures is done in Fuzhouhua (another subdialect of Northern Min); in northern Anhui and Taiwan, Hokkien is spoken. At its height some 350 years ago, the Three in One had followers in several major cities of the empire.

Lin Zhao'en and his contemporary Li Zhi (1527–1602) were described by the Ming literary critic Zhu Yizun (1629–1709) as "the two strange extremists of the Min region."[17] It is interesting that Li's cultivation of truthfulness led to suicide, while Lin's similar rejection of status quo Confucianism resulted in his eventual apotheosis at the head of a popular religious movement. Already in Ho Qiaoyuan's *Min shu,* written in 1612 and printed in 1621, we read that the Three in One has spread all over Fujian: "In Pu[tian], from the mountains to the seas, . . . there is no one who does not worship him. Up north, Yan[ping], Jian[an], Ting[zhou], Shao[wu] [prefectures], and to the south, Jin[jiang], An[hui], Qing[xi], Zhang[zhou] [prefectures], all have Three Teachings Halls, wherein his image is worshipped."[18] In 1671 Lin Xiangje commented on the Three in One, then at its peak: "The Teachings of my great uncle [Lin] Longjiang flourish in the present day provinces of Wu [Jiangsu], Yue [Zhejiang], Yan [Beijing], Qi [Shandong], and Yuzhang [Jiangxi]. Today the Master's temples cover the empire, so that within a single commandery, [temples are built that are] towering and beautiful, with gold and gemstone [ornaments] sounding and sparkling, with carved tiles and delicately patterned bricks, gazing at one another every few miles."[19]

Prohibited along with other religious groups accused of being related to the "White Lotus movement," such as the Zhaijiao and Longhua groups during the Qing's Yongzheng and Qianlong periods (1723–1795), the Three in One movement went underground. The opening salvo of this prohibition occurred in 1716, when an adherent named Zhu Kun was apprehended for the abduction of a young woman. An edict ordered the destruction of Three in One temples.[20] According to adherents, many temples at that time attempted to avoid destruction by changing themselves into "academies" (*shuyuan*). Iconographic details of Xiawuni, Lord Xia (Lin Zhao'en), were changed and

[16] For a discussion and classification of Northern Min dialects, see Yuan (1960). Further information on Puxian dialect can be found in "Putian Fungyan zhi," a draft manuscript for inclusion in a district gazetteer assembled in the 1960s but never published.

[17] Zhu Yizun, *Jingzhiju shihua,* j. 14, p. 43.

[18] He Qiaoyuan, *Minshu* (preface 1612, printed 1629) j. 129, p. 31 (Fujian Provincial Library).

[19] Lin Xiangje, *Ouliziji,* 1947 manuscript (Fujian Provincial Library). The author's use of the term *jun* (commandery) is a conscious archaism.

[20] Accounts of this incident are widespread in the Three in One, but there does not appear to be any documentation of this abduction. See Lin (1992).

he appeared in Confucian dress, much like the statues of Zhu Xi (1130–1200) in regular Confucian academies. In 1788 the compilers of the *Siku quanshu* ordered that Lin's writings be destroyed.[21]

The situation gradually eased up, so that an observer at the end of the Qing dynasty could write:

> The Three Teachings are practiced in the two regions of Putian and Xianyou. In all twelve subdivisions of Putian, . . . almost every village has a Three in One temple. There are especially many in Huating and Hushi. . . . As for the worship of the Three in One in Xianyou, almost the entire district takes part in it. You can practically call the Three in One the district's religion. Every village has to have a temple. No matter who they may be, whenever a family has troubles, they all invite Three in One Masters to resolve the issues. Every year on the 16th of the seventh month, the date of the Founder of the Teachings' birth, over ten groups per village carry banners and beat drums and gongs, playing as they march along and proceed to the ancestral temple on East Mountain [in Putian City] to present incense (*jinxiang*). This goes on without a pause for over a month."[22]

Another observer at the turn of the century, the last Putian metropolitan graduate (*jinshi*) Zhang Qin, made the following comment in his study of the various god cults of the area: "Today in the two districts of Putian and Xianyou, temples devoted exclusively to the Master number several hundred. The smoke of incense is always renewed and never ends."[23]

The Three in One was revived at the end of the Qing dynasty and during the Republican period. The key figures in the revival were Chen Zhida (d. 1872) and his disciple Liang Puyao, personal name Junlong (d. 1904), who carried on after Chen's death. These two men, based in the Wubentang (Hall of the Realization of the Fundamental) north of Hanjiang, organized large-scale republication projects and salvaged the bulk of the tradition. Most of the printed books and many of the manuscripts I collected were published by these men or their successors in the early Republican period. A second group gathered in the Hansantang (Hall of the Encompassment of the Three [Teachings]) inside Putian and included Zhang Qin, Guo Sizhou, and Chen Wenbing.

The revival of the Three in One in the 1980s and 1990s rivals that of the late Qing and Republican periods. Although many books, manuscripts, inscriptions, carvings, and ritual implements were destroyed during the Cultural Revolution, the current level of activity of the Three in One in the Putian and Xianyou region suggests that it is the most systematic organization in the area,

[21] *Siku quanshu zongmutiyao.* Franke (1972) notes that while the editors gave the *Linzi quanji* a scathing review, it was not banned, whereas the *Sanjiao zhengzong tonglun* edition of Lin's works was banned (see appendix 1). Zheng (1988: 233) quotes the review of the *Linzi quanji.* Berling (1980) mentions a decree prohibiting the Three Teachings issued in 1744.

[22] Guan Foxin, *Putian shihua* (1966), draft manuscript, Fuzhou Shifan University Library.

[23] Zhang Qin, *Kaoli zhengsu baocun shenshe shuodie,* undated blockprint.

capable of mobilizing thousands of people and hundreds of vehicles on the festivals of the god Xiawuni (Lin Zhao'en). Indeed, their social and cultural resources far surpass those of regional cults to local gods, ancestral lineages, and possibly even the local government.

I attended the rituals held to commemorate the birthdate of Lin Zhao'en at the Honorable Confucius Temple atop East Mountain within Putian City in 1989 and 1993. During the four or five hours I stayed at the temple on each visit, roughly one hundred tractor-drawn carts loaded with about twenty worshipers each drove up the steep road to the temple. Each group carried banners, baskets of offerings, and, most importantly, a wooden model of a temple containing a small statue of Lin Zhao'en and an incense burner. The groups were invariably accompanied by an instrumental troupe, who played on their gongs and sona (an oboe-like instrument) and led the group before the temple. They would bow before the temple, place incense in the main burner, and set out offerings and incense on the inner altars. Meanwhile, the model temples were placed on the central altar for the duration of their stay. Some groups included ritualists who would join in the rituals being performed inside the temple. The incense burner brought by the temple was recharged with incense ash from the main temple. In addition, every visitor asked for and received a *Zheng qi* (Orthodox Breath) talisman, with a small amount of incense ash wrapped inside it.

Clouds of incense filled the air, pierced with the sound of gongs and sona. The temple was a sea of people, struggling to get to the various altars. In the midst of this tumult a serene, solemn ritual was being performed at the center of the temple by ritualists dressed in blue or yellow gowns. The visiting groups and the individuals made contributions to the main temple that totaled well over 100,000 *renminbi* by the end of the celebrations. Many of the groups were fed dishes of vegetarian noodles, and the side buildings of the temple had been converted into a bustling, chaotic kitchen. After waiting for their incense to burn away, the groups gathered their statue and renewed incense burner and departed. Most visits lasted about one hour. At the high point of the day, some twenty or thirty groups crowded into the temple simultaneously. The temple committee carefully registered each visiting temple and its contribution. Not every temple visits every year, but in 1992 close to five hundred temples sent groups of representatives. Many of the worshipers were women, from young teenagers to older women. The musicians were generally male, as were the keepers of the model shrines and the ritualists. One group of temple committee members that received the visitors was made up entirely of women.

At one point, a procession of some three hundred people arrived on foot, representing the City God Temple of Putian. They brought with them assorted musicians and drum-cart and cymbal troupes. They also carried a twenty-foot-long stick of incense decorated with a brightly painted dragon. This would burn for four days, throughout the celebrations. This visit from a major popular temple demonstrates the respect shown and the links between popular cults and the Three in One.[24] The renaissance of the Three in One is part of a much larger phenomenon of the reinvention of traditional cultural forms in China, the significance of which is still little understood.

The development of the Three in One can therefore be divided into five phases. The first phase covers the period from the gradual establishment of the Three in One through the Ming–Qing transition (1570–1670). In this phase Lin Zhao'en and a group of low-level scholars developed a vision of the unity of the three teachings, the unity of Chinese culture. They developed techniques of self-cultivation and an organizational structure to reproduce their vision through initiation, scriptural study and recitation, and ritual practice. As will be seen below, the movement spread rapidly in the first hundred years, gaining support from a wide range of social classes. Literary and historical works by Three in One adherents during this period provide insights into the sense of self-transformation they felt the new movement provided. These developments arose during a period in which literati were actively forming new organizations to fill a power vacuum in local society created by the increasingly overextended nature of late imperial local government. Their moral vision arose in response to increasing commercialization of society, and their organizational structure provided an opportunity for individual adherents to perform and display their morality.

The second phase was a period of clandestine organization under Qing dynasty bans (1670–1820). Some scholastic activity continued, primarily in the field of inner alchemy and self-cultivation. Many temples survived by disguising themselves as local academies. Fragmentary evidence shows the continuation of temple construction and some evidence of continuous ritual activity in particular temples throughout this period. Nevertheless, the paucity of sources from this 150-year period makes this phase something of a black hole.

The third phase (1820–1949) begins with the decline of official control in the buildup to the Taiping Rebellion. The complete fracturing of local society during this period into feuding multisurname, multivillage alliances indicates an escalating incapacity on the part of the Qing government to control local society. Through documents, oral histories, and other materials gathered through fieldwork in many villages of the Xinghua area, this book will examine the variety of ways in which the Three in One worked its way into the villages of Xianyou and Putian during this phase. The writings of late Qing literati and Republican adherents suggest that these people turned to the Three in One as a vehicle to resist first the decline of morality and social chaos of the late Qing, and later the inroads of Western modernization, May 4th cultural iconoclasm, and Republican antisuperstition campaigns and modern nation-building. By this time, the Three in One had clearly divided into two

[24] Under the auspices of the McGill University–Putian CASS Xinghua Popular Culture Resource Centre, Professor Zheng Zhenman and I have organized a survey of ritual activity and temple organizations in over six hundred villages of the Putian, which will provide further data on the interactions of the Three in One and local cults.

major ritual traditions, one relatively orthodox and maintaining a Confucian style, the other far closer to Daoist and popular religious practice. These developments were in part a legacy of the diversity and clandestine nature of the second underground phase.

The fourth phase runs from 1949 to the 1970s. There is some evidence of Three in One activity into the 1950s, and of underground activity in the early 1970s. But by and large the tradition went dormant or underground, in uncanny ways reworking aspects of the earlier (third) underground phase.

The fifth phase involves the widespread, large-scale renaissance of the Three in One most clearly expressed through the reconstruction of over one thousand temples that has taken place in the 1980s and 1990s. There is now an active Three in One temple in almost every village of the Putian and Xianyou plains. The worship of Lin Zhao'en as the god Xiawuni is thus the most widespread cult in the Xinghua area.

SYNCRETISM AND HYBRIDITY

Lin Zhao'en's effort to meld the Three Teachings into a unified Xia religion was part of a much larger moment in Chinese intellectual and social history. The earliest efforts to combine the Three Teachings can be traced back to the Six Dynasties period. Imitation, competition, and court-sponsored debates and attempts at systematization and codification were all aspects of the continuing process of "syncretism" (Kohn, 1995). In fact, many of these efforts turn out to be barely concealed efforts to reassert the supremacy of one of the triad. Indeed, by the beginning of the Ming, Ming Taizu (1328–1398) had already declared his own version of syncretism to be official policy.

Roughly contemporaneous with Lin Zhao'en were several major figures in the Ming merger of the Three Teachings. Each school developed its own spin on syncretism. Disciples of Wang Yangming's Confucian school of mind, such as the founders of the Taizhou school, preached Confucian texts in the marketplace, and organized social movements. Other Confucian iconoclasts became extreme individualists, like Li Zhi (1527–1602) and He Xinyin (1517–1579). Neo-Confucians such as Xue Dachun (1586–1660) and Jiao Hong (1540–1620) also stressed the need to reach beyond the confines of their own system of thought. Their approach has been termed "compartmentalism" (Ch'ien, 1986).

Buddhist reformers such as Hanshan Deqing (1527–1602) and Zhu Hong (1535–1615) organized large-scale lay Buddhist movements (Yu, 1980; Brook, 1993). The profound impact of Daoist philosophical and alchemical traditions on Ming society has long been recognized (Liu, 1970; Seidel, 1970). Less well studied, until recently, was the role of figures like Yuan Huang, a commoner with a Confucian heritage and a medical doctor (Brokaw, 1991). The interplay of the intellectual currents that swept through these individuals reveals the complexities of the interactions between the

Plates 2 and 3. Confucian, Daoist, Buddhist, and Three in One gods and sages: from a set of paintings for use in Three in One ritual seen at the Naishengtang, Xianyou

Three Teachings at the time and the potential for new fields of discourse arising out of colliding streams of cultural change.

Lin Zhao'en's own philosophic efforts at syncretic systemization are generally considered to have achieved rather modest results. Several scholars have examined his debt to Wang Yangming's subjectivist philosophy of the essential sageliness of the individual Heart-Mind (Mano, 1979; Berling, 1980; Zheng, 1988a; Lin, 1992; Ma and Han, 1992). In his effort to demonstrate the relationship among Confucian, Daoist, and Buddhist concepts, Lin seldom provides more than an equation of terms. There is little sustained analysis of the correspondence of concepts embedded within their original philosophic or theological system. Moreover, the underlying call for a return to Confucian morality, and an acceptance of the social order, sharply differentiates Lin's writings from those of millenarian sects of the time (Berling, 1980; Brook, 1992). Millenarian tendencies can, however, be detected in the writings of some of Lin's disciples.[25]

Syncretism in terms of doctrinal equivalencies is perhaps less significant than the fact of joint worship of representatives of the Three Teachings, which actually occurred independently at a popular level in many areas of China in the Ming, if not before (Brook, 1993). As we will see, these tendencies were taken to an extreme in certain branches of the Three in One, where as many as sixty figures, including Confucian and Three in One sages and an assortment of local gods, came to be worshipped in one temple.[26] Several recent studies have focused on forms of resistance that find expression in rituals created through religious synthesis under conditions of colonialization or other forms of alien domination (Taussig, 1980; Comaroff, 1985). As Stewart and Shaw (1994: 10) point out, "where religious observance is inseparable from other social processes, we lose the ability to differentiate syncretism from other sorts of cultural bricolage and hybridization." One could view the efforts of Lin Zhao'en and his disciples as a process of religious synthesis employing a consciously syncretic discourse designed to carve out a new trajectory of individual self-cultivation and cultural renewal under conditions of hegemonic domination from a rigid Confucian system. This sees the movement as a kind of syncretism from below and fits rather well with the period of persecution under the Qing and the contemporary struggle against both Communist state power and the world capitalist cultural system. Viewed another way, the literati and merchants who jointed the movement saw themselves as carriers

[25] Most references to Maitreya Buddha, or the Third Dragon Flower Assembly, etc., are "postapocalyptic," in that Lin Zhao'en has already manifested the Dao, and now his followers can attain it in their own lifetimes through inner alchemy and moral conduct. One text, however—the *Zhuozu baojing* (Precious scripture of the patriarch Zhuo) from the Baiyundong (White Cloud Cavern), does mention the Wusheng Laomu (Eternal Mother), a figure often mentioned in millenarian contexts.

[26] Liturgical manuscripts such as the *Xiangyang shuyuan Ru Dao Shi Shengdan* (Sacred birthdates of the Confucian, Daoist, and Buddhist [deities worshipped at the] Xiangyang Academy) list 152 different dates celebrated annually, with 8 more feast days for gods worshipped on side altars. See appendix 6.

of cultural meaning imposing a syncretic vision from above onto local society. However, the "return to Confucianism" via Daoist inner alchemy and Buddhist meditation quickly became encompassed by a ritual tradition closely modeled on Daoist and Buddhist liturgical frameworks. At some levels, this provided a form of resistance, a unique tradition that could be viewed as superior to stale, formulaic, hypocritical Confucian rites, particularly at the level of community organization and ritual expression. Yet prestige within the Three in One tradition tended to go to those who achieved success in self-cultivation, rather than specialists in ritual. The re-inscription of Confucian values undermined the potential subversion, placing the Three in One in an ultimately conservative position as a force of Confucian morality in local society. Nevertheless, the emphasis placed by the Three in One on self-cultivation and its insistence on self-organization at the local level for the performance of communal rituals draws on a deep-seated liberal, even radical potential within Confucianism to challenge social and individual values.

Over time, the Three in One developed more and more forms and potentials, building upon new options arising in late imperial China. From the discussion above, we see that the Three in One emerged in the third phase of Xinghua culture outlined above, just at a moment of systemwide transition. Each particular Three in One temple or community responded to these vectors of change through a process of forced selection and exclusion, determining their relationship with both the tradition of the Three in One and the society in which they lived. Thus, paradoxically, the drive to unification of the Three Religions, or the underlying desire to reunify Chinese culture through a movement to bring the pursuit of Confucian sagehood to Chinese society as a whole, led in many ways to the elaboration of a multiplicity of distinctly different forms of Three in One groups, which continue to transform and interact with new economic, political, and cultural forces sweeping through Southeast China. Yet at another level it could be said that the Three in One was itself absorbed by the powerful unifying forces of evolving Chinese popular culture. The underlying principle that the more manifestations of *ling* (spiritual force) in a community the better remains a potent source of flexibility and creativity in China.

The Three in One movement was hybrid from the start. Mixing and matching elements of different religious systems, and carried forward by low-level local intellectuals, the movement sought to achieve a revitalization of Confucian sagehood through individual self-cultivation and group ritual practice. The goals of this movement, launched by lowly local scholars eager to develop a practical mysticism, were ultimately to reverse the tide of social and moral decay and to achieve the reunification of Chinese culture, the re-creation of the golden age of classical antiquity. By utilizing a widely shared language of Confucian values, the Three in One attempted to construct an *organic* hybridity out of the multiple, diverse chaos of divergent religious traditions and everyday religious activity. This effort led to a fusion, or homogenization, of the Three in One with other local cult practices and ritual traditions, and ultimately to the development of what can be seen as a communal, ritual practice with its own local, counterhegemonic discourse. Yet, at the same time, by "returning to [the fundamentals of] Confucianism," the Three in One was issuing an even more radical challenge to latter-day, socially entrenched, Confucian hypocrisy. This challenge, framed in the same terms of widely shared Confucian values, revealed an *intentional* sense of hybridity, which "enable[d] a contestatory activity, a politicized setting of cultural differences against one another dialogically" (Young, 1995: 30).[27] The Three in One contributed to the creation of a sense of local cultural difference by working within and upon the potentialities of social organization in late Ming and Qing Xinghua local society. This involved the continual fusion with localized cultural forms, the growth of a distinct ritual tradition, and the gradual integration of the Three in One into local communities. This establishment of cultural difference has resulted, paradoxically again, in yet another level of the intentional sense of hybridity, which provides the potential in the contemporary setting to use the language and practices of radical Confucian self-cultivation to challenge the legitimacy of the state and the party as well as to respond to growing pressures toward capitalist cultural homogenization.

As Robert Young (1995) has pointed out, hybrid cultural formations inevitably rely upon theories of desire and heterosexual sexuality. Lin Zhao'en theorized that spiritual power (*ling*) becomes incarnate at the moment of biological conception in the sexual joining of men and women. The forces of power/desire within the sexual act are immediately recuperated by naming it *ren* (humanity), identifying it with the underlying substance that transcends differentiation, and channeling it into two directions simultaneously. One direction is the path of return to nondifferentiation, through the gradual refining of the forces of the body back to their "original elements" and then back to the void that subtends them. Even the void must be shattered at the culmination of this trajectory of spiritual enlightenment. The other, equally vital trajectory channels sexuality, desire, and material/spiritual power into the patriline. Conception produces *ren* (humanity) and leads to filial relations between fathers and sons (*xiao*). More and more sons lead to the need for the hierarchical ordering of brothers through ritualized relationships (*li;* rites and propriety). Relations between (male) friends require a principle of order and organization (*zhong;* loyalty) enabling *zhi* (orderly governance), and so society is regulated. Nevertheless, as we will see, the flows of the Three in One have not been confined by Lin's desire to channel the flow of desire into spiritual illumination and an idealized patriarchy. Overflowing restraints established by its founders, the Three in One continues to flow in unexpected directions, and many are swept into its trajectories and its whirlpools.

The bifurcated channeling of desire within the Three in One arises from an underlying problematic that polarizes the field of action of the movement in

---

[27] Young is here summarizing Mikhail Bahktin's (1981) notion of linguistic hybridity and examining its applications to cultural theory in the work of Bhabha, Stuart Hall, and other cultural studies theorists.

each phase of its transformations. These are the polar attractors of *sheng* (Confucian sagehood) and *ling* (immediate, efficacious spiritual power).[28] The Confucian sage embodies cosmic harmonies, exemplifies moral conduct, and lives his life as a ritual dance of righteousness (Finagrette, 1972; Hall and Ames, 1987; Taylor, 1990). *Ling* is the irruption of supernatural power or efficacity into actualized resolutions. *Ling* can be channeled through ritual acts or spirit possession.[29] Early adherents of the Three in One aspired to a model of Confucian sagehood, which would be recognized and emulated at the highest levels of local society. Yet, over the long run, the Three in One would have much more success, and expand far more rapidly into village life, than at the level of gentry society and scholarly academies. In village life, the model of the supernatural power of local gods, and the ability of ritual specialists and spirit mediums to channel that power, became a powerful magnet for the potentialities of the Three in One. At the level of village life, Lin Zhao'en would become for many a powerful local god who could be appealed to through offerings, incense, and prayer, and who could speak through miracles and divinatory poetry.

Lin's effort to confront what he saw as the hypocritical, formalistic Confucianism of his day with a vision of Confucian sagehood revitalized by Daoist inner alchemy and Buddhist meditation rested on a quasi-materialist theory of desire and supernatural power. He struggled to reconcile the model of the Sage with the combined potentiality of Buddhist enlightenment and the supernatural power of a Daoist deity. At a philosophic level, this was his response to the impasse between the Cheng-Zhu Neo-Confucian School of Principle and Wang Yangming's School of Mind. At the level of social action, the effort to organize a movement devoted to reconciling these contradictory modes of

[28] *Chambers Science and Technology Dictionary* (New York: Chambers, 1991) explains that magnetic poles "cannot exist" but are "deduced from the direction" of charged movements within the field, the globality of whose material conditions the polarity expresses in terms of potential.

[29] Stephen Feuchtwang (1977: 605) distinguishes models of supernatural power in official, Daoist, and "popular" religion: "One can move from popular religion into the Taoist as well as into the official religious traditions. The two shared a common ground of metaphysical speculation. But it is in Taoism and not in the official religion that the metaphysical categories of this cosmology are applied as real forces. In the official religion, the notion of a hierarchical structure in the moral universe is consistently displayed. This notion is anthropomorphized as it approaches popular religion, for the metaphor of bureaucracy becomes increasingly elaborate as the spirits of men who have died take on greater and greater powers and the representations of gods are themselves treated as having power. The distribution of this power is through a hierarchy, that is to say by *delegation* through ranks from the top. The image of bureaucracy is applied to the universe of Taoist religion, too, and with it the attribution of spiritual powers to the spirits of the dead—again as Taoism approaches popular usage. But between Taoist religion and the popular religion—the former in its application of transcendental metaphysical categories: the latter in the use of the concept *ling* in particular—an alternative relationship is added to that of delegation, it is the diffusion and concentration of power in any spot of time or space as a center appropriately oriented to the greater arrangement of power on a transcendent plane. The ultimate center at the most transcendent plane is known as the great unique (*t'ai-i* and its synonyms). One may call this a process of *identification,* and it is common to Taoist religion, alchemy, and geomancy."

spiritual power led to confrontation and paradoxical results. Even within his own lifetime, most scholars and officials viewed as completely unacceptable the image developed together with his disciples of Lin as a modern-day enlightened (successor to) Confucius possessed of supernatural powers. Nonetheless, for many individual adherents of the Three in One, these polar tendencies of spiritual striving functioned as mutually contradictory but nonetheless irresistible magnets. The tension produced by these polar attractors underlies the entire range of Three in One practice from scriptural study and individual self-cultivation, on the one hand, to ritual practice and guided spirit mediumism, on the other. At the level of social groupings and movements, these tensions set the internal limits of the range of strategies adopted in the Three in One's striving for self-definition, autonomy, and positions of social control within local Xinghua culture. At each phase in its transformations, the Three in One movement has been torn between these tendencies, as it confronted new external circumstances and absorbed and transformed new forces. Unable ever to resolve these contradictory impulses, the Three in One continues to struggle to invent new potentialities for itself and for Xinghua culture as a whole.

ORGANIZATION OF THE BOOK

The first chapter raises theoretical issues concerning the nature of ritual experience and the construction of subjectivity. It also sketches an outline of the major historical phases in the local culture of the Xinghua area, briefly examining the central ritual complexes that defined each phase. The second chapter examines the elements of an exemplary life trajectory, a "kinetic geography" developed within hagiographic accounts of the life and apotheosis of Lin Zhao'en.[30] These accounts make use of narrative devices such as dream portents, stages of alchemical progress, and mystic signs along with a constant tension between spiritual attainment and official harassment to reveal the pattern, meaning, and promise of Lin's life. The third chapter examines the reasons behind Lin's success in establishing the Three in One in the face of official suspicion and opposition. This chapter goes on to describe the early schisms in the movement, based on contemporary documents, and describes the principle disciples, as well as the social basis for the rapid spread of the movement.

Chapter 4 explores the unique system of internal alchemy developed by Lin Zhao'en and practiced by all initiates into the Three in One. This chapter also includes an examination of the scriptural heritage of the Three in One and a discussion of the early liturgical texts. Chapter 5 traces the revival of the cult over the late Qing and Republican periods up to 1949 and the network of temples within the different branches of the movement. This chapter trans-

[30] See Dean and Massumi (1992) for the concept of kinetic geography, where it is developed in relation to political leaders.

lates and analyzes the surviving corpus of epigraphy related to the Three in One. It also includes a brief discussion of the spread of the Three in One to Taiwan, Singapore, and Malaysia. Chapter 6 discusses the ritual traditions of the Three in One, examining in turn religious organization, initiation, rules of association, ritual pantheons, ritual calendars, ritual texts, liturgical music and dance, visualizations and spells, the role of space and time in ritual, gender roles in ritual, and the economics of ritual.

Chapter 7 analyzes the range of cultural roles played by the Three in One in contemporary China by examining a range of different kinds of relationship between Three in One temples and their surrounding communities. Several individual life histories of practitioners of the Three in One, based on textual and oral historical sources, are discussed. Chapter 8 focuses on the tendencies and potentialities of the Three in One in contemporary China, first discussing forms of contemporary outreach developed by the Three in One, such as newly circulated regulations, textbooks, and simple expository dialogues. This chapter goes on to examine the paradoxical roles of intellectuals, government agencies, and outside groups in contesting and legitimizing the cult in contemporary China. The conclusion discusses the current status and future prospects of the Three in One and returns to the question of the nature of ritual experience in the construction of subjectivity. The appendices provide information on editions of Lin's writings, summaries of his doctrines in scriptural form, translations of liturgies and popular scriptures, and data on early disciples and temple networks.

Readers interested in issues such as the role of ritual in contemporary Chinese popular culture and localism and resistance may find the discussion in chapters 1, 7, 8, and the conclusion most provoking, while the accounts of the historical transformations, inner alchemical traditions, and ritual traditions of the Three in One in chapters 2 to 6 are more descriptive. The historical and doctrinal information in these middle chapters nonetheless informs the approach to ritual and cultural processes outlined in the first chapter and discussed further in the final chapters and the conclusion.

Research into the Three in One has uncovered several tensions, traces of which appear throughout this book, such as that between Confucian sagehood and the irruption of supernatural power. Another tension arises between institutional history and the effort to find a new set of concepts to describe individual experience within ritual. There is a tension even between vocabularies, for the first chapter attempts to sketch out a model of the "individual" as a contingent, charged point of contact of a range of forces: social, political, economic, cultural, and libidinal. The "individual" that emerges from this model is not the self-conscious, self-contained subject. Instead, an "individual" can be a person, a group, an abstract assemblage of forces, or all of these in a temporary, continent coalition. Yet several chapters of the book contain descriptions and analyses of historical figures and their actions and statements. A related tension emerges in chapter 1 between the description of ritual-events as a philosophic category and this concept as part of a historical process.

Tensions surround the need for typologies to classify aspects of the Three in One in the context of a framework that emphasizes the contingent balance of forces in particular contexts. Finally, there is a tension between the presentation of local cultural difference and efforts to relate this to some understanding of "Chinese Culture." One of the most interesting aspects of the Three in One is that it was one of many responses to new demands for unity arising out of a widespread sense of increasing social and cultural fragmentation in late imperial China, yet the unity it sought to impose generated a multiplicity of local differences. The presence of these tensions in the following chapters is designed to bring out or embody the agonistic relationship between imperial models of power and the local configurations described in this book.

· C H A P T E R   O N E ·

Ritual-Events

THEORIES of religion and ritual often begin by assuming a self-contained individual who performs a self-contained ritual, which is said to embody timeless truths of the self-contained culture. In the passages that follow, I begin with an analysis of ritual-events in the middle, rather than at either end, of the self-confirming binary divide of self and society.

RITUAL-EVENTS AND THE INTERCORPOREAL

An immensely intricate and hierarchical social order developed within China with certain empirewide ritual forms, several midlevel, transregional ritual and performance genres, and a plethora of discrete regional, or localized, ritual traditions. Ultimately, a model of the body in Chinese ritual systems would have to take into account the determinant mechanisms of local culture, as well as the impact of imperial models of ritual practice. For different periods in Chinese history, in different regions, it would be useful to map out changing arenas and apparatuses of power. These arenas and apparatuses are developed for the induction of bodies into various formations of subjectivation that work within certain parameters of repeatedly performed identification—within the family, the lineage, the village, the culturally defined region, the economically oriented market region, the socially differentiated class membership, and the political administration. Many of these levels were established through rituals. Certain rituals mark and perform entry into specific groups over the life cycle. Others, like exorcisms of the possessed, reinscribe one or more of these formations of subjectification. Many celebrate the presumed divine sanction of these naturalized "identities" and relationships.

As a general illustration of some of the processes discussed above, one might look at the example of a Chinese festival centering around a ritual for the birth date of a local god. Such events have been gathering force, increasing in number and intensity over the past fifteen years in Southeast China. Many children and young teenagers have grown up in a world increasingly inscribed with ritual celebrations. Imagine a small child witnessing the range of physical and emotional expression taking place. Inside the temple, and outside on stage at crucial moments in the liturgy, Daoist priests perform the stylized gestures of imperial court audiences, complete with intricate dance, the manipulation of court tablets, kowtows, presentations of memorials, offerings of tea, etc. Outside the temple, the mediums present a range of what defines extreme behavior, including grimaces, mudras, trance dance, hyperventilation, screams and cries, transformation into animal modes, and body mutilation. On stage, the entire range of stock character types, human situations and moral dilemmas, and stylized embodiments of emotional states is represented. Before the altars, villagers kneel and burn incense, present offerings, and pray fervently. Village headsmen perform dignified movements of kneeling and offering inside and outside the temple. Performing arts troupes highlight gender roles with cross-dressing and lewd songs and dances. A tremendous variety of food offerings, incense and smells of all kinds, smoke, color, and sound flow through the charged space of the ritual. Like physical forces, these flows have an impact upon the bodies of the participants, transforming them and forcing a reactive response. A tremendous range of culturally specific bodily gestures and embodied registers of intensity is presented for emulation and improvisation. The child may grow up to be a medium, a village representative, an actor or actress, or a villager burning incense in the ritually prescribed fashion. The child gradually develops an understanding of or an ability to perform or respond to this repertoire of physical gestures and trajectories of intensity. Such a process could be viewed metaphorically as the irrigation of the ritual body, creating channels of intensity and trajectories of gesture, voice, and rhythm. In such processes, opportunities abound for the mixing of flows, the transformation from intensity to intensity, or the pursuit of lines of flight from cultural processes of iteration and citation (see Butler, 1990; 1992; for analyses of flows of force in ritual, see Gil, 1989).

An example from the philosophy of science can provide a mode of conceptualizing this problem. Gilbert Simendon (1989; 1992) has analyzed the process of individuation of living organisms, individuals, and social collectives. He argues that an individual is generated out of a complex metastable field of preindividual forces, potential forms, and possible coalescences of matter. The moment of individuation is determinative in physical processes, such as in the formation of a crystal. Even after attaining the consistency of energy, form, and matter that constitutes a crystal, the crystal continues to interact with its milieu, in order to maintain its consistency. In the case of living organisms, the realm of virtuosity Simendon refers to as the *preindividual* is carried along throughout the living being's lifetime of continuous individuation. Thus, attaining a particular identity is only one, and but a temporary, aspect of a continuous interaction with the milieu, and a continuous process of individuation drawing upon the virtual, or preindividual, realm. Many of the forces that move through a living being undergoing these processes may be described as *transindividual*. This is particularly the case with regard to the establishment of an individual identity vis-à-vis a social collective. Social collectives, such as the Three in One, can themselves be said to take part in a process of individuation, or the actualization of virtual potentials. This way of examining issues may help us to conceive of the processes by which the Three in One spread through the Xinghua region. Examining the Three in One in this way enables us to avoid assigning it, or the individuals within it, a fixed identity, or attempting to tease out a set typology. Rather, one can try to think of these processes in their process of self-definition, a process beyond an atomistic, self-conscious model of thought or perception, including preindividual potentiality, transindividual vectors of change, and a constantly changing milieu. This implies that institutional developments are inadequate as an explanatory framework in and of themselves, but also that the discourse or rhetorical realm opened up by the Three in One cannot be interpreted as either adequate in and of itself (transparently meaningful) or a direct, if distorted, reflection of an underlying institutional or class nexus. Instead, we will have to examine the gap between institutional formations and social milieus and the rhetorical structures of discourse, the gap between things and words, to seek to examine the forces at play in between, the forces of desire, or the transformative creative force of actualization of the virtual at work in the complex process of individuation.

TABLEAU 1: TRANCE AND GROUP POSSESSION AT THE CROSSROADS

At an intersection on the edge of a city a neighborhood temple is celebrating a festival in honor of its gods. A procession is returning to the temple, and a large crowd has gathered at the intersection, completely blocking traffic to all but the palanquin of the gods. As these emerge into the street the crowd presses forward. People hang out of windows, and hang upon each another, responding to the movements of the god's sedan chair. This ornate, carved, heavy wooden seat is carried on poles by eight men, four in front and four behind, all of whom are in trance. As the sedan chair approaches the temple, it begins to spin clockwise, moving faster and faster, until, with blinding speed, it suddenly reverses directions and spins in the opposite direction. The crowd thrills and moves closer, forming a tighter circle. The sedan chair changes direction again, and again, moving at impossible speed. Spirit mediums in trance follow the sedan chair into the street before the temple, some as young as eight or nine, young men with skewers through their cheeks, who, excited by the sight of the temple and sensing the excitement of the crowds, begin to cut themselves with sharp swords, or flail themselves with maces. Blood runs down their faces. At the sight of this, the crowd begins to buckle and sway, groaning and crying out over the noise of exploding firecrackers. Several individuals in the crowd enter into an intense trance, and race forward to join the mediums in the center of the intersection, dancing and hopping, their eyes rolling backwards in their heads.

TABLEAU 2: THE END(S) OF A PROCESSION

At the end of a procession, four different forms of music are playing simultaneously in the temple and its courtyard. A brass band plays martial tunes inside the temple. A traditional instrumental ensemble plays songs of offering before the altar of the gods. Outside on the stage, a troupe of girls in red dresses and black hats dances to disco music. Simultaneously, on the steps of the temple, the Eight Officers are shouting out strange hoots and whistles. Firecrackers explode in the courtyard between the temple and the stage. Sound is one of the most saturated of the sensory stimuli. The overpowering sound of exploding firecrackers makes rock music seem obsolete. From one point of view, the ritual space is differentiated by distinct musical forms and sonic blasts. From another perspective, the forms of sound interpenetrate one another, pulling the listener first toward one form, then toward another. This sensation of pulling is sometimes physically acted out by mass movements of the crowd, shifting from one source of sound to another. The pull of the trajectories of sound, the vectors or planes opened up by timbers and pitches, traverse individual bodies in the crowd, moving the individual in different directions simultaneously.

These sensory distortions are inevitably accompanied by affective investments. The channeling of affects through the repeated participation in rituals generates kinetic geographies and affective parabolas. These grooves of habitual movement, emotion, and intellection, and their interactions, are carved out by ritualized, re-iterated behavior. A specific constellation of sensation and emotion is generated. But ritual is always excessive, whether by virtue of the resonance (tension, redundancy) of codes striving to circumscribe and channel desire, or because the sheer excess of forces sweeping through a particular individual cannot be contained.

The spinning sedan chair of the gods in the first tableau was a whirlpool of affect and intensity, drawing in the crowd, and then transmitting waves of affect intercorporeally back through it, erupting into intense trance possession in certain individual bodies in the crowd. The four different groups of musicians in the second tableau are multiple whirlpools, or nuclei of expression, in a single ritual-event.

The crowd in the tableaux moves as one body, even when it eddies into and between different nuclei of expression within the commotion. In the first tableau, these movements include the circle formed within the intersection, the tightening of the circle as it closes in upon the sedan chairs, and the outward spiral of the irruption of trance and spirit possession. In the second tableau, there was the milling and swirling movements of the crowd. The crowd moving as one body expresses the *intercorporeality* of ritual-events.

The intercorporeality of the crowd enables the rapid transfer of affect/intensity between and through individual bodies. Other movements within the crowd parallel the transmission of affects from body to body. These are the operations of *infracorporeal* states of preindividual intensity, potential fields of intensity such as spontaneous possession and imperviousness to pain of self-mortification. The range of intensity is an expression of the infracorporeality of potential states of experience.

A nucleus of expression is multidimensional: each actual formation that enters into it, directly (as a part of its coding) or indirectly (bleeds between nuclei in the commotion), such as music, dance, drama, recitation of liturgy, posters, patterned and coded movements, clothing—constitutes a dimension. Each of these dimensions in turn is a multidimensional block of space-time.

A nucleus of expression is synaesthetic—each of its dimensions implicates all five senses—plus proprioception—the senses are synthesized differently, each nucleus implicating one or some more directly than others. Where the same sense is dominant in two different nuclei, it should not be assumed that it is operating in the same mode. There are many visions involved in ritual, not just Vision or the Gaze; a multiplication of the senses—different visions, tactalities, etc., and shades between.

The multidimensionality of the nucleus of expression is in the in-betweenness of bodies—the intercorporeal—all of their possible ways of affecting and being affected as a collectivity. The multidimensionality of the intercorporeal is affective/intensive. The affective/intensive field is the *positive unconscious.*

Behind these tableau there lie, of course, linearities and structurations. The linearities include temporal orderings; liturgical developments and the spread of cults; deifications; the progression of the particular ritual from which the nodal image was taken; economic, historical, political, hydraulic changes. The structurations are both horizontal and vertical, spatializing orderings such as the system of nested hierarchies of the temple, gender, age, novitiate/master divisions; temple, lineage, village, local party, central state configurations, including the superposition of the spirit-world imperial hierarchy on the ritual locale.

The word in Chinese for "society" is *shehui.* Etymologically, this means the assembly of the altar of the earth. The term was used in ancient and medieval times for assemblies of territorial cults and guild associations. Chinese communities in most rural areas, and in many city wards and neighborhoods, still maintain a local temple dedicated to a god. The assembly of the temple on the festival of the gods is a form of assemblage, a collective machine for the production of ritual-events.

Chinese society is a hotbed of associational assemblages. In rural communities many of these are based within temples. Many are functional, pooling resources for the organization and performance of a ritual-event, or pooling shares in investments, partnerships, or temporary alignments. Even within such hallowed institutions as the Chinese lineages, or even the Chinese family, associational assemblages form autonomously and dissipate with rapidity.

RITUAL-EVENTS AND THE POSITIVE UNCONSCIOUS

TABLEAU 3: GRANDSTANDS OF THE GODS

A small village holds a ritual. Carved, painted wooden god statues, dressed in embroidered robes, from temples near and far, and from individual home altars, are invited to attend the ritual. These statues are arranged in bleachers within the temple. Many different deities are represented, with multiple versions of the same gods and goddesses in different shapes and sizes. An altar set up inside the temple, to which these gods are serving as witnesses and invited guests, is elaborate and visually overwhelming. Paintings of the Lord of the Three in One are flanked by images of the host of Confucian sages, Daoist immortals, buddhas and bodhisattvas, and saints of the Three in One. The rituals, performed by ritual special-

Plate 4. Six mediums possessed by gods on a stage before a crowd at the completion of a village group initiation ritual in the Jiangkou area, Putian.

ists in embroidered robes, involve elaborate imitations of court audiences, along with theatrical exorcisms and purifications and Buddhist recitations. Some twenty different rites within the overall structure of the communal sacrifice (*jiao*) are performed in succession, including a distribution of blessed food for the universal deliverance of hungry ghosts (*pushi*). The ritual music ranges from stately and refined to martial and exhilarating. The musicians play the drum, gongs, sona (oboe), and strings. Most of the musicians are also trained ritualists, particularly the drummer, who sets the rhythm of the ritual. The ritual dance is led by one of the five to nine officiants, the singing by another. The Three in One scripture master presides over the central rites, including recitation of spells and visualizations of self-transformation into various Buddhas and the Golden Body of the Lord Xia. Scriptures are recited, some dedicated to the local gods, some to the Lord of the Three in One. Tea and incense are offered to the gods. A large array of documents drawn up for each ritual is read aloud at the appropriate time and then burned (transformed). Each day sees six or seven two-hour-long rites performed, usually with half-hour breaks in between, starting at one or two in the morning and often continuing past midnight. Sleep patterns are completely disrupted, as sleeping and waking states merge together. The prescribed, formalized actions of the ritual appear more and more as a form of dreamwork.

The ritual space of the altar is a space of transformation of forces. Sensations and intensities are captured, intensified, and transformed by the complex, coded space of the altar. The complexity and contradictory nature of the competing stimuli and affects result in a fragmenting of the unity of the individual that is then swept up in multiple trajectories of sound, sight, taste, touch, and smell. Different equations are developed between different senses along these distinct and multiple trajectories. Sensations cross registers: thus the fragrant smoke rising from burning sticks of incense form words visible to the gods. Ritual acts by priests and mediums recombine the senses and the realm of intensity in different ways. Visualization of the gods of the body is not a step-by-step perusal of iconographic elements, but a physical, material process of dancing, bowing, chanting, and traveling in spirit through cutting winds and shining stellar palaces. Identification of one's own body with a variety of gods requires the utterance of spells and mantras (true words) that enable a different sensorium and experience of intensity. The flow of qi (breath) into and around the body of the ritualist and out into the purificatory water sprinkled by the priest over the altar and the participants in the ritual enables a transformative power over material objects—the altar expands before the eyes, the offerings are covered with sweet dew that releases a piercing fragrance, the spirit money in one's hands changes into white gold.

The ritual-event is replete with a multiplicity of different planes or vectors of sensory and intensive stimulation, which constantly cross registers, moving from body to body. This multiplicity is mirrored at the level of consciousness by a taboo on contradiction in the representation of the deity. Three in One scripture masters and Daoist priests worship the local god in his "true" form as an avatar of a high Daoist stellar god. Community representatives worship the god that has endorsed their power and position in the community. Outside the temple, and sometimes erupting inside of it, spirit mediums are possessed by the god and may address commands to the crowd of worshippers, or pronounce on various issues. Contradictions between these different representations are not allowed to surface. The issue is not logical coherence but the multiplicity of spiritual manifestations. The more forms supernatural power takes, the better.

This vision of continual transformation and multiple manifestation of supernatural power unsettles any unity of meaning or representation. Just as the individual involved in a ritual is subject to forces and vectors of transformation through the powerful tensions of the elements of the ritual structure and the call of competing, disorienting sensory stimulation, so too spiritual power (*ling*) manifests in continuous transformation. The multiplicity of the "positive unconscious" can be seen in the presence of a positive taboo on contradiction— any representation of the supernatural is accepted. The positive unconscious is not confined to a model of individual self-consciousness, or the Freudian symbolic unconscious. Similarly, the intercorporeal and the realm of intensity (the infracorporeal) are not limited to a model of atomistic individual subjectivity.[1]

[1] Michel Foucault discusses the "positive unconscious" in his analysis of shifts in modes of seeing and knowing in the introduction to *Les Mots et les Choses* (1970) (translated as *The Order of Things*).

The synaesthetic nature of ritual is also brought out in the liturgical texts. The following passage from a Daoist liturgy shows the importance of the role of sound. Here primordial sound coagulates into the original glyphs of the sacred revelatory scripture, traversing registers of sensation (the aural to the visual). But these glyphs can only be described as being beyond representation:

> Behold! The Three Energies (the original trinity proceeding from the Dao) suddenly coagulate, creating a point of viridian incipience on high. The Two Principles (Yin and Yang) separate, taking for the first time the shape of the Great Ultimate (*taiji*). Pure sound was as yet unheard, the stars were not in their place, when suddenly the energies from the Three Regions gushed forth, producing the Eight Notes of Harmony. [These sound energies] coagulated in the center of the Great Vacuity, as billowing clouds, constantly intermingling, wheeling and turning above the Purple Empyrean. Now floating, now sinking, in accordance with the norm (*ke*), being neither smoke nor dust, neither vapors nor steam, [these sound energies] formed characters ten thousand years square, sounding with the Eight Notes, expressing the essence of the Three Energies, the subtle manifestation of the Five Elements. Oh Great Tao of the Jade Aurora, manifesting itself visibly in the Real Void! This Heavenly Perfected and the Ancestral Beings, paying homage to this revelation, copied it. [These writs] were tortuous and spiraling, clustered and weird. Some called them "Real Writs," others name them "No resemblance." (Translated in Schipper and Wang [1986: 203], from the *Suqi xuantan ke* [Ritual for the vesperal communication], nineteenth-century manuscript, Schipper collection; Ofuchi, 1983; 290.)

In a Taoist ritual, the synaesthetic transformations (from cosmic sound energies to divine signs) described in this text are understood as direct transformations of cosmic forces, rather than as mere metaphors. This approach to cosmic transformation and the transmutation of energy can be extended to the analysis of the intercorporeal and infracorporeal flow of forces between bodies in ritual-events. Anyone who has attended a highly charged village festival in Taiwan or China will sense what is meant by the reference to a level of experience that overspills the individual and generates a multitude of new planes of experience among the assembled crowd: a proliferation of multiplicities that can be analyzed as new sets of relations, new collective bodies undergoing innumerable transformations, new collective subjectivities constructing themselves.

We can view the ritual-event as a process of self-expression, as the performance of autonomous organization, as a positive expression of the welling of the self-organizing forces of existence, but one that falls back upon, at the same time that it contests, boundaries of self, community, and state. The difference into which the ritual leap falls back is the event. What transpires? A reaffirmation of linearities and structurations, but with something having happened, a modification of them. The ritual is a pulsing, it is stroboscopic—continuous and discontinuous. A ritual-event works through a self-modulation of the realm of intensity.[2]

RITUAL-EVENTS AND RITUAL TRADITIONS

Given this approach to ritual-events, how can we relate such processes to the development of a ritual tradition within a religious movement such as the Three in One? Lin Zhao'en and his circle of early disciples put together a set of elements drawn from different traditions and organized around a central problematic. They linked a regime of inner alchemical meditation with a developing set of rituals based on scriptures and liturgies incorporating Three in One philosophy but modeled on earlier Buddhist and Daoist liturgical frameworks. They tied inner alchemical practice to public ritual performance. But they went even further by urging a transformation of everyday life according to Confucian modes of conduct. Participation in group study and discussion would assist adherents in interpreting their circumstances and acting correctly, thereby influencing others by their example. Initiation and subsequent master–disciple relations would aid the adept in advancing through the stages of the inner alchemical process. Group meditation and group ritual performances would consolidate and channel the spiritual striving of the Three in One collectivity and sweep other members of the surrounding community into its trajectory. A variety of techniques for autonomous organization were developed to support the expansion of Three in One groups from study cells through the construction of temples to the establishment of permanent ritual units with regular, group meditation and ritual performances.

The combination of Confucian ideals and concepts with certain elements of Buddhist and Daoist liturgy meant designing a ritual tradition that would generate ritual-events that would operate in specific registers of intensity on specific communities or collectivities. However, as implied in the discussion of ritual-events above, the collective subjectivity of the founders of the Three in One was itself constantly undergoing modification due to external circumstances and the play of transversal forces. As Three in One groups increased, fragmented, schismed, and transformed in reaction to internal organizational contradictions, new contexts and pressures, and above all the impulsion of their own problematic, the quest for Confucian sagehood *and* supernatural

---

[2] A ritual-event is an assembly or assemblage that gathers forces, objects, and people into an *expression-event*. Expression is a self-fulfilling process—no thing or meaning or symbol is expressed. The process of expression expresses only itself. Its apparent "objects" (signs, meanings, persons, agents, subjects, etc.) are inert, residue—its persistence, its past, its arrested force. A ritual-event is its own subject, and the semiotic and nonsemiotic elements swept up in it are its partial objects. The human participants in a ritual are part-objects and part-subjects. Fragments of consciousness, trained, habitual, reflex behavior, vectors of intentionality and desire are all absorbed into the rhythmic refrain of the ritual-event, which strives toward its own expression. This discussion of the ritual-event is drawn from an ongoing collaborative project on the philosophy of ritual with Brian Massumi.

spiritual power, the range of ritual-events generated within the Three in One movement increased and diversified. As the Three in One transformed, it changed far beyond what Lin Zhao'en or his circle of disciples would have recognized. These unintended transformations are also the subject of this book.

For certain individuals and groups participating in these traditions, it would be appropriate to talk in terms of strategies of ritualization (Bell, 1992). The founding circle of Three in One leaders can be understood in this way. They devised a range of specific rituals for individual and group practice while at the same time extending the reach of Confucian models by stressing the ritualization of everyday life. But an emphasis on self-reflexive participation, subjective interpretations, individual empowerment, and the attainment of a sense of identity already implies an underlying model of the self-conscious individual actor/agent. Such an approach runs the risk of overstating the role of the individual in ritual. The different levels of identity achieved through participation in a ritual-event may be best seen as an after-effect or residue of tumultuous transformations. In fact, participation in the Three in One is often described as a gradual movement from one phase to another, from one dimension to the next, through deeper dimensions of understanding and illumination, leading to freedom from an everyday sense of self.

What is important is not so much what Lin Zhao'en thought as what were the potentialities that were opened up by the problematic he and his disciples developed. What were the ritual machines that were generated by their questions, and what were the collective assemblages of semiotic and nonsemiotic elements and forces that experienced them? The following section examines the way in which elements and forces drawn from distinct ritual traditions can coexist over time, phasing in and phasing out into new arenas and apparatuses of power.

PHASES, PLANES, AND VECTORS

Drawing on the work of Daniel Stern on the development of infants, Felix Guattari (1995) elicits the implication of Stern's conclusion that infants develop in phases, but that the skills and modes of perception and interaction developed within each phase are not overcome or resolved at each higher level but subsist in a growing pool of potential. The skills and modes of perception and interaction of any one phase when viewed together can be seen to open up a kind of plane of consistency in a virtual realm. These skills, interactions, and resources phase in and phase out, overlaying one another in complex ways through their actualization within any particular event.

The coexistence of phases can be further examined in relation to a virtual realm. Pierre Levy (1995: 13–14) follows Gilles Deleuze in differentiating the virtual from the actual, and the possible from the real.[3]

_____

[3] Deleuze develops his understanding of the reality of the virtual as virtual through his reading of Bergson, and his notion of the limitations of possibility through a critique of Leibniz in *Difference and Repetition* (1994: 208–221).

The word virtue comes from the medieval latin *virtualis,* which itself came from *virtus,* force, power. In scholastic philosophy, the virtual is that which exists in power (*puissance*) but not in actuality. The virtual tends to actualize itself, without being subsumed by its effective or formal concretisation. The tree is virtually present in the seed. In rigorous philosophical terms, virtuality is not opposed to the real, but to the actual: virtuality and actuality are simply two different manners of being. . . . The possible is already completely constituted, but it holds itself in the wings. The possible realizes itself without any change in its determination or its nature. It is a phantasmatic, latent real: it lacks only existence. . . . Contrary to the possible, static and pre-constituted, the virtual is like a complex problematic, the node of tendencies or forces which accompany a situation, an event, or object or any kind of entity and which calls for a process of resolution: actualization. This complex problematic belongs to the entity under consideration and constitutes one of its major dimensions. The problem of the seed, for example, is to make grow the tree. The seed "is" this problem, even if it is not only that. This is not to say that it "knows" exactly the form of the tree that finally will spread its leaves above it. Starting with its own constraints, it must invent the tree, co-produce it with the circumstances that it encounters. *On the one hand, the entity carries and produces its virtualities:* an event, for example, reorganizes an anterior problematic and is susceptible to receiving varied interpretations. *On the other hand, the virtual constitutes the entity:* the virtualities which inhere in an entity, its problematic, the node of tensions, constraints, and projects which animate it, the questions which move it, are an essential part of its determination. (italics in original)

This book seeks to explore the problematic of the Three in One, and to examine the ways in which it invented itself in relation to the external circumstances it encountered. Rising out of a specific historical juncture of social, philosophic, and libidinal forces, the Three in One represents a collective social and spiritual striving within a field traversed by polar attractors of sagehood and spiritual power. Throughout its transformations, the Three in One encountered a wide range of specific power formations. Although state suppression could be extensive, it was generally sporadic and ultimately incapable of eliminating the spread of the Three in One. The key transformation in local society was the decline of the state, the commercialization of society, and the rise of local power formations based in gentry alliances, transforming lineages, and newly evolving temple networks. More recently, transnational flows of capital and religious groups have added further complexity and potentiality. This process of actualization as self-invention is an ongoing process, and the continual invention of cultural forms recharges the virtual with new potential.

In chapter 2, hagiographic accounts of Lin Zhao'en's life are analyzed in terms of phases, planes, and vectors. Each phase of his life opens up new planes, created by emerging vectors and the interaction of forces, that create new spaces for the actualization of virtual potential. In many ways, Lin's own approach to the merging of the Three Teachings, discussed in chapter 3, can also be seen as an effort to expand individual access to the forces and potentials within these teachings by pointing out their interconnections and mutual reinforcements, as well as the unexpected spaces they open up when used in conjunction with each other. The phases of alchemical experience, discussed in chapter 4, although presented as a serial progression through distinct stages, can also be understood as involving the progressive opening up of new spaces at various phases in the process (initiation, establishment of the basis, and attainment of the ultimate principles). Each of these phases opens the practitioner to a new relationship with the virtual. The chapters on the historical unfolding of the Three in One emphasize the multiplicity of its concrete actualizations within an ongoing problematic. Chapters 7 and 8 discuss the problematic of the Three in One in the contemporary context, and the conclusion develops a model of four overlapping spaces opened up by groups like the Three in One: the spaces of the earth, of territory, of networks, and of collective experimentation.

RITUAL AND TIME: MULTIPLE TEMPORALITIES AND HISTORICAL MEMORY

If rituals are, as Levi Strauss said, primarily machines for the suppression of time (see Leach, 1970; Gil, 1989), we can nonetheless map the return of the repressed in the multiple temporalities that ritual-events generate. Ritual-events can also be examined as apparatuses for the containment of forces and the imposition of certain boundaries of identity. There are many examples of these processes in the rituals of Xinghua culture. Imperial ritual and official rites assert the cyclic nature of time, and the role of the emperor and his delegates in moving time forward into another repetition (Zito, 1984; 1993; 1994).[4] Daoist ritual works with a deconstruction of time, reversing the flow of time into a world prior to time, while at the same time performing a revelation and destruction of cosmic texts that complete an immense cycle of time, enacting the emergence of immanent multiplicity (Schipper and Wang, 1986; Schipper, 1993). Both imperial and Daoist ritual forms work with a variety of written forms, inscribing or revealing the structure of the cosmos.

Local cults work differently, in Feuchtwang's (1992) analysis, employing the (re)distribution of incense and fire to burn simulacra of value (spirit-money) to make a claim about the possibility and efficacy of communication between the god (a deceased human being) and the living community protected by it.[5] A similar collective representation of the continued power and

---

[4] In addition to establishing a specific temporality, imperial ritual works to generate relations of hierarchical encompassment through the centering carried out within ritual action by the emperor and his representatives. See the analysis of the structural and symbolic logic of imperial ritual in Zito (1984; 1994) and Hevia (1994; 1995). Operations upon time are inseparable from relations of power.

[5] This may not be so absolute a distinction, as many cults develop written documentation, from spells and invocations to spirit writing, scriptures, and liturgies. Thus the role of writing in

potential protection of the dead underlies the ancestral cults, but in that case the role of inscription is again crucial (on ancestral tablets, on gravestones, and in lineage genealogies).

All these ritual processes suppress the irreversibility of time by reducing time in different ways to spatial forms (Gil, 1989; chap. 1). In their respective contexts—the imperial court, the altar of heaven, official shrines and altars at the provincial and district levels, the city god temples, the temples of local deities, lineage halls, Three in One temples, and individual homes—they drew individuals into the preparation and performance of rituals in ways that marked and empowered their identities.

The suppression of time is also the institution of a statement of historical meaning. By fixing a source of spiritual power in a biographical/hagiographical past, one could commemorate it while performing the continued expression of its power in the present. Feuchtwang (1992) points out that rituals of local cults depend on two aspects of the collective representation of the continuity between the living and the dead, namely, the protective and the demonic. The unrequited dead in particular are presumed to be ever eager to attack the living. At times, ritual specialists, such as Daoist priests, Buddhist monks, or Three in One masters, must be brought in to exorcise the demonic forces that threaten the community. This is done by recourse to a military metaphor of command, capture, control, and destruction (Lagerwey, 1987a; 1987b). Regardless of whether the spiritual power of the god is felt to be protective or threatening, the collective representation of the deity's power after and over death founds the cult.

Each household is involved in several overlapping ritual spheres based on its membership in territorial subsystems, kinship units, and local cult subsystems (Feuchtwang, 1992). Wilkerson (1995) has explored the economies of debt, rights, and prestations within these partially overlapping ritual circuits. Duara (1988) has developed a typology of forms of social organization for villages in northern China, based on cult and lineage variables, generating what he has termed the cultural nexus of power. The local cults to which households belong often form a localized nested hierarchy, but they usually also extend beyond the immediate locality via pilgrimages to the founding temple of one or more major local cults. Such pilgrimages can be based on division of incense networks originating in the founding temple. These networks need not be parallel to either the administrative spatial hierarchy or the regional marketing structure (Sangren, 1986). Any individual is therefore likely to be involved in different ways in several different cults, and in several different ritual spheres, depending on gender, class, age, and education. One may be involved as either a participant, a member of the audience, or someone included

---

local cults is highly significant. See Schipper (1985), where he argues that ritual masters and spirit mediums perform a vernacular version of rites modeled on (whether parallel or opposed to) classical Daoist liturgy. Schipper also has argued that Daoism can be understood in this context as "the written tradition of popular cults." See Ding and Zheng (1993) for a discussion of the effects of written texts and the official canonization of such sources on local cults.

or excluded from official rites. Each of these cults and ritual traditions contains its own contested historical claims. Faure (1986) has demonstrated that priority in claims to landownership is a crucial dimension of lineage membership, with major consequences for interlineage and intralineage development.

When we examine a local culture over time, we can identify changing ritual orders with complex, shifting institutional arenas, which suggests that any one individual would be simultaneously transfixed by several overlapping ritual orders themselves undergoing vectors of change. As Jacques Le Goff (1980) remarked, there were "as many different collective notions of time in a society as there were different social groups." Given the complexity of individual involvement in multiple social groupings activated by ritual practices, one can also see how any one individual would have been caught up in many different machines for the production of time. Time moves at different speeds, sweeping fragments of individuals and partial understandings along varied trajectories. Initiation into the Three in One adds another set of ritual practices (both group and individual) to the multiple ritual orders any particular individual would be swept up in through the course of everyday life. The Three in One built new ritual machines by assembling parts and pieces of different ritual traditions. These ritual machines generated new temporalities and opened up new spaces. They also produced new power relations within the spaces they occupied and transformed.

The particular coalescence of flows (consistency) that takes place in any given ritual is unique. Thus new ritual forms, or a new balance between ritual forms in a particular period, could present an entirely different set of relations with the surrounding context. Indeed, such historical changes could be quite complete. Similarly, rather than insisting upon any essential nature of the individual, or the a priori status of any particular process of the formation of individual identity, one could view participation in a ritual, or a particular ritual tradition, as an abstract technology of the self.

RITUAL AND ALCHEMY: THE RITE WITHIN

Elsewhere I have referred to Daoism as the alchemy of Chinese society. I also mentioned that most Daoist rituals have at their "secret" core another, internal ritual (Dean, 1993). There is no end to ritual action. The central role of internal alchemy in ritual practice and individual self-cultivation within the Three in One will be examined in chapter 4. Here I would simply like to call attention to Marcel Mauss's remarks on the techniques of the body:

> I don't know whether you have paid attention to what my friend Granet has already pointed out in his great investigations into the techniques of Taoism, its body techniques, and breathing techniques in particular [1930]. I have studied the Sanskrit texts of Yoga enough to know that the same things occur in India. I believe precisely that at the bottom of all our mystical states there are body techniques which we have not studied, but which were studied fully in China and

India, even in very remote periods. . . . I think that there are necessarily biological means for entering into "communication with God." (Mauss, 1979; 122)

Lin Zhao'en developed an elaborate, nine-state process for transcending the self and the void. The Heart Method contains the following nine stages:

The First: "Put the *Gen* [Hexagram] in the Back" (Fixing one's concentration in the back and stilling all thought).

The Second is called the revolution of the heavens. Imitate the *qian* and *kun* [hexagrams] in order to establish the Ultimate.

The Third is called penetrating the passes; [the brightness] penetrates the limbs and apertures to refine the body.

The Fourth: Rest it in Earth and sincerely cultivate humanity in order to form the hidden elixir.

The Fifth: Gather from heaven and earth to collect the drugs.

The Sixth: Coalesce the spirit in the cavity of vital force.

The Seventh: Free yourself from birth and death by embodying heaven and earth.

The Eighth: Transcend heaven and earth to embody the Great Void.

The Ninth: Break up the Void in order to realize the ultimate principle.

These stages are explained in detail in chapter 4. The nine stages are often discussed within the Three in One in terms of three phases: *liben* (initiation, literally "establishing the basis"), *rumen* (entering the gate), and *jize* (attaining the ultimate principles). Each phase places the adherent into a different relation with the cosmos. Initiation opens the way to self-cultivation. "Entering the gate" involves passing through the first several stages and gaining control over inner breath and the visualization of light within the body. "Attaining the ultimate principles" involves passing beyond a sense of self, space, time, form, and the void. The goal of this process is the mystical unity of the heart-mind with the fundamental substance of the universe, which is empty and void, yet beyond differentiation (thus it cannot be characterized as empty or not empty). This inner alchemical tradition is still central to the everyday practice of members of the Three in One today. It is also central to Three in One ritual practice, as will be shown in chapter 6.

PHASES, PLANES, AND LOCAL HISTORY

It is not possible to do more here than summarize in a very preliminary way the development of the Xinghua local culture by proposing a set of phases, marked in each case by an emergent constellation of key ritual practices and institutions.[6] This development involved transformations of the physical and

---

[6] Readers will no doubt feel uncomfortable with the lack of extensive documentation of the historical processes discussed in this chapter, but the inclusion of such sources would have exceeded the limits of this book. For sources, see Dean and Zheng (1995). For further information on some of these issues, see Dean (1993; 1995).

social environment that provided the ground (*arena*) for the contesting of symbols and the performances of cultural (and individual) unity (what might be called *apparatuses of capture*). These phases should not be seen as separate historical periods. Rather, each phase marks the emergence of a new plane of consistency. Each phase opens up new pools of potential that subsist through the other phases, although each new phase involves a new assemblage of forces. Speaking in very general terms, in each phase the center of ritual activity appears to have shifted over time from Buddhist monasteries to lineage halls to popular temples. These institutions developed distinct arenas for the performance of rituals—halls of merit within monasteries, ancestral halls and academies, elaborate temples with large public courtyards and theatrical stages. Yet these arenas and apparatuses build upon one another, enlarging the cultural repertoire of Xinghua local culture, while actualizing a particular constellation of forces, arenas, and collective assemblages at any specific time.

Some evidence for these changes can be drawn from table 1, which shows epigraphical inscriptions from the Xinghua area.[7] Note the preponderance of Buddhist inscriptions in the early centuries, the rise of ancestral hall inscriptions in the fourteenth to sixteenth centuries, and the rapid rise of popular temple inscriptions in the eighteenth to twentieth centuries. Of course, the rise of one sphere of activity does not imply the complete collapse of the others. On the contrary, note the revival of ancestral hall inscriptions in the eighteenth century or the sudden rise in official shrine inscriptions in the fifteenth and sixteenth centuries. Other spheres of ritual activity appear to remain relatively constant over time, such as the Confucian temple inscriptions. Many individuals would have been involved in several spheres simultaneously. A fuller documentation and interpretation of these shifting arenas of ritual activity will have to await further study. What is useful to bear in mind here is the notion that not only did different arenas for ritual activity rise to prominence at different times, effecting shifts in the ritual center of gravity of the local culture at the time, but the rituals performed within these arenas themselves underwent continuous modification.

I have termed these ritual performances "apparatuses of capture"—the capture and temporary consolidation of social, economic, political, and libidinal forces by cultural forms. These changing cultural forms can be understood as transformers, or transducers, constantly modulating forces in society. By examining some of the structurations underlying ritual-events in a specific locale over time, we can disrupt the presumed solidity and immutability of "Chinese culture" and raise the possibility of an approach combining a philosophy of ritual with an archaeology of shifting ritual formations in Chinese popular culture. By examining the spread of the Three in One in the context of long-term transformations in local cultural forms, we can see which cultural resources and trajectories the Three in One attempted to seize hold of, and

[7] The figures given in the chart are only one possible classification of the epigraphical texts in Dean and Zheng (1995), many of which refer to multiple arenas of ritual practice.

TABLE 1
Distribution of Inscriptions by Category over Time

Century	8, 9, 10	11	12	13	14	15	16	17	18	19	20
Confucian Temple	0	2	6	5	7	6	5	4	3	4	0
Official Shrine	1	0	6	5	1	10	15	6	3	6	1
Ancestral Hall	0	0	1	6	9	16	24	3	18	4	3
Academy	0	0	2	0	1	0	5	1	1	7	0
Daoist Belvedere	0	0	1	0	0	1	0	0	1	4	0
Buddhist Siyuan	6	8	5	5	5	4	1	14	7	8	5
Earth-God Altar	0	0	0	0	0	0	3	0	2	8	0
Popular Temple	0	0	6	8	3	2	5	9	19	46	18
3 in 1/Sectarian	0	0	0	0	0	0	0	2	0	5	4
Other	1	0	1	5	3	5	4	1	3	1	4

Source: Dean and Zheng, 1995.

which in turn transformed the Three in One. The very terms "cultural form," "ritual form," and "ritual order" are, however, inadequate to describe the processes at work in a ritual-event. Form implies stasis, whereas ritual-events are a process of becoming. "What is real is the *change of form: form is only a snapshot view of a transition*" (Bergson, 1983: 302).[8]

PHASE ONE

This first phase in the establishment of a Han Chinese presence in the Xinghua area was a piecemeal process involving the founding of Buddhist monasteries in remote settings and isolated settlements by small groups of immigrating surname groups and their dependents and attendants. The Buddhist monasteries gradually cleared lands and established monastic estates. The earliest recorded monastery in the area was the Golden Immortal Monastery, founded in 558. Several Buddhist monasteries would be established in the Tang and under the Min empire (Schafer, 1954). In 568 the Chen dynasty briefly established a district government in Putian. The Sui dynasty reestab-

[8] In an inspired effort to move beyond static conceptions of form and content, Mikhail Bahktin (1990: 256) describes how a "fragment of content" detaches itself from the "unity of nature and the unity of the ethical event of being. . . . [W]hat is detached and . . . irreversible is the event of striving, the axiological tension, which actualizes itself thanks to that without any impediment, and becomes consummated." Guattari (1995) suggests that this irreversible striving is central to the autopoetic process whereby collective assemblages of partial objects and partial subjects create their own collective subjectivities.

lished Putian District in 589 and again in 607 after it had collapsed in the interim. The Tang Putian District was established in 623. The Xinghua Commandery was founded by the Song dynasty in 973.[9]

The early Han settlements in the Xinghua area, perhaps dating as far back as the late Han or Six Dynasties period (Bielenstein, 1959), tended to be high up in narrow valleys within the mountains. Local tradition relates that the eight major surname groups of the Xinghua region immigrated during the Yongjia period of the Six Dynasties. It is more likely that these groups moved in gradually over the early Tang period, after having in many cases first established settlements in the Min River area around Fuzhou (Clark, 1995). Conflict and tension with early inhabitants of the Xinghua area, primarily the She ethnic group, remained a factor into the late Ming and Qing dynasties. Only after having consolidated their hold on the mountain valleys did the Han Chinese settlers gradually expand their settlements to the narrow seacoast. There they began the building of small-scale earthen dikes to protect stretches of mud flats cleared by small groups of people. Only when a large enough number of such minor dikes had been established around the mouth of one of the mountain streams did the possibility arise of linking them into a total irrigation system with a continuous stone dike along the sea with sluice-gates for connected irrigation channels that controlled the flow of water throughout the system. The construction of such irrigation systems was usually the work of government officials responding to requests from groups of single-surname settlers and their dependents. The government of the Min empire and the Northern Song frequently turned to the Buddhist monastic estates in the area, which were efficient economic machines capable of extensive infrastructural construction (see Gernet, 1995). These estates had been active in the building of roads and bridges in the area. They were also directed toward regional irrigation projects. This first phase of the development of the four great Xinghua irrigation systems was marked by the establishment of temples dedicated to the government officials or their representatives responsible for organizing the large irrigation projects. These cults of water deities indicate the central government's strong role in local society. These shrines to the founders of the irrigation systems often received an official government cult.

Local gentry in Putian had begun by this time to look both to the court and to local society as an arena for action. This phase saw the spread of acade-

---

[9] Population figures for the Xinghua area are unreliable, since they often were affected by changes in the tax registration system. The *Putian xianzhi* (1968 reprint of [Qianlong] *Xinghuafu Putian xianzhi* [1758]) provides various figures for the early period: 62,157 households in the Song Taiping Xingguo period; 55,227 in Yuanfeng 3; 72,363 households in the Yuan. Song dynasty households tended to have low populations, generally around 2.4 persons to a household in the Fujian region. The Ming Wanli total population figure given is 148,756. The figure for 1552 (during Lin Zhao'en's lifetime and prior to the pirate invasions) is 166,730. The 1562 figure of 147,316 indicates the effects of the disturbances. Ming population figures are often distorted by complex efforts to avoid exact registration on the tax roles. This problem is even more pronounced in Qing dynasty population figures. Lineage genealogies reveal that whole lineages sometimes managed to register as a single household.

mies and cults to early Lixue philosophers. It was also the phase during which
settlement groups began to modify the ancestral worship system to allow for
the development of lineage halls and localized forms of ancestral worship.
During this phase, however, the majority of such halls were still established
under the guise of Buddhist halls of merit, within which local ancestors could
be worshipped by professionals (Zheng, 1992). There are also records from
this phase of village-based temple festivals, known as *shexi*. One gets a sense
from these records of the role of Buddhist and Daoist rites in village life, and
various mixed formations of local god cults and ancestral ritual.

PHASE TWO

The second phase of the development of the irrigation system, from the late
Southern Song to the mid-Ming, was a phase in which the land opened up by
the initial major reclamation and irrigation efforts became filled up, and conflicts began to develop over the distribution of water and resources within the
system. This phase was characterized by a proliferation of local cults marking
local identity. Many of the early official cults to the water deities now began
to be contested. Early gazetteers and stone inscriptions record the process of
imperial recognition or canonization of a host of local deities. The *Song
Huiyao jigao* records over twenty-four acts of official recognition, canonization, or promotion of local gods in the Xinghua area. Successive gazetteers
provide a total of the presentation of 114 titles to fifty deities within 150 years
from 1107 to 1256, covering the reigns of Song Huizong and Gaozong and
Song Lizong. In Putian District fifty-nine titles were bequeathed to twenty-
three deities; in Xianyou, thirty-seven titles went to seventeen deities, while
for the inclusive unit of Xinghua Prefecture, an additional eighteen titles were
bequeathed to ten deities. This effort to rank and recognize local gods by no
means could contain the process of the expansion of the local pantheon. Beyond this group, many other gods and goddesses are mentioned in the
gazetteers, literati writings, and stone inscriptions from this phase. This is the
first phase for which we have records of multiple village processions (*raojing*).

The government reaction at the beginning of the Ming was a severe effort
to curtail local cults. Certain later gazetteers record discomfort with the proliferation of cults. The Jiajing Xianyou district gazetteer (*Jiajing Xianyou
xianzhi*) claims that many such cults are illegitimate and licentious. The list
in that district gazetteer is sharply reduced from seventeen deities to only six.
This early Ming gazetteer's exclusive attitude may reflect early Ming efforts
to reform and systematize official worship of popular cults. This reformist zeal
led to two efforts to stamp out licentious cults in the area. In 1465 Prefect
Yue Zheng "destroyed licentious cults" and in 1519 Prefect Lei Yinglong "destroyed over four hundred temples" (some accounts state that the total was
eight hundred). Such efforts were nevertheless the exception rather than the
rule. Subsequent gazetteers would revert to a broader set of criteria of legiti-

macy, namely, clear evidence of imperial canonization, inclusion in early local gazetteers, and evidence of widespread and time-honored popular support.

Another sign of the growing independence of local cultural forces in this phase was the seizure of land by lineages and the government from Buddhist monastic estates. This has to do with the evolution of ancestral worship in Southeast China, particularly the rise of a cult of the Fujian founder in addition to the original ancestor buried far away in the central plains of China. New forms of ancestor worship centered around the tombs of the Fujian pioneer ancestor, the house of that local founding ancestor, and, eventually, the establishment of ancestral halls where the lineage founder, the Fujian founder, and other meritorious ancestors were worshipped. Later developments include the proliferation of branch ancestral halls and the inclusion of more and more categories of ancestors. Ancestral halls were openly established in this phase. Many literati composed statements on the acceptability of these breaches with tradition, arguing that ritual arises from the meaning of the acts of worship, and thus transformations in ritual conduct can be justified in terms of intent (*li yi yi qi*). Much of the debate over ancestral worship appears to reflect two phases of immigration into the Xinghua area. The early lineages who had arrived in the Northern Song were challenged by newly arrived lineages in the Southern Song. The former tended to emphasis the viability of extending ancestral worship beyond the classical model, which allowed the worship of only five generations of ancestors put forward by Zhu Xi. Newly arrived and newly successful lineages at first upheld the classical model, but as time went on they too felt constrained by it and also argued for modifications.

As these lineages began to expand, they became the principal agents of major land reclamation and irrigation maintenance. A good example of this is the extensive Mulan irrigation system, which was begun by Lady Qian (who was drowned in the midst of her labors) and completed by Lord Li. Temples were erected to these figures near the top of the dam, along with a temple to fourteen families who had participated in the construction. The subsequent history of the irrigation system revolves around the suits and countersuits between the descendants of Lord Li and those of the fourteen families over who should have what proportion of control over the tax-free lands dedicated to the maintenance of the system (*Mulanbi zhi*).

The government and the lineages began to take over Buddhist monastic landholdings. By the end of the Ming Buddhist landholdings had declined from 30 percent in the Song to a mere 3 percent (Tian, 1990). The major infrastructure of the area had been completed, and the government now viewed the Buddhist monasteries as a drain on social and fiscal resources. The lineages had by then openly established their own ancestral halls and no longer felt a need to mask their breach of traditional ancestral worship restrictions under a Buddhist robe (Dean and Zheng, 1993). Abandoned by both of the major forces in society, the Buddhist monasteries lost morale and rapidly declined. A stream of bonzes flowed into local society and frequently found their way into temples devoted to local gods. These communal temples usually had rather small endowments, just enough to cover annual birthday festivities and the meager upkeep of a resident temple-keeper.

The changes in the fortunes of Buddhist monasteries, lineages, official shrines, and popular temples during this phase were all strongly affected by the reforms of the first Ming emperor. The effects of his policies were felt for many years and perhaps merit consideration as a separate phase in local cultural development. His efforts to establish the *lijia* system of local control and mutual responsibility and to standardize the official cult of the altar of the soil and the grain, the city god, and the register of sacrifices to government-approved orthodox cults had a strong impact on local cultic expression. He also forced the reorganization of large Buddhist monasteries and enlisted Buddhist monks and Daoist priests into the state bureaucracy. Yet within fifty years of these reforms, many of the official altars to the soil and the harvest had been co-opted into a local pattern of expanding centers of ritual activity.

What this suggests is that although the *lijia* system of the early Ming was gradually disintegrating, the *she* that had been officially founded in the administrative subcantons or *tu* levels continued to provide an organizing framework for local social and cultural self-organization. The *she* began to mutate from a government shrine into a fundamental building block of the local temple system. This process of mutation can be seen in the process of the founding of new villages or the branching off of new villages from earlier ones. These new villages were often still registered under the original *li* name. Nonetheless, as population expanded, new settlements were formed. These new settlements sought to found branch *she* altars as the symbolic basis of their new territory, but many, for one reason or another, were not able to do so.

In much the same way that the classical model of ancestral worship was stretched and appropriated to allow for the evolution of lineage halls worshipping an expanded set of founding ancestor, Fujian pioneer ancestor, and then any number of successful ancestors and branch founders, so too the official system of worship at the altar of the soil was also transformed into a vector of local cultural differentiation. Other in-migrating people, especially those Minnan residents escaping extensive pirate raiding in the Ming, brought along their local gods. These gods were sometimes jointly worshipped with the gods of the local *she* in larger temples called *miao* or *she-miao*. Over time, the importance of these *she-miao* expanded. A hierarchy of ever more magnificent temples developed: *miao* (temple), *gong* (palace), *dian* (grand hall), *guan* (belvedere). A single large temple might house several *she* and over a dozen gods. People in the Putian plains began to conceive of their *she* and *miao* as part of wider spiritual precincts known as *jing*. To this day villagers give their addresses in terms that range from *she* to *miao* to *gong* to *jing* to *li*.[10] The level of *jing* is particularly significant. As a boundary defined by re-

---

[10] Several formularies in the comprehensive list of Three in One documents entitled the *Wubentang guitiao* call for the initiate to indicate their address in terms of province, district, *li*, township, *jing* (spiritual territory), and Three in One *tang* (Hall). See appendix 5 for the contents of this collection.

ligious processions between several villages, it represents the evolution of a local conception of spatial identity. It may have evolved from Daoist notions, for this is the term used in Daoist ordination certificates. In any case, we sense here a complex layering of historical and institutional arenas of identity, changing over time but retaining some connection to their earlier meanings.[11]

Phase Three

The third phase begins in the mid-Ming and extends to the mid-Qing. This is the phase in which Lin Zhao'en and his disciples established the Three in One. In the Xinghua region, the reclamation of land from the sea continued, along with the expansion of the irrigation systems. The phase was marked by the consolidation of lineage control and growing competition between and within local cults. This was also a phase characterized by the spread of commercialization. Fujian merchants had begun to pursue interregional coastal and international trade in the Song dynasty. Periodic Ming official bans on trade had a drastic effect on the local economy. Nonetheless, interregional trade, whether overland or coastal, was an important feature of mid-Ming Xinghua life. Xinghua is situated between the provincial capital Fuzhou to the north and the great port city of Quanzhou to the south. Although the Quanzhou port declined in the Ming (Skinner, 1985), there can be little question that widespread processes of commercialization had begun to deeply transform the Fujian economy over this phase (Rawski, 1972). This phase saw the rapid rise of the cult of Mazu, Goddess of the Sea, whose mother temple is just off the Putian mainland on Meizhou island (Li, 1979; Xiao et al., 1987; Jiang, 1992). The spread of her cult indicates the expansion of coastal trade, first along the Fujian coast and then into southeastern China and Southeast Asia.

The spread of commercialization had several unintended effects. Social tension between absentee landlords, managerial landlords, tenants, and bondservants would explode into open conflict over this phase. Social mobility expanded as wealth brought new powers to merchants. The examination system was unable to absorb increasing numbers of candidates into the civil service. A growing population of literate men and women had to look elsewhere for employment, entertainment, and enlightenment. As social dislocation increased, fundamental questions were raised about the nature of society, the cosmos, and role of morality. These issues took form in the debates between

---

[11] For further information on these topics, see Dean (1997). As an aside, it is interesting to note that on Taiwan from the seventeenth century onward large-scale landlords sponsored the opening up of swaths of land and settled them with migrants. The Qing taxation system did not require the imposition of the *Li* subadministrative territorial unit (except in the Penghu Islands). Instead, it used a cash basis in land relations, a more capitalist set of relations, without the historical layering and complexity (also apparent in the realm of lineage development and gentry culture). This means that it is easy to ready *she* (tudigong) on Taiwan simply as the lowest level of a one-dimensional hierarchical scale, rather than in relation to overlapping and contradictory institutional developments and historical conceptions.

Ming official interpretations of the Cheng-Zhu school of Neo-Confucianism and the school of the Heart/Mind, led by Wang Yangming. Wang opposed the orthodox approaches which advocated a tireless search for principle in external things. In its place, he proposed innate knowledge of the good (*liangzhi*), arguing that all men have the potential to become sages. Many of his followers, such as the Taizhou school radicals, lectured to crowds in the marketplace and at temple fairs.

As the Ming population expanded, the government found itself increasingly incapable of maintaining the same level of control over local services. Defense became a pressing problem as the coastal area of Fujian became a ripe target for massive pirate raids. The raids only intensified, and Putian and Xianyou were sacked several times in the late 1500s. In the course of this devastation, the major lineages of the area were severely damaged (Vermeer, 1990).

In this phase the expanding population of the Xinghua region began to put impossible demands on the local ecological/cultural system. Paradoxically, at that same moment a new systemwide center emerged in each irrigation system to resolve conflicts that would have torn these systems apart and brought down mutual destruction, while at the same time local, village-based ritual took on new comprehensiveness as well. During this phase a nested hierarchy of temple processions developed in many of the irrigation systems in the area. The temple committee of the highest temple in each irrigation system, for example, the Eastern Peak Temple of the Jiangkou Jiuliyang irrigation system, developed mechanisms for the mutual preservation of the system. Aside from mechanical distributions of responsibility with collective adjudication, the symbolism of the hierarchy of processions establishes a systemwide cultural emblem of identity and individuation. The intense struggle over water rights in the coastal irrigated area demanded some internal mechanism for adjudication short of all-out lineage warfare. In the Jiangkou irrigation system, the Donglaisi[12] was put in charge of the irrigation system. The members of this temple committee were drawn from the directors of the Belvedere of the Eastern Peak. The latter temple had been established in the Yuan but rebuilt in the Ming. From this time onward it functioned as the highest level of the interlocking temple networks in the area. All of the temples in the Jiangkou plain joined in the five-day procession of the Belvedere of the Eastern Peak each lunar New Year. These village temples also participated in local processions between associated or neighboring villages. They also held processions in their own village. Thus, each of the temples of the nine villages that had gradually formed into the neighborhoods of Jiangkou Town first held a procession in its own corner of the town, then went on a joint procession around the town with the other eight temples, and finally joined in the regional procession led by the Belvedere of the Eastern Peak. When social relations in Jiangkou dis-

---

[12] The Donglaisi is now a temple-monastery complex with adjoining shrines dedicated to Daoist, Buddhist, local, and Three in One gods. This is still the central coordination spot for the booking of theatrical groups who perform at the many temples of all the villages in the area on the birthdays of the gods.

integrated into open conflict, the combatants were made to stand before the banner of the Belvedere of the Eastern Peak and speak the truth. The decision of the committee was irrevocable.

This phase can be seen as involving the development of local forms of self-government, financing and regulating of local infrastructure and cultural activity. The single-whip tax reform, the curbing of overseas trade, the rise of piracy in the area, coastal evacuations, the decline of the major lineages, and the growth of population all led to the gradual abdication by the central government of concrete support of local infrastructure and social regulation. Into this vacuum arose a midlevel gentry formation, capable of mobilizing major irrigation repair projects not because they were deputized by the government to do so, but because of their networks of contacts within and across the various irrigation systems.

Once the pirates finally were cleared away, partly by supreme efforts on the part of Qi Jiguang (1528–1567), the empire was already on its last legs, and the Qing conquest of China had begun. The infamous coastal evacuation of 1660–1680 forced villages to move inland some 50 li at certain points along the coast, further disrupting the already battered lineages in the area (Vermeer, 1990). After peace was enforced and the ban lifted, the remnant lineages scrambled to reclaim their lands. Much, however, had already changed. The grand lineages were destroyed, and the effort to rebuild the lineages was forced to proceed along contractual lines, rather than relying on hereditary privilege. The rapid commercialization of the coastal area, which had initially been exploited by the lineages as a means of diversification of their capital holdings, now provided the ground rules for the reconstruction of social relations in this area (Zheng, 1992).

This fundamental shift had a number of unanticipated consequences. Lineages discovered that they were transforming into economic partnerships rather than highly hierarchical organizations. Lineage landholdings could not be controlled by customary law to the degree that had been possible before the widespread commercialization of property relations. Minor lineages were able to negotiate land purchases with increasingly independent households within the disrupted lineages. The minor lineages also began to form alliances among themselves against the major local lineages. Temples dedicated to local cults emerged as the best place for this kind of supralineage activity. Even the major localized lineages in the Putian area discovered that their main ancestral halls were no longer adequate to the complex new social relations within and beyond the lineage. They too established major temples to local gods, often right next door to their main ancestral halls.

What social possibilities did the popular temples embody and provide in late Ming and early Qing Fujian? In contrast to lineage organization, where hierarchical principles are intrinsic to internal organization, popular cult temples develop nonhierarchical, transverse flows of communication and coordination outside of government lines of interference. These flows are embodied in incense-division networks, which operate with relatively flexible and nonhierarchical principles. The temples in the network all acknowledge the precedence of the founding temple from which most took incense to found their own temple. Other temples in the network can spawn lower-level temples as well. However, all temples in the network can return to the founding temple and are treated on an equal basis. Status within the system is won by competitive gift-giving, and donations are carefully recorded and carved on steles lining the walls of the founding temples (Dean, 1993; chap. 2).

In addition to providing a versatile regional networking potential, popular cult temples also took on new dimensions within village social organization. Membership in a temple is theoretically open to all in the community, in marked contrast to the kinship ties underlying lineage orders. Membership in a temple committee, moreover, commanded considerable social prestige. Temple committee members were often called upon to contribute large amounts of personal income to the activities of the temple. This sort of personal sacrifice was repaid in social standing and a seat at the central decision-making body of the community. Here again, commercial prosperity or merchant status was no obstacle to membership. Temple property was considered to be communally owned, and temple activities were expected to be paid for by everyone in the village on a per capita basis. The stone inscriptions gathered in the Putian region also provide evidence of literati being brought into the sphere of temple committees, either as sponsors of restorations and rituals or as consultants in matters of ritual, or for communications with the government, or as full-fledged members of the board. This latter role was often assumed after retirement from office when the official was back in his hometown.

As temples became the preeminent decision-making center of village life, they began to take over responsibilities for social services, including irrigation, in the area under their influence. Of course, as Prasenjit Duara (1988) has shown for North China, in some villages the temple organizations were dominant, while in others lineage organizations remained most influential. Generally speaking, there are three basic types of social organization discernible in the Jiangkou area. In one type the village is primarily a single-surname village. A lineage hall remains but generally is in complete disrepair. There is, however, an active temple. Tasks and roles within the temple are determined on the basis of rotation and priority of marriage. Special rituals for different gods that are worshipped are assigned by divination at the beginning of the year. In effect, every adult male in the village directly participates in a ritual and thereby reproduces the symbolic sphere of the common pantheon. A second type of social organization includes multiple lineage villages or neighborhoods that share a common temple. In this case, respective lineages of residential sectors are represented in the temple by a distinct god, and those groups take responsibility for the rituals and sacrifices and theater performed on the birthdays of their gods. A third type of social organization, more common in the older, mountainous region, includes multiple-lineage villages in multivillage alliances, with a major temple representing the coalition.

If membership in temple committees and multivillage alliances was based primarily on territorial considerations (rights to landownership—which Faure has shown to be crucial to lineage membership as well), participation in organizations such as the Three in One represented a different associational principle—translocal, voluntary association. The Three in One quickly developed its own branches and systems of division of incense in this phase, expanding even during the early years of the Qing takeover. Midway through this phase of Xinghua culture, the Three in One fell under Qing government suspicion, along with several other religious groups.

PHASE FOUR

The fourth phase, from the end of the Qing through till Republican times, saw the disintegration of the system, and a descent into widespread feuding. Feuding parties, made up of broad coalitions of villages known as White, Black, or Red Banners, retained a connection to various cults and included a range of ritual activities. Martial arts self-defense corps, secret societies, and multitemple alliances that divided along the segments of the irrigation system all evolved ritual forms while struggling within a collapsing social and governmental order.

Philip Kuhn (1990) has pointed to the soul-stealing scare of the Qianlong reign as one of the last spasms of autocratic control in the Qing dynasty. This is exemplified in the government attitude to the Three in One at that time, in terms of both local prohibitions and the order for the destruction of Lin Zhao'en's writings by the editors of the *Siku quanshu*. The decline of state power, intensified commercialization of society, the cumulative effect of long-term local militarization, population pressure, and the decline of the large lineages and religious institutions all led by the turn of the nineteenth century to the formation of new arenas for the production of truth at the local level.

The geographically determined nested hierarchies of temple systems that had developed within the irrigation systems of the Putian plains now divided up into a patchwork of multiple village alliances. In general, the pattern was one of several small single- or multiple-surname villages forming an alliance to withstand higher-order single-lineage alliances. Both groups established popular temples as bases for their internal cohesiveness. The feuds were "modes of regulating conflict in which the principle parts are played by the accuser and the accused, according to recognized rules, and not by a judicial authority" (Asad, 1993: 90). Under these circumstances, feuding becomes an end in itself, a shifting marker of social relations. Recall that the usual term for the festivals of the local gods is *yinshen saihui* (*competitive* assemblies to entice the gods). Much of the tension between different clusters of feuding coalitions of villages can be seen as forms of ritualized violence and competitive ritual excess.

The only time the feuding alliances could be unified was in opposition to the state. During the Taiping Rebellion, local groups organized the Small

Knives revolt in Xiamen and the Lin Jun revolt in central Fujian. Lin Jun was able to coordinate with Xinghua Black and White Banner alliances to lay siege to Putian and then capture Xianyou city for a short time. The government turned to local gentry such as Chen Chiyang, who organized local militias against the insurgents. Chen Chiyang later organized a massive repair of all four of the major Putian irrigation systems. He is representative of the new powers taken on by local gentry at the end of the Qing dynasty. Other local gentry played significant roles as mediators between the government and the ritually defined alliances of villages. One such figure was Zhang Qin, the last Putian *jinshi*, who was called to Beijing to assist in Yuan Shikai's enthronement rites. Zhang was a tireless spokesman for the Three in One and a respected mediator of disputes within the branches of the movement.

A wider view of the data on feuding coalitions in this phase would contrast the irrigated plains with the rocky coastal areas and with the hilly, mountainous areas unreached by irrigation. In this view a picture of widening class differences could be worked into our discussion. Based on differences in access to irrigation and other ecological factors, these three areas developed widely varied social organizations over time. In the case of the Hugong mountain region bordering the Nanyang irrigation system to the south, local forms of popular religion, especially Ming loyalist forms of so-called secret religions (in this region arguably an open dimension of popular religion), were an important register of local discontent. In the last years of the Qing and in the Yuan Shikai era, this area was the base for a rebellion led by a local figure who called himself the Sixteenth Emperor. On two occasions his forces sacked Putian City. These groups became involved in local feuding and in multivillage alliances as well. Although further analysis remains to be done, it appears that the "Sixteenth Emperor" received organizational support from the "closed-door" religious groups that were widespread in the area.

PHASE FIVE

A fifth phase, beginning with the formation of the People's Republic and the subsequent campaigns against religion ("feudal superstition") culminating in the Cultural Revolution and the post-Mao reinvention of tradition, continues to this day. It is still too early to determine the central ritual forms of this phase, but the evidence of the last ten to fifteen years suggests that a brief phase of revolutionary political ritual form is giving way increasingly to a reassertion of traditional forms, in an entirely new context.

This fifth phase in the local cultural history of the Xinghua region is already upon us, with powerful flows unleashed by the implosion of the state, the resurgence of "tradition," and the deterritorializing impact of multinational capitalism. The infrastructure of the irrigation systems, buttressed during the 1950s and 1960s, is now under attack. Deforestation, industrial pollution, an explosion in construction, and a breakdown of command structures all are putting impossible demands on the ecology of the area. Yet, simultaneously, village-level and, increasingly, regional ritual systems are being restored. According to a survey of several hundred villages in the irrigated Putian plains, the average village has six temples, each housing on average fifteen deities. Something like 45 days of ritual performances take place on average in each village every year. Some villages hold over 250 days of theater and ritual a year. Children in rural Putian have now reached adolescence in a world marked increasingly by temple festivals and ritual performance of cultural difference. Of course, these same years have seen the rapid expansion of multinational capitalism into Southeast China. It is still too early to discern the boundaries, or the significance, of the collision of flows at work in this phase. We can only begin to map the process of the melting of some powerful institutions, the sedimentation of attitudes and identities induced through repeated rituals, and the lines of tension in play in the contesting of the value and legality of these ritual forms.

Each of the phases briefly outlined above involves a different set of relationships among the elements of the local culture: between the central or local government and the locality; among the Buddhist monastic estates, the lineages, and the popular cults; between the communities living along the segments of the irrigation system; between the rival or parallel ritual traditions; among the gentry, the government, and the commoners; between the inside and the outside; between the forces circulating through the regions, some captured, some translated, some intensified, and others diverted. Each phase was marked by a new set of central arenas with their own developing ritual forms—official shrines and village festivals in the first phase; ancestral halls, contested cults, and differentiated processions in the second; hierarchical processions involving large segments of the irrigation system in the third phase, along with the transcendence of lineage structures by popular cult temple systems marked in some areas by village-based rituals of collective spirit medium training; a patchwork of lineage feuds and secret religions and secret societies constituted by discrete ritual forms in the fourth phase. The fifth, most recent phase has seen the rapid reconstruction of temple systems and a much slower rebuilding of lineages, along with the increasing impact of transnational capitalism.

Each phase involved the development of apparatuses of capture or individuation, such as various rituals within different arenas with multiple levels of ritual interaction. They also engendered a discursive practice in the textual production of local literati, forever reinterpreting classical practice in light of local variations. Confucian ritualists, Daoist priests, Buddhist monks, Three in One adherents, marionettists, and other ritual specialists, along with playwrights and other writers, similarly forever reinterpreted local cults and practices and the utterances of spirit mediums in terms of "classical" or "universal" models. We need to grasp the forces underlying the production of these documents, which themselves acted as utterances that played an immediate political role in local life in different phases. Most of these discourses developed around or within new ritual practices and contributed to new forms of authorized thought and behavior. In the realm of material culture, builders, stone carvers, artists, actors, and cooks also actively participated in the elaboration of their local culture.

Each phase of Xinghua local culture takes on its form and consistency from different kinds of highly charged festivals, replete with powerful forces sweeping through the community and the bodies of the participants. These ritual-events need to be analyzed on a case-by-case basis to examine the flow of affects and intensities circulating within them. Ritual form may be the leading element in the channeling of affect (intensity and sensation) in the elaboration of local culture. These minglings of bodies with physical and supernatural forces proceed by phases. These phases are linked not dialectically, but through a process of self-organization. Self-organization leads to the channeling of flows, which over time leads to sedimentation in more or less supple structures, in some cases leading to rigidification in long-lasting institutions (political hierarchies, power-monopolizing lineages). Yet even rigid structures slowly flow, can mutate, or become re-incorporated into new self-organizing processes (DeLanda, 1992). The phases outlined above indicate different mechanisms of individuation at work, shaping particular bodies and subjectivities. This suggests that individual subjectivities are constructed in relation and in reaction to the forces moving through the environmental and sociocultural fields. These forces are gathered into particularly intense relations in the course of those rituals that dominate specific phases. Analysis of the channeling of affect in ritual can therefore assist in mapping the processes and phases of local cultural self-differentiation. The transitions from one phase to another are moments of significant systemwide hesitation before dangerous bifurcations. They are not teleologically determined, dialectically impelled, or logically necessary. Lines of flight appear all the time, and bifurcations lead to distinctly different formations. Rituals machines phase in and out, modulating a growing pool of potential for the reinvention of ritual forms and the channeling of human and cosmic forces.

THE SYNCRETIC FIELD

Diagrammatic flowcharts could be drawn of the field of forces (the pool of potential) active in each of the different phases of Xinghua local culture, *or across all of them*. A diagrammatic overview of the syncretic field of potential opened up by the Three in One *across the phases* of Xinghua local culture might be mapped in the following way: An irregularly shaped, multidimensional force-field is opened up around and between the polar attractors of *sheng* (Confucian sagehood) and *ling* (spiritual power) by the attraction and mutual repulsion of those centers. This force-field is stretched between the limits set by Confucian processes or apparatuses (the Confucian machine) and shamanic ecstatic practices (the shamanic machine). The *sheng* center of attraction is characterized by forces of fusion that manifest in the arenas of the nested hierarchy of the local cultural system—the *miao, gong,* and *dian* (temples, "palaces," and "grand halls"). The *ling* center of attraction is characterized by fission, pulling forces toward the *she* (altar of the soil), the smallest communal unit. A vertical, transversal, territorializing line connects the hierarchical cluster of units with the localized territorial units, constantly struggling to regather the local altar/community into the nested hierarchy. Certain lines of flight nonetheless emerge out this line, accelerated by passing close by the *ling* center of attraction (the irruption of shamanic possession). A second horizontal line of deterritorialization crosses the field, composed of capitalist flows (homogenized consumer culture), nationalist flows (modern nation state and citizenship), and communist flows (cultural revolution). A complex knot of lines forms on the syncretic field in the vicinity of the *sheng* center of attraction. This is the knot of interiorization, self-cultivation, inner alchemy. Lines extend from this knot to Buddhist apparatuses (Three in One inner alchemy makes explicit links to Buddhist meditation and cosmology).[13] The syncretic field is made irregular by the pressure of formations such as the local lineages, the irrigation system, and the varying pressures of supralineal hierarchies linking the region to the imperial government. These formations set the limits within which the syncretic field can move or expand. Of course, many lines link these formations with points on the syncretic field.[14]

This diagrammatic flowchart of the syncretic field of potential should not be conceived of as a two-dimensional, structural model. Rather, it is multidimensional: a constantly changing flowchart of a transforming force-field. Not only the centers of attraction, but all the various arenas and apparatuses and centers or nuclei of attraction that compose the field generate different dimensions. Within the multidimensional space opened up by the syncretic field, various strata overlay one another. These are the strata (spaces or planes) of the earth, of territory, of networks, and of collective experimentation. Specific arenas can be located on different strata, although many lines link arenas from stratum to stratum: earth god shrines on the stratum of the earth, lineage halls and Confucian temples and official shrines on the stratum of territory, popular cult temple systems on the stratum of networks, Three in One halls on the stratum of collective experimentation.[15] These strata interpene-

[13] The Buddhist monastic estates themselves had gone from being the machine that opened up the Xinghua region to a beyond within. Now a marginalized group absorbed into Chinese society, they had nonetheless managed to make their ritual machines central to ancestral worship and communal expiation of the unworshiped dead (*pudu*); see Teiser (1988).

[14] The multidimensional field opened up by Daoism overlaps in many respects the syncretic field of the Three in One. A comparison of ritual techniques indicates, however, that the Three in One altar and ritual practice (including visualizations) represent a considerable simplification and streamlining of the complexities of Daoist ritual technique. Thus the Daoist field would involve a far more involved intensive realm, and more complex knotting in relation to other formations. The emphasis within the Three in One was on the routinization and regularization of ritual practice, inner alchemy, and everyday moral behavior. See chapter 6 on ritual traditions.

[15] These spaces/strata are discussed further in the conclusion.

trate one another, so specific ritual apparatuses active within particular arenas work simultaneously on different levels.

It is crucial to note that each Three in One ritual-event *actualizes* the syncretic field of potential in a *singular event* by folding the entire field into itself and redistributing it in a new way.[16] The multitude of ritual-events of the Three in One combine into a vector of change, carrying the syncretic field of potential forward into new actualizations and new configurations. The diagram is not a structural model of reversible codes, or a model of possible formations. The ritual-event actualizes the syncretic field of potential. Without the ritual-event, the diagram has no existence.

RITUAL AND CULTURAL DIFFERENCE

This flowchart of shifting phasings in the ecological-individuating apparatuses of the cultural development of the Putian plains suggests a break with the traditional, static, homological model of the role of ritual in Chinese culture. In that model, imperial ritual is the model of modeling, and the principle of homology descends from the court to the fief to the family. Kinship ritual is presumed to be modeled on imperial court ritual. The government is presumed to work through institutional homologies via the ritual sacrifices at the alters of soil and grain of each district, the city god temples, and the shrines to officially recognized and canonized local deities. Imperial ritual modeled and performed principles of hierarchical encompassment. Yet many features of local geography and evolving local cultural power relations determined the ways in which this system of homology would be incorporated and co-opted by local cultures. This is more than saying that every homology of the center at the peripheries runs the risk of achieving too great a local independence and striving for a life beyond the limits of a copy. Rather, this view challenges the scope of the homological imperial model (and its easy acceptance in a West determined to demonstrate the passivity and abjectness of Chinese culture). To challenge such a fundamental principle of both the Chinese discourse of *li* and the common Western model of Chinese ritual is to raise the possibility of a multivocal understanding of Chinese culture from below. Rather than seeing all local cultures at all times rising to a common level of unity in a vision of inevitable centrality of the cosmic role of the Chinese emperor, perhaps we can imagine a vast variety of locally rooted and constantly changing conceptions of cosmos and individuality, rising out of local and immediate contests of power and metamorphoses of bodies. This does not mean that the cosmos looks different according to where you are situated in it, as in functionalist readings of Chinese religion, but rather that the cosmos itself is constructed and subject to change, along with the individual, and that the changing set of

[16] This process can be visualized drolly as in animated claymation, where figures are constantly reabsorbed into a blob of clay from which new figures are generated and redistributed.

perspectives on a changing cosmos can never be encompassed in a single system.

When we look at the culture of the Putian plains in its development over time, we are struck by the differences from and the similarities to something like the *negara* of Bali, described so poetically by Clifford Geertz (1980). Geertz describes a theater state, where the performance of rituals of competitive prestige constructs and circulates political power. He contrasts this form of political organization with the patrimonial state, the manorial state, or the despotic state of the Asiatic mode of production. The latter inevitably recalls images of the hydraulic empire of Karl Wittfogel (1957), and the model of imperial control at the rural level sketched out by his student, Xiao Gongquan (Hsiao, 1960). Several authors have demonstrated the important and long-term role of the state in major irrigation projects in the Yellow River, Yangze River, and Tongting Lake regions. In the Xinghua area a wide range of levels of government involvement and forms of local control was manifested in varied modes of ritual construction of local power relations. In the Xinghua area there was no simple answer to the politics of the irrigation system, and local communities were neither as smooth a category of sluice-gates in the flow of ritually constructed power as in Geertz's model of Bali, nor as rigid and isolated as the terror-stricken villages of Wittfogel's model, quaking in the shadow of the despot. Instead, the communities themselves transformed over time in relation to each other, to the irrigation system as a whole, and to the state and its representatives.

Other scholars have described nested hierarchies of temple networks in Chinese communities (Sangren, 1986). In the Xinghua region, the profusion of gods provokes another set of questions. What were the ideological ramifications of such abundance? The gods worshiped in the different temples appear to be drawn from a common set, a locally defined pantheon, some Daoist in origin, others local deities, others fairly recent fabrications like Sun Wukong, Ju Bajie, and members of the Yang Jiajiang. Local Daoist priests, marionettists, playwrights, and literati had played a part in elaborating the complex mythology linking these figures together.

Daoist and other ritual specialists and knowledgeable writers had played a key role in composing scriptures for the local deities and recent additions to the popular pantheon. These scriptures share standardized features, usually revealing the local deities' esoteric identity as one of the higher emanations of the Dao. They also rehearse the legend of the god, usually in the dramatic frame of an interview before the Heavenly Worthy of Primordial Commencement (Yuanshi Tianzun). The god's miracles and otherworldly promotions, posts, and powers are detailed with care (see Ding and Zheng, 1993). As we will see below, the ritual specialists of the Three in One have preserved many such scriptures dedicated to popular gods and may well have composed some of them. Much of this material finds its way into the abundant local ritual theater repertoire, which has separate genres for the ritual repayment of vows, for exorcistic rituals designed to ward off children's measles, for the festival of the hungry ghosts, and for marriages and celebrations of longevity (Dean, 1993). The material is reworked again in the spells, chants, and invocations taught to the young mediums in initiation ceremonies. Literati embellish the columns and lintels of temples with antithetical couplets (*duilian*) that draw upon this material. Frescoes reproduce the legends on the walls of the temples. Stone inscriptions in the temples provide a lasting testimonial to the god's power. Songs and stories of the gods circulate among the people. Divinatory poems of the gods bring them into interaction with individuals seeking advise about every aspect of day-to-day existence. Spirit-medium-produced spirit writing allows the gods to continue to tell their own stories, and to continue to add new revelations. Most importantly, the gods themselves are carried through the streets on their birthdays. Most temples in the Xinghua area hold either a Daoist ritual or a Three in One ritual, with theater, and a procession for a god at least once a month, not counting the major festivals of the year.

Clearly, a rich knowledge of the legends and interconnections of the gods is instilled in the minds of the residents of the Xinghua area through their strong, multiple ties to the temples and rituals of their culture. The common pantheon provides a symbolic sphere of unity despite the constant divisiveness over water rights. At the very least, the local ritual calendar is well-known to everyone in the area. In the Jiangkou area, the nested hierarchy of temple networks within the community works with this shared cultural knowledge by placing the Rensheng Dadi, Great Emperor of Humane Life, god of the Eastern Peak, and among the highest of the gods in the local pantheon, at the center of the most all-encompassing procession around the entire plain.

Unique rituals were also developed locally. Daoist priests in the Jiangkou area wrote liturgies for an elaborate set of rites of ordination for spirit mediums connected to local temples. These mediums were in fact trained by elder spirit mediums, not by Daoists. Nevertheless, the Daoists made themselves central to the process by issuing certificates at the conclusion of the training, and by inducing the new mediums' first public trance. Another set of examples includes the elaboration of Daoist liturgies and rites to accompany local cults to the Measles Headquarters, dedicated to Zhang Gong and Chen Jinggu. Similar combinations of human theater or marionette theater and Daoist liturgy were developed around rites of thanksgiving, requiem services, exorcisms of plague demons, and the Mulian cycle in the Pudu (feast for the hungry ghosts), which is celebrated in the Xinghua region not at the usual time in the seventh lunar month (Zhongyuan pudu—7/15), but on the fifteenth of the tenth lunar month (Xiayuan pudu), at the Festival of the Lower Prime. The entire range of Three in One ritual, examined in chapters 4 and 6, is a remarkable instance of the elaboration of a ritual tradition within a local culture.

We are dealing here with the central media and modes of communication and creation of the local popular culture. This is not an unchanging, self-contained system, but an open-ended, continuously evolving cultural network employing a great variety of textual and ritual media.[17] Indeed, one could argue that toward the end of the Qing dynasty, the ecological limits of the system were surpassed, due to extreme population pressure. At that point, villages divided up into a set of feuding alliances, known as the Black Banner and the White Banner alliance. Yet even in this descent into generalized feuding, the alliances were organized around the temples, with the White Banner associated with Mazu and the Black Banner with Zhang Gong. Clearly, however, the worship of the popular pantheon was no longer providing an avenue of resolution of social conflict. For the current phase as well, a closer examination of the spaces of local cultural production, the forces at work in that production, and the media (texts, bodies, stones, music, theater) swept up into the production will lead to greater understanding of rural popular culture in China.

In general one can suggest that a close examination of rural popular culture, both in traditional times and to a surprising extent even today, reveals cultural forms built around religious rituals and ritual arenas (monasteries, ancestral halls, cult temples) engaged in ceaseless strategies of contesting local histories. There are countless instances of the popular appropriation of imperial codes or ritual codes or hagiographic codes for purposes of local self-definition. The transformations of the Three in One ritual tradition, as it interacted with different social contexts and developed in different ways, are an example of a vector of cultural transformation. Similarly, the elaboration of a complex local pantheon with its own ritual traditions in the Xinghua region should be seen as paradoxically both the evolution of a local unity and the successful attainment of cultural difference.

[17] See Cedzich (1995) for an example of complex transformations within a single cult.

The Apotheosis of Lin Zhao'en

LORD OF THE THREE IN ONE

The Lord of the Teachings is named Lin (taboo name) Zhao'en. His personal name is Mao xun. His courtesy name is Longjiang (Dragon River). His Daoist name is *Zi guzi* (he who makes himself into a valley). Late in his life he attained enlightenment. Thereupon he called himself *Hunxu shi* (Master Chaotic Void) and *Wushi shi* (Master of No-beginning). His students first called him *Sanjiao xiansheng* (Master of the Three Teachings). Later they called him *Sanyi jiaozhu* (Lord of the Three in One). They also called him *Xiawunishi Daotongzhongyi Sanjiao dushi da zongshi* (Master Xiawuni, Great Patriarch and Great Savior of the World, the One who is in the Center of the line of the Three Teachings).

Thus begins the *Sanyijiaozhu Xiawuni Linzi benxing shilu* (The true record of the activities of Master Lin, Xiawuni, Lord of the Three in One [hereafter *True Record*, or *TR*]). This account provides a year-by-year description of the activities of Lin Zhao'en from his birth in 1517 until his death in 1598. The book was written by his chosen successor, Lu Wenhui (1564–1618), known as the First Transmitter, edited by the Second Transmitter, Chen Zhongyu (1598–1655), and revised and printed in 1655 by the Third Transmitter, Dong Shi (1624– ca. 1688).[1]

In the verse of Lu Wenhui:

The veins of the Way always transmit the truth
On the Black Rock of Eastern Mountain a Unicorn appeared
Out of Chaos comes the (third) five hundred dragon tree assembly of Maitreya
 Buddha
Confucius, Laozi, Śākyamuni all join in one body.

(*TR* 3a)

What did this extraordinary being look like? According to the preface of the *True Record:*

The Lord of the Teaching's appearance was severe, full of spirit, and outstanding. His eyes both revealed and concealed. The left was a tortoise and the right a

---

[1] Biographical information on Lu Wenhui, Chen Zhongshu, and Dong Shi himself is given by Dong Shi in an appendix to the *True Record* (Taipei Three in One temple 1964 reprint of a 1939 Xiangyang Academy edition of this work, completed in 1655, pp. 68a–70b). The Taipei temple reprinted an edition provided to it by a Malaysian temple. An edition reprinted in 1939 survives in Putian (Putian Provincial Library and/or Putian Museum Library collection). See Franke (1972).

phoenix. His complexion was dark like a dragon, his gait was martial and steady like a unicorn. Inside his left eye there were four red spots. Around the eye up to the temple there were three more red spots, making a total of seven. The red spot between his eyebrows was sometimes hidden and sometimes visible. The top of his head was like an infant's, his breath moving in and out of it. On his back were eight black marks. His ears were large and the lobes hung down. His belly was white and his body was thickest. Whether walking or sitting, laughing or talking, he was a concealed Maitreya Buddha. (*TR* 2b)[2]

In 1613, fifteen years after Lin's death, Lin's disciple Lu Wenhui had an image of his Master carved and set up in a temple called Yaodaoci. Lin Zhao'en was now definitely a god. Special rituals, commissioned by Lu and written by Chen Zhongyu, were performed before his statue.

This is not the end of the story, however; it is only the beginning. Shortly after Lin's death, and possibly beforehand, his immediate circle of disciples began to quarrel among themselves over the succession. Several efforts were made by different individuals to establish their own collections of their Master's works. Another important measure was the writing of their own version of the life of Lin Zhao'en. At least eight such accounts were written between 1599 and 1655. Five are either lost or remain undiscovered. Only three are available, though rare. These are the *Linzi shixing* (True acts of Master Lin [henceforth abbreviated as *TA*]) of Zhang Hongdu, written in 1599; the *Linzi nianpu* (Chronological biography of Master Lin, henceforth *CB*) of Lin Zhaoke (1610); and the *Linzi benxing shilu* (True record) of Lu Wenhui, Chen Zhongyu, and Dong Shi, completed in 1655.

Zhang Hongdu was considered one of the Four Attendants of Lin Zhao'en. His account pays close attention to the dating of Lin's books and essays and the spread of the Three Teachings beyond Fujian province. Zhang presents Lin's teachings as "establishing their foundations" in the Confucian bonds and values. Lin used Daoism as the "gateway," from the cultivation of the heart and the refining of the nature to the forming of the elixir and the issuing forth of the spirit. He used Buddhism as the "ultimate principle," from the realm of forgetting the body and the spirit to the region beyond consciousness and knowledge. All these led in Lin's view to the "shattering of the void" and the attainment of nirvana. Zhang Hongdu's preface is dated 1599, the year following Lin's death. His account of Lin's last days is particularly poignant.

[2] Lin's iconography includes heraldic animals like the turtle, phoenix, dragon, and unicorn, symbols of the four directions. The seven red spots around and above his eyes suggest the star palaces of the Big Dipper, source of cosmic power and protection. The top of his head resembled an infant's soft spot, because his inner alchemical transformations had made an opening through the cranium through which he could breath the Primal Breath of the cosmos. The eight black spots on his back are undoubtedly the eight hexagrams of the *Book of Changes*. His long earlobes resemble those of the Buddha, as did his expansive belly. The body of the Buddha is similarly covered with sacred signs.

Lin Zhaoke, Lin Zhao'en's cousin, set out in his 1610 account to deny the deification of his relative.[3] Lin Zhaoke belonged to the official class and was no doubt concerned about the imperial government's attitude toward the cult forming around Lin Zhao'en. He wrote his version of Lin's life in response to a now lost version by Weng Wudao. According to the *Linzi menxian shilu* (True record of the sagely disciples of Master Lin), written by Dong Shi and published in 1672:

> Weng Yao. A man of Putian Qingjiang. He collected a *Linzi nianpu* (Chronological biography of Master Lin), which was very detailed. This work includes descriptions of healing by exorcism and worship of the Heavenly Dog. But this is not Master Lin's teaching of the Middle Way of Perfect Rectitude. Much of the material in the preface is coarse and vulgar. This is perhaps because Weng left Confucian studies early and had no real hand in them, so he declined into uncultured ways.

Dong Shi has kinder words for Lin Zhaoke:

> Lin Zhaoke, personal name Xueming, courtesy name Rongmen. A cousin of Lin Zhao'en. He served as district magistrate of Anqing. He was excellent at the Classics. When he read Weng Yao's *Chronological Biography* he detested its uncultured aspects and so corrected them in his own *Linzi nianpu* (Chronological biography of Master Lin). Events are recorded sparingly in terse language. Fuzhou scholars reprinted the original. Lin Zhaoke also excerpted Master Lin's writing into the *Wuni zhenti* (The truths of Wuni). (*Linzi menxian shilu*, 22b)

As other scholars have traced Lin's life and deeds in some detail, I will concentrate here instead on the religious themes that create hagiography out of biography through a comparison of three biographical accounts. Lin Zhaoke's *Chronological Biography* presents the most straightforward version. Zhang Hongdu's *True Acts* includes several hagiographical elements, particularly the narrative of alchemical transformation. The *True Record* adds other hagiographic elements, including a series of episodes linking Lin Zhao'en with Maitreya Buddha.

As noted by Delehaye (1961), hagiography combines biography, panegyric, and moral instruction. The drive to create an ideal portrait excuses any omission of unnecessary details. There is a tendency to substitute abstract forms for individual types. One often encounters the borrowing and transmission of legendary themes and the artificial grouping of incidents and persons. In this genre, the supernatural is only impressive when combined with the miraculous. Most hagiographies include three parts, treating the signs leading to the

---

[3] Lin Zhaoke obtained his *jinshi* degree in 1574. He was appointed as a secretary in the Bureau of Rites, then promoted to vice-director, and finally became the minister of justice. Later he took a position as prefect of Jianzhou. He subsequently retired to his home in Putian, where he lived for over twenty years, writing commentaries to the poetry of Chu Yuan, Li Po, Tu Fu, and Wang Wei, as well as to the *Zuozhuan*. He also wrote *Yuzhou* (Cosmos), *Duoshi* (Much knowledge), and other works. His biography is included in the *Xinghua Putianxian zhi*.

birth of the saint, his life and death, and the miracles that follow his death. In the case of the hagiographic representations of the life and death of Lin Zhao'en, there is less emphasis on the miracles following his death. This may be due to the fact that these accounts, written shortly after his death, portray his life as a successful alchemical process. They culminate in a vision of Lin as a realized being, in union with the original substance of the universe. Thus his hagiography serves as an inspirational text, holding out the promise of similar enlightenment to his followers. Rather than regarding the accounts of Lin Zhao'en's visions as delusions and his followers and biographers as superstitious, we should instead seek to understand these texts in their own terms, and look for the elements of the image of the Lord of the Three in One that Master and disciples were creating together.

Several narrative devices weave in and out of the versions of Lin's life in both the *True Acts* and the *True Record*. These include one series made up of miraculous signs, prophecies, and dreams, such as the Unicorn dream, the Dice dream, the dream of the Supreme Emperor, and the dream of realized Buddha-nature. A second series of visions, found mainly in the *True Record,* includes the vision of Maitreya at the birth of Lin, the vision of the Dragon King, the all-important vision of Maitreya in his sixty-second year, and the vision of the Buddha in his seventieth year. A third series, found in both accounts, traces the stages of Lin's inner alchemical transmutation, from the comments of his Daoist associate Zhuo Wanchun, through the attainment of inner and outer elixirs, through to their union in an alchemical transmutation, and on to the growth of an immortal embryo in the final year of Lin's life. A repetitive tension that propels the narrative forward is that established between official suspicion and divine vindication. Each spiritual advance is countered by a worldly setback. Yet the underlying narrative suggests that any degree of official suspicions can be overcome, just as the Three Teachings can be realized in one man.

This chapter follows these interwoven strands of hagiography in Lin's sacred biography in chronological progression. This has the advantage of bringing out the tension within the text between Lin's spiritual and alchemical progress, and the distrust and suspicion his growing influence aroused in official eyes. Chapter 4 will reconsider these materials from the perspective of the evolving relationship between Lin and his disciples that lead to the formation of the Three in One religious movement. Wach (1962) pointed out that it is the relationship *between* the Master and his disciples that generates a particular kind of religious movement. We will see how Lin's image was elaborated by both the Master and his immediate disciples.

BASIC BIOGRAPHY

Lin Zhao'en was born in 1517 in Putian into a very prominent, large family, with many relatives serving as officials, and many others studying to become officials. Lin was an outstanding student and passed the first of the civil service exams to become a *xiucai* (scholar) at the age of eighteen in 1534.[4] A collection of his student essays was later assembled by Tian Rucheng,[5] the superintendent of schools in the Putian area. Soon after this Lin married, but his wife died within a year. This was to prove the first of a series of tragic family deaths. He remarried in 1538. In 1539 his grandfather, Lin Fu, died, and in 1544 his father, Lin Wanren, died. In 1546 his uncle Lin Wanchao died, shortly after passing the last and most arduous of the exams to become a *jinshi* (advanced scholar).

In 1547 Lin Zhao'en took the next round of exams and, to everyone's complete surprise, failed. At this point something inside him cracked. He had been to visit Luo Hongxian, a famous student of Wang Yangming, to ask for a funerary inscription for his recently deceased uncle. Perhaps he discussed genuine self-cultivation, as opposed to rote Confucian book-learning, with the philosopher. Upon his return to Putian he announced that he was quitting his Confucian studies. He refused to heed the demands and threats of the director of studies. He refused to behave according to conventional social standards.

Around this time Lin was visited by a wandering Daoist named Zhuo Wanchun. The two became inseparable. They drank and wrote poetry together. They slept out under the stars together. Zhuo introduced Lin to Daoist internal alchemy, as their joint collection of poems and conversations, the *Xuanyu lu*, attests. Around this time Lin records having met a mysterious Master who taught him the Confucian inner alchemical "Heart Method" of "stilling the *gen* hexagram in the lower back."

Before he could devote himself fully to the practice of this method, Lin found himself embroiled in a confrontation with the new director of studies, Zhu Heng (1512–1584).[6] Lin refused to heed Zhu's summons to return to the Confucian academy and instead burned his Confucian hat and robes before the gates of the school. Eventually a compromise was reached whereby Lin would remain on the school register but not take exams.

Lin had already, in 1551, accepted his first eleven disciples, and in 1554 he outlined a course of study for them in the hall he had built under the shadow

[4] Chinese calculations of age add a year for the time in the mother's womb, and everyone grows a year older each New Year's. Months refer to lunar months.

[5] Tian Rucheng, *zi* Shuhe, 1526 *jinshi,* began his career as a secretary in the Nanjing Bureau of Justice and was promoted to Jiangxi assistant administration commissioner and ultimately to the post of assistant education-intendant censor for Fujian. He wrote several books, including *Dan jiwen, Xihu youlanji, Tian Shuheji,* and *Liaoji.* See his biography in *Ming shi,* j. 287.

[6] Zhu Heng (1512–1584), *zi* Shinan, *zi* Weiping, *hao* Zhenshan, from Wan'an, 1532 *jinshi,* first served as district magistrate of Youxi and Wuyuan, then as secretary in the Bureau of Justice. He was promoted to section director, then transferred to the post of Fujian assistant education-intendant censor. Later he was made provincial administration commissioner for Shandong, and in 1560 he was promoted to right vice censor in chief at court. There his forthright character led to clashes with Zhang Juzheng, and he was forced into retirement early in the Wanli period. He wrote the *Daonan yuanweilu* and a *Collected Works.* His biography is included in *Ming shi,* j. 223, *Mingshi liejuan,* 78.

of a pagoda built by his grandfather. Soon, however, they were all caught up in the series of pirate and bandit raids that overwhelmed Putian from 1556 to 1563. During this phase, Lin emerged as a leader of the local gentry and a protector of the poor and suffering. He drew upon his family's extensive resources to provide food and shelter for the dispossessed. He offered to sacrifice himself to save the city when Hunan-Guangdong mercenaries turned against the city residents they were supposed to be protecting. He sent his disciples to gather, bury, or cremate thousands of corpses of people killed in the raids. He composed funerary documents and performed religious rituals for the souls of the dead.

Lin emerged from these trying times as an exemplary local gentry and an established religious leader. From 1563 to his death in 1598, he traveled around Fujian and southeastern China lecturing, establishing temples, and writing, constantly writing. From 1567 on, his disciples carved and printed several different collections of his writings. In 1572 he had to expand his school in Putian. He wrote new regulations, openly emphasizing the key role of his heart method for the first time. Over the next fifteen years, he wrote elaborate commentaries on some of the main works of the Chinese philosophic tradition, including detailed exegeses of key Confucian classics, Daoist scriptures, and Buddhist sutras. Some of his disciples spread the faith to Zhejiang, Jiangxi, Anhui, Nanjing, and Beijing. A group of the Hanlin academicians wrote him from Beijing in 1596, asking for advice on his heart method. But Lin was already preparing for his death. His actions grew restricted, he no longer spoke, he meditated constantly. Surrounded by disciples, he died in 1598.

HAGIOGRAPHY

To move now from mere reality to the intriguing realm of the supernatural, we must return to the beginning. Or rather, before the beginning. According to the *True Record*, the moment of Lin's conception was marked by Lin's mother *dreaming* of a revolving *elixirlike* (pill-shaped) bright moon, which flew into her bed-curtains. She became pregnant.

> Birth: Mingde 12, a *dingchou* year (1517). An old prophecy stated, "In a *dingchou* year, Maitreya Buddha will descend into this world and be born." On the 16th of the seventh lunar month, at the yin hour (3 to 5 A.M.), people saw a brilliant light illumine the heavens. An unusual fragrance spread over everyone. And thus was born Master Lin, Xia Wuni, Lord of the Three in One. (*TR* 5b)

Lin Zhaoke's account of these auspicious events fails to mention Maitreya Buddha and also significantly fails to allude to anything resembling an elixir. Instead, he recounts Lin's mother's dream:

> The moon descended into her womb and she became pregnant. The full moon shone brightly and an unusual fragrance quickly spread through the entire house, and thus Master was born. (*CB* 2a)

Plate 5. The birth of Lin Zhao'en, from a temple mural in Xianyou (many such murals show thirty-six scenes from the life of Lin Zhao'en)

Several themes central to the hagiography of Lin Zhao'en can already be seen in these opening remarks. The themes of prescient dreams, visions of the gods, and alchemical elixirs are all present in this account of Lin's birth. These are followed by other standard hagiographical topics. Many of these would not be out of place in a standard biography in the dynastic histories. Lin was of course a child prodigy, and no less significant a visitor than Wang Yangming, principal thinker of the Neo-Confucian School of the Mind, supposedly came to visit the Lin residence:

> 1520. Master Wang Yangming came to visit (Lin's grandfather) Lin Fu. Lin had the Lord of the Teachings brought forward. Master Wang Yangming said, "This lad's rich appearance is highly unusual. I suspect that he will not be successful in the civil service examinations. But his accomplishments later in life will greatly exceed my own. (*TR* 6a)

Although this encounter is most improbable, there was a strong connection between Wang Yangming and Lin's grandfather, Lin Fu. The two had been imprisoned together for their criticisms of the court and had worked closely together in suppressing Yao uprisings in Guangxi. Lin Fu's collected works include poems he wrote to Wang while they were both in jail. They are said to have passed the time discussing philosophy. Their relationship may explain the importance given to Wang's philosophy of the Mind in Lin's education, overseen by his grandfather.

Not only was Lin's childhood physiognomy exceptional, so was his conduct. After a comment on his aptitude for studies, we find the following:

> 4 years old: 1520. . . . Whenever he discovered someone desecrating images of the gods, he would shout out and stop them. This must be because of his heaven-sent nature. (*TR* 6a)

> 13 years old: 1529. . . . Whenever the Lord of the Teachings went out, he took silver in his sleeves to give out to the poor. His mother, thinking he was foolishly wasting the money, reproached him. He replied, "My family has been wealthy and noble for generations. The Way of Heaven [opposes] evil conduct. Why should I not use my extra [wealth] to supply what other people are lacking?" His mother took him seriously [after that]. (*TR* 6a)

After passing his initial exams, Lin began to catch the eye of local scholars and school superintendents. In 1540, at the age of twenty-four, he was selected by Superintendent Tian Rucheng and ordered to compose works in imitation of the ancient classics. Around this time he went to Jiulihu (Nine-Carp Lake), a scenic spot in the Xianyou mountains with a Daoist temple, a lake, and a waterfall. Inside the temple is a dream-chamber, still used to this day. Visitors burn incense and prepare for incubation. The dreams can predict the future or suggest cures for illness, rather like those at the shrine to Aesculapius at Epidaurus (Delehaye, 1961: 154). Lin dreamt that a Perfected Being appeared and said to him, "As for the deeds of the Unicorn, this is the age in which they will show forth [in your writings]."

Lin's first son was born in 1543, and the next year his father died. His father had begged his sons to pay back his debts, which amounted to over 1,000 in gold, and they complied with his wishes. At the age of thirty, in 1546, Lin prepared for the next round of civil-service examinations in the Confucian Classics. These were the provincial exams held in Fuzhou, the capital of Fujian. His family sent someone to Jiulihu for a dream that would reveal the outcome of the exams. The dream was most peculiar. The first two dice each came up with a 4, and the final dice rolled for a long time before coming up with a 1. This case of 4:4:1 was interpreted positively by the family as signifying that Lin would come first in the exam of all eight regions of Min (Fujian).

Unexpectedly, Lin failed the exams and renounced the profession of Confucian studies, fixing his will on the study of *xin, sheng, xingming* (the heart, the body, and the store of life force—or original nature and destiny). The *True Record* states, "for years he was as if mad or drunken, he seemed beside himself and crazed." He rushed after every Daoist master, high Buddhist monk, or Neo-Confucian sage he could find, begging them to enlighten him.

The entry for 1546, the year Lin failed his exams, also states Lin did in fact eventually meet the "enlightened master" he sought. The sources are rather confusing on who this master was and where and when Lin met him. In this case, Lin Zhaoke's *Chronological Biography* provides more information than the *True Record*. The *Chronological Biography* first quotes Lin Zhao'en's own *Xinsheng zhizhi* (Direct pointing to the mind as a sage), written in 1564, where he recounts his long and difficult pursuit of the Way:

> Within ten years, I was fortunate to meet an enlightened master who pitied and instructed me. He pointed directly to this sagely mind, and all the words he spoke to me were from the *Four Books* and the *Five Classics*. He said, "Since the time of Confucius and Mencius these books have been obscured by interpretations and have remained unclear to this day." Moreover, he repeatedly discussed for me the subtle principles regarding stilling in the back and moving in the chamber. When he was about to leave, he spoke to me again, saying, "You are not an official. If you do not have the means to verify this, who will be able to follow and believe it?" "Verify it with [curing] illness. If illness is cured, they will believe." "But how am I to cure people's ills?" The master said, "When you were young did you not recite the writings about the fullness of the body and the plumpness of the countenance? A full body comes from a broad mind, and plump countenance is rooted in the mind. Even more the yellow center (*Huangzhong*) of the *Book of Change*, when regularizing influence reaches the cavities of the body, is sufficient to extend its wondrous effects to the four limbs. You need only maintain your resolve and do no more violence to your vital force, and illness can be cured." "I beg to inquire the method." "Medicine is the will, and the method rests firmly in your own mind." (Translated in Berling, 1980: 68–69)

We will return to an analysis of the implications of this passage for the evolution of Lin's heart method in chapter 4. For the moment it is interesting to note that Lin Zhaoke went on to provide another clue to the timing of this event:

> The Master once told [me] Zhaoke that when he went up to Guangliu, in the region to the right of the river, with the remains of my uncle Wanchao, Duke of Lanzhou, he met an extraordinary person by the side of the road. This person transmitted correct secret instructions to him. Therefore he said that this was a matter of "being fortunate to have encountered an enlightened master." (*CB* 6b [518])

Since Lin Wanchao (1543 *juren*, 1538 *jinshi*) died in 1547, the encounter must have occurred just after that time.

In 1548 a student of divine signs, Zhuo Wanchun,[7] a wandering Daoist,

---

[7] In addition to the *True Record* and the other biographies of Lin Zhao'en, other sources on the life of Zhuo Wanchun include the *Fujian tongzhi*, j. 263, *Ming Fangwai;* the (Wanli) *Xinghua fuzhi*, j. 26; the *Gujin tushu jicheng, Shenyidian*, j. 258, *Shenxianbu liejuan*, j. 35, and the hagiographical manuscript entitled *Zhuozu zhenren zhi* (Record of the perfected being, the ancestor Zhuo [Wanchun]). See also Zheng (1988a: 87–92).

followed the unmistakable indications to Lin's door. Both the *Chrono-logical Biography* and the *True Record* records this example of divine prognostication:

> [T]he Little Immortal observed the *qi* moving toward the Lord's home. The Lord had just stepped out. Zhuo asked Lin's mother, nee Li, "How is it that auspicious clouds circle the room? Most certainly an extraordinary event has taken place." Lin's mother replied, "Could it be that my son will pass the exams?" "That would not be exceptional enough." "Perhaps my daughter-in-law will give birth to a noble child?" "That would not be exceptional enough." "Well what would be exceptional enough?" "This is definitely a matter of someone attaining the Dao. That's why these auspicious clouds are so thick." At this Lin's mother said, "Are you trying to tell me that my second son who has given up his studies is going to attain Dao?" The Little Immortal nodded his head again and again. (*TR* 10a)

When, after a few moments, Lin Zhao'en returned home, Zhuo Wanchun saluted him and burst into laughter. According to the *True Record,* Lin tested him with a demeaning arithmetic question and then challenged his ability to compose linked verse. Later, feeling that he had insulted a true Daoist, Zhuo invited him back and asked for an explication of the Dice Dream. The Little Immortal explained, "This is a matter of ninefold transforming elixir. You will realize it for yourself before long" (*TR*). In Lin Zhaoke's *Chronological Biography,* Zhuo Wanchun's comment reads as follows: "This is a matter of the ninefold elixir. The perfected beings are promoting you." At this the Master suddenly understood." (*CB* 7a)

The Little Immortal went on to quote a verse of alchemical poetry:

> Carefully reflect on the Iron Man that comes in the night,
> Long life without death is man-made.

He went on to explain that the elixir is not the product of one person alone. Only because Lin's family had accumulated seven generations of merit, and because Lin had renounced his Confucian studies and studied Daoist myster-ies, could Lin now expect to attain the Dao. Then he burst into a mantic verse:

> Dragon River was once a good scholar
> Today we invite each other to pace the Jade Altar
> He's casting his past away and following the flow
> If he weren't a Daoist how could he do it? (*CB* 7b; 518)

The *True Record* includes Lin's own poem composed in response:

> Floating, flying beyond the clouds, an idle man
> In Buddhist cloths, Daoist shoes, and a Confucian hat,
> Everyone on the street calls me a madman (*dian*)
> But the characters for mad include two characters for "true."

Zhuo Wanchun and Lin Zhao'en were inseparable for several years. In 1549 they traveled to the Buddhist temples in Fuzhou together. Lin also studied

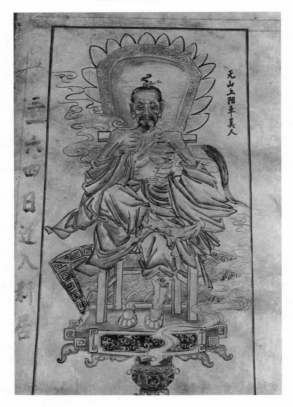

Plate 6. Zhuo Wanchun, the Daoist companion of Lin Longjiang (temple mural from Xianyou)

Daoist diet and breath control for several months before renouncing it as not the way to the ultimate principles.

The following year, 1551, marked a major turning point in Lin Zhao'en's life. Although he had been expounding the Dao for some time, he had never taken disciples. At this point, eleven followers, starting with his good friend Huang Zhou, received special instructions in the heart method and took up discipleship. All versions of Lin's life state that Lin decided to test the marvels of his heart method by curing illness. He stated to Huang Zhou, "This hunting [for followers by means of curing illness] will reveal only a relatively minor [aspect of the] power [of the method]." They then transmitted the method to Huang's teenage daughter, who had trouble with her eyes. Soon she was cured.

The *True Record* elaborated the reasoning behind this trial cure, attributing the remarks to Lin:

> The Great Way has long been obscured. The Sacred Teachings are difficult to illumine. If we do not, at the beginning, make use of the extraneous aspects of the

heart method to test it a little on the poor and the sick who have had results from taking medicine, taking the teachings regarding the heart and the nature of the three Masters, and quickly explicating them, then who will believe it? Thus we will not keep this to ourselves, but instead we will rely on the expelling of disease to attract them. When they know that they can overcome disease by means of the heart method, then they will begin to believe in the Dao and they can be built up by means of the heart method. (*TR* 10b)

The text goes on to discuss the reasons for the success of the heart method over all forms of disease, a topic we will turn to below. Both *Lives* then converge to state that after disciple Huang Zhou's daughter was cured, the next person they approached was retired Minister of Justice Liu Xun. Lin Zhaoke describes in detail the stratagems adopted by disciple Huang Zhou to ensure that Lin Zhao'en would accept the sincerity of Liu Xun's request for instruction. Was this because Lin did not want to get mixed up with officials, or was it part of an effort to render his teachings more mysterious and precious still? In any case, the cure was efficacious, and Liu Xun saluted Lin as his master. Lin Zhao'en had secured his first disciple of high official rank (albeit retired).

He would need this kind of support the following year, when Superintendent of Schools Zhu Heng demanded that he return to the academy. This was the occasion for the burning of his Confucian scholar's robes. He dressed in commoner's clothes and returned to the protection of his late grandfather's estate and burial ground, the Eastern Mountain of Putian. He sent a provocative message in response to the official summons, claiming that he was content to be "an illiterate villager." When Zhu Heng insisted that Lin deliver lectures at the academy, Lin refused, saying, "Formerly when I was in the academy you could summon me. Now I am in the mountain groves and you can no longer summon me. If you want to see me, you will have to visit me in an official capacity."

This was a total provocation, and Zhu Heng sent officers to bring Lin in. After a long argument, Lin suggested a way out of the dilemma in which he would remain on the academy roster but not compete in the examinations. Lin remarked, "When I was letting my feelings go amongst mountain groves, I was a student in hiding, hiding among the mountain groves. Today, in response to your instruction, I return to scholastic dress and take my place amongst the students. Yet I will not strive to compete in the exams. This is a matter of a man of the mountain hiding, hiding in the academy." Zhu Heng was pleased with the compromise and later read and admired Lin's writings, thus becoming another friend with official rank.

In 1553 Lin Zhao'en printed his first book, entitled *Linzi* (Master Lin), and the following year he outlined his regulations for study at his private academy, located in a retreat built by his grandfather Lin Fu on the Eastern Mountain, which he renamed the Zongkongtang (Hall of the Honorable Confucius). These regulations have been translated by Judith Berling (1980: 75–77). They outline a Confucian course of study aimed at the traditional examinations but emphasizing moral cultivation, proper behavior, social courtesies, and camaraderie. As Berling notes, these regulations make no mention whatsoever of the heart method, which Lin was using to win disciples at the time. Clearly, he was seeking to project a public image as an acceptable Confucian teacher. His essays over the next few years dealt with the intricacies of Confucian ritual. He also began composing the first of his *Shuwen tiangao* (Manuscripts of memorials to Heaven), later collected and printed with a 1561 colophon. Another collection from this period is the *Jiugao* (Early manuscripts). An essay entitled *Shanren* (Mountain man) enabled him to put his own interpretation on his compromise with Superintendent Tian.

Huang Daben, an early disciple of Lin's, wrote a preface to the *Linzi*, which describes the behavior of Lin and his disciples in this early stage:

> In the autumn of 1553, several tens of gentlemen were roaming with Master [Lin]. In addition to discussing the heart-mind and [underlying] human nature, Master Lin expounded the unity of the Three Teachings, the failings of common academic approaches, and the means by which heaven, earth, and the sage could unite as one. When discussing Buddhism, he pointed out the errors of Chan meditation. When discussing Daoism, he pointed out the worthlessness of "circulating the breath." When discussing Confucianism, he pointed out the narrowness of the division into separate schools of thought. Toward his disciples he spoke of brotherliness; toward officials, he spoke of loyalty. And he ordered us from time to time to recite passages such as the Eight [Forms] of Filial Piety and the Nine Thoughts from the *Analects*, as well as Mencius's passage on "Niushan is what I want," etc. Sometimes we climbed high to clarify our feelings; sometimes we sang out to nurture our good intentions. Casual and calm, he did not act proud or arrogant. The gentlemen were all delighted and felt that they had found something to believe in (*yigui*).

In the 12th month of 1555, pirates raided Putian City. Lin dispensed food and funds to the defenders of the city. The following year, in the aftermath of a plague, he began gathering corpses and providing coffins for their burial. Lin's reputation as a teacher and moral leader began to rise, but not without exciting some envious attacks from other gentry in the city. In the 4th month of 1559, several thousand pirates overran Fuqing and began to move on Putian. Lin organized several other Putian gentry to sign a contract with a band of Hunan-Guandong troops temporarily stationed in Putian, offering them 1,000 in gold should they drive back the pirates. The troops defeated the pirates and Lin presented 100 in gold, but other gentry withheld their portions. The troops seized Lin, led him out onto the military exercise ground, and beat him with sticks. They demanded that he gather the funds from the other gentry. Lin did not cower and instead denounced them, saying, "Formerly we contracted with you for a sum of 1,000 in gold, asking that you pacify the city. Now you have indeed driven back the pirates, but you have gone on to plunder all about. This is unruly! It is impermissible. Though I die, I will never give in" (*TR* 15b). Upon hearing this, the other gentry were greatly moved, gathered the funds, and paid the troops, who finally left the city. The new superintendent of the schools, Hu Tinglan,[8] was so impressed with this that he ordered a colored banner made and paraded around the city in honor of Lin.[9]

The second month of 1561 saw the death of one of Lin's disciples. Lin established a particular form of mourning for him, which became the standard for his disciples.

That winter pirates again besieged Putian, and plague broke out within the city. Bodies were everywhere, and there were not enough coffins to go around. Lin dispatched over 70 disciples to gather over 1,200 corpses, with instructions to bury them on Taiping Mountain. He composed a "Corpse-Gathering Song." The *True Record* details several other occasions in 1562, 1564, and 1565 in which Lin dispatched disciples to gather corpses. The governor of Fujian sent funds to aid him in his work in 1562 and publicly commended him. Lin commissioned Buddhist monks and Daoist masters to perform religious services for the dead. He also composed his own petitions for use in these services and may have personally directed some of them. Lin was coming into his own as a religious teacher. The *True Record* evidences this shift with the following notice:

> 1562. 3rd month. The pestilence vapors were particularly strong in the city. Demons and evil beings constantly appeared and disappeared. Once they met the Lord chanting in the night, and they climbed up the Eastern Mountain, and ran off together to avoid him, saying, "The Master of the Three Teachings has come." From this time onward, all those suffering from plague or disease begged for deliverance from the Lord. The Lord only wrote out the words "When one's Dao is high, dragons and tigers submit; when one's merit is weighty, demons and spirits show respect." The sick all were cured without medicine. The Lord's writing of the *zhengqi* (Orthodox Breath talisman) began at this time. (*TR* 16a)

In the 6th month of 1562, Lin escaped the heat in Tianxinlou (Heart of Heaven Tower) and wrote the *Sanjiao huipian* (Joint chronicle of the Three Teachings), detailing in chronological order the history of philosophic ideas and interpretations of the Three Teachings throughout Chinese history.[10]

In the 8th month counterpirate expeditions were carried out by General Qi Jiguang. Lin donated 30 *mu* (5 acres) to a shrine dedicated to the general, complete with a statue of the hero. But Lin predicted a month later that the pirates would return and devastate the city. He composed a treatise on the de-

---

[8] Hu Tinglan, from Zengcheng, a 1550 *jinshi*, had himself been actively involved in defending Putian against pirate raids (see *Fujian tongzhi*, j. 130).

[9] He Qiaoyuan provides an account of this event in his *Minshu*, j. 129, *Lin Zhao'en juan*, in which he states that the great lineages of Putian had offered to pay 1,000 to the mercenaries, who wiped out the invading pirates. The lineages then reneged and planned to scatter, but Lin came forward with 500 on his own to settle the issue. Later, after a successful pirate raid laid waste to Putian, Lin provided several hundred more to pay for coffins and medicine.

[10] This book is analyzed in Berling (1980: 200–204) and Zheng (1988a: 152–155).

fense of the city, calling for the formation of local self-defense corps, but the other gentry did not accept his views.

The *True Record* includes a curious episode from the 9th month of 1562. A medium lad had won a great following in the city, claiming to control the handles of fortune, misfortune, life, and death.

> The Lord said, "Is the city lost? It will rise up if it listens to people, but it will fall if it listens to spirits. Instead of funding the policies of the wise and defending it with the courageous, they are entranced by evil spirits into casting money after [spurious] profits. Is this not foolishness?" And then he wrote in large characters on his gate, "The Orthodox Breath of the Master of the Three Religions is here. Therefore anyone who has unorthodox breath will instantly be melted away." When the medium lad saw this he fled. (*TR* 17a)

Here we see Lin publicly declaring his religious powers in a duel with a spurious spirit.

Lin's misgivings about the pirate raiders were fulfilled when the city was overrun on the 9th day of the 11th month of 1562. He escaped from the north gate. According to the *True Record,* the pirates had heard of him and wished to see him. When they learned of his escape, they sent representatives into the Three in One hall to worship the images there. They also set up a banner before the memorial shrine built to honor Lin for his defense of the city in 1559. They ordered that these buildings not be burned.

> The dwarf pirates had been in the Putian area for over eight years, so they could speak the local dialect. They knew all about the good and evil deeds of everyone in the city. . . . They worshipped his image and protected his official shrine. At that time they massacred countless people, but no one in Lin's family was hurt. (*TR* 17a)

Lin's brother Lin Zhaogao managed to escape through the burning city with the *Joint Chronicles of the Three Teachings* in one arm and his mother on the other. Lin Zhao'en was delighted and ordered that land should be sold to provide for the cost of printing the book in 1563.

Lin launched into another round of corpse gathering, cremations, and funerary rituals for the restless dead. Expenses were paid for by the sale of his own land. These activities continued in 1564.

> In response to many requests, [Lin performed funerary rituals and] delivered the wandering spirits from the Putian and Xianyou region. He used alcohol to purify the roads. Thereby the survivors did not sicken from pestilence, and the dead had their spirits settled. And after these great battles, there was peace for over twenty years. (*TR* 18a)

All these deeds won Lin considerable praise from officials. Some, including Geng Dingxiang (1524–1596), a leader of the Taizhou school, then serving as superintendent of education in Fujian, went so far as to recommend him to the throne for promotion. This was rejected because there was no precedent for selecting a "recluse" for office.[11]

In 1564 Lin Zhao'en was 48 years old. He drafted his *Xinsheng zhizhi* (Direct pointing to the mind as a sage), in which he outlined his heart method, but he refused to allow the book to be printed while he was alive (the book was first printed by his disciples in 1590). This same year Lin Zhao'en received news of an elixir:

> Prior to this time the Lord's Purple-gold elixir had not yet been warmed to a state of perfect yang. Patriarch Lu [Dongbin] of Chunyang then manifested in the southern Quanzhou region. He hid the elixir among some medicines in the market and transmitted the secret formula to one of the Lord's disciples named Yang Zhizhai. This man came to Putian to tell the Lord about this, and the Lord was astonished to hear the news. But in the end Zhizhai did not in fact understand the formula. He went to look for [Lu Dongbin] again, but he couldn't find him. So we understand that the Great Way is a true Mystery. (*TR* 19b)

Lin Zhao'en spent the following year, 1565, working on several versions of this new understanding of himself in relation to the original substance of the universe. These include the *Bentijiao* (Teachings on the original substance), the *Xiayu* (Sayings of Xia), and other works. According to the *True Record,* the inspiration for the use of the word *Xia* came in a moment's illumination:

> When the Lord was writing the *Sayings of Xia,* he had just put down the draft but had not yet selected a title. While sitting in meditation he suddenly glanced at the top of his bookmark, where the words Xiayu were marked. So he named his book the same. The use of the word Xia began with this. Only in 1584 did his disciples revere the Lord with the title Master Xiawuni. (*TR* 20a)

Further organizational work was in order. Lin created a new uniform for his disciples. He drafted a set of regulations for Buddhist and Daoist disciples. He continued with his writing, traveling to Fuzhou to find time to write.

The *True Record* includes an interesting item under Lin Zhao'en's 51st year, 1567:

> A fisherman caught a huge turtle. Lin Yi announced this. The Lord ordered him to purchase it. Their carriage had not yet reached the Jinzhou pagoda when suddenly a stinking wind blew around them. Everyone was curious about this and finally released the turtle into the river. The turtle turned back its head and refused to depart. The Lord used his pen to write several sentences on its back. Then it

[11] Geng Dingxiang, *zi* Cailun, *hao* Qutong, was born in Huangan in Hubei. The memorial can be found in *Geng Tiantai xiansheng wenji,* j.2.16b. See also *Ming shi,* j. 221.5b; *Mingru xue'an,* 35.1a, and *Ming Biographies.* The conservative Taizhou scholar Guan Zhidao (1536–1608) classed Lin Zhao'en as a member of the school, albeit with reservations (see Berling, 1980: 222). A number of contemporary scholars have seen connections between Lin Zhao'en's Three in One and the Taizhou school (see Berling, 1980: 53, 54, 68, 222).

quickly sped away. The next day in the middle of the night wind blew and waves surged into the room. Suddenly a god in official hat and clothes appeared. Two gods holding banners followed behind him. They circled the Lord three times, then kowtowed on the steps before him and left. Wang Xing and Li Dai were startled and asked who they were. The Lord replied, "This was the Dragon King of the North Sea. On account of his having sent rainstorms, many boats were harmed and many lives were lost. The Jade Emperor demoted him into a turtle so that he could repay his former karmic debts. Yesterday the reason why the turtle hesitated and would not leave was that it was afraid that our good deed would not be counted without some human documentation. So it asked me to write a few lines of explanation. Now the Jade Emperor has pardoned his crimes, so he came especially to thank me. (*TR* 21b)

This is a classic example of the "throw it back tale," and a clear hagiographic embellishment to the story of Lin's life. This legend also occurs in Zhang Hongdu's *True Acts*.

That same year Lin Zhao'en traveled to the Wuyi Mountains in northwest Fujian, and to the Jianyang area. He criticized the breath control and meditation techniques being taught in these areas by local religious leaders. This was a sign of his growing confidence in his own powers as a religious leader. One monk whom he criticized followed him back to Putian and became his disciple.

Lin visited Nanjing in 1570, where he was received by great crowds. He left some disciples behind to transmit the teachings. The following year he was in Fuzhou in the 10th month. A disciple named Wei Heming dreamt that the Shangdi, the Supreme Emperor, had asked the Lord (Lin Zhao'en) to "return" in order to take charge of the Three Teachings. Lin Zhao'en proclaimed his willingness to die, so long as the truth of the Three Teachings continued to spread after his death.

That same year the great ancient camphor tree behind Lin's academy showed renewed signs of life. The *True Record* recalls an ancient prophecy from an immortal who lived in the Eastern Jin dynasty: "1,210 years after this immortal disappears, at the dragon-flower assembly [of Maitreya], 800 perfected beings will meet." The timing indicated the late Ming, and later calculations of the number of Lin's close disciples came to 800 (*Mensheng shilu*, pref.).

In 1572 Lin Zhao'en expanded his academy in the first month of the year, adding side halls for Buddhists and Daoists. As with the new uniforms he had created a few years before, the architectural renovations were intended concretely to symbolize the Three Bonds and the Five Constant relationships of Confucianism.[12] He rewrote the regulations, this time strongly emphasizing the centrality of the heart method. In the 4th month of the year he traveled

---

[12] The Three Bonds are the bonds that tie a prince and subject, a father and son, and a husband and wife; the Five Constancies are *ren* (benevolence), *yi* (righteousness), *li* (propriety), *zhi* (knowledge), and *xin* (sincerity).

to Jiaoyang, where the poor and the infirm flocked to him to receive training in the heart method. The next year he traveled to Jiangxi.

In 1574 Lin wrote his lengthy interpretative commentaries on the *Four Books*. He explained his desire to return to fundamental Confucianism in another *Memorial* to Heaven.

His fame as a healer had spread far and wide. In 1575 he was summoned to aid Surveillance Commissioner Zhu Guanyu,[13] who had fallen ill while traveling to Yanping. Lin protested that he had not entered official gates for thirty years. Nevertheless, Lin was forced to go see the official and quickly instructed him in the heart method. The illness soon dissipated, but Lin withdrew, refusing rewards. The official sent a placard declaring that Lin was an "excellent scholar-gentry."

The following two years were taken up with further writing projects. In 1577 he also built a temple to Shangdi, the Supreme Emperor (a Daoist deity), on the top of Maixian Cliff in Xianyou.

In 1578 he traveled to Xinan, where he helped cure the child of a rich family. Thousands came to worship Lin, exciting the suspicion of the magistrates of the cities of the region. One of them, named Lu, accused Lin of taking in too many disciples. Lin replied that his teachings were without class or category; whoever took refuge in them was welcome. "Confucius and Mencius are an open book," he insisted.

That same year (1578) Lin Zhao'en had a vision identifying him as Maitreya Buddha:

> In the ninth month the Lord of the Teachings was on a boat in a river in Jiantang (Hangzhou). In the night there appeared a top, emitting five colored lights of great brilliance, and descending from the void to demonstrate that Maitreya Buddha had incarnated. It proclaimed: "I am the Commander who opens the Heavens, the Great Master who performs the Law. From the nonbeginning onward I have been but one person. Śākyamuni [Buddha] and I stand shoulder to shoulder. All the limits [of the universe] are beneath me. I now manifest in order to fill Shakyamuni's position. This is the third dragon-flower assembly [called to] save mankind and the heavens." (*TR* 28a–b)

The shining top's remark has become the beginning of the *Bentijing* (Scripture of the original [or fundamental] substance [or body] of the cosmos perhaps the single most important scripture of the Three in One (see chapter 4). This vision confirmed Lin's role as a religious leader. As we might expect, neither Zhang Hongdu's *True Acts* nor Lin Zhaoke's *Chronological Biography* makes any mention of the Maitreya Buddha. Their entries for Lin's 62nd year, 1578, provide no record of a shining top falling out of the void.

Shortly after this episode, the *True Record* predictably shifts to the tale of Lin's persecutions. He fell once again under official suspicion. This time it was

---

[13] Zhu Guangyu, *zi* Deming, *hao* Wenlu, from Xiangfu, Henan, 1544 *jinshi*, first was appointed as a secretary in the Bureau of Revenue, then promoted to the position of censor. He served as regional inspector of Shanxi, Guiyang, and Zhejiang.

the Kaifu (Area Commander) Liu Siwen,[14] who sent an invitation to Lin while he was staying in Fuzhou in early 1579. The invitation was rejected by one of Lin's disciples, Lin Junjiao, who stated, "My Master does not accept invitations from those who are not his disciples." This enraged Liu, who ordered Lin's arrest. The messenger who brought the news stated that Lin was likely to be beheaded. The dozen disciples around Lin trembled with fear. Some pretended to be sick, others slipped away with 100 in gold meant to be used for printing scriptures. Only Wang Xing traveled through the "star-filled night" from Minqing and demanded to die in Lin's place. Lin dressed him in new clothes, and the next day Wang marched bravely into the yamen, fully expecting to die. Liu asked who he was, and why Lin took disciples. Wang took the opportunity to explain how disciples were accepted into Lin's organization. He carefully outlined the vows to heaven and even showed Liu one of the forms that are burnt during an ordination ceremony. Liu revealed that he was suffering from illness. Wang had him burn incense and take vows. He transmitted the heart method and within moments Liu was feeling relief. Liu was soon feasting Wang and calling him *Xiansheng* (Master). Later he sent offerings to Lin and sought further instruction.

At the end of that year, 1579, Lin wrote out his *Jiuxu zheyan* (Selected sayings on the Nine Stages), a programmatic description of the process of the heart method from simple meditation to complete enlightenment. The next year while Lin was in meditation something peculiar happened, according to the *True Record:*

> Suddenly there was a thing that went from the top of his head straight down into his spirit chamber. It was round like an elixir-pill. The Lord felt most strange, but did not know what to make of it. A week or so later he traveled to the Shangsheng Buddhist Monastery. The Perfected Being Zhang Sanfeng had disguised his name as Tao Wenyu. He came to see the Lord. He told him, "This is called the black-iron elixir. It is extremely rare. It depends entirely on one's own merit. If ones' merit is inadequate, how could one attain the ultimate?" Then he imparted the subtle meanings of the five phases to the Lord. These are recorded in the *Xuange* and the *Xuantan* (Mystic songs and Mystic conversations), which the Lord recorded and carved. (*TR* 29b)

This passage goes on to state that Zhang Sanfeng[15] explained to Lin that his progress in refining the elixir was a matter of working away former causes from an earlier kalpa. The *True Record* remarks:

> Later, in 1584, when Master Lu gathered and composed the *Bentijing* (Scripture on original substance), this fact was borne out. There is also a register of the names

[14] Liu Siwen, *zi* Ruzhi, was from Mengjin district in Human. A 1556 *jinshi*, he first served as a censor in the Hunan Circuit. In 1562 he was appointed as regional inspector of Yunnan, and later of Jiangxi. In 1571 he was made assistant minister of the Court of Judicial Review within the central government and finally attained the position of Nanjing minister of revenue. His biography is in the *Fujian tongzhi*, j. 129, and the *Lantai fajianlu*, j. 17.

[15] Sources on Zhang Sanfeng are analyzed in Seidel (1970) and Zheng (1988a).

of 800 earthly immortals. Some are still under investigation, and their names are advanced or removed in accordance with the findings. There are those who have not yet worshiped the Lord, or who are as yet unborn. Their names are there too. There was an ancient prophecy that stated, "How could the meeting of the 800 be by chance? 1,240 years from now, those who have sharp points on two parts of their heads will be saved. Thus will people begin to believe that there is a great immortal hidden south of the river." (*TR* 29b–30a)

This passage further reveals that Zhang Sanfeng frequently came to visit Lin Zhao'en at night. Sometimes he was accompanied by the Immortal Lad of the Kingfisher Lake. Of all Lin's disciples, only Wang Menglong could see him. Unfortunately, this disciple fell in for worldly pursuits and did not attain immortality.[16]

The following year, 1581, Lin was invited by Buddhist monks to an abandoned temple on Gushan (Drum Mountain) near Fuzhou, to exorcise evil spirits said to haunt the premises. His arrival on the spot did the trick (*TR* 30a). In the summer Lin traveled to the Wuyi Mountains and then on to Ninghua. Almost the entire city came out to bow before him. Upon his return to Putian, he stayed in the Shangshengsi and wrote lengthy commentaries on the Heart Sutra and the *Changqingjing* ([Daoist] Scripture of constant quiescence).

Later that year he helped heal a lay Buddhist named Zhu Youkai. His cure reveals interesting aspects of his theory of the origin of disease, which will be discussed below. Again Lin was busy building or repairing temples, this time major local Buddhist temples such as the Nangshansi and the main hall of the Meifengsi in Putian. The next year, 1582, he built a Jade Emperor Hall for the Xuanmiao Guan (the Daoist Temple of Dark Mystery). He ordered Zhu Youkai and others to act as the directors of the temple committee. He also restored the halls to the Three Pure Ones, Zhenwu (the Somber Emperor of the North), the Emperor of the Eastern Peak, and Wenchang.

In 1583 he continued his writings, producing some of his most penetrating essays, such as *Mengzhong ren* (Man in a dream). That year he felt ill and was repeatedly urged by a spirit to "travel to Hunan and Guangdong." The spirit also remarked cryptically, "Rosy mist descends from the mouth of the Green Yang Cavern." Lin learned that there was a cave of this name in the Wudang Mountains, so he set out by boat from Fuzhou:

> No sooner had they left the city when a sudden thunderstorm broke out. Wind and waves pounded against the boat. From within the Lord's belly a pellet of true Yang red, bright as the sun, emerged and was washed by the waters. It restrained

[16] Zhang Hongdu's *True Acts* condenses the description of Lin's inner alchemical elixirs by describing an encounter with Zhang Sanfeng in this year in which he explains that Lin has already been working on his own "purple-gold elixir," and that what he has just experienced is in fact the "black iron" external elixir, which arrives spontaneously (TA 24b). His account also includes a passage on the alchemical transformation of 1583 that is identical to that in the *True Record*.

the heavens and calmed the earth. This is perhaps a matter that goes beyond the power of words to describe. A moment later he was asked about it, but he simply got into another boat and set off as before. The wind and rain, thunder and lightning were all gone. They reached the opposite shore and saw the three words "Green Yang Cave" carved on the rock. The Lord was surprised by this. The disciples quickly asked him what it meant. He said, "The thunder and the lightning just now was transforming of my golden elixir. This is the meaning of 'Travel to Hunan and Guangdong' (lit., the broad lake) and 'the descent of the rosy mist.'" Thereupon he turned back and rowed south. He stopped at Hong Wenyi's thatched cottage. He piled stones before the door and stayed inside for over twenty days with door sealed. The sun was blazing, and it was unbearably hot. Yet at night it was extremely cold. Suddenly a person came and told him to drink water, and in one sitting he drank tens of gallons. His spiritual *qi* shone forth. (*TR* 31b)

This passage describes Lin Zhao'en's alchemical transformation. The elixir is within him, the body is the containment vessel, and the thatched hut is the crucible. The splitting up of bright red yang and the subsequent washing in cold water, followed by the repeated procedure in the hut, all suggest the cyclic transformations of the elixir.

The year 1584 marked a turning point in Lin's life. He gathered some eighty-seven essays and manuscripts he had written up to that point and edited them into two collections, the *Shensheng tongzong* and the *Fei fei Sanjiao* (Repudiations of repudiations of the Three Teachings). A disciple named Huang Fang built the first Three in One shrine at Mafeng. The *True Record* goes on to list over twenty Three in One shrines that were subsequently built during Lin's lifetime (see table 2 in chapter 3). Lin also donated funds to purchase land to support the sacrifices at the Confucian temple.

Once again, the *True Record* brings us quickly back face to face with harsh reality by quoting in full the text of a proclamation prohibiting the Three in One and ordering the burning of Lin's books and the destruction of his Three in One halls issued in 1585. We will examine the specific charges leveled against Lin in the following chapter. The whole incident arose because various officials vied with one another to invite Lin to visit them. When Regional Inspector Yang Sizhi's[17] casually written invitation was rejected, he denounced Lin to Censor-in-Chief Dan Yangbi, who was passing through Putian. Yang posted a proclamation denouncing Lin and his teachings and ordering the burning of blocks of his recently printed collected works. But after Yang saw Lin's works being burned in Putian, he felt remorse, claiming that he had only intended to put Lin in his place, and that the books were for the

[17] Yang Sizhi, *zi* Yuanshu, from Xiangfu in Henan, received his *jinshi* degree in 1574. He was first appointed censor of the Shenxi Circuit and finally achieved the post of vice minister in the Court of Judicial Review. See *Fujian tongzhi*, 1898 ed., j. 96:5b, and *Ming shizong*, j. 52. Yang had asked Chief Minister of the Bureau of War Chen Rui (a 1553 *jinshi*) to arrange a meeting with Lin. Lin rejected the invitation but at the same time accepted an invitation to meet with Area Commander Chao Kehuai (1565 *jinshi*), further humiliating and enraging Yang Sizhi.

most part morally uplifting. The burning had been the result of too zealous a reading of his proclamation.

But these political difficulties did not get in the way of Lin's spiritual evolution, according to the *True Record*. In the 7th month of that year, 1585, Lin went again to the Wuyi Mountains:

> There his belly gave forth a sound like distant thunder. On the 15th of the month, Śākyamuni Buddha descended from the Heavens. He handed over the power of control to the Lord. This is the meaning of what is called "compelling the things left undone by Śākyamuni" and "the total attainment of the dharma and its power." (*TR* 37b)

Lin was not too disturbed by the official attacks launched against him. He claimed instead that if the charges reached the court they would entail an open discussion of the true principles he upheld, and that they would thereby serve to bring his principles to the attention of many people. He claimed that his own activities could be carefully cross-checked by reference to the *Memorials to Heaven,* copies of which he kept, dating back to the first one in 1541. He composed his treatise *Wusheng lun* (Essay on nonlife) at this time.

The following year, 1586, was his seventieth. The pressure of visitors was becoming extreme, and as there was no place to put them up, he had his disciples build a dormitory and a Dharma Hall on the foundations of Duke Cai's home. He continued with his writing, composing a series of five alchemical poems to help break people from their delusions regarding alchemy. The following year we find further evidence of Lin's spiritual growth:

> In the 2nd month (of 1587) the Lord received news that something unusual had happened. He entered the room to look into it and all he saw was billowing purple breath, spreading across the room. It went out and dissipated. Then he felt that the six voids were unobstructed. He did not know what made his body a body, or what made his spirit a spirit. At the time the Perfected Being of the Kingfisher Lake wrote a poem to clarify this event, in which he explicated that the body experienced in this way was the body of nonbeginning, and the spirit was the spirit of nonbeginning. The state of unconsciousness and unknowing, without thought or concern, was the substance of the prior heaven. All forms and images, all stillness and movement, were but the action of the prior heaven.

Not unexpectedly, this illumination was followed by another round of accusations leveled against him, this time by Lin Fan, a *xiangshi* (student in the local government school) who accused Lin in connection with a Buddhist priest allegedly keeping poisonous insects in order to poison people. These accusations led to a warrant for his arrest and a summons into the yamen, this time before the newly appointed District Magistrate Sun Jiyou.[18] This official

---

[18] Sun Jiyou, from Yuyao in Zhejiang, received his *jinshi* degree in 1586 and served as district magistrate of Putian from 1587 to 1592. See *Fujian Tongzhi* (1898), j. 132:11a, and *Putian xianzhi*, j. 7:32b.

quickly discovered that this was a matter of jealous slander and treated Lin with great respect.

Meanwhile, later the same year (1587), Lin's disciple Zhu Youkai had been spreading the Teachings in the Jian'an region. There a Zhejiang magician drew a picture by planchette in a spirit-writing seance of the "Three Teachings Joined in One." He said to Zhu Youkai:

> Recently all the spirits in audience in the heavens saw that the Jade Emperor was worshipping an image of the Three Teachings Joined in One. This must be your Master of the Three Teachings. [This image] should be transmitted and worshipped. Youkai and some friends plotted to print the image secretly. But the Lord did not dare have his name printed at the top. He said, "The Confucian Master Chungni grasped the one in the Center, he is the Great Patriarch of the Saintly Teachings who Saves the World. The Daoist Master Qingni holds fast to the Center and attains the One, he is the Great Patriarch of the Mystic Teachings Who Saves the World. The Buddhist Shakyamuni who returns to the One within the Void is the Patriarch of the Chan Teachings Who Saves the World. As for the one who has with his writings opened up their writings, he is the one who has unified the Three in One." Thereupon the disciples began to call Lin the Lord, Lord of the Three in One. (*TR* 41a; also in *TA* 34b–35a)

We see another example of Lin's caution in this passage. While he avoids public exposure as a World Savior, he manages to inform his disciples that this is in fact exactly what he is. The following year (1588), Li ordered the printing of his *Milejing* (Maitreya Buddha sutra).

> For this was the time when Maitreya Buddha would take command of the world. Formerly, when the Lord had been staying at the Zhuqisi (Bamboo Ridge Monastery), Maitreya Buddha had personally appeared before the Lord and asked him to write his scripture. The Lord let fly the brush and soon completed the work. The concluding gatha goes, "Maitreya Buddha is my body. Maitreya is my heart. My body is indeed Maitreya's body. My heart is indeed Maitreya's heart. Maitreya and I are not two different bodies, Maitreya and I do not have different hearts. . . ." Only then did the disciples realize that the Lord had in fact truly manifested as Maitreya and that the Great Dragon Flower Assembly was not empty talk. While the Lord was sitting in meditation he saw a crystal pagoda in the heavens descend into his breast. He beheld the thousand Saints all return into his one chest. Then the crown of his head gave off light, completely illuminating the limitless dharma-realms. Every one of his 84,000 pores emitted endless beams of light. (*TR* 41b)

That same year Lin completed his interpretive commentary on the *Daodejing* (The book of the Way and its power). He had now completed commentaries on all the major classics of the Three Teachings. This completed his detailed reinterpretation of the Chinese philosophic and religious tradition, beginning with a chronological survey of early truths and subsequent misinterpretations (*Joint Chronicle of the Three Teachings*), and concluding with textual exegeses of the preeminent works (in his view) of each tradition. He remarked that these would form the ladder of the Three in One, and that they were suitable for recitation in ritual. That winter a unicorn appeared in a flash of lightning on Mount Wuhou. The unicorn would reappear in the 4th month of 1598, the year of Lin's death, in Jiangkou (*TR* 41b).

The entries in the *True Record* for 1589 consist entirely of the texts of letters written to Lin by officials and disciples, and his letters written in response. These letters illustrate the extent of Lin's influence on his times. Many inquire into the workings of the heart method. Zhang Hongdu's entries for this year relate several examples of Lin's skill in selecting geomantically efficacious sites for graves of his followers and their families. Lin decried the excesses that geomancy could lead to and tried to put a check on geomantic activity among his followers. Nonetheless, on one occasion he had two pagodas built at the eastern seaboard of Putian district in order to balance the *fengshui* of the entire Xinghua area (*True Acts* 36b).

The following year (1590) Lin was active again in famine relief in Putian, winning the commendation of a large number of officials. Soon, however, Lin was once again the victim of jealous slander. Moreover, a bandit chief named Chen Wenzhang attempted to capitalize on the growth of the Three in One movement by claiming that he was the *Sanjiao disanzi* (Third son of the Three Teachings). District Magistrate Sun captured him and discovered the truth and posted a proclamation decrying the attempt to defame Lin Zhao'en. Meanwhile, Lin's spiritual progress continued:

> At this time the Lord had already entered deeply into the dharma realm. The sarira (relics of the Buddha) that he had attained already included the 8,400 [of Shakyamuni], but he also knew that there were other sarira in the land of fundamental emptiness that he had not yet explored. The Pratyekabuddha had met the Lord in a former kalpa. This Buddha spoke through Weng Menglong to the Lord: "Old Lin, you are the one whom Śākyamuni indicated would come to bring this dynasty back to the true Yang. You will rebuild the universe (*zai zao qiankun*) and support humankind and all things. In this way immortal spirits comprehend the mysteries and join with the Great Void as one body. Without cultivation or manifestation, without birth or death. Upon this they return to the land of the fundamental emptiness. How could there be enough sariras for this? However, those outside the Way regard this [state] as one of complete separation. The common and ignorant think that it is death. Probably you weren't aware of this, old Lin." The Buddha proceeded to present Lin with a poem as a proof of what he had said. (*TR* 57b)

The following year (1591) Prefect Lu Yijing (from Guichi in Anhui, a 1562 *jinshi*) built a military station on the former grounds of the Yongfusi Buddhist monastery, which had been burned down during the pirate raids. Lin sent the Buddhist monk Mingfeng to complain to the district magistrate, who in turn notified the provincial supreme commander and grand coordinator. These officials authorized the rebuilding of the temple and the removal of the barracks to the military exercise grounds. Lin also had a pagoda built in Lupu. After obtaining all levels of official permission, he ran into difficulties when workers refused to go beyond the fourth floor. Lin got official permission to proceed and completed the project. Later he donated the rents from some of his land to the district government to help support official sacrifices at the shrine to the virtuous antipirate General Qi Jiguang.

That same year Lin's cousin, Zhaoke, was traveling by boat near Fuzhou when a strange wind almost overturned the boat.

> On board was a Xinan man who had long since worshiped the Lord. He took out the Orthodox Breath talisman that he always kept hanging at his side and worshiped it in the open. The boat then settled down and Zhaoke realized that Lin's dharma power was beyond comprehension. (*TR* 58a)

In 1592, in the 4th month, Lin had the Yucangxi bridge built for over 100 in gold. Then, in the 10th month, his disciples held a major Lanpen (Ullambana) Ritual.[19]

> First they held a Purificatory Dragon Flower *jiao* Sacrifice to Prolong Life, seeking to repay their ancestors. Next they held a Water and Land Ritual in order to deliver the souls of each disciple's seven generations of ancestors, along with all the souls of their relatives on the male and female sides. This was a means for people to resolve their obligations and release themselves from their entanglements. Everywhere this ritual was performed, the good results were immediate. People far and wide respectfully did similar rituals. (*TR* 58b)

Earlier that year Lin had a vision regarding the fate of his own ancestors, according to the *True Record:*

> In the first part of the 1st month, the Lord was sitting at the side of the Three in One Hall. His foot was hurt. Suddenly he got up despite his foot and rushed into his chambers. Zhu Fengshi was at his side and sent a lad in to see if he was all right. [Lin] asked him, "Did you know that I have a reason [for acting thus]?"

---

[19] Yunqi Zhu Hong (1535–1615), a contemporary of Lin Zhao'en and an active Buddhist reformer, describes the Lanpen ritual in the following way: "The ritual of feeding the burning mouths (*yankou shishi*) was first instituted by Ananda and was included in the teachings of the Yogacara school. The yoga teaching came to be propagated by the two masters, Vajrabodhi (d. 741) and Amoghavaraja (d. 774), of the Tang dynasty. It could command gods and spirits and move mountains and oceans, its majestic power being beyond human imagination. After it was transmitted for a few generations, there was no one capable of inheriting it. The ritual of feeding the hungry ghosts was the only one preserved. [In performing the ritual,] one makes signs with the hands (*juiyin*), recites spells orally (*songzhou*), and enters into a trance (*zuoguan*). Because the three acts must coordinate with each other, it is called yoga [i.e., a yoke]. This is indeed not at all easy to do. Nowadays few people are proficient in employing mudras and dharanis, not to mention the ability to enter a trance. Since this is the case, they cannot achieve correct coordination. Once coordination is lost, then not only will they not be able to help sentient beings, they will also end up harming themselves. . . . You must believe me when I say that it is indeed not at all easy to perform such a ritual" (translated in Yu, 1980: 184–185). For a recent description, see Pang (1977) and Ofuchi (1983).

Zhu replied that he did not know the reason. The Lord said, "I just saw my late father and mother, along with a great many of my relations and ancestors, coming down out of the sky. I didn't dare remain seated, so, ignoring the pain in my foot, I rushed into my room. Today I have delivered the souls of my ancestors from father on up to the forty-eighth generation. All of them have been reborn in heaven." (*TR* 59a)

In 1593 some of Lin's disciples assembled a simplified version of his writings and had it printed. In the 9th month of that year Lin had yet another spiritual experience:

On the fourth day of the 9th month the Lord went into samadhi from the *chen* hour onward. He came out of it about midday. In a dream he heard, "I do not speak a word, yet the myriad dharmas are born in me. My foot does not take a step, yet I am everywhere throughout the ten directions. When I point to heaven, heaven completes me. When I point to the earth, earth pacifies me. When I point to the sea, the billows of the sea are everywhere calmed. I have no disease of the body. Every family tends toward the good and has no disease of the heart. Great joy and blessing, the earth has reached Supreme Peace." (*TR* 59b; based on the version in *True Acts*, 33a–b)

In the 12th month Lin composed the *Daotong zhongjing* (Scripture of the one in the middle of the Way). Master Lu Wenhui collected the text and took down oral instructions on the Chart of the Great Void of Prior Heaven, the Chart of the Ultimate Principle of Posterior Heaven, the Chart of Heaven, Man, and the Earth, and the Chart of the Roundness of Heaven and the Squareness of Earth.

In 1594 Lin worked again to help the hungry, donating seventy-two ounces of gold to the government. He also established granaries on behalf of the government and went on to donate 100 shi of grain to the Longbo sheyi Granary. But in the fifth month of the year there were food riots in Fuzhou, and the blocks to some of Lin's writings were burned in the resulting fires.

In the 10th month a disciple of Lin's named Cai Jing went to Jinling (Nanjing) to spread the faith. He was well received, and a hall was built in the Sanshanheng. In the 12th month an order was received from the Ministry of Rites to purchase all rare books in the land. Provincial and district authorities pressed Lin to give them copies of all his writings, but many had been lost, or the blocks had been destroyed. Therefore Lin asked Lu Wenhui to re-edit his collected works, sorting out books and essays included in earlier collections such as the *Shenxue tongzong*, the *Fenneiji*, the *Fenzhe, Biaozhe,* and the *Yuezhe shiyu*, and reorganizing them into the thirty-six volumes of the *Linzi sanjiao zhengtong zonglu*. The collection was grouped into four cases. Lu also followed Lin's instructions and selected his writings into thirty-six juan of the *Xiawuni jing* (Scriptures of Xiamuni), in twelve volumes.

On the night that the collection was completed, a round light shone forth and the Dipper Mother descended. The Lord prepared his hat and clothes and led Master Lu in prayer and worship. Then he said to him, "The auspicious manifestations of this evening are in response to your completion of the collection." Master Lu then worked all through the night and finished the text. The Lord was delighted: "My scriptures are today finally complete, my writings are today finally finished." They were carved and printed in response to the official request. (*TR* 61a).

> 1595: District Magistrate Chen repeatedly but unsuccessfully prayed for rain. He invited Lin Zhao'en's aid, saying: "I receive the grain and emoluments of the entire prefecture. You receive the praise of all the four directions. Although our rank and titles differ, people's expectations of us are identical. Now as for the golden elixir [leading to] thunder and lightning, this is something I believe you can accomplish. The maintenance and nurture of harmony at the center is the responsibility of us all." The Lord accepted his invitation and set up an altar in the Fengshansi. Within three days the rain poured down. (*TR* 62a)

This act culminated Lin's role as a model gentry. By relying on his inner alchemical powers, Lin was performing a task normally reserved for a district magistrate in the role of an officiant within a cosmic imperium (Levi, 1986; Zito, 1987).

But Lin felt that the end was near, and he interpreted a white nimbus circling the sun on the 23rd day of the 2nd month of 1596 as a sign of his imminent death (just as an earlier such astrological configuration had been interpreted as a sign of the death of Śākyamuni). Later that year, on the occasion of his eightieth birthday, over eight thousand disciples from all over came to offer congratulations. Meanwhile, Lin's alchemical powers had achieved the final breakthrough:

> Three round marks appeared on the Lord's forehead, red as cinnabar. The crown of his head opened up and he breathed in and out through it, just like an infant. Wang Lu asked him about it and the Lord replied, "This is what is called 'the three flowers gather at the crown of the head' and the 'five breaths doing homage to the origin.' Men of the Dao transform their breath by refining their essence. They transform their spirit by refining their breath. Then by refining their spirits they return to the Void and go straight to the place just like an infant. This is what is meant by 'the gate of heaven splits open and the inner elixir shoots forth its radiance.'" (*TR* 64b)[20]

In the 9th month Lin began a final tour of the Three in One Halls in the area. Early the next year he had Lu Wenhui compose a condensed version of his works and his scriptures to facilitate the popularization of his teachings. In the 4th month he composed a few lines of inspired verse to include in his scriptures. By the 11th month he knew the end was near.

He ate and drank in his room, and he composed songs and verses. Sometimes he

---

[20] Zhang Hongdu's *True Acts* states that it was Zhang himself who proposed this alchemical interpretation of the changes to Lin's face and head (*TA* 40a).

forgot where he was. Even when people he had known for a long time came to see him, he could not recall their names. But when he spoke with them, he always gave them what they sought. Once, while seated, he began to kowtow and said to Master Lu, "Confucius, Laozi, and Śākyamuni all came to ask me to take over the Three Teachings and deliver the disciples of the Three paths. I am about to return. . . . After I return, the Way will belong to you, take care of it!" (*TR* 65b)

Lin Zhao'en chose a religious death:

1598, 14th day of the 1st month, at five in the morning, heavenly music sounded and a golden light shown forth. The Lord quietly folded his hands in salute and passed away. His body remained soft, his hair turned black again, his coloring remained good. Before long his arm fell and his hand opened and then closed again. At the time the only ones around him were some dozen disciples, including Master Lu, Lin Zhaoke, his grandson Jiyue, and some others. When news of his death spread, his disciples came rushing from all over and cried out in sorrow as though they had lost their own parents. Over ten thousand people came to weep. His relatives wore mourning for three years. . . . [His funeral was conducted] on the 28th day of the 1st month of the following year. His [eldest] grandson, Jiying, carried the Lord's soul banner from Wenfu li to Shimen Mountain. As for the gentry, landowners, scholars, and commoners who had received the Lord's aid, all of them came from far and near to attend the sacrifice and hold the cord guiding the hearse. Over seven thousand people attended the funeral. The ritual was completed and the grave finished by the 4th day of the 2nd month. (*TR* 67a)

LINES OF NARRATION

Sorting out the hagiographic elements in this account of Lin Zhao'en's life, we have seen the role of dreams and prophecies: the unicorn dream of 1540, the Dice Dream of 1546, the disciple's 1570 dream of the Supreme Emperor, and Lin's mystical Dream of Supreme Peace of 1596. The evolution of the elixir and the attainment of enlightenment also underlies the narrative of the life of the Lord of the Three Teachings in the *True Record* (and the *True Acts*). Lin first receives information about a "purple-gold" (internal) elixir from the immortal Lu Dongbin in 1564. He experiences the black-iron (external) elixir and has its significance explained to him by the immortal Zhang Sanfeng in 1580. He finally pairs inner and outer elixirs and undergoes alchemical transformation in 1583. The inner alchemical process is only completed in the year of his death, 1598, when he completes the construction and liberation of the immortal embryo. These moments correspond closely to developments in Lin's writing on inner alchemy. Lin composed the *Direct Pointing at the Mind of the Stage* in 1564, the *Selected Sayings on the Nine Stages* in 1579 and the *Illustrated Inner Landscape of the Nine Stages* in 1583. These sources are analyzed further in chapter 4. The themes of the purple-gold and the black-iron elixir had all been prefigured in Zhuo Wanchun's 1548 interpretation of the Dice Dream.

Plate 7. Lin Zhao'en surrounded by his spiritual guides and disciples. Note the three bodies in one hovering above him.

Despite these unifying narrative elements within the hagiographic account, in looking back over Lin's life it is clear that unpredictable external events played a major role. In 1555, within five years of the time that Lin first accepted disciples, and just one year after he had drawn up his first set of regulations for discipleship, massive pirate raids struck Putian. Over the course of the next ten years, repeated attacks would occur. We have seen how Lin responded to these events, offering to sacrifice himself to save the city, dispensing funds to help the destitute, and burying and conducting services for the unattended dead. These charitable and religious acts provided a natural and acceptable outlet for his growing religious organization.

One can also follow the careful development of an image of Lin as a religious figure, starting with the marvelous signs around his birth, then his destined encounter with Zhuo Wanqun, and on to his use of the Orthodox

Breath talisman against disease, false mediums, and pirates. The respect accorded him by the "dwarf pirates," who were often Chinese, rather than Japanese, confirmed his growing reputation. His power over pirates was similar to his power over demonic spirits and disease, as the use of his Orthodox Breath talisman and his casting out of heterodox spirit mediums indicates.

The dreams and portents gradually give way to full-scale visions that mark Lin as an embodiment of Maitreya Buddha. These include the vision of Maitreya at the birth of Lin in 1517, the all-important vision of Maitreya in 1578, the vision of Śākyamuni Buddha in 1585, the vision of Buddha nature in 1587, the encounter with Pratyekabuddha in 1590 (via a medium), the vision of the deliverance of his ancestors in 1592, and the experience of samadhi in 1593.

Episodes like the 1567 throwing back of the turtle and the statement of thanks by the Dragon King fall into the category of the legendary tale. The miracles effected by Lin's Orthodox Breath talisman in 1591 and earlier during the pirate raids on Putian could be classed as mirabilia. These legends and miracles are woven into the image of the deified Lin Zhao'en.

The account in the sacred biographies also enable us to follow the development of the Three in One organization. He first accepted disciples in 1551–1553, drew up regulations for them in 1554, and outlined rituals for their comportment in 1558. His organization gained considerable legitimacy by its charitable and religious work during the raids. In 1565, after the pirate raids abated, Lin drew up new regulations for his expanded organization. This time the heart method was put in a prominent position, in recognition perhaps of the increasing importance to Lin of inner alchemy. In 1566 he developed special uniforms for his disciples. He began accepting donations from his disciples in 1567, published a set of his collected writings, and built larger quarters for them in 1572. He began organizing large-scale temple construction projects, which required the raising and spending of considerable sums of money. He began traveling to spread his teachings in 1569, and he sent disciples to five provinces. In 1578 he expanded the Zongkongtang, designing a particular architectural configuration to symbolize the unification of the Three Teachings into One. He expanded his missionary work for the Three in One and began accepting "travel money" in 1580. In 1584 he first allowed Three in One shrines to be built and began to organize the printing of his collected works. This was the first year that he allowed his disciples to call him Master Xiawuni. Both these innovations followed shortly after his alchemical breakthrough of 1583.

Serious questions were raised about the size and nature of his organization in 1578 and 1579, and in 1585 he withstood a major official attack on his character, his writings, and his organization (see chapter 3). Yet in 1586 he was able to expand his headquarters, building dormitories to accommodate the increasing number of disciples. In 1587 he endorsed the image of himself as a triple body composite of the three masters of the three teachings suggested by a Zhejiang magician. Thereupon his disciples referred to him as the Lord of the Three in One. The year 1587 was therefore a year of profound significance in the development of the Three in One (pace R. Huang, 1981).

Lin's reputation was spreading widely, and several Hanlin academicians wrote to him in 1589. In the early 1590s Lin and his Three in One organization were involved in famine relief, geomantic readjustments of the entire Putian region, bridge building, temple construction, large-scale religious services, the provisioning of granaries, and successful prayers for rain. The year 1597 saw the publication of another version of his collected works, which included the *Bentijing* (Scripture of the original substance) and the *Milejing* (Maitreya scripture). Both these sources present an image of Lin as a realized being, on equal footing with the Buddha.

Many Three in One temples are currently adorned with frescoes illustrating some of these images and the very hagiographic episodes highlighted in the preceding account of Lin Zhao'en's life. The oldest I have been able to locate are in the Ruiyun Shuyuan in Duwei in Xianyou. This is an incomplete set attributed to Li Xia, a renowned painter of the area who died in 1933.

The lines of narration within the accounts of Lin Zhao'en's life weave in and out of four phases. Each of these phases can be conceptualized as distinct vectors (or series of events) composed of multiple interlocked social, economic, and libidinal forces converging to open up a plane of social interaction. The first phase, from Lin's birth in 1517 to his failure at the examinations in 1547, saw the formation of a promising Confucian student, the scion of a wealthy family within a major, well-connected lineage, being groomed for an official career. The second phase, from 1547 to 1551, while brief, was crucial to the subsequent changes in Lin's life. He rejected the conventional vector of Confucian studies leading to an official career and turned instead to a quest for mystical experience, involving radical philosophic questioning and experiments with various forms of self-cultivation. The third phase went from 1551 to 1563, from his acceptance of disciples to his actions during the pirate raids on Putian. This series of events follows from the decision to establish a school, to transmit techniques of meditation and self-cultivation, and to lecture on the unification of the Three Teachings. Extraordinary events such as the pirate raids pushed Lin and his disciples to the forefront of a new sector of local gentry, responding to emergency situations beyond the control of the state. Lin came to the rescue of the city, interceding with mercenary troops, offering to sacrifice his own life for the city, leading his disciples in social welfare operations and in the gathering and burial of thousands of abandoned corpses. The fourth phase, from 1563 to 1598, saw the gradual development of a religious movement from the school that Lin had established in the 1550s. In this phase the internal series includes (a) the development of Lin's historical critique of the separation of the Three Teachings, and his demonstration of their fundamental unity and (b) the development of Lin's alchemical experimentation and the codification of his system into the Nine Stages of the heart method. External events that had an impact include (1) the growing official suspicions concerning the Three in One religious orga-nization, (2) the needs and expectations of growing numbers of disciples; and (3) complications arising from the evolving organizational complexity of the burgeoning Three in One movement. Lines emerging from each of these phases create resonances, contradictions, and connections between phases. For example, Lin said that his mystical searching phase lasted nearly ten years, which suggests that it lasted well into the period of pirate invasions and may have come to a close with his decision to follow through with the develop-ment of a religious organization. These phases and planes ultimately combine into a life trajectory, a kinetic geography of a religious leader, channeling the senses, perception, and knowledge of his followers into a new configuration, blazing a new path to enlightenment. As he also provides the techniques of self-cultivation and is at any rate credited with the rituals and organizations of the Three in One, it is not surprising that his image and the sound of his name should guide the adherents of the Three in One along the way to realization of the *benti,* the fundamental unity of the substance of the universe.

The Early Disciples

BY THE TIME Lin Zhao'en was forty-seven, in 1563, he was a religious teacher with a large following. There is considerable debate as to just how Lin viewed his own role. Much of the doubt is generated by certain of Lin's own writings, which attack "delusions" and avoid any indication that Lin was veering toward divine status. But in his disciples' minds there was little doubt that they were in the presence of more than just an erudite Confucian scholar. Many believed that they were blessed to be in attendance on a divine Confucian sage, a living Buddha, a Daoist immortal. This chapter explores how they constructed a god out of a man.

Lin Zhao'en's Three in One organization developed slowly, in a complex interaction between the development of Lin's vision of the unification of the Three Teachings and his inner alchemical progress, the needs and desires of his disciples, the suspicions of the local government, and the support and recognition his charitable and religious work gained from the community. The Three in One expanded from a handful of disciples in 1550, to the thousands who attended his lectures during his travels beginning in the 1570s, to the seven thousand who participated in his eightieth birthday, and the over ten thousand who attended his funeral in 1598. The *Mensheng shilu* lists the names of over 130 disciples but gives a figure of 800 disciples at the end of Lin's life. The *Jinling zhongyitang xingshi* provides some three dozen other names. Many more names could be gathered by compiling the names of the donors and collators recorded at the end of each *juan* of the many different editions of Lin's collected works.[1]

OFFICIAL SUSPICION

How did Lin Zhao'en succeed in establishing a private academy that developed into a widespread religious organization? This organization came to fulfill many social functions traditionally performed by the provincial- and district-level representatives of the imperial government. We have seen that Lin was frequently the object of official suspicion and attack. He had, however, considerable support from his influential family, as well as from a num-

---

[1] The *Jinling zhongyitang xingshi* gives brief biographies of two merchants: Tai Zhaoquan, from Kuaiji, a merchant renowned for his fairness, who never cheated his gentry customers and was active in bestowing coffins on the poor; and Xu Yangchi, from Putian, another merchant who was befriended by all the gentry and literati.

ber of officials, including some who had initially set out to destroy him. But the most important source of support was that of his disciples and followers.

We have seen several instances in the preceding chapter of official condemnation of Lin Zhao'en and his activities. The reasons for this lie in the government's suspicion of extragovernmental organizations and their potential for political disruption. When such organizations were guided by messianic principles, the government was even more weary of the prospect of fanatical insurrection. J. J. M. De Groot has described the evolution of the Confucian orthodox rejection of such organizations and their heterodox (by definition) ideologies. He provides a translation of the "Law against Heresy and Sects":

Prohibition against Religious Leaders and Shamanic Practices

ARTICLE 1

Religious leaders or shamans, who, pretending thereby to call down heretical gods, write talismans or pronounce them over water, or carry round palanquins [with idols], or invoke saints, calling themselves orthodox leaders, chief patrons, or female masters; further, further, all societies falsely calling themselves Maitreya Buddha White Lotus communities, or the Teachings of the Bright Reverend One, or School of the White Cloud, etc., together with all that answers to practices of the Left-hand [i.e., deviant] Way or the extreme measure (*Yiduan*); finally, they who in secret places have images, and offer incense to them, or hold meetings which take place at night and break up by day, whereby the people are stirred up and misled under the pretext of cultivating virtue,—shall be sentenced; the principle perpetrators to strangulation, and their accomplices each to a hundred blows with long stick, followed by a lifelong banishment to a distance of three thousand miles.

ARTICLE 2

If anyone in the army or amongst the people dress or ornament the image of a god, and receive that god with the clang of cymbals and the beating of drums, and hold sacrificial meetings in his honor, one hundred blows with the long stick shall be administered, but only to the principals.

ARTICLE 3

If the village chiefs, when privy to such things [as detailed in art. 1 and 2], do not inform the authorities, they shall receive each forty blows with the bamboo lath. Services of prayer and thanksgiving [for harvest] in honor of the common local gods of the Soil, performed in spring and autumn respectively, do not fall under these restrictions.[2]

---

[2] Ter Haar (1992: 124) translates a late Ming commentary to *Article One* as follows: "[There are] different societies fraudulently proclaiming themselves [the Teachings of] Maitreya from the West, the White Lotus Society of Master [Hui]yuan, the [Teachings] of the Venerable of Light of Mani [Manichaeism], and the White Cloud tradition of the Buddha." This shows that de-Groot's translation should have distinguished between Maitreyan teachings and White Lotus societies.

Ter Haar (1992) has demonstrated how this law against the "heterodox way" (translated above by deGroot literally as "the Left-hand Way") gradually overtook an earlier prohibition against *yaoyan* ("heterodox teachings").[3] DeGroot (1971) provides a list of bloody attacks on and suppression of various sectarian groups over the course of the Qing dynasty. Other scholars have offered various explanations of this history of persecution (Naquin, Overmyer, Shek, ter Haar, Ownby).

The fullest record of official suspicion of the Three in One during Lin's lifetime is the 1585 proclamation by Regional Inspector Yang Sizhi. Interestingly, the entire text is included in the *True Records*. As mentioned above, Yang had felt slighted by Lin Zhao'en and had attempted to present a memorial calling for his impeachment to the court via Censor-in-Chief Dan Yangbi, who was passing through the area. The censor-in-chief responded acidly:

"[Although] I have not met this Lin of the Three Teachings, I've heard about his gathering corpses [for burial] and his aiding the poor. In his academic lectures he shows an exhaustive knowledge of the classics. He has had a good reputation in the central Min area for a long time. Should your memorial be sent up to court, we'd have to bring down the Nine Chief Ministers and the [Ministers of the] Six Boards to debate with him. Today in this province there are many who approve of him. Should your memorial be rejected, this will merely further strengthen his reputation. Wouldn't it be better simply to issue a proclamation prohibiting the [Three in One]? That will be enough to disperse his followers."

The text of the proclamation runs for five pages (*True Record*, 24b–27a) and is written in an accusatory and mocking tone. The document can be summarized as follows: Lin is referred to as a *yaoren* (heterodox man). He is said to have gathered together thousands of disciples. His heterodox writings craftily conceal their profound perversity. He confounds the age and bewitches the people. He spoils the name of the orthodox teachings. Not content to trick the followers of just one of the teachings, he has declared that all three return to one teaching, and that he is the master of the three teachings. He has named his hall the Three Teachings Hall and yet has again divided it into three (chambers) to confound the ignorant. Even the ignorant realize that there are three religions, and that the Confucians study in the state-run Confucian academy, while Buddhists and Daoists all have their bureaus (within the government). Yet he claims to have refined all the teachings. Such false claims must be rectified. Why must he set up his writings as *jing* (classics; scriptures)? The ancients did not refer to their own writings as classics, nor did they call themselves saints. They did not seek to sell their works in the marketplace. Not only does Zhao'en call his works "saintly," he also calls them a "unification of the schools." This false claim should be recti-

[3] Ter Haar (1992: 123–130) points out that the earlier prohibition of "heterodox teachings," based on precedents in the Tang and Song legal codes, was included in the area of the Ming penal code dealing with disorder and banditry (*Daming jijie fulie*, 18: 6b–7b) and prescribed beheadings for leaders and followers alike. The prohibition against the "heterodox way" quoted above was a new addition to a different section of the laws concerning transgressions of ritual (*Daming jijie fulie* 11: 9b–12a [934–939]).

fied. Moreover, one set of books is given the demonic title of *Disputing Disputes on Confucianism,* which should also be rectified. In general, it appears that his underlying ambition is to outdo the Duke of Letters, Zhu Xi (1120–1200). Another devious trick is insisting that his followers take an oath of allegiance, and only then consenting to see them. Even people who are seriously ill, and who have been misled into thinking he can bring the dead back to life, have to take the vows before being granted an audience. The same holds for those desiring to learn his geomancy. After transmission of vows they are expected to have complete faith in him. This is a crafty means to ensnare people. And he is clever about it. When one first sees him, a gift of fruit and a little money is adequate. Then your name is inscribed in the record books of the initiates. Incense is burned, talismans are written, spells are chanted, while the vows are sworn. Then a pictorial image is given out and one is ordered to worship it. One must uphold a vegetarian diet. One may not discuss the secrets of the teachings even with one's parents. If this were an orthodox teaching, why couldn't one discuss it with one's parents? Thus upon first initiation one has already broken the law with regards to one's parents. The burning of incense and swearing of vows beguiles people into a willingness to perform magical acts of the Left-hand Way. Last year he traveled through northern Fujian, Jiangsu, and Zhejiang, gathering together thousands of disciples who crowded the cities, meeting at night to recite scriptures and worship buddhas. All kinds of suspicious people follow him. Whoremongers, gamblers, lictors, and yamen runners all are accepted as disciples. Is this something the Duke of Letters would have done? Formerly, when Putian was sacked, he dispensed coffins to bury the untended dead. His family was extremely wealthy, and he had been storing up wood in his Three Teachings Hall for just such an occasion. Later he compared himself to Wen Wang, who also buried the untended dead. So it was all done for selfish reasons. Yet this was enough to persuade some *shidafu* (literati) to become initiates. They have never carefully examined whether he deserves their respect. The proclamation concludes that Lin's writings would have been considered extremist and heretical by Confucius and Mencius, and that they pose a threat to contemporary society. The Three Teachings Hall and the writings of Lin Zhao'en should be burned. A report on the investigation will subsequently be posted in the Minglun Hall of the Confucian Temple, and in places where people congregate. All his heterodox disciples should scatter and disappear. Literati should cease falling for his tricks and return to the orthodox Way.

Regional Inspector Yang ordered Funing Circuit Intendant Wang Shimao (1536–1588)[4] to post the proclamation. He posted it at the Fujian Coastal Defense Station. Lin's followers asked how they should react, and he told them to post the proclamation on their own doorways, arguing that government persecution would only force the truth of the Three in One out into the open. After the proclamation had gone up, Lin came back from a trip to Jian-

---

[4] Wang Shimao (1536–1588), *zi* Jingmei, *hao* Linzhou, 1559 *jinshi*, was the younger brother of the renowned poet Wang Shizhen. He ultimately attained the position of vice minister of the Court of Imperial Sacrifices. Wang wrote the *Minbushu,* an important source on Fujian history.

ning. Yang sent Prefect Li Bofang, Vice Prefect Guan Xueyin, Assistant Prefect He Biao, and Jietui (Judge) Zhu Zhihe as a group to check up on him. Zhu gathered up the blocks to his writings and the sign-placard of the Three Teachings Hall and burned them in the district schoolgrounds[5] to fulfill Yang's orders. At that point Yang seems to have realized that he had gone too far, noting that copies of Lin's works were already widely distributed, and that it was useless to attempt to destroy them. In fact, Yang's efforts seem to have had little effect on the growth of the Three in One. Judge Zhu, according to Zhang Hongdu, subsequently felt such shame over his conduct that he resigned his position and led his entire family to become initiates in the Three in One.[6] Although Lin was again called in for questioning in 1587, the charges were quickly dropped.

Compared with the sort of persecution handed out to other religious leaders and religious groups (Ter Haar, 1992), Lin's treatment was relatively mild. But in time the Three in One would suffer by association with the label of the "White Lotus movement." One of the first to make such an accusation was Xie Zhaozhe (1567–1624):

> There are now in the world a kind of person like those "who eat vegetables and worship devils" and [followers] of the White Lotus teachings: these are all ritual methods descended from the Five Pecks of Rice bandits. They are everywhere, misleading the masses without end and causing calamities and disturbances. . . . Moreover, within the central Min area there are the magical practices of the Three Teachings, which arose from [the teachings of] Lin Zhao'en of Putian. . . . He taught people to heal diseases with the *genbei* method, and because it was somewhat effective, his disciples followed after him like a cloud and transmitted [his teachings] to one another, and so there are a great many in my province who believe in him. After [Lin] Zhao'en's death, a preaching hall was established at his place, and on the first and fifteenth of each moon, people assemble there and burn incense. Later they added the use of talismans and registers, communal sacrifices and prayers, exorcisms and the capture of demons. All these are connected with the Yellow Turbans and the White Lotus [Teachings]. . . . In his old age [Lin] became ill and developed a mental illness; he could not differentiate between water and fire. He was insane [suffering from a mania] for a year and then he died. How could he really have been in possession of [true] magical arts? . . . Nowadays his disciples cover the cities and towns of the prefecture. Among them are worthy people no different from literati and gentlemen. But a few wicked and degenerate [followers] avail themselves of the curing of illness for private advantage; they practice malicious banditry and cheating and there is nothing they will not do. How do they differ from heterodox shamans and shamanesses? (Translation based on Franke [1973] with modifications.)

[5] Zhang Hongdu states that the books were burned at the Three Teachings Hall (TA 31b).

[6] According to the *True Record* and the *True Acts,* when Yang was later serving at court he attempted once again to denounce Lin Zhao'en, but the latter was defended by the far more powerful Zou Yuanbiao (1551–1624), leader of the Tonglin party. On Zou Yuanbiao, see *Ming Biographies,* 1312–1314.

Xie made further disparaging comments about Lin that were quoted by the editors of the *Suku quanshu tiyao* in their negative assessment of the *Linzi quanji* (Collected writings of Master Lin):

> Lin Zhao'en, from my own Puyang in Fujian, considered himself to be learned and an accomplished writer. He was able to cure disease with his *genbei* method. Those of his disciples to whom he transmitted his method did not absorb his teachings and vainly set about summoning down demons and capturing ghosts. Strictly speaking, they are shamans, for what good is it to spend all day seizing the hundred ghosts? Nevertheless, the followers of his teachings increase each day, and many of them are wicked, false, deceitful, and thieving. I fear that some day [they will] cause a disaster in these parts no smaller than those caused by the Yellow Turbans and the White Lotus. (*Siku quanshu tiyao*, j. 125, *zajia*)

As Ter Haar (1992) has shown, the fear of anything associated, accurately or not, with the White Lotus teachings could lead to severe persecution (see chapter 5 below).

FAMILY BACKGROUND AND SUPPORT

To see how Lin Zhao'en had the room to maneuver under the paranoid surveillance of the state, we need to examine his family background. Dong Shi commented on the family support provided by Lin's grandfather and many years later by a grandson:

> The Three in One Hall on East Mountain was formerly the place where the Master's grandfather, the General Wugong, kept his study. After he had retired from official duties, he had a pagoda built here and called himself Old Woodsman of the Eastern Mountain. Inside [the pagoda] there were written four large characters, "The Woodsman's Cottage of Eastern Mountain," written by Panou Li Xiang. The Master established his academy here many years ago. After his death, his students built a shrine there to worship him. This was repaired in 1629 by the Master's grandson, [Lin] Qisong. In 1653 the disciples invited Master Chen of Hunan to the hall to illumine the Way. At this time they again reworked the old foundations, so that the veins of the Dao could transmit forever, with [new chambers] distributed to the right and left. In 1655 they invited . . . [Dong] Shi [to the hall]. (Preface to Poems on the Eight Scenic Attractions of East Mountain, included in *Dongshan jicao*, 1.35)

These remarks by the Third Transmitter, Dong Shi, demonstrate that Lin Zhao'en made use of his family's official background and resources when first establishing his academy. They also reveal that at least some members of his family continued to support Lin's efforts long after his death. Behind his grandfather's study, at the top of East Mountain, located on the northeast edge of Putian city, stands a stone pagoda and Buddhist temple, also built by Lin Fu. The pagoda is one of the major sites of the city. Lin's family members had many accomplishments to their credit and offered a strong network of support for Lin's innovations.

Lin belonged to an extended lineage known as the Jiumu Lin (the Lins of the Nine Prefects), so named because nine sons of the Fujian pioneer ancestor Lin Pi (fl. 752) had served as prefects in the Tang dynasty, and one of the eight great surname groups said to have immigrated into Putian in the Jin dynasty, in 308 (*Putian xianzhi,* 35; Vermeer, 1990; Clark, 1995). Lin descended from the line of the Duanzhou Prefect Lin Wei, eldest son of Lin Pi. In the nineteenth generation one Lin Hong (*jinshi* 1401) settled in Putian and served as district magistrate and later as a prefect.

> In the Ming at every provincial examination Putian took half of the places of all Fujian, and at the Metropolitan examination they always won one-third of the places above the quotas. Few areas in the realm could match their ability to have successful *jinshi* among the grandfather and grandson, father and son, elder and younger brothers, and cousins within one family. (Translated in Berling [1980: 62] from the *Bamin tongzhi*)

Tan Qian was even more specific:

> In Putian, from the *gengxu* year of the Hongwu reign period (1370) to the *xuzi* year of the Jiajing reign period (1528), out of over fifty examinations, there were 1,111 *xiangju* (prefectural graduates), 324 *jiabang* (first-place graduates), 2 *zhuangyuan* (principal metropolitan graduates), 4 *taohua* (third-place metropolitan graduates), 1 *huiyuan* (principal graduate), and 25 *jieyuan* (principal prefectural graduates). In the Song dynasty, there had been over 790 *jinshi* (metropolitan graduates) and over 640 special mentions in the various examinations, with 5 *dakui* (principal graduates) and 6 prime ministers.

According to tables in Parsons (1969), the successful degree holders from Putian also managed a high rate of office holding. Putian was responsible for 494 officials during the Ming dynasty. This figure easily surpasses that of any other local area of particular political significance in the tables. Of this number, the Lins of Putian produced one-seventh, with 71 office holders who held 128 official positions over the course of the Ming dynasty, with at least one member holding office during all reign periods from Yongle through Chungzhen (1403–1644), with the exception of Chingtai and Tianxun (1450–64). The Chen and Huang surname groups of Putian also maintained an astonishing record of success in the imperial service.

Fourteen of Lin's direct ancestors over the preceding six generations beginning with Lin Hong had obtained degrees and served in office, mostly as prefects, district magistrates, or professors and instructors in Confucian schools (see chart in Zheng [1988a: 23–24]). Those who had attained the highest positions included his grandfather, Lin Fu, who attained his *jinshi* degree in 1504. He served in the Ministry of Justice, then was imprisoned for offending the eunuch Liu Jin. Later he was appointed prefect of Yuanzhou, and later of Ningbo. In 1522 he was appointed administration vice commissioner of Guangxi. While there he won the respect of Wang Shouren for his administrative and military abilities. Both were actively engaged in putting down minority rebellions. Wang mentioned Lin in several memorials. Lin Fu wrote a poem to Wang entitled "Discussing the *Yijing* with Wang Yangming While Incarcerated." Shortly before passing away, Wang recommended Lin Fu for his own position, as regulator-general (supreme commander) of Guangxi and Guangdong. Shortly after Wang's death in 1529, Lin Fu lost his position due to a defeat suffered by his subordinate officers and returned home to Putian.

Four of Lin Fu's five sons held office, Lin Wanren, the father of Lin Zhao'en, being the only exception. Among Lin Zhao'en's brothers and cousins, six obtained degrees, and five held offices such as prefect, district magistrate, and secretary in the Nanjing Ministry of Revenue and the Ministry of Justice in Beijing. Of this group, five also wrote books and collected works. Lin Zhao'en, being a radical Confucian, put great emphasis on family and lineage and composed several works on ideal lineage ritual. He also carefully arranged for his own burial in the family mountainside cemetery in Huatingxian. Four of his younger brothers—Lin Zhaoju, Lin Zhaogao, Lin Zhaojing, and Lin Zhaozhi—were among his earliest disciples, receiving instruction in the heart method in 1551–52. Lin Zhaoke, his cousin, also received initiation as a disciple of Lin, as did other relatives.[7]

SUPPORT FROM CONTEMPORARY SCHOLAR-LITERATI

In addition to his immediate family and the extended lineage, Lin also received support from influential admirers and readers all across the country. These included prominent intellectuals like Geng Dingxiang (1524–96), who recommended him for office; Zou Yuanbiao (1551–1624), who defended him at court; He Xinyin (1517–79), who went to visit him in 1561;[8] several members of the *jinshi* class of 1586, who corresponded with him; He Qiaoyuan (also a 1586 *jinshi*), who wrote a favorable biographical sketch of Lin; and Yuan Huang (1533–1606), who commented that "When I read the Classics in my early years there were many passages I could not understand. But each time I looked up the collected writings of Lin Zhao'en, everything

[7] It is also true that some of Lin's relations scoffed at his teachings and considered him an embarrassment (Zheng, 1988a).

[8] The timing of this visit is questionable. He Xinyin is quoted in the *True Record* as having said several extremely flattering things about Lin Zhao'en's efforts to unify the Three Teachings into One. In his own writings, he was less enthusiastic about Lin. See his letter *Shang Qi Mentao dashu*, where he describes a visit to Lin and his conclusion that Lin's views were unexceptional. The date of the visit is given as 1559 in the *True Record* and in the *Chronological Biography*. He Xinyin's own writings and his flight to Fujian to avoid persecution in 1562–63 suggest a later date for the encounter. He Xinyin is worshiped alongside Lin Zhao'en in some temples in Southeast Asia (see Franke, 1972).

became at once perfectly clear."[9] Guan Zhidao (1536–1608) offered a luke-warm assessment. Huang Zongxi's (1610–96) biography of Lin (translated in Franke, 1973) is more equivocal, although he too sets out to defend Lin against distortions of his doctrines.[10]

Yet Lin's views were scarcely known by many of the most influential con-temporary literati.[11] Zheng Zhiming (1988: 231–239) suggests that Lin's status as a mere *shengyuan* made it difficult for higher-ranking literati to as-sociate with him. A *shengyuan* was still a commoner in the eyes of the law, without any of the privileges of a *jinshi*, not to mention those of an official. Zheng goes on to argue that Lin's charitable activities could not be fully legitimized by the local authorities because they suspected him of harbor-ing plans to develop a religious organization. Therefore he was not listed in the regional gazetteers under the categories of *yixing* (righteous behavior) or *xiangxian* (local sage). In fact, Lin's very biography was expunged from later editions of the district gazetteer.[12] Yet his efforts to become a religious leader were held in check by his own Confucian models; thus Lin never became a wonder-working figure. Zheng concludes that Lin's efforts to penetrate popular culture with a practical version of Confucian morality

[9] These remarks are taken from Huang Zongxi's biographical essay on Lin Zhao'en. For fur-ther information on Yuan Huang, see Brokaw (1991).

[10] Huang Zongxi shared Xie Zhaozhi's feelings about the dangers of inner alchemy: "Xie Zhaozhi said that Lin Zhao'en became insane and died, and his pupils said too that in his late years there was something in his breast blocking it up and that he could not bring out a single word. He did not even know the names of those around him from morning to evening. That was the evil resulting from his dealing with *jindan* (metalic elixers)." Translation based on Franke (1972) with minor alterations. Complete translation and original text of the *Lin Sanjiao juan* (Biography of Lin of the Three Teachings) in Franke (1972).

[11] Contemporary figures such as Li Zhi (1527–1602), Hu Zhi (1517–1585), Yang Qiyuan (1547–1599), Jiao Hong (1540–1620), Luo Rufang (1515–1588), He Xinyin (1517–1579), Tao Wangling (1562–1608), Du Long (1542–1605), Yuan Zongdao (1560–1600), Yuan Hong-dao (1568–1623), Du Wenhuan (d. 1640), Yunqi Zhuhong (1535–1615), and Hanshan Deqing (1546–1623) scarcely mentioned Lin Zhao'en in their writings and their letters. A typ-ical example is Du Wenhuan, who in his preface to *Sanjiao huizong* quotes Huang Guancan as saying, "As for the Three Teachings, they have each been transmitted separately, but nowadays one Mister Lin in Putian has begun to combine them into one, but I am unable to obtain a deep understanding [of his efforts]" (quoted in Zheng, 1988: 53). However, a small number of offi-cials interested in Lin's heart method did correspond with him in 1589. These include Huang Hongxian (1541–1600), who attained the rank of tutor (academician reader in waiting) and vice supervisor of the Household of the Heir Apparent, and was the author of an account of Korea (*Chaoxian guoji*). Other scholars wrote to Lin around this time requesting permission to be his disciples in inner cultivation. These include Yuan Zongdao (mentioned above), Wang Tu (1557–1627; see *Ming shi* j. 212, *Ming shi liejuan*, j. 75), Wu Yingbin, Xiao Yunju, Wang Keshou, Yu Shizhang, and others (see Zheng, 1988: 68–72).

[12] Franke notes that Lin's biography appears in the *Minshu* (1630), the *Fujian tongzhi* edi-tions of 1684 and 1737, and the *Gujin tushu jicheng* of 1726, but that it is absent from the *Fu-jian tongzhi* edition of 1829/1868 and the *Putian xianzhi* of 1758 and its later supplementary editions of 1879 and 1926. Zhang Qin did include a biography in his draft 1945 *Putian xianzhi,* as well as a defense of the Three in One in his official report on local cults entitled *Kaoli zhengsa baocun shenshe shuodie.*

and Confucian self-cultivation/enlightenment failed because his teachings reached only local intellectuals, whereas his influence on popular religious behavior was far more limited. Moreover, even as a philosopher, his sources were often limited, and his efforts to combine three complex religious systems were often arbitrary and self-contradictory. Nevertheless, Lin was struggling to produce a third alternative to Zhu Xi's "broad learning" and Wang Yangming's "innate knowledge of the good," and his vision of a renewed Confucian morality seems to have found many echoes in contemporary popular culture.

Yet we will soon see that Lin's influence quickly spread beyond a small circle of "local intellectuals" and "local officials" with whom he came into contact. Moreover, Zheng's analysis represents Chinese popular culture and popular religion as largely static, primarily concerned with personal benefits, and motivated by a search for support from or protection against supernatural or miraculous powers. While a good case can be made for the vitality of a "shamanic substratum" within Chinese culture and religion (van der Loon, 1977), this does not mean that popular culture and religion remain unaffected by regionally differentiated economic, political, and social changes. As pointed out in chapters 1 and 2 above, the local culture of the Xinghua region was deeply influenced by Confucian thought and morality through its local lineages and their rituals, and those of its schools, academies, official shrines, and Confucian temples. Lin's Three in One movement drew from a wide acceptance of Confucian modes of thought and action, while it rode the wave of late Ming and early Qing social changes in the Xinghua region that saw popular god temples develop beyond and above the scope of extended lineage organizations throughout the Xinghua region.

EXPANDING ROLES FOR LOCAL GENTRY

Zheng Zhiming (1988: 239) makes the interesting suggestion that Lin Zhao'en represents a new level of lower gentry active between officialdom and popular culture. He suggests that this group was struggling to break away from an increasingly rigid version of official Confucianism, as seen in the compilation of the *Sishu daquan* (Great compendium of [commentaries] on the Four Books), the *Wujing daquan* (Great compendium of [commentaries] on the Five Classics), and the *Xingli daquan* (Great compendium on human nature and cosmic principle). One might add that in local terms, such figures can be seen to be responding not only to the rigidity of official thought, but also to an empire-wide crisis in the examination system, and to the local crisis of lineage control. Of course, it is one thing to argue for innovations in the elite having an impact on the masses, and it is another to show how a new vector of change emerges at the meeting point of social forces, sweeping philosophic discourses along while transforming the terms of analysis as well as the form and content of the social forces themselves.

The late Ming imperial government apparatus was overstretched at the local level. At the same time, one notes the decline of Buddhism and of Daoism, the rise of lineages, and the rise of the role of the "model gentry," who would respond to emerging social crises by mediating between the imperial administrators and local groups. There was a need for this emerging gentry class to be able to articulate some kind of theoretical and liturgical basis for the popular merger of Three religions, as can be seen in the proliferation of novels and plays with these themes at this time.

Nevertheless, this new kind of mediating role raised the suspicions of local officials like Yang Sizhi. Yet Lin's role as a model local gentry was vindicated on several occasions. For example, Governor Yi Daotan was planning to visit the Xinghua region but desisted when he heard news of the scattered corpses in the area. He received reports on Lin's efforts to gather and bury the corpses of the unattended dead from district educational authorities and proceeded to investigate. Professor Liu Shirui submitted a report in support of Lin Zhao'en's efforts, going so far as to recommend his promotion to office. As a result, Lin received prizes from Regional Inspector Pan Huang and Prefect Lu. The *True Record*, 19a, provides a list of those who built a shrine to commemorate his bravery.

HEALING AND MIRACLES

Lin Zhao'en gained renown as a healer and a worker of miracles. Beginning with his cure of his disciple's daughter, Lin's heart method became known as the "cure that required no medicine." A theory of disease is proposed in the *True Record*:

> [Lin] repeatedly dreamt that hundreds of men and women came to him, begging for gold and silver. The Lord explained to them the means of repaying debts to the wrongfully dead (*yuanzhai*). He ordered them to contribute funds to generate good merit, and their illnesses were immediately cured. In general, those illnesses that cannot be cured by doctors are for the most part caused by the entanglements brought on by debts to the wrongfully dead. The means by which the Lord was able to cure serious illnesses without the use of medicine were all a result of the broad light shed by his divine powers (*shentong*). This was all on account of teaching people how to disentangle themselves from former injustices. Thus he ordered them to wash away former transgressions, to do good deeds in order to eliminate their own adversities, to forward good causes in order to make up for their own misdeeds. In this way what disease could not be cured? Thus for the entire category of disease and pain brought on by various kinds of unprincipled and unfair conduct, such as debts incurred through causing the death of another person, or the turning of one's back on righteousness or being ungrateful for the mercy [of parents], or the leveling of other's graves on account of the business of divination, or being rude to spirits by cursing and swearing, only the Lord

was able to completely illuminate and disentangle their [causes]. (*TR* 50a, note on the year 1584)

Lin secured his reputation as a healer by paying visits to (and curing the diseases of) General Qi Jiguang (1528–1588) in Fuzhou. They exchanged correspondence, met to discuss philosophy, and maintained a friendship that would last twenty years. Lin would later sponsor a shrine in Qi's honor. Other officials he cured included Zhu Guangyu and Liu Siwen. Lin's method of curing led to the compilation of the *Linshi quebing gongfu* (Master Lin's art of healing), which is included in the *Yanjian milu* (Secret record of ease), edited by Chen Meigong (Berling, 1980: 138, n. 118).

The *Jinling zhongyitang xingshi* also provides several case studies of the curing of disease. Zhen Lai, the author of that text, comments on the role of the heart method in the spread of the teachings. Ma and Han (1992: 737–783) suggest that Lin's healing method was what won him support from the "masses," extending the reach of the Three in One beyond the circle of local intellectuals and officials around Lin, and setting the stage for the development of the Three in One into a full-fledged religious movement. They quote Zhang Hongdu's *True Acts:*

> Whosoever was impoverished and ill, even including those who could not walk, supported themselves on canes and came to him. Even those who were orphaned and alone, barely capable of being human, all crawled their way to him. . . . [Lin taught them all the rudiments of the heart method, and of] all these impoverished and sick people, there was not one who was not overjoyed and did not kowtow [to him], congratulating themselves on having received a [new] life. (TA 21)

LIN'S SOCIAL VISION

Lin's social vision was a utopian Confucian vision of the restoration of the perfection of the golden age of Tang, Xun, and the Three Dynasties. He based his belief in the possibility of achieving such perfection on the underlying goodness of human beings. He identified the Confucian virtue of humanity (*ren*) with the seed of life (*xingming zhi zi*) created by the mixing of male and female semen and blood (*jingxue*). This identification enabled him to elaborate a method of inner self-cultivation of this spark of life-force, or humanity, which he referred to as the elixir (*dan*). This elixir or spark of life/goodness is itself based on heaven and earth, which are in turn based on the void.

Ren (humanity/seed of life/spark of goodness/the elixir) is also the root of social relations. *Ren* leads to filial piety (*xiao*). The union of husband and wife produces the father-and-son relation, or *xiao* (note how women disappear in this and the following equations). The father-and-son relationship leads to the relationships between brothers, which require *li* (ritual/property/hierarchical relations and prescribed actions). Relations between brothers lead to relations between friends. The proliferation of such relations would lead to chaos without the imposition of a ruler, and this necessity underlies the development of loyalty (*zhong*).

Lin's unification of the Three Teachings was designed to provide a philosophic or cosmological basis for his social program, and a step-by-step, practical program of self-cultivation leading to sagely illumination for the individual practitioner. But Lin believed that self-cultivation was a gradual process. In the meantime, one should endeavor to abide by Confucian values and modes of conduct. Thus he outlined a series of social reforms that would be conducive to the individual pursuit of sagehood and the attainment of social harmony. His program included a discussion of several of the most pressing issues of his day. Thus we find, for example, an early discussion of communal self-defense, essays on the rectification of ancestor worship, suggestions on the redistribution of monastic lands to assist in the reintegration of Buddhist monks and Daoist hermits into his ideal society, and essays on a revival of the well-field system to assist the destitute. As we have seen above, Lin was actively involved in charity work, public granaries, burial of the unattended dead, and so forth. These aspects of his religious role have remained an important part of Three in One activity to this day.

He Qiaoyuan commented on Lin's social vision in the following appraisal:

> Lin Zhao'en, *zi* Maole, was from Putian. He devoted himself to Confucian studies and also had a penetrating knowledge of Daoism and Buddhism. He wished to combine these into one path and unite them in a return to the Confucian way. Contemporaries called him the Master of the Three Teachings. Zhao'en said:
>
> > As for the age of Tang, Xun, and the Three Dynasties, in those times people completely carried out the bonds and constancies, and people completely carried out the four occupations. In this way people had no separate Ways. No one spoke of "My Confucianism," "My Daoism," or "My Buddhism." [Viewing things] in this way, the Daoists [can] return to Confucianism, and the Buddhists [can] return to Confucianism. In this way the expression "the Three Teachings" in reality is but the one teaching of Confucianism. I have long wanted to write an essay to submit to the Court [asking it to order] followers of Daoism and Buddhism to cultivate their Daoist and Buddhist teachings, but at the same time to take wives and have children, to enter the population registers and the tax registers, and to view their residence within Buddhist monasteries and Daoist belvederes as we Confucians look upon our Confucian temple schools. But they should also accept and make use of our Confucian *Classic of Filial Piety* and the *Analects*, etc., as well as the rites of capping, marriage, requiem, and sacrificial worship. I wish [thereby to ensure] that there will no longer be vagrants, and that people will no longer abandon their human relations, and that the bonds and constancies will all be maintained, the four professions will flourish together, and no one will claim to be separate and beyond the reach of human relationships, [so that we will] thereby ascend to the age of Tang, Xun, and the Three Dynasties. . . . People ask me, "What you say, is this possible?" and "I consider this to be but empty words."

[In fact] Zhao'en's teachings reached to everyone from the gentry and the scholar-literati to the impoverished in the marketplace. He also considered that it would be difficult suddenly to change the ignorant. Therefore he first led them on by techniques such as the "moving within the chamber [meditation and visualization]," the nine-stages [of inner alchemy], the curing of illness, and prognostication. He caused their Heart of the Way to arise gradually, and he ridded them of external concerns. The books he wrote in tens of thousands of words were all concerned with this alone. Scholars south of the [Yangzi] River, both *fangnei* (within the limits; i.e., orthodox, Confucian) and *fangwai* (beyond the limits; i.e., Daoist, Buddhist, iconoclast), all faced north and took him as their master. In the Jiajing period, Putian city fell, and [even] the thieves avoided touching [both] the Filial and Virtuous Chen Maolie and the Master of the Three Teachings [Lin Zhao'en]. (*Mingshancang*, j. 96)

Lin did in fact write the *Nijuan Dao Shi renlun shugao* (Draft memorial on human relations of Daoists and Buddhists), in which he suggests specific measures for the reintegration of Buddhists and Daoists into society. In these memorials, which a disciple persuaded him not to submit to a court saturated with Daoist and Buddhist influences, Lin accuses Buddhist monks, Daoist masters, Buddhist nuns, Daoist nuns, and prostitutes of disrupting the very equilibrium of heaven and earth by renouncing familial obligations. In *Liu-mei tiaoda* (Replies on six items for improvement, 8 pp., 1556), he suggests a redivision of the 60 *qing* of lands belonging to the Nanshansi (South Mountain Monastery), the largest monastery in Putian, located just to the south of the city, as an example. Lin had stayed at this monastery during his early phase of mystical searching, practicing meditation and the recitation of Buddhist sutras. He had also keenly observed the economy of the monastic estate, which was one of the five greatest Buddhist monasteries in Fujian. Lin argued that Guanghuasi monastery, the largest monastery within the Nanshan monastic complex, could be run with only eight monks, while Nanshansi as a whole would need only thirty, each of whom would be given fifty *mu* and assigned a prostitute with whom to raise children. This would leave forty *qing* that should be redistributed to impoverished local paragons of virtue (one hundred *mu* each). Such people would be an excellent choice to run the monastery, just as several exemplary Song virtuoso had done (such as Zhu Xi, who served as abbot of the Wuyi Chungyuanguan). Not so virtuous officials who had been sent home in disgrace should each receive one hundred *mu*, which would give them a basis to reform themselves. Grain from the remaining lands should be distributed to students in the Confucian schools, and to those who had spent their lives studying without success in the exams, so as to encourage the local literary scene. Additional reserves could be distributed in the event of natural disasters. Of course, Buddhist and Daoists would be subsidized for marrying and raising children and expanding the registered population. Lin concluded that if such a redistribution were envisioned for all the monasteries of Putian, ten times the benefit could be attained, whereas if this were an empirewide policy, then the lands and rental incomes could be measured in the billions.

As several scholars have pointed out, while Lin was extremely well versed in the Confucian classics and very knowledgeable about the different schools that had evolved within Confucianism, his notion of Buddhism and of Daoism was in fact quite limited.[13] His comments on Buddhism were primarily restricted to the Chan tradition. With regard to Daoism, he confined most of his comments to the school of inner alchemy, although his dealings with practicing local Daoist priests surely forced him to confront a very different aspect of Daoism. At one point he commented on this discrepancy:

> The Song text *Yanyi Taimoulu* states: "The teachings of the yellow caps [Daoism] began with the Han Zhang Dao (Way of Zhang [Daoling] in the [latter] Han dynasty)." Thus they all had wives and children, and even though they lived in temples and belvederes, they were no different from commoners. Later the abbots, for selfish reasons, secretly registered within their own family the names of

[13] Lin Zhao'en's *Sanjiao huibian* includes brief comments, arranged chronologically, on over one hundred figures associated with the Confucian tradition, sixty-five Daoist figures, and sixty-two Buddhists. His writings call for a return to the founding classics of the Confucian tradition, but he referred to the works of the major Song Neo-Confucians as well. According to Zheng Zhiming's count (Zheng, 1988: 112–257), those Song Neo-Confucians to whom Lin referred over ten times in his works include Shao Yong (1011–1077), Zhou Dunyi (1017–1073), Zhang Zai (1020–1077), Cheng Hao (1032–1085), Cheng Yi (1033–1108), and Zhu Xi (1130–1200). Less frequent references (5–10) were made to Xie Liangzuo (Shangcai) (1050–1103), Yang Shi (Guishan) (1053–1135), and Lu Jiuyuan (Xiangshan) (1132–1180), whereas others, such as Luo Zongyan (Yuzhang) (1072–1135) and Zhen Dexiu (1178–1235), are mentioned more than once. As for Ming Confucian scholars, Lin rarely referred to others besides Wang Yangming and Chen Baisha. Lin hoped to "return to the Way of Confucius" before there was such a thing as Confucianism in order to avoid the shortcomings of both the Zhu Xi school and the Wang Yangming school. However, despite his efforts to distinguish his gradualist approach, his insistence on the work of the inherently virtuous nature in the process of self-cultivation places him much closer to Wang Yangming's Heart/Mind School. As for Daoist texts, Lin refers by name most frequently to two Ming commentaries to the *Daodejing:* the *Laozi jicheng* of Xie Hui (completed in 1530) (31 references), and Wang Dao's *Laoziyi* (total of 25 references). Lin also refers to Lu Xubai's *Laozitongyan* (7), Wu Cheng's *Daode zhenjingzhu* (4), Cheng Zhu's *Laozi lun*, Cheng Wenjian's *Yi Lao tongyan*, Su Che's *Laozije*, Yan Junping's *Daode zhiguilun*, Sima Guang's *Qianxu*, and the *Ming Taizu yuzhu Daode zhenjing*. Conspicuously absent are references to the so-called Neo-Daoist writers of the Six Dynasties, such as Wang Bi. Other Daoist texts Lin mentions by name include the *Zitong huashu*, the *Changqingjingjing*, the *Yinfujing*, the *Huangtingjing*, the *Lingshujing*, the *Cantongji*, the *Tianbao jinjing lingshu shenjing neijing*, and the *Xishengjing*. Usually when Lin referred to Daoism he was referring narrowly to inner alchemy, as his selection of Daoist figures in the *Sanjiao huibian* also attests. Lin's comments on Buddhism are similarly primarily restricted to discussions of the schools of Chan Buddhism. Lin refers, by name to the *Diamond Sutra*, the *Heart Sutra*, and the *Platform Sutra* but also mentions the *Yuanjiejing* (Sutra of comprehensive enlightenment), the *Mituojing* (Maitreya sutra), the *Śūrangama*, the *Vyuharāja*, and the *Vimalakīrti* sutras. It is interesting that Lin cites only the *Dahuiyulu* of Da Huizong Gao Chanshi (1089–1163) out of the voluminous *yulu* literature. This monk was active in urging Song *shidafu* to avoid personal enlightenment and instead to persevere in their obligations to the state. The one Buddhist figure singled out for the highest praise in Lin's writings was Hui Neng.

those seeking refuge and thus admitted them. Song Yizu despised this and ordered that no temple or belvedere within the empire could maintain dependents. Thus the lack of wives and children within Daoism began with Song Yizu. Daoist texts state: "Renouncing wives is not Daoism," and yet there are those who consider renouncing wives to be Daoism. Is this not a corruption that must be repudiated? As for the avoiding of grains and the emphasizing of hunger, residing in quietude and cutting oneself off from the common, all these also are not the Way and should be repudiated (*Dao Shi shihuan*).

Lin was certainly well aware of the existence of the Zhengyipai (Orthodox One) school of Daoism, based in Longhushan in Jiangxi and recognized by the Ming court. This was a hereditary priesthood of ritual specialists that conferred titles and registers on Daoists who visited their headquarters or their branch offices, paid fees for ordinations, and demonstrated an adequate knowledge of ritual methods. Lin noted that the Zhang Daoling's "sons and grandsons have had descendants up until the present without a break." Lin was also involved in repairing the Xuanmiaoguan, the site of the Putian Bureau of Daoist Affairs, and the City God temple, both of which were most likely staffed by local Zhengyi priests.[14] These Daoists, in addition to those Buddhist monks who specialized in ritual, performed most of the rituals in demand at the local village level. Yet, for the most part, in his discussions of Daoism Lin drew upon Daoist inner alchemical writings, while he criticized the unfilial lifestyle of the adherents of the Quanzhen (Complete perfection) school, which had adapted a monastic lifestyle within official Daoist belvederes, and which was particularly widespread in northern China. Nonetheless, the Daoists who had the greatest impact on Lin included "wandering Daoists hermits" such as Zhuo Wanqun. This kind of religious figure did not fit easily into any institutional framework. Operating by means of loosely knit master-disciple networks, they traveled widely in pursuit of enlightenment, spreading techniques of self-cultivation as they traveled.[15] Yet even if they avoided family obligations, they would never escape Lin's moral censure.

Although he was critical of their human relations, Lin applauded the uplifting aspects of Buddhism and Daoism, arguing that their attention to otherworldly techniques (*chushifa*) was an important balance to the usual emphasis within Confucianism on this-worldly techniques (*shijianfa*). Although he denounced superficial understandings of concepts and practices such as magical techniques (*fashu*), longevity (*changsheng*), talismans and spells (*fuzhou*), confession of sins (*chanzui*), prayers for divine intercession (*rangqing*), alms-

---

[14] Lin would also have been familiar with the Bureau of Buddhist Affairs, which had been established in the Meifeng Monastery in Putian in the early Ming. See Yu (1980) for an account of the decline of this bureau over the Ming and the rise of the sale of blank ordination certificates and other corrupt practices. See also Tian (1990) on the decline of Buddhism over the Ming. See Brook (1993) on the uses of Buddhist sponsorship by gentry groups during the Ming.

[15] Lin included in his writings a satirical song entitled "A Song to Shatter Delusions," ostensibly by Zhong Liquan, on the 3,600 false paths of Daoism, which mentions a wide array of inner alchemical and ritual practices (*Pomi*).

giving (*bushi*), karma (*yingguo*), reincarnation (*lunhui*), and heavenly palaces and the underworld (*tiantang diyu*), he accepted the emphasis on good behavior such notions enjoined, and he provided a metaphysical interpretation of these concepts in terms of Confucian enlightenment. At a more fundamental level, he agreed with the Buddhist notion of the equality of all beings and the ability of all beings to attain Buddha-nature. This corresponded to his belief in the underlying equality and goodness of human nature, and his conviction that everyone could attain Confucian enlightenment. For Lin, "every man is a Yao and a Shun."

Even if Buddhists, Daoists, and prostitutes who contravened familial ties could be reintegrated into society, it would still be necessary to reaffirm the basic models of familial and lineage ritual. Lin wrote nine charts and essays on these topics, with detailed discussions of ritual conduct and paraphernalia. Some scholars have interpreted these essays as an effort to ensure the continuity of classical ritual even among fragmented or divisive lineages or impoverished social circles (Ma and Han, 1992: 829). His uncle, Lin Yuntong,[16] wrote an antiphon to the work entitled *Zong Kong Tang* (Hall for honoring Confucius), in which he commented on the sense of responsibility for ritual practice felt by the local gentry:

> Putian is commonly called the Land of Ritual. I was born late, yet I also wished to record the refined achievements of the former generations, which in general were simple, elegant, and truly calm. The four ritual [complexes; i.e., capping, marriage, requiem, and sacrifice] of the people mostly respect the forms established by the Duke of Letters (Zhu Xi). They are abundant yet not extravagant, and their substance accords with their form. How is it, then, that they should have become excessive and extravagant, leading to the current situation, wherein it is difficult to restrain them? I personally have lamented this, and after recently retiring from office, I considered getting together with three or four gentlemen to take charge of this matter. Then I got hold of and read this essay and felt as though I had found something that completely matched my desires. [The essay] deliberates on what is appropriate in ancient and modern [rites], [and] following the principle of according with human feelings, it deletes errors and strikes the mark. It is accurate and usable. I once discussed it with several literati over a banquet, and all approved of it without a single shake of the head. Thus I believe it accords with people's hearts. Therefore I strongly endorse it, for if this [rectification of ritual] is not the duty of my group (*dang*) then whose duty is it? That is why I wrote this antiphon. Zhao'en is one of my grandchildren; he has studied the ancients and is a good writer. This essay is most appropriate to the times. Recorded by the Lin Yuntong, the Farmer of the Purple Hat Mountain Withdrawn Studio.

[16] Lin Yuntong, *zi* Ruyu, *hao* Tuizhai, posthumous name Duanjian, received his *jinshi* degree in 1526 and rose to the position of Nanjing minister of works. He was the author of the *Tuizhai wenji* (Collected works of the Withdrawn Studio), the *Yaozhou yaji* (Elegant collection from Yaozhou), and the *Dushuyuan shiji* (Collected poems of the Reading Garden).

Lin's efforts to revive the "family rituals" of Zhu Xi (Ebrey, 1991a; 1991b) in his early writings represents one of the most paradoxical dimensions of his legacy. For as we shall see in chapter 6, his disciples gradually elaborated an entire range of new rituals "in accord with human feelings" that would be absorbed by Xinghua local society even as they transformed it.

Lin's vision of social harmony was closely modeled on Zhang Zai's *Ximing* (Western bronze inscription), which he quoted favorably several times. Lin agreed that "the people and I are born of the same womb. If I have material possessions, I [should] share these with them." In the essay *Jingtian* (Wellfield), Lin advocated the revival of this ancient system of the distribution of property, arguing that this system would ensure that everyone from commoner to gentleman, from ruler to official, would have enough to live on.

Fundraising from Disciples

When the Lord was first expounding the Way, all the expenses came from his own purse. In 1567 he announced that his funds were inadequate. His disciples then begged that he accept their ritual offerings. For without this how could the teachings be spread throughout the four quarters. In 1580, due to the fact that the ritual offerings were inadequate, his disciples begged him to accept travel money or additional gifts. For without this how could the teachings be spread throughout the four quarters, transforming all under heaven for ten thousands generations? The Lord then began to accept gifts. The *Zongli* (general manager) carefully recorded them. Each contribution was kept by the *Si* (lit., the bureau, probably the temple committee treasurer). [These funds were used] either for the carving of blocks and the printing of books, or to assist the poor and sick. (*TR* 23b–23a)

Lin Zhao'en was clearly able to raise considerable financial support for the printing of his writings, the construction of temples, and a wide range of charitable and religious work.[17] He made it very clear in his daily vows and petitions to heaven, of which a number are preserved in his collected works, that he would not accept gifts or seek personal profit from his position. All funds he accepted were carefully recorded in two parallel account books. One vol-

[17] As seen in the accounts of Lin Zhao'en's life, his charitable activities began in earnest with the pirate invasions of Putian in the 1560s. According to the *True Record*, Lin donated private land, hired priests and laborers, and coordinated government funding efforts to pay for the gathering and burial of corpses. The total number of corpses gathered given in the *True Record* is 22,800: 2,200 in 1561, 15,000 in 1562, 4,800 in 1563, and 800 in 1564. According to a reckoning by Putian Professor Liu Shirui, Lin also used private funds to establish trusts and public granaries, distributed food and medicine to the needy (sometimes on a daily basis to the destitute), provided 1,300 coffins free of charge, paid for 240 tombs, donated over 30 in gold to schools and scholarships, paid for the costs of over 100 soldiers, built a shrine to General Qi Jiguang and endowed it with 43 mu of land, feasted the defenders of the city, buried over 3,000, and cremated over 20,000 people killed in the disturbances. He announced that his private funds were exhausted in 1567.

ume was kept in the home of a disciple named Chen Daoqiing; the other was available for public inspection, presumably at the Zongkongtang. A few of his petitions to heaven dating from 1564, 1569, 1570, 1571, and 1572 provide precise figures on gifts accepted and expenditures on temple repairs and charity work (Berling, 1980: 85–86, translates two such documents). The figures mentioned in these documents are not large—in one, sixty-two ounces of silver are divided between construction costs and charity. In another, gifts of over one hundred ounces of silver in 1569 for the construction of an academy are returned with the excuse that the timing was not right (Lin only agreed in 1584 to the building of Three in One temples beyond his own center, the Zongkongtang, on Dongshan in Putian City). This public accounting of income and expenditures is still standard in Three in One temples, and indeed in most other temples dedicated to popular deities in Southeast China.

Regardless of the continued suspicion and occasional suppression of Lin Zhao'en's fledgling movement, the Three in One continued to attract disciples. Extensive records of the early transmissions and temple construction and proselytizing activities have survived. From them it is possible to get a picture of the schisms that developed between the early disciples.

THE FOUR ATTENDANTS AND THE THREE TRANSMITTERS

Lin Zhao'en's principal disciples are usually described by members of the Three in One as the "Four Attendants and the Three Transmitters" (*sipei sanchuan*). In some Three in One temples one finds the Four Attendants grouped around the central figure of Xiawuni, the deified Lin Zhao'en. The four are Lu Wenhui (1564–1618, *zi* Yanzheng, *hao* Xingru), Zhu Fengshi (*hao* Xuhui), Zhang Hongdu (*hao* Yilin), and Lin Zhijing (*hao* Danle, *hao* Zhenming). They will be discussed in turn below. The Three Transmitters are Lu Wenhui, Chen Zhongyu (1589–1655, *zi* Jujing, *hao* Juhua), and Dong Shi (born 1624, *hao* Zhian). Evidence suggests that there was a struggle for succession among the disciples after Lin's death. The line of transmission excluded Lin Zhenming, who nevertheless remained very active in southern coastal Putian. The current surviving branches of the Three in One suggest an early split that has left its traces to this day.

There are good reasons why the transmission stayed in the hands of the Three Transmitters. They had the education, the background, and strong social and economic support. Nowadays the center of their ritual tradition is the populous coastal region from Putian to Jiangkou, centering in Hanjiang. In these areas the Three in One is nowadays still the best organized, initiation rituals are strictly observed, and a scholastic tradition as well as an esoteric inner alchemical meditational tradition are still maintained. By contrast, Lin Zhenming's home village was a poor fishing community built on a hillside overlooking Meizhou Bay, with a view of the island housing the ancestral temple of the Heavenly Empress Mazu. Lin returned to this village after Lin

Zhao'en's death, carefully guarding his master's oral transmissions concerning the *Gen Bei* inner alchemy method. He built the Yuexiuci there in 1590 (*True Record* 21). The Three in One developed rapidly, mixing with local cults and absorbing local Daoist and Buddhist ritual traditions. The result was a popular religious movement completely integrated into the local socioreligious organization. Testimony to the vitality of religion in a harsh environment, this small village now boasts five major temples and several smaller shrines. Buddhist and Daoist temples, local god cults, and sectarian cults like the Xiantianjiao (The Way of Former Heaven) thrive side by side and continue to intermingle. The richness and complexity of the ritual traditions developed by this branch are one response to the bookish traditions of the Putian branches.

Lu Wenhui (1564–1618) was one of the Four Attendants, and the First of the Three Transmitters. According to Dong Shi's short account of the Three Transmitters, appended to the *Linzi benxing shilu* (True record of the actions of Master Lin), Lu began work as Lin Zhao'en's principal editor in 1594, assisting in the compilation of one of the major collections of Lin's works, *Linzi sanjiao zhenzong tonglun* (Master Lin's discussions on the combination of correct principles of the Three Teachings). After Lin's eightieth birthday in 1597, when he became increasingly feeble and lost the ability to speak or to greet visitors, Lu acted as his spokesman. Lu also edited the *Xiawuni jing* (Scriptures of Xiawuni), the *Xiawu jingxun* (Explications of the scriptures of Xia), the *Jiuxu neijing tu* (Illustrations of the inner landscape of the nine stages), and the *Sini jinglue* (Summary of the scriptures of the Four Teachers).

From Dong's account we learn about the personal relationship between Lin Zhao'en and Lu Wenhui. Initially, when Lin had gone to Fuzhou to work and meditate in the Jie Jie Shi ("Double Borrowed Hall"), he held a fast for seven days and emerged with the premonition that someone named Lu would succeed him. The man turned out to be living in Fuzhou, married to the daughter of the Honorable Lin Guoning. Lin made repeated efforts to interest him in his teachings, all of which met with failure. Then Lu's father fell ill, and Lu went to Lin for help. When he learned about the Method of Healing in the Heart, he finally realized the profundity of Lin's teachings. Now it was Lin's turn to refuse him, but Lu made persistent visits, until Lin finally took him into his own family. There he had Lu, who was a good writer and versatile calligrapher, help compile the scriptures of the Three in One movement.

Lin instructed him day and night, until Lu was enlightened. The *True Record* relates how Lin composed a scripture, the *Daotong zhongyi jing*, in order to transmit the Method of One in the Center to Lu on January 4, 1594. "The night the scripture was completed a round light shot forth, gleaming like jade. The Master called it the Cavern Heaven of Jade Florescence." Soon after this Lin ordered Lu's writings to be included in the collection of his works, supposedly compiled in response to a plea for rare and lost books from the provincial government, responding in turn to a request from the capital. Lin is said to have remarked that Lu's writings could "Open up those things that the Lord of the Religion (i.e., himself) had not yet opened up." Just before his death Lin announced several times that Lu should succeed him, quoting visits from the Daoist Immortal Zhang Sanfeng confirming Lu's predestined role. Just as he felt death drawing near, he taught Lu a gatha containing the essence of the method of Unifying the Dao.

Despite all these signs, there were a number of rival claims to the succession immediately after Lin's death. According to Dong Shi, people who had received a couplet or held a brief audience with Lin suddenly claimed to have his secret instructions. Lu, by contrast, had the scriptures he had edited and those he had written to his credit. The original blocks from the final approved edition had been kept in Qingjiang, but these had been "put into disarray by jealous [rivals?]." So Lu was forced to re-edit and recarve the collection once again, adding in some of his own works. Lu Wenhui served with the title of Great Master of the religion, First Disciple of the Center and the One of the Three Teachings, Continuer of the Unified (Tradition) of Master Xiawuni for twenty years. Lu's activities included considerable travel, editing, and writing. His own works include the *Zhongyi xuyan* (Introduction to the Center and the One), prefaces 1598 and 1599, the *Xing ling shi* (Poems on the spiritual luminosity of human nature), preface 1600, and the *Linzi benxing shilu* (True record of the activities of Master Lin), which Dong Shi edited in 1655 (see below). Other works attributed to Lu include the *Xiaxin ji* (Collection of the essence of [the Way of] Xia) and two ritual texts, the *Fangsheng yiwen* (Liturgy for the releasing of living beings) and the *Sanhui chanwen* (Litany of the Three Assemblies). The latter is modeled on Buddhist confessional litanies.

In 1608 Lu Wenhui built the magnificent Yaodao Temple in Hanjiang. He restored the temple in 1613, built a Hall for the Assembling of Scriptures, placed a statue of Lin as Lord Xia in the hall, "and worshiped at its side." Lin's apotheosis was thus accomplished a mere fifteen years after his death. The building stood until 1993: it housed dormitories for the No. 6 Middle School. It was the largest temple of the Three in One to have survived from the Ming dynasty. (See chapter 5 for an account of the misadventures leading to the destruction of the temple.) Lu's successors, Chen and Dong, both repaired and enlarged the building (in 1644 and 1660, respectively). Dong Shi wrote a detailed description of the temple. The text of this inscription reads as follows:

> Twenty miles outside the city of Putian, the area at the base of the Huang Mountain in Hanjiang is called the "Jade Island." There are lychee groves in profusion, and it is a magnificent site. It towers over the city like a mountain, and trees stand on top of it, specially raising their verdancy as though spreading forth a canopy. In 1608 the First Transmitter, Lu Wenhui, selected a favorable site at the base of Lychee Root Mountain and built a shrine to revere the Great Master Linzi. Therefore, scholars call it the "Great Founding Temple." The temple is magnificent and imposing, its walls are tall and broad, and there is truly nothing about it that could be improved. In the grounds to the east and west, he planted over one hundred

dragon-eye trees. In front and behind along the path he planted a dozen lychee trees. The proceeds of these fruit trees were to go to the spring and autumn ritual expenses. In 1644 the Second Transmitter, Master Chenzi, rebuilt the gateway, enlarged the courtyard, dug a pond, built a stage, and built a bridge over the pond. Outside he built a pentachrome wall to preserve the extent of the temple [lands]. In the autumn of 1660 I built a temple on the top of Lychee Root Temple to revere Confucius, Laozi, Śākyamuni. Thus by returning to the origins of the Dao I was able to illumine the meaning of the harmony of the Three Teachings. As for the Sages of the Three Teachings, they came forth in the Zhou dynasty, they divided ways in the Han, Tang and Song, and then they united in the Ming. From the time of the Three Saints it was over two thousand year until my Master Linzi came forth. He conjoined the heart of the Three Saints in a point of utter purity and concentration, in order to tie together this unification of the Dao of the Three Gateways. Now as for this being the work of a single man, how could he not be the only one since Creation to achieve this? What other reason could I have to build this hall than on his behalf to enable sages, worthies, and gentlemen to understand that by which the Three Teachings join as One? My Master Linzi created this to start with, and there are students of the Dao to complete it in the end. That is why the transmission of the Central Unity, and the construction of Temple Schools, is considered the foundation of the schools and academies of the world—this too is my aim. As for the aid offered by the two Immortals [Zhang] Sanfeng and [Zhuo] Shangyang, my Master Linzi has already appended their writings to his *Discussions on the Combination of Correct Principles* in order to transmit them to the world. Therefore I built the Tongwei and Wushan temples to honor them. At this time, those who joined in my aim and assisted with acts of merit included Chen Dapi. Others raised contributions to help the construction along. [The honorable] Susheng and Yuying contributed gold to complete it. After everything was completed, I carefully recorded how all those who started it began and how those who finished it completed it in the end. This too is a matter of seeing people who never existed before since the beginning [of time], and great affairs that have never before taken place since creation now starting to happen. The sages to come can carry on this work, and students to come can start up again. I humbly yet crudely record the gist of it, in order to record the date, but I dare not go on speaking of this. If one wishes to see a more eloquent account that would be adequate to add luster to the past and enrich the future, then that will have to await the arrival of gentlemen [like yourself]. (*Dongshan jicao;* Dean and Zheng, 1995: 209–211)

The second of the Four Attendants was Zhu Xuhui, about whom little is known. His *Xinhaijing* (Scripture on the ocean of the heart) has survived. This work, modeled on Buddhist sources, is a beautiful prose-poem on the "oceanic consciousness." Zhu's temple, the Taihuci, was built in 1592 and is probably the oldest surviving Three in One temple. The temple has been recently restored, after serving as a government grain warehouse. In the Republican period the temple housed the village school, while the gods of the

Three in One and several popular deities were worshiped in the back and side halls.[18]

The third of the Four Attendants was Zhang Hongdu. He wrote the *Linzi benxing jilue* (Summary record of the activities of Master Lin) and annotated editions of the *Four Books*. His major role in the Three in One was as a missionary to the north. Ma Xisha and Han Bingfang (1984; 1992) have explored the expansion of the Three in One religion north to Nanjing and Beijing under the separate leadership of one Wang Xing and Zhang Hongdu (later succeeded by the "mad monk" Zhen Lai). According to the *Jinling zhongyitang xingshi* (True activities of the One in the Center Temple of Jinling [Nanjing]),[19] Zhang Hongdu was "perfectly filial toward his Master, and after observing three years of mourning, he renounced his properties and business and devoted himself to printing the works of [Lin]. He traveled north and south of the Yangze, and on to Nan Zhili to spread the teachings." In 1610 he made it to Shuntian (Beijing), where he built a Three in One shrine on the Yuhe Bridge. Zhang's teachings attracted the attention of an official named Zhu in the Ministry of Works, who assisted him in bringing along large numbers of students and worshipers. Zhang died soon thereafter in 1614, and the temple was left without a keeper. It was subsequently sold and made into the Beijing Putian Huiguan (*Jinling zhongyitang xingshi*, 2a–3b).

Zhang Hongdu plays a very different role in his home village of Xihong, set deep among paddyfields along a stream in Huangshi to the east of Putian City. Originally the village was on the seacoast, but the entire Putian plain has been continually extended for centuries and the sea is now miles away. Zhang is revered in this village as a protector god. There is talk of a Zhang religion, Zhang jiao, and a large body of legends about Zhang and his disciples circulates. A large temple has just been built on the site of the original Yuxici, first constructed in 1593.[20] This temple now houses some forty gods, with Xiawuni at the center, flanked by Zhang Hungdu, Lu Wenhui, and Li Mingdeng (a disciple of Zhang's with a shrine in the village). The others have been drawn in from several other temples, destroyed during the Cultural Revolution. In this village the process of restoration or reinvention of traditions is speeding up the assimilation of the Three in One with other popular god cults. The following legend is indicative of Zhang's position in the minds of the villagers:

During the Qing, the villagers were unable to pay their taxes, and the venal magistrate sent troops to burn down the village. Warned in advance, the villagers fled,

[18] The temple is located in the same village that reveres a medium named Zhu, whose life closely resembles that of Mazu (Li Xianzhang, 1979).

[19] The *Jinling zhongyitang xingshi* is included in an early edition of the *Linzi chuanji* (Complete collected works of Master Lin), preserved in the Beijing Library and the Gest Library, Princeton University, editions of the *Linzi quanji*, in the second half of the last *juan* (*juan* 36) of the collection (overlooked in Berling's otherwise comprehensive listing of the contents [Berling, 1980: Appendix E: 258–259]).

[20] The Yuxici was first built in 1593, according to the *Linzi nianpu* (Chronological biography of Master Lin), 1610, reprinted in Mano Senryu (1979).

leaving a few old men in the village. These men lit fires in every hearth, which made the troops hesitate to attack. Eventually the wood ran out and the fires dwindled. The incensed troops, realizing they had been tricked, charged into the village and began setting fires and tearing down the temple. When they started ripping up the courtyard in front of the temple, arranged then as now in the shape of the Eight Hexagrams, they unearthed a talisman Zhang had planted under one of the bricks. The talisman immediately flew up into the heavens, stirring up great winds and bringing down torrential rains. The soldiers fled in terror, and the village was saved. (Interview in Hongdu, October 1991)

This image of the disciple of Lin Zhao'en acting as a protector deity for his own village recalls Weller's (1994) discussion of the underlying potential for resistance within popular religion.[21]

The fourth of the Four Attendants was Lin Zhenming. Lin Zhenming was born in the village of Yuexiu, described above. He represented the greatest threat to the line of transmission of Lu Wenhui, Chen Zhongyu, and Dong Shi (see below). Lin returned to his home village of Yuexiu after Lin Zhao'en's death. He had already built the Yuexiuci there in 1590. Lin wrote the *Dingwu benji* (Basic annals of [the period between] the *Ding* [year] and the *Wu* [year] [lost]), the *Mingxiaji* (Collection on illumining Xia, preface, 1598), the *Longhua biejuan* (Informal account of the Dragon Flower Assembly), and the *Zhuowushiji* (True meaning of the Great Wu Lord). Judith Berling has discussed the *Mingxia ji* (Berling, 1980, 224–226) and remarked on the continuing divinization of Lin Zhao'en, the inclusion of Daoist elements, and the claim to Lin Zhijing's central role in continuing the tradition of the Three Teachings.[22] This latter point is strongly emphasized in the colophon by

---

[21] Zhu Weigan, in his *Fujian shigao* (Draft history of Fujian) (Fuzhou, 1986, 2: 605–606), presents material on the attack on Xihong and the salvation of the city by a divine wind. He claims that the incident began when a tax collector named He Jie spotted a villager from Yang Wei, who had fled there to avoid the vicious government reprisals in 1859 for lineage feuds between White Banner and Black Banner village coalitions in 1856. The tax collector informed on the man, and troops were sent to arrest him. Xihong villagers repulsed the troops. Then the magistrate of Putian, named Liu, led local troops to punish the village. The villagers defeated the troops and injured the magistrate. He reported to Fuzhou, and the army was sent to destroy the village. But as Liu was about to attack, a great wind arose, blowing over to stone commemorative archways in front of the magistrate's troops. He fell to his knees and prayed to the gods to stop the storm and begged the villagers to control their resentments. As a compromise, the central halls of each home were torn down, so the magistrate could report that the town had been flattened. Zhu does not mention that Zhang Hongdu was the god to whom the villagers prayed for protection.

[22] The *Mingxiaji* is arranged in question-and-answer form. Lin Zhenming refers to Lin Zhao'en throughout as Lord of the Teachings. Issues covered in the first section of the book include the one drop of true yang, the heart method, the beginning with the *gen* hexagram in the back, the proportions of the micrososmic body, the earthen crucible of inner alchemy, the Yellow Court, true water and true fire, the heavenly pipes, the yin and yang within the body, metallic crystals and jade liquers, metallic elixers, mercury within cinnabar, daogui, the qi of the former heavens, the formation of an (immortal) embryo in the purple-gold cauldron between the kidneys (the zhenchuchu), embryonic breathing, the fire phases (said to be simply the natural formation of the elixer), the ninefold transformations and the seven recyclings (Lin explains that

Weng Hui to the *True Meaning of the Great Wu Lord* (this is in fact Lin Zhi-jing's godly title). Weng claims that Lin was the only disciple to receive the correct transmission, and Lin makes a similar claim on page 3. Weng's enthusiasm for the book knows no bounds. "It would be difficult to come across this text in 100,000 kalpas. My generation must hear of it and, moreover, worship and uphold it." The book is largely a commentary on the Nine Stages, based on Lin's purported secret instructions from Lin Zhao'en. The *Informal Account of the Dragon Flower Assembly* also refers to Lin's possession of secrets from the Master. But Lin accuses Lu Wenhui of having been instructed by the Master to publish his *Huiyu* (Discussions in the assembly), along with his collected works. Lin hints that Lu had ulterior motives in withholding the book from publication. "Over ten years later, I published the book, unable to stand by while secrets perished." The *Huiyu* makes up half of the book and is concerned mainly with underlining the identity of Lin Zhao'en with the Maitreya Buddha. This had been a favorite theme of Lin Zhao'en's in his last years, as his *Milejing* (Maitreya scripture), *Bentijing* (Scripture on the original substance), and several of the *Xiawu Scriptures* reveal.

The second of the Three Transmitters, Chen Zhongyu, inherited the position from Lu Wenhui. In 1609 Lu had ordered Chen to compose a Lanpen Liturgy (*Ullambana*). He repeatedly had the ritual performed, employing Chen's new liturgical text. Master Lu remarked, "This is also a major event for the Three in One Religion." In 1617 Lu built the great Ancestral Hall and put a more splendid statue of Lord Xia in it. In the 11th lunar month, he sent Chen Zhongyu to Fuzhou to hold a Lanpen Ritual. As Chen was composing the *Memorial* for the service, he suddenly felt worried and rushed back to Hanjiang, where he found Lu in a precarious state of health. Lu pointed at Chen and said, "The transmission of the Way of the One in the Center and

---

the emotions are the gold that must to returned to its origin), the opening of the mystic pass (Lin states it is not a real opening; rather, it is an opening with neither inside nor outside), the openings of the breath and the wellsprings and sea of qi, the hun and the po souls, the refining of the elixir (Lin emphasizes that the heart is the elixir), the joining of inner and outer elixirs, life and death, the crack of thunder and lightning that opens up the crown of the head, the Gate of Lifeforce (coccyx) and the Gate of Nature (niwan point in the brain), the lead (the single point of True Yang [metal]) and the Rivercart (the fire within water), the Ancestral Breath, the birthing from the womb, the boundless Buddha, the true scripture of inborn nature, Buddhist terms such as the mastering versus subduing the heart, annihilation vs. samadhi, fixed mind, wisdom, the manifestation of the inner nature, emptiness, Western paradise (to be found within the body). Lin Zhenming relates most of the discussion of alchemical terms back to the drop of true nature, or humanity, within the heart. Yet it is clear that inner alchemy was an obsession with his interlocuters. Lin Zhenming points out that the *gen* hexagram in the back method preceded Lin Zhao'en, citing passages from Zhu Xi. There are frequent quotes from the *Cantongji* and the *Huangtingjing,* as well as quotes on the alchemical instructions of Xiwangmu to Han Wudi (6b). Several passages comment on the alchemical workings of the microsocmic body—noting the vertical and horizontal meridians, and the endless flowing in the Yellow Chamber of the Milky Way and the Yellow River. These insights are drawn from the *Hua To nezhaotu* (Hua To's inner vision chart). Longevity is linked to the uninterrupted flow within the meridians. Inner and outer elixirs (8b).

the Unification of the Dao is now upon you, my disciple." Chen tried to refuse, but when Lu finished speaking, he grasped Chen's hand and died.

This succession also provoked a storm of controversy. Several rivals published books proclaiming their right to carry on the tradition. Chen withdrew to the coastal village of Songdong, but gradually his influence grew, and people came to regard him as the legitimate successor. According to the *True Record* (71–73), Chen's father had been a disciple of Lin Zhao'en and had built a shrine to him at Mafeng, in Putian. Lin had tried to communicate abstruse doctrines to him, but he had been unable to comprehend them. Lin said, "Your descendant will complete these teachings for me. "That very night Chen's mother dreamt that she heard Heavenly Music and saw a great general descending from heaven with a baby in his arms. The baby accepted books from Lin Zhao'en and announced his desire to save mankind." His salvific urge was so great that he could not abide to wait the full-term pregnancy and so was born prematurely at seven months. At sixteen he was taken in by Lu and had an enlightening experience. He gave up his other activities and devoted himself to learning the stages of inner cultivation of the Three in One: entering the door, establishing the base, and reaching the supreme principle. He composed *Litanies* and earnestly repented his former wrongdoings. At the age of twenty-one (nineteen by Western reckoning), Lu had ordered him to write the *Ullambana Scriptures* (actually ritual texts) and other liturgies and litanies. This he did, reputedly within a month's time, surprising and delighting Lu. Lu had him recite these scriptures everytime there was a Great Assembly (of the Three in One), and all present had to admit that they had never heard the like. Lu also had Chen put his *Poems on Awakening the Heart* to music and sing them at the assemblies. At home Chen's father sang and he harmonized, leading some neighbors to consider them insane. Nevertheless, Chen's musical abilities may have enabled him to write new lyrics to melodies he found in other current religious traditions. Several liturgical works attributed to Chen have survived in use in different branches of Three in One ritual practice (see list of sources: liturgies). Chen therefore may have developed the principal framework of Three in One liturgy, borrowing from Buddhist and Daoist ritual traditions in the area.

Chen was only twenty-nine in 1617 when he attempted unsuccessfully to avoid the position of Second Transmitter.[23] His age and juniority was definitely a factor in the difficulty he experienced in achieving recognition, as would be the case for Dong Shi (see below). He built the Songdong Temple and repaired the Dongshan Temple in Putian, the Yaodao Temple in Hanjiang, and the Xiangyang Temple in Jiangkou. He printed and re-edited missing texts, or added new material as in the case of the *True Record*. Several ritual texts still in use by various Three in One branches are attributed to him. (See manuscript list below.) Evidence for his eventual recognition was his role

---

[23] Such efforts to appear to refuse positions of power and influence, gifts, or other offerings are common, even expected, gestures in Chinese culture.

in the reburial of Lu Wenhui in 1645, when he led a procession of several hundred adherents of the Three in One from all the afore-mentioned temples as well as the Aofeng Temple to worship at the new gravesite.

Dong relates in the *True Record* (73–75) that Chen told him in 1655 that he would have to complete editing of the *True Record* for him. He announced, "My deeds are complete and my merit full. I now place the heavy responsibility of the Three Teachings on Student Dong. Now, all of you, on a certain day, hold a *jiao* ritual to send me back to the True." Dong Shi wrote several works that provide rich documentation on the development of the Three in One. In addition to his work editing and enlarging the *True Record of the Activities of Master Lin* quoted above, he wrote the *Sanjiao menxian shilu* (True record of the sagely adherents of the Three Teachings; *Preface* by Dong Shi dated 1672, two afterwords by disciples also dated 1672; 1910 reprint) and the *Dongshan jicao* (Collected grasses of the Eastern Mountain). The first work provides short entries on 137 followers of Lin Zhao'en, then lists 49 men who built various temples. It includes entries on two Daoists and nine monks. In this work we find attacks on two of the Four Attendant Disciples, namely, Zhang Hongdu and Lin Zhijing:

> Zhang Hongdu, *hao* Yilin, *zi* Shengzi. When he was young he pursued Confucian studies. When he entered the doors [of the Three in One] he made great progress. Later he grew weak with drinking. Master Lin saw this and repeatedly scolded him. In the end he became a jealous lowly person. What a pity. His *Linzi benxing jilue* (Summary record of the activities of Master Lin) is worth looking at. (15b)

In the entry on Lin Zhijing we learn that when Master Lin was held by a venal official (probably Commissioner Yang Sizhi), Lin Zhijing withheld his large private store of gold and someone else had to substitute himself for Lin. Next he criticizes Lin Zhijing for his choice of words in the title to his *Dingwu benji* (Basic annals of [the period between] the *ding* [year] and the *wu* [Year]). Dong felt, no doubt along with many contemporaries, that the term *Basic Annals* should be reserved for use only in the chronology of an emperor.

> [This was a matter of] not knowing how to honor [Master Lin] and instead causing him trouble. How could this be permitted? As for his disciples, Weng Wenfeng, Wu Shang, Weng Man, Wu Yiguan, etc., they write talismans and concoct medical recipes. They invoke ghosts as though they were gods, falsifying the Great Dao to further their basic greedy interests. They rely on eliminating disease as the source of nurturing one's destiny. They perform all kinds of heterodox practices in order to confound the world and fool the people. [They are the sort that] the people of the world hold their noses at and that the Superior Man does not even countenance. (22a–b)

Dong Shi is alluding to the fact that the disciples of Lin Zhenming had already established a rival ritual tradition that claimed to derive from the Three in One. This branch would come to be known as the Mingxia pai, or the Weng pai. The founding temple is the Yuexiuci. As mentioned above, the Yuexiuci is today surrounded by several temples to various cults, with a flow of ritual texts and worshipers between them. The Daoist gods mentioned in the *Mingxiaji* (Yuhuang shangdi, Sanguan dadi, and Xuantian shangdi), are housed in a side hall of the temple. In the main hall Lin Zhao'en is flanked by Dizang zunwang and Lingguan dadi. The eastern hall is devoted to Guanyin, with Weito and Jialan at her side. The western hall is devoted to Lin Zhenming, flanked by Confucius and Wenchang. The temple is also known as the Mengxiaci, which is one name of the branch founded by Lin. The other name is the Wengpai. Lin Zhenming's tomb is also in the village.

Another major temple of the Wengpai is the Jiangdongci in Zhongmen, farther down the coast toward the Xianyou border. This temple has been recently rebuilt. The central altar contains six long, thin spirit tablets, each two feet high. These provide the names and titles of a separate order of transmission of the Three Teachings, that of the Wengpai: The first, *Sanjiao dichuan Yuexiu Zhenming Lin shi xiansheng shenwei* (Spirit tablet of Master Lin of Yuexiu, first transmitter of the Three Teachings), is for Lin Zhenming. The others are for his successors, down to the seventh, with the fifth transmitter missing. The second transmitter is here named Weng Wudao, the third is Weng Yiyang, the fourth is Lin Hengshan. The fifth is missing possibly because of the disturbances brought on by the forced coastal evacuation of this area in the early Qing dynasty. Alternatively, the missing tablet may be an indication of the force of the prohibitions against the Three in One in the Qing Yongzheng and Qianlong periods. The sixth tablet commemorates Chen Maoshan, and the seventh is for Zheng Xuegui. A stele still in the temple, written by the seventh transmitter, Zheng Xuegui, in 1898, explains the name of the branch:

> In 1897 I traveled here from Dongshan, to pay homage to the ancient site of Master Weng of our Way. This Master (the second in the line of transmission) received the Dao from Master Lin Zhenming. He deeply obtained inspiration from Lin's method [of healing in the] heart. Now the Mingxia branch takes its name from the writing of Master Lin. But because the Great Master, Ruler of the Three in One Teachings, was surnamed Lin (i.e., Lin Zhao'en), and Master Zhenming shared the same surname, so the branch did not dare use Lin for its name, and instead named itself Weng. This demonstrates their respect and is an important aspect of the ability of the master of my branch to carry onward the lifeline of its Dao. (Dean and Zheng, 1995: 351–352)[24]

OTHER CONTEMPORARY DISCIPLES

Dong Shi's *Linzi menxian shilu* (True record of the sage disciples of Master Lin) provides the names of 137 early disciples of Lin Zhao'en. Fifty-two of the 137 figures introduced separately are said to be men of the Putian Xianyou

[24] The discovery of the tablets and this inscription was first reported by Lin Guoping and myself in Ding and Lin (1989, 1992).

area. Some 57 entries give no place of origin, but in over half of these cases the likelihood is strong that they too were from Putian. The recorded origins of the other disciples is as follow: Songjian 4, Zhangnan 3, Ninghua 3, Minxian 2, Fuzhou 2, Quannan 2, Chu 2, and 1 of each for Tiantai, Lu Xindu Shaowu, Minqing, and Huizhou. Forty figures held official posts. Many of these were local officials who had various contacts with Lin and had finally formed a favorable impression of him. Some had gone on to take vows. Another group is made up of Hanlin academicians or well-known philosophers or recluses who corresponded with Lin late in his life. The most important officials who can also be considered as genuine disciples include Yu Shizhang, Wang Keshou, and Xu Wanren. Other disciples important to the social standing of the Three in One include Lin Zhao'en's uncles, cousins, and brothers, such as Lin Jingmian. The professions of the majority of the disciples are seldom clearly indicated, but three or four were fishermen or farmers, and a similar number were Buddhist monks or Daoist priests.

The *Linzi menxian shilu* also provides some information on the early schisms in the Three in One, including an attack on Lin Zhenming's tradition:

> It is not a matter of whether or not he had the method transmitted to him. However, why is it that he carved (and printed the work) only after Master Lin had died, and not while he was still alive? If we were to try to ascertain his intentions, they would amount to nothing more than an effort to stand out as better than his fellow disciples. Moreover, Master Lin himself said that the matter of eliminating disease was merely a minor proof of the workings of the Way. Now that [the heart method] is [widely] believed in by the people, there is no longer much need to discuss it. (*Menxian* 18a)

The following entry sheds some light on the succession issue and at the same time reveals the wide social range from which Lin accepted his disciples:

> Huang Longqing, Hao, Yongwo. A man from Duotou in Putian. He made his living as a fisherman when he was young. He was brave and headstrong and liked to fight. Once when he was drink he injured a man. He escaped from punishment by staying in the deep mountains, where he repented for his crimes for over ten years. He heard something of Master Lin's Way, and so he begged to be accepted as a disciple. As soon as [Lin] spoke, he was enlightened. Master Lin was surprised. He explained, "I am a criminal. I wish to become a house slave of the Three Teachings, in order to pay back the evil crimes I have committed in this life." He made daily progress in his studies. [He acted like] an ignorant but dedicated servant. After Master Lin had passed on his alms bowl (i.e., chosen his successor and died), he begged to speak, stating, "The Way of the Master has a successor. If there is anyone who wishes to serve as attendant to the Way, he should take Master Lu as his Teacher. I serve the Great Patriarch of Yaodao (Jade Island), and though I am but an insignificant weed, I dare not rest for even an instant." (*Menxian* 46a)

Another entry on a Buddhist monk reveals something of the possessiveness of the cult for one of its own. For although the thought of Lin Zhao'en was consciously syncretic and open to many influences, at an institutional level the religion was exclusive, jealous, and competitive.

The Buddhist monk Huixing (Haoran) left his home at an early age and went to . . . mountain monastery. His *hao* is Haoran. Master Lin ordered him to spread the Teachings. At that time, the foundations of the Zhijie Bridge in Hanjiang were about to be built. Haoran worshiped and prayed and the tide did not rise for three days. [After the repairs the foundations?] stood three feet above the water. People passed the word about his divine powers. People of the neighborhood set up a shrine to him. . . . [Haoran] said that he wished to return to being a Buddhist Chan Master. Thereupon Master Lin cursed him. When he went out the door blood began to pour without end from the seven openings [of his head; i.e., eyes, ears, nostrils, mouth]. Haoran was greatly frightened. He closed the door and did penance for three years. Master Lin admitted him again.[25]

THE EARLY SPREAD OF THE THREE IN ONE

Dong Shi's *Linzi menxian shilu* also provides the names of a number of other disciples who were sent to spread the faith beyond Fujian to different parts of China. Nanjing was the first and most important of these sites.[26] The *Jinling*

[25] I located the Gongde ci in Hanjiang where a statue of Monk Huixing (Haoran) is still revered to the left of the statue of Lord Xia. A stele in the courtyard of the temple describes the construction of the bridge in great detail. See Dean and Zheng (1995: 183–184).

[26] Lin Zhao'en was himself very active in transmitting the Three in One. He traveled to the following places on the dates indicated to spread his teachings.

1567: 2d month: Fuzhou Jinshansi; 6th month: Minhou Xuefengsi; 12th month: Wuyi Mountains and Jianyang
1568: 2d month: returned to Putian; 4th–7th months: Fuzhou
1569: 2d–8th months: via Wuyishan to Jiangxi Wannianxian
1570: 2d month: to Lianjiangxian Danyang; 6th–8th months: Nanjing (Jinling)
1571: 9th–12th months: Fuzhou
1572: 4th–9th months: Shaowu, and back to Putian via Fuzhou
1573: 2d–5th months: Jiangxi Nanchang
1575: 2d–6th months: Fuzhou and Yanping
1576: 10th month: Xianyou
1577: 4th–9th months: Guangdong Xinan, Meilin, and Hangzhou in Zhejiang
1578: Spring: Fuzhou area (Hongtang, Nantai)
1579: 2d month: Fuzhou; Summer: Wuyi Mountains, then on to Ninghuaxian until 8th lunar month
1583: 4th month: started out by boat for Wudangshan from Fuzhou; turned back at Shuikou
1585: 4th month: Wuyi Mountains; headed for Nanjing but stopped in Jianning's Baiyunsi; returned to Putian in 9th month

Lin also sent disciples to spread the teachings. According to Zhang Hongdu's *Linzi xingshi*, Wang Xing, an effective healer, was sent to Xinan where he built a temple. In 1571 Chen Biao was sent along with Li Zhang to Fuzhou, where they built a Sanjiao huiguan and a cemetery and attracted thousands of worshipers. In 1585 Lin sent You Sizhong and Zhang Hongdu to Jinling, where they attracted hundreds of worshipers. In 1589 Zhu Youkai was sent to Xinan. In 1593 Zhang Zisheng spread the teachings to thousands in Linjiang Prefecture.

zhongyitang xingshi (True activities of the One in the Center Temple of Jinling [Nanjing]) provides further information on the Three in One groups in Nanjing and the spread of the faith to the Jiangxi, Huizhou, Jiangsu, and Beijing areas. Lin Zhao'en had stayed in Nanjing for three months in 1570, and he sent followers to continue to spread the teachings to Nanjing in 1576. Zhang Hongdu had established a temple there while en route to Beijing (about 1610). In 1616 Chen Biao, *hao* Daquan, a *xiucai* from Yuhu in Putian, went to Nanjing, where he debated Three in One doctrines with considerable success. He stayed in Nanjing for three years before accepting an invitation to teach in the Wuyi Mountains until his death at eighty-five.[27]

The next Three in One disciple to take up work at the Nanjing temple was the "mad monk" Zhen Lai, *hao* Liaoxuan (Comprehends Mystery), a native of Shuinan in Putian. His original surname was Zhu, and he had been Lin's servant from an early age. He single-mindedly practiced the heart method with some success. At the age of twenty he married, but his wife died three years later, and he became a wandering monk. For fifteen years he visited famous mountains, caves, monasteries, and masters all across China. All this searching only confused him further, and finally he settled at the age of forty in Xishan at Yuzhang (Jiangxi Nancheng), where he returned to intensive practice of the heart method. His results attracted a large following and support from the local gentry. With their aid, he printed certain works of Lin Zhao'en and built the Longquan Monastery.

In 1610 Zhen Lai spent several months together with the renowned scholar and statesman Zou Yuanbiao, *zi* Nannie (1551–1624), in the Jiangxi Lushan area. Zou then invited Zhen Lai to teach in his home town of Jishui, where he had established the Jenwen Academy. Zou praised the teachings of Lin Zhao'en as "a school of thought with both substance and function, which can serve as a bridge between this world and the other world." He went so far as to promise to print Lin's entire collected works, though it is not certain whether this promise was fulfilled. Thousands of his followers in the Jishui area were taught by Zhen Lai (JL 4a).

In 1612 Zhen Lai accepted the invitation of the Zhejiang Xinan scholar Wang Rufeng to teach at Huangshan in Anhui. There Zhen Lai found many Three in One shrines, which had been built by his associate Wang Xing, and many followers, including "*shidafu* (literati), second-degree candidates, first-degree candidates, and *shanxin zongjiaozhe* (good believers in the ancestral teachings)" (JL 4b). Zhen Lai moved on to Hangzhou and Suzhou before settling in Nanjing in 1616. Zhen Lai found the temple that Zhang Hongdu

---

[27] Shortly after Lin's death, Chen Biao and Wang Xing, two of his closest disciples, went to Fuzhou and built five shrines there, where they printed some of Lin's works. They were shown respect by "literati and intiates new and old in the four prefectures of Yan[ping], Jian[an], Ting[zhou], and Shao[wu]." Wang Xing, *zi* Zhengang, later went on to the Huizhou area, where his fame as a healer attracted many followers. He built several Three in One halls in the Huizhou area and printed some of Lin's writings. He later took up residence at Huang Shan, before returning to Putian in his eighties.

had built near the Zhenzhu Bridge in a state of disrepair, about to collapse, and with almost no activity. By 1621 Zhen Lai had raised the funds to build a large temple, the Jinling Zhongyitang (One in the Center Temple). On the day of the consecration of the temple, great crowds gathered, and Grand Secretary Zhou Rupan composed antithetical couplets while Shangdong Censor Zhang Jimeng sent an inscribed plaque.

The *Jinling zhongyitang xingshi* gives a detailed account of the activities of the temple from its founding in 1620 until 1631. During this period, Zhen Lai organized large-scale relief operations for the destitute, dispersing over thirteen thousand coffins and purchasing plots for them in several cemeteries around Nanjing. The Three in One also conducted requiem services, swept the graves on Qingming, and held services for the dead on the Middle Prime (7/15) rites of Universal Deliverance. Clearly, the temple had become a major social service and religious center.

Zhen Lai notes that nine out of ten adherents were attracted to the Three in One through a desire for better health. The heart method was a means of curing disease without medicine, and it won a wide following. Zhen Lai provides several case histories of people cured by using the heart method.

The *Jinling zhongyitang xingshi* also praises the contributions of Xu Wenpu (*zi* Zuoheng) toward the printing of the *Linzi quanji* (Collected writings of Master Lin). This edition is still extant in the Zhejiang Provincial Library (Ma and Han, 1992: 753, n. 2).

> The carving [of the blocks] began in 1629 and was finished in the autumn of 1631. [The edition] came to forty volumes with over 3,000 pages, with over 1,500 blocks. The number of juan and the table of contents are all included in Xu Zuoheng's colophon. The expenses came to 300 jin (silver). [This edition] is based on the original drafts hand written by the Master during his lifetime. Not a single character has been changed. . . . (I) Zhen Lai, have inspected the printing. (*JL* 22b–23a)

Xu Wenpu was also responsible for introducing the Three in One to several of the eunuchs stationed at the Ming Imperial Tombs at Nanjing.

A final entry for the year 1631 describes a meeting of 110 members of the Three in One led by Zhen Lai at which several senior initiates made testimonials about their personal experiences within the Three in One (see chapter 7). Zhen Lai strongly emphasized the importance of regular practice of the heart method for internal self-cultivation. For external behavior, he recommended the use of *gongguo ge* (ledgers of merit and demerit) (this genre of *shanshu* is discussed in Sakai, 1960; Brokaw, 1991).

> As for the method of [registering] merits and demerits, there was no one who did not reverently believe in and practice it. Therefore [the temple] printed some thousand volumes and distributed them in all directions, wishing that those who read them would use them. Then good deeds would accumulate, and bad deeds fade away. Some formed associations to practice [the use of the ledgers] together,

gathering on a monthly basis to record their merits and demerits in accordance with the ledgers. They felt this to be a help in polishing the pearl of the heart-mind and the body. (*JL* 33b)

Having described Zhen Lai's activities in Jinling, we can now consider a popular novel, the *Sanjiao kaimi guizheng yanyi* (Romance of the Three Teachings exposing delusions and returning to the truth), in one hundred juan, by Pan Jingruo, which was printed in 1627. This text, which was declared heterodox and ordered to be destroyed shortly after its publication in Nanjing, has been preserved in the Tenri University Library in Japan. Judith Berling (1985) has analyzed the book as a fictional embodiment of the philosophy of the Three in One movement. This interpretation is cast into some doubt by the reaction the novel provoked in Three in One circles when it was first published in Nanjing:

> In Tianqi 7, ding mao (1627), in the 3rd month, a publisher who frequented the bookstalls, named Yan Jiunie, and a rascal of a writer, named Pan Jiuhua, together edited the *Romance of the Three Teachings That Exposes Delusions*. Each edition had eight volumes. They flipped through the *Shuihuzhuan* (Water margin) and the *Xiyouji* (Journey to the West), in order to borrow passages. They have degraded the orthodox and insulted the sagely. This is a left-hand Way that deludes the masses. These are heterodox words that are uncanonical. They went so far as to use the Master of the Three in One's name, his *zi* and his *hao*, at the beginning of the book, relying on his fame to reap a profit. This is like fish-eyes mixed with pearls, not distinguishing the heterodox from the orthodox. When they saw this book, the hearts of the multitudes were enraged. Thus they wanted to take the matter to the courts. [Yan] Jiunie, etc., knew that they were in the wrong and feared punishment. They said that they were willing to rely on the writings of the gods to see what should be done. Xie Ji, Zhou Jinglian, Xu Tong, etc., requested a decision at the Chaotian Temple. All of the [printing] blocks of the *Romance* were brought out and smashed and then burnt. Pan Jiuhua ran off and disappeared. Then an official document was posted as proof, stating that should anyone in the future attempt to print the book, they would be held accountable. (JL 17b)

Despite the negative assessment given the novel by the leadership, the novel does indeed point in a satirical way to many key issues that galvanized the Three in One in its early years. Berling has described these concerns as the management of moral capital. Indeed, many of the members of the Zhongyi Temple in Nanjing were merchants, and, as we have seen above, the Jinling Three in One movement sponsored the publication of ledgers of merit and demerit, perfect instruments for calibrating one's moral capital. Moreover, there is a sense of urgency, or ceaseless striving, built into the heart method itself. The notion that one can create one's own universe (*zizao qiankun*) is central to the Three in One vision, whether this be an inner universe created by successful meditation or a social utopia created through moral example. This impetus can be understood in the context of the many changes that were affecting Chinese society at the time. Turbulent social changes in the late Ming included rapid urbanization, rising commercialization, expanding population pressures, increased social dislocation and social mobility, sharpening class conflict, rising failure rates in the examinations, the centralization of the taxation system, escalating crime, social conflict, piracy, warfare, a declining state apparatus, and expanding opportunities for local gentry and scholars to assume positions of leadership in local society.

At the beginning of the Qing dynasty, the Three in One was still active in Nanjing. Dan Qian wrote in his *Zelin Zazu,*

> Lin Zhao'en of Putian cured illnesses with his *genbei* method and had a swarm of followers. He was extremely well versed in the various writings and wrote the *San-jiao huibian* (Collected edition of the Three Teachings) in several *juan.* He developed a mental illness, went mad for several years, and then died. Nowadays there are two shrines in Nanjing where his disciples worship him. (Quoted in Ma and Han, 1992: 755)

To return to developments in Putian, we turn to Dong Shi's *Collected Grasses of the Eastern Mountain,* another important source on the development of the Three in One in the early Qing. The collection contains his "Preface to My Fiftieth Birthday" and so must have been written after 1674. The collection consists of a dozen short philosophic essays, followed by a collection of prefaces, records, letters, eulogies, and inscriptions, as well as five-character regulated verse, five-character ancient-style verse, seven-character regulated verse, seven-character quatrains, and seven-character ancient-style verse. Especially valuable are the entries on the rebuilding of the Yaodaoci (pp. 1.51–52), the Xiangyangci (pp. 1.41–43, and 1.51–52), the Dongshansi (pp. 1.36–37), and the buildings and activities of the Fuzhou temples. Equally fascinating are the discourses on the meaning of the *Yulan Pen* ritual, the attack on the mediumistic practices in the Three in One in Xianyou, comments on the Three in Ones interaction with Buddhist organizations, and the discussion of the god statue of Lin Zhao'en as the "residence of the god" (see below, on ritual traditions and scriptures).

Several epistles and eulogies, particularly the one for his mother-in-law, reveal Dong to have been a deeply emotional man. He could also be extremely paranoid, especially when it came to the issue of his right to be the Third Transmitter of the Teachings. We hear again about Chen's secret instructions and learn in excruciating detail about his self-doubts and initial refusal to accept the position. These sources name many of the other men who lost out to Dong, most of them his seniors. We get a sense of his connections among the powerful figures in the Three in One in Xianyou and Fuzhou, and his efforts to guide them in reigning in the increasing popularization of the Three in One. The colophons to this work by two of his disciples, written in 1677, equate Dong Shi with Mencius, just as Dong had done for Chen Zhongyu.

A few years after assuming the title of third transmitter, Dong Shi decided to set his own mark on the largest Three in One Temple, the Yaodaoci, built by Lu Wenhui. In the inscription quoted above we can see the processes lead-ing to the continuous expansion of supplementary shrines to figures associ-ated with the Three in One. In 1608 Lu Wenhui had built the magnificent Yaodao Temple in Hanjiang. He restored the temple in 1613, built a Hall for the Assembling of Scriptures, placed a statue of Lin as Lord Xia in the hall, "and worshiped at its side." Lin's apotheosis was thus accomplished a mere fifteen years after his death. Lu's successors, Chen and Dong, both repaired and enlarged the building (in 1644 and 1660, respectively), each adding new temples to the complex.

Dong Shi also made repeated efforts to rebuild the temple his father had built across the Jiangkou bridge just across the Putian, Fuqing border. These efforts resulted in repeated frustrations but reveal something of the relation-ship between family- or lineage-based temple building projects and the new organizational locus of temple building available to Dong Shi through the or-ganizational matrix of the Three-in-One:

> I am a Qinjiang man. If you cross the long bridge from Qinjiang, you are in Fu-tang territory. The land to the north of the bridge belongs to Futang, and to the south to Puyang. My father first tried to open up [some land] from the Wangs of Futang in order to built a Great Teacher Master Lin Shrine in Xiangyang. Because this space rested between the Fu[tang] and Pu[yang], this was resisted by the Wang lineage. Therefore my father sold land and raised 100 in gold to buy the Xiangyang property. He built the shrine in 1629. Now the marvels of this tem-ple were clear to all. The origin of the mountain against which it rests is the Thatch Hall, where formerly Zhu Xi and Wang Yangming discussed the *Book of Changes*. Later people wrote in seal script the characters "Ziyang caotang" (The Thatch Hall of Purple Yang [Master Zhu Xi]), and so the mountain received its name. Now Xiangyang is at the foot of Thatch Hall mountain, so the area is close to the Way of Confucius. Although the mountain is small, it twists into lying shape, with its back to Zimao (Purple Hat) and overlooking Qinjiang (Brocade River). The Three Platform [peaks] rise up and stretch into the sky. The water of the Brocade River flows on, circled and fed by the ocean and by streams. If you add in the Long Bridge as its armor and the three settlements as its clustered stars, then truly one can say that its marvels are clear to see. My father toughed it out here for sev-eral years, and then one day a flood caused a disaster. The wood and stones couldn't withstand it, and all turned into fish and dragons and swam off. My fa-ther extended his every effort to raise money, convinced that the work must be completed. The shrine was rebuilt and my father passed away. At the time I was only ten years old. Some dozen of his disciples were able to keep the place in good condition. In the winter of 1653 I sold land for over 200 in gold, in order to build a pagoda for viewing the worship. As soon as I had finished this project the hal-berds and spears [of Qing armies] swarmed all over, and during those twenty years, I left home and wandered about without a perch. In 1655 I accepted the position of third transmitter from Master Chen of Hunan. I expounded the Way and seldom made it back to Xiangyang. Who would have thought that in winter

of 1666 pirates and refugees wantonly camped in the shrine. As fast as a crane flies up, the eaves of the temples were destroyed in flames. Alas, when I recall this, how can I help but feel my liver and gall bladder torn apart? In 1667 I passed by Xiangyang when returning from Fuzhou, and Wang Zhaolong said to me, "Formerly your father and you, Patriarch, wished to establish the Shangyang temple but did not succeed. Later we divided off into the Aofeng Temple, but now the Aofeng Temple has been moved, and so we have invited the statue of the Great Teacher back to the Pagoda for Viewing the Worship, waiting for the day when you will rebuild the shrine. For the affairs of the world go from unity to division and then back to unity again. A descendent's carrying out [his ancestor's] wishes, how could this be a mere coincidence?" I replied, "Oh my, it is possible to support the Great Dao with bare hands, but it isn't possible to conduct such a large act of merit with bare hands." Wang said, "The materials for the beams and rafters are all ready. Wouldn't it be better if you didn't worry too much? Now all the disciples in Minzhong (the Putian Xianyou region) are within your gate. You certainly do not lack for men. Don't be embarrassed to stick out your tongue, for thus the Xiangyang shrine will be rebuilt." I said, "Oh, my! My position vis-à-vis the disciples is based on what I have in my heart. If I were to borrow my three-inch tongue to accomplish an act of private merit, well, that is something I just cannot do." Wang said, "Tell me one place where you are not in the process of building shrines. Now Xiangyang is indeed the place where your ancestor first established a shrine, and fortunately now you have a weighty responsibility of carrying out the Way and leading it, and because of this, Xiangyang is looked up to by those on all four sides. How could it be that a father's wishes are not complied with, and a father's affairs are not completed. Those who feel responsible desires will laugh at this." I said, "Oh my! Before I arrived here, the long hard labor of my father was reduced to cold ashes. How could I feel any different than the pain I am in now? Fortunately Heaven has not cast us off, we still have the Pagoda for Viewing the Worship which escaped the flames. A great many pillars and beams standing inside it could be used for rafters and beams. Now as for carrying on my father's wishes and completing his affairs, of course I know all that. What I am unhappy about is [your] not realizing that I am unhappy about this. I realize how deep such a crime is, and that being scorned for this is inevitable. But still in the end I cannot tell people. Knowing that I can't tell people, and yet forcing myself to tell them, this is nothing more than hoping that the various sagely and virtuous [disciples] will expunge the guilt and remove the cause of scorn for this most unfilial son." [Dong] Shi writes this preface with repeated bows. (*Preface to the Reconstruction of the Xiangyang Shrine*, in *Dongshan jicao*, 1.41–43.) In the winter of 1669, I, Dong [Shi], led disciples from Fuzhou, Puyang, and Xiansi to rebuild the Xiangyang Shrine. By the spring of the following year [1670], the work was complete, and we held a sacrifice before the First Teacher Master Lin. (*Dongshan jicao* 1:51–52)

Note the tension here between Dong Shi's carrying out his filial or ancestral obligations and his desire to avoid being perceived as exploiting his position as leader of the Three in One. The Xiangyang Academy was built by Dong's father on land originally belonging to another lineage. Here we begin to see the possibility of the Three in One as a new force in local society, gathering a multitude of voluntary adherents into a building machine. "Tell me where are you not building shrines and temples?" This was a force that could stand up to, and eventually surpass, local lineages. But the issue of continuing his father's vision suggests that the Three in One could also infiltrate into lineage structures and ideologies, building on established bases in local power relations. Dong Shi went on to compare the construction of the shrine to progress in self-cultivation within the framework of the Three in One, extending an analogy from the *Book of History:*

> Formerly when Master Lin taught people, he used the bonds of propriety to establish the base, and this was the foundation of my Teaching. He used the regarding of one's true nature as the "entrance into the door," and this was the Hall of my Teaching. He used the [transcendence of] emptiness as "the ultimate principle," and this was the ridge pole of my Teaching. For a hall without a foundation cannot get started, and without a ridge pole it cannot be completed. (*Dongshan jicao* 1:51–52)

The architectonic metaphor of the Three in One Hall was an appropriate one for the active expansion and rebuilding of the Three in One after the destruction caused by the Qing takeover and the Ming resistance. However, all was not as unified as Dong Shi would have liked. According to another passage in the *Dongshan jicao,* within a few decades of the death of Lin Zhao'en, the Three in One had already undergone many unwholesome changes:

> Last year, in the winter, the Xianyou disciples came to Putian asking for instruction. They presented me with what they had [already] learned, and I said to them, "This is in fact the method of eliminating disease, particular to the teachings of Master Lin. However, this is still but a matter of "hunting [a convert] by means of a relatively minor power." This was not something Master Lin was content with. Master Lin said, "The elimination of disease is but a minor proof, only one means of working the Dao. Now that it is [widely] believed in, it is appropriate no longer to discuss it." Now how is it that Master Lin would say that one should not discuss the elimination of disease and the salvation of people, which are the fullest means of practicing humaneness? This is nothing more than [his] worrying that people would [be caught up with the] minor uses of the Great Way. Moreover, as time goes on, the more [the teachings] are transmitted, the more they lose the truth. The ignorant take the elimination of disease to be Master Lin's Way, and reciting of scriptures and litanies to be Master Lin's Teaching. Those who have not slid into shamanic curing are few indeed. The [Xianyou] disciples agreed with me. This year in the fifth month, they invited me to their city to explicate the greatness of Master Lin. At this a great number of scholar-gentry from within the city heard of this and gathered round, and a great many came from outside the city as well. (Preface to the Xianyou city Three in One Hall Ullambana Ritual, *Dongshan jicao* 1.31–32)

Dong Shi spent many years in Xianyou, attempting to set things straight. The following excerpt describes the reconstruction of a temple in the city:

As one enters Xianyou City's western quarter, Shuwu, to the east there is the Golden Lotus Tower, and to the west a river runs by. There are residences there too. Formerly, Bishan Liu Huaru had his home there. During the Chengshen reign period (1630–1644), Huaru turned his home into a shrine in which the Great Teacher Master Lin was worshiped. At that time the locally selected *jinshi* Dai Hongheng felt deep concern [for the shrine] and wrote a placard reading "Three in One Shrine." During the revolts of 1655, troops and commoners settled inside the shrine. Fortunately, Lin Zhaokai, Dai Jingwang, Wu Mingyao, and Liu Shiji forcefully preserved and protected the shrine. In 1659 [Lin] Zhaokai and the others invited me to the temple to expound upon this Way and lead in later sages. I stayed here three years and held two Ullambana Rituals and thrice presided. Very numerous were those who came to join the Three in One, seeking a way to climb higher, whether they were scholars, farmers, artisans, or merchants. However, the size of the temple was inadequate, with only one *mu* of land, and it was always filled with wind and dust and smoke and fire. . . . But I don't want the disciples to search about for land and buildings. We will create the universe (*zao qiankun*) from here. Thus what people now call wind and dust and smoke and fire will be changed into a mountain dragon and a starry Dipper. A temple of a single *mu* will be transformed into a magnificent temple. The masses will compete to take part in setting up columns and rafters and then will discuss the merits [of the Masters] and establish the sacrifices. (Preface to the Record of the Construction of the Xianyou City Great Teacher Lin Shrine by Contributions, in *Dongshan jicao* 1.36–37)

Dong Shi's *Record of the Xishan Shrine,* discussing the rebuilding of the Xishan Three in One temple in Fuzhou in 1663, is significant in two respects. First, it too reveals the extent of the destruction of coastal temples of all kinds following the coastal evacuation at the beginning of the Qing takeover of Southeast China. Second, the text provides an intriguing classical precedent for the expansion of the cult through the establishment of side-altars to Lu Wenhui and Chen Zhongyu:

Formerly, in the Bamboo Grove Hall of Quiescence, worship was offered to the utmost Saint and First Master Confucius. Those [worshiped] around Confucius were first the Four Saints, and then the seventy-two disciples, in estimation of their [perfected] hearts. At first this was the fashion of only Song scholars, but when Zhen Dexiu was made Guozi jijiu (National Sacrificer), he made this the fixed rule of the Academy, so that nowadays all the schools and academies in the empire worship them. Now, my Master Lin introduced the utmost attainments of the Saint Confucius's study to his disciples. [Lin's disciples] numbered 800. Therefore at that time shrines were spread out throughout the area. For example, in the Central Min area, the Aofeng, Jibi, Jinding, and Nanchan shrines were built during the Ming dynasty. At that time one could say that they were filled with scholars. After the destruction brought on by soldiers, these have unavoid-

TABLE 2
Spread of Construction of Three in One Temples in the First Sixty Years
of the Movement

Date	Location	Site/Name of Temple	Founders
1584	Putian	Mafeng	Huang Fang
1585	Putian	Hanjiang Shangshengsi	Su Huang, Lin Ziming
1588	Putian	Yaotai	Lin, Li Mengxiong
1589	Putian	Meijian	Lin Hong
1590	Putian	Yuexiu Mingxiaci	Lin Zhenming
1590	Putian	Tangxia	Chen Jie
1592	Putian	Chongbing	Zhang Mou, Zhang Yuanfu
1592	Putian Houzhu	Shuinan	Zhu Fengshi
1593	Putian	Yuxi	Zhang Zisheng (Hongdu)
1594	Nanjing	Sanshan jie Guozijian	Cai Jingjun
1594	Putian	Qingjiang	Li Yingshan, Huang Dayin
1595	(4) Putian	Chishan	Zhou Qiming
1596	Putian	Guqing Xingtou	Lin Qing
1597	Putian	(5) Fenggu Linzhai	Li Mingwu
1598	Putian	Shicheng	Lin Chengyi
1598	Xianyon	Fengting	Wang Kefang
1598	Putian	Anminpu	Chen Tianyu
1598	Fuqing shangzepu	Huabeili	Wang Xing
1600 (1598)	Putian	Zhu Dun	Lin Yingbin
1600 (1598)	Xianyou Wukuntou		Li Sheng
1600 (1598)	Xianyou	Nanpo	Chen Qishen
1600	Xianyou	Hanxing	Cai Yanjiao
1600	Fuqing	Aofeng	Wang Xing
1600 (1602)	Gutian	Yidushuikouzhen	Wang Xing
1600	Minqing	Fangxiou	Wang Xing
1600	Jianning		Wang Xing
1608	Minxian Tangyu	Zhideli	Wang Xing
1600	Nanzhili Xiuningxian	Huizhoufu Meilindu	Wang Shishu, Wu Yingzheng
1601 (1600)	Putian	Chengjiang	Lin Yanxun
1601	Fuzhou	Sanshan Hongtang xiawu	Chen Tiansi, Yu Yanliang
1601	Zhejiang Jiangshanxian	Chuzhoufu Nianbadu	Xu Liangcai, Mao Sixin
1601	Jiangsu	Songjiangfu Nanmen	Chen Qixian, Jiang Yunlong
1601	Jiangsu	Songjiangfu Beimen	Chen Qixian, Jiang Yunlong

TABLE 2   (*Continued*)

Date	Location	Site/Name of Temple	Founders
1602	Putian	Dongshan	Chen Daozhang
1608 (1600)	Putian	Hanjiang Yaodaoci	Lu Wenhui
1610	Beijing	Xuntianfu Yuheqiao	Zhang Hongdu
1611	Putian	Lindun	Lin Zongtai, Chen Dabiao
1611	Huian	Fuyang	Chen You
1611	Huian	Chongwusuo	Li Yukun
1614	Putian	Nantai Houpu	Cai Yanjing, Ye Fuqing
1621	Nanjing	Zhenzhuqiao	Zhen Lai
1630	Putian	Shangyang	Dong Yingjie
1630	Putian	Songdong	Chen Zhongyu
1637	Fuqing	Aofeng	Wang Kai
1630–44	Xianyou	Xiguan	Liu Huaru
1663	Sanshan	Yushan	

The *Menxian shilu* allows us to add a few others to the list.

	Ninghua		Huang Qingjiang
	Shuyuan		Li Yinglin

The *Dongshan jicao* mentions other temples built before 1668.

	Fuzhou	Zishan
	Xianyou	Dongxi
	Xianyou bishan	Ruiyun

ably turned into deserted, smoke-filled wastelands. In the spring of 1663 the Fuzhou disciples built a shrine on Zishan especially to worship Master Lin. They set up [altars to] the first transmitter, Master Lu, and the second transmitter, Master Chen, to the east and west. The committee in charge of these matters consisted of Pan Xian, Lou Wenshao, Pan Shikai, and some dozen others. Within less than seven days the temple was complete. . . . Who knows if, after a hundred generations, this too will not become the fixed rule of the Academy, as was the case with Bamboo Grove Hall of Quiescence? (*Dongshan jicao* 1.50–51)

TEMPLE BUILDING AND THE DIVISION OF INCENSE

Sources such as the *True Record* list the earliest Three in One temples established. According to the True Record, as early as 1569, when Lin Zhao'en was on his way to Wudang shan and was stopped by weather and roads in Jiangxi, two Hong brothers asked if they could build him a lecture hall (*shuyuan*), offering over 200 ounces of gold for the project. Lin told them that not enough people yet believed in the teachings, and that they should wait until the time was right. The first mention of construction projects financed by the Three in One occurred in 1564 and involved renovations to a Buddhist monastery called the Fengshansi in Jinling (Nanjing). Lin sent the Buddhist monk Mingfeng and a Daoist priest named He Zuo to oversee the project. An official based in Nanjing, the Duxuan there, was a relative of Lin's and helped finance the renovations. It was not until 1584 that Lin agreed to allow Huang Fang to build a Three in One shrine in Mafeng, Putian. Recall that this was also the year marking the culmination of Lin's inner alchemical quest.

In these early shrines (*shengci*—shrines dedicated to the example of living exemplary figures), images of Confucius, Laozi, and the Buddha were joined by an image of Xiawuni, Lin Zhao'en. We do not know if images or statues of Lin were worshiped during his lifetime. Recall the episode in 1587 when a follower named Chen Youkai encountered a magician in Zhejiang who described Lin as the Lord of the Three in One and prepared a woodblock image of Lin in this role. Lin permitted this usage among his disciples. It is likely that these events mark the successful creation of an apotheosized image of Lin Zhao'en as the god Xia Wuni. By the time of his death in 1598 over twenty temples had been built. This number would expand to over fifty by mid-1600s, despite the Qing Manchu invasion.

Inner Alchemy, Scriptures, and Liturgies

THE THREE IN ONE had divided into three or four branches by the early Qing. The "orthodox" mainstream tradition was in the hands of the three transmitters, Lu Wenhui, Chen Zhongyu, and Dong Shi. (This tradition would be reclaimed at the end of the Qing dynasty by Chen Zhida and Liang Puyao, founders of the Wuben branch.) Lin Zhenming had established a separate branch, which became known as the Weng branch, or the Mingxia branch. Both the mainstream tradition and the Mingxia tradition spread into Xianyou. Meanwhile, groups like Zhen Lai's Three in One branch in Nanjing were still active in the early Qing, while other offshoots, such as Zhang Hongdu's temple in Beijing, appear to have been absorbed into broader institutions such as the Putian Huiguan (Putian Nativeplace Association).

All the branches of the Three in One initiate new adherents into the *Kongmen xinfa* (Confucian heart method), also known as the *Genbeifa* (*Gen* hexagram in the back method), developed by Lin Zhao'en. These initiations are graduated, with further secrets of the technique dispensed when the adept has gone through the necessary preliminary stages. Many temples organize meditation groups for the group practice of the heart method, and this is still one of the strongest attractions of the tradition to young people and outsiders. The heart method is widely perceived as leading to good health. The secrets of the methods of inner cultivation vary to some extent from one branch of the tradition to another, and often from one temple to the next within the same branch. An important subdivision of Three in One literature consists of the secret manuals explaining the heart method.

The establishment of the heart method was a central component of the creation of the Three in One movement. Lin Zhao'en saw the heart method as a practical means to channel what he believed was the material basis for spiritual life, the drop of supernatural spiritual power and humanity achieved at conception. The heart method was to be the principal means for an individual to attempt to reconcile the quest for Confucian sagehood with the pursuit of supernatural spiritual powers. This chapter outlines the heart method and the early scriptures and liturgies of the Three in One. A subsequent chapter will show how the meditation system is integrated into the ritual tradition. Alchemy here joins with ritual practice in the Three in One technology of the self.

The heart method is given its fullest early expression in a hitherto little known text, the *Jiuxu zheyan neijing tu* (Chart of the inner landscapes of the selected sayings of the Nine Stages), written by Lin Zhao'en and edited by Lu Wenhui in 1583 (see Lin, 1985; 1992). A variety of other alchemical texts, commenting on aspects of the heart method, continue to circulate within the Three in One in Xianyou and Putian. Certain texts by Lin Zhenming contain extensive commentary on inner alchemy.[1] The *Sanjiao jintan fahui jue* (Secret instructions on the flowering of the golden elixir of the Three Teachings), Dong Xizu, 1722, manuscript copy dated 1917, consists of long passages of alchemical verse, and a detailed description of the *Sanjiao jiuzhuan huandan jue* (Secrets of the ninefold transformed elixir of the Three Teachings). I also photographed a collection of secret instructions (*mijue*) for ritual use that highlight the role of internal alchemy in ritual practice (see below). More recent texts, such as the *Sanjiao chuxue zhinan* (Pointers on beginning study of the Three Teachings) by Chen Zhida and the *Jiuxu yaojue xuzhi* (Necessary information of the essential secrets of the Nine Stages), a manuscript photocopied by Lin Guoping, provide further details and interpretations of the heart method (Lin, 1992).

Many techniques of inner alchemy evolved in China over the centuries. The basic principles of this system have been outlined in a number of studies (Sivin, 1980; Needham, 1983; Baldrain-Hussein, 1984; Robinet, 1989, 1990, 1993; Boltz, 1983). The basic concepts are as follows. The human body is made up of three components: the Primal Breath, the Primal Spirit, and the Primal Spermatic Essence. Conception occurs when the blood of the woman mingles with the sperm of the man. The embryo breathes the Primal Breath until it is born, after which time it breathes in the stale breath of the created world. To restore one's ability to breathe the Primal Breath, it is necessary to reverse time, and the usual outward flow of generation. This often involves reversing the flow of the breath by mingling it with saliva and swallowing, followed by complex, guided visualizations of the conjoining of the breath, the sexual energy, and the spirit. By refining the breath, sexual essence, and spirit within one, one can give birth to an immortal embryo and through this process return to the undifferentiated state prior to time. The refining of these forces within the body is often described in terms of an alchemical process, utilizing imagery from "external" alchemical experimentation. The body is often pictured as containing three elixir fields: one in the head, the other centered in the heart, and the lowest beneath the navel. Other commonly used terms are the five elements (or phases), the yin and yang polarities, the hexagrams of the *Book of Changes,* and the fire phases (referring to the generation of heat in specific parts of the body through intense concentration). Different systems of inner alchemy mobilize these elements into different models and processes. Many seek first to combine the breath with the sexual energy, and then to cause the spirit to be refined by these combined and purified forces.

Lin Zhao'en's heart method developed out of this larger tradition. According to Lin Zhao'en, *xing* (underlying nature) and *ming* (life force/di-

---

[1] These include the *Longhua biezhuan* (Alternative account of the Dragon Flower [Assembly]), preface, 1610, the *Zhuowu shiyi* (True meaning of [Master] Zhuo [Wanchun]), and the *Mingxiaji* (Collection on illumining Xia), 4 juan, Lin Zhenming, preface, 1598.

rection) originate in the shapeless void. They begin to divide at birth once incarnated in human form: "The *xing* is then *ji* (encased) within the flesh of the heart, and it is called the *shen* (spirit). The *ming* is encased within the navel and the kidneys [respectively], where it is called the *qi* (vital energy; breath) and the *jing* (spermatic essence; sexual fluid)" (from *Direct Pointing to the Heart as a Sage*). Elsewhere Lin summarized the inner alchemical process: "Refine the *jing* to transform it into *qi*, [then] refine the *qi* to transform it into *shen*, [and then] refine the *shen* to return to the void" (*Zhengzong tonglun*, j. 30, *Xugao*).

Lin Zhao'en's heart method is a graduated progress made up of nine stages. These nine stages are divided into three phases, namely, "establishment of the basis," "entering of the gateway," and "attainment of the ultimate principle." The first step consists of the rites of initiation (see chapter 6), involving the recitation and burning of a Memorial to Heaven and the initial transmission of the outline of the heart method, as well as detailed instructions on the initial stage.[2] The initiate is also given a mantra, usually "*Sanjiao xiansheng*" (masters of the Three Teachings), to repeat while following the initial meditations and visualizations. Moreover, "entering the gate" implies a reorientation of the adept's life in terms of Confucian modes of being. Lin Zhao'en explained that there are actually four phases in this process:

> [When one has] "established the basis," only then transmit to them the "entrance to the gateway." The "entrance to the gateway" in this teaching consists of all the phases from the first, "use the *gen* hexagram in the back to still thought," to the sixth, "coalesce the *shen* (spirit) to form the *yang* elixir." When one reaches the seventh stage of "embodying heaven and earth" and the eighth stage of "embodying the great void," it seems as though one has attained [the ultimate]. But because these stages are still [attained] by means of active effort (*gongfu*), this is still not the end. Only after an initiate has attained this point can one discuss the ultimate principle with them. The ninth phase of "shattering the void" is the ultimate pinnacle of this teaching. (*Selected Sayings on the Nine Phases*)

Thus Lin actually distinguishes four phases: (1) taking vows; (2) working through inner alchemical techniques in stages one to six; (3) casting off conscious striving, leading to escape from time (stage 7) and space (stage 8), and finally (4) smashing the void—moving beyond all differentiation into enlightenment.

As seen above, Lin Zhao'en's hagiography in the *True Record* is at one level the account of an inner alchemical process. The actual process of the elaboration of Lin's heart method seems to have taken many years. The "mysterious master" who transmitted the "Confucian heart method" to Lin around 1547 appears to have transmitted only the first two of Lin's nine-stage inner alchemical oeuvre. These were the *genbei* (*gen* hexagram in the back) and the

---

[2] The current text of the Memorial to Heaven is very similar to the standard form translated in Berling (1980: 81–86).

xingtian (moving within the courtyard, later identified as the *zhoutian* [revolution of the heavens] stage). Since Lin fell in with the Daoist wanderer Zhuo Wanchun the following year, it is likely that he learned several more inner alchemical techniques from him, which he may have ultimately incorporated into his Nine Stages.[3] Lin used his rudimentary heart method to cure the daughter of his first disciple, Huang Zhou, in 1550. It was not until 1561 that Lin wrote the essay *Direct Pointing to the Heart as a Sage,* in which he discussed various aspects of the heart method: "Begin it with the *gen* hexagram in the back, and the movement in the courtyard. Complete it with the [attainment] of the original substance of the void. This therefore is the means by which the gentleman can avoid leaving the heart-mind and still achieve Sagehood. This is a gradual [process] of learning." The year 1561 is the same year that Lin printed a collection of alchemical poems attributed to Zhang Sanfeng, the ubiquitous Daoist of the late Ming (Seidel, 1970).[4] Perhaps Zhuo and Zhang are to thank for the breakthroughs in the elaboration of Lin Zhao'en's heart method. Be that as it may, both Zhuo Wanchun and Zhang Sanfeng are often placed in altars to either side of Lin Zhao'en in temples of the Mingxia and Sanyi branches of the Three in One.

In 1579 Lin wrote the *Nine Stages* essay, and the *Inner Landscape* was completed in 1583. The system had reached completion. Also in 1583 Lin himself is recorded as having undergone a particularly intense alchemical trans-

[3] The *Zhengtong zonglun* contains the *Wuyan lu* (Record of sayings that awaken), which contains several dialogues between Zhuo Wanchun and Lin Zhao'en. In these dialogues we find discussions on inner alchemy, covering the dimensions of the human microcosm, the importance of the *gen* hexagram in the back, the formation of an inner elixir by coalescing of the spirit, the movement of the elixir upward through the three elixir fields, and various details of the fire phases.

[4] The dates and deeds of Zhang Sanfeng are still disputed (Seidel, 1970). From writings attributed to him it appears that, like Lin Zhao'en, he emphasized the merger of the Three Teachings as well as the importance of Confucian values and conduct in everyday life. Lin included the *Xuange* (Mystic songs) and the *Xuantan* (Mystic conversations), ostensibly by Zhang Sanfeng, in his *Zhengzong tonglun.* The poems refer to several key concepts in the Nine Stages, such as the role of the *xinjing* (the quiescent heart) in the creation of the elixir. One verse reads: "One must first coalesce the spirit and have it enter the cavity within the cavity, silently it returns to its root and ripens at the center. When the center is ripe the embyro grows." This passage recalls phase 6 of the heart method. Another passage reads, "Begin by gathering the one dot of true mercury within the body, and have it return to one's true place of exit. This inner medicine is called the purple gold [elixir]. Continue [one's practice] and there spontaneously forms in the great void a dot of true mercury. Take it and cause it to mix together with the purple gold inner medicine. This external medicine is called the black iron. Thus the purple gold is the yin elixir, and the black iron is the yang elixir." This passage closely parallels the description of the yin elixir in phase 4 and the yang elixir in phase 6. Lin remarked in his preface to the *Mystic Conversations* that "As for the *Mystic Songs,* they put first the cultivation of the body and the refinement of the nature. . . . Peeling away *yin* and purifying *yang,* they depict the laborious actions required of those dwelling in the world. These are all the gradual teachings of the mystic way. As for the *Mystic Conversations,* these show that the *waijing* (outer realm) always comes without [conscious] striving. And as for the 'cavity within the cavity,' the 'growing embryo dwelling in restfulness,' and the 'purple gold and the black iron,' are these not the ultimate attainments of the mystic path? If scholars can sincerely view these writings in this way, then the Way under Heaven will no longer be hidden."

formation. The following year he is said to have completed the *Bentijing* (Scripture on the original substance), translated later in this chapter.

Judith Berling has given a careful analysis of Lin Zhao'en's heart method (Berling, 1980: chaps. 5–6), examining Neo-Confucian philosophic debates on terms used by Lin Zhao'en as well as certain antecedents in Daoist inner alchemical literature. She concludes that Lin made use of inner alchemical terms but always interpreted them as cosmic processes, rather than employing the terminology of the alchemical laboratory.[5] Materials discovered in Putian and Xianyou enable us to take a closer look at the concrete visualization techniques transmitted to Three in One initiates along with the more publicly available text of Lin Zhao'en's *Nine Stages*. In these texts the emphasis is on the visualization of colored "pearls," which are to be circulated within the breath around the body. The texts contain a considerable amount of technical inner alchemical terminology. The first twenty pages of the *Inner Landscape* provide charts and explanations to illustrate the parts of the body and the processes required for the alchemical transformation. For example, on page 3, in a passage entitled "the essential instructions concerning the commencement of the transmission of the method," we find the following description of the alchemical properties of the body:

> The lungs, liver, heart, spleen, and kidneys are all quite close to one another. The [point] of origin is beneath the navel, and the Niwan is in the center of the head. The Heavenly Palace is located in the Gate of Heaven; the Main Gateway and the Cranial Gateway are located at the top center of the cranium. The Courtyard of Heaven is also located between the eyebrows. The Upper Jade Pillow is at the back base of the cranium. The tongue has four openings. Two of them connect to the heart, the other two to the spleen. The throat has two tubes: one connects to the lungs, the other to the stomach. The latter is used for taking food and drink. The *po* souls are in the lungs and the *hun* souls are in the liver. The *shen* (spirit) is in the heart. The Yellow Chamber is below the navel, opposite the Gate of Life. The Scarlet Palace [the heart] is above the navel a little bit. The Sea of Blood is between the two nipples and is called the *dan zhong*. The Sea of Breath is 1.3 inches below the navel. The space between the nipples is the Sea of Blood. Blood circulates and the breath follows it. There, wherein the blood and the breath reside, determines the distribution of yin and yang. The breath is the origin of life. Blood is the Master of Destiny. The intermingling of breath and blood are Father and Mother of Man. They cannot be lost. There are Upper, Middle, and Lower Elixir Fields; all are within the Sea of Breath. The two kidneys are at the back of

[5] Berling relies primarily on Lin Zhao'en's 1561 *Xinsheng zhizhi* (Direct pointing to the heart as a sage) and his 1579 *Jiuxu zheyan* (Selected sayings on the Nine Stages), along with other writings, to explicate the system. The former text contains scattered references to several points that are grouped into a graduated series of stages in the latter text. The latter text appears to transcend the vision of the former with its emphasis on shattering the void in the final stage. Readers unfamiliar with inner alchemical terminology may wish to consult Berling's analysis of the stages. Taylor (1990) discusses Neo-Confucian traditions of meditation leading to enlightenment, and Gregory (1987a) describes various Buddhist meditation systems.

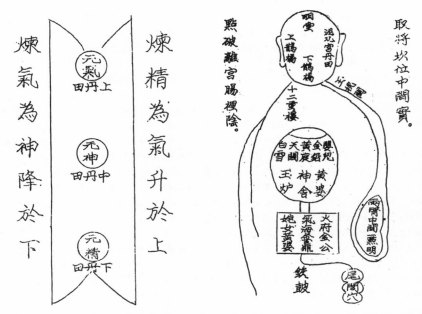

Plate 8. Images of the alchemical body from the *Chart of the Inner Landscape of the Nine Stages. Left:* Chart of the three elixir fields and the interactions of breath, spirit, and sexual energy. *Right:* the principal parts of the alchemical body including the Illumined Hall in the head and the Yellow Court in the abdomen

the waist. The spermatic essence (*jing*) is in the kidneys. The bladder is below the belly and is the point of exit of urine. The Kunlun (Magic Mountain) is located at the topmost protruding bone at the back of the top of the head. Others say it is the protruding bone at the top of the spine. The brain is the sea of marrow. All marrow circulates through to the anklebone (*rui*); thus, from the top of the head to the base of the coccyx, it is produced within the spinal column. The anus is the valley mouth. The anklebone is in the "eye" of the foot. The flowing fountain (*yongquan*) is in the center of the base of the foot. The five viscera, the six cabinets, the hundred bones, the nine passageways, the meridians, and the blood vessels are all interconnected, linked one to the next without any separation. When the heart is stirred it moves; when it is calm, it rests. The Gate of Destiny, the Heavenly Emolument, and the Three Furnaces, [these are where one] who accumulates enough *qi* leaks it out. The student must be calm and still; his heart/mind must not have stray thoughts and must not charge away. Establish the controls, and lock tight the monkeys of the mind and the horses of the will.

This passage is followed by several epigrams and various diagrams on the alchemical process. Having discussed and identified the parts of the body and their principal alchemical properties over several pages, the text turns to a practical account of the Nine Stages. A full translation of the passages on the

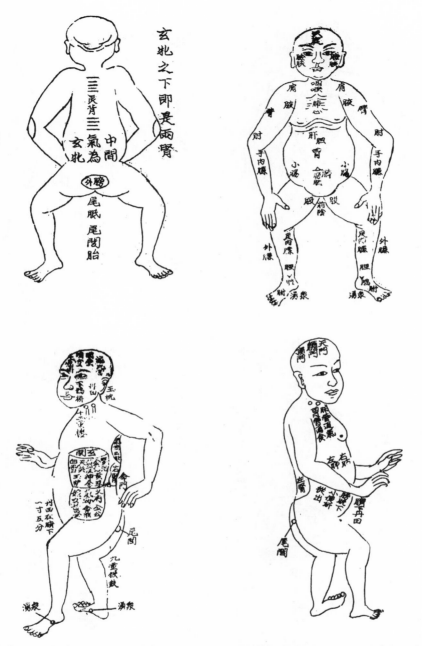

Plate 9. Images of the alchemical body from the *Chart of the Inner Landscape of the Nine Stages* from the front and back and left and right. Note the position of the *gen* hexagram in the back in the upper lefthand image.

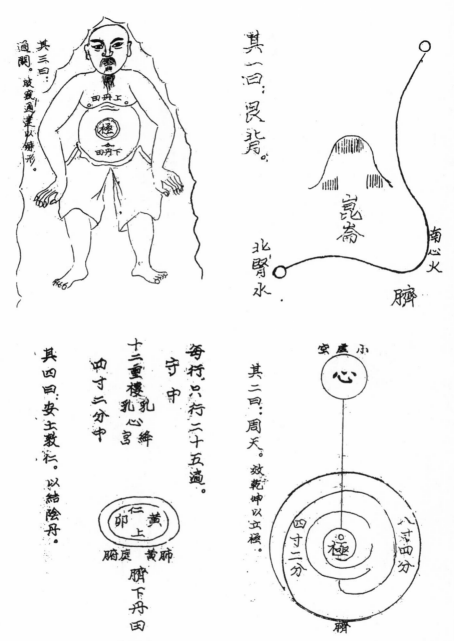

Plate 10. Images of stages 1, 2, 3, and 4 of the heart method from the *Chart of the Inner Landscape*. See appendix 2 for detailed explanations of the stages.

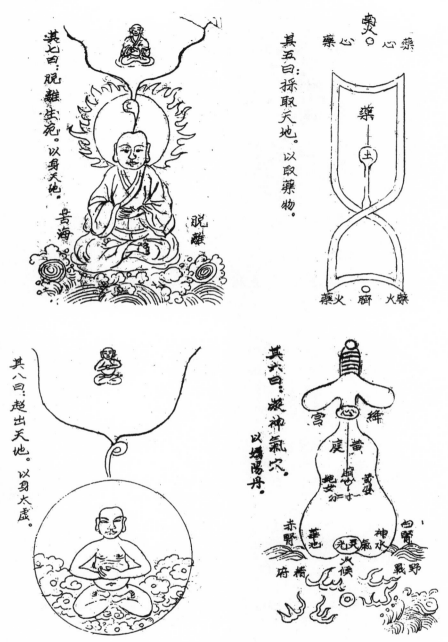

Plate 11. Images of stages 5, 6, 7, and 8 of the heart method from the *Chart of the Inner Landscape*. See appendix 2 for detailed explanations of the stages.

Plate 12. "Shatter the Void to Experience the Ultimate Principle." Image of stage 9 of the heart method from the *Chart of the Inner Landscape*.

Nine Stages is provided in appendix 2. It is difficult to summarize the heart method in simple terms. The first stage involves concentrating on a point in the back until all thought is gone. The commentaries describe the location of this point. The second stage calls for one to visualize an orb of white light at this point, and then to visualize it revolving in a wide circle centered at this point. The light revolves vertically in a circular clockwise direction from the heart to the navel and back again. This revolving of the light is interpreted as a mingling of the sexual energy with the breath. Mastery of these two stages enables the adherent to cure illness by focusing visualization of light and heat on the afflicted area of the body.

In the third stage the orb of light is guided all around the body along a set routing. The fourth stage brings the light back to the center, where it is absorbed into a crucible visualized in the shape of a lotus flower. This is identified as the joining of the adept's spirit (*shen*) with the mixture of breath and sexual energy that has already been accomplished. The fifth stage involves visualizing the rising and falling of the pearl of light from the heart chamber to the navel nine times as in an alchemical process. This process generates considerable heat within the body. It is interpreted as consolidating the mixture of the spirit, the breath, and the sexual energy. In the sixth stage, the light, now visualized as a fiery red light within a white light, is moved to the point between the kidneys. This is explained as moving the inner yin elixir into position to allow it to merge with the coalescence of external spiritual force, the external elixir. In the seventh stage, this is achieved and visualized as a red and white pearl emerging from the waist, rising to the head, and sinking back down to the navel. This is explained as a conjoining of inner yin elixirs and an outer yang elixir. This begins a process of give and take between the microcosmic body and the macrosom. This stage frees the adept from time (birth and death). The eighth stage also calls for the visualization of pearls of light: black, white, and red, exiting from the back, flowing into the forehead, and descending down again, eighty-nine times. Chen Zhida explains that this is an image of the rising up of the Primal Breath within the practitioner, which joins with the Great Void to form the divine pearl of the Primal Spirit, what Lin Zhao'en calls the *sarira* (a relic of the Buddha) ray of light. This stage enables the adept to merge microcosm and macrocosm with the Void, freeing the adept from space (transcending heaven and earth). The ninth and final stage calls for the smashing of the void, and freedom from all differentiation. The body is visualized as the Golden Body of the Lord of the Teachings (see the Scripture of the Fundamental Substance below). A black pearl is visualized in the Sea of Breath (the lower elixir field). This transforms into a white pearl that rises up beyond the forehead, expanding infinitely along with the adept.

It is worth mentioning that adherents of the Three in One maintain that very few practitioners are able to go beyond the fourth stage. Those who get to the sixth stage are considered truly advanced. Those who have attained the seventh or higher levels are revered as enlightened sages of the tradition. Many say that Chen Zhida and Liang Puyao in the late Qing were the last to have attained the ninth stage of the heart method. Mastery of even the first two stages allows one to preserve one's health and physical well-being. One sixty-year-old man who looked forty explained that his good health was a result of a lifetime of practice of the heart method. He also explained that he could help others who were ill, although the best method was to teach them to practice the heart method themselves. He went on to say that he could use the heart method to knock a spirit medium out of a trance.

When we compare Lin's heart method with standard Daoist systems of inner alchemical self-cultivation, we notice several distinctive features. In general, the first six stages of the heart method follow relatively standard Daoist inner alchemical techniques, with some significant variations. The seventh, eighth, and ninth stages show a strong Buddhist influence. The first major variation is that although Lin discusses interactions between fire (associated with the *kan* hexagram) and water (associated with the *li* hexagram) in the area between the two kidneys and the heart, the point of initial concentration is assigned to the *gen* hexagram in the back, rather than to the more common *dantian* (elixir field) in the center or front part of the body behind and below the navel. Berling (1980) has shown how the *gen* in the back point had been identified in Neo-Confucian discussions by Wang Gen and Luo Hongxian, the disciples of Wang Yangming. Second, the traditional use of guiding the *qi* in the "gathering of [or between] *yin* and *yang*" is usually a vertical transfer of forces between the three elixir fields within the body, whereas for Lin Zhao'en this becomes a horizontal process at the level of the navel and the back. Third, Lin rejected the special practice of still sitting, or fixed periods of meditation, arguing instead for the integration of the heart method into everyday life. Fourth, although Lin Zhao'en utilized basic techniques of visualization (of brilliantly colored "pearls" of light), he rejected the regulation of breath, and particularly the reverse flow of breath, *niqi* (i.e., the swallowing of breath and its forced reverse passage within the saliva). Lin countered this with his notion of *xunqi* (flowing with the breath), as he countered *jingzuo* (quiescent sitting) with *jingxin* (the quiescent heart).[6]

Another key feature of Lin Zhao'en's heart method is its urgent sense of striving, its drive for self-transformation. Each stage prepares the adept for the next, in a fervent expression of belief in the notion that the individual adherent (*zizao xingming*) personally creates his own nature and life force, as Lin put it in his *Addendum to the True Meaning of the Primal Spirit*. The stages of the alchemical process divide into various phases. "Establishing the basis" involves initiation into the movement and a reorientation of the adept's life in terms of Confucian modes of conduct. "Entering the door" involves gaining control over processes of concentration and guided visualization and the circulation of sexual energy, breath, and spirit within the body. Once these abilities take on an automatic quality, however, the practitioner must cease self-conscious striving. At that point one simply awaits the arrival of the "external elixir" and prepares for the final phase, the "attainment of the ultimate principles," wherein self, time, space, and the void are smashed to pieces, and enlightenment is achieved.

SCRIPTURES

The *Bentijing* (Scripture of original substance) is the most frequently recited scripture in the Three in One tradition. Portions of the scripture are incorporated into all kinds of ritual texts. In light of its importance to the Three in One, I translate the scripture below, occasionally making reference to the annotated commentary prepared by Liang Puyao in 1888.

---

[6] Contrast the more complex visualizations enjoined in Shangqing texts of medieval Daoism discussed in Robinet, (1993) or the Liandu visualizations discussed in Boltz (1983), and even the less elaborate visualizations in use in contemporary Daoist ritual in Taiwan discussed in Schipper (1993) and Lagerwey (1987).

The Lord of the Three in One Xiawuni's Scripture
of Original Substance[7]

I am the Commander who opens the Heavens, the Great Master who performs the Law.[8] From the nonbeginning onward I have been but one person.[9] Śākyamuni [Buddha] and I stand shoulder to shoulder. All the limits [of the universe] are beneath me. I now manifest in order to fill Śākyamuni's position. This is the third dragon-flower assembly [called to] save humankind and the heavens.

Within heaven and earth and beyond heaven and earth, what place is not the void? What place is not the spirit? What place is not the breath? What place is not me?

The Golden Body of the Lord of the Three in One Xiawuni[10] has already written the beginnings of the eight hexagrams of the *Book of Changes*. Has already attained Nirvana and extinguished life and death. Has already become the Great Patriarch King of the Nine Heavens and the Great Dharma King of the Nine Lands [of China].

The Pearl in the Treasury was recommended by all the Buddhas. [This was] the moon orb that flew into the curtains [of the bed], illuminating the Three Masters. What is it that the Three Masters all must return to Confucianism? Only because the laws of the world are what the world requires. Thus one can avoid the profound and the shallow, and the Way is no different from this. Then one can on entering [the home] be filial, and when leaving be brotherly. Do not be too close nor too distant.

Drill through the Kunlun [Mountain peak, i.e., the cranium] to make a hole. Set up the Ultimate Principle as your foundation. Mingle with the two wings [of Yin and Yang] as your means of fulfilling your talent. Lay forth the four images (metal, wood, fire, and water) as your standard.

When gold and iron mix together, Yin and Yang are paired together, then two

---

[7] A fuller edition of this text, the *Linzi Bentijing shilue* (Master Lin's scripture of the fundamental substance, with brief commentaries), with a preface by Liang Puyao dated 1888, begins with a passage defining the fundamental substance that reads as follows: "The fundamental substance is the substance of what was spontaneously. It is without birth or death, without beginning or end, without above or below, without distant or near, without inner or outer, without ancient or modern; it has always been like unto itself and that is all. Void and empty and that is all. And as for the scriptural, it is the constant. With words [which speak of that which is] like unto itself and void. Neither present nor absent, not reached by the realm of the senses. Soundless and odorless, it lasts throughout the myriad kalpas and never diminishes."

[8] The *Linzi Bentijing shilue* remarks that this "I" is the "I that is not I," the "I that contains the ten thousand things," etc. The preface of this work comments that contemporary (i.e., late Qing) Confucians do not examine the underlying meaning of the scripture, simply dismissing Lin Zhao'en for claiming to be Xia (great), and misunderstanding that the "I" of this scripture is the "I that underlies all things." Moreover, the comments about being the "Commander who opens the Heavens, etc." were all spoken to Lin Zhao'en directly by Maitreya Buddha.

[9] The *Linzi Bentijing shilue* comments that the Great Void has neither beginning nor end and yet is the origin of heaven, earth, humankind, and the myriad things. As they all share this origin and the one breath that unifies them all, they are but one person.

[10] The *Linzi Bentijing shilue* interprets this golden body as the "great body which is not the body" and as the Primal Breath and Primal Spirit of the fundamental substance.

pearls will shine forth, shining into six voids. How even are the two Reverend Ones. They are granted imperial honors as distinguished guests.

The dharma and the powers are all attained. The thousand billion trikaya golden bodies move to reside before the Great Ultimate and take up their position before noncommencement. The one person within all one million can activate the one million spirits. Those of heaven are called heavenly spirits. Those of earth are called terrestrial spirits. The seventy thousand spirit generals and the seven million nine hundred thousand spirit soldiers, how mighty are their powers. How surging is their spiritual strength. They are constantly around me protecting me.

The Golden Body of the Lord of the Three in One, Xiawuni, gives heaven and earth their regularity; gives the sun and the moon their brilliance; gives the four seasons their orderliness; gives ghosts and spirits their abilities.

At the sound of the order, it is like thunder and lightning. If there are any heavenly demons, terrestrial demons, human demons, material demons, mountain demons, water demons, bird demons, beast demons, and all demons that belong to the grass or to the trees, which one of them is not struck with terror. Which one is not defeated, so that its gall bladder is smashed and its body torn asunder and crushed into dust.

Golden Body, Golden Body, Golden Body of the Threefold Marvelous Dharma [Trikaya]. The hundred thousand million Golden Bodies. The breath that is not breath. The spirit that is not spirit. Constantly filling up the dharma realm. What place is not me? The Original Substance of the Lord of the Three in One Xiawuni. What place is not me? The Golden Body of the Lord of the Three in One Xiawuni.

Om. Jinchilin. Yuchilin. Hum.[11] I obey the commands of the most reverent of Noncommencement and Chaotic Origin that Opened up the Heavens.

The scripture begins by casting Lin Zhao'en as a cosmic commander, equal in rank with Śākyamuni Buddha, and fulfilling Buddhist prophecy by being reborn in the final age of the dharma. The second paragraph proclaims the unity of all things within the fundamental substance. Thus all things are within the Golden Body of the apotheosized Lin Zhao'en. The third paragraph equates Lin with Confucian sages of antiquity, Daoist immortals, and realized Buddhas of the past. The fourth paragraph relates the birth of Lin Zhao'en (the pearl in the bedcurtains) and explains the need to uphold Confucian values in everyday life. The fifth and sixth paragraphs summarize the inner alchemical process. Drilling through the Kunlun point (at the top of the cranium) allows the immortal embryo to mingle with the primordial forces of

---

[11] The *Linzi Bentijing shilue* interpets the "Om" as the sound of the opening up of the cavity of the Dark Pass within the body. The Jinchilin and the Yuchilin are interpeted as the golden ford and the jade liquid (seminal essense and saliva) conjoined within the cavity of the Dark Pass. This thus symbolizes the union of fire and water. The "Hum" is explained as the expansion throughout all external space of the *haoran zhengqi,* the billowing orthodox breath. Jinchilin and Yuchilin are sometimes represented as attendants standing beside Lin Longjiang on a Three in One altar.

Yin and Yang. Merging of gold (inner elixir) and iron (external elixir) enables the two pearls (perhaps the eyes visualized as the sun and the moon, or the black and white pearls mentioned in the visualizations of the Ninth Stage [see appendix 2]) to illuminate the microcosm/macrocosm. With this process completed, all powers are attained (cf., paragraphs 7, 8, and 9). The myriad golden Buddha bodies take up their positions, protecting the practitioner, who has power over the demonic multitudes. The practitioner realizes that he too is part of the fundamental substance of the universe, the golden body of the Lord of the Three in One. The scripture ends with a mantra and a prayer.

Lin also wrote a *Milejing* (Maitreya scripture). Although less commonly recited now, it helps clarify the question of Lin's own self-conception of his religious mission. Lin begins by mentioning the association between Maitreya Buddha and the Song monk Budai (Clothbag, d. 912), who supposedly could contain the void in his sack.[12] Lin demonstrates that this was just a "borrowed name" for a nameless vastness. After demonstrating similar paradoxes in Daoist and Confucian texts, he goes on:

> My body is not large, yet my body fills the dharma realm. My belly is not large, yet my belly contains the dharma realm. My body fills the dharma realm, thus it is smaller than its own belly. My belly is larger than my body, for it contains the dharma realm. When my body stretches it is still small, for my body first attains completion in its hair follicles. When my belly stretches it is still large, for it contains the void. The void is empty, yet it is not empty between heaven and earth. What is not empty between heaven and earth is empty within the void. The void is not empty when it is in the hair follicles. The hair follicles are not empty, yet they are empty within the void. The void, heaven and earth, the hair follicles, which of these are empty and which are not? Which are empty in emptiness, and which are not empty and [yet still] empty? Which are not empty yet within emptiness and which are empty within the not-empty?

The scripture goes on to expose the paradoxical nature of the concept of emptiness, employing a Nāgārjunan negation of negation. The series of negations then take up the issue of the paradoxical emptiness of the body and its part. Nevertheless, the passage concludes with a rapturous affirmation:

> The revered Maitreya Buddha is my body. The revered Maitreya Buddha is my heart. My body is Maitreya Buddha. My heart is Maitreya Buddha. Maitreya and I are not different bodies. Maitreya and I do not have different hearts. Maitreya's body is no different than mine. Maitreya's heart is no different from mine.

The scripture concludes with the opening passage of the *Scripture of the Fundamental Substance,* translated above.

Lu Wenhui, working under Lin Zhao'en's order, compiled the *Xiawuni-jing* (Xiawuni scripture) in thirty-six juan in 1585. This entire process of trans-

---

[12] Overmyer (1976 : 151, n. 60) mentions the legend of the monk Budai and his identification with Maitreya in popular iconography.

forming Lin's writings into scriptural form merits close examination. Lu later composed a four-juan condensed version of the scriptures, entitled *Xiawuni jing chuan* (Essentials of the Xiawunijing). Later again, he further narrowed down the essence of the teachings into a single juan entitled *Xiawunijingxun* (Essence of the Xiawuni Scriptures). The recitation of these scriptures can be prolonged from one day to seven days depending on which version of the scriptures is being recited (see chapter 6).

The twelve scriptures, each divided into three juan, that make up the *Xiawunijing* are:

1. *Xiazongchijing* (Scripture of the General [Principles] upheld within the Xia [Teachings])
2. *Xia xunshijing* (Scripture of the Xia interpretation)
3. *Rulaixing jing* (Scripture of the Tathāgatha nature)
4. *Zhongmiaoxuanjing* (Scripture of the multitude of miraculous mysteries)
5. *Dachengshijing* (Scripture of the time of great completion)
6. *Fanshenchengjing* (Scripture of the turning over of the person to complete sincerity)
7. *Dushizhengyijing* (Scripture of the salvation of the world by the Orthodox One)
8. *Zhongheweiyujing* (Scripture of the nurture given by positioning oneself in the central harmony)
9. *Mingguang puzhaojing* (Scripture of the universal radiance of the bright luminence)
10. *Zuishangyichengjing* (Scripture of the most high single [Mahāyāna] path)
11. *Tongxuanjizejing* (Scripture of the cavernous mystery of the ultimate principle)
12. *Daotongzhongyijing* (Scripture of the unity of the Dao in the One in the center)

The fourth and fifth scriptures both have prefaces dated Wanli *jiawu* (1594). Both prefaces make reference to Lu Wenhui's work in editing the scriptures. A summary of the contents of these scriptures can be found in appendix 3.

Dong Shi made some interesting observations on the Xiawuni scriptures in his "Preface to the Scriptural Admonitions":

After Yao and Wu, Confucius was the only person whose words could be carried for ten thousand generations. After Confucius, the only person whose words could be carried on for [another] ten thousand generations was Master Lin; for who else could it have been? . . . My Master Lin saw what it was that made Confucius a saint; he made his heart into the heart of Confucius. He saw how Confucius had become a saint, and he also saw that every person for all time could also become a Confucius. But this small, dancing heart is hard to preserve, so [Master Lin] spat out phrases to make scriptures, which are sufficient to stand as an instruction to a myriad generations. . . . Teacher Lu Xingru, the true first transmitter of Master Lin's teachings and the patriarch of subsequent students, in order to compose a ladder to sainthood, assembled those phrases Master Lin had used to exhort his disciples, along with the most pithy passages, coming to a total of fourteen [and adding in] four passages of questions and answers to disciples, and three hymns from the [Poems on] *Spiritual Luminosity* and the *Greatness of the Way within the Heart*. He called his collection the *Linzi jingxun* (Master Lin's scriptural admonitions), in the hope that it would stir up later students. In the spring of 1649 I read a collection of these early admonitions, having got hold of an old manuscript, and I found the words solemn and the meaning profound, so I ordered it to be recarved in order to extend its influence. In the winter of 1651 Yi Taiji, Zhuo Rusi, and Zhu Dingle completed the reprinting at the Gold Mountain [Shrine] in Xianyou City. This is what is called being kept like a treasure in a famous mountain and having someone to pass it on to. (*Preface to the Scriptural Admonitions,* in *Dongshan jicao* 1:29–31)

Another important liturgical text composed by Lu Wenhui was the *Longhua sanhui chanwen* (Litany for the third assembly of the Dragon Flower). This text casts Lin Zhao'en as a god, the Lord of the Three in One, who provides techniques for self-cultivation and salvation and dispenses forgiveness for transgressions. The text begins with a hymn on the Lord of the Three in One's boundless oath to save all souls. Obeisance is called for to the Great Masters of World Salvation—Confucius, Lord Lao, Śākyamuni, Lord of the Three in One, all past, present, and future saints and sages of the Three in One, and all immortals and mahasattvas. All these deities are invited to act as witnesses to the confession. After a passage extolling the spiritual powers of the Lord of the Three in One, the text alternates between obeisances before the statue of the Lord, followed by eight-line verses on sins that have been committed and which must be confessed, followed by hymns on the spiritual powers and specific responses of the Lord to particular transgressions. The transgressions include failure to follow the stages of advancement within the Three in One, disloyalty and unfilial behavior, discarding family for personal spiritual pursuits, lack of compassion for others, sexual desire and pursuit of wealth, drunkenness and violence, killing of living beings, swearing or speaking evil, revealing of secrets of the teachings, cheating, pride, impurity of motives, failure to search for enlightenment in the scriptures, lack of determination, lack of resolve, actions entailing karmic resolution and rebirth, physical illness, natural catastrophe, incomplete tranquillity, and incomplete insight into former karmic entanglements. The litany concludes with an oath and a closing hymn.

Several ritual texts, including some scriptures and litanies, were composed by other disciples of Lin's. These include the *Xinhaijing* by Zhu Fengshi, one of the four attendants. This scripture is closely modeled on Buddhist sources. Even the beginning scene is modeled on the audience with the Buddha common at the beginning of many sutras, although here Lin Zhao'en replaces the Buddha, while his disciples play the role of the celestial host attending a court audience. Master Zhu Fengshi breaks rank to relate the devastation caused by flooding, and the extreme suffering of the masses. Lin explains that this is a result of actions taken by the Shuiguan Dadi (Great Emperor of the Water Office) as a direct result of the sea of karmic entanglements. The only solution is to comprehend the sea of the heart, or the sea of dharma, which is in fact the sea of Buddha nature. The scripture goes on to describe and name the principal gods of the major seas, rivers, streams, and paddyfield ditches. Many of these designations are drawn from Buddhist texts. The tides of the sea are then compared to the flow of the breath in meditation. Thus control of the breath leads to the calming of the seas. Having explained this principle, a decree from the Jade Emperor is issued to the chief dragon deities (nagas) of the seas, who rejoice in its command for tranquillity. The scripture concludes with several hymns (gatha) addressed to the souls of the drowned, calling them to the shores of salvation.

Another example of derivativeness from Buddhist and Daoist ritual texts is the writing of liturgies by Chen Zhongyu for the *Lanpen* ritual. Several texts for this ritual attributed to Chen are still extant. Many are still in use within the manuscript collections of both Wuben ritualists in the Hanjiang and Putian areas and Mingxia ritual specialists in Xianyou (see bibliography). These include liturgies for specific aspects of the Complex Lanpen ritual: the invitation of saints to their seats at the altar, the presentation of offerings, the deliverance of hungry ghosts, and the resolving of the entanglements of the dead and the living. Various titles are found on these texts, such as *Jinjiao daqing sheng anwei* (Great invitation to the saints to take their positions at the altar for a complete sacrificial offering), *Sanjiao longhua jiaodao jingong yiwen* (Liturgy for the presentation of offerings at a Three Teachings Dragon Flower sacrificial offering and prayer meeting,) *Sanijao lanpen dahui yiwen* (Liturgy for the great assembly of the Three Teachings Lanpen), *Jieyuan yiwen* (Liturgy for resolution of entanglements), *Sanjiao jingong yuankeyiwen* (Complete liturgy for the Three Teachings presentation of offerings), *Gongyang yiwen* (Liturgy for offerings), and *Xiajing Heshu Luotu* (The river writ and the Luo chart of the Xia scriptures) (cited in Lin, 1992: 180). Chen Zhongyu also composed one of the first sets of regulations for assemblies of the Three in One, the *Chenzi huigui*, which is discussed in chapter 6.

The process of textual codification of the new liturgy of the Three in One can be seen in the writings of Lu Wenhui, Zhu Xuhui, and Chen Zhongyu. Lu reworked Lin Zhao'en's writings into scriptural form fit for recitation. Lu Wenhui's *Litany* positioned Lin as a deity who has a solution to every transgression, time and again providing the means of redemption and salvation. Zhu closely modeled his *Heart of the Sea* scripture on Buddhist sutras, casting Lin in the role of the Buddha, and his disciples as the celestial host. Chen Zhongyu works Lin Zhao'en and his teachings into his versions of the *Lanpen Ullambana* liturgy. In each place where one would expect from Buddhist or Daoist versions of these texts to find the Buddha or Lord Lao evoked, we find instead an evocation of Lin Zhao'en. Chen incorporated some of Lin's and Lu's hymns into these liturgies and composed many more himself. These didactic or praise verses crystallize the Three in One cosmology and pantheon. The underlying structure of the ritual is otherwise untouched, and there is every likelihood that ritual actions and gestures were similarly copied with minor, but significant, variations. The inner visualizations, mantras, and spells that accompany these rites appear, on the other hand, to have been more fully worked out, as they are framed as an extension of the inner alchemical heart method (see chapter 6).

With scriptures, liturgies, and litanies completed, temples constructed, and images of Lin Zhao'en worshiped with offerings of incense, tea, and fruit (vegetarian offerings offered to Buddhist deities), the Three in One had achieved the status of a parallel ritual tradition. No doubt it took some time to rework all the important liturgical texts of the local culture. From the basis established by Lu Wenhui, Zhu Xuhui, and Chen Zhongyu, the Three in One liturgical repertoire has continued to expand. Liturgies specific to the Three in One have been developed for most of the rites normally performed in the Xinghua area by other ritual specialists, such as Buddhist monks or Daoist priests. All the major categories of ritual are covered: (1) communal sacrifices on annual festivals or on the birthdays of gods and Three in One sages; (2) the ghost festival (celebrated in the Xinghua area most fervently on the Lower Prime date of lunar 10/5, rather than on the Middle Prime [1/15]); (3) rites of consecration of god statues, temples, and halls; (4) daily offerings in temples; (5) requiem services; and (6) minor rites of celebration of longevity, marriage, and exorcism of illness for individuals or families (including *kaojun* [feasting of spirit soldiers], *guoguan* [traversing the passes] prophylactic rites, and *shoubing* [retrieving of fears that afflict children]). Currently many teams of ritualists keep an average of eighty or ninety liturgical manuscripts and scriptures on hand for ritual use. This provides a good indication of the range of rituals they are capable of performing.[13]

We have little definite evidence of the work in this field of the Weng branch, under the leadership of Lin Zhenming. This group is likely to be one source of the fusion of the Three in One with local cults. For the next major step beyond the elaboration of a parallel ritual system in the integration of the Three in One with communal organizations was the absorption of local deities into Three in One ritual. This involved, at the textual level, the writing or copying of scriptures dedicated to local gods, and the elaboration of a range of documentary forms and celebratory rites addressed to these deities. At the level of ritual action, it was only through the physical absorption of local cults into Three in One temples that the Three in One was able to become part of community-wide processions. Such processions form a different kind of text, one written by the collective movements of the community (see chapter 1).

---

[13] Lists of 250 titles of the liturgical manuscripts photographed or photocopied in the course of research leading to this study can be found in the bibliography under "Liturgical Manuscripts." Lin Guoping (1992: 179–182) lists the titles of 113 Three in One printed books (including multivolume edited works) and manuscripts. Of these, 79 are manuscripts.

In fact, in only a very few temples does the statue of Lin Zhao'en participate in processions. But when the local Three in One temple houses a number of local gods on side altars, these are usually taken on procession on their feast days. This entire process of fusion is likely a result of the clandestine period under the mid-Qing dynasty ban, when many temples supposedly transformed Lin Zhao'en's image into that of the Jade Emperor, claiming that the temple was Daoist.[14] The bulk of the scriptures of this kind that I have located are within the Mingxia tradition.

Scriptures to Popular Local Deities

In the Mingxia tradition, new scriptures and liturgies were written or adapted from Daoist and popular sources for the following local or regional gods, if not more:

1. Sima Shengwang
2. Tian Gongyuanshuai
3. Tianhou (Mazu)
4. Yang Taishi
5. Qitian Dasheng (Sun Wukong)
6. Zhang Gong
7. Chen Jinggu
8. Ciji Zhenjun (Baosheng Dadi, Wu Tao)

Scriptures dedicated to more widely worshiped deities and Buddhas were also composed or copied:

9. Xuantian Shangdi
10. The (Wuxian) Five Manifestations
11. Guanyin
12. Dizangwang (Ksitigarbha)
13. Yaoshiwang
14. Guan Shengwang (Guan Gong or Guan Di)
15. Wenchang
16. The Three Officials (of the Heavens, Earth, and Water)
17. The Emperor of the Eastern Peak
18. The Ten Kings of the Underworld
19. The Gods of the Northern Dipper
20. The Jade Emperor

While some of these scriptures are copied directly from Daoist or Buddhist sources and can be compared with versions of these scriptures in the respective versions of the official canons of these traditions, many of the scriptures dedicated to local gods had not been absorbed into one of the canons. I have

---

[14] Some temples are said to have transformed Lin's statue into Confucius and claimed that the temple was a private academy, dedicated to the study of the Classics.

argued elsewhere that the extent to which a local cult has achieved a textual dimension (chants and invocations, locally circulated scriptures, liturgical texts dedicated to the deity, and acceptance into the official canon) may indicate the degree to which that cult had transcended its local origins and was operating at a different level. Thus the composition of such texts marks a major transformation of a cult from a locally based oral tradition (usually of spirit possession origin) to a participant in a wider cultural universe (Dean, 1993).[15] In the case of many of the Three in One scriptures, we can see clear signs of Daoist or shamanistic origins, with little or no veneer of Three in One doctrine. The Three in One has managed to preserve and utilize crucial texts of the local culture, which might otherwise have disappeared.

The uses of these scriptures provide examples of the process of transformation of popular beliefs and ritual traditions within the Three in One. For example, the two main branches of the Three in One Religion adopted dramatically opposed approaches to the god of theater, Tian Gongyuanshuai. The conservative branch abstained from any theatrical performances altogether and instituted commentaries and lectures on the scriptures of Lin Zhao'en in place of theater. This branch was made up of wealthier, better-educated city dwellers. The rival branch, founded by Lin Zhenming, spread among poor illiterate villagers and fishermen along the rocky coastal area and in the rough mountains of the Xinghua region. This branch preserves a legend of a cosmic battle between Lin Zhenming and Tian Duyuanshuai, in the course of which Tian was defeated and forced to submit to Lin. Thenceforth he agreed to serve as a trainer in music, dancing, and ritual for the initiates of this branch of the Three in One. His image is worshiped on a subsidiary altar in all the temples of this branch of the Three in One.

The scripture of Tian Gong Yuanshuai translated in appendix 4 illustrates the nature of these texts. They follow the basic layout of such texts in the Daoist canon and the Buddhist tripitaka. Formally, the scripture closely resembles many such scriptures written to popular deities (see Boltz, 1986).[16]

---

[15] The Tian Gong Yuanshuai scripture forms a part of the collection of manuscripts of the Zhandouci near Fengting, Xianyou. The recent date of the copying of this manuscript does not necessarily indicate a recent date of composition. So many scriptures, liturgical manuscripts, and precious books and inscriptions were destroyed in China during the Cultural Revolution that the continuity of manuscript traditions has been shattered. Fortunately, a tremendous resurgence of traditional local popular culture and religious observances throughout Southeast China and elsewhere around the country has resulted in a great amount of copying of surviving manuscripts. The temple I found these manuscripts in had gathered them from all over the Xinghua region. In many respects, this scripture is part of a tradition of scriptures written to popular deities beginning at least in the fifteenth century.

[16] On the cult of Mazu (Tienhou), see the important research of Li Xianzhang (1979) and the studies by the late Xiao Yiping, a great local historian of Putian. Academic conferences have been held on the goddess in Putian in 1988, 1990, and 1991. Research on the distribution of Mazu temples in China is being published in the *Haiwai jiaotong yanjiujuankan*, 1988 issue. Mazu scripture recitation societies survive in Putian, and their scriptures are somewhat different from the one Boltz analyzes. Watson (1985) discusses the variety of interests the cult has served in different areas.

The scripture begins with several songs and spells (1a–2b) in heptasyllabic verse, followed by a prose summarization of the nature and title of the god (2b–3a). Third, there is an invocation composed of four character lines (3b). The scripture per se begins on page 4a with the title, after which comes the usual scene of the gods in audience before the Jade Emperor (4b–5a). The Great Officer of Heaven presents a memorial detailing the woes of the world (5b). The Jade Emperor takes pity, recalls Tian's qualities, and commands him to approach the throne (6a). He is ordered to descend to earth, bringing salvation and exorcising disease and evil (6b). The efficacy of the scripture is then extolled at length (7b–10b). Next we find the Precious Appellation of the Jade Sovereign (10b–11b). At this point the heavenly audience breaks up with the gods singing a song in praise of Tian (12a–13b). Concluding remarks are followed by a short synoptic hymn (14a–14b). The final portion of the scripture is made up of passages extolling the miraculous powers of the scripture.

The description of the circumstances surrounding the presentation of the memorial by the Great Officer of Heaven (5b) offers an unusually detailed account of popular views on the supervisory techniques of the gods. Particularly interesting is the account of punishment of evil deeds via a procession of gods of pestilence on the 22d day of the 2d lunar month. Most likely the continual repetition of the procession has created a ritual paradigm that generates a mythological interpretation. That plague and disease are forever returning only serves to set the stage for Tian Gongyuanshuai's spectacular descent and role as Exorcist and Savior. But the scripture assures us that whoever possesses it can cause this miraculous descent of protection by recitation and offerings to the god whenever necessary.

The description of the god in this scripture combines aspects of the joyful, pleasure-loving god of theater known from Quanzhou marionette sources (see Dean, 1994) with the frightening picture presented in the *Daofa huiyuan*, c.233.6b–7a, 236.3a, 237.1b, 4a), and discussed by van der Loon (1977). In this Ming dynasty Daoist source, Tian appears as a white-faced, smiling god, with the characters *ruyi* ("as you like it") painted on the side of his mouth. He carries a golden box in his hands. He is one of the Four Crazy Generals, a Master of Illustrious Virtue like the powerful Marshall Zhao Gongming, with whom he is associated. In the scripture (translated in appendix 4) he is described as "having a great general whose body is like white jade. His hair is like the blades of a drill. His eyes are like striking lightning. His teeth are like spearpoints." This is a description of the White Dog General who accompanies the god. Furthermore, Tian Gong Yuanshuai "commands the awesome power of the Bureau of Pestilence." But we read later that he was "utterly talented in literary and marital arts." Moreover, we learn that "with his red face and mustache, he was the flower of them all." The god statues in Putian temples show a young man with a red face, a thin mustache, and wavy lines at the side of his mouth left by the drooling crabs. But Generalisimo White-tooth, who is frequently represented in an adjacent hall, is a

white dog with sharp fangs. The red and white faces refer to the seemingly
contradictory qualities of drunken jester and frightening exorcist.[17]

[17] The god of theater, or a version of him (he is also commonly represented in Southeast China
as Lei Heiqing, or sometimes as Tang Minghuang), has been worshiped in Fujian since at least
the Song dynasty. Troupes of Fujianese marionettists numbering over three hundred performed
in the Southern Song capital at Hangzhou. Outside the north gate of Putian in Fujian, a stele
from the Ming erected inside a temple to the god lists the names of over twenty-five theatrical
troupe leaders (Dean and Zheng, 1995; 241–242). In fact, whether or not due to the worship
by theatrical troupes, the cult of the god has spread throughout Fujian. In many areas, the god
is now worshiped as a local protector deity, quite distinct from his role in consecrating theater.
Puxian theater has a vast repertoire and an ancient pedigree. It is a vibrant tradition to this day,
with over 160 troupes and about 50 marionette troupes in the two districts of Putian and Xianyou. Each of these troupes of course worships the god Tian Gong Yuanshuai. It is likely that
the vast repertoire of Putian theater presided over by Tian Gong Yuanshuai would reveal significant regularities of performance of certain repertoires for different occasions such as the god's
birthday, annual festivals, and family rituals. The important thing to recall here is that for the vast
majority of the dramatic troupes and performances, theater is an offering to the gods. It has an
inherent ritual dimension. Piet van der Loon (1977) incisively revealed the deep connection
between entertainment and exorcism in the Chinese theatrical tradition, noting that the forces
of good almost always triumph over evil in these traditional plots. Beyond this general observation, we can find genres that have evolved a closer relation to ritual. There are five plays in the
Puxian repertoire that are closely related to rituals designed for critical moments in an individual's life, including the life crisis rituals of birth, initiation, marriage, and death. These plays include the Beidouxi for the difficulties of childbirth and infant disease; the Lufuxi (measles headquarters play) for childhood disease, especially measles; the Yuanxi (repayment of vows play) for
giving thanks after great success; the Wuhuangxi (the five emperors plays) for deadly disease or
plague; and, of course, for death itself, the first great ritual drama of the Chinese tradition, the
Mulian plays. Each of these plays must be performed in tandem with a ritual performed by a
Taoist priest or Buddhist monk. When I arranged to videotape these plays in Putian, I first had
to go into the mountains with the help of local connections to find a troupe that still maintained
a living tradition of performance. Then I had to find a temple and a group of Taoists because the
group would not consider performing the plays without a ritual. Local Taoist and Buddhist priests
have developed liturgical texts to accompany all these performances—or is it the other way
around? In most cases the plays include ritual sequences within themselves that parallel or echo
and reinforce the rituals performed by the Taoist or Buddhist or Sanyi Xiansheng, Master of the
Three in One. Thus we find the *guoguan* ritual for Beidouxi; a more elaborate *Lufu jiao,* with
separate Taoist liturgies and also including a *guoguan* rite, for the Lufuxi; a full-scale Taoist *jiao*
for the *yuanxi;* and a variety of *gongde* and *pudu* rituals for the Mulian plays.

The Yuanxi, or theater of the repayment of vows, tells the story of the god of theater, Tian
Gong Yuanshuai, in great detail. The Song empress is ill and the emperor promises to wear a
cangue and do penance to save her. His prime minister intercedes, recommended that his son
wear the cangue instead. His son is none other than the god of theater, who was utterly bored
with life in heaven and insisted on being born on earth. The god persuades the emperor to have
everyone in the empire wear the cangue—everyone else, that is. The dramatic crescendo is
reached when the god, who has been rewarded with free rein of the imperial palace, has fallen
asleep after getting himself roaring drunk. In his stupor, he is found by the imperial princess, who
paints his already very red face with crab designs. When he wakes up he cannot wash off the color
or the designs (in fact, the head of the marionette is switched while a curtain is hung up to block
the view). He is informed that he cannot return to his original role as third son of the Jade Emperor, but instead must become the god of theater and amuse himself forever by performing the
Records of the Grand Historian, the *Shiji*. The marionette god is then brought into the temple

The scriptures and the liturgies listed in the appendices are a working collection of ritual specialists of the Three in One. The elaboration by the ritualists of the Three in One of a parallel and rival ritual tradition to that of the Buddhist monks and Daoist priests in the area, a tradition heavily imitative of these rivals, is an extremely significant phenomenon. One can point to the fact that participation in these rituals did not require membership in a hereditary priesthood, like the Daoist ritual specialists, or the abandonment of family ties required to join the Buddhist orders. Anyone could become a member of the Three in One, so long as they upheld the oaths, worshiped the deified form of Lin Zhao'en, practiced his heart method of inner cultivation, and, in the case of the Mingxia branch, received instruction from his divine assistant, the god of theater. This branch of the Three in One provided people without powerful bureaucratic or lineage connections a new form of social organization, within a new liturgical framework. In the rapidly commercializing society of Southeast China in the late imperial period, this kind of social formation provided prospects for moral and social advancement to disadvantaged groups. In a society where flows of money were unseating bureaucratic and hereditary power structures, social hierarchy was in turmoil. The possibility of direct investment by the poor and powerless in an open liturgical framework implies an appropriation and co-optation of traditional symbols and forms of the reproduction of cosmic power. For these initiates, the god of theater had become a personal tutor in the arts of ritual, a friendly guide leading them through the paces to immortality. The god has changed from a constrained symbol of inversion in a functional reading of his role in ritual to a symbolic agent of transformation (Dean, 1995). It comes as no surprise that this branch of the Three in One was fiercely criticized by the mainstream, con-

---

to pay his respects to the local gods. The play continues with the wealthy patron who ascends the stage wearing a cangue. The marionettes tease a lot of money out of him and his family before obtaining a pardon from heaven and the removal of his cangue. Then a Taoist priest ascends the stage and leads him in worshiping the five directions. This play is full of humor, poking fun at the very god that the marionettists themselves worship, in a fascinating series of inversions and reversals of everyday hierarchy.

This play used to be performed quite often in the 1920s and 1930s, sometimes by actors rather than by marionettes. It was performed again two years ago in Hanjiang by a wealthy Overseas Chinese businessman. Some of these plays and their associated rituals can be linked to individual life crisis occasions while simultaneously generating a communal dimension. This is obviously the case for the Mulian plays, which are always performed during the Lanpen Pudu rituals, held in Putian in the 10th lunar month rather than the 7th. The sending off of a King of Pestilence boat is also usually performed during a Wangye jiao, or large-scale Taoist exorcism of plague spirits. Even the *guoguan* can be performed on behalf of all the children in a community. It may be useful to consider that communities have their own crises, one of which is what Stephen Feuchtwang calls the "annual apocalypse," the crossing over into the New Year. The ancient Nuo ritual exorcisms were developed to drive out the evil spirits and make the New Year safe and prosperous for the community. Every New Year's in the northern Putian plains, exorcistic dances and processions are performed that are locally referred to as "Carrying out the Nuo exorcism." These ritual dances are performed by bands of men who have undergone a secret initiation. See Dean (1993) for more information on these topics.

servative branch for its dramatic exorcisms and its reliance on talismans, spells, and spirit possession. Indeed, of the gods who spoke most forcefully through its adherents, none was more formidable than Field Marshal Tian.

LITURGIES FOR MINOR RITES

Other scriptures and liturgical manuscripts show the ways in which the Three in One responded to domestic concerns around childbirth and childhood disease. The *Xiajiao huer duolounijing* (Xia teaching dharani scripture to protect children), an undated but fairly recent manuscript in the collection of ritualists of the Chengsan Shuyuan in Xianyou City, lists the Sanskrit derived names of fifteen ghostly spirits that afflict children with the following diseases: raspy throat, rashes, crossed-eyes, croop, spasms, drooling, uncontrollable laughing, loss of appetite, clenched fists, biting of the tongue, uncontrollable weeping, refusing to let go of their mothers, strange signs, fearfulness and crying, and sobbing. The practitioner is told to tie a five-colored thread into 108 knots while reciting the secret names of the ghost-spirits, and then to rush outside and tie them up in all directions. Offerings of incense, flowers, lights, and rice are then to be presented to the Buddha dharma kings. The text goes on to explain a simple method women can use if they are unable to give birth, since evil spirits are to blame for miscarriages and death in childbirth. Evil spirits go so far as to destroy the concentration of men and women during intercourse, so that they cannot conceive. The method consists of the woman fasting and purifying herself on the eighth and fifteenth days of the month, then at midnight praying to the Buddhas of the ten directions, and then placing a small amount of mustard grass on the top of her head while reciting the *dharani* incantation provided in the text. The spells in the text are guaranteed to protect children in peace and quiet. The scripture draws upon Buddhist sources, making little mention of Three in One doctrine or deities aside from its title, and an opening verse in Three in One style.

Another text devoted to issues of childbirth and childhood disease is the *Mingxia rangguan duxian yiwen* (Mingxia liturgy for the overcoming of [difficult] passes and deliverance from danger), also in the collection of the Chengsan shuyuan in Xianyou City. This text draws upon Lushan Daoist/shamanic sources but includes frequent references to Three in One deities, especially the Xiawu Patriarch (Lin Zhao'en). Underlying the liturgy is astrological lore and a theory of the range of threats each child must confront in his or her life. The liturgy begins with a series of Daoist and Buddhist purificatory spells such as the *Jinguang shenzhou* (Divine spell of golden light, translated in Lagerwey [1987a: 86–87]). Next several powerful goddesses of the thirty-six temples (of the Sannai [Three Sisters] Cult) are invoked, with a list of the locations of their temples (primarily in northern Fujian, beginning with the Linshui Temple of Chen Jinggu in Gutian). Fifty more goddesses arranged in various categories are then invoked, including the goddesses of the Southern and Northern Dippers, and those attached to the courts of Tai-shan and the local city god, and all goddesses on ritual towers, bridges, and local temples and roads. A second group of fifteen goddesses is those responsible for spreading (and thus for checking) disease: these diseases include measles, pox, colds, fevers, and dysentery. Other goddesses are in charge of childbirth, breastfeeding, the internal organs, the mouth and the tongue, good fortune and the dispersal of disaster, the transmission of ritual requests, the selection of male offspring, etc. The text goes on to invoke the thirty-six goddesses in charge of each third of each month, and then the animals associated with the Chinese zodiac, concluding with a list of the twelve dangerous passes: those of spring, summer, autumn, winter, the four seasons, longevity, the Ghost Gate, the Gold Lock, the swift cry, the General, the Heavenly lament, and the Mainstays of Heaven. The goddesses are invited to partake of an offering and then asked to "embody the sincerity with which the Master of the Teachings (Lin Zhao'en) delivered the world. Observe the true meaning of the offerings offered by the sacrifiand. Today, on behalf of the *jiaozhu dizi* (disciple offering the sacrifice), eliminate the immediate affliction and get rid of the source of sorrow." Spells to transform the offerings into food fit for the goddesses follow. The goddesses are then asked to bolster the *qili* (strength of the breath) of the sacrificiand and to assure that that particular pass of adversity and its related affliction never again attack the child. After more offerings, the goddesses are asked to guard mother and child in all seasons and at each of the eight annual nodes. Next chants are given to accompany a passing over of four bridges, one for each season. The description of each bridge includes passages on the Hundred Flower Garden, where the souls of children are kept prior to conception. Celebratory hymns are then sung, and a memorial is recited and burned, along with offerings of spirit money and flowers to the goddesses. The latter are then sent off to conclude the liturgy. The text also gives a list of some forty offerings to be prepared for the ritual, including tea, wine, noodles, cooked rice, fruit, vegetables, vegetarian dishes, flowers, the five sacrificial meats, thirty-six bowls of rice, and varieties of spirit money. As we will see below, the preparation of ritual offerings is a crucial, but often overlooked, aspect of the performance of gender within the performance of ritual.

The Three in One in the Qing and Republican Eras

THE FORTUNES of the Three in One were to fall dramatically during the Qing Yongzheng and Qianlong periods (1723–1795). As mentioned above, the Three in One movement was prohibited, along with other sectarian religions accused of being related to the White Lotus movement.[1] A number of accounts point to a prohibition of Three in One temples in 1716. Legend within the Three in One has it that this was in response to the abduction of a young woman by an adherent named Zhu Kun. To avoid destruction, many Three in One shrines are said to have transformed iconographic details of Xiawuni, Lord Xia (Lin Zhao'en), into that of Yuhuang shangdi, the Jade Emperor (Lin, 1993: 135), or Wenchang Dadi. Many temples changed their nomenclature from "shrine" or "hall" to "academy." The late Qing Putian writer Guo Fulin stated, "Lin Zhao'en was worshiped in the Yuhu shuyuan (Jade Lake Academy). . . . At the beginning of the Qing, when Three in One temples were being destroyed, many were changed into Wenchang [academies]. [Now] the Wenchang [statue] in the Wenchang Pavilion next to the Fengshansi (Phoenix Mountain Monastery) wears Three in One sandals, and this academy being named Wenchang is also evidence [of this change]" (*Jiyushanfang shiji,* quoted in Lin [1993: 135]).[2] Whatever the truth of these accounts of the destruction of temples, in the Qianlong period compilers of the *Sikuquanshu* ordered that certain editions of Lin's writings be destroyed.[3]

This process of suppression should be seen in a larger context. As ter Haar has shown (1992), the term "White Lotus Teaching" was attached as a pejorative label to many religious groups and movements in Qing China as justification for suspicion and suppression. In the 1720s a series of investigations and aborted rebellions of Luojiao or Zhaijiao followers took place in south China. In the 1740s several more such outbreaks occurred, including some

---

[1] The Qing government's draconian policy on so-called heterodox teachings (sectarian movements) was outlined in a memorial submitted in 1647 by Lishi geishizhong Lin Qiyuan. See *Donghualu,* Xunzhi 3, 6th month. However, this was a period in which the pacification campaign in Fujian was still under way (see Wakeman, 1985).

[2] Another late Qing source adds, "There had been a Three in One shrine to the north for a long time, but one year in the Kangxi period it was ordered to be destroyed, and after that no one dared to rebuild it" (*Fujianzhai biji,* quoted in *Shanmin suibi,* juan 5).

[3] *Siku quanshu zongmutiyao.* Berling (1980) mentions a decree prohibiting the Three Teachings issued in 1744. Franke (1973) points out that the passage on the *Linzi quanji* from the *Siku quanshu tiyao* quoted in chapter 3 did not specifically call for the destruction of the text. Lin Guoping (1993: 136) argues that certain of Lin's writings were destroyed, citing Zhang Qin's 1945 draft *Putian xianzhi, juan* 22, *Yiwenzhi.* From the large number of variant surviving editions (see appendix 1), it would appear that the prohibition had limited impact.

large-scale rebellions in northern Fujian, and deeply disturbed the court. In 1748 the Laoguan Zhaijiao led a rebellion of one thousand people that was put down within five days. In 1748 a search revealed the presence of Luojiao, Dachengjiao, Jintungjiao, Yizimen, and Guanyinjiao groups in Putian, Xianyou, and many other districts of northern Fujian. Seventy-three Luojiao Scripture Halls and Vegetarian Halls were found. These groups survived persistent efforts to stamp them out. Between 1727 and 1895, thirty-nine such events led to arrests and the filing of criminal records (Ma and Han, [1992: 392–405]). Despite such efforts at suppression, groups like the Three in One, the Longhuajiao, Jintongjiao, Xiantianjiao, and Yaochidao managed nonetheless to flourish in the Xinghua region.[4]

A considerable gap remains in our understanding of the transformations of the Three in One over the mid-Qing period. We have seen Dong Shi vigorously attacking the failings of the followers of Lin Zhenming, the Wengs, situated to the east of Putian City. We have also seen him bemoaning the decline into shamanistic healing of the Three in One in Xianyou, to the west. During the period in which the Three in One went underground, one can only assume that these divisive tendencies took over. From another point of

---

[4] These different religious movements spread into Fujian over the course of the Qing dynasty and faced many of the same persecutions and circumstances as the Three in One. Wang (1994) shows that the transmission of the Jingtongjiao into Putian occurred in 1622, with the founding of the Shudetang by Cai Wenju (1584–1654). Cai was converted from the Longhuajiao by the founder of the Jintongjiao, Wang Zuotang (1564–1629). The Jingtongjiao later divided into three branches in Putian. Wang provides a list of successive patriarchs of the main branch of the Putian Jintongjiao and shows that the transmission to Taiwan took place in 1725. (Other sources suggest a date of 1683.) I was taken to visit the Jintongjiao Temple at Caizhai Dingcuo, just south of Putian City, by the Three in One adherent and splendid painter Zhu Shengying. Jintangjiao members allowed me to copy several important scriptures, including the *Kai Jintangjiao shu* (Preface on the founding of the Jintangjiao), circa 1910; the *Gufo zongpai* (Ancestral charts of the former buddhas); *Caigong chushi* (Birth of Master Cai), circa 1811; *Sanji genyuan xingjiao shiji ji* (Record of the deeds and travels of the root and origin of the Three ultimate limits, 1987 reprint of a 1930 Taiwanese edition); *Zhushi Laoye jiangfan jiapu* (Family register of the living master who descended to earth), circa 1894; and *Xuanhua baochan* (Precious litany of the suspended flower). The Jintangjiao currently has over 130 temples in Putian. The small village of Longhua in Huangshi Township has over ten Jintangjiao temples, and the entire population practices the teachings and eat only vegetarian meals. The Longhuajiao was derived from the religious movement founded by Luo Qing (1442–1527) (see Overmyer, 1976).

The Longhuajiao was founded in the Putian area in Yongzheng period (1723–1735) with the establishment of the Yiyuantang in Duotou, Hanjiang. Zhang Qin estimated the number of temples in the Republican period at around 320. Current estimates (*Putian zongjiaozhi chugao*) are around 100. Stele inscriptions from the Jindetang in Duotou can be seen in Dean and Zheng (1995: 320–321 and 329–330). The Xiantianjiao traces its origins back to Huang Dehui (1662–1722), founder of the Hongyangjiao. His successors established the Qinglianjiao but changed its name to the Xiantianjiao around 1850 after suffering Qing persecution (Overmyer, 1976; Topley, 1963). The Fujian founder of the Xiantianjiao was Li Daosheng (fl. 1860). The first major transmission into the Putian area took place in the Guangxu period (1875–1908) under the direction of Ouyang Deyuan. He helped found over forty temples with several thousand adherents. Of these, only twelve remain active today. The Yaochidao has two active temples in the vicinity of Longhua Township in Xianyou.

view, this black hole in the history of the Three in One can be seen as a period of tremendous richness and diversity.

Various sources suggest that the Three in One continued its activities in the Yongzheng and Qianlong periods in a more or less clandestine fashion. Lists of heads of temples at major Three in One temples show only occasional disruptions through this period.[5] The process of the division of incense and the establishment of new temples appears to have continued, although concrete evidence of the establishment of new temples begins again only in the 1840s. One of the most important of these was the Wubentang (Hall of the Realization of the Fundamental), established in 1846. The founders of the Wuben branch in late Qing repeat many of the accusations made by Dong Shi in the 1660s as part of an effort to reestablish unified central control over the Three in One. They attempted to further this goal by republishing a number of the early works of the Three in One.

Many texts were, however, written during the long period of obscurity prior to the late Qing and Republican revival. These included the *Sanjiao jintan fahui jue* (Secret instructions on the flowering of the golden elixir of the Three Teachings), written by one Dong Xizu in 1722, which circulated in manuscript. This period is most likely the time in which the Three in One borrowed heavily from local Daoist and Buddhist ritual traditions, developing its own liturgical corpus.

By the Daoguang period, Three in One texts were again being openly (re)printed. One example is the *Yangzhenji* (Collection on cultivating perfection) in two volumes, with a preface dated Qianlong *dingmao* (1747 or 1807), and a postscript to (re)printing dated Daoguang 15 (1835). By the Guangxu period, the Three in One had already come back into the open. Chen Zhida (d. 1872) organized the Wubentang and published several texts, with the aid of his disciple Liang Puyao (d. 1904). Subsequently, the Hansantang in Putian became a center of printing and spirit-writing activity through the late Qing and Republican periods.

DIVISION OF INCENSE

To determine the organizational forms employed in the transmission and development of the Three in One, this section will discuss the division of incense from a founding temple to a branch temple, and the ritual transfer of a seal

[5] According to a manuscript dated 1895 in the Zhuguangci in Bangtou, Xianyou, the order of transmission of the Mingxia (Weng) line into Xianyou was as follows: Lin Zhao'en—(1) Lin Zhenming; (2) Weng Wudao; (3) Weng Yiyang; (4) Zheng Biyan; (5) Lin Qingshan; (6) Chen Hengshan; (7) Chen Xiushan; (8) Chen Shengshan; (9) Weng Fuchu (who brought the Mingxia to Xianyou, where it was transmitted in 1650 to a Shengyuan named (10) Chen Yukun, who transmitted to the founder of the Zhiguangci, (11) Lin Yechuan. The following are the successive leaders of the Zhuguangci temple: (1) Lin Yechuan, (2) Huang Shiji, (3) Lin Qiren, (4) Chen Renxiang, (5) Chen Libo, (6) Chen Mingwang, (7) Chen Jinjiao, (8) Chen Zhenti.

and incense to the new temple. Individual temples scattered throughout inland Xianyou were founded by Lin Zhao'en and certain of his disciples. The
Menxian shilu lists some forty-eight disciples who built close to fifty temples,
the majority in the Putian and Xianyou region. Other sources enable us to
compile a total list of some sixty temples that had been built by 1666. Lu Wenhui, Chen Zhongyu, and Dong Shi continued to found temples in Putian and
Xianyou, as did Weng Wudao, Weng Yiyang, and others. Some of these figures are represented on the altars of these temples, accompanied by a statue
or image of the local founding patron. These temples went on to send off
branch temples, some of which have also continued to grow offshoots.

In Xianyou City, two temples stand at the head of the line of transmission
of the Sanyipai and Mingxiapai, respectively. These are the Jinshanci and the
Daxingci. The Jinshanci was founded in 1598. An extant stele bears the following inscription:

> The Master was a product of Putian. His name was Lin [taboo personal name]
> Zhao'en, sobriquet Dragon River. He was the second brother in his family. Lin
> was sincere in his studies and hard working. He desired to follow in the footsteps
> of the sage philosophers. He lectured on the Saintly Writings (the Classics), ad-
> vocated ideal social relations, established his opinions, and wrote books. He was
> good to people. During the pirate raid on Putian, he gave everything to bring
> peace and security to all the people. In Xianyou he gave to the hungry, built roads,
> gathered corpses of the unburied, gave out wood for coffins, and so the people
> of Xianyou considered him to be most virtuous. In 1598 the gentry Lin Shaoyun,
> personal name Zhaokai, built a one-room shrine in Wenfeng within Xianyou City
> to honor Lin Zhao'en's merit. Now in the third year of the new emperor's reign
> (1664), Lin Zhaokai and others have torn down the old temple and rebuilt a
> shrine with three chambers and two side chambers. Fortunate they were to meet
> with the approval of Circuit Intendent He Bing, the Prefect Li Ying, the District
> Magistrate Gu Dai, and the Commandant Qian Long, all of whom contributed
> to the cause. Construction began in the 7th lunar month of 1663 and went on
> to the 5th month of 1664. Total costs came to over 800. There were towering
> rooftops and carved walls, and carved image for worshiping. The virtue of the
> Master could uplift the coiled mountains and carp waters and be transmitted for-
> ever without end. The shrine has 3 mu, 8 li, of land, and its rice is registered in a
> household under the name of the Gold Mountain Shrine located in the Li [yi-
> dong]. General Manager Liu Huaru, Chen Gaochu, Wang Shuqing, Cheng Yuan-
> guang, and Wang Juren, all shared in the glorious enterprise and so indeed should
> have their names recorded for posterity. Thus it is recorded in 1664 at the mid-
> autumn festival, an auspicious occasion. Stone placed by the people of Xianyou
> City. (Dean and Zheng, 1995: 434)

In Xianyou the Jinshanci sent off the following major branch temples: to
the east (Bangtou) the Yushanci, Puguangci, and Pumingci, the Leshanci in
Laidian, and to the west the Zongshanci in Jinjing in Longhua.

The Yushanci (Jade Mountain Shrine) is the major branch temple of the

Sanyipai in the Bangtou region east of Xianyou City. Over one hundred temples are said to have branched off from it, each of them with the character "Jade" or the character "Mountain" in their name.[6] The Yuhuici is its main branch temple. According to a manuscript from the Yushanci dated circa 1885, the temple was founded in Kangxi 6 (1667). The manuscript lists certain of the successive generations of leaders of the temple and notes that a charitable estate was established in trust for the temple, probably in the Guangxu period.

Rituals of division include the *qingxiang* (requesting of incense) and *jiaoyin yishi* (transmission of the seal ritual). The new leadership of the new temple is selected by divination blocks from among the Jinggong (Wendao). These are secret transmissions. The Wudao (ritual performances) of the Yushanci are renowned. On the three most important ritual occasions—the Three Primes (1/15, 7/15, and 10/15)[7]—they will send ritual specialists to their branch temples if those temples do not have enough people to perform the rituals. By the same token, if the Yushanci holds a large ritual, their "Disciple shrines" *dizici* all will send representatives to take part. Some will send *jingshi* (who will be allowed a special ritual performance time). There will also be performances of theater for several days. People throughout the Three in One temple system, and indeed anyone who wishes to, are free to visit the Yushanci. The Yushanci is well known for its efficacious divination blocks: on the 1st and 15th of each lunar month, many people go to inquire about such things as building houses and undertaking marriages.[8]

[6] In the Bangtou area one can continue to trace the process of the division of incense from the Yushanci to the Yulinci. This history has been recorded in a manuscript handbook dated 1885 from the Yushanci in Bangtou: In the Qianlong period the Linshanci was established by Fujiao Zhang Zhengang. In 1879 the Yushanci Temple sent representatives there to act as assistant teachers (*fujiao*). Also in the Qianlong period, the Yulinci was built by Lin Yiliang. It was rebuilt in Tongzhi 1 (1862) by Zhutan Zhang Leifeng. In Daoguang 29 (1849) the Shufeng Jinfengci Golden Peak Shrine was opened by Futan Zhang Leifeng. In Tongzhi 5 (1866) the Qianxi Yumingci was opened by Zhutan Zhang Leifeng. Also in the Tongzhi period a branch temple was opened in northern Putian Jiangkou Dongcaicun called the Shunzhongtang (Hall for Conforming to the Central).

[7] See Stein (1979) for a discussion of the origins of the rites associated with these nodal points of the year.

[8] Several Three in One temples make use of the *Sanyijiaozhu lingqian (lu yu Dongshan zuci cungao)* (Numinous divinatory poetry of the Lord of the Three in One, recorded at the ancestral shrine on East mountain). This is a set of eighty-four quatrains, with five characters to line. The poems are sometimes straightforward and sometimes allusive, referring to historical figures. Many expound conventional morality and point to the constant supervision of human behavior by the gods. For example: "The blue heavens can't be cheated / Three feet [above the head] are the gods / Power is in your hands to employ / but who can avoid thinking of the consequences?" There is occasional reference to Confucian, Buddhist, and Daoist themes, but little explicit mention of the Three Teachings, save for the final poem: "Do not commit any evil / carry out only good deeds / With all your heart take refuge in the Three Saints / and your name will be recorded in Six Heavens." Each poem has a commentary, first interpreting the general sense of the poem and then relating the poem to specific areas such as business travel, geomantic issues, marriage, pregnancy (the maleness of the fetus), fame and fortune, and illness.

The Puguangci and the Pumingci were both also founded early on from the Jinshanci. The Puguangci in Xiaming village claims to have over eighty branch temples in Laidian, Jiaowei, Huian, and Taiwan. On the festival for the hungry ghosts of the Lower Prime, the Xiayuan lanpen pudu, their 180 ritualists divide into many small groups and go to different villages over the festival to perform ceremonies. They are a form of ritual corporation.

The division of incense of the Mingxiapai in Xianyou is described in a 1948 manuscript from a ritual specialist based in the Daxingci. The Daxingci in Xianyou was founded in Wanli 16 (1588) by Mao Jinlian. Although it is claimed that Mao studied with Lu Wenhui, it seems that at some point quite early on, the temple switched to the Wengpai. Currently the following figures are worshiped in the temple: Principal deity: Lord of the Three in One, Zhuo Xiaoxian (Lin Zhao'en's Daoist friend), Daoist Immortal Lu Tongbin; the Four Attendants have here been changed to include Lin Zhenming, Weng Wudao, Zhu Xuhui, and Lu Wenhui (excluding Zhang Hongdu but allowing room for the founder of the Wengpai). The local gods Wuxian lingguan and Tian Gong Yuanshuai are worshiped in side halls.

The manuscript claims that a total of 280 temples branched off from the Daxingci.[9] The Zhuguangci in Bangtou is said to have branched off from the Daxingci in 1650 (according to an 1885 manuscript in the Zhuguangci). The Daxingci manuscript lists 20 other branch temples and goes on to list another 14 temples that had branched off from these temples. It is noteworthy that over 80 temples sent representatives to the consecration ritual of the restored Daxing temple held on September 14–16, 1990.

If the claims in these sources are accurate, the Jinshanci and the Daxingci account for over 180 and 280 branch temples, respectively, thus accounting for virtually all the 475 temples in Xianyou Country. Of course, a degree of exaggeration is to be expected in these claims. A few other Three in One temples in Xianyou were established directly by Lin Zhao'en and his disciples, such as the Qixingci (Seven Star Shrine) in Fengting (founded in 1598) and the Jinshan shuyuan (Mirror Mountain Academy) in Lindou village, Feng-

---

[9] The manuscript lists the following twenty branch temples: within Xianyou city, Xiajie Xianshengci (Worthies and Sages Shrine), Tianditan Baosongci (Shrine of the Precious Pine), Zhishansi Zunshengci (Revered Sage Shrine) within the Monastery of Complete Goodness, and Shimatou Zhuzhenci (Shrine of the Pearl of Pacification). East of Xianyou were the Xueshengci (Shrine for the Study of the Sages), Baixia village Zhuguangci (Shrine of the Pearly Radiance— on which see below). West of Xianyou were the Xiamatai village Shusheng tang, Yuanxinci (Shrine of the Original Heart) in Cangxi village, a shrine in Dukou village, Zhongshanci (Bell Mountain Shrine) in Zhongshan village, Yuyuanci (Shrine for the Replenishing of the Origin) in Cangxi village, Kaiyuanci (Shrine of the Commencement of the Origin) in Shangban village, and Xinxingci (Heart and Nature Shrine) in Yunzhu village. South of Xianyou was the Shrine of Transformation, Ruifengci (Shrine of the Auspicious Peak) in Donglin village, Kuishengci (Literary Sage Shrine) in Oucu village of Gaiwei, Naishengtan (Hall of the Patient Saints) in Dongping village, Longshengci (Shrine of the Dragon Sage) in Xiajiang village, Ruiauci (Shrine of the Radiant Mystery) in Guyang village, Yangxinci (Shrine for the Cultivation of the Heart) in Kangjie village, and Yishengci (Shrine of the Righteous Saints) in Liupanjie. North of the city was the Peishanci in Wanfugong village.

ting. These temples also claim to have founded scores of other temples in the Xianyou and coastal Putian and Hui'an areas.[10]

THE REVIVAL OF THE THREE IN ONE IN THE LATE QING AND REPUBLICAN PERIODS

There are four inscriptions from the late Qing and early Republican period that shed light on the nature of the Three in One during the transition from the from late Imperial China into the modern period. The first, from the Yaodaoci in Hanjiang, describes the organization of rituals at that venerable cult center. The second, from the Hansantang in Putian, describes the efforts of Chen Zaizheng and Liang Puyao to spread their version of Three in One traditions. Chen was based in a temple in the Hanjiang area called the Wubentang (Hall of Illumination of the Fundamentals), and this is the name of the branch of the Three in One he founded (see below). Chen and Liang wrote several introductory tracts on the Three in One, such as the *Sanjiao chuxue zhinan* (Pointers on elementary study of the Three Teachings) and the *Zhengtong yizhilu* (Record of easy to understand [principles] of the Orthodox School). The second inscription, from the Shande Zongkongtang near the City God Temple in Hanjiang town, is by Zhang Qin, the last Putian *jinshi,* who will be mentioned below as a mediator for disputes over ritual orthodoxy within the Three in One. This inscription reveals the attitude of the literati at the end of the Qing toward the Three in One. The third inscription, from a modest village-level temple, describes the concrete processes through which the Three in One inserted itself into popular religion during this period.

[RECORD OF RITUAL ASSOCIATIONS BASED AT THE JADE ISLE ACADEMY]

Master Xingru (i.e., Lu Wenhui) founded the Yaodao Academy to propagate the orthodox tradition [of Master] Xiawu, to save human beings and ghosts, and so that the moisture of his teachings would always be renewed and shine brightly, etc. Fortunately, he received secret instructions and obtained the true transmission of the One in the Center. [We] desired to offer fragrant incense to our ancestors and sustenance for the orphaned ghosts, but without a fixed income, this would easily become a rule practiced in absentia. This was the reason for the establishment of the Ullambana Association. This association is made up of twenty-five families, who provide funds that raise interest. [These funds] not only were used to repair the shrine and to purchase ritual implements, but also were invested in seven mu (1.2 acres) of paddy fields. These lands were divided into five shares, named Humanity, Righteousness, Propriety, Wisdom, and Trustworthiness. The

---

[10] A number of Three in One temples in Xianyou appear to have been founded by local patrons, who are worshiped on side altars as founding patrons (*tanyuezhu*). These temples tend to avoid allegiance with either the Mingxiapai or the Putian mainstream tradition, referring to themselves simply as Sanyipai (Three in One branch). This process indicates the potential for autonomous organization of temples at the village level within the Three in One.

Plate 13. Chart of the transmission of the Three in One at the Zhuguang Shuyuan (Pearl Radiance Academy), from its founding in 1667

care of the fields was rotated around the shares. Annually, on each of the two holy days of the Upper Prime (lunar 1/14, Lin Zhao'en's birthday) and the Middle Prime (7/16, the date of Lin Zhao'en's death and attainment of the Dao), as well as on the Lower Prime Feast for the Deliverance of the Hungry Dead (10/15), four thousand wen (over U.S. $100) would be handed over for use by the Master of the Altar. These expenditures were rotated as well. Any remaining funds were used for ritual offerings to the ancestors. Each family would be given [an equal share of] the remaining funds, so that all could feast the ancestors and pray for blessings for their children and grandchildren. The declaration of the association has been engraved in stone to last forever, for with a few words we can reveal the origins of our cause. [There follow the names of five groups of five families each, organized according to the share titles listed above. There are several different surnames in each grouping. Recently discovered inscription reported in *Hanjiang wenshiziliao*, 1994.]

This inscription reveals the economic underpinnings of a temple within the Wuben branch of the Three in One. A pool of twenty-five unrelated families joined together to provide the means of ritual production for the major festivals of the tradition.

Record of the Beginning and End of the Recent Construction of the Hall to Contain the Three Teachings

Text composed and Sealscript heading written by Initiate Chen Daoshi, characters reverently written by Initiate Chen Zuyin.

It is said that as for any [major] act of construction, this can hardly be said to begin on the day [of the actual building], but instead there must be an earlier origin. Looking at the process of the construction of this hall, it would appear to have started in 1915, but in fact its origins go back to 1899 in the Qing dynasty. For over ten years the hall was moved to and fro. It we did not probe into its origins, would this not be like enumerating allusions while forgetting their references? When we think back to the spring of 1899, this was the first time that the Great Immortal Master Who Carried Forward the Teachings [Zhang Sanfeng] came south. His palanquin sojourned in the east hall of the Putian City Temple. He was worshiped at the Leshan Hall. At that time Su Daokuan, He Daodian, Guo Daojin, and Zheng Daoyuan worshiped together before the incense burner, praying without stop. [The immortal Master then] brought salvation [in the form] of the raft that crosses the stream of confusion of this vulgar world. Moreover, he explicated the Xia [Three in One] method of self-cultivation. Masters and disciples were deeply moved, and they were firmly united at that time. The disciple Zheng Guoxi was the first to be initiated. Our good friend Zhu Daoyi swore to take the propagation of the Teachings of Xia as his life's work. When circumstances arose, he resourcefully led the way. He dragged Master Liang Puguang up to the city to expound the orthodox teachings of the Wuben [branch]. As soon as Master Su heard [Liang's words] he became enlightened and agreed to take on the task of immediately setting up an altar. Since there were financial difficulties, he first reverently set aside an incense room in his Fengshan residence and named it Zongben (Hall of Ancestral Origin). It was dedicated to preserving the Wuben line. This was thus the conception period of this hall. That year, in the winter, the Great Immortal again came south to the city and selected by divination some land inside the Martial Temple in the south of the city. [The Immortal Master] declared he would descend on the 11th day. An altar was set up and a ritual for the saving of ghosts and living men was performed. The expositions and poetry caused those in attendance to feel uplifted. Scholars and literati seeking his transformative touch crowded through the doorway, and so this became the site of the temporary ritual headquarters. Prior to this time, the Ritual Mater Huang had built the Mingshan Temple in Xiawu Lane [in the residence of?] the younger brother of the Ming Censor Duke Lin Niantang. Those who sought supernatural protection often received strange writings, but because the time was not right, he relied on the writings of talismans and curing of disease as a device to lure people to the faith. In 1900, after the Wu festival, Great Immortal Chen first visited the Martial Temple and then led his associates to the Mingshan temple to take over services there and to save those [in need]. They reunited [around] the incense burner and established order. Grand Ritual Master Zhao gave it the name Hansan (Containing the Three [Teachings]) and held a seven-day ritual of the recitation of litanies. The very best ritualists from every hall were invited, and it was the finest gathering of talent of the day. Who would have thought that when it comes to splendor and decline, gathering and dispersing, each follows the other. For ten years after 1903, how swiftly the time passed. Had it not been for Lin Fuzhi, Lin Weijin, and Shi Xinjun, who continued looking after it, then how could the Mingshan Temple and its various buildings have become the transitional resting place of the hall. In 1913 Zhu Daoyi took charge of ritual matters of this hall. He called together those who specialized in the ancient studies and again examined the mysteries. As for those who had repented, he led them to repent again. Those who had not cultivated themselves he led in group cultivation. The banners and drums sounded forth again, and people flocked in droves. His colleagues decided, in order to spread the Way, to set up a fund to build a temple, and so they obtained the present land, and laid out the pattern of its broad foundations. The main hall was completed in 1915. The next year the Former Philosopher Hall and the Hall for Assembling the Ancestors were built. By 1917 the eastern and western towers were complete. In 1919 the main gate and the lecture hall were built. In 1925 the meditation hall and the extra buildings were completed. Those who oversaw this work from start to finish were You Zhiyuan, Fang Zhijia, Zheng Yuanqin, etc. It took about ten years to complete the construction, at a cost of some 8,000 in gold. [The hall was] magnificent and awesome; it faced south, in a central geomantic and calendrical location, and it established foundations that will survive a myriad kalpas. A place of surpassing spiritual power, where bananas and mulberry will forever [demonstrate] reverence. In the extra land around [the temple] there is still room for enlargements. To the southeast the road is the border. To the west the grass field of the Martial Temple is the border. Later on the sages will continue to flourish, each having furthered the standards of their forebears. That successors should shine forth, this is indeed what the founders envisioned. We have carefully recorded the origins of the hall and depend upon those to come. The incense and [lamp-]oil properties of the temple are appended below: One store-front located outside the Sicheng gate to the left, number 17. One river field of 1 duan 9 fen at number 20, of Lin Hechung at the river's edge. 1927, 3rd month, fruitful dawn, carved by Initiate Guo Qinggao. (This stele now stands in the Pu-tian Number One Middle School; Dean and Zheng [1995: 364–365])

This inscription provides information on the organization of the Three in One at that time, and its close relationship with spirit mediumism (a practice still widely used today). The Great Immortal Master is said by members of the Eastern Mountain Ancestral Shrine to be none other than Zhang Sanfeng. He was able to inspire the group of friends to join the Three in One. Later, after listening to Liang Puyao lecture and Zhang Sanfeng return again to write el-egant poems through the planchette, members of the group determined to build a temple.

Zhang Sanfeng, Immortal Chen, and Immortal Huang all played an im-portant role in a thirty-year series of mediumistic utterances recorded in the *Zhenjia bao zhengyi* (True collection of the treasures that vouchsafe the home), 4 vols., and the *Zhenjia bao buyi* (Supplement), 2 vols., published to-gether in 1935. This text presents 380 messages from forty different gods, each carefully dated, from 1899 to 1928, mostly at either the Wuben tang or the Hansan tang. This source provides a rare glimpse into the day-to-day workings of a Three in One temple at the end of the Qing empire and on into the Republican period (see below).

STONE INSCRIPTION ON THE CONSTRUCTION OF THE GOOD AND VIRTUOUS HALL OF THE VENERATION OF CONFUCIUS IN HANJIANG, WRITTEN BY ZHANG QIN

Confucius established his teachings and his writings are known, but his Way of Human Nature is seldom achieved. Of his seventy disciples, those who under-stood were few indeed. Zi Si wrote the Way of the Mean and began to illumine the Way of Human Nature. This was transmitted to Mencius. After Mencius, for over a thousand years there was no transmission. In the Song the Confucian scholar Shao Kangjie obtained the principles of the *Yijing* from the Daoist philosophers, and Lu Xiangshan used Chan principles to take part in meditation. In this way the theory of the unification of the Three Teachings was completed. In the midst of the Ming, Master Lin Longjiang of Putian came forth and greatly expanded these principles, leading the lingering shortcomings of the Daoists and the Buddhists back to Confucianism. At the same time, he dispensed with the use-less prattle of Confucian scholarship and concentrated on the Way of Human Na-ture. Thereupon, several hundred years of struggles between adherents of dif-ferent schools were unified and made mutually intelligible, Now Confucius's teaching was suspended between those of Daoism and Buddhism, and, like the sun and the moon, there was nowhere that it did not shine upon. This is not my individual point of view, but a clear case of timeless truth. The Way of the Three Teachings of [Lin] Longjiang was truly transmitted solely to Master Lu [Wenhui] of Hanjiang. The Yaochi (Jasper Pool) and Yaodao (Jasper Island) Shrines were both built at that time by [Lin] Longjiang's disciples. Now after three hundred years, they are collapsing into decay, yet who will restore them? Now Huang Ziqi and Huang Shengsan were also refined initiates of [Lin] Longjiang's. The *Yijing* states, "When the bell is struck in the palace, the sound is heard outside." The *Shijing* states, "When the crane cries on the Nine Mounds, the sound is heard in the heavens." Words and sounds call forth a rapid response. I had not seen Huang Ziqi, and Huang Shengsan for over ten years. In 1936 the Shande Zongkong tang [Hall of the Excellent Virtue of the Patriarch Confucius] was completed. Huang Shengsan asked me to record it and said he would carve my words on a stele. I agreed. I discovered that the origins of this hall go back to Huang Qizong. He learned the principles of the Three Teachings in 1865 and set up an altar in his own home to worship Master Lin Longjiang. More and more initiates joined him, so he initially contributed two pieces of land and, together with Huang Dezhou, etc., built a three chambered hall as a place to lecture on the Way. Thirty years later, Huang Shengsan carried on his work, and initiates became even more numerous. His fellow initiates, Huang Qitai, and Huang [two characters missing], etc., expanded the land of the hall and enlarged the hall. In 1914 they built a three-room structure to the south of the hall. They built a passageway all around, and thus the temple gradually took full shape. In 1918 Shengsan and Huang Daosheng, Huang Benshan, Kang Dadao, etc., again raised funds to build a Great Hall and gateway. Lin Longjiang's statue was now worshiped in the Great Hall. On the foundations of the original hall they built a storied tower to worship Zhuo Wanchun, and they called this the "Small Nonmountain." They also built a pavilion for worship in front and dug a pond below it, and planted flowers and trees all about. Thereupon red and green changed hands, and all were grandly and radiantly reflected in the heart of the water, the pools of the river. I traveled there late with Huang Shengsan, and when we reached the temple, I found that it was ever enlarging. Thus I realized that Huang Shengsan's study of the Way of Human Nature must also be progressing each day. Shengsan has [progressed] indeed, and I feel great remorse. My own father worshiped the Three in One all his life long. On the day of his death he wrote me a letter instructing me in the Three Teachings. I have raced about all my life foolishly and have not been able to penetrate the Way of Master Lin Longjiang. I did read through his writings and found that his teachings were none other than the [theory] of the correct relations of minister, younger brother, and friend. His efforts did not leave behind everyday activities. His profession did not transcend the constancy of scholar, farmer, worker, and merchant. This was in fact the Way of Zi Si in his *Doctrine of the Mean*. Yet those who delight in the strange and seek after the peculiar have developed [the Three in One] into dealings with gods and spirits, [writing] scriptures and litanies that are inferior even to those of the Daoists and the Buddhists, etc. If one strays even slightly from the teachings, even a minor discrepancy can cause one to be a thousand miles off: this is something one must beware of. Without the true Way throughout the empire, it is impossible to forbid these deviations, and so false teachings will delude the world. Unfortunately, these teachings are not like floods or wild beasts, [rather] they are poisons that will flow for a hundred generations! Correct the Way of the world and one will correct the hearts of men. The renaissance of the nationality must commence with correct education. I still admire Huang Shengsan for his efforts. In 1938 this stone was set up by the initiates of the Shande Hall of Hanjiang. (This stele stands in the Shande Tang in Hanjiang: Dean and Zheng [1995: 369–371])

This inscription reveals the extent of support the Three in One still commanded from traditionally educated literati at the end of the Qing and through the trials of the Republican period. We find that Zhang Qin's father was a lifelong adherent. On his deathbed, he instructed his son to examine the writings of the tradition. Zhang Qin finds them to be basically similar in essence to the Confucian Classics but bemoans the unorthodox developments in the Three in One, presumably at the hands of those like the Weng line mentioned above. For many literati, the Three in One represented a viable response to the challenges of Western science and Western culture. Zhang Qin makes just such a claim in the passage on the Three in One in the gazetteer of Putian he compiled, and a report on temples and popular cults for the Republican government. He is best known, if not notorious, for having served as a ritual consultant during the imperial coronation of Yuan Shikai.

STONE RECORD OF THE INCENSE AND LAMP-OIL PROPERTIES OF THE EASTERN UNICORN SHRINE

The Donglinci (Eastern Unicorn Shrine) was founded by Wu Yihe, who raised contributions and had it built in the Manchu Qing dynasty in 1910, in order to worship the Lord of the Three in One. After it was completed people recommended that Yihe should be the leader or organizer of the worshipers. However, that year the expenses [of construction] were immense, and there was scarcely any money left over. At that time [six characters missing] thought that since the Dafu Association still had some leftover funds, they might well be used by the temple, and a contract was signed with the association to that effect. Fortunately, many approved, and so an account was set up and transferred to Yihe. He felt that these people had established endless merit, so he set up several Patron Spirit Tablets to praise their lovely commitment. After this the Teaching of the Way expanded, and the amount of money contributed was increasingly abundant. Discounts the annual average ritual expenditures on incense and lamp[-oil], by 1939 the accumulated funding was quite large. The monk [two characters missing] called together the group of patrons and their descendants and recommended the purchase of a strip of private land in the Hanbian area, totaling 2 mu, 1 fen, to be used as the incense land for the temple. These lands would temporarily be supervised by Yihe. The following year it would be necessary to prepare for the offerings for the Upper, Middle, and Lower Prime birthdays of the Lord of the Three in One and the sweeping of the grounds, and to prepare numerous offerings to place before tablets of the patrons, in order to reflect sincerity and reverence. Now after Yihe attained his hundredth year [i.e., after his disease], an appropriate person should be selected to supervise these properties. Moreover, it is impermissible for Yihe's descendants to seize or usurp these lands for their own purposes. Fearing that there would not be any proof of these words, they were specially carved on a stele and placed inside the temple, so that this would be known for all time. 1944 in the 5th month. (This stele is set into the wall of the inner chamber of the Donglinci in Dongjiacun: Dean and Zheng [1995: 371–372])

This inscription, from the Donglin Temple in Dongjia village of Huangshi Township, relates to the actual circumstances of the expansion of the Three in One into village religious life and social organization. Here we see a group of adherents making use of funds belonging to a spirit association probably dedicated to another god in the same temple. Such associations are usually self-help groups organized around a particular deity that pool funds for common needs. Unfortunately, the name of the god is illegible on the stele. The members of the spirit association are here transformed into patrons of the Three in One and worshiped on the altar and during the principal annual rituals.[11]

SPIRIT WRITING

The Three in One has made use of a wide variety of media in its effort to proselytize. Although neither as exclusive nor as single minded as Christian missionary groups, the Three in One has attempted to spread its vision and enhance its membership through public lectures (often coinciding with ritual performance) and the publication and distribution of various texts. These may include the scriptures and historical writings of the founders of the Three in One, or they may include more recent testimonials to the continuing efficacy of the tradition. These latter include collections of texts inspired by spirit-mediums.

Outreach under the Qing ban on the Three in One must have been secretive. The force of the ban may have gradually withered away, to judge from scattered dates of temple construction and restoration through the mid to late Qing. The growth of the Three in One ritual tradition no doubt contributed to its spread through Xianyou and coastal Putian. Lists of temple committee heads, or *Zhangjiao*, at certain key sites (Zhongmen's Jiangdongci and Bangtou's Zhuguangci) indicate a largely unbroken ritual tradition. Not until the Republican period, however, was there to be a renewed effort to spread the Three in One teachings openly. Probably the most effective means for spreading the teachings were the murals painted on temple walls outlining the miraculous deeds of Lin Zhao'en. The affordability of Three in One ritual was also a factor in its growing acceptance in Putian and Xianyou. Lectures on Three in One scriptures often accompanied ritual performances. Detailed instruc-

---

[11] Another stele listing Three in One temple properties is the *Qixingci juantianbei* (Stele listing contributions of land to the Seven Stars Shrine) in Fengting (Dean and Zheng [1995: 473, and plate 27]).

tion on inner alchemy and ritual practice were provided to anyone who was willing to undergo initiation.

The Republican period was a time of unprecedented expansion in the Three in One. A great many sectarian groups also flourished during this time. In the Putian area, as seen above, the primary figures in the Three in One were Chen Zhida and Liang Puyao, based at the Wubentang, with support from figures at the Hansantang in Putian City. Chen and especially Liang played an important role in the *Zhenjia bao zhengyi* and *Zhenjia bao buyi,* mentioned above. Such texts are highly performative. Such texts have a long history in Chinese religious literature (Kleeman, 1994); for an account of their production, see Jordan and Overmyer (1986). This particular text begins with a brief account of Zhang Sanfeng and two local gods, Hu Zhenren of Jiuhua Mountain near Putian, and Chen Zhenren of Mount Hu, east of Putian. The following gods are listed in order of the frequency of their appearance:

Lord Huang of Mount Ming, 72
Zhang Sanfeng, 56
Perfected Chen of Mount Hua, 48
(nameless) Immortal Masters, 38
Xuantan Zhao Zhifa, 29
Zhuo Wanchun, 25
Perfected Hu of Mount Hu, 17
Lu Dongbin, 15
Zhu Hufa, 12
Zhongjun, 7

This source provides a rare glimpse into the workings of the Three in One temple at the end of the Qing empire and on into the Republican period.[12]

THE SPREAD OF THE THREE IN ONE INTO TAIWAN AND SOUTHEAST ASIA

The spread of Xinghua people into Southeast Asia is a fascinating story. The earliest indications of trade between Xinghua and Indonesia date back to the Song dynasty. An extant stele, entitled the *Xiangying miaoji,* now kept in the Putian City Museum, was located in the former Eastern Peak Temple behind the Yuan dynasty Sanqing dian ([Daoist] Temple of the Three Pure Ones), built in 1007. These contracts continued and expanded, culminating in the famous South Seas expedition of the eunuch admiral Cheng He, who stopped in Putian at Meizhou Island to pray to the goddess Mazu for a safe journey. The sharp increase in piracy from the mid-Ming onward, together with the expansion of Western imperialist powers into Southeast Asia, led the court to impose a ban on overseas trade that had a severe impact on the

[12] I have located similar texts, though in manuscript form, from other Three in One shrines. One of these, an untitled manuscript from a temple in Jiangkou, recorded poems transmitted in the Republican period. It had recently been updated.

Xinghua region. The coastal evacuation in the early years of the Qing dynasty exacerbated the difficulties of overseas trade. It was not until the Daoguang era that population pressure and the opportunity for overseas employment began to lure Xinghua residents to migrate to Malaysia, Indonesia, and Singapore. Malaysia's tin mines and rubber plantations were the initial attraction. Later, the Xinghua community would choose to specialize in the transportation industry. This was to turn out to be a very sound investment.

The example of the founder of the cycle trade, Mr. Yeou Kee (1872–1929), is indicative of the general pattern. He moved to Malaysia at an early age from Dongyuan cun in Putian. He apprenticed to an engineer and later set up a cycle repair store, which expanded into a pedicab empire. He invested his fortune in the rubber tree plantations. By the time of his death, the overwhelming majority of the pedicab and cycle repair trade was in the hands of Xinghua residents. With the rise of the automobile and motorcycle, the Xinghua community moved into auto sales, manufacture of spare parts, and repairs. A tremendous boost came when local governments decided to invest heavily in public transportation. Many public transportation companies were run by Xinghua people. To this day in Singapore, over 60 percent of the public bus, automobile, motorcycle, and taxi business is in the hands of Xinghua immigrants.

In addition to bicycles, tires, and automobile and motorcycle spare parts, the Xinghua community was involved in the following industries: local products, electrical products and soldering, mixed goods, clocks and watches, foreign goods, banks, finances, movies, building, nurseries, taxies, pedicabs, public bus companies, plastics factories, electrical wire factories, stone polishing factories, battery factories, production of cooking spices, soy sauce, oil lamps, rice noodles, management of hotels, restaurants, bars, beauty salons, insurance companies, shipping companies, import-export, and fishing. Xinghua immigrants also became lawyers, doctors, professors, accountants, and engineers.[13]

[13] The first Xingan Huiguan in Southeast Asia was founded in 1897 in Taiping, Malaysia, and had over one hundred members in 1970. The Singapore Xingan Huiguan was founded in 1920, and the Hongwen School was founded shortly afterward. A building was purchased in 1930. The war suspended activities in the 1940s. After the recovery, the school expanded to over a thousand students and forty teachers. In the 1970s a new building was purchased, financed in part by a series of theatrical performances used to raise funds. There are now four different Xingan Huiguans in Singapore, and this splintering appears to reflect the impact of Christianity upon regional associations. Added to this is the government planning policy calling for the eradication of the localized residential areas in downtown Singapore and the centifugal diffusion of native-place communities into the various new skyscraper housing developments around the island.

The Penang Xingan Huiguan was founded in 1932. Since there were only a few pedicab companies and the rest of the Xinghua immigrants were laborers, it was at first difficult to purchase an office building. Only with the assistance of Master Huizong of the Guangfu Monastery was it possible to raise the funds to purchase a former temple for the use of the huiguan.

The Kuala Lumpur suburb of Brickfields is the site of the Selangor Xingan Huiguan, founded in 1935, with a membership in 1970 of over thirty thousand. This represents the largest concentration of Xinghua peoples overseas, and it is no accident that directly across the street from

Wherever a sizable Xinghua community establishes itself, a native-place association (*huiguan*) is built, and sooner or later there is sure to be a Three in One temple established. Wolfgang Franke (1972, 1980) noted the existence of four Three in One temples in Singapore, fourteen in Malaysia, and two or three in Indonesia. On a 1993 recent visit to Singapore and Malaysia, I found that the Singapore temples had slowed down in terms of ritual activity, while those in Kuala Lumpur were still very active. The principal temple in Kuala Lumpur is the Sanjiaotang, located just across the street from the Xingan Huiguan. The photographs of four deceased founders of the teachings hang in the temple. The scriptures of this temple are said to have been copied from an even earlier temple in Klang (Pacheng), probably the Zongkongtang (described by Franke, 1972). A recent plaque in that temple (dated 1994) celebrates the seventy-fifth anniversary of the temple, which would date its founding to 1919. The temple serves as a base for the training of younger ritualists.

---

the Xingan Huiguan is the largest and most active Three in One Temple in Malaysia, the Sanjiaotang. It is also worth mentioning that Selangor is the site of the founding of the Selangor Cycle Dealers Guild in 1911, and that the membership of this guild in 1970 was over two hundred. Another major commercial association in the area is the Selangor Motor Parts Traders' Association, which was made up of over fifty-six companies in 1970.

Other Xinghua Huiguans in Malaysia include the Sibu Xinghua Puxian Gonghui (founded 1937). This area was settled in 1911 by two groups of Xinghua immigrants totaling 141 people sponsored by Reverends Brewster and Chen Bingzhong. By 1970 there were some ten thousand Xinghua residents in Sibu. The Kuching Xingan Huiguan (1946) developed out of the local fishing trade. By 1970 there were over six thousand Xinghua residents of Kuching, and their fishing association had some two hundred boats while their automobile association included over sixty companies. Other Xinghua associations include the Perak Ziyouche Automobile Association (founded in 1939) and the Perak Cycle and Motor Dealers Association; the Malacca Xingan Huiguan (1945; membership in the hundreds in 1970); Kelantan Xingan Huiguan (1951); Seramban N. S. Shing An Association (1954); Kuantan Hin Ann Association (1954; membership in 1970, 226); Klang and Coast Hin Ann Association (1957; membership in 1970, 285); Trengganu (Persatuan) Hin Ann Huiguan (1967); Hock Phor Sean Association Kedah and Perlis; and Bahu Pahat Fu Pu Xian Huiguan (1970).

The following list of local associations sponsoring the publication of the Singapore Xingan Huiguan illustrates the continued importance of the transporation industry: Singapore Cycle & Motor Trader's Association, Singapore Motor Tire Dealers Association, Licheng Club, Nanyang Putian Huiguan, Singapore Bicycle Dealers Association, Singapore Trisha Owners Association, Singapore Kang-Tau Ong Clansmen Association, Singapore Puzhong Gaoping Gonghui (founded 1947), Singapore Taxi Transport Association, Singapore Xinghuayin Tiandao [Protestant] Church (founded in 1911 by the Protestant missionary Brewster, who was active in Putian, where he founded several churches, a school [Zheli zhongxue, later Putian Number One Middle School], and a hospital), and Hock Puoh Sang Communities Union (1947).

The list of companies outside Singapore who supplied advertisements and contributions to finance the publishing of the *Singapore Xingan Huiguan zhi* provides a map of the spread of Xinghua companies and industries across Southeast Asia. There are companies from Bateu Pahat, Muar, Kluang, Malacca, Seremban, and Kuala Lumpur. From West Malaysia, there are Kuala Kangsar, Taiping, Butterworth, Penang, Kedah, Klang, Ipoh, Teluk Anson, Kuching, and Sibu. From East Malaysia there are companies from Kelantan, Trengganu, Kuantan, Sabah, and Brunei. Seven cities in southern Thailand are also represented. In Indonesia, the largest concentrations of companies are from Djakarta and Medan.

The pudu rituals held at the Sanjiaotang each lunar 7/15 feature a toppling of the tower (*daota*) ritual for the deliverance of women who died in childbirth from the Blood Pool at the very lowest level of the Chinese Underworld (see Seaman [1981] on the significance of the blood bowl ritual, and Dean [1990] for a brief description of the ritual as it is performed in Putian). In this rite, paper figurines representing the deceased are gradually raised on a rope up the tower as the priests destroy ten gates of the underworld, smash ten bowls, and finally smash the blood basin at the base of the tower itself, after mourners have consumed the red liquid in it. In one ritual that took place in 1992, forty-seven 15-foot towers, each decorated with some forty-two paper deities, were toppled and then destroyed before a crowd of mourners. The entire parking space before the temple was transformed into an eerie underworld.[14]

Since 1995 was a year with an intercalary month (the 8th month was repeated), large-scale pudu rituals were performed again in the 7th month of that summer. Interestingly, the Three in One pudu rites in Malaysia are now attended by Overseas Chinese from Minnan, Chaozhou, and Guangdong areas, in addition to Xinghua émigrés. Hokkien is increasingly used in ritual contexts. Moreover, the performance of the pudu rite in the 7th month is an aberration from Xinghua custom, for there the pudu is performed in the 10th month. Thus by adapting to the customs of other Chinese ethnic communities in Southeast Asia, the Malaysia Three in One has been able to expand and thrive. Three in One ritual masters print name cards offering ritual services and listing their beeper numbers. The pudu rites are advertised in local newspapers well in advance, and proceeds are substantial.

Not only are Three in One ritualists active in Malaysia, contemporary Malaysian Huaqiao investment in the Three in One within China has soared since travel back to China became possible for Malaysian Chinese in 1991–93 (see section above on the economics of ritual).[15] The most telling instance of the central role of the Three in One in the Xinghua communities of Malaysia comes from the Fupuxian Huiguan in Klang. This brand-new building is equipped with a conference room, a bar, a disco, a workout room, a sauna, and an auditorium. But the top floor is equipped with practice space for young students of Three in One ritual. Tables are arranged in a *bagua* formation, with flags indicating the names of the hexagrams. Students learn to dance between the hexagrams in complex group choreography. They are provided with robes, and organized practice sessions are offered three evenings a week. The ritual masters are from the nearby Zongkongtang, which maintains a cohort

[14] Kenneth Cheong of the National Museum of History in Singapore has begun documenting the ritual traditions of the Sanjiaotang in Kuala Lumpur on videotape. He recorded the 1993 *daota* rite described in the text, as well as the 1995 diannual Pudu ritual at the Jiulidong in Singapore.

[15] The Malaysian government had refused to allow travel while the Chinese government continued to support the Communist guerrilla movement in Malaysia. With the surrender of the guerrilla forces, this obstacle was removed.

of twenty ritual specialists. Over a dozen students are undergoing training, which was 80 percent complete in the summer of 1995.[16]

THE THREE IN ONE AND THE JIULIDONG IN SINGAPORE

Franke noted the existence of four temples in Singapore with strong connections to the Three in One. He also noted that the Jiulidong (Nine Carp Cavern) was the most important Xinghua temple on the island. This temple has divided incense to found two other branch temples in Singapore, and three more in Indonesia (Medan, Sumatra). Franke conjectured that this temple had developed from a local tradition influenced by the Three in One, but worshiping the Immortals Lu, Xie, Wang, and Chen. This ritual tradition is known as the Qiongyao sect and involves the group ordination of spirit mediums and their incorporation within the spirit medium troupe of the temple. Franke provides translations of two steles in the Jiulidong in Singapore dating from 1948 and 1954, respectively. Both steles remark on features unique to popular religion in Xinghua, such as the cult of the Nine Immortal He brothers at Nine Carp Lake, a temple by a waterfall in the Xianyou mountains visited by Lin Chao'en and still famous for its dream oracles. The inscriptions also make mention of Mazu, Zhuo Wanchun, and Lin Longjiang (Lin Zhao'en). The 1948 stele notes that "On an island (*sic,* should be *bandao,* or peninsula) in the sea to the southeast [of Putian City] is [the fortified city] Puxi. There lived the Elder Holy Immortal Lu [Shiyuan], and the masters Xie [Yuanhui], Wang [Chengguang], and Chen [Shande]. They together cultivated the Qiongyao xiandao (Immortal Way of Rosegem Jade)."

The same stele goes on to note that "Then in the autumn of 1945, at the time the Anti-Japanese War was won, the Cavern [Temple] was completed, and it was decided to hold a pudu every ten years (each jia year) in order to commemorate these events." The 1954 inscription makes it clear that Three in One ritual masters performed at the diannual festivals: "This year we have invited trustees from in and outside the [Qiongyao] Doctrine, have trained scriptural masters of the Three Teachings, and have assembled former Mulian actors. . . . [We] will record fragrant names of the Scriptural Masters [of the Three in One and] the actors.

According to one of the leaders of the spirit medium cult at the temple, Mr. Huang, the first rituals at the Jiulidong were performed by Daoists. There is also a Japanese occupation. The 1954, 1964, 1974, and 1984 *fengjia* pudu rituals were all performed by Three in One scriptural masters (Tanaka, 1991). The 1994 ritual, however, was performed simultaneously by Daoists masters and Buddhist monks from Putian. Since the local Puxian opera troupe had disbanded, marionettists were also brought in from Putian and attempted to perform on stage as actors, with somewhat mixed results.

[16] My thanks to Mr. Huang Qingyi, general manager of the Fu PuXian Huiguan in Klang, for his conversations with me on the situation of the Three in One in Malaysia.

A third, and more recent, inscription entitled *Chongjian libei* (The setting up of a stele to commemorate the reconstruction [of the temple], dating from the 1980s, provides further information on the Qiongyao ritual tradition. There we read an account derivative of the earlier inscriptions of the arrival of the Nine Immortal He brothers at Nine Carp Lake, and their subsequent attainment of immortality. The local deities Tian Hou (Mazu, goddess of the sea, whose birthplace and place of ascension are in and around Meizhou Island in Putian), Zhuo Wanchun (the Daoist friend of Lin Zhao'en, separately worshipped at the Jiulidong), and Lord of the Teachings, Lin Longjiang, are all referred to. The inscription goes on:

> These immortal sages have been recorded in the Register of Sacrifices, and temples [dedicated to them] have been built throughout Southeast Asia. Later [these cults] were transmitted into Shiting, and the former sages within the village decided to propagate and spread the teachings, and so they first established the Shangfang Temple. Then they raised funds and built a cavern temple across from the Shangfang Temple, which they called the Nine Carp Cavern. The ritual method of Rosegem Jade worships the Great Realized Immortals Lu, Xie, Wang, and Chen, the Nine elderly immortal He brothers, the Realized Being Zhuo [Wanchun], and the arrayed saints, both civil and military. The [spirit writing] planchette saves the world and its awesome spiritual power manifests miraculously. These saints, the incense burner, and the supernatural planchette were first brought south to the temple by Huang Wenjing in 1935 when he worshipped and received the carriage of these gods from a boat from back home. Now they have spread their ritual method all over Indonesia.

Based on field work at the original Jiulidong in Shiting, Jiangkou xiang, Putian, and in the vicinity, I would suggest that this cult was an offshoot of village-based group spirit-medium initiation rituals, which can be found only in the northernmost section of Putianxian in Jiangkou Township (see chapter 1, phase 3). The involvement of the Three in One ritual tradition in the Singapore Nine Carp Temple is probably due to the coalescence of Xinghua cultural traditions in Overseas Chinese community settings.[17]

[17] For a detailed description of the role of Taoist liturgy in relation to spirit-medium initiation in this area, see Dean and Zheng (1993). Beginning in the late Ming, the Jiangkou region of northern Putian developed a unique cultural ecology featuring a large number of temples with multiple deities representing all different social groups in the villages—lineages, neighborhoods, spirit-associations, etc.—all tied together within an ancient irrigation system. Each god worshiped in each temple must have a medium, so once every generation young men are selected for three rounds of training in chant, trance, and dance. They are also taught how to write talismans and perform healing exorcisms. Before they enter the temple for initiation, they take part in a Taoist ritual, where they are instructed as to their vows and prohibitions and receive certificates of initiation from the priest. This certificate is called a certificate of the Great Ritual Institute of Mount Lu (*Lushan Dafayuan dudie*), where Chen Jinggu received her training in the magical arts. These certificates are renewed once every New Year by the Taoist priest in an annual ritual. These rituals can be dispensed with by a group ritual that is sort of a preparatory funeral, informing the gods and the underworlds that the mediums have become eternal servants of the Tao. While the majority of these spirit medium initiations are related in local practice to the Lushan Dafayuan

This example of the shifting roles of the Three in One ritual tradition in relation to the spirit-medium initiation cults of the main Xinghua temple in Singapore shows how cultural forms continue to be negotiated and contested in a multicultural setting.

THE THREE IN ONE IN TAIWAN

In addition to being brought to Malaysia, Singapore, and Indonesia, the Three in One also accompanied the Xinghua community that migrated to Taiwan. A 1986 stele in the Longshantang (Dragon Mountain Hall), which faces the railway tracks along Lane No. 1 of Chung-shan North Road in Taipei, states that in 1914 a worshiper from Ditou village of Huian Country, Fujian, named Chen Zhaoxing brought some of the incense from the Dragon Mountain Hall of that village to Taiwan. The Ditou village temple was itself a branch temple of the Honorable Confucius Temple in Putian. The stele (translated in appendix 9) goes on to relate the history of the temple. A major event is the transmission of Lin's scriptures from Malaysia to Taiwan in 1969.

The Xia religion in Taiwan now counts four or five temples, including the Longshanci in a market on Senlinlu, Taibei. (Zheng Zhiming [1990a] provides a list of the temple committee members and the names of the ritual specialists of these temples.) At some of the temples, young people are being taught to perform certain rituals, using Hokkien rather than Puxianhua.[18] In addition to these temples, the Xinghua Nativeplace Association of Taiwan plays an active role in maintaining Xinghua cultural activities within Taiwan through the sponsorship of festivals and processions, and by preserving cultural and business connections with Putian and Xianyou.

THE RETURN OF OVERSEAS THREE IN ONE GROUPS TO CHINA

Starting in the late 1980s, Malaysian and Taiwanese Three in One groups have been successful in raising funds for the reestablishment of the Three in One

---

(the Great Ritual Office of Mt. Lu), a certain number trace their origin to the Qiongyao Dafayuan, based in the Jiulidong in Shiting. One principal deity in this ritual lineage is Xuantian shangdi, but the Immortal Lu Shiyuan and his associates, the immortals Xie, Wang, and Chen, are in the fact the prime objects of worship and the most active figures in the local medium cult. This cult appears to have declared its independence from local tradition due to the power of its spirit-writing-medium cult. A brief printed scripture distributed by the Qiongyaotang in Singapore states that the gods originated in the vicinity of Puxi fortified city near Meizhou Bay. The birthplace of the immortal masters has recently been revealed to the leader of the Singapore Jiulidong altar association in a dream, and a temple is being built near Puxi at a cost of some 600,000 Singapore dollars.

[18] The adherents perform funerals and commemorative rituals, wearing the same blue gowns and conical white hats with blue tassels worn by adherents of the Mingxia branch in western Xianyou and the Malaysian adherents who brought copies of Lin Zhao'en's *Xiawunijing* and other writings to Taiwan in the 1980s.

tradition in the Xinghua region. In 1992 they supported the construction of a Lin Longjiang Memorial Hall to the side of the East Mountain Ancestral Shrine. A sum of approximately two million RMB was then raised toward the purchase of the military barracks in front of the shrine. These will be torn down and the original overall layout of the shrine will be restored.

Nonetheless, the return of Overseas Chinese delegations from Three in One groups has resulted in a degree of confusion, reflecting the difficulty of organizing such a diffuse religious tradition with so many local variations. No doubt the investment of such large funds also puts strains on the leadership abilities of the local leaders of the Three in One. Thus, for example, Taiwanese groups that trace their roots back to northern Huian were asked on one occasion to assist in efforts to perserve the Yaodaoci. This beautiful temple, dating from the late Ming and with many original beams and architectural features, stood in the middle of the athletic field of No. 6 Middle School in Hanjiang. The Taiwanese Three in One negotiators were unable to persuade the local authorities to preserve the building. Frustrated with this impasse, local Three in One adherents began posting big-character posters denouncing the authorities. This led to a quick and irrevocable decision to demolish the temple in 1994. It is fortunate that such breakdowns in communication among Three in One adherents, lobbyists, and the authorities are now far less common than before. In 1995 representatives from Malaysian Three in One groups supported a conference organized by the Putian Folklore Association on "The Academic Study of Lin Longjiang." This group, together with Taiwanese Three in One groups, continues to support the publication of Three in One texts, the performance of rituals, and the training of Three in One ritualists, both in Fujian and abroad.

Ritual Traditions of the Three in One

THE EVOLUTION of a ritual tradition that would parallel and in some places actually replace the local ritual traditions of Buddhism and Daoism was a crucial aspect of the development of the Three in One.[1] This process began, as we have seen, with the writing of the *Bentijing* and Maitreya scriptures by Lin Zhao'en and the reworking of Lin's philosophical essays into scriptural form by Lu Wenhui in 1597. Lu actually reworked Lin's philosophic writings into three different sets of scriptures for recitation. The next stage was Lu's composition of Buddhist-influenced litanies. Then Chen Zhongyu composed liturgies in imitation of the Buddhist-based *Yulan pen* ritual texts, along with other liturgical texts modeled on Daoist ritual texts. Zhu Xuhui also composed a scripture that is clearly modeled on Buddhist imagery. These texts, along with the *Bentijing* (Scripture of the original body), the *Milejing* (Maitreya scripture), and various versions of the *Xiawuni Scriptures,* form the basic liturgical materials of the Three in One. With this set of largely Buddhist-based liturgical texts, the rituals of sacrifice and worship of the Master borrowed from Confucian academy ritual, along with ritual exegesis of classical texts, and the Daoist-inspired heart method, the Three in One would have had a fairly complete ritual tradition that might have satisfied local literati with a primary interest in self-cultivation and advanced study of the Confucian Classics.

This was manifestly not the interest of Lin Zhenming (who probably could not have found many literati in the coastal region where he lived). Lin and his disciples developed a further set of scriptures dedicated to the gods of local popular cults. They also elaborated scriptures and rituals in imitation of Daoist liturgy. Thus we find liturgies for the *fazou* announcement ritual, the *qing shen* invitation of the gods, various rituals of audience and offering, and rituals for the deconstruction of the altar and the sendoff of the gods. A complex set of documentary forms has been developed, again paralleling and in some cases superseding those used by the local Daoists and Buddhists. These texts and ritual practices later had a certain influence on the development of the more mainstream Three in One ritual traditions.

By the late Qing, the Three in One had developed two rather distinct ritual traditions. For the sake of simplicity, we will call these the Wuben and the

---

[1] Several people I spoke to in a number of locations in Xianyou pointed out the marked decline in the number of Daoist masters in those areas and noted that Three in One ritual masters were now the only alternative for most ritual occasions. This is not to say that someone could not invite a renowned Daoist master from farther away, but that for everyday occasions and regular ritual-events, Three in One ritualists would do the job.

Plate 14. Mingxia ritualists at the Dongshan Zongkongtang

Mingxia ritual traditions. In Xianyou, the Sanyipai, a more loosely organized branch of the Three in One, developed an intermediate and somewhat independent range of rituals. The differences between the Mingxia and the Sanyi traditions appear to be based on different lines of transmission, and minor differences regarding ritual observances. Thus we hear from members of the Sanyipai in Xianyou that unlike members of the Mingxiapai, they do not worship the local god of theater, Tian Gongyuanshuai. This is said to be due to the legend that links this god to Lin Zhenming and the Mingxiapai. (Yet this god is worshiped in certain Sanyi Three in One temples in Fengting—perhaps for other, local reasons.) The members of the Daxingci Mingxiapai claimed they worshiped the Daoist Immortal Lu Dongbin instead of the Immortal Zhang Sanfeng, generally associated with Lin Zhao'en and the Three in One. Another example is the prominent place accorded by the Mingxiapai to the recitation of the *Yushu jing* (the Daoist scripture of the Jade Pivot Star). They claim that Lin Zhenming was this star in a former existence. Lacking this conviction, the Sanyipai ritualists do not start each ritual with a recitation of this scripture. For similar reasons, adherents of the Sanyipai claim not to keep a scripture dedicated to the god of theater. Generally speaking, these two traditions have developed a set of rituals for individual rites (rites of passage, initiation, and minor exorcisms), family-based ritual (especially requiem services, also birthday celebrations, and marriages), and community-level ritual (birthdays of the gods of the Three in One, birthdays of the local popular gods, Yu-lanpen feasts for the hungry ghosts).[2]

RELIGIOUS ORGANIZATION: INITIATION

A ritual specialist in the Wuben tradition explained the initiation process in the following way.[3] New initiates must be introduced by three members. They undergo an initiation ceremony in which they fill out a report listing the "diseases of their hearts" *xinbing* (*shijie qizhang*). After washing and purifying themselves, they straighten their clothes.[4] Then they kowtow nine times before the image of Xiawuni and bow three times to the master controller (*zongchi*) or the handler of the teachings (*zhangjiao*). Then they kneel before the god and recite an "initiation report" and a "report on an oath to uphold the prohibitions." These documents are then burned. Next, the master controller recites the rules of the teaching (*jiaogui*). He next transmits the method of stilling in the back (*genbei xinfa*). Initiates pay a symbolic fee (in Qing times this was eighty-one *wen;* currently the fee is one *mao* RMB). This is referred to, according to Lin Zhao'en's formulation, as "establishing the

[2] Several accounts of the Daoist ritual tradition in Taiwan and Southeast China now are available, along with some descriptions of Buddhist ritual practice (Liu Zhiwan, 1974, 1984; Ofuchi, 1983; Saso, 1978a; Schipper, 1993; Lagerwey, 1987a; Kamata, 1986; Welch, 1967, 1968, 1972; Pang, 1977). Schipper (1975) provides the Chinese text and a detailed description of the Daoist division of lights (*Fendeng*) ritual, with color plates, charts, and musical scores. Lagerwey (1987a) provides an introduction to the arrangement of the Daoist altar and the preparations for rituals. He outlines the basic program of liturgies for the living, *Jiao* (Offering), and *Gongde* (Liturgies for the dead). He also gives a detailed account of five central rites within the Jiao, and three within the requiem service. These sources provide a background and a framework for comparison with the Three in One rituals described below. My account will, therefore, not seek to be exhaustive, but rather will touch on general features of the Three in One ritual tradition.

[3] The late Chen Zhaojing (d. 1992) was a learned man, a lawyer, a lifelong adherent of the Three in One, and a most courteous gentleman. He worked assiduously to promote the Three in One—most importantly, in his view, by editing and helping to republish the complete works of Master Lin, as well as gathering many important documents, books, and liturgical materials of the tradition. In the collating of classical texts, he worked with Xu Shiyang, who commanded wide respect in Three in One circles for his achievements in inner alchemy. Mr. Chen worked in a ritual context as the secretarial assistant, compiling the voluminous documents that would be used in the ritual. Mr. Chen led me to the Wuben temple and to the graves of Chen Zhida and Liang Puyao. He gladly let me make copies of his collection of liturgies and formularies for documents. He also took me to a teaching seminar organized by the Three in One in which two ninety-year-old gentlemen explicated the text of Master Lin's commentaries to the *Four Books* to a group of men in their sixties, seventies, and eighties. A select group of younger men in their forties were also allowed to attend and assist the elders during their five-day seminar.

[4] The Wuben branch ritualists generally don a simple blue cotton gown and go bare-headed. Mingxia and Sanyi ritualists were either yellow, white, or blue gowns. A variety of different ritual caps are worn, especially by the chief ritualist, including various forms of a five-petal cap modeled on Buddhist headgear. Some Mingxia ritualists wear a conical white hat with a red tassle, recalling Manchu court haberdashery.

basis" (*liben*). The following steps are "entering the gate" (*rumen*) and "making principles ultimate" (*jize*).

The second step requires a similar ritual and the burning of another [*Great*] *Report*. This ceremony was traditionally conducted by the general coordinator, who would give the advanced initiate a ritual name, *faming*, and transmit the advanced inner alchemical "method of the heart moving in the courtyard" (*xingting xinfa*). The initiate would give sixty-four *wen*. Further progress would no longer be marked by a ritual. The advanced initiates often gather together to meditate and do *qigong* and inner alchemy. Younger people are gradually being trained in the ritual techniques. These include regular days of offerings (only vegetarian offerings) and scripture recitation, followed by group meditation.

There are slight variations in the texts of the initiation reports used by the different branches of the Three in One.[5] In general, they are somewhat simpler than the different sets of initiation vows for Confucians, Daoists, and Buddhists composed by Lin Zhao'en (translated in Berling, 1980: 111–116), yet they incorporate many phrases from these formative versions. The Wuben vow is as follows:

MALE INITIATION VOW

I, Three in One *menren* (male initiate) So and So, have earnestly divined to choose an auspicious day, fasted and purified myself, and presented ritual gifts of introduction, desiring to become an initiate of the Lord of the Three Teachings. I request the transmission of the Confucian heart method. I will take the Three Bonds and the Five Constancies as my everyday standard. I will realize the instructions concerning being filial upon entering [the home] and brotherly when departing. I will carry this out everywhere so that my studies will illumine the substance [of the teachings] and be fit for application. One must be clear about the distinction between rectitude and profit. I must be censorious of evil depravities. I must carry forth the Bonds and Constancies. I will definitely be the most serious of men, and there is no form of licentious evil that I will not chastise. As for breaking the Bonds and Constancies, being disloyal and unfilial, being neither a scholar, a farmer, a craftsman, or a merchant: If I should fail to distinguish rectitude from profit, or be unreproving of belligerent dispositions or uncensorious of depravities, then I would be a sinner against Confucius. How could I establish myself in the space between heaven and earth? I must revere and keep the illumined instructions I receive, and conscientiously carry out the heart method that is transmitted to me. I dare not speak of [these secrets] even to relatives within my own home. If there be any leaks [of secrets] let Heaven judge me. To this end I reverently present this petition, which I bring forward with fear and trembling.

[5] The initiation vows of certain Mingxia Three in One temples are less directly derived from Lin's early models. They tend to include lists of prohibitions, such as those given later in this chapter. They also often have the initiate call upon the aid of the Lord of the Three in One, the Great Patriarch Who Saves the World, as well as the "various immortal masters of this hall" and the "[guardian deities] of this hall who protect the dharma and the Dao."

1. I vow to daily scrutinize my faults and to repent of them thoroughly.
2. I vow that each day I will maintain a fast for one meal.

Year, month, day, Name of Three in One initiate, who burns incense and forwards this document with a hundred bows.

The Vow for Female Initiates is similar but adds injunctions that are deemed gender-specific:

I, Three in One *xinnu* (female believer) So and So, have earnestly divined to choose an auspicious day, fasted and purified myself, and presented ritual gifts of introduction, desiring to become an initiate of the Lord of the Three Teachings. I request the transmission of the Confucian heart method. I will take the Three Bonds and the Five Constancies as my everyday standard. I will realize the instructions concerning the Three Forms of Obedience and the Four Virtues. I will be filial and respectful to my father- and mother-in-law, and harmonious with my sisters-in-law at all times. Raising silkworms, spinning hemp, and weaving clothes will be my regular occupation. In movement and at rest I will serve them with the Middle Way. [I will] carry this out everywhere so that my studies will illumine the substance (of the teachings) and be fit for application. One must be clear about the distinction between rectitude and profit. I must be censorious of evil depravities. Now carrying forth the Bonds and Constancies is definitely the most important human affair. If I should fail to distinguish rectitude from profit, or be uncensorious of depravities, or break the Bonds and Constancies—then I would be a sinner against Confucius. How could I establish myself in the space between heaven and earth? [The remainder is the same as for male initiates.]

According to members of the Wuben branch, every generation of Three in One initiates ideally should see the rise of a realized Master who could transmit the Teachings to the next generation. The realized Master's name is connected with one of the characters in a "transmission poem" obtained via planchette and accepted by Chen Zhida (*Xianre xianshi*). In this poem, Liang Puyao began the Pu generation and transmitted to the Dao generation, but there has not yet been a realized master in this generation to take up the word "Dao" as part of his sobriquet (*hao*).

RELIGIOUS ORGANIZATION: DISTRIBUTION OF DUTIES

The Wuben tradition distinguishes among four categories of initiates. These are the general coordinator (*zongchi*), the master who controls the Teachings (*zhangjiao*), the protector of the Teachings (*Hujiao*), and the more general category of fellows in the Way (*Daoyou*). Due to the dislocations of the revolutionary war and the Liberation period, in particular the Cultural Revolution, there has not been a general coordinator in over sixty years. Each temple selects its own *zhangjiao* and small group of *hujiao* from among its *Daoyou*. The last traditional rituals for the promotion of a *zhangjiao* conducted by a *zongshi* were performed over sixty years ago in the Hansantang in Putian City.

According to the manuscript from the Daxingci in Xianyou City written in 1948, the following positions were distinguished in the Mingxia tradition:

Zhangjiao Shi (1): master who controls the Teachings: in charge of the training in inner alchemy; also takes part in collation of ritual texts

Bingjiao shi (1): master who carries out the Teachings: person responsible for all matters having to do with the temple; receives all visitors

Fusi jiaoshi (deputy master of the Teachings) (1): a deputy to the preceding two masters

Zhu tanshi: chief altar master (1): director of ritual activities and chief instructor in liturgies, scriptures, song, and recitation

Futan shi: deputy altar master (1): assists chief altar master

Shizuo (aide to the master) (1): assistant to the assistant, commonly known as the third altar master; responsible for ritual matters

Dong Shizhang: general manager (1): assists in internal activities of the temple; also assists the *Bingjiao shi.*

Zhangjiao shi: protector of the Teachings (1): in charge of the training of the female members of the temple in inner alchemy

Bingjiao shi: in charge of all internal matters of the temple involving women

Fusi jiaoshi: assistant to the two preceding positions

Dongshi zhang: assistant in all internal matters of the temple regarding the female members, and in aiding the male membership

In addition, the text mentions other positions, including spirit-medium writers and temple committee members. The text also states that in the Republican period there was a great upsurge in Three in One activity and it was necessary to augment the previously quite abbreviated administration of the temple with the list of ranks above. In 1947 the god Zhou instructed the Mingxia to add the position of *fujiaoshi,* as well as to establish a temple committee (*dongshihui*) and to initiate a women's ritual and alchemical order. The position of *shizuo* was created in recognition of the contribution of one Lin Youyu, later the *zhu tanshi* of the Daxingci, who in the Guangxu period has produced a beautiful edition of the scriptures and liturgies of the Three in One. The bulk of the text consist of a listing of the people who filled various of these positions in different periods in four closely connected temples, including the Daxingci in the Republican period. We also learn of the major rituals they performed during that period, and some of the remarkable events that transpired. These include the time a *zhangjiao shi* who was a *juren* passed away. The next day his spirit entered the ever-alert planchette and communicated his presence. It was determined that he had been promoted in the celestial bureaucracy, and in recognition of this accomplishment he was made the guardian spirit of one of the Three in One temples. Another time a spirit who usually spoke through the planchette actually possessed one of the Three in One officiants and dispensed medical recipes to the sick and suffering.

The process of selection of an individual for a particular post is detailed in the Daxingci manuscript. First a list of candidates is nominated by acclaim and then put before the gods for selection by divination. The candidates must already have an advanced knowledge of inner alchemy and generally have exhibited good conduct. Once approval of the candidates has been obtained from the god, one officiant assigns each of the names a number. He then is sent into a room at the back of the temple. A second officiant casts divination blocks for each number, and a third announces the numbers and records the results. Whichever number gets the most favorable casts of the divination blocks is assigned a particular job. Then the officiant who had been in the back room comes out and announces the names that correspond with the numbers. An announcement is drawn up, indicating the number of successful tosses for each candidate. Then a ritual is performed to present the new officiant to the gods.

RULES OF ASSOCIATION

We also have the text of the *Huigui* (rules of association) written by Chen Zhongyu. He provides sample forms for the *Gaotian shugao* (Memorial to Heaven). Such memorials are no longer commonly used in the Three in One, but the inclusion of this form in the 1986 reprint of the *Rules of the Association* may help revive their use. We learn that Dong Shi held assemblies on the 6th of each month. A brief appended outline of the initial worship of the Saint's ritual for contemporary use reads as follows:

1. Entire congregation solemnly stand. Perform three bows toward the statue of the Lord of the Religion. First bow. Second bow. Third bow.

2. Sing one stanza of the Poems to Awaken the Heart.

3. Recite Master Lin's Commandments (also known as the *Poem to Illumine the Nature*):

> Don't let evil thoughts arise
> don't do evil things
> The Master of the Three Teachings
> Taught us so.
> If we do otherwise
> our hearts will die
> What sorrow should the heart die
> Worse than if the body dies.
> We dwell on earth but 100 years
> who can avoid death?
> If the body dies but the heart lives
> then this is not dying.

4. Extinguish all entanglements (Meditation).

5. Ritual completed.

Other rules of association are included in the *Sanjiao Yizhilu* and other sources. Lin (1994) lists three different sets of prohibitions that are in use within the Three in One. In the set adopted by Hanjiang temples, there are twelve clauses:

1. The initiate must uphold the statements in the Memorial of Initiation and the Five Don'ts: (1) Don't use the words of the sages for personal advantage; (2) Don't disrupt the social bonds by lying or meandering; (3) Don't seek fame and honor through scholarship; (4) Don't discuss illicit ideas or intervene in other people's private matters; (5) Don't disturb the course of study, which must proceed in sequence.

2. Speaking strange words, spirit possession, spells, and prognostication are all forbidden.

3. Prostitution, gambling, and drinking are forbidden.

4. Covetous tricks for personal gain are forbidden.

5. Initiates should not take part in rituals of celebration or requiem in the homes of those who are not initiates. One should not accept excessive gifts or payments for rituals conducted (for initiates). Ritualists may accept a roll of cloth and a fan, but no other cash or gifts, with the exception of transportation costs and sacrificial items. Three meals a day during the ritual are the responsibility of the host, but these should be simple vegetarian repasts.

6. Costs for rituals on the birth dates of the gods should be shared equally by all the initiates on a voluntary basis, and not be forced. Costs for the construction or repair of temples should be contributed voluntarily without any pressure.

7. The recitation of scriptures should not influence agricultural work; thus attendance is voluntary. The costs of scripture recitation should be borne voluntarily by participants.

8. Offerings for gods' birthday rites should be vegetarian and simple.

9. The Three in One temples should not be used as cafeterias.

10. Vestments and rites should accord with the times.

11. Each day one should fast for one meal. Before eating, one should reflect on one's conduct and words of the day before.

12. The transmitted techniques of the heart method should not be leaked to even the closest relative.

The Jiangdongci in Dongzhuang Township (a Mingxia temple) printed the following *Six Vows* and *Twelve Prohibitions* in 1982:

1. I will think over all my past mistakes and vow never to do such things again.

2. I will respect the illustrious teachings of the Three in One and be correct in word and deed, and strive to improve myself. I will not serve ghosts or spirits, or speak of strange things, or do anything forbidden by the teachings.

3. I will uphold the national constitution and the laws of the government, acting as a good citizen, and break no laws.

4. I will believe in the true teachings with perfect sincerity. My words and my thoughts will be united, and I will not secretly contravene the teachings.

5. I will carefully follow the saintly instructions, valuing the three bonds and the five constancies day and night, and keeping the five words *ren, yi, li, zhi, xin* (humaneness, righteousness, propriety, wisdom, and trustworthiness) in my heart at all times.

6. I will carve the four mercies in my heart. Heaven and earth mercifully give birth to beings and nurture humankind, and so we must be good. Chairman Mao Zedong mercifully governed the country and provided peace for the people, and so the people must show him loyalty. Father and mother mercifully raise their children, so their children must demonstrate filial piety toward them. The Master mercifully taught his students, and we must show reverence in return.

The Twelve Prohibition are (in summary): (1) Prohibition of licentiousness. This is the first of all evils. A man cannot be licentious and be a *junzi* (gentleman). A woman must be chaste in order to be a proper lady. (2) Prohibition of theft. Theft of others property sullies the heart. Similar explanations are given for prohibitions against (3) killing, (4) lying, (5) covetousness, (6) insincerity, (7) sloth, (8) deviousness, (9) graft (and other such conduct, the consequences of which will be visited upon one's descendants), (10) bizarre conduct or speech, (11) anger and hatred, and (12) dreamlike delusion and blindly following one's passions. Several other similar sets of "six" or "ten" prohibitions are posted in Three in One temples in Xianyou.

RITUAL PANTHEONS

The ritual pantheons of the various branches of the Three in One tradition are as rich and complex as the liturgical and meditational techniques. For example, a typical Mingxia liturgical manuscript, the *Xiajiao sanyuan qijian qingshen yiwen* (Ritual text for the invitation of gods and the installation of an altar of the Three Origins of the Xia Teaching), invokes the following twenty-eight gods or groups of deities: Confucius; Laozi; Śākyamuni Buddha; Xiawuni (Lin Zhao'en); Yuhuang shangdi (Jade Emperor); Yanluo Wang (King Yama); Dongyue rensheng dadi; Shuibu (Water Bureau Gods); Milefo (Maitreya); Guanyin; Dizang; Zhang Sanfeng; Zhuo Wanchun; Wenchang; Beidou qixing wang (Seven Gods of the Northern Dipper Stars); Guandi; Leisheng tianzun; San Guan (Three Offlcials of Heaven, Earth, and Waters); Lu Wenhui; Lin Zhenming; Zhu Xuhui; Zhang Hongdu; Chen Zhongyu; Weng Wudao; Dong Shi; Weng Yiyang; the 800 lofty sages (Lin Zhao'en's initial circle of followers); all the sages.

Here the disparate teachings and traditions are all embraced to the point that Dong Shi (the third transmitter of the mainstream branch) is sandwiched between two patriarchs of the Weng branch that he reviled in his *Menxian shilu*. The order in which these gods are invoked is significant. Note that Lin Zhenming (founder of the Weng branch) comes after Lu Wenhui, but Weng Wudao (the successor to Lin Zhenming) comes before Dong Shi.

Ritual Texts: Liturgical Manuscripts

More work remains to be done on the analysis of the liturgical texts and ritual practices (including meditational methods and spirit-medium seances) of the Three in One. The manuscripts listed below provide a starting point for that study. Among them we find ritual texts for the celebration of the birth and death date of Lin Zhao'en, several of his disciples, and many local gods. There are ritual texts for funerals, tenth month pudu feasts for the Hungry Ghosts (*yulan pen*), consecrations of god statues, and communal *jiao* sacrifice rituals. Particularly interesting are the scriptures to local deities, which provide a great deal of otherwise unavailable information on their cults, powers, and iconography.

A typical active Three in One altar will have in its possession a set of approximately 80 to 90 liturgical manuscripts. In the course of fieldwork, I have come across several substantial collections of scriptures and liturgies of the Three in One. These include the Sanyipai collection of the Zhandouci: 85 texts; Mingxiapai texts from the Daxingci in the personal collection of a ritualist: 90 texts; Naisheng tank texts: 92; and Qixingci texts: 66. Another large collection (60–80 texts) belonging to the Shandetang consisting of Hanjiang Zuci and Wubenpai texts was kept in the late Chen Jiaojing's home in Hanjiang. The following comments are based on a preliminary analysis of these sources and notes on Three in One rituals that I have attended. These scriptures and liturgical manuscripts are listed in the bibliography. These collections contain the following categories of liturgical manuscripts: scriptures, rituals of communal sacrifice, requiem services, Lanpen rites, miscellaneous rites, collections of spells, talismans, music, and dance choreography.

Ritual Time (1)

Chapter 1 discussed the various modes of temporality generated within a single ritual-event and the efforts of different ritual traditions, such as Imperial Confucian ritual or Daoist liturgy, to control time. The Three in One, by merging many of these different ritual traditions, has created its own mixture of speeds and generated its own distinctive temporalities. The Three in One developed a range of rites of passage, prophylactic rites, and rites of affliction. Van Gennep, who developed this schema, noted that this classification of rites is itself

> rhythmic in the sense that it begins by considering the human life, the principal
> object of our interest, from its beginnings to its end; then the cycle of the year,
> and lastly the manifestation of various activities diverging in direction yet all ra-
> diating from Man as the center of energy. This rhythm, which is rectilinear in the
> first data series, then cyclic in the second, is alternating in the third. For here the

action is direct from subject to object, then rebounds back from object to subject. (van Gennep, 1937, quoted in Turner, 1986: 235)[6]

The rituals of the Three in One can also be classified in these terms. Life-cycle rites have been developed to celebrate marriage and deal with death. Many rites relate to the annual cycle, as it has been conceived in China, where it includes the New Year and the Festival of the Hungry Ghosts. Lin Zhao'en's own date of birth and death correspond closely to the Upper Prime Festival (which has been absorbed into the Lantern Festival) and the Middle Prime Festival. Similar commemorative anniversaries have been established for many cults observed within the Three in One. Birth and death dates for the Four Patriarchs (of Confucianism, Daoism, Buddhism, and the Three in One), the Four Attendants, the Three Transmitters, and a host of local and empirewide deities are celebrated at Three in One temples. Although not exactly rites developed in relation to seasonal changes, these annual observances transform each year into an intricate patchwork of ritual moments. These commemorations are a collective assertion of the meaning of particular gods in relation to the Three in One tradition within Xinghua culture. Prophylactic rites and rites of affliction (and subsequent thanksgiving) have also been developed to respond to the threat of illness or the outbreak of disaster.

As an example of a life-cycle ritual, we might examine a liturgy for marriage. The Three in One Wuben branch performs a wedding ceremony based on a liturgy and employing a memorial. Although the *Family Ritual* of Zhu Xi contains a liturgy for marriage, it certainly makes no room for Buddhist or Daoist elements (Ebrey, 1991a). These ritual traditions in fact often make do with a simple Bai Tian Gong (Worship of Heaven) ritual for marriages. The Three in One liturgy indicates an even more comprehensive engagement with domestic life. The manuscript begins:

> This one dot [of spiritual power] which emerges from the void, how could it but be that which was prior to the division of Qian (Heaven) and Kun (Earth). In the Great Void and the Great Nothingness, there spontaneously dwells the pure

---

[6] Van Gennep further subdivided the category of rites of affliction into a tripartite structure of rites of separation, margin or limen, and reaggregation. Victor Turner developed this insight by characterizing ritual process in general as having a four-part processive form composed of breach, crisis, attempted redress (through ritual and symbolic action), and outcome (climax or satiation). Turner focuses on the third stage, the stage of redressive ritual and symbolic action. In Turner's analysis of ritual, the liminal moment of communal equalization in the redressive ritual phase is equated with antitemporality, the denial of time. Turner notes two forms of antitemporality: the perennially sacred and the perennially sacreligious. Both are based on an intuition of eternity. "The complex temporality of all the social and cultural processes I have been discussing demands a moment of experienced eternal life as its cognitive and ontological counterstroke, the factor constitutive of processual meaningfulness." Yet the manipulation of time in Chinese ritual suggests an even more complex awareness of multiple modes of temporality. Moreover, Turner's analysis of antitemporality shares a common problematic refusal to consider coevalness (Fabian, 1983).

essence of the Chaotic Radiance. Contained within this cavity, it is called the Rulai (Tathāgata; the self-so which is and will be). Heaven, earth, and humankind share it. Preserve it and you can advance to be a sage. Lose it and you will sink into bestiality. It is the key to emerging from this [realm] and entering that one. Can one not but be careful of it? All must become enlightened by the Lord of the Three in One:

> The veins of the Dao have transmitted their Truth
> On the Black Rock of East Mountain a Unicorn appeared.
> The Chaotic Radiance shines in the 500-year Third Dragon Assembly
> Confucius, Laozi, and Śākyamuni merge into a single body.

> The Lord of the Three in One made a boundless oath
> To save the Three Thousand [Beings] and the Great Kalpa
> In the Dharma Realm incense wafts and all prostrate themselves,
> Returning to Confucianism, Buddhism, and Daoism.

Several Buddhist protector deities are next invoked, and then a number of Daoist spells are recited (for the purification of the hall, the bodies of the practitioners, and heaven and earth). Next the *Poem to Illumine the Nature* (translated above) is recited, and a pledge to return to the enlightened, the correct, and the pure is uttered. A *Hymn of Incense* is sung, and then the text continues:

> Confucius, Laozi, Śākyamuni, and Xiawuni are the Four Patriarchs. Their merit surpasses the Three Realms. Their heart fills the Six Voids. Vastly they spread out the unity of the Thousand Saints. Awesomely they erect the standards of the Hundred Kings. Their divine powers are beyond measure, and their merit is limitless.

Next the following are invoked: Confucius, Laozi, Buddha, Xia Wuni (He who illuminates the return to Noncommencement of the Three Teachings—Brightly shine the two pearls in the Noon Heavens—the Dao United, unified through the Center—the Great Patriarch of the Three Teachings who Saves the World). This group is followed by the Jade Emperor, Hou Tu, Maitreya Buddha, Guanyin, Leisheng Puhua, the Three Officials (of Heaven, Earth, and Water), the Astral Gods of the Northern Dipper, Zhang Sanfeng, Zhuo Wanchun, Marshal Zhao Xuantan, Lu Wenhui, Zhu Xuhui, Lin Zhenming, Zhang Hongdu, Chen Zhongyu, Dong Shi, Chen Zhida, and Liang Puyao. The inclusion of the latter in the list suggests that the liturgy was composed around the end of the Republican period. Finally the Dharma Protector nagas, the former Xia sages, the city gods, earth gods, the gods worshiped on family altars, and all the gods mentioned in the various scriptures and litanies are invoked, as well as all the past, present, and future Three in One sages. Then the following memorial is read:

To the Spirits of heaven and Earth:

> So and so, of such and such a Three in One temple of the People's Republic of China, together with the members of his family, etc., all burn incense and bow a

hundred times, earnestly memorializing the completion of a marriage in response to heavenly aid and spiritual blessing. May this be a matter that plants good fortune and extends life. The rites emphasize the Bonds and the Constancies, and [Becoming] Husband and Wife is the floresence of human relations. With poetry and song, zither and lute, the capping of marriage is the source of the Kingly Way. These words are to record that So and So (male) selected this date to carry out the rites of marriage, singing out the Enticement of Zhou poem (the first of the poems in the *Book of Songs*). On this day he reverently invited all his friends within the Three in One to his home to set up a sacred space of the Way, to prepare water and offer flowers, recite scriptures and perform litanies, all in order to reverently inform the spirits of Heaven and Earth, and to display the earnestness of his heart. I beseech the [gods] to observe this with their merciful light, that my humble home and family will extend forever like the tangled vines of a melon plant. I present this memorial with the utmost of trepidation.

Date . . . Hall . . . Three in One adherent so and so, together with his entire family, etc, burns incense and bows repeatedly, while offering up this memorial.[7]

This is followed by a recitation of the *Scripture of Fundamental Substance*. Offerings are presented, and then the gods are thanked for having come to act as witnesses to the marriage and are sent off to return to their respective palaces. They are beseeched for blessings as they depart. A final hymn concludes:

The Four Patriarchs return with the Sages and Saints of the Three Teachings. They uphold the Dao like the Sun in the Heavens. Order this initiate's home always to be upright. I today swear that I will never backslide. Prostrating to all ten directions I will be able to enlarge my humanity (*ren*). Being humane, I will not seek only to refine my own nature but will search everywhere for signs of mercy. Where in the Void is there not the Dharma Body? Where is there a speck of dust in the Void? People all have a nature of the Void. All people have a body of the Merciful Revered One. Everyone will return [to the Way]. Everyone will believe deeply! Everyone will enter the Three in One. Forever and ever, world without end.

The liturgy suggests a simple ritual structural process involving (1) the establishment of an altar; (2) the invitation of the gods; (3) presentation of the memorial to the gods, asking for their blessings for the marriage; (4) recitation of scripture; (5) offerings to the gods; (6) send off of the gods; (7) deconstruction of the altar. The ritual also inscribes itself within the Confucian temporality of the patriline ("may my humble home and family . . . extend forever like the tangled vines of a melon plant"). Yet the recitation of the *Scripture of Fundamental Substance* and several comments in the liturgy re-

---

[7] This memorial is taken from the *Wuben guitiao* (Regulations of the Wuben Hall) list of formularies for memorials and proclamations. The reference to the People's Republic reveals that the formularies have been updated for contemporary use. The memorial is burned after being recited.

garding the need for initiates to devote themselves to self-cultivation and the expansion of the seed of spiritual power and humanity point to alternative temporalities—the time of inner alchemical self-cultivation, and the time of active moral striving. Reference is made at the beginning of the liturgy to the time and space before the division of heaven and earth, wherein glows spontaneously the chaotic radiance. If this is an image of antitemporality as noted in Turner and Turner (1986), it is one that is paradoxically the very basis of human conception (the dot of spiritual power) and thus of temporal progression, as well as being the final object of the search for enlightenment.

Appendix 6 provides two lists of the rituals performed on an annual basis by the Three in One ritualists who belong to a particular temple that has absorbed a large number of local gods. The list of the Jade Pool Academy in Hanjiang, a center of Wuben branch activity, posts 34 ritual events a year. Of these, over a third are rituals dedicated to the founder and disciples of the Three in One. The second set, from the Mingxia branch in the Seven Star Shrine of Fengting, calls for 69 rituals each year to be held at the temple. Many more popular gods are included in the list. The list does not include the rituals performed at other satellite Three in One shrines by ritualists in the temple, nor does it include rituals performed for families or individuals. Furthermore, this list does not include spirit-writing sessions, which can be arranged upon request virtually every day. The *Xiangyang shuyuan Ru Dao Shi shengdan* (Sacred birth dates of the Confucian, Daoist and Buddhist [deities worshiped at the] Xiangyang Academy) lists 152 different dates celebrated annually, with 8 more feast days for gods worshiped on side altars.

RITUAL TIME (2A): RITUAL STRUCTURES OF THE WUBEN BRANCH

The following is an outline of the ritual tradition of the Wuben branch. The *Xiawunishi Sanyijiaozhu pudu famen jinshu sheke chuandao kaijing shuofa guitiao* (Carefully recorded regulations of the Ritual Gate for Universal Deliverance of the Lord of the Three in One, Master Xiawunishi for the establishment of the liturgies, the transmission of the Way, the reciting of scriptures, and the preaching of the Law) (preface, Guangxu 9 [1883], undated manuscript copy from the Shandetang in the collection of Mr. Chen Jiaojing) provides an overview of the ritual documents used in the Wuben tradition of the Three in One (see below). In general, rituals in the Wuben tradition may be divided into two categories: *xishi* or *jingyan* (auspicious events, or scriptural recitations), and *sangshi* or *chanyan* (requiems, or Recitation of Litanies). The ritual tradition is further divided by Three in One practitioners into the following categories:

1. *Jieyuan* or *Jiexie* (Rituals for the atonement of past wrongdoings) Considered to be auspicious events, these rituals can sometimes be rites of thanksgiving upon the recovery from illness

2. *Anqing* (Setting in place the auspicious) Rites for the temporary setting of god statues on an altar prior to their consecration

3. *Kaiguang* (Opening up to the light) Rites for the consecration of god statues and temples

4. *Gaojun* (Announcement of completion) Rites for the announcement of the completion of the construction and consecration of a temple

5. *Chanxiu shoujie* (Practice of the confessional litanies and acceptance of the prohibitions) Rites for the promotion of a *zhangjiao* to a higher level

6. *Baoben* (Responding to one's origins) Rites for the repayment of one's obligations to one's ancestors; primarily requiem services

7. *Pudu* (Universal deliverance) Rites for the salvation of the hungry and homeless ghosts, performed in the Xinghua region primarily at the *xiayuan* (Lower Prime), the 15th of the 10th month, rather than at the *zhongyuan* (Central Prime), the 15th of the 7th month, as in Minnan regions and many other parts of China.[8]

Most of these rituals are variations on the following core set of scripture recitations:

1. *Kai jingxun* (half day)
2. *Kai sinijing* (one and a half days)
3. *Kai xiawu cuanyaojing* (two and a half days)
4. *Kai Xiawujing* (three, five, or seven days and nights)

For example, the *Kai jingxun* for a Baoben ritual begins in the early afternoon and includes the following rites:

1. *Jiantan* (establishment of the altar)
2. *Zhaohun* (summoning of the souls)
3. *Jianzu* (offerings to the ancestors)
4. *Xiao sini* (recitation of the abbreviated Scripture of the Four Ni Sages)
5. *Jingxun* (recitation of the Essence of the Xiawuni Scriptures)

---

[8] The order of rites for a Xiayuan Lanpen ritual held at the Zongkongtang (Dongshanci) in 1989 was as follows: Jingtan (Purification of the Altar), Qigu (Opening Drums), Qijian (Opening Construction of the Altar), Sini (Four Teachings Scripture), Sanguan (Three Official Scripture), Shierguan (Twelve Luminences Scripture), Zhaohun (Summoning of the Souls), Rujing (Confucian Scriptures), Yuzhu ([Taoist] Scripture of the Jade Pivot), Diamond Sutra, Jingxun ([Selected] Admonitions from the Xiawuni Scriptures), Xieengong (Offerings to Give Thanks for the Grace of the Gods), Beidou (Scripture of the Northern Dipper), Chaocan ([Morning] Audience Hymns), Mituo (Amita Sutra), Pumen (Pumen Scripture), Yangfan (Raising of the [Soul Summoning] Banner), Dizang Shiye (The Ten Karmic Scripture of Ksitigarbha), Shi Wang jinjing (Presentation of Respects to the Ten Kings [of the Underworld]), Zhonggong (Noon Offering), Shuichan (Water Litany, in three parts), Xiayuanchan (Litany of the Lower Prime), Zhongshi (Middle Dispensation [Feeding of the Hungry Ghosts]), Fazou (Sending the Memorial), Xuepen (Blood Bowl Scripture), Shuideng ([Sending of the] Lamps on the Water), Xiaojing (Scripture of Filial Piety), Jiulian (Rite of Nine Lotuses), Jifu (Sacrifices to the Master), Gongling (Offerings to the Spirits), Beidou (Scripture of the Northern Dipper), Wanke (Concluding Liturgy).

6. *Sanhui chanwen* (recitation of the Litany of the Threefold Association of the Dragon Flower Assembly)

7. *Pushi* (universal distribution of food to the hungry ghosts)

8. *Wanjian jianzu* (evening offering to the ancestors)[9]

In addition to the performance of rituals featuring extensive recitation of scriptures, the Wuben ritual tradition occasionally concurrently holds *jiangjing* (explications of the scriptures/classics) sessions, which are reminiscent of the activities of the Ming School of Mind philosophers. During one such multiplex ritual event at the Ruiyun shuyuan (Academy of Auspicious Clouds) in 1988, the explication of scriptures was conducted simultaneously with a standard ritual (*daochang*) held at a nearby temple. Three elderly Three in One adherents took turns reading from the *True Record*, the *Collected Drafts from the Eastern Mountain*, and short passages from the *Linzi sanjiao zhengzong tonglun* (Master Lin's discussions on the combination of correct principles of the Three Teachings). Passages were first read out, explained, and then related to the current situation of the Three in One. There were three interrelated themes raised. The first concerned the elevation of the virtuous character of all adherents. The second concerned the need for initiates to respect the teachings of the Lord, to combine inner cultivation and refinement of outer conduct, to elevate and improve their virtue, and not to asso-

---

[9] The order of rituals in the *Kai sinijing* is as follows: (1) *Jiantan* (establishment of the altar); (2) *Kai sinijing* (recitation of the Four Ni Scriptures); (3) *Jinbiao* (presentation of the memorial); (4) *Zhaohun* (summoning of the souls); (5) *Jianzu* (offerings to the ancestors); (6) *Xiaojing* (recitation of the Classic of Filial Piety); (7) *Daodejing* (recitation of the Way and its power); (8) *Jingangjing* (recitation of the Diamond Sutra); (9) *Wugong* (Noon offering) with chanting of the thirty-six hymns; (10) *Jingxun* (recitation of the essence of the Xiawuni Scriptures); (11) *Sanhui chanwen* (recitation of the litany of the Threefold Association of the Dragon Flower Assembly); (12) *Pushi* (universal distribution of food to the hungry ghost); (13) *Wanjian jianzu* (evening offering to the ancestors). If the Sini rite is being used for a Yulan pudu, the Xinhaijing (Heart of the Sea Sutra) is added. For the requiem service for a woman who has died in childbirth, the Xuebenjing (Blood Pool Sutra) is recited. This rite requires a *zongchi*, or at least a *zhangjiao* or *zhutan*, to preside, and eight initiates to assist.

For the *Kai xiawu cuanyaojing*, the sequence of rites takes two days, requires the participation of twenty-five initiates, and begins at midnight: (1) establishment of the altar; (2) presentation of the memorial; (3) summoning of the souls; (4) offerings to the ancestors; (5) recitation of the Scripture of the Four Ni Sages; (6) recitation of the essence of the Xiawuni Scriptures, in four parts; (7) recitation of the litany of the Threefold Association of the Dragon Flower Assembly; (8) universal distribution of food to the hungry ghosts; (9) evening offering to the ancestors.

For a *Kai Xiawujing* rite, the sequence takes three days and nights, eight *zhangjiao*, and twelve or twenty-four assistants. The sequence of rites is: (1) establishment of the altar; (2) presentation of the memorial rite for major services; (3) summoning of the souls; (4) offerings to the ancestors; (5) recitation of the full text of the major Confucian, Daoist, Buddhist, and Xia scriptures; (6) recitation of the litany of the Threefold Association of the Dragon Flower Assembly; (7) universal distribution of food to the hungry ghosts for three, or five, or seven successive nights, followed by (8) evening offering to the ancestors. The text points out that any ritual lasting longer than nine days and nights would exhaust the ritualists as well as the sponsors and their guests.

ciate with those who would bring disgrace to the Three in One. The third point was to firm up their beliefs, to carry out the teachings of the Lord, and to promote the official recognition of the Three in One by the government at every opportunity (Lin, 1994: 17).

RITUAL TIME (2B): RITUAL STRUCTURES OF THE MINGXIA BRANCH

The Mingxia branch of the Three in One has an even richer liturgical tradition than the Wuben branch. Borrowing extensively from local Daoist ritual traditions, they distinguish between communal sacrifices (*jiao*) and requiems (*chan*). In the terms of the Three in One, the Wuben branch practices *wendaochang* ("civil" rituals—i.e., scripture recitation), while the Mingxia branch performs *wudaochang* ("martial" rituals—i.e., rituals featuring dance movements, music, elaborate ritual actions, etc.). The sequence of rituals for a Mingxia *Qingcanhui* (Assembly of Auspicious Praise for the day of attainment of the Dao by Lord Xiawuni) held on lunar 7/16, 1994, in the Sanyijiao Minghemiao (Brilliant Lotus Temple) near Fengting, Xianyou, was as follows:

DAY 1

    1. *Qijian* (Establishment of the altar)
    2. *Sini* (Recitation of the Sinijing)
    3. *Sanguan* (Recitation of the Scripture of the Three Officials)
    4. *Zhongyuan Diguan chizei baochan* (Recitation of the Precious Litany of the forgiveness of sins by the Official of the Earth on the Central Prime)
    5. *Rujing* (Recitation of the Confucian Scripture)
    6. *Yushu* (Recitation of the Jade Pivot Scripture)
    7. *Xiawu jingxun* (Recitation of the Abstract of the Xiawu Scriptures)
    8. *Jingangjing* (Recitation of the Diamond Sutra)
    9. *Xuantian Shangdi jing* (Recitation of the Scripture of the High Emperor of the Dark Heavens)
    10. *Xiaoshi* (Minor distribution [of food to the hungry ghosts])
    11. *Beidou jing* (Recitation of the Northern Pole Scripture)
    12. *Jingong* (Presentation of offerings)

DAY 2

    1. *Shengxing yiwen* (Liturgy for the presentation of sacrifices and offerings)
    2. *Sanjiao zhushou yiwen* (Three Teachings liturgy for birthday congratulations)
    3. *Wugong* (Noon offering)
    4. *Dizang Rensheng daye yiwen* (Liturgy of the Lord of the Underworld)
    5. *Jieyuan yiwen* (Liturgy for the resolution of conflicts)

A typical three-day ritual (requiem) performed by the Mingxiapai would involve the following:

DAY 1

    1. *Yushu jing* (Scripture of the Jade Pivot)
    2. *Yuhuangjing* (Scripture of the Jade Emperor)
    3. *Sanguanjing* (Scripture of the Three Officials [of Heaven, Earth, and Water])
    4. *Sinijing* (Scripture of the Four Sages)
    5. *Lingguan Tiansheng Jing* (Scripture of the Divine Official, the Heavenly Sage)
    6. *Zitongjing* (Scripture of the God of Zitong [Wenchang dijun])
    7. *Guansheng jing* (Scripture of the Sage Guan [Gong])

DAY 2

    1. *Kai jingchan* (Opening up of the scriptures and litanies)
    2. *Zao chao* (Morning audience)
    3. *Yuhuang can* (Praise poem for the Jade Emperor)
    4. *Jinggong* (Offering ritual)
    5. *Jingxun* (Recitation of the essence of the Xiawuni Scriptures)
    6. *Yanshen* (Feasting of the gods)
    7. *Pushi* (Universal distribution of food to the hungry ghosts)
    8. *Qi wufu* (Prayers for the five happinesses)
    9. *Zhudeng* (Blessing of the lamp)
    10. *Baidou qifu* (Worship of the Dipper stars and prayer for good fortune)
    11. *Song shen* (Send off of the gods)

DAY 3

    1. *Zaochao* (Audience ritual)
    2. *Dagong* (Offering ritual)
    3. *Sheng tian* (*chaodu*) (Ascension to heaven, in a requiem service)
(the latter could involve a *Jiulian* [Nine Lotus] ritual, depending on the cost and complexity of the ritual)

A typical Mingxia requiem service would involve the following rites:

    1. *Jingyan* (Stilling of the altar)
    2. *Fazou jinbiao* (Announcement of the document and presentation of the memorial)
    3. *Gongyin qingshen* (Welcoming of the gods)
    4. *Anwei* (Settling into place of the gods)
    5. *Shoujiao* (Receiving of instructions)
    6. *Ranghua* (Flowers of prayer)
    7. *Songnian Dongyue Wenchang* (Recitation of the scripture of the God of the Eastern Peak and Wenchang)
    8. *Zhaohun* (Summoning of the spirit)
    9. *Oianta* (Dragging of the tower)
    10. *Songnian Sanpin* (Recitation of the Three Categories)
    11. *Pushi* (Universal Distribution [of food to hungry ghosts])
    . . .

17. *Jiulianjing* (Recitation of the Nine Lotus Sutra)
18. *Dizangjing* (Recitation of the Ksitigarbha Sutra)
19. *Ji jiaofu* (Offerings to the sedan chair bearers)
20. *Gong Zu* (Offerings to the ancestor)
21. *Huaqiao* (Transformation [by fire] of the sedan chair)
22. *Beidoujing* (Recitation of the North Pole Scripture)
24. *Songshen* (Send off of the gods)

The Mingxia ritual tradition includes elaborate pudu (ulambhama) rituals, usually performed around lunar 10/15, the Lower Prime. There are also rites for consecration (*kaiguang*), gods' birthdays (*shengdan*), and thanksgiving (*xie tiandi*). The most complete ritual troupes within the Mingxia branch claim to be able to perform a six-, seven-, or eight-day *Lianghuang can*. The most complex ritual usually performed is the five-day *Wuzhe dahui* (first yin then yang). There is also the four-day-long version of the *Yulan penhui* involving first yang rites and then yin rites.

In rites such as the *Wuzhe dahui,* the ritualists first beat the drum, then set up altar tables. Next they explode firecrackers, burn spirit money, and perform music (three drumbeats and three blasts of the *sona* oboe). The ritual begins with the establishment of the altars. This is followed by the purification of the ritual space (*qingjing*). Then comes the *dianhu shima* (the lighting of candles and incense and the feeding of [paper] horses) during the *fazou* (announcement of the memorial) or *jinbiao* (presentation of the *biao* memorial). This involves sending off three *han* (rectangular, boxlike paper envelopes) addressed respectively to the Jade Emperor, the Great Emperor of the Eastern Peak, and the Lord of the Three in One. Various other documents are also set off (*Fa guanwen, tudi tie,* etc.). An Invitation to the Gods is then addressed to the Jade Emperor of Heaven; the Three Officials of Heaven, Earth, and Water, the city gods, the earth gods of the canton and the local altar of grain, the Three Transmitters and the Four Attendants, and the adherents of the Confucian, Daoist, Buddhist, and Xia paths.

RITUAL SPACES (1)

Ritual space can be conceived in several ways.[10] At the most immediate, it involves a body or a group of bodies moving through prescribed gestures and

---

[10] Ritual space is not composed of fixed places or set fields. These places are made into space by the movements that pass through and transform them (vectors, trajectories, temporal changes). Space is practiced place (De Certeau, 1984), created by the forces that collide and are constrained to move within and through it. A number of theorists have underlined the importance of a differentiated approach to space. Henri Lefevre (1991) isolates material spatial practices (experience), representations of space (perceptions), and spaces of representation (imagination) and then discusses these three dimensions in terms of accessibility and distanciation, the appropriation and use of space, the domination and control of space, and the production of space. Bourdieu (1977: 89) comments that it is through the "dialectical relationship between the body

patterns within a field configured with symbols charged with cultural meanings. Each body opens up space by actualizing one vector out of the virtual sum of all motion. These movements open up space by charging space with the forces moving through the bodies of the participants. A good example of this is the group dance of the Three in One ritualists discussed below. Another simple instance is the establishment of an altar within a temple or in a private home, which reconfigures the relationship of spaces and forces within the architectural structure. At another level, the spatial layout of the altars and gods within a temple is a permanent arrangement of ritual space that channels the flows of worshipers in and through the temple.

The participation of Three in One groups in rituals that take place in public spaces of a village (or occasionally in a village ritual procession) is yet another form of the generating of ritual space. At yet another level, Three in One temples are involved in a complex spatial relationship with the other sites of charged power in the community. They are also involved in various nested hierarchies and spatial networks of temples. Circuits of shared ritual activity or interaction between sets of Three in One temples constitute another level of ritual space. These spatial links between temples and across communities can take place in either an incense-division line or a circuit fashioned by the sharing of ritual resources. In the latter case, key annual rituals will be performed over several days in different locales to allow an adequate number of ritualists to be drawn together for each ritual-event. These spatial relations often are reaffirmed by joint participation at the consecration of a new or

---

and a space structured according to the mythico-ritual oppositions that one finds the form par excellence of the structural apprenticeship which leads to the em-bodying of the structures of the world, that is the appropriating by the world of a body thus enabled to appropriate the world." These approaches tend, however, either toward a universalized conception of space or to a narrowing of the scope of transformative spatial operations (the transformation of space) into a "durably installed generative principle of regulated improvisation" (Bourdieu, 1977: 163). For the purposes of this study, the concepts of deterritorialization and reterritorialization in the works of Deleuze and Guattari (1989) provide more flexible tools for the analysis of the specific historical situation of the Three in One. The Three in One constantly exfoliated new spaces through ritual-events in a fluctuating field of power relations. Imperial power declined during Lin Zhao'en's lifetime, then was consolidated in a new way under the early Qing emperors, and then continued to evacuate certain local arenas of power relations throughout the late Qing. This had less to do with dynastic cycles than with fundamental transformations of the economy and the nature of imperial taxation and local control. Subsequent efforts to appropriate ritual spaces by the modernizing nation state in the Republican period met with innovative forms of resistance (see Duara, 1995; chap. 3). Into these shifting grounds, the Three in One deterritorialized elements of Confucian, Daoist, and Buddhist ritual machines, and reterritorialized them in new contexts. In terms of the analysis of ritual events outlined in chapter 1, ritual space is opened up with ritual-events by the fields generated by the attractive force of the various synaesthetic and intensive nuclei of expression. These nuclei of expression are regions of collective being. A nucleus of expression borders itself by constituting a center of attraction that delimits a space-time synaesthetic region. Within this region created by the center of attraction, some of the actual formations sharing the same ritual space are excluded or filtered or backgrounded. The center of attraction is the product of a technology of attention (a sensorial/desiring capture of bodies, a fascination or seduction, an induction of a "passion" as in Spinoza's *Ethics* [Curley, 1994]).

newly repaired temple. Annual or semiannual incense-presentation processions by almost all local Three in One temples to the Honorable Confucius Hall on East Mountain in Putian or to the gravesite of Lin Zhao'en or other major figures in the Three in One tradition (i.e., Chen Zhida's tomb near the Wubentang) provide another spatial network based on a central node. Another space opened up by ritual is that of the ritual marketplace. This section goes on to consider the spaces opened up by the circulation (and immolation) of ritual documents, and the spaces of visualization. Finally, the section returns to an examination of liturgical dance, where many of these spaces are synthesized and produced.

RITUAL SPACES (2): THE RANGE OF THE RITUAL MARKET

As mentioned above, another dimension of ritual space concerns the spatial links between temples or teams of ritualists based in particular temples. Each of the temples we have discussed has a certain ritual scope, an area, or a set of temples with which it maintains ritual ties of different kinds. These may be ties based on the division of incense, or they may be ties of mutual aid, or they may represent a ritual clientele, or a local ritual cycle. Certain groups of ritualists based in temples such as the Yushan and Puguang temple in Bangtou, or the Daxing temple in Xianyou, or the Qixing and Zhandou temples in

CHART I
Arrangement of an Altar for a Requiem Service in the Wuben Tradition

Prior Heaven (the unformed world)
The Void
Scriptures and Litanies / Ten Halls of the Underworld / Buddhist Heavens / Three Daoist Officials of Heaven, Earth, and the Waters / Protector of the Faith
The Auspicious One
Dashi (demonic representation of Guanyin)
Dragon Flower Assembly
Table of the Supreme Ultimate, also the Table of the Scriptures
Original Substance
Three Realms
Latter Heaven (the revealed world)
Each Family / Liang Puyao / City God / Treasures of the Xia Tradition / Golden Portals of the Star Palaces / Principal Sacrifier / Chen Zhida / Gods of the Cantons and Earth God Temples
For more elaborate rituals, the numbers of gods in each level can be expanded.

CHART 2
An Altar Laid Out for a Mingxia Qingcanhui

Top of Front Altar:
Patriarch of the Central Xia
Realized Being, Zhuo (Wanchun); Confucian Masters
Assembled Saints of the Scripture Altar; Assembled Saints to Whom
Offerings Are Made

Middle of Front Altar
Guanyin Dashi
Xietian Dadi, Immortal Master Yu
Immortal Master Zhang, Immortal Master Jin

Deities at the Front of the Front Altar (listed from left to right):
Ciji zhenjun (Baosheng Dadi); the Great Man Zuo; the Great Man Li; Tian Gong
Yuanshuai; the Great Man Guo; the Great Man Wan; the Three Wangye; the Great
Man Jin; the Great Man Yu; Guangze zunwang; Princess Baihua; Princess Yang;
Princess Yuan

Left Altar
Master of the Theater; Master of the Communal Sacrifice

Right Altar
Reverent Spirits of the Taisui, Who Revere the Three Teachings

Back Altar/Front (listed from left to right):
Dashi, ershi (Messengers); the Brilliant King (Earth God) of the Li (Subcanton); the
City God; the General Who Protects the Ritual and Protects the Way;
the Naga Who Protects the Dharma; the Saintly King Jialan

Back of the Back Altar:
Xuantian Shangdi;
The Great Emperors of the Three Offices (of Heaven, Earth and Water); the Great
Emperor of the Earth

Outside in Front of the Temple:
The Dashi Who Opens Up the Teachings

Fengting, offer their ritual services to a wide range of communities in their
vicinity.

A manuscript from the Fengting Zhandouci entitled *Pu Xian Hui gecun
gongshe pu* (Record of the temples and community shrines of each village in
the Putian, Xianyou, Huian) list sixty-one temples and communal shrines
where Three in One ritualists based in that shrine perform rituals on an annual basis. Most of these are in the surrounding area, with sixteen just across
the county line in the Eleventh Du of Hui'an County and fourteen in the adjoining Tangan Township. Each address is given in the following form: *xian*
(county), *xiang* (township), *li* (traditional subcantons established in the Ming
dynasty), *cun* (village), *gong* (main village temple), *she* (altar of the soil marking a specific neighborhood or community). Some addresses also list the *jing*

Plate 15. Painting of Lin Zhao'en and disciples upon a boat, saving souls, for use in ritual. Yellow envelopes in front of the painting are invitations to gods to visit the altar (from a Wuben rite in Hanjiang).

(local spiritual precinct covering an alliance of several village temples) and, if the temple is in a city, the *pu* (ward).

These are by no means all the temples with which the Zhandouci maintains relations. For one thing, all of these are temples or communal shrines dedicated to local gods, rather than other Three in One temples. The Zhandouci has many other ritual exchanges with other Three in One temples. Moreover, the Three in One ritualists of the Zhandouci are not the only ritual specialists invited to the temples on their list. The existence of a set of temples in which they operate does suggest, however, that they have captured a corner of the ritual market in the area and are performing rituals for a wide variety of local village temples. Daoist priests in this area keep similar handbooks, and it would be interesting to attempt to map out the respective range and frequency of the rituals performed by these traditions. There is nothing to prevent simultaneous, parallel performance of rituals by Daoists, Buddhists, and Three in One Masters. Indeed, such an occasion would be especially renowned. It is in fact this capacity for duplication and repetition that allowed the Three in One to develop a parallel ritual tradition in the first place.

Another aspect of ritual geography was referred to earlier in the discussion of the division of incense. Certain Three in One shrines maintain a cycle of rituals within a set area in which they all participate, by hosting the rite or by sending representatives or officiants. Such events are announced by invitation cards, which are often posted in the shrines to inform the initiates. Some shrines keep posted lists of the dates and locations of the major rituals performed in their expanded ritual area, such as the Feast of Deliverance of the Hungry Ghosts.[11]

RITUAL SPACES (3): THE PRESENTATION OF INCENSE

While the movement of troupes of ritual specialists from particular temples to a wide range of community temples represents a scattered centripetal flow-chart of spatial relations, the presentation of incense by Three in One temples at the grave of Lin Zhao'en and at the Dongshan Zongkongtang is a centrifugal flow of massive proportions. Several hundred temples make these pilgrimages annually at the birth and death dates of Lin Zhao'en (lunar 1/16 and 7/15, respectively). The 1948 manuscript from the Daxingci in Xianyou gives an account of a ritual presentation of incense pilgrimage that Huang Chengyi participated in during 1928. We read that in 1928 the Dongshanci held a great assembly attended by two to three thousand representatives from over many Three in One temples. Buddhist and Daoist delegates were also present. A delegation of twenty-four people led by a juren named Xiao Heyi proceeded to the Dongshan Zongkongtang from the Daxingci, stopping at major Three in One temples along the way. When they arrived they began to perform a ritual. They were stopped, and people claimed that their ritual was unorthodox. The disputing parties went to the last Putian *jinshi*, Zhang Qin, for mediation. He examined the ritual texts and declared that their ritual was indeed orthodox. Subsequently, the leader of their delegation was made the chief master in charge of the ritual for the entire celebration.

As mentioned in the introduction, current celebrations on the birthday of Lin Zhao'en (1/16) at the Dongshanci Zongkongtang are exuberant events. Delegations come from all over, mostly in tractor-carts, carrying their incense

---

[11] Thus, for example, the Wubentang maintains a list of some twenty-five temples in the Hanjiang and Jiangkou area with which it collaborates on a series of rituals around the major nodes (the Three Primes: lunar 1/15, 7/15, and 10/15). Ritualists from the Wubentang join the scattered ritualists at these smaller temples to ensure a ritual quorum. This pooling of resources extends to sharing of expenses, expertise, ritual documents, and, of course, human relations (*renqing*).

burners in a small wooden replica temple. This is placed on the altar in the temple while they burn incense, set out offerings, make contributions to the main temple, collect talismans, and set off firecrackers. Often they are accompanied by a musical troupe. Finally, they retrieve their spiritually recharged incense burners and return home to further celebrations. Delegations come and go all day, numbering in the hundreds. Elaborate ceremonies are also performed on the death date at the tomb of Lin Zhao'en in Huating.

RITUAL SPACES (4): THE CIRCULATION OF RITUAL DOCUMENTS

Yet another dimension of ritual space is established by the production and oblation of a wide range of ritual documents. Ritual documents proliferate in Chinese village life, and the Three in One has added its own set to those circulated by Daoist priests, Buddhist monks, Confucian masters of ceremony, lineage halls, sectarian groups, spirit-writing associations, temple committees, and a vast array of other local specialists whose trade involves some ritual manipulation of texts (geomancers, medical practitioners, carpenters, theatrical troupes, musicians, etc.). Ritual documents are circulated and consumed in many different forms and media. Most of the documents are burnt, it is said, in order to transmit them to the gods.

The liturgical manuscripts explicitly state that the smoke of incense rises to the heavens and attracts the gods. The representation of the gods as inhabiting contiguous realms (the heavens, the underworld) that can be reached by scented smoke, or by transformation by fire (*hua*) expands the parameters of space and fundamentally affects the orientation of the individual bodies generating space through their ritual gestures and movements. Communication between these spheres is achieved via the burning of talismanic messenger, (paper figurines) and texts, or by the revelation of scripture, or through spirit-writing or possession. This communication, when regularized, routinized, and ritualized, is modeled on court protocol. Moreover, the most powerfully charged texts are often indecipherable talismans or unintelligible spells or mantras. These texts are oversignifying: they represent an excess of signification, an overflow of spiritual power, which cannot be contained but can be redirected for immediate and local uses. The sacrifice of texts interrupts the downward flow of signification of the bureaucratic metaphor. The downward flow of meaning is at once interrupted and yet immediately reconnected to the creation of a multitude of local meaning. The sacrifice of texts, like the burning of spirit money, is a form of the sacrifice of meaning.[12]

[12] Detailed materials on the ritual documents in use in the Wuben branch can be found in the *Xiawunishi Sanyijiaozhu pudu famen jinshu sheke chuandao kaijing shuofa guitiao* (Carefully recorded regulations of the Ritual Gate for Universal Deliverance of the Lord of the Three in One, Master Xiawunishi, for the establishment of the liturgies, the transmission of the Way, the reciting of scriptures, and the preaching of the Law), with appendices listing the formularies for proclamations and memorials for initiation (*rujiao*), celebratory rites (*qingcan*), scriptural recita-

RITUAL SPACES (5): VISUALIZATIONS AND SPELLS

Yet another ritual space of the Three in One is that opened up by visualizations. Through the practice of the heart method, the inner alchemical body is first elaborately visualized and explored and then shown to be a microcosm of the universe. For purposes of ritual, this microcosmic/macrocosmic link is crucial to the efficacy of the actions. Recall, however, that the final stages of the heart method require liberation from space (heaven and earth) as well as time (life and death). The paradox of nondifferentiation in spatial terms is expressed in terms of "merging with and then smashing the Void."

Although Three in One ritual visualizations and spells are somewhat less developed than those in use in the local Daoist tradition (see the illustration of a Daoist ascending to the star palaces of the Jade Emperor from a visualization handbook from Xianyou in Dean [1993: 49]), there is nevertheless a considerable overlapping. Many spells and visualizations were, however, originally developed for the process of internal alchemy (discussed above) and probably later applied to ritual practice. *Zhangjiao* at certain ritually active shrines keep secret a booklet of instructions (*mijue*) with mantras and special talismanic designs for use in ritual. These texts also provide the main officiant with a set of instructions on visualizations that should accompany the various ritual acts in which he is engaged. I was given permission to photograph one such anthology, entitled the *Sanjiao xinfa*. This text is a manuscript copy by a disciple of the Huibei (Northern Hui'an district) Fuyang Zongzhengci (Shrine of Ancestral Orthodoxy). The copy is in the collection of the Jingshantang (Mirror Mountain Hall) in Lindou village (see discussion of this temple in chapter 7). This temple was among the first founded by Lin Zhao'en and has been the source for many more branch temples, particularly during the Republican period. During that period, it was a major center of ritual practice in the coastal Xianyou area. A set of printed liturgical texts, dated 1926 and distributed from the Xianyou Scriptural Preservation Association—conceivably located in the Jinshantang (Gold Mountain Hall)—survives intact at this remote temple.

The text of the ritual meditation manual consists of 102 pages. The first pages described the qualifications of a *zhangjiao*, which primarily concern morality and integrity, as opposed to external fame, wealth, or position. Admonitions on the accurate composition of ritual documents follow. Next, some twenty pages are devoted to charts of different kinds of ritual spaces, such as charts 1 and 2 above. These include charts for *Sanyuan qingcan anhua* (flower charts of the positions of gods for Three Primes celebratory rituals in denom-

tions (*kaijing*), and announcement rites (*qiwen*), mentioned above. This text provides model forms for copying out proclamations (*bangwen*), memorials (*shuwen*), and documents (*die*) for a wide variety of purposes. These are summarized in appendix 5. A set of formularies for use in rituals dedicated to local gods in the Mingxia traditions is included in manuscripts listed in the bibliography. The preparation by hand of this elaborate ritual paperwork is an important and time-consuming part of every major ritual-event.

inations of three, four, and six). Charts for the setting out of altars for communal sacrifice (*jiao*) and penitential requiems (*chan*) are followed by *Beidou zhifu* (North Dipper planting of good fortune), celebratory rites of the Upper, Middle, and Lower Prime days (1/15, 7/15, and 10/15). Ksitigarbha Ullambana rites (*dizang lanpen*) with accompanying charts for the opening of the Way [for the deceased] by means of the Three Scriptures (*sanjing kailu*), the layout of a ritual space for a newly constructed Three in One Hall, and the dotting of the eyes for the illumination of the gods rite, and finally charts for elaborate *Longhua* (Dragon Flower) communal sacrifices and requiem services.

The remainder of the text consists of instructions and incantations for use by *zhangjiao* in the performance of these rituals. First we are given the opening sequence of prayers and visualization for use in the purification of the altar and the sending off of memorials and announcements to the gods. This is followed by instructions a wide variety of heart methods, or spells and visualizations to accompany and/or accomplish specific rituals acts.

The first set of methods relates to the liturgy for the presentation of the memorial (*Jinbiao yiwen*). This rite includes a preparatory rite called *Qijian anxiang* (initial construction of the altar and the setting in place of incense). The text of the announcement is provided. The ritual begins with the *heart method for the purification of the heart.* The main officiant visualizes his "seven apertures as clear, open, and clean. His complete sincerity is fixed in place. Completely concentrated and undistracted, for him time has come to a standstill. This is what is known as using thought to stop thought, in order to seek out the heart." By means of the heart method for the purification of the mouth, he visualizes that his breathing and sound and the breath of his mouth, throat, tongue, . . . and teeth are all cleansed so that no filthy breath will affront the saints. In the *heart method for the purification of the body,* the officiant visualizes that his five organs, even apertures, and four limbs are all originally breath of the fundamental Dao, which is eternally overbrimming. Ritual vestments must be kept clean so that not a speck of dust could sully them. Realizing that his heart and body have been purified, he then turns to the purification of his intentions through the *heart method for the purification of the three callings.*

Thereupon, the officiant, holding a stick of incense, bows toward heaven and invites the local tutelary deity, as well as those of the subcanton and the vicinity, and settles them in place in the western altar. After replacing the incense stick in the burner, he again lights three sticks of incense and reads the Earth God document (*die*). As the troupe of ritualists intones the *spell of the Earth God,* the main priest makes a prayer, stating that "I am upholding the orders of the Lord of the Teachings. All the gods pertaining to the nearby streams and mountains and altars of grain and soil all find your seats, and solemnly protect the sacred space (*daochang*). After that, transform the altar into a vast space, and ensure that the offerings are laid out neatly. The realm of the altar must be solemn, fit for the arrival of the saints. Sit still in your seats without moving."

Next, by means of the *heart method for the invitation of all the gods who protect the Dharma*, the officiant, holding incense, bows to the heavens eight times and reverently invites the generals who protect the Dao, messengers who oversee the fast and the scriptures, the gods of the day and of the altar, and all powerful spiritual forces in the vicinity to the altar to pool their strength to exorcise demonic sprites. They are also asked to protect the scriptures and the altar. The incense stick is returned to the burner.

This is followed by the *recitation of the Scripture of Original Substance* and the *invitation of water heart method*. After paying homage to the image of the Lord of the Teachings, the ritual master should use a sprig of "peach" to write in the air six talismans over the small container of water on the altar. These talismans are variations on simple cosmic diagrams representing Confucianism, Daoism, Buddhism, Heaven, Earth, and Mankind. Each symbol is accompanied by a spell: "This is the water of wisdom"; "This is the water of the gods"; "This is the water of ritual." (Certain of these talismans and spells are also used in different rituals to call down sweet dew, others to purify the sacred space, others to transform spirit money.) After the six talismans have been drawn in the air over the small, shallow vase of water, the characters "Spirit water illumines and purifies" are drawn too. Next the sprig is rotated three times to the left over the water, then inserted back into the vase. At this point, the officiant raises the vase up high and stands straight. He carefully envisions water rising up through the souls of his feet to his anus (or coccygeal channel; see Needham, 1983: 5.5: 203). From there it moves between the two kidneys three times. Rising along the spine, it moves through the Kunlun Pass (crown of the head) to enter the Niwan Palace. From the Cranial Gateway (Dingmen) and the Seal Terrace (Yintang), the waters flow down the Storied Tower (the trachea) into the Vase where they bubble up. In one's heart one thinks, "This water was drawn from the well of the Jade Capital on the Kunlun Mountains. It is completely pure. This is no ordinary water."

After this he begins to sprinkle water from the vase with the talismanic sprig. These actions are known as the *heart method for purification [of the altar]*. The main officiant, holding the vase of water, visualizes in his heart-mind that the water is divine water. Then, solemnly carrying forth the heart method of inner alchemy, he takes the sprig from the vase and first lustrates himself. Second, he cleanses "all the dirt between heaven and earth to make it pure for the carriages of the high saints. Third, he purifies the four corners and entranceways of the altar. Fourth, he purifies the tables and chairs, the fruits, tea, wine, and offerings. Fifth, he purifies the drummer and the woodwind players on the left and right. Sixth he lustrates the family of the chief sacrifiand. Seventh he purifies the team of ritualists and their assistants. Eighth, he purifies the storerooms, the stove, and the guests and helpers. Ninth, he purifies the well, the kitchen, the stage, and all props and utensils. Tenth, he purifies the nearest stream."

This is followed by the *heart method for the praying with incense,* in which the officiant kneels in front of the altar with a lit stick of incense and visualizes the smoke of incense curling and twirling throughout the ten directions straight up to the abode of the high saints. Next he returns the stick of incense to the incense burner, takes a bowl of liquor, and kneels with it before the altar. Then he pours a libation on the ground, visualizing that "the breath of the liquor rises from the ground at the center of the altar to the headquarters of the heavens, while simultaneously sinking to the headquarters of the earth and the waters. Thereby the saints and spirits of the three realms and the ten directions are all able to enjoy the breath of the liquor and be attracted to the altar."

This is followed by the *heart method for the universal summons*, which involves the reciting of a spell. Music sounds forth while the chief officiant bows and leads the retinue in kneeling and worshiping. Then he carries out the *heart method of the transformation of the body into the golden radiant [body]*. At this time he "imagines his body suffused with golden light, as eternal as the constant Dao. A man of complete sincerity can move material things. Above he can invite the saints to descend [to the altar]. In the middle realm he can look over the coming and going of the talismanic messengers. Below he can subdue demonic beings. If he be lacking in sincerity by a single hair, the golden glow will dissipate."

Next the officiant employs the *heart method for the transformation of foodstuffs* in which he sprinkles the offerings with divine water and visualizes the incense and offerings increasing infinitely. Next, employing the *heart method for the [summoning of] sweet dew*, he sprinkles the offerings again with the "waters of Confucian kindness and wisdom," transforming their taste with the sweetness of divine dew.

This is followed by the *heart method for invitation of the saints*. As the chief cantor (the deputy to the chief officiant) intones the phrase "The Lord of the Teachings is the Great Patriarch who saves the World," the main priest kneels and one by one visualizes the saints descending into their places at the altar. When they have taken their places he uses the *heart method for the providing of offerings*. Clasping his hands together in salute and then kneeling down, he invites the saints to partake of the offerings and bows to each three times in a row.

With this the purification of the altar and the invitation of the saints is complete. The manuscript next describes the visualizations, spells, and talismans that accompany the *liturgy for (the establishment of) an announcement of the memorial rite*. In this rite, the officiant reads out the memorial of invitation to the saints, sends out a universal invitation (*zhuang*), and presents the memorial and the accompanying documents (*guan*). First he performs the *heart method for summoning the talismanic officers* by setting his mind on inviting down to the altar the talismanic officers attached to the day of the rite, and the talismanic officers of three realms and the five directions of the assembly of the Four Masters (Confucius, Laozi, Śākyamuni, and Xiawuni). Then, standing in the center of the altar, he grasps the various ritual documents. He has certain ones burned to transmit them to the gods. He completes the invitation, the summons, the offering, three libations of wine, and the rewarding of the messengers before sending them off. The *heart method for sending off the talismanic officers* consists of the silent recitation of the spirit spell to transform the paper spirit-horse, "The *Qian* prime divided into images [split into the lines of the hexagrams of the *Book of Changes*], the Heavenly Horses let flow the essence. Should it [merely] revolve, it will not form bones, [but] upon combining, it will take shape. It transformed into eight steeds, who rode the radiances and flew upward. Take my divine water and rise high to Highest Purity (Taiqing)." He then writes three talismans.

Next the officiant performs the *sacred spell for the transformation of money:* "Heaven has a star of wealth, Earth has a spirit of wealth. Yin and Yang are the forge that creates success. In heaven and on earth, the most high communicate. Today I refine [the elixir], so that strings of cash and white [gold] are distinguished clearly. Qian. *Yuan heng li zhi. Om. Kun lu zhi di po a.*"

This is followed by the *heart method for the feasting of the gods.* The officiant places incense before the standing envelopes with the names of the invited gods inscribed upon them. He places incense on the altar of the sacrifice and of the scriptures. He also places incense before the paper horsemen who represent the talismanic officers. He reverently prostrates himself and worships. When the acolytes reach the line "the altar is purified, the gauze compartment is refined and solemn," he then stands up and joins in the worship. He beseeches the rules of the saints to command the [attendance] of the great gods. When the Reverent Taisui Astral God and other gods have all assembled and he has completed his offerings to them, the officiant picks up the papier-maché horse decorated with flags. He turns first to the Green Emperor in the East. While the deputy master of the altar intones the spell for the elimination of catastrophes and the [attainment] of good fortune, the chief officiant kneels and worships to the east, earnestly praying that the gods will provide to the patron of the sacrifice and his family or associates good health and well-being and eliminate adversity. After this the officiant moves up to the Fire Bureau of the Red Emperor of the South, and on to the White Emperor of the West, the Black Emperor of the North, and the Yellow Emperor of the Center, praying in a similar fashion in each quarter. As the deputy master intones, "The Five Stars array their lights," the officiant bows toward the north, east, south, center, and west. After making this round of bows, he reverently presents incense and flowers, then transforms spirit money and spirit horses by consigning them to flames.

These are the opening rituals of purification and invitation of the god.[13] Many other instructions on the meditations to accompany different ritual acts

[13] These could be compared with Daoist rituals of purification and invitation. Daoist ritual as practiced in Fujian and Taiwan generally involves a far more elaborate summoning of the Talismanic Officers, which are conceived of as gods within the body (Ofuchi, 1983; Lagerwey, 1987a; Schipper, 1993; Saso, 1978a, 1978b).

are included in the text and outlined in appendix 8. The following sheds further light on processes of visualization in Three in One ritual practice:

The *heart method for the Liturgy of the Universal Distribution [of Nourishment to the Hungry Ghosts]* begins with the invitation of the Lord of the Teachings onto the raised stage/altar by means of a silent gatha: "The Buddhas of the ten directions, with that one step, allow me to ascend the lotus flower precious dais." While reciting these lines silently, the officiant climbs onto the stage. There he sets out sticks of incense. Then as acolytes chant hymns, he kneels and silently recites the *Scripture of the Fundamental Substance*. Then he transforms the ritual space into an area vast enough to accommodate the hosts of orphan ghosts. He transforms the food to provide for this ghostly multitude. Only after having formed a very clear picture of these transformations does he rise. This is followed by a sequence of rites and accompanying visualizations, namely, the purification heart method, the heart method for the invitation of the Buddhist saints, and the heart method for the invitation of the Seven Future Buddhas. The latter process involves a series of visualizations. First the officiant sings out the [gatha of the] Precious Name of the Lord of the Teachings while visualizing that his body is the very body of the Lord. When he sings the Precious Name of the Humane Emperor, he visualizes his body as that of the Humane Emperor of the Underworld. When reciting Guanyin's Holy Name, he visualizes himself as Guanyin, and so on for Pumen Buddha. The recitation of the Three Officials (of the Heavens, Earth, and Waters) Gatha leads to a visualization of the illumination of the pathways of the Underworld. The Gatha of the Five Directions is accompanied by a visualization of the Buddhas of the Five Directions descending into the altar and showing forth their powers. He murmurs the spell "O mi ni hum" in each direction.[14]

LITURGICAL MUSIC AND DANCE AND THE GENERATION OF RITUAL SPACE-TIME

Distinct configurations of space and time in Three in One ritual emerge through liturgical dance and music. The musical traditions of the main branches of the Three in One are quite distinct. The Mingxia tradition has developed its own tunes and has its own instrumentation. The music of the Sanyi tradition and the Wuben tradition is much more derivative of the local regional opera, Puxian opera. The *Zongji keyi chu* (General collection of the song-tunes to the various rituals), a manuscript in the working collection of the Zhandouci near Fengting, Xianyou, provides notation for several tunes. Many of these are similar to the tunes and instrumental suites performed in

---

[14] A sizable number of Sanskrit-derived and pseudo-Sanskrit spells have made their way into Three in One ritual texts, such as the ubiquitous *Om mani padme hum* mantra. These mantras play a major role in the pudu texts attributed to Chen Zhongyu, the second transmitter.

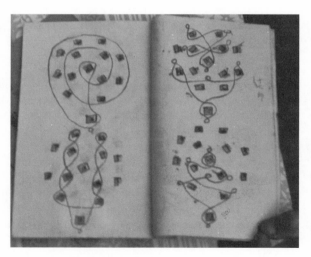

Plate 16. *Above:* The Orthodox Breath/Energy talisman. *Below:* Bird's-eye view of group ritual choreographic patterns from a *Huace* (Flower patterns) manuscript

the local *shiyin bayue* (ten sounds eight musics) instrumental ensemble music (Lin Chengbin, 1995).[15]

Another set of materials relates to the choreography of ritual dance in the Mingxia tradition. Texts entitled *huace* (flower-patterns) provide a bird's-eye view of the patterns to be traced by the procession of ritualists. These patterns trace certain shapes or illustrate abstract patterns, or certain figures such as the eight trigrams, or the character *shou* (longevity). Individual bodies are moving elements in a flowing line that traces patterns in space.[16]

The Three in One developed a range of ritual machines that open up space-time continuums through the performance of ritual-events. These machines combine parts and elements drawn from Confucian, Daoist, and Buddhist ritual to create a new alignment of the senses, capturing and channeling external and internal forces into the gestures, visualizations, incantations, and patterned, rhythmic movements of the disciplined bodies of the ritual participants. The liturgical texts of the Three in One contain stage directions, calling out to be recited, chanted, enacted. Some call out to be burnt and transformed. These texts overreach themselves, pointing to the synaesthetic flow of nonlinguistic elements that extend them into new spaces, new temporalities.

EARLY THEORIES OF RITUAL IN THE THREE IN ONE

Dong Shi's *Dongshan jicao* discusses several aspects of ritual behavior, providing justification for particular rituals, for the recitation of scripture and litanies, and for the worship of god statues. Dong provides a theory of ritual:

[15] Lin Chengbin (1995) notes the presence of the following tunes in both Three in One and *shiyin bayue*, basing himself on a Qing dynasty Qianlong period manuscript from the Juyingci (Shrine of the Gathered Heroes) in Kangbei village, Daqi Township, Xianyou. This text listed over two hundred tunes, including *Zuidiqin, Furongchen, Lanhuamei, Wanpailing, Xuang hudie, Xiao taohua, Zhuyunfei, Yiduoqiao, Zaoluopao, Qintingfang, Jiangtou jingui, Xi honghua, Chunjiang ci, Wang guxiang, Xiu huali, Gu tailun, Wugeng duan, Qi Yan Hui, Wu Jiaqi, Yan'er le, Putianle, Xiu ting zhen, Gun baigua, Yijiangfeng*. Instrumental suites included *Shangxia lou—nanci bai* and *Puochenzi—Yujia ao—Tieyingdeng*. Lin claims the *gongchipu* notation is very skeletal, lacking in ornamentation common in *shiyin bayue*, and thus may represent an earlier phase in the development of local music. Instrumentation is also more sober in Three in One ensembles than in *shiyin bayue* troupes. The question of the influence of Puxian theater on both these forms has yet to be adequately studied.

[16] This genre of group processional ritual dance is widespread in the Xinghua region. I have located similar materials in the collections of Daoist priests and spirit-medium altar associations (*tanban*). The earliest text discovered so far is a *huace* from the Daoist altar dated to Daoguang 29 (1860). Daoist texts related to the issuing of certificates to altar associates in northern Putian also date from the Daoguang period. *Tanban* manuscripts of a more recent date refer to these dance patterns as dancing the Nuo exorcism (*xingnuo*), and they are performed at Yuanxiao (Upper Prime Festival, around lunar 1/15) and during group initiation ceremonies. There is a reference to *xingnuo* in the Fengting Township gazetteer, but it is unclear whether this refers specifically to *tanban* dances led by spirit mediums or if it is merely a scholastic expression for the more common dance of the demons (*guizi wu*), a masked dance troupe frequently featured in New Year's processions throughout Xinghua. For further details, see Dean and Zheng (1993).

At one point, several gentlemen asked me, "The establishment of the Ullambana ritual has its origins in the Buddhist ritual texts. Formerly Master Lin also carried out [this ritual]. Since he did this, could you explain the meaning of doing it?" I replied to them, "This is nothing more than my imitating the filial piety practiced by Maudgalyāyana, who repaid his [debts to his] origins, in order to carry out my own filial piety. Next, by means of resolving obligations and untangling knots, I can carry out my righteousness. Next, by means of broadly uniting good [Karmic] causes, I can carry out my righteousness. Next, by means of broadly uniting good [Karmic] causes, I can carry out my humaneness. But all this is but one [minor] matter within the Teachings as a whole. Those who are excellent at embodying [these virtues] and carry them out [in ritual] have the Teachings within them as well as the Dao. What is the principle of this? If you push the meaning [of this] in order to extend humaneness, then the humaneness of my heart is born. Once the humaneness of my heart is born, then it can produce the perfected humaneness of all the ages under heaven, and thereby broadly carry forth my humaneness. [Similar arguments follow for righteousness and filial piety.] But if one does not embody these virtues and carries out rituals, then the Teachings are lost and so is the Dao. . . .if one is doing things in vain with empty words, you end up destroying the meaning of the words, and create a frivolous attitude. [Such people] carry out the tricks of [religious] masters and shamans and claim to be able to gather a great crowd of people who burn great clouds of incense. This is absolutely unnatural. Most realize that if the Dao is illumined then the heart is correct, and if the heart is correct then nothing you do will be incorrect. (Preface to the *Xianyou City Three in One Hall Ullambana Ritual, Dongshan jicao* 1.32–33)

Dong Shi goes even further in another text:

THE 1666 JINSHAN [GOLD MOUNTAIN (SHRINE)] ULLAMBANA RITUAL

Having something that is of benefit to the Teachings, but when carrying it out instead bringing harm to the brilliant Teachings, this is something that has gone on forever. . . . For example, there is the issue of the Ullambana ritual. Formerly Mulian used it to save his mother, but it is hard to use it to save one's brother. Now one needn't discuss the humaneness of saving one's mother or one's brother. However, when one flatters nameless ghosts, good customs do not ensue. When one piles up phrases and uses one's heaven-sent resources to seek after profit and paradises, and when one's considerations extend so far as to those to whom one is unrelated, then what is in name compassion is in reality sheer cruelty. What appears pure on the surface is venal within. The thoughtlessness of all this is profound! Since this shrine was built in Xianyou City in 1653, four or five years have passed without the celebration of an Ullambana ritual. I was not worried by this, nor was I delighted to hear that the disciples plan to hold it now. What is the reason for this? I am afraid that the multitude that follow the flow [of common custom] will in fact cause harm to my illustrious and orthodox great teachings. If there are those among the disciples who on entering can be filial to their parents and friendly to their elder brothers, and on leaving can illumine the seriousness of righteousness and profit, then the defense against disgrace rests within the square inch of the heart. [Such people] will support the old, teach the misguided, and in every matter seek the truth. If everyone thus moves toward the true, what use is there in reciting the scriptures? If the Great Heavens are already pleased, what point is there in speaking the Dharma? Moreover, the ghosts and gods will have no worries. Whereas what does not please me now pleases me, and what I did not worry about now worries me. Thus on the question of whether or not the Ullambana ritual can change local customs and rectify people's hearts and maintain the worldly [moral] teachings, I dare say that it neither increases these things nor fills in any insufficiency in them. Indeed, such would be unnatural! This is my preface. (*Dongshan jicao* 1.45–46)

Another passage in the collection discusses the recitation of scriptures:

ESSENTIAL POINTS ON THE UPHOLDING OF SCRIPTURE

Scripture is the verification of my heart. Therefore one can comprehend the meaning beyond the words. From one sentence to and 100 million, although I know that this scripture was not written by me but by saints, sages, immortals and Buddhas, and clearly shows the aspect given it by its family of origin, yet still it is as though there were no words or sentences at all. When it is like this, one can be said to be excellent at upholding the scriptures. The next best are those who uphold the scriptures in accordance with which they dare not allow anything outside it in. From one sentence to one hundred million, if it speaks of retribution, then they understand retribution; if it speaks of cause and effect, then they understand cause and effect; if it speaks of wisdom and enlightenment, then they understand wisdom and enlightenment. Although [dependent on] words and phrases, still they too can be said to be excellent upholders of the scriptures. But if one does not understand wisdom and enlightenment, retribution and cause and effect, but merely seeks after benefit of rapidly attaining paradise and languishing there, then from one sentence to one hundred million, it is all a waste of their bones. Falsely performing good deeds (*gongguo*), falsely looking for the other shore from [words written on several sheets of paper] they then enter into demonic and heterodox ways. Such people look as though they are into the scriptures, but their hearts are miles away, and their heterodox thoughts and dissolute dreams never cease. From one sentence unto one hundred million, they do not see what the scriptures are saying; they are myriad kalpas and cycles of reincarnation away from the saints, sages, immortals, and Buddhas. They are destined to be reborn as hungry ghosts and dumb beasts. (*Dongshan jicao* 2:25–26)

Another passage in the collection provides a theory of religious representation:

A TEXT ENCOURAGING THE THREE IN ONE HALL TO SWEEP THE FLOOR

Burning incense and sweeping the floor is a happy matter for Buddhists, and sprinkling and sweeping back and forth is a great rule of Confucian studies. For who does not know that the heart is like the ground, and the ground is like the heart? If the heart and the ground are bright, then whenever you look among

heaven and earth and the ten thousand things, all are in the realm of purified actionless action. Now people like me are middling to lower quality. If we are in a
place where the dust piles up, getting more and more year after year, then it finally will pile up into a mountain. But if we can sweep away the dust and get rid
of the dirt, every day for a month, every month for a year, then who knows but
we might be able to build a bright and illumined heaven, an earth of purified actionless action. Now today in the midst of a cleansed ritual space, the manifestation of the mighty golden body [of the Lord] could be [taken] either one way or
another way. If it is [seen] one way, then the golden body is nothing more than
a wooden puppet or an earthen slab. It cannot be considered in terms of the meaning of the three marvelous dharmas (*trikaya*). But if it is [taken] the other way,
then the essence does not leave the spirit, and the spirit does not leave the breath.
The Dharma body is just like the image of the Master, it is the residence of the
gods; it is also just like the *daochang* (the "sacred space" of a ritual), who would
tolerate a single thing (speck of dust) within it. (*Dongshan jicao* 2:5–26)

This passage could of course be taken to refer to self-cultivation, as well as to
the literal sweeping away of dust in a temple or ritual space. Similarly, the statue
of Lin Zhao'en is only an idol if it is not understood as a "manifestation of the
mighty golden body"—or a physical form of the triple body of the Buddhist
Trikaya (Buddha, Sangha, and Dharma). Issues of idolatry and imagery were
hotly debated in Confucian academies and other sites of official worship, where
the issue was whether or not to represent Confucius, or the city god, or an ancestor. God statues would seem to be quintessential fetishes, upon which are
projected the collective powers of the individuals in the cult. Yet in this passage Dong insists on interpreting images at several levels simultaneously. The
"dustless floor" is equated to the "golden body" of the Lord of the Three in
One, which is again linked to the "dharma body" of the individual practitioner.
These spaces are again equated with the "sacred space" of ritual. This awareness of and ability to maintain a multiplicity of references suggests a sophisticated reflexive awareness of the power and potential of religious imagery.

Yet another aspect of religious ritual, the recitation of litanies, or confessional texts, receives the following justification from Dong Shi:

I only find it bizarre that the Confucians of the present day all feel a taboo against
the use of the words *chanhui* (repentance) and consider it to be pedantic non-
sense. For because of this there is nothing that they fear, nothing that frightens
them, leading them to be disloyal, unfilial, inhumane, and unrighteous. They destroy the bonds and turn against constancy. Is this not a matter of Confucius having harmed people? Now as for the Buddhist and Daoist sort, they have already
broken with social bonds and constancy. If these are the teachings of Śākyamuni
and Laozi, then when they talk of repentance, is this not but vainly fixing up
empty phrases for other people, in order to inveigle their money and to get something to eat and drink? Is this not a matter of Śākyamuni and Buddha harming
people? My Great Teacher, Master Lin, established the ritual texts in order to save
the world and opened up the door of repentance first of all. When my master

[Chen Zhongyu] received the Second Transmission, he was able to spread these texts onward. Was the meaning of this not simply to bring the Confucian of this time, within the context of the Three Bonds and the Five Constancies, to an understanding of what is to be repented so as to repent the more, and to an understanding of what must be cultivated so that they can cultivate the more? (All this) to the point where they reach [the level of] Confucius and only then to stop. Truly this was a matter of bringing the Buddhists and Daoists of this time, within the context of the Three Bonds and the Five Constancies, to an understanding of what must be cultivated so that they can cultivate the more? [All this] to the point where they reach [the level of] Confucius and only then to stop . . . causing the stream of the Three Teachings to . . . respect Confucius's Three Bonds and Five Constancies . . . and to construct the perfect Way of Confucius, Śākyamuni, and Laozi, and only then to stop. (*Dongshan jicao* 1.33–34)

THE ECONOMICS OF RITUAL

In chapters 2 and 3 we examined the way in which the financing of the Three in One expanded from Lin's personal and family funds, to donations from disciples for travel and printing costs, to large-scale contributions of cash or private property for the construction of temples. With the establishment of a network of temples, regular expenses for rituals were gathered either on a fee basis or as voluntary or, in some villages, required communal contributions. Major expenses included the restoration of temples, which took place when possible approximately once every sixty years, and special printing projects.

A portion of a manuscript entitled the [*Sanyijiao*] *Guitiao* (Rules and Regulations [of the Three in One], dating from the Guangxu period, provides explicit prices for the different rituals performed by the ritualists based in the Wubentang, north of Hanjiang, at that time. For the initial initiation, the fee was 81 wen. For the second-stage initiation, involving the recitation and burning of a document called the Greater Testimony to Heaven, the fee was 64 wen. For the third and highest level of initiation, the *Chanxiu shoujie*, the fee was 1,600 wen for the services of the *zongchi*, 640 wen for the two *hujiao*, 640 wen for the two *zhangjiao*, and a similar amount for other officiants, up to an additional 1,600 wen. For birthdays of the gods, each officiant should receive 81 wen. For an offering ceremony, in addition to 48 wen for the composition of the required documents, the five officiants (*zhangjiao*, two *hujiao*, and two *Daoyou*) should divide a fee of 800 wen. For requiem offering services, the documents cost 120 wen, and the services by five officiants cost 1,200 wen. More complex requiem services would require 480 wen for documents and 480 for scriptures. These funds were to go to the Wubentang, where they were to be recorded in an account book and used for the printing of scriptures or the preparation of ritual offerings.

For a basic rite of scripture recitation, the *zongchi* receives 160 wen, while the *zhangjiao* and the eight other officiants each receive 81 wen. The basic fee for a *Kaijingxun* rite is 240 wen for scripture recitation and 240 wen for the preparation of documents. For a *Sinijing* rite, the rate rises to 480 each for scriptures and documents, with a 20-wen surcharge for documents summoning the souls of the dead in the case of requiems. For a *Kaijingxuan* rite, the fee is 1,200 wen for scriptures. For a *Kai Xiawujing* rite of three days duration, the fees are 3,600 wen each for scriptures and documents. An additional 1,200 wen should be prepared for the *zongchi* (480) and the eight *zhangjiao* (240). A total of twenty-one officiants take part in this kind of rite. For a five-day *Kai Xiawujing* rite, the rate rises to 6,000 each for scriptures and documents, with an additional 2,000 or 2,400 to be divided between the *zongchi* (800), the *zhangjiao* (400 each), and the other officiants, totaling eighteen or twenty-four. For the largest-scale, seven-day *Kai Xiawujing* rite, the fees are 8,400 wen for scriptures and documents, with an additional 2,800 or 3,920, with 1,120 going to the *zongchi*, 610 to the *zhangjiao*, and the rest to the contingent of thirty-six officiants.

The *Guitiao* goes on to provide an item-by-item list of expenses for different kinds of documents: for celebratory rites of thanksgiving, the memorials cost 240 wen, the preface to the *Xiawunijing* (which must also be posted) costs 48 wen, and the instructions (also from the Xiawu Scriptures, and also posted for the ritual) cost 32 wen. Large red proclamation posters cost 100 wen, as do other proclamations, though black (requiem) proclamations cost only 24 wen. Memorials for announcement, offering, and distribution of food rituals, along with documents to summon souls, total 100 wen. Passes and passports for the dead cost 100 wen. If a pentachrome proclamation is drawn up and posted, it costs 240 wen.

Certain features of the memorials (*shuwen*), passes (*guan*), notices (*zhuang*), and proclamations (*bangwen*) of the Three in One deserve mention. Many of these documents routinely request that the blessing of the ritual extend to the owner of the house (*cuozhu*) or the owner of the land (*dizhu*) upon which the ritual is taking place or the Three in One hall is built. There is also regular mention made of those with whom one had grievances or enmity over business dealings (*yuanchou yeze*). Both of these features reveal the social class in which the Three in One operated—that of rentier rather than landlord—and the increasing commercialization of society in which the Three in One expanded.

Contemporary costs for Three in One rituals vary from place to place around Putian and Xianyou. They are, however, invariably said to be lower than the costs of hiring Daoist priests of Buddhist monks. For a simple ritual of a single day's duration, a figure of 500 renminbi is standard. For a more elaborate ritual involving over ten officiants and musicians performing for three to five days, a sum of 3,000–5,000 renminbi is standard. Daily wages for ritual specialists seldom exceed 30 to 50 RMB. Patrons are, however, expected to provide food and lodging (usually in the home or the temple), and many of the offerings are taken home by the ritualists by way of payment.

The income of the main temple of the Three in One, the Zongkongtang, has expanded from roughly 50,000 renminbi in the early 1980s to 136,382.78 for 1994.[17] That year's expenses came to 83,363 RMB. Of course, the major investment of the 1980s and 1990s involved the reconstruction and repair of the temples of the Three in One tradition. In the case of the main centers of the tradition, the Zongkongtang on Dongshan in Putian and the temple beside the grave of Lin Longjiang, Malaysian and Taiwanese Overseas Chinese contributions have been substantial in the 1990s.

With the lifting of the ban on Malaysian Chinese visiting China, Malaysian Huaqiao investment in the Three in One began in earnest. The following amounts (in RMB) give some indication of the nature of these contributions:

Lin Longjiang Memorial hall	130,000
Reclamation of front temple of Zongkongtang	190,000
Paving of road to tomb of Lin Longjiang	86,000
Yushanci (Bangtou)	20,000
Yuhuici (Bangtou)	10,000
Sanjiaotang (Houtang)	10,000
Mingxiatang (Xixucun)	5,000
Mingxiaci (Banwei Yangmeicun)	5,000
Zongkongtang (Houjiao Shimen)	5,000
Yangxiatang (Fengting Xiajie)	5,000
Yushanci (Laicucun)	3,000
Fengshanci (Xianyou)	3,000
Hushanci (Fengting)	3,000
Meizhou Tianhougong (because Lin Moniang is a relative of Lin Longjiang)	10,000
Total	466,000

These figures are substantial, but they amount to only a fraction of the sums raised within the thousand temples of the Three in One in Xinghua. For example, the Zongkongtang on Dongshan has matched the 190,000 RMB amount raised overseas for the reconstruction of the front temple (currently a military barracks). During the terrible floods in the Anhui region in the early 1990s, the Zongkongtang raised 150,000 and donated it to the government relief operation.[18] The reconstruction of the thousand temples of the Three in One has cost at least 15,000,000 RMB. The annual performance of everyday worship, major annual rituals, and rites for individuals and communities within the Three in One represents an enormous figure.

[17] Lin (1994: 26) provides details on various forms of income in the posted annual accounts for the Xiangyang Academy for the year 1988, which totaled 51,058.95 RMB.

[18] This contribution was acknowledged with an official letter of thanks from the agency responsible for the coordination of the relief effort. The letter is posted in the office of the temple committee of the Dongshanci Zongkongtang.

Several sections of this book have touched on the economics of the Three in One ritual tradition, from its early formative stages, to the organization of annual ritual expenses in local temples, to the costs of the reconstruction and expansion of the tradition in recent decades. The spread of the Three in One into Southeast Asia has demonstrated its adaptability to local customs. Recently Overseas Chinese and Taiwanese Three in One groups have taken part in a larger phenomenon of the "reexporting" of "traditional culture" back to China. These groups are actively involved in renegotiating the meaning and value of "traditional cultural forms." These examples of local management of ritual traditions demonstrate the versatility and flexibility of local autonomous organizational forms in Chinese society. The Three in One is distinguished by its ability to transcend lineage and village ties, to create a transregional, transnational organizational network. The Three in One in Xinghua is most likely capable of mobilizing more human and capital resources than even the local government. The Three in One is a remarkably successful instance of the local management of culture in Southeast China and Southeast Asia. This tradition is uniquely well documented, with a continuous ritual practice that augments historical study.

The economics of ritual of course involves far more than the financing of temple construction or ritual performances. Systems of exchange underlie entire cultural systems (Sahlins, 1985). Notions of debt, belonging, property (physical, symbolic, and intellectual), and personhood are all implicated in any full discussion of the economics of ritual (Mauss, 1979; Strathern, 1992; Wilkerson, 1995). Here I would only like to raise one issue. In the context of the rapid economic development of the southeastern Chinese coast over the past decade and a half, the economics of ritual implies an interruption of the "normal" flow of capital and human resources into investment in agriculture, manufacturing, and speculation (or into narrowly defined social services). Yet this flow is immediately reconnected into the performance of ritual excess. Through the performance of ritual-events, capital and human resources are rerouted and reconnected with multiple flows of texts, bodies, sounds, food, offerings, and so forth. A generalized redistribution occurs, with ritual consumption becoming an end in itself. A ritual-event consumes itself. Of course, many provisional ends are served, including the assertion of status and leadership within the community. Yet ultimately the ritual consumption represents not only the actualization of latent potentialities within the community but also an investment in the community through the invention of new potentialities. The renowned *guanxi* system operates to some extent in similar ways, although it is usually viewed from the point of view of individuals investing in their own relationships, confident that they will receive more than they put in, in a process of continuous escalating (or deepening) interaction.[19] Capi-

---

[19] Mayfair Yang (1994) differentiates a "feminized," traditional, rural, ethical discourse of *ren-qing* (human relations) from a more "masculinist," postrevolutionary, instrumentalist discourse of *guanxixue* (guanxiology), but she argues that both forms coexist within a less masculinist alternative gift economy that subverts the hierarchical, homogenizing state model of control.

tal and resources diverted into ritual excess represent a major expression of trust in the potentiality of the community. This is a historically specific community, composed of innumerable specific networks of interaction, not a reified, abstract reservoir of changeless values.

RITUAL AND THE PERFORMANCE OF GENDER

The Three in One emphasizes a traditional, Confucian, patriarchal morality, with gender roles for men and women strictly confined to heterosexual relations within the patriarchal family structure. Yet tens of thousands of women have been initiated and practice inner alchemy, scripture recitation, and liturgy (see table 3 below). Three in One doctrine specifically rejects the abandonment of family ties for life in a nunnery. However, several Three in One temples have organized women's groups, who practice group meditation. A number of women's liturgical troupes have been formed and hold positions of authority in their communities. Classes in Three in One teachings for women were established in major temples in the Republican period (see chapter 7). Unfortunately, evidence on the role of women in earlier periods is lacking. Negative evidence includes the lack of significant mention of women in early accounts, including the *Menxian shilu* or the *Jinling zhengyitang xingshi*. When women are mentioned, it is usually in the context of men carrying out filial obligations toward them, or Three in One leaders healing women from disease (e.g., the daughter of Huang Zhou, Lin's first disciple).

Any amount of fieldwork, however, yields a distinct impression of the majority participation of women in ritual-events. Although rarely in the position of ritual specialists, women nonetheless make up the majority of participants.[20] They prepare and bring offerings to the temple, burn incense, pray, cast divination blocks, consult oracles and spirit-mediums, purchase talismans, and participate in incense-bearing groups, often singing songs together as they escort their temple's incense burners to the pilgrimage destination. Often these women understand their ritual roles on such occasions as representing their patrilinial families. Nonetheless, the experience of group activity, whether as liturgists, pilgrimage groups, or preparers and presenters of ritual offerings, brings women into collective assemblages that open up spaces potentially quite distinct from domestic or patrilinially defined roles (Huang, 1993). Moreover, involvement in temple activities and decision making, and performance as liturgists and reciters of scripture, provide positions of power and authority to some women in the Three in One. Finally, the individual or group practice of inner alchemy allows for individual exploration of the self and the cosmos, potentially transcending gender roles.

[20] When confronted with this fact and questioned about it, women often deny that there are mostly women about, indicating that they see themselves primarily as representatives of their patrilines (Anderson, 1996).

Since the Three in One developed a corpus of rituals for individuals and families, such as requiem services, marriages, and exorcisms of childhood diseases or potential adversities, their sphere of activity enters into the domestic arena. There Three in One rituals reinscribe gender, for, as Barlow has suggested, gender roles are largely defined by ritual performance within parameters of kinship categories (Butler, 1990, 1992; Barlow, 1993; Anderson, 1996).[21] As Freedman pointed out (1978: 173), women are responsible for routine offerings made to ancestors at the domestic, family level, whereas men perform rites in the extra-domestic, ancestral hall. Certain gender categories are, however, challenged by some areas of Three in One ritual performance. A few women connected to the Three in One have become spirit-mediums. Rather than merely contacting the dead or speaking in the name of lowly deities, as implied in some accounts of Chinese female mediums (Potter, 1974; Kendall, 1985; but see also Ahern, 1975; Sangren, 1984; Wolf, 1992), these mediums are possessed by powerful martial women warrior goddesses, such as the female Yang Jiajiang. Their standing in the community is high, and they command considerable respect and attract major funding.

In general, although the doctrine and some of the liturgy of the Three in One appear to reinforce Confucian gender roles for both men and women, certain aspects of Three in One practice provide limited means to challenge static gender roles. In this respect, the role of women in the Three in One represents an interesting response to the decline of socialist constructions of "gender equality" over the past fifteen years, which can be seen in the decline of the Women's Federation in some areas into a mere extension of the single-child enforcement agency. This ideological and institutional decline has left open the representation of women to Western capitalist imagery. Women's roles in the Three in One thus can be seen to contest to some extent both static Confucian representations of gender and socialist or capitalist representations as well.

[21] Barlow cites Chen Hongmou (1696–1771) on this point and concludes, "Chen Hongmou's definition of nu, fu, and mu makes it clear that while (good) women in the jia did effect social relations outside the family, no position existed for female persons (or male persons, for that matter) outside the jia's boundaries" (Barlow, 1993: 257). She follows Elizabeth Cowie in defining kinship not as a system of exchange but as a "production line of subjectivities." Barlow also links the production of gender identities to ritual: "Li—behaviors, rituals, or normative manners—were what, for the most part, protocol consisted of; they provided guidance for appropriate, proper, good, and efficacious self-preservation. Prescribed, normative behavior, and gendered experience were inextricable" (p. 260).

Current Cultural Range of the Three in One

THIS CHAPTER first reviews the renaissance of the Three in One since 1979 and discusses statistics on the number of temples and initiates in the movement. Then a series of case studies are presented to explore the range of forms of the relationships between particular Three in One temples and their surrounding communities in the Xinghua region. It is possible to broadly distinguish three basic kinds of interactions: (1) small groups of believers isolated from the community; (2) groups on a par with other temples dedicated to local deities; and (3) temples that have become the center of the community, often by absorbing all the local gods and functions of the other popular cult temples. In some cases, there are significant local variations. The chapter concludes with a discussion of several individual life histories of Three in One adherents.

CONTEMPORARY BRANCHES OF THE THREE IN ONE

The principal branches of the Three in One active today are the Zucipai (Ancestral Temple branch), Wubenpai (Enlightened Origin branch); Hongdupai (Hongdu branch, also known as the Zhang Religion); Mingxiapai (Enlightening Xia branch, also known as the Weng branch); and Sanyipai (Three in One branch). These can be divided into two major groups. The Zuci, Wuben, and Sanyi branches, and to a certain extent the Hongdu branch, all accept the Three Transmitters Lu, Chen, and Dong. The Mingxiapai maintains its own tradition descended from Lin Zhenming.

The Zucipai is centered in Putian around the Dongshanci. Its members strictly observe only what they believe to have been Lin Zhao'en's teachings and do not revere subsequent disciples. The Dongshanci was formerly closed inside a military compound, and the main center of Zucipai activities was an altar in a nearby private house.

The Wubenpai is strong in the Hanjiang area and up into the Jiangkou region. The Wuben temple was the site of Chen Zhida's revitalization of the Three in One cult at the end of the Qing. His soul tablet is worshiped in the temple, along with that of his disciple, Liang Puyao. Chen's tomb is nearby.[1] Chen and Liang wrote several introductory tracts on the Three in One cult, such as the *Sanjiao chuxue zhinan* (Pointers on elementary study of the Three Teachings) and the *Zhengtong yizhilu* (Record of easy to understand [princi-

---

[1] Franke (1972) provides a photograph of a large grouping of Three in One adherents around the tomb taken in the 1920s.

ples] of the Orthodox School). Chen and especially Liang played an important role in a thirty-year series of mediumistic utterances recorded in the 1935 *Zhenjia bao zhengyi* (True collection of the treasures that vouchsafe the home) and the *Zhenjia bao buyi* (Supplement), discussed below.

In recent years the Wuben and Zuci branches have regrouped in the restored founding Zongkongtang temple on Dongshan inside the north gate of Putian City. This group emphasizes individual cultivation. Its rituals are primarily directed at family-level rituals for members of the organization. Thus their temples preserve a distance from the gods of popular religion. As a result, they are seldom able to penetrate into the central decision-making sector of village society. Their temples remain aloof from most other village-level, temple-based ritual (with the exception of the yulanpen ritual for the hungry ghosts). They maintain close connections with a set of nearby Three in One temples, visiting each other on the occasion of one of the annual rituals of the Three Primes (1/15, 7/15, 10/15), taking part in inaugurations of newly built or restored halls, and so forth. Thus these temples and the groups that participate in them are involved in a supravillage-level organization.

The Hongdupai, based in Xihong village, suggests the potential for extreme localization of the Three in One teachings, as it is basically a single village cult dedicated to a local god (Zhang Hongdu), with a small number of branch temples in villages where Xihong residents have emigrated. By contrast, the Mingxiapai has managed to spread its unique traditions over a wide area of coastal Putian and inland Xianyou, adopting Buddhist and especially Daoist ritual methods and gradually overwhelming all other traditions. The Sanyipai, which traces its origins to the Three Transmitters, Lu Wenhui, Chen Zhongyu, and Dong Shi, has also developed a roughly parallel ritual tradition and penetrated into local-level social and cultural forms throughout the Xianyou area. The differences between these two branches appear to be based on different lines of transmission, and minor differences regarding ritual observances. Generally speaking, these two traditions have developed a set of rituals for individual rites (rites of passage, initiation, and minor exorcisms), family-based ritual (especially requiem services; also birthday celebrations), and community-level ritual (birthdays of the gods of the Three in One, birthdays of the local popular gods, yulanpen feasts for the hungry ghosts).

The Sanyi branch is a far more diffuse group, representing a middle ground between the Zuci branch's fundamentalism and the Mingxia branch's hybridization. Individual temples scattered throughout inland Xianyou were founded by Lin Zhao'en, Lu, Chen and Dong. Some or all of these figures are represented on the altars of these temples, invariably accompanied by the local disciple or first abbot or temple head. These groups are much more susceptible to suggestions from the Zuci and Wuben branches as to the need to reorganize the religion and seek official recognition. They have recently begun inviting elder scholastic figures from the Putian and Hanjiang region to present lectures. These take the form of scriptural commentary and can last for three days. Rituals are simultaneously carried out at an altar set up across the courtyard from the lecture platform. These rituals are often performed by Sanyi branch members together with visiting Mingxia groups.

Three in One adherents distinguish between civil teachings (*wenjiao*)—various forms of inner alchemy, often practiced in a group under the direction of an advanced teacher, and some scriptural recitation—and martial teachings (*wujiao*)—the performance of ritual, dance, music, and singing. Generally speaking, the Wuben tradition is known for the *wenjiao* and the Mingxia and, to a lesser extent, the Sanyi branches are known for the *wujiao*.

In Xianyou the Mingxiapai centers around the Daxingci in Xianyou City and the Zhuguangci in Bangtou Township. The latter has many branch temples in the eastern part of Xianyou. The Daxingci has branch temples to the west in Longhua and Daji townships in the narrow Xianyou valley. The Sanyipai is based in the Jinshanci in Xianyou City and in the Yushanci in Bangtou. There is an extensive Sanyipai incense division network in Bangtou. The Sanyipai is also active in the mountains north of Duwei Township, in the far western part of Xianyou.

THE THREE IN ONE IN PUTIAN AND XIANYOU IN THE 1980S AND 1990S

In Putian and Xianyou great efforts have been made over the past fifteen years to reunify the Three in One. This began with the building of the Shimenci (Stone Gate Shrine). Next to the recently repaired grave of Lin Zhao'en in Huating County south of Putian, a new temple has been built. The Shimenci symbolized the resurgence of the Three in One for the third time in its four-hundred-year history. The arrangement of gods within the temple and the schedule of ritual observances of birth dates of the deities symbolize the forces that are pushing the disparate branches of the Three in One together. The Shimenci attempts to incorporate many of the major branches and to revere the important disciples worshiped by those branches. They recognize not only the traditional Four Attendants, referred to as the Upper Four Attendants, but also another set, the Lower Four Attendants. This latter group includes Dong Shi, Chen Zhida, Chen Zhuhua, and Liang Puyao. Although they are attempting to embrace a wide range of practices of different branches, a bias toward the Putian traditions is evident in their exclusion of the Weng branch (see below). Rituals are held on the following dates:

Lin Zhao'en: 1/14 (death); 7/16 (birth)
Lu Wenhui: 11/3 (birth)
Zhu Huixu: 1/16; 4/16
Zhang Hongdu: 1/15; 7/28
Lin Zhenming: 4/4; 6/16
Dong Shi: 2/9
Chen Zhida: 10/27; 2/13
Chen Juhua: 2/26; 4/15
Liang Puyao: 7/18

The grave of Lin next to the temple makes it an obvious pilgrimage point for all the branches of the religion. Thousands of followers arrive from all over the Xinghua region. Rituals are conducted by nine to sixteen Masters throughout the day. Theatrical performances are offered. Particularly ardent believers generally perform a Great Ritual Salute at the grave, consisting of nine kowtows and eighteen bows. Three in One adherents usually perform a four-bow salute (to the four *Ni*, the gods or sages of Confucianism, Daoism, Buddhism, and Lin Zhao'en [Xia Wuni]). Outsiders simply perform the usual three-bow salute. Offerings include cakes, fruits, tea, and flowers (i.e., pure vegetarian offerings). These activities last from the 1st to the 15th of the first lunar month of the year.

In 1988 the Ancestral Shrine of Lin Zhao'en was finally recovered from the military and promptly rebuilt, largely with local funds. This is now a center of the reunification effort. The core of the temple committee appears to be made up of the Hanjiang-based Wuben branch leaders, working together now with the Zuci branch elders. More recently, representatives from Xianyou have been added. In 1989 an academic conference was convened by the leaders of the Three in One. This was a way of gaining official acknowledgment of the religious movement and seeking legitimation through scholarly discussion of what had been a taboo topic a decade earlier. Moreover, the Ancestral Shrine has begun organizing "advanced seminars" on the explication of the scriptures and philosophic writings of Lin Zhao'en. This tradition goes back several years and began in the Hanjiang area, site of the Wuben Hall. In 1989 I attended a seminar in which the two ninety-year-old adherents provided a word-by-word, phrase-by-phrase explication of Master Lin's commentary to the *Four Books*. In the early 1990s representatives from the Wuben tradition traveled to Xianyou to give lectures on the scriptures, often on raised stages opposite the altars around which a Mingxia-style ritual was being performed. In 1993 the Ancestral Hall initiated a series of seminars that attracted some one hundred attendants. The idea was to cultivate a group of adherents to take over the transmission of the philosophic and exegetical tradition, now resting precariously in the hands of a few elderly gentlemen.

The Ancestral Hall also organized surveys of all extant Three in One temples and issued a formal set of guidelines to each temple. They also loosely coordinate the presentation of incense from these far-flung temples. The Ancestral Hall has staged fund-gathering drives to support the reconstruction of the hall itself and also various charities, such as disaster relief during the 1991 Anhui floods.

The following figures are based on surveys conducted in 1987 and 1989, respectively, by the Ancestral Shrine on Eastern Mountain, Putian, of the Sanyijiao. The name and village of each temple are listed, so the final figure of 1,044 temples seems reliable, although in many places Lin Zhao'en may be added to other local gods on an altar. My impression is that these are for the most part temples in which Lin Zhao'en (as Xia Wuni) is the main god. There are thousands more temples devoted to other popular god cults in this area. The number of male and female adherents varies wildly from the first to the second survey. In the first survey, male adherents almost always outnumber females. In the second, females often outnumber males. Perhaps the first survey focused on initiates (menren), while the second counted either all family members of initiates or all those who occasionally visited the temples. Neither set of figures can be considered completely reliable, although the total number of temples is likely to be quite accurate, as addresses and the names of the temple leaders were also provided in the survey. The first total of 55,106 adherents in some 757 temples would mean an average of over 70 adherents per temple, which seems high, but may reflect different levels of interaction between the Three in One and the community in different areas. The second total of over 500,000 in 1,044 temples would mean 1,000 adherents per temple. This may be an accurate estimate of the general population per temple, but it is unlikely to reflect numbers of initiates. This figure may well be a result of a desire on the part of the Ancestral Shrine to win government acknowledgment of the size, importance, and status of the Three in One as part of their campaign for government recognition as a legitimate religion. Irregardless of the actual number of initiates, it is clear that the Three in One is extremely widespread through the Xinghua region.

According to a rough survey of fourteen temples in ten townships with a combined membership of 527 people conducted by Lin Guoping in 1988, 63.5 percent of adherents were male, and 36.5 percent female. By profession, 85.4 percent were farmers, 1.8 percent were workers, 5 percent were students, craftsmen made up 3.2 percent, government employees and officials made up 3.4 percent, and professionals made up 1.2 percent. In terms of literacy and educational level, 26.7 percent were illiterate, 54 percent had an elementary school education, 19.3 percent had graduated from high school, and 0.14 percent had graduated from university. By age group, 15 percent were under thirty, 37.4 percent were between thirty and sixty, and 47.5 percent were 60 and older. Some 29.4 percent had been initiated prior to 1978, and 70.6 percent after (Lin, 1994). Fieldwork confirms the impression from various documentary sources that entire families are raised within the Three in One, with children undergoing initiation more or less as a social obligation. As they progress in inner alchemy and group ritual, the more interested and activist individuals take on greater responsibilities within the Three in One collectivities.

Case Studies

The following case studies examine the role of specific Three in One temples in a variety of villages and urban communities. They are arranged into three categories, but, as will be explained below, this is not intended as a strict typology.

TABLE 3
Distribution of Three in One Temples in the Xinghua Region

Township	Temples	Men		Women		Total	
Putian	24/ 32	588/	960	387/	1,000	855/	1,961
Hanjiang	27/ 72	1,068/	3,786	973/	3,541	2,041/	7,368
Wutang	9		872		911		1,783
Jiangkou	39/ 18	1,242/	2,551	656/	1,827	1,898/	4,328
Huangshi	44		22,098		18,301		41,399
Huating	29/ 30	643/	3,796	367/	3,541	1,029/	7,337
Hushi	46/ 46	2,539/	5,762	1,954/	5,055	3,662/	10,917
Quqiao	28/ 23	1,887/	5,088	666/	5,356	1,763/	10,444
Lingchuan	40/ 52	3,418/	6,423	1,954/	5,055	3,662/	13,712
Beigao	42/ 30	560/	655	570/	611	1,130/	1,266
Dongzhuang	29/ 20	367/	1,255	662/	1,596	1,010/	2,851
Meizhou Island	2/ 2	130/	240	30/	460	160/	700
Pinghai	13/ 12	1,213/	4,262	433/	4,550	1,646/	6,832
Dongqiao	38/ 33	2,989/	4,280	1,179/	4,552	4,163/	8,832
Zhongmen	28/ 33	740/	32,355	352/	38,115	1,092/	70,470
Daitou	20/ 36	1,508/	14,351	715/	12,473	2,223/	26,824
Xitianwei	14		801		985		1,786
Nanri Island	4		122		5		127
Putian	398/510	26,012/112,976		10,117/114,363		28,043/227,339	
Xianyou	24/ 21	814/	5,958	744/	4,985	1,558/	10,943
Bangtou	55/ 86	3,899/	30,872	1,588/	26,406	5,429/	57,278
Fengting	35/ 43	1,342/	3,635	563/	5,927	1,905/	11,562
Jiaowei	39		9,626		6,228		15,857
Duwei	39		10,246		2,376		17,622
Longhua	30/ 32	1,250/	4,413	808/	3,006	2,068/	7,419
Yuanzhuang	17/ 15	808/	2,883	200/	4,907	1,108/	7,770
Xiyuan	7/ 12	220/	2,779	164/	2,723	384/	5,502
Shufeng	12/ 18	475/	4,956	266/	4,589	741/	9,497
Daji	53/ 50	1,777/	23,437	1,143/	21,197	2,924/	44,634
Laidian	48/ 52	2,553/	21,126	2,016/	18,124	4,569/	39,250
Fengshan	2/ 1	45/	80	30/	80	75/	160
Shexing	14/ 9	435/	1,800	268/	1,448	783/	3,248
Xiangqi	2/ 2	35/	400	29/	400	55/	800
Zhongshan	2		820		730		1,550
Shicang	4		915		850		1,965
Youyang	3		1,011		615		1,625
Gaiwei	47		12,219		10,812		23,031
Xianyou	475	/138,545		/119,768		/258,313	
Fuqing	2		486		377		863
Pingtan	1		50		70		120
Fuzhou	2		1,200		1,000		2,200
Huian	25/ 54	205/	11,631	346/	12,160	557/	23,791

TABLE 3 (*Continued*)

Township	Temples	Men	Women	Total
Total Number of Temples and Adherents				
Putian	510			
Xianyou	475			
Fuqing, Fuzhou,				
Huian	59	13,367	12,707	26,074
Total	757/1,044	34,890/265,309	20,716/248,123	55,106/513,432

CATEGORY ONE: SMALL SEPARATE GROUPS

These include groups that are distinguished by class (whether higher or lower) as well as those that chose to differentiate themselves from village ritual for their own reasons. These different kinds of relations between the Three in One groups and village religion indicates the flexibility of the tradition: its ability to accommodate different cultural levels.

Jade Pool Academy in Hanjiang

The membership of the Yaochi Shuyuan in Hanjiang is drawn from a select group of primarily elderly, literate gentlemen. They arrange study groups in which the eighty-year-olds instruct the seventy-year-olds on the significance of Lin Zhao'en's commentaries to the *Four Books*. The cultural level of these adherents is quite high; many of them can quote the Confucian Classics at will. They are actively engaged in a serious program of self-cultivation. They also perform rituals for the members of the group. The temple has a temple keeper, and neighbors occasionally come in to burn incense.

The Shrine for the Obtaining of Dew of Heping Village

The membership of the Hepingcun Delinci consists of a small group of generally impoverished, displaced, or marginal men and women in Hepingcun in Fengting who gathered together to build a small shrine to the Lord of the Three in One. They perform simple rituals there but rely mostly on the spirit possession of one of their group by Tian Gongyuanshuai to attract people to the temple. Through the Three in One they are able to band together and perform their aspiration for a moral life-style, while at the same time providing a setting for communication with the gods.

Multiple Three in One Temples of Gold Mountain Village

Jinshancun is located on Xinghua Bay below Hanjiang in Huangshi Township. The village has some four thousand residents in seven major surname

Plate 17. Altar of the Naishengtang (Hall of the Patient Saints) in Laidian, Fengting, showing Zhang Sanfeng and Zhuo Wanchun on either side of Lin Longjiang

groups, including Zhu, Weng, Lin, Xu, and Zheng, as well as many miscellaneous surnames. There are a great many temples in this village, including the major Jinshangong (Gold Mountain Temple), which is the principal temple in charge of villagewide ritual activity, and the Lingyundian (Temple of the Spiritual Clouds). The latter has steles dating from Jiaqing 9 (1804) and Xuanfeng 5 (1855) (Dean and Zheng, 1995: 267, 319). These inscriptions reveal the role of individual families in supporting a particular temple over several generations. In this village, individual families or groups have established more than eight Three in One Temples, including the Mingyue, Mingxia, Zongkongtang, Hanyitang, and Qingyuntang. Several small shrines of the Longhua "secret religion" have been established in the village. These include the Longhuatang, Deshanan, Deyuan Tang, Dafutang, Benyuantang, and Guanghuatang (formed out of the merger of the five other, now defunct temples).

Hall of Ancestral Jade in Licu Village

Zongyutang is located in Licu village in Jiangkou. The village has a population of about two thousand, mostly of the Li surname. The Li ancestral hall is in nearby Xindun village and was founded in the Qianlong period (see Dean and Zheng, 1995: 231, 254). The village has several temples, such as the Weixiandian, Fengyidian, and Fuxingtang. The Weixiandian is the main ritual center, and it organizes a great number of rituals around its multiple god cults. The major annual rituals, such as *yuanxiao,* are organized by this temple. The entire population of the village participates in these rituals. The Three in One temple, by contrast, has a far narrower membership. A stele in the temple dated Guangxu 31 (1905) records that the temple was founded in that year by one Li Yanglong. The stele goes on to list twelve patrons surnamed Li, and one each surnamed Guan, Chen, Liu, Huang, Weng, and Pu. Members of the temple state that the founder came from Xihong village in Huangshi (center of the Zhang Hongdu cult). The temple is now in the process of rebuilding. About one hundred members of the families descended from the founders still participate in this temple. There is an active spirit-writing group. The writings of the gods have been recorded in a manuscript mostly written in the Republican period but recently updated.

Commentary: These Three in One temples all enjoy a minority relationship with the wider village community, but the principles of membership are different in each case. They range from groups defined by their high literacy and interest in self-cultivation to groups thrown together by economic adversity who assist one another and proclaim their status through rituals and spirit-mediumism. The temples may reflect the interests of a single family over time, or of the descendants of a group of founders drawn from multiple surnames.

Category Two: Equal Level with Popular Temples

There are many instances in which the Three in One temple is on a level equal to that of the temples of the local popular cults within the village structure. In perhaps half the villages of Xianyou, the Three in One temple is at least parallel in size and influence to any other temple in the village. Moreover, due to the systematic nature of its organizational structure, its regular schedule of ritual activity, group inner alchemical practice, and training of new initiates and ritualists, the Three in One temple is at least as active as the other popular temples.

Shrine of Universal Enlightenment in Puming Village

This temple in Bangtou was built in Wanli 38 (1610). It was restored in Qianlong 19 (1754) and in Daoguang 16 (1836). The *Regulations* of the temple emphasize two parallel activities: transcendence of the world (*dushi*) and salvation of the world (*jishi*). This indicates an equal emphasis on self-cultivation and assistance to others (through ritual and charity work). The village is composed entirely of the Zheng surname. Lin Longjiang's old family home, belonging to an uncle, is said to be there. Lin is said to have stayed there in the Jiajing period. In the Wanli period one Zheng Zhongyi turned Lin's old home into a Three in One temple. (Some villagers say that it was originally a tax or rent collection warehouse belonging to Lin Longjiang's family.) Initiates practice primarily the civil Way of meditation and recitation of scriptures (*wendao*), rather than active ritual performances known as *wudao*, the martial Way. That is to say that two or three times a month they practice the heart method of inner cultivation, based on the Confucian injunction to examine oneself three times a day. These practices benefit the initiates themselves, but initiates can also use their *qigong* to help cure others.

The gods worshiped in the temple include the Lord of the Three in One seated in the center next to Yuhuang Dadi, the Jade Emperor; Huang 1, Huang 2, Zhuo Zhenren, Zhou Xianshi, and Sima Shengwang. There are said to be over forty branch temples, including the Pulinci nearby. Others are in Yuanzhuang, Zixiao, Laidian, and Gaiwei; in the mountains of Shufeng and Zhongshan; and in Hui'an and Singapore.

Nearby there stands the Ziyangtang (Gong), a local temple dedicated to Mazu, Dashigong, Chen Ma, Wu Ma, and Guangong Dadi. This temple holds a *bao'an* ritual for the protection of the community in the 2d and the 8th month of each year. They celebrate *yuanxiao* on 1/8–12. The temple committee of the Ziyangtang is drawn from the committees of Pumingci (within Dongqiao village) and another nearby Three in One temple, the Zhusanci in Xiazhu village. This committee decides which *zhang* (extended household— in this area equivalent to a branch of a lineage as well as a production brigade—literally extended architectural complexes with up to 108 rooms) will begin the procession by casting divination blocks. Three leaders are selected: one for the Chen lineage, one for the Zheng, and one for the mixed surname group. An overall *shezhang* is also selected, along with *gongzhang* workteam leaders. Ritual expenses are supported by temple lands (*gongtou tian*) consisting of over 10 mu. On the occasion of a large *bao'an jiao*, a four-day Three Audience Daoist ritual is held and there are nine successive performances of theater.

Universal Unicorn Shrine in Qiwei Village

The Pulinci is located in Qiweicun in Bangtou. In the Pulinci are a *zhangjiao* and twenty initiates, about a dozen of whom can do rituals. This is the main Three in One temple in the village, and it is linked to the Yan lineage, which is the major lineage in the village with some three-thousand people, divided into four branches. According to their lineage genealogy, dated Qianlong 19 (1754), the ancestors of this branch of the Yan lineage moved to Qiwei village from Yongchun in 1490. They also have an ancestral hall called the Linqingtang, which is one hundred years old. The Yan lineage members live in massive, palace-style (*gongting*) extended houses. The entire village is composed of about a dozen such large family homes (*zhang*), each of which is equivalent to a *fang* lineage branch, and a production unit (*shengchan dui*).

In the nearby Meiqigong Temple, built in Jiaqing 5 (1800), restored in Xuanfeng 1 (1851), and restored again in 1986, the following gods are worshiped: Zhanggong, Dashi Gong, Anding Gong (Xianggong), and Shengmu Keshi niangniang. All but Xianggong proceed on 1/15. On 10/15 a *bao'an jiao* is held. The temple had over ten mu of temple lands, the proceeds of which were rotated between the four branches of the Yan lineage to cover ritual expenditures.

Dragon (Flower) Assembly Shrine in Tangbian Village

The Longhuitang (Hall of the Dragon [Flower] Assembly) is located in Tangbian village in Duwei Township west of Xianyou. The village is divided into six groups (*zu*), five of which are branches of two separate Wu lineages. These five groups originally set up the Hougong (Back Temple, also called the Longjinggong [Dragon Well Temple]), dedicated to Mazu and Fazhu Ma. The sixth group was made up primarily of the Li surname, and they established the Qiangong (Front Temple) dedicated to Dashi and Ershi. That temple later collapsed, and all the gods and groups are now represented inside the Hougong, which rotates ritual activity between the six *zu*. The Longhuitang has some twenty-five initiates, of whom eighteen can perform rituals. Currently the Ancestral Hall of the Wu lineage has been moved inside this Three in One temple. Originally the Panggui Wu lineage had three branch ancestral halls in the village and counted some twenty-five generations, while the Huitang Wu kept an ancestral home for lineage ritual. Now all these lineage halls have collapsed. In 1988 the Wu lineages performed a lineage reunion (*huizu*) ritual in the Longhuitang. Major village rituals are handled by the Longjinggong, such as the 8th month *baoan* rituals and the annual two-week pilgrimage to the mother temple of Mazu on Meizhou Island. Several god associations (*shenminghui*) connected to the temple all had land. There was also gunpowder land (*qiangban tian*) for the costs of the processions. These lands were also known as festival lands (*jieri tian*).

Commentary: These three examples are rather complicated. In the first case, the Three in One temple is a well-established community center whose temple committee members also sit on the committee of the village temple and share in decisions involving villagewide rituals. In the second case, a single-surname village has a Three in One temple and a village temple. Both appear to be of equal size and influence. In the third case, the Three in One temples' fortunes are changing with the changing ritual orders in the community. The branches of a slightly smaller lineage have joined together within the Three in One temple, while the gods formally worshiped by different lineages have all been absorbed into the increasingly powerful village temple. These examples suggest that the Three in One temples, village temples, and lineage halls are always involved in a ceaseless contesting and performing of power within their communities.

CATEGORY THREE: COMPLETE TAKEOVER

Shrine of Universal Splendor in Xiachaiqiao Village

There are several surnames in Xiachaiqiao village, the major ones being Liu, Zheng, Yan and Liang. In all there are only two hundred people in the village; the population has dropped since Liberation. Each lineage has ancestral halls in other villages. The Three in One temple, the Pushengci, is a branch of the Puguangci. This temple has now become the village temple. As such it had been endowed with more than twenty mu of shrine land (*citian*). Each mu provided 150 *jin* in rent. These land rents covered ritual expenses, irrigation, policing, theater, and a local school (*minxiao*). There is a *shezhang* in charge of public affairs and expenses. Inside the village each lineage has a lineage home (*zucu*). Ancestral worship takes place at these locations on 7/15. Moreover, each lineage had some lineage land: three mu for the Zheng; two *mu* for the Liang; only 4 *fen* for the Liu. Each student got the proceeds of six *fen* to support their studies. Formerly some families would invite Daoist priests to perform rituals, but now everyone invites Three in One masters. Divination and prayers are nowadays all done in the Three in One temple.

There is a temple in Dawangcun, adjoining Xiachaiqiao village, called the Shengxinggong. It is dedicated to Zhanggong, Dashi gong, Furenma, and Sima Shengwang. Originally, at an even higher regional ritual circuit level there had been a temple in Qiwei village, but this was destroyed in a flood and later divided up into four separate temples, one of which was the Shengxinggong. This latter temple holds major annual rituals at *yuanxiao*, on lunar 10/10 (a *bao'an* ritual), and on the lunar 7/23 birthday of Zhanggong. Other small villages that take part in this temple's ritual circuit rotate the performance of the *yuanxiao* festival and ritual over a two- or three-day period between 10/7 and 10/15. When Xiachaiqiao village takes part in the Shengxinggong rituals, it does so under the auspices of the Pushengci. Financing for such involvement is also drawn from the Pushengci land rent.

Pearly Radiance Shrine in Baxia Village

There are some four thousand people living in Bangtou's Baxiacun, which was originally a port town on the Lai River. It is now a township center. The major surname groups are Huang, Chen, Lin, Ou, and Cai. Major village rituals as well as most family rituals are handled through the Three in One temple, the Zhuguangci, founded in 1650. This is an important Mingxiapai temple. There are a few other temples in the town, such as the Guanyinge, the Tianma Monastery, and the Longxinggong, where Jin Daren is worshiped. Local legend has it that a Three in One (ritual master) fought and beat this god in a magical battle. That is why the Zhuguangci now is in charge of his procession. There is also a Xingxingge dedicated to Mazu. The latter's procession is also organized through the Zhuguangci. The Zhuguangci claims to have established over 130 branch shrines in Xianyou and Putian. There is an active group of ritualists, numbering sixty to seventy, based at the temple. Forty of these are elderly and thirty are younger men.

Seven Star Shrine in Putou Village

The Qixingci, located in Putou village in Fengting, Xianyou, was founded in Wanli 26 (1598). This Three in One temple is now joined together with the community shrine of the earth god (*she*), the village temple (*gong*), and a larger village temple (*dian*). The Qixingci is said to have branched off from the Yushanci in Bangtou; others, however, say that Lin Longjiang personally founded it (because the Beidou North Pole Star fell to the Earth there). According to this legend, Lin Longjiang carved his own image and left it there, so this temple's image is the truest. He also is said to have planted a cinnamon tree there. This temple has opened several branch temples, including the Zhandouci, the Linshangong Xiujiaocun Yuheci, and the Shangqingcun Hongyunci.

The village is made up of a large Lin surname group of some thirteen hundred people; other surnames include the Huang, Yu, and Zheng, with a combined population of three hundred in all. The village lands originally belonged to a large Buddhist monastery, the Huiyuansi. Local legend has it that the geomancy was only good for monks, not for villagers. This area was known as the Quan'an Zhuang (Buddhist Estate): The villagers got the lands after the temple collapsed in the Qing dynasty.[2] The monks had struggled unsuccessfully over water rights with the powerful Fengting Xie lineage. The Lin surname group were originally from the nearby Kentou village and were probably tenants of the Buddhist Estate. Together with the Doumen village Wu lineage, they jointly built a temple called the Ancanggong in which they principally worshiped Mazu, Sima Shengwang, and Yanggong Taishi. Later the Lin and the Wu lineages fought over water and divided up the temple—the Lin lineage took Mazu (and added in Sima and Taishi); the Wu lineage now just worships Sima Shengwang. At some point the Lin lineage moved into Putou village. Eventually they divided into two branches, the Shangcu and Xiacu, each with its own ancestral home.

In Putou village there was already a Shunjidian (Temple of Harmonious Aid), which had originally been a Buddhist monastery and later became a Confucian academy. Then a plague devastated the village, so members asked the Jade Emperor of the Lingyundian (Temple of the Surpassing Clouds) located on the highest point in the Putian plains, the summit of Hugong Mountian, to come and suppress the plague. Therefore they worship the Jade Emperor in this temple and divided incense from the Lingyundian.

---

[2] This monastery was completely destroyed during the Cultural Revolution but has been completely restored since. For further information on the history of the Huiyansi, see the inscriptions in Dean and Zheng (1995: 460).

All of these temples and their gods were gradually absorbed into the Three in One temple. The gods are now worshiped in halls adjacent to the central hall of the Qixingci. This is the central point of organization for the ritual activity of all the groups worshiping these different gods. Thus on lunar 5/16 they organize a pilgrimage to present incense to the Lingyundian. During that time there are theatrical performances for two to six days. The ten headmen are selected by divination. On lunar 1/19 there is a procession around the spiritual precincts of the community; on lunar 3/23 Mazu's birthday is celebrated. On lunar 4/26 Yang Taishi is offered a one-day Daochang (ritual). On the Three Primes (1/15, 7/15, 10/15) a two-day Daochang is held, with the *zhongyuan* (Middle Prime) festival being especially exuberant, celebrated with theater. The birthdays of the gods are organized by rotation through the eight neighborhoods, most of which are lineage clusters.

The Three in One masters in the Qixingci can perform rituals, and they go to many temples in the area to do them. An initiate goes through the following phases of study: (1) scripture recitation, (2) instruments, (3) ritual choreography, (4) talismans, spells, and secret language (the latter are known in full only by the principal altar master and the deputy altar master). Initiates study the heart method of inner alchemy for the most part every day. A controller of the Teachings directs their practice; they also learn secret words (*miyu*).

"Grasping the Central" Shrine in Kennai Village

Kennaicun in Fengting is divided into two parts, called the Upper and Lower Ancestral Houses; each part had its own temple. In the Beishangong the following gods were worshipped: Guangze Zunwang, Tian Gong Yuanshuai, Yanggong Taishi, Jiayou Shenghou, Shenggong, Zhan Xianshi, Mashi Jiangjun, Jinying Jiangjun, Heshan Jiangjun, Jinshi Jiangjun, Shegong (2), Shema (3), Mashen Jiangjun, and the Huwei Jiangjun. In the other temple, the Peiyuantang, these gods were worshiped: Jixiang Dajiang, Jixiang Shizhe, Huwei Jiangjun, Ciji Zhenjun, Zhang Gong, Wenchang Dijun, Kuidou, Heimian Jiangjun, Wencao Wupan, Zhang Diye, Fuhu Zhushi (Huang Niepan), and Yingling Bozhu (Cai). Both temples were torn down in the 1940s, and the gods were put into a Three in One temple called the Zhizhongci (also referred to as the Zhizhong Shuyuan). At this temple a conglomerate group of gods are worshiped, including at the center the Lord of the Three in One, Zhuo the Daoist Immortal, Zhang Sanfeng, Chen Gong Shenghou, Xuantian Shangdi, Yuhuang Dadi, Sanguan, Zhengxun Shenghou, Mazu, Guanyin, Shijiamoni, Laozi, Confucius, Sima Shengwang, Chen Jinggu, Chenshi Dashi, Li Tiekuai, Luo Daye, Shegong, Shema, Nan Beidou Xingjun, and Mazu's two generals. Most important of the popular gods are Ciji Zhenjun, Chen Gong Shenghou, and Yuhuang Dadi. The Three in One ritualists perform rites on their birthdays and on the Three Primes. This village also takes part in the larger Zhu Zai ritual circuit.

Mirror Mountain Academy in Lindou Village

The Fengting Lindoucun Jingshan Shuyuan is a large Three in One temple said to date back to the late Ming. The village is made up of a single surname, with 800 Chen lineage members there. Of this number, 750 are at home. All are said to be *mentu* (literally, initiates). The *tanzhang* (altar director) is forty-two years old; his father was also *tanzhang*. In the temple the following are worshiped: the Lord of the Three in One, and the Daoists Zhuo and Zhang on one side and Tian Gong Yuanshui (Xianggong) on the other side. The temple makes a pilgrimage every 7/16 to Dongshanci (the Ancestral Temple in Putian) to present incense. The entire village greets the delegation upon its return with a god's palanquin and then circles the village. In the larger ritual circuit to which they belong, the Dongcai 53 village unit, their palanquin (in which the Lord of the Three in One sits) goes first. They claim that the temple was established by Lin Zhao'en in person, and that they have the oldest set of Three in One scriptures and a Ming dynasty palanquin. They do not practice the nine-stage heart method. But their god (Lin Zhao'en) is most effective in divination. Each 1/14 they hold a major *daochang* (ritual). They are famed as a martial Way (*wudao*) village and claim to have established various branches of ritual tradition. They also claim to be in the same tradition as the Qixingci of Fengting and the Yuhuici.

POLAR ATTRACTORS AND GROUP STRATEGIES

These brief case studies have been presented in what may appear to be a rather schematic typology ranging from (1) minority sect with an emphasis on study and self-cultivation to (2) alternative center of ritual activity and group meditation to (3) comprehensive community center for all major social and ritual activities. It would be preferable, instead, to view these instances as points on a spectrum stretching between polar attractors that indicate the range of actualizations of the potentiality of the Three in One in the Xinghua region. One pole consists of the tendency toward embodiment of the model of the Confucian sage. This pole stresses cultural unification, a reintegration and reinvigoration of contemporary Confucian patriarchal society by a radical return to the spirit of the early Confucian sages. The other pole is modeled on the immediacy of spiritual power, the ability to command forces of the cosmos, and can be seen in the apotheosis of Lin Zhao'en into a god within the Xinghua popular pantheon.

The Three in One was caught between these tendencies, yet the social standing of its founders and followers, the social changes that affected it, and the forces that traversed it all assured that neither tendency would overwhelm the other. The low-level local intellectuals who founded the Three in One had little impact on mainstream philosophic movements of the Qing, which

Plate 18. Three in One offerings on the birthdate of Lin Longjiang (from Putian)

tended, on the contrary, to move away from an experimental approach to Confucian self-cultivation toward scholastic evidential research (Elman, 1984). The arena for the display of morality and exemplary behavior on the part of Three in One groups became the village community, particularly after the Qing dynasty bans. Some groups remained closer to an ideal combination of study of the classics, self-cultivation, and exemplary behavior supported by separate status in the community. But this result may have been equally due to the strength of other groups active in the same areas, such as academies, poetry associations, local cult temple committees, community spirit-medium altar associations, or other lay Buddhist and "sectarian" groups, not to mention Buddhist monks and Daoist and other ritual specialists. Some groups fused more completely with village religious life, where efficacy in the performance of rites was a concrete demonstration of the powers of self-cultivation. It is by no means clear that the communities described above represent any general or inevitable pattern of transformation. The astonishing range of Three in One temples and communities in the Xinghua region is a vivid illustration of the principle of multiplicity within processes of individuation.

Nevertheless, several concrete strategies for the attainment of social control, or at least autonomy as a viable social and religious group, can be discerned in these case studies, and in materials in earlier chapters on the founding of Three in One temples. One of the principle means of achieving these ends was the development of an economically viable ritual tradition open to those willing to undergo initiation into the heart method and training in ritual practice. Many Three in One adherents were communal activists looking for a group in which to invest their energies and display their good intentions. Such groups could function to train their members in decision making, sharing complex tasks, and group processes. Armed with these skills, Three in One members could join or become more active in other groups and institutions. In many cases we can see groups of Three in One initiates entering into and merging with lineage formations at the village level. By obtaining leadership positions within these lineages, Three in One groups could control a good deal of village life. These strategies were already apparent in the reconstruction of the Xiangyang Academy by Dong Shi. In the case studies presented in this chapter, the most extreme instance of a merging of the Three in One with lineage power formations is found in the single-surname Lindou village, where the hereditary head of the sole lineage is concurrently the altar master of the Three in One temple. Here the Three in One, village religion, and ancestral worship have been melded into one, as can be seen in the village procession in which the statue of Lin Zhao'en leads the alliance of fifty-three villages in the area. In Kennai village, the Three in One temple has served as a bridge between the two main branches of a single lineage, which had earlier been divided. But in multisurname villages such as Putou (Seven Star Shrine), the Three in One has merged with the major lineage, even while serving as a framework for multisurname unification and village coordination. Much the same could be said of the Zhuguang and Puming academies in Bangtou, although in these cases, other village networks based in different cults and temples, or a more equal distribution of strength between different lineages, serve to contain the influence of the Three in One in the community.

Looking farther back in time, note the tendency in the early period for founders of Three in One shrines to donate their personal homes to be transformed into temples, rather than appealing to the community for a communal construction project. The stele inscription from the Yaodao Academy and the Dongjia inscription detail modes of pooling resources and establishing trust funds for ritual functions. Liturgical texts also make reference to various forms of self-support practiced by members of Three in One groups. These modes of self-help were drawn from models developed by the wide range of autonomous associational groups that flourished in Chinese society, including brotherhoods, spirit associations, joint investment groups, lineages that had transformed into joint stock companies, and secret societies. These associations developed different techniques for self-governing and the division of labor. Some relied on hereditary transmission of offices or selection of successors by a master, while others employed combinations of divination, rotation, voting, consensus, and selection by acclaim. Many Three in One groups experimented with these models.

Another strategy altogether was to seek official patronage or at least official recognition, as seen in the Kangxi period stele inscription at the Jinshan Shrine in Xianyou. At the other end of the social spectrum, groups of marginalized, displaced people have been able to attain a degree of recognition through their involvement with the Three in One, as can be seen in the spirit association of Heping village, which gradually institutionalized itself as a side temple within the framework of the larger village temple. Groups like the highly cultivated elder gentlemen of the Yaochi Academy in Hanjiang suggest that in such a developed and complex urbanized setting it was far more difficult for the Three in One to establish broad control over village or urban ward religious activities. In these areas strong, extended lineages with lands in the villages and shops and ancestral halls in the urban areas proved relatively impervious to the Three in One, except on an individual level. Thus in these areas the Three in One attempted to appeal to a gentry ideal of Confucian sagehood and moral excellence. One sees examples of this ideal and evidence of its appeal in Zhang Qin's stele inscriptions.

In the Republican era, spirit-writing associations (mentioned in stele inscriptions from the Hansantang) provided a powerful organizing strategy. The combination of a supernatural guided seance with primarily Confucian messages was a potent instrument in the reinvention of the Three in One at that time. This may have been one of the most successful efforts within the transformations of the Three in One to balance the polar attractors of Confucian sagehood and supernatural spiritual power. The spread of the Three in One in the late Qing and Republican periods was phenomenal. Although it is difficult to judge precisely, my impression is that the movement may have gone from some one hundred temples in the early Qing, through a long, slow expansion to perhaps two to three hundred temples by the Daoguang period, and then begun to accelerate to four to five hundred by the end of the Qing, with perhaps as many as five hundred more temples established in the Republican period. Some temples have declined, and some new ones have been founded recently, but the past decade and a half has primarily seen the stabilization of the Three in One at a level of approximately one thousand temples. Clearly, the Republican period saw the most rapid expansion, and I suspect that spirit-writing was the motor of this process. The diversity of these strategies and the groups that pursued them, as well as the historical specificity of the circumstances of these struggles for power or autonomy, suggest that we should by all means avoid reifying the Three in One.

INDIVIDUAL LIFE HISTORIES WITHIN THE THREE IN ONE

The polar attractors of Confucian sagehood and immediate spiritual power affected the life trajectories of many individuals involved in the Three in One. We have already explored the phases and patterns in the hagiographic account of Lin Zhao'en's life and examined statements by his disciples, especially those of Dong Shi on his relationship to the Three in One movement. This chapter explores various other individuals' life histories. The first set of testimonials is drawn from the *Jinling zhongyitang xingshi*. These statements were made on the occasion of a gathering of the Nanjing Three in One adherents held in 1614, which resulted in a decision to print ledgers of merit and demerit (*gongguoge*). The second set of sources is from the records of a major Mingxia branch temple in Xianyou during the Republican period. Finally, a set of vignettes of a contemporary ritualist, a temple committee member, and various spirit-mediums concludes the chapter.

The "Mad Monk" Zhen Lai records that he held a meeting in the Jinling Zhongyitang on the 14th of the 1st lunar month of 1631 that was attended by over one hundred initiates who burned incense and worshiped. After the ritual, Zhen Lai addressed the assembly, asking them to reflect on the fact that such rituals had been held successively for nine years in the Zhongyitang. What did all this ritual activity mean to the people present, he wondered. All of them had studied the teachings of the Master and had received instructions in the secrets of the heart method, but had they believed what they studied, practiced the heart methods, and improved their virtue? Several people then spoke up at once, "wagging their old wives' tongues," crowding forward, and all shouting at the same time. Only a small group remained kneeling, earnestly seeking instruction. Zhen Lai told them,

"Within never leave off practicing the heart method. Thereby the *yin* world will be refined. Externally be conscientious in practicing the ledgers of merit and demerit. Thereby all karmic entanglements will dissipate. Moreover, don't think about the past, but put your mind to finding 'convenient means' in the moment. In the future you must deliberate even less. What is crucial is that the 'work [of inner alchemy]' be tight (*jinmi*). Do not allow any idle moment to creep in. Then extraneous thoughts will have no way to enter. This is what is meant by 'being conscientious.' If you disciples all work at it, you will attain it."

[Tao] Minqi then said, "How can we but admire our teacher's lesson?" [Xie] Zaizhi said, "We should practice the Nine Stages of the heart method, storing up spirit and breath in order to invest (*zi*) them in our nature and destiny (*xingming*). Externally, we should uphold the ledgers of merit and demerit, in order to differentiate good and evil. Maintaining this simultaneous inner and outer cultivation is what is meant by the expression 'to reach the other shore you need a raft.' Only when one has achieved a state of doing neither good deed nor demerit, and being without a heart/mind or a ritual method, can one say that the other shore has been reached and the boat abandoned."

[Zhou] Rengshu said, "Daily make up for your former mistakes, without worrying about how people act. If you can obtain a concentrated heart, then you can cultivate your nature. Earnestly repent and confess, and thereby gradually cultivate [yourself]. Suddenly you will be enlightened. This is what is called the Pure Land. Thus headaches and professional struggles are all fundamentally empty. Follow both the [way of] man and [the way] of the Dharma, and thus neither misfortune nor good fortune will be your master." [Xu] Qingyu said, "Every day we are seized by our feeling or our senses, tossed this way and that within the world. Thus people in their everyday relations feel constrained and confused. If you are willing to examine yourself carefully, you will begin to comprehend [this]. Understanding [this], you will return to the key and [re]unite with your fundamental virtue."

The entire assembly listened to these testimonials with all their heart, not leaving all night long. A method of calculating merits and demerits was instituted, and there was no one who did not believe in it. Thereupon they printed a thousand volumes [of this ledger] and distributed it all around. They hoped that readers would carry out the [recommended actions] and thereby accumulate excellent merit for themselves, while their evil deeds would fade away. Some formed associations to practice the [ledgers] together, meeting every month. They recorded their experiences with merits and demerits, taking this to be an aid in the polishing of their hearts and bodies. (*Jinling zhongyitang xingshi, xia juan,* 31b–33a)

Yet in a sense the meeting and these testimonials prove ambiguous. As Zhen Lai remarked elsewhere, out of every ten people who take up the heart method, only one or two keep up with it (*xia juan,* 20a). Individual spiritual progress cannot be regulated or routinized. But to Zhen Lai and his disciples, it seemed that moral conduct could be codified by means such as the publication and regular utilization of the ledgers of merit or demerit. The regulation of moral conduct held out the promise that the performance of merit would lead to the rewards of social recognition.

Many of these ambiguous contradictory tendencies surface in the *Daxing-shuyuan yangeji* (Record of the development of the Daxing Academy), a 1948 manuscript that contains two autobiographical statements, both entitled *Gui-jiao jingli lueji* (Summary account of [my] experiences within the [Three in One] Teachings). These accounts by Huang Chengyi and his friend Chen Xingben enable us to get a very close picture of how individual practitioners gradually rose through the ranks of the temple hierarchy, as the two friends, both based in the Daxingci, worked in different capacities for various temples in the Xianyou area over a period of forty years. The most important halls with which the initiates and ritualists of the Daxingci interacted were the Xuan-huaci (Shrine of the Mysterious Transformation), Baosongci (Shrine of the Precious Pine), Chanxintang (Hall of the Heart of Zen), and Peishanci (Shrine of Prepared Goodness). The Baosongci was eventually absorbed into the Zhuzhenci, leading to a new transmission of liturgies and scriptures. What follows is a translation of the accounts of these two leaders of the Daxingci between the years 1917 and 1945.

A Summary Account of My Experiences within the Teachings of the [Three in One], by Huang Chengyi

I have researched the fact that my ancestors have for generations been initiated into the Three in One. In 1917, when I was twenty-seven years old, my classmate and friend, the *kuisheng* (provincial candidate with distinction) Tang Fubin, began teaching at the Zunshengci (Shrine for Revering of the Saints). Those days,

my friends Cai Mingji, Yu Xingqi, Wei Caiyu, and I frequently went to the Zunshengci to study [ultimate] principles with Master Tang. Tang often pointed out
to me that his ancestor had been the patron founder of the shrine. Therefore I
was initiated with Tang as my witness at the Zunshengci. At the time, I considered initiation to be merely a social obligation, and I didn't think anything about
it for quite some time.

It was not until 1925 that, with my friends Yan Yuanfu and Wei Caiyu as witnesses, I went to Hou Zhang village to visit Zheng Shiling (Bide). . . . At this
time, activities at the Daxingtang had died away. With Zheng Bide at the lead,
Yan, Wei, and I went to the Daxingtang and reorganized its activities. So it was
that this year at the Qingming festival it was decided by divination that Wei Caiyu
(Name in the Way: Daozun), would be zhangjiao (controller of the Teachings),
Cai Cengjing would continue as bingjiao (deputy), and I was entrusted with the
task of shizuo (deputy assistant altar master) and was given the Name in the Way
of Chengyi (he who carries on the One). At that time Zheng Shiling taught me
mystic visualizations and the secrets of inner alchemy (lit. elixirs). In the 4th lunar
month of that year (1925) I requested that I be given full responsibilities for my
post. But after being given the job I felt that I was inadequate in ritual matters
and asked to be let go. Zheng Shiling urged that I be put in charge of secretarial
matters and the writing of documentary forms for ritual purposes.

In 1926 the Daxingtang planned to hold a *Wuzhe dahui*. Therefore, Zheng
Shiling ordered Yan Yuanfu to take pledges and gifts to the Xuanhuaci and to invite the god Great Reverend Master Zhou from the Xuanhuaci to the Daxingci
to look after the pudu rite. At this time I "grasped the brush and followed the
movements of the planchette" (i.e., took up the role of interpreter of the seance).
I continued this work for over twenty years. Later that year I was reinitiated at
the Xuanhuaci. In accordance with the instructions of the Great Reverend Master Zhou, Fan Qianyi transmitted the elixir secrets to me.

From 1927 to 1928 I assisted at performances of the *Wuzhe dahui* at each of
the following branch shrines: the Chengshantang, Naishengtang, Fenchici, Hui-
shanci, and Meishanci. I was invited to act as a member of the organizing committee and to handle secretarial matters. In 1926 and 1928 both the Xuanhua
and the Daxing temples held *Wuzhe dahui*. [Later on] in the spring of 1940 the
Xuanhua temple also held a *Yulan shenghui*, and in the autumn of 1946 the same
temple held a *Sanqi pudu* (General Assembly of the Adherents). I was entrusted
with the duties of general manager for all these events, as well as taking care of all
secretarial matters.

In the spring of 1927 I accepted the order to go with Fan Qianyi and Xiao
Pingxie and some twenty-four adherents to take part in the Regional Great Assembly of the Xia Teachings at the Ancestral Shrine on East Mountain. In this
meeting Xiao Pingbi and I were responsible for making offerings and representing the Daxingci and Xuanhuaci. We read a statement that had been composed
by planchette in the words of the Great Master Zhou.

In 1938 every sector of Xianyou held a *Lichan dahui* (Great Assembly for Worship and Penitence). I was made general manager and put in charge of secretar-

ial matters. In 1946 in the autumn and winter, the Feishan, Xuanhua, and Mei-
shan temples held a great assembly. They had prepared a lecture stage beforehand.
I lectured on the Classics from the stage all night long. In the spring of 1938 I
went to Wanfugong village to raise the ridge-pole of the Feishantang and assisted
in the activities of the consecration services. The beams were raised in the autumn.
At Mid-autumn Festival a consecration ritual was held. During the offering of sacrifices I acted as one of the presenters of offerings and as lecturer on the scriptures. From *bingyin* to *xuzi* the temples of the Xia teachings all over Xianyou district frequently held *Daoqi dahui* (Great Assemblies of the Nodes of the Way). I
was often invited to speak on the scriptures. In 1940 I helped Wu Ruiying build
the Zhongshantang in Kuitang village. In the summer of 1945, in accordance
with an order from the Great Master Zhou, I went to the Feishantang where the
planchette instructed that I take up the position of *zhangjiao* at the Xuanhua and
Daxingci temples with the Name in the Way of Rengzhao (Still Shining). It was
decided by divination to send up a memorial [about this] at the Xuanhuatang on
lunar 6/9 and to request a seance at the Daxingci on 6/10. On 6/12 I sent up
another memorial at the Feishantang. I 1946 I took complete charge of all the
affairs and secretarial matters for the *Sanqi pudu* and General Assembly of Adherents held at the Xuanhuatang.

   In 1934 I had followed Fan Qianyi's lead in going to the homes of all adherents to participate in the *Daoqi yuehui*, taking charge of the recitations and lectures. In the summer of 1935 I established a Daode Zixiu Yexueguan (Night
School for the Self-cultivation of the Way and Its Power) and lectured on the
scriptures there. I also established the Yangxing Yaofang (Pharmacy for the Cultivation of [Underlying] Nature), Xiao Heyi acted as director of the pharmacy,
and I served as deputy director. We were tireless in our efforts to produce medicines to distribute to the needy. In 1948 I took charge of establishing a Female
Teaching group at the Daxingci. At this time I regularly gathered and recopied
Daoist books relating to inner alchemy. I collated various editions of liturgical
texts. I frequently instructed and trained people in the performance of ritual and
the composition of documentary forms and ritual memorials, never resting noon
or night. I always practiced inner alchemy without ceasing. Yet somehow I was
distracted by "dust and demons," and I was frequently invaded by everyday duties, so it was hard for me to achieve enlightenment regarding the mystic key
within the inner work, and my external affairs were completely without accomplishment. When I think deeply about this I feel shame, and I am embarrassed
when I examine myself. It is only by virtue of my single-minded belief and dedi-
cation of my life [to the Three Teachings] that I have been able to avoid heavy
illness and enjoy an old age. In conclusion, after being initiated into the teachings, I was fortunate to encounter the protection and instruction of the Great
Master Zhou. Thus I say: "My parents gave me life, my Reverend Master taught
me!" and "The Way of Heaven is hard to match, the Space of the Way is hard to
find." True indeed are these words. Therefore the merit of the Great Master is
enormous and immeasurable. Thus I have recorded my experiences in the hopes
that the sages and philosophers who succeed me in the Way will follow the cor-

rect Way and not fall into false paths far from the Way. All who are ignorant can still achieve enlightenment. The true key is their hope.

A Summary Account of My Experiences within the Teachings of the [Three in One], by Chen Xingben

My family, in former generations, moved in the Ming Hongwu period from Quanzhou to Xianyou City's River Channel Lane (next door to the Daxingci).[3] Only at the end of the Qing did they move to Jixing Lane off Yongzheng Road. Being so close to a saintly locale, for generations my ancestors entered into the Xia path [of the Three Teachings]. In the Late Qing my revered grandfather, the Honorable [Chen] Yang, entered the religion at an early age. He studied scriptures and liturgies, taking charge of secretarial matters and the copying of scriptures, and frequently printed Daoist texts and scriptures with the former *bingjiao* of the Daxingci, Zhang Daoxue. He was praised by fellow adherents for this work.

In the early Republican period, my revered father [Chen] Deming followed in his father's footsteps and entered the Three in One early, and so from his teenage years through to his old age, he was very experienced in the Xia Way's liturgies and every aspect of its rituals. He assisted in establishing the Zhuzhenci. Together with my former father-in-law, Zhang Xintian, he helped build the Shifengci (Stone Peak Shrine) and assisted in repairing the Rusong Nunnery. He was even more active in charitable work. He assisted in disaster relief, gathered unburied corpses, repairing bridges and roads, dispensing medicine. He also helped organize the ritual affairs of the Xiashantang (Misty Mountain Hall). He helped out in all kinds of charitable work, and in all matters he extended every effort. Although at this time I was but a teenager, and still in the midst of my studies, I was able to assist my father in some of these activities. This was one phase.

In 1933, on the deserted foundations of the Rusong Nunnery, the Baosongtang was built. When the positions were chosen by divination, my father was selected to be the *zhangjiao,* and I was selected for the position of *shizuo,* and so I took my training at the Daxingci. That year at the Mid-autumn Festival we held a consecration ritual, and at the same time we were blessed by the descent of the Great Master Zhou and the Great Master Immortal Zhang Tianyi, who one after another gave their instructions [by planchette]. That same year, in the winter, the Great Master [Fan] Qianyi personally transmitted the secrets of the elixir to me, saying that I should at the same time keep up [ritual activity]. His instructions were very exhaustive. Shortly afterward, in the Baosongtang and the Nanglitang, I kept active. Each time there were lectures [on the writings of Lin Zhao'en], [there was also] the giving of aid to the impoverished and the giving out of medicine to the ill. All kinds of charity work made rapid progress at that time. In no time the temple was beautiful and complete, solemn and tall, and adherents filled the halls of the temple. This was another phase.

---

[3] On a visit to this home in 1992, I was shown a Ming dynasty land deed belonging to the family that contained the lines "west to the outer wall of the Daxingci as the outer limit [of the property]."

In 1934 I took part in a Night School for self-cultivation of the way and its virtue as a registered student. In the summer of 1935 I rotated positions and went to live in the Daxingci. I learned a lot from Great Master Zhou's messages. Under Great Master [Fan] Qianyi's instruction, I studied the elixir method of the inner work. I also studied liturgy and scripture to great avail. In 1936 the Baosongci was taken over and turned into a school, so the Baosongci was temporarily moved into the Daxingci. The former *zhutan,* Fan Kongzhou, had died, and I temporarily took over all instruction of ritual performance. That same year, in the autumn, I led [a group of] adherents to the East Mountain Shrine in Puyang to present incense and worship the Sainted [Lin Zhao'en]. At the mid-autumn celebrations at the Daxingci, the Great Master Zhou descended to take part in the diannual celebration. I was in charge of these rituals. I also took part in the ritual [purification-]pacification of the hall and assisted the former Altar Master Peng Chengyi. I carefully took up the job of carrying out the duties of the liturgies and rituals of the communal sacrifice, and the rites were the most solemn and splendid of that period. In the spring of 1937, Deputy Altar Master Li Xingxiu went overseas. His deceased father had asked him to raise funds overseas, and he sent back a sum of money. At that time, the Zhuguangci collapsed, so the entire sum of money Li Xingxiu had sent was used to repair it and make it as good as new. The Baosongtang and the Zhuzhenci were combined and renamed the Zhuzhen Baosongtang. The temple was beautiful and filled with adherents. All the affairs of the temple, including rituals and charity work, were my responsibility. The fame of the temple spread far and wide. This was yet another phase.

In 1938 I was invited to the Feishanci to teach liturgy and ritual practice. I was tireless at this task. In former years Altar Master Fan Kongzhou taught the external rites of liturgy, and Qin Qinfang taught the singing and drumming at the Xuanhuaci. Both of these masters passed away in 1940, and I received the sincere invitation of Altar Master Huang Debiao and accepted the order of Master Qianyi to go, together with my friend in the Way, Zheng Zucan, to teach and transmit liturgies and scriptures at the Xuanhuatang. We made some innovations and our accomplishments were clear. That year in the spring I was responsible for the Yulan [pudu] ritual and ritual documentation. The scene at the hall was magnificent. This was yet another phase.

In the spring of 1942 I received an invitation from the male and female religious officials and various disciples, and with Master Chengyi's permission (lit., at his order), I went to the Yuanxinci (Shrine of the Wellspring of the Heart) to teach and transmit liturgy and take charge of ritual practices. I refused to accept any remuneration and spared no effort. I struggled to transmit the veins of the Way. In the summer of 1945 I accepted an invitation from Altar [Master] Chungguang of the Zunshengci (Shrine to Revere the Sage) to teach ritual practice there. In the autumn of 1946 I accepted the invitation of Feishan[ci]'s *zhangjiao* Yang Zhiyi to take charge of ritual documents and altar arrangements for a [large-scale rite], the *Wuzhe dahui,* and to teach ritual practice [at the shrine]. In the autumn of 1946 the Chengsan (Hall for Carrying on the Three [Teachings]) and the Xiansheng (Former Sages Hall) held a Longhua *Wuzhe dahui* ritual. The temple committee members received instructions from the Perfected Being Zhang (Sanfeng—probably by planchette) to invite me to take charge of all the ritual documentation. I edited the entire set of liturgical texts into a set of volumes [for the ritual] and organized the entire ritual. I worked myself to the limit at this, and my efforts were praised by the entire temple committee and by representatives of all the branch temples of the Daxingci. This was another phase.

In the summer of 1945 Assistant (i.e., Third) Altar Master Huang Chengyi succeeded to the post of *zhangjiao* [vacated at the death of Master] Shangyi. The position of assistant altar master was vacant. I accepted the order to be promoted to the post of assistant altar master of the Ancestral Daxing Hall. In the summer of 1947 the newly appointed deputy altar master of the Daxingci, Cai Mingyi, organized the initiates to ask me to teach them external ritual practices, saying this would be most beneficial, and that they had many shortcomings in this area. So in the winter of 1948 I directed a *Sanqi pushi* at the Xuanhua[ci] and another at the same time at the *Feishan[ci] dahui*. . . . I also helped conduct *Yulanpenhui* at the Zunshengci and the Yuanxinci. All these efforts were successfully completed. [At this time we] received indications regarding inner alchemy [via the planchette] from the Great Master [the Immortal Zhou]. [Zhangjiao] Qianyi transmitted [illegible character] revered [one's?] instructions. Qianyi's literary output was lectured upon by the Honorable Xiao and Huang [Chengyi], who together clarified several points. This was another phase.

In conclusion, I regret that the roots of my Dao are too shallow, and that my character and talents are too common, so I could not become enlightened about the mystic key, or make shine the inner work, or [achieve more] than one-ten-thousandth of the secrets of the elixir. But from the time I received my initiation at the Daxingci onward, I worked hard at teaching scriptures, external rites, and liturgy. I raced about to the various branch shrines and temples to train younger adherents. I made my contribution to the ancestral hall (Daxingci), however minor this contribution may have been. . . . The deep sources of my Way broadly deliver those good people who believe in it. I personally have inclined toward devoting myself to the Teachings. This has been my personal inclination and sincere aspiration. I recall that the Revered Great Master Zhou transmitted a message stating that Ten Philosophers would appear. The assembled sages [of the Daxingci] eagerly anticipate that there will be worthy successors who will fulfill the merciful heart of the Great Master in saving the times and saving the people. The veins of the Way will be transmitted forever. This is my deepest hope. Therefore I composed this brief account of my experiences within the Teachings.[4]

Several vectors emerge from these autobiographical accounts. These include increased ritualization, increased emphasis on communication with the gods, and increased popularization of the Three in One teachings. As seen in

[4] A concluding passage following these two autobiographies comments that major figures such as Lin Youyu in the Daxingci in the Republican period had taught disciples in eleven different shrines, that they never took any money for their efforts, and that they also performed requiems and auspicious rituals for individual families.

the case studies above, while a few sectors within the Three in One still emphasize the importance of inner cultivation, in most communities in Xianyou the Three in One is chiefly influential as a publicly oriented ritual tradition. Huang Chengyi was cognizant of this tendency, as he indicated in the preface to the *Record of the Development of the Daxing Academy:*

> I have often observed that the shrines and academies of the Xia path that are so abundant in Xianyou are the crowning glory of the prefecture and the entire coastal region. Yet those who are intitiated into the Teachings, although full of belief, still vainly worship [as though worshiping] spirits in order to obtain peace and security. They study external ritual, singing, dancing, and the minutiae of ritual practice, to please the common masses. None of them work on the study of *xin, shen, xingming* (heart-mind, body, and human nature, i.e., self-cultivation) or practice meditating in stillness to protect their life. They go so far as to divide into different branches and groups, practice the Left-hand Way and peripheral teachings, mistakenly transmit secret elixir recipes, and devote themselves to the performance of ritual, relying on their spreading fame to seize a profit for themselves. They turn their back on the marvelous meanings of the teachings of the Lord. Their errors are so uncanonical that the government look upon them as a type that should be severely eradicated.

With regard to the increasing emphasis on contacting spiritual powers, the autobiographies reveal the central role of spirit-writing by planchette in the Three in One in Republican times. The chief means by which leaders of the Daxing Academy extended their control over branch shrines such as the Hall of Mystic Transformations was by sending a statue of the god Great Master Zhou to the branch shrine. The god was consulted through planchette for all major decisions regarding rituals, and many texts recited in ritual were composed by the god through spirit-writing. The god's decision also determined the selection of people for different positions within the temple leadership. Moreover, communications from the god via spirit-writing frequently revealed that various deceased members of the Daxing Academy temple committee had been assigned to serve as protector of the altar gods in smaller branch temples. This increased reliance on spirit-writing is also seen in the *Zhenjiabao* thirty-year record of seances at the Wuben and Hansantang discussed above. The stele translated above on the role of the Great Immortal (Zhang Sanfeng) in the founding of the Hansantang also demonstrates the central role of spirit-writing in this period.

The "popularization" of the Three in One in the Republican period refers to its increasing role in social services and welfare. The Daxing Academy became involved in the dispensation of medicines, rice, coffins, and free burials of the untended dead, along with the performance of group rites such as the *Lanpen pudu* and the *Wuzhe dahui*. The most significant event of this kind was the massive ritual of deliverance for the local and Overseas Chinese martyrs of the Anti-Japanese War held in 1938 by the leaders of the Daxing Academy. These ritual-events expanded the influence of the Three in One, while its increasing involvement in social services caused it gradually to merge with a new, broader conception of "local customary practices," downplaying its specificity as a religious group.

CONTEMPORARY ORAL HISTORIES

The Zhandouci is near Hepingcun in Fengting, Xianyou. The shrine was originally built in the 1930s, inside the home of a ritualist. The current leader of the Zhandouci, one Mr. Zheng, was a leader of a Xinghua Red Guard faction that fell into disfavor. Discouraged and futureless, he returned to his home, where he devoted himself to the study of Chinese herbal medicine. After a few years he was approached by elder Three in One adherents, who noted his good work as an herbalist and encouraged him to study the heart method and ritual practice with them. After several months of secret tutelage, the group decided to perform underground Three in One rites in private homes (mostly requiem services), beginning in 1972. The group went public in 1978, with Mr. Zheng now its leader. They quickly developed a wide following by offering rituals at a low rate for individuals who were making up for the lack of rituals during the Cultural Revolution. The explosive reconstruction and repair of Three in One and popular god temples in the area led to more demands for ritual services. The Zhandouci ritualists honed their skills in song, dance, and ritual performance while building up a set of liturgical manuscripts (see bibliography). Many of the temples they consecrated maintained relations with them, inviting them back on an annual basis to perform rites of celebration of the birthdays of the gods of the temples. The group became prosperous and decided to build a new Three in One temple. The Minghemiao (Brilliant Lotus Temple) was built over six months in 1992 for a cost of approximately 100,000 RMB (U.S. $12,000). Many supplies and much of the labor were volunteered, so actual costs would likely be double that amount. This is within the average cost range for the construction of a new house in this area. The temple was consecrated with a large ritual attended by representatives of many Three in One temples, who left commemorative mirrors and inscriptions. Mr. Zheng is now a respected elder and is considering retiring from ritual work to take up Chinese medicine once again. Considerable stores of herbs have already been stockpiled within the temple, so it is likely that he will continue to work within the framework of the temple and the Three in One.

One of the leaders of the temple committee of the Dongshan Zongkongtang in Putian, a Mr. Lin, was a military man who had joined the Communist party. In his forties he fell ill and learned the Three in One heart method. The success of the technique led him to learn more about the doctrines and rituals. He quietly took his initiation and began looking for a chance to disengage himself from the party. This opportunity arose when he was hospitalized in the same room with the local party secretary. He implored the secretary to allow him to retire from his military position and from his party post. His request was granted, and he was able to devote himself full-time to the activities of the Dongshanci Zongkongtang. His connections in local military and party circles have proven to be a major asset for the Three in One, for the Zongkongtang has been reclaimed bit by bit from a military barracks over the past fifteen years. Mr. Lin has put his administrative skills to work in organizing a reunification movement within the Three in One, along with the temple reconstruction project, appeals to the government for official recognition as a religion, work on the organization of an international conference, relations with Overseas Chinese Three in One associations, large-scale ritual celebrations, and publication projects (the collected works of Lin Zhao'en, as well as the *Xiawunijing* in four volumes, have been printed recently). He has also initiated over two hundred new adherents and participates in rituals and meditation. He is a member of the temple committee, consisting of fifteen representatives of different regions of Putian and Xianyou, and concurrently a member of the Overseas Chinese Three in One Association, which has about twelve members.

SPIRIT-MEDIUMISM

In addition to providing a framework for self-cultivation and the ritual practice of individual adherents, a number of Three in One shrines also feature spirit possession. This is the case in a newly built and very large Three in One shrine in Xianyou. The woman around whom the temple has been built is possessed by the Yang Jiajiang female warrior goddesses (see the introduction, "Scene 2"). This woman tells an interesting story about her transformation into a spirit-medium. When she first became possessed her husband dragged her away from the temple. Two days later she fell in the kitchen and struck her head. She had to be hospitalized. In the hospital she had visions of Lin Zhao'en and Guanyin coming to visit her, encouraging her to continue as a medium. But when her husband discovered she was at it again, he dragged her away a second time. Two days later their son fell off his bicycle and broke his leg. The woman secretly returned to acting as a medium but was caught by her husband a third time. Then, two days later, his brood of young pigs all died. That was the last straw—he had had enough. He accompanied his wife to the small shrine where she had been possessed, knelt, and burned incense, praying for the god's protection. Since this time her reputation has continued to grow, and the temple where she works is one of the largest Three in One temples in Xianyou.

Another example of spirit possession in the Three in One tradition is that found in the Heping village temple in the Fengting area. A group of former longshipmen had been thrown into extreme poverty by the decline of the small harbor in the village. They formed a small Three in One shrine along the lines of a *shenminghui* (spirit association for mutual aid) and cast lots to see which of them should be the medium. An elderly gentleman was selected,

Plate 19. Altar of the Zongxingtang, showing the goddess Yang beside the central figure of Lin Longjiang

and he has since often been possessed by Tian Gongyuanshuai. Gradually the influence of this small group grew in the village, and they moved into a side room of the village temple, which became a Three in One shrine. Since one of the group was an old widower, he eventually took up residence in the temple and served as the temple keeper for the entire village temple (the main shrine was dedicated to Sima Shengwang and Mazu). Thus the group gradually attained a relatively permanent status in the village, and they lead rituals on the birth dates of Lin Zhao'en, Tian Gongyuanshuai, and other gods associated with the Three in One. These rituals are attended by a large number of village families on a voluntary basis. Individuals who seek supernatural assistance or advice can ask the medium to attempt to be possessed by the god, who then responds to their questions.

In general, almost every Three in One shrine or temple is equipped with a forked stick for spirit-writing seances, although the practice seems to have subsided from a high point in the Republican period. Spirit possession is now even less common in the Three in One as a whole, and so far I have not found any evidence of people being possessed by either Lin Zhao'en or his main disciples. These activities must be seen in context. Almost every village cluster in the Xinghua area has an active spirit-medium temple, often quite small, and frequently referred to as a *dong* (cavern). These temples operate on an ad hoc basis, when people come to ask for advice about illness or business or family matters. Most work with a combination of planchette and direct possession.

In addition to these small temples, a variety of specialists concentrate on mediumistic encounters with the dead. In the Xinghua area, these mediums are referred to as *qianwang* (guiding the dead). They usually work out of their homes. The Three in One has relatively little mediumism when compared with the distribution of such cavern-temples and other specialists in spirit possession active in the area.

After all, spirit-mediumism is an extreme form of the manifestation of supernatural power (*ling*). In most Three in One contexts, this is too extreme a form to balance with the pull toward Confucian modes of sagehood. This tendency to avoid complete identification with village god cults can be seen elsewhere. Instances where Lin Zhao'en's statue is taken on a procession around the spiritual boundaries of the village are extremely rare, in striking contrast to the hundreds of gods in the thousands of temples of the Xinghua region who process quite regularly.[5] So far, the spirit-writing that drove the Republican-period expansion of the Three in One has not made a major revival. The following chapter explores the potentialities of the Three in One in contemporary China and examines certain strategies that specific groups are pursuing.

[5] Village processions involve carrying the god on a sedan chair in a place of honor in the procession. In contrast, during a presentation of incense (*jinxiang*) procession or pilgrimage to the Dongshan Zongkongtang or other sites sacred to the Three in One, small statues of Lin Zhao'en are carried along within portable, model wooden temples and then set on the altar.

The Three in One in Contemporary China

ONE SECTOR of the current Three in One leadership is involved in a concerted effort to reorganize the entire movement in order to unify and standardize the tradition, thereby enhancing their control and, they believe, making the Three in One more acceptable to the state. Official recognition as a religion is a cherished political objective of this group. Several obstacles stand in the way of this goal, having to do with both the complexity of the Three in One and the rigidity of official definitions of religious groups. Nevertheless, the leadership committee based in the Dongshan Zongkongtang continues to submit requests to the government; conduct surveys of the movement; gather, edit, and republish scriptures and early historical texts; organize study groups and teams of ritual and managerial consultants; and issue documents to the one thousand temples connected to the movement. This chapter first examines several texts related to this process. The first of these is the *Xiajiao guizhang jielu* (Prescriptions, ordinances, and rules of the Xia Teaching), a document drawn up by the Dongshan Ancestral Shrine temple committee and distributed to every Three in One temple in the fall of 1989. Second, we examine inexpensive mimeographed broadsheets, distributed to appeal to younger and less educated people, which are passed out at temples and in inner alchemy instruction groups. A related set of materials includes printed primers on the philosophy and regulations on the Three in One. Finally, we examine the rise of "conferences of the gods" and other contemporary arenas for the contestation of the meaning of the Three in One in contemporary China.

The following regulations were issued by the Dongshan Zongkongtang leadership committee and can be seen posted in most Three in One temples in the Xinghua area.

XIAJIAO GUIZHANG JIELU (PRESCRIPTIONS, ORDINANCES, AND RULES OF THE XIA TEACHING)

In order to carry on the unification of the Way given in the orthodox teachings of the Xia Teachings, and to urge initiates to rectify their hearts and refine their bodies, personally carry out the teachings, and to rectify corrupt practices, set straight the attitudes of the [Three in One], and especially to [act] in accordance with the scriptural writings of the Xia school, respecting the laws of the current authorities, carefully examine the following prescriptions, ordinances, and rules:

1. Initiates into the Xia religion must be obedient to the leadership of the party and the government, observe the laws and policies of the nation, and carry out normal religious activities.

2. Uphold the principle of voluntary admittance into the religion. Anyone desiring initiation should fill out an Initiation Proclamation and carry out the initiation formalities, including the initiation ritual. The witness should recite the contents of the Initiation Proclamation and transmit the heart method. After having been initiated, one must demand of oneself to act in accordance with the Proclamation and diligently practice inner work (inner alchemy).

3. Adhere to orthodox self-cultivation, and do not engage in activities such as discussing the demonic and speaking of the bizarre, engage in spirit possession, the recitation of spells or the writing of talismans, divining people's fates, or determining good fortune and bad luck, healing illness by writing talismans, or any other actions that lead to the destruction of the regime of the [cultivation] of the "heart-mind, body, and human nature." Even more should one prohibit using the aforementioned techniques to act ostentatiously, swindle, and deceivingly steal the property of the masses. Even when taking part in [acceptable] religious activities of the religion, one may not accept money or gifts.

4. One should "establish one's base" in the regular four professions, and not delight in idleness and despise work, abstaining from proper employment. [Avoid] participating in prostitution, gambling, and drinking in order to avoid sinking into the stream of criminals and misfits.

5. Increase unity! Fellow members should respect the elderly and care for the young, befriending their siblings. When they have done well they should be acknowledged, when they make mistakes they should be counseled, when they are ill they should be looked after, when they are in adversity they should save one another. Do not have people trying to outwit one other, or claim one thing before a person and then deny it behind his back, or develop divisions and spread rumors that lead to incidents.

6. Uphold the unification of the religion, and do not form cliques and factions, each setting up its own banner, and each going its own way.

7. The shrines [and halls] of the Xia religion should be peaceful, pure places for the discussion of scriptures and the performance of [rituals]. It is not permitted to gamble inside them or gather for drinking, to play majiang or poker, to gossip about people, or to discuss illusory, confusing, or filthy matters, in order to avoid dispute and damage to the spirit of the religion.

8. Each shrine [or hall] should keep accounts of any income [contributed]. These accounts should be publicly displayed every month or seasonally, so that the community all are informed and to hold them up for public approval.

Each shrine [or hall] must uphold and observe these regulations together. They may not lapse from them. If there are those who disobey them, then depending on the gravity of the circumstances, they should be given appropriate instruction. If the infractions are extremely serious then they are no longer considered initiates, and we will support the government authorities in carrying out strict punishments.

This document is typical of the reunification movement launched by the leadership committee of the Zongkongtang on East Mountain in Putian.

Their goal is government recognition of their status as a religion. In many ways, their actions continue the tendencies toward unification and orthodoxy exhibited by the Four Transmitters in the Ming-Qing transition and the Wubentang and Hansantang groups in the Republican period. The constant refrain of these documents is the need to uphold morality, avoid corruption, and, above all, prevent the pull of supernatural power as manifested in spirit possession, the writing of talsimans, or divination. For the leadership groups in the Three in One, supernatural power can move all too rapidly from the upright to the demonic.

BROADSHEETS

In an effort to present the basics of the Three in One to farmers and urban dwellers with only rudimentary education, several methods have been explored. These include ritual performances, public explication of scriptures, murals outlining the life and deeds of Lin Zhao'en, and the publication of a range of pamphlets and broadsheets on the Three in One. The following dialogue was written in simple Mandarin and lithographically reproduced on cheap paper:

EXPLANATORY ANSWERS ON THE ESSENTIALS OF THE THREE TEACHINGS

A: Ah Lin! Today I'm feeling bored, I'd like to hear your news. I'm going to ask you something and I want you to give me a careful answer.

B: OK! Go ahead.

A: The "Three Teachings" you're always talking about, where did it come from anyway?

B: Ah Xie, have a seat and listen. The founder of the Three Teachings was born in the Ming dynasty. He was born in Zhengde 12 (that is, 1516 [*sic*]) on the 10th day of the 7th month in the yin hour. He was named Lin Zhao'en, his *zi* was Yuele, he was also known as Longjiang (Dragon River), and his Daoist name was Ziguzi. His family lived in Chizhu Lane of Putian City, in Fujian Province. He was clever as a child and loved to study. He pitied the poor and the weak. When he grew up he didn't take an official position, and he gave up the scholar-literati profession and dedicated himself with all his energy to philosophical research. He combined the three families of Confucianism, Daoism, and Buddhism into one family, and he wrote the world-famous *Zhengzong tonglun* in thirty-six *juan*. He also wrote the medical *qigong* text "The Nine States."

A: How many religions are there anyway?

B: There are a lot of religions in the world, but five of them have received the most attention.

A: Which five?

B: The greatest was the Saintly Teaching. This was our Chinese ethnic traditional religion. From the Spring and Autumn and the Warring States to the Ming and

Qing period, there was not a single emperor who did not revere it as the Way and use it to bring harmony to his household and rule the empire. [He goes on to introduce Daoism, Buddhism, Christianity, and Islam.]

A: Since there are these five religions, what need is there for a Three Teachings?

B: Creation and decline are the unchangeable rule of the universe. Because the development of fresh, new things meets the needs of the times, [Lin] made use of the professional theories of the former [religious leaders] and added new elements and made revisions, so that the result would be even more beneficial. Therefore the heavens endowed him and the [Three Teachings] were born.

A: Why is it called "Three Teachings"?

B: The name of the Three Teachings is due to its reverence for three ritual teachings; that is, Confucianism, Daoism, and Buddhism. . . .

A: Since according to you there are five major religions in the world, why is it that the last two are not revered, but only the first three?

B: It's like this. The first two religions were Chinese ethnic historical traditional religions. The next only entered China in the Tang and mixed with the others, and was similar in principles with the others, as it was a relatively progressive religion. The last two only recently entered China, and since Lin Longjiang was born in the Ming, he couldn't have heard the names of these religions, nor understood their principles, so he would not have known to revere them.

A: As you put it, there really were objective [reasons] for this situation, and that's why there are five religions but only three religions are revered. I'd like to ask another question. Given that there are three religions that are revered, which is the most important?

B: Returning to Confucianism and revering Confucius is the most important.

A: Why should one "return to Confucianism and revere Confucius"? Why not "return to Daoism and revere Laozi"?

The text carries on in this way, explicating basic terms and tenets of the Three in One, such as the Confucian virtues, the Three Bonds and the Five Constancies, and basic terms from the alchemical method. An interesting obsession of the text concerns bodily movement. Proper posture when seated or standing and deference when moving in groups of people is strongly emphasized. This recalls the tenth chapter of the *Analects,* where Confucius's body is described externally from many different angles. Texts such as these are distributed free of charge to interested visitors at Three in One halls.

Some of the larger temples, and occasionally small ones as well, distribute short collections of Three in One texts, including chronological biographies of Lin Zhao'en and primers of Three in One philosophy such as Chen Zhida's *Sanjiao chuxue zhinan* (Pointers for the beginning study of the Three Teachings).[1] These books provide the text of the Initiation Proclamation, the *Scrip-*

---

[1] Several different editions of this text have been printed by various Three in One temples. I collected two copies both mimeographed on coarse paper and stapled together. One version from Zhongmenxian was bound together with a copy of the *Zhuozu Zhenren zhi* (Hagiography of the Perfected Being, Ancestor Zhuo [Wanchun]). As in many such publications, the collators are listed at the back of the volume.

ture of Fundamental Substance, a short introduction to key themes and methods of the Three in One by Chen Zhida (emphasizing the heart method, and the mantralike recitation of the phrase *Sanyi jiaozhu* [Lord of the Three in One]), and finally a section on the basic outline of the nine stages. The beginning student is urged to begin with these texts and the basic practice of the heart method, and only then attempt to read the True Scriptures of Xiawu and the works of Lin Zhao'en. Moreover, in the continued practice of the heart method, it is essential to find a master to guide one's progress. If one does this, then "one's work [of inner self-cultivation] will be pure and easy, the body of the Dao will manifest. It will not be difficult to become an Immortal and a Buddha." But initiates are warned against "speaking of the demonic and the bizarre, and healing by means of talismans," all of which "lead one to abandon the true study of the arts of cultivation of the "heart-mind, body, and human nature."[2]

CONFERENCES OF THE GODS

Another form of outreach and legitimation for the Three in One has taken the form of academic conferences. Somewhat bizarre ritualistic academic conferences have been held to commemorate the birthdays of several of the major popular gods of the Minnan area in Fujian over the past decade. It is worth examining the role of the government, the intellectuals, outside sponsors such as Taiwanese and Overseas Chinese temple organizations, local sponsors, and the local temple committees involved in these conferences.

As noted in chapter 4, scriptures dedicated to popular local deities like Xia Wuni (Lin Zhao'en), Tianhou (Mazu), or Baosheng Dadi (the Great Emperor Who Preserves Life), who got their start in Fujian and whose cult later spread to Taiwan and Southeast Asia, usually begin with a conference of the gods. The assembled immortals gather in ranks before the throne of the Most High Lord Lao (or the Buddha, or Lin Zhao'en) to hear a memorial from an august celestial dignitary. The memorial details the recent horrors of life in the "dusty world" down below and urgently implores the Most High to remedy

---

[2] A more elaborate version of this kind of primer is the *Sanjiao zhengzong yizhilu* (Record of easily comprehended [aspects] of the comprehensive unification of the Three Teachings), edited by the Hansantang (Shrine of the Embodiment of the Three [Teachings]) and published in 1921 (with a preface by Guo Sizhou). This book provides the chronological biography of Master Lin written by Lin Zhaoke, followed by a selection of essays by Lin Zhao'en, such as *Xinxing* (On the heart-mind and human nature), *Mengzhongren pian* (The man in a dream), *Shi chushi pian* (Essay on leaving the world while in the world), *Puomi pian* (Essay on breaking down delusions), *Yijie liyu* (Plain and simple explanations), *Jienung koutou* (Playful explanations of common expressions), *Lunyu zhengyi zheyao* (Selections from the correct interpretation of the Analects, the *Cunsheng guitiao* [Regulations to be carefully observed (for the constant practice of the heart method)], the Regulations of the Hansantang, the Regulations for Initiations, Regulations for the Explication of Scriptures, [Principles for the Performance of] Rituals of Offering, and formularies for the Announcement of the Prohibitions and the Announcement of Initiation.

the latest round of debauched behavior and self-destructive immorality practiced by blind humans. At that point the Most High calls upon an immortal in the far-flung celestial bureaucracy. The immortal is hastily summoned to court and awaits his orders. Soon he is informed of his mission, given sacred texts and spiritual powers, and sent down to enlighten the masses. The remainder of the scripture shifts focus to detail the benefits to be gained by a recitation of the scripture: it will cure illness, ensure fruitful yields, and provide protection from demonic assault.

Scriptures such as these have recently been recited, or at least quoted, in officially recognized conferences held in Fujian and sponsored by Taiwanese adherents of the cults of the very gods lauded in the texts. Chinese intellectuals, who for decades had been told to avoid any mention of these elements of "feudal superstition," are now searching for materials on the history of the cults, sometimes even becoming consultants for temples dedicated to these gods. And this curious academic ritual is just the tip of an iceberg, or should one say volcano.

I was frequently reminded of this image of an assembly of the gods when I attended a series of conferences on the gods of Fujian held in Xiamen, Zhangzhou, Quanzhou, and Putian between 1985 and 1993. These included two conferences on Lin Zhao'en (1987, 1995), three conferences on Mazu, three on Baosheng Dadi, one on Kaizhang Shengwang (Saintly King Who Opened Up Zhangzhou: Chen Yuanguang) (for more information on these cults see Dean [1993] and ter Haar [1990]). Other conferences held during this period deserve to be mentioned, such as the conferences on Cai Xiang and Zhu Xi, both sponsored by their respective lineages. More recently conferences have been held on a number of other gods, goddesses, and illustrious lineage members.[3]

These conferences were all officially approved, especially those involving scholars from overseas. They were all presided over by local officials, sometimes from the local city-level bureau of culture or the political consultative congress (*zhengxie*), or by the party secretary, the mayor, the propaganda department, or the United Front people. Aside from these figures, who approved the holding of the conferences, the conferences were also attended by a large group of intellectuals, usually numbering about fifty, including full professors, associate professors, lecturers, and local scholars from the regional academic organizations under the control of the *zhengxie*. Then there was another group made up of sponsors (usually Taiwanese members of temple committees connected to the respective cults) and local·figures connected to the founding temples. Following the format of most Chinese conferences, the conferences of the gods included an opening ceremony, where the top-ranking local officials and university professors spoke, then several days of small-group presentations, leading to a final conference where reports on the small-group presentations were

---

[3] A conference was held in 1995 in Gutian around the cult of Linshui furen. See Berthier (1988) for background and analysis of this cult. See the bibliography for published papers from a number of the Mazu and Baosheng Dadi conferences.

made and invited speakers presented papers. The conferences were usually followed by a tour of the sites connected to the cult. These tours, and the conferences as well, were tantamount to an official stamp of approval on the cult, and so the conference groups were met with great fanfare when they arrived at the founding temples. Moreover, selected conference paper volumes have been published by the organizers of these meetings.

There were many taboos and prohibitions surrounding these conferences. The local officials began each conference by denouncing the feudal superstitious nature of the cult in question and suggesting instead a commemorative approach to the cult deity, who should be lauded for their contributions to society (of their times) and their enduring example to later generations. This kind of euhemeristic treatment will no doubt bring to mind the ceaseless efforts of Confucian officials to rein in heterodox cults (*yinsi*) over the ages. But the situation for the intellectuals was even more complex. Many of them had been forced for years to ignore the importance of these cults for the local history of Fujian. Now they were being asked to present papers on these gods with very little material to work with. The gazetteers were turned inside out, but only a few references could be found. These were stretched and bent into several conference papers. The slim materials on the developments of the cults on Taiwan available to the mainland intellectuals became grist for the mill of many a paper. Any reference, no matter how minor, in the writings of local literati could win an enterprising academic a ticket to a conference, with several days of free meals, a set of materials, and a commemorative attaché case. Sometimes, local level scholars had the advantage, in that they had been storing away local historical materials for years. A few of them were keen supporters of these new developments. Nevertheless, the scholarly content of most of the papers presented at these conferences has not been significant. But the degree of government acceptance and confirmation of the cults has been extremely significant.

CHINESE GOVERNMENT SUPPORT

The Chinese government clearly hopes to exploit the Taiwanese and Overseas Chinese interest in the cults of Fujian to entice investments and build up "unofficial links" with Taiwanese and other nongovernmental groups. On the other hand, the government feels that it is confronting an unpredictable force. Governmental groups were involved in planning the first international Mazu conference in 1990. Before it was held, however, a local meeting was called, and materials were carefully worked up for presentation at the larger conference.

The Chinese government and the Communist party attempt to regulate religion through the Bureau of Religious Affairs. At the district level, this organization is incorporated into the Division of Propaganda. The organization has been responsible for the implementation of savage attacks on religious organizations at various times over the past fifty years. The Three in One has been no exception, with the main temples taken over by army units or used as grain warehouses throughout the Cultural Revolution. The officials of the Bureau of Religious Affairs are also responsible for maintaining surveillance over these groups during periods of relatively lax control. Older officials in the bureau tend to be violently antireligious. I have argued that the very definition of religion adopted in China through Marxist and Leninist sources is a Western construct ill-suited to the Chinese case (Dean, 1993). The history of state relations with religious groups is a chronicle of misunderstanding and the abuse of power.

The government, however, is not monolithic, nor it is insusceptible to pressure from outside groups or from retired cadres. Moreover, there has been a certain amount of confusion generated by the competing claims of different divisions of the government. Thus the Taiwan division of the United Front must compete with the Tourism Division, and the latter has to compete with the Cultural Division, and both of these with the Religious Affairs Division, and all of these with the party secretary and the people responsible for long-range economic planning and development. These issues frequently complicate the local coordination of policy toward a major cult center. The case of the Mazu temple on Meizhou Island is a good example. There, large amounts of money are being donated to the temple committee, run by the capable woman Lin Ah-be. Local officials did not dare demand a share of these funds for fear of blocking the flow. Lin Ah-be has no doubt been quick to play on their fears. Meanwhile, other government bureaus located an overseas investor called the Libao Multinational (apparently now transformed into the Tati Corporation), to whom they ceded "development rights" on the island for ten years, effectively giving over control for a series of what have so far turned out to be empty promises regarding the construction of hotels, apartment blocks, and other facilities. Meanwhile, another pool of money has been used to establish a Mazu research foundation, headed by the man in charge of the Putian Zhengxie. So this powerful faction also has an incentive to discourage direct government intervention in the temple funding process.

TAIWANESE AND OVERSEAS CHINESE SUPPORT

Taiwanese support has been behind the majority of the "conferences of the gods." The Beigang Chaotian gong Mazu temple has issued a colorful pamphlet boasting that it was the sole sponsor of the Second International Mazu Conference, held in 1991. The intense rivalry between Mazu temples on Taiwan has found in the Fujian connection a new playing field full of interesting possibilities (see Sangren [1988] on the Taiwanese Mazu temples). For example, the Dajia pilgrimage to the Chaotian gong in Beigang is well-known in Taiwan. The entire pilgrimage lasts a week and is conducted on foot, in costume, with several elaborately carved and immensely heavy sedan chairs bearing the Dajia gods. In 1987, however, rather than visit Beigang, the Dajia pilgrims decided instead to return to Meizhou. In this way, they greatly enhanced their status on Taiwan, not least for their audacity. But the Dajia pilgrims went one step further. They "discovered" the original birthplace of Mazu in Gangli village of Zhongmen Township, overlooking Meizhou Bay. By supporting the still disputed claims of the temple there to be the mother temple of the cult, the Dajia pilgrims put themselves in a new relationship with the newly anointed founding temple. The other Mazu temples on Taiwan were quick to react. Not only did they too contribute to the Gangli temple, but they also found other means of reasserting their rivalry. In addition to supporting the Second Mazu Conference, the Beigang Chaotian gong also sponsored the reconstruction of various parts of the Meizhou temple (which had been completely destroyed in the Cultural Revolution). In response, the Lugang Mazu temple lost no time in building a pavilion midway up the hill behind the temple. Inside the pavilion is a large poster of the god statue from Lugang. They also sponsored the construction of an immense statue of the goddess at the highest point on Meizhou Island, which ensures that every visitor will walk past the pavilion and the Lugang Mazu temple.

LOCAL SUPPORT

One conference of the gods where local support was most clear to me was the Lin Longjiang Academic Conference. The cult has been struggling since 1979 to regroup and obtain official recognition. With the support of about two dozen temples in Malaysia and Singapore, along with three or four in Taiwan, the leaders of the cult managed to repossess from the military the ancestral temple of the cult on East Mountain in Putian City. They did their own surveys of the cult, reprinted scriptures, and sought to standardize ritual practice. In an effort to secure government support, they convened a conference in 1987. The conference was rather bizarre. It was paid for entirely by the Three in One. Approximately sixty-five speakers attended, including professor Li Shiyu from the Tianjin Academy of Social Sciences and Professor Liu Huisun from Fuzhou Normal University. Perhaps a dozen other university teachers attended. Others were members of local-level research organizations, high school teachers, medical doctors, painters, and poets. All the local assistants at the guest house they booked, which belonged to the military, were members of the cult. After being severely lectured to during the opening ceremony by the chairman of the Putian Political Consultative Congress, who warned them against performing any acts of feudal superstition, they went on with the conference. Several elderly gentlemen with long white beards lectured on the Four Books and the Five Classics and on the importance of inner cultivation in the modern age. Many of these men were retired lawyers, teachers, even local government officials or military men. Indeed, the wealth of local connections these cult leaders maintained goes a long way to explaining their success in holding the conference. Nevertheless, rumor had it that one high-level official complained that Putian would soon be known as the feudal superstition capital of China if similar conferences were allowed to go on.

A second conference on the Three in One was held in Putian in February 1995.[4] This time Overseas Chinese support from Malaysian Three in One groups was the obvious reason for the conference. The conference revolved around the presentation of large wads of cash to the temple beside the tomb of Lin Zhao'en. The funds were to be used to build a concrete road from the Fuzhou–Xiamen highway up to the site of the tomb. Official sponsorship was muted, with the principal officials in attendance being a deputy administrator from the Putian City government and the deputy of the Putian branch of the Overseas Chinese Association (an official in the United Front Division). A local representative of the People's Consultative Congress also attended. Organization was provided by the Putian Folklore Association (connected to the group officially organized to rewrite a regional gazetteer). This kind of ad hoc association can operate more freely than an official branch of the local government or the party. They now sense a potential for organizing more such conferences around the visits of major donor groups of Overseas Chinese from Southeast Asia. Academic content was marginal, with brief papers from local scholars. Local performance troupes, by contrast, were magnificent and so numerous that by the middle of the performances in front of a stage upon which the Overseas Chinese and government officials sat, the crowd and the performers converged upon one another and forced the conclusion of the procession. The high point of the conference came when the Overseas Chinese representatives passed funds to the temple committee chairman, who was so overcome he could only dance about, speechlessly waving the money over his head. Perhaps he realized that he had not been invited to speak at the conference. Indeed, several guests hinted that it would still be a long time before the people would be allowed to speak for themselves at an event like this. The implication appeared to be that there was little room for commentary between the show of official support and overseas capital.

CONTESTING SYMBOLS OF SPACE AND TIME

Let us now move beyond the conferences on the gods to discuss other instances of the manipulation of popular religious symbols into representations

---

[4] An article in the *Putian Meizhou ribao* (February 25, 1995) mentions the presentation of 243,000 RMB, of which 200,000 was donated by Mr. Zhang Delin of Kuala Lumpur, 32,000 RMB by the Zongkongtang of Klang, and 10,000 RMB by the Zhuxingci of Port Klang. A mimeographed volume of essays was prepared for the conference entitled *Putianxian shouju Lin Longjiang Minsuwenhua xueshu yantaohui lunwenchi* (Collected essays for the First Putian County Academic Conference on the folklore and culture of Lin Longjiang), edited by the Putianxian Minsu Xuehui (Putian County Folklore Association) and the Houjiao Shimenshan Zongkongci Dongshihui (Temple Committee of the Honorable Confucius Shrine of Shimen Mountain in Houjiao).

of state authority. One way in which this happens is when the basic cultural emblems of space and time—the traditional seasonal festivals—are transformed into national festivals. Clearly, however, these official celebrations are at the same time contested (celebrated differently or appropriated) by local groups for their own purposes (Wang, 1992). The points where these festivals are celebrated become rival maps of the power networks energizing the locality.

Of course there are some spaces that belong to the government, and that the government can reclaim with the aid of modernized traditional festivals. Governmental buildings, public highways, schoolyards, auditoriums, and so forth all are swept up into the official celebration. All these celebrations reaffirm the organic links between the government and its units (*danwei*). Thus we find parades of representatives from these units, particularly schoolchildren and their teachers, following brass bands and floats advertising local industries and companies. These parades are a prominent feature of Lantern Festival during the Chinese New Year's celebrations. The processions are forced by their numbers, and the use of trucks and large vehicles, to move along the major highways that have been carved through or around the older, narrower city streets.

But the cities had a different spatial organization that is beginning to reemerge. This was the traditional ward system, and each ward had its own temple. In Quanzhou there were thirty-six ward temples, with seventy-two temples for subdivisions of the wards.[5] In the past ten years, many of these temples have been restored (Wang, 1995). An alternative map of the circuits of power within the city is revealed during the traditional seasonal festivals of the gods, particularly the Lantern Festival, when different temples around the city visit one another. Quanzhou is rather unique in having a cultural ministry that has sought to protect and even support or co-opt some of the traditional community structures. Even there, urban development threatens to destroy communal relations. In general, there appears to be a growing and perhaps irreversible gulf between urban and rural symbolic systems. Children and young teenagers in the villages have now spent their entire lives punctuated by increasingly elaborate village festivals, while kids of a similar age in many cities have little or no contact with this realm of symbolic experience.

The Three in One is able to activate a Xinghua-wide network of incense division. Moreover, the Three in One leadership and rank-and-file are often also deeply involved in other cults and communities. They have longstanding ties with the other, smaller sectarian groups in the area, such as the Longhuajiao, Jintongjiao, Xiantianjiao, and Yaochidao,[6] not to mention links with Guanyin

---

[5] Wang Mingming (1996) has shown that the ward system began as a State-sponsored centripetal administrative model, but that it was co-opted by local communities into a centrifugal model of local differentiation. Similar co-option of administrative institutions and structures, and contestations of the meaning of spatial forms, played an important role in the transformations of the Xinghua cultural area. See Dean, 1996, on the mutations of the *li* and the *she* in Xinghua.

[6] See chapter note 88.

scripture recitation groups, or Mazu associations made up primarily of women. Thus the networking is by no means only a nested hierarchy, but a rhizomatic tangle of underground connections.

In addition to providing an alternative organization of space, popular religion also provides a second calendar underlying the cultural self-definition of the locality. This is the calendar of the birthdays of the local gods. Every locality has a different local pantheon, built up out of the legends and efforts of successive generations. Ritual specialists, artists, playwrights, actors, marionettists, musicians, local literati, stone masons, carpenters, wood-carvers, and paper-cut artists all work to celebrate their local culture, putting the collective representatives of local symbolic value into textual and visual form. The effort of the government to step in and hold the "conferences of the gods" in time with the birth dates of the gods represents an effort to co-opt these defining moments in the rhythm of local time into a political statement. Thus it was not surprising that the first conference on Lin Longjiang was held close to his birth date in the first lunar month.

In fact, the Three in One has a particularly strong relationship to the annual cycle of rituals. The central rites of the birth date and ascension date of Lin Zhao'en (1/14 and 7/16) correspond miraculously with the dates of the Upper and Middle Prime (1/15 and 7/15). The Lower Prime (10/15) is often the date of the *Lanpen* rituals in which Three in One ritual troupes specialize. This is no doubt a marvelous coincidence rather than an attempt on the part of the founders of the Three in One themselves to co-opt or piggyback upon some of the key moments of the ritual calendar.

STATE FESTIVAL/LOCAL FESTIVAL

As soon as the government touches it, a local cult transforms into a distorted image of an official state organ, with brass bands, dancing lions and dragons, bands of schoolchildren, or old folks' disco-dancing aerobics groups. The spontaneity of the local festival and the traditional underlying structure are missing. Fortunately, these events, although somewhat grotesque, are limited to those rare occasions when representatives of the government deign to visit the cult centers with an approving air. This temporary appropriation of the cult's symbolic space is played out in a formalized fashion. Such distortions are by no means a recent phenomenon. State appropriation of local cults has often led to sudden extreme changes in a cult's structure and potentialities. These new dimensions could be and invariably were again appropriated for local uses.[7]

The local festivals of the cults raise another important spatial issue: the question of scope of cult activity and their interface with the state. Many villages were linked into ascending regional hierarchies. Each level of the hierarchy

---

[7] See Ding and Zheng (1989) for a discussion of the relationships among the state, Daoism, and local cults.

could be marked by a regional association, often symbolized by a common cult. In other words, a village would first hold a procession around the village to affirm the spiritual territory of the god. Next the village would join in a procession linking several villages in a local association. Finally, the village would join in a grand procession linking several regional associations under the common symbol of a major regional cult, like the city god of Hanjiang, or the Humane Emperor Who Records Life of the Temple of the Eastern Peak of Jiangkou, or the Jade Emperor in the Temple of the Towering Clouds on the top of Hugong Mountain, the highest point in the Putian plains. These processions could involve between 36 and 108 villages. The last of these grand processions took place in the 1930s. Many of the lower-level processions had been restored, but the larger spatial claims of the higher-level cults continued to run up against the local government's claims to oversee the major roads and public spaces of the area. Innumerable stories were told of the last-minute intervention, sometimes quite heavy-handed, of the state in large-scale processions. Standoffs between officials and Overseas Chinese or their local representatives had become a regular feature of these events. Without a far more accommodating attitude on the part of the authorities, this issue will remain a flash point for the growing contradiction between official mass culture and local cultural forces.

In 1993, on the 4th day of the 9th lunar month (October 18), the Humane Emperor of the Eastern Peak, seated in his massive, ornately carved sedan chair, began his procession around the entire extent of the Nananbi irrigation system in Jiangkou Township. Palanquins of the multitudinous local gods of the fifty-two villages in the irrigation system joined the spectacular procession, which lasted for three days. A perfect circle of time (sixty years) had been completed since the last such procession, and by means of completing the circuit the gods had reinscribed their hold on their territory: their spiritual precincts had been reclaimed.

A similar process began in 1989, when the Three in One retrieved the Honorable Confucius Hall on East Mountain in Putian from the military. Plans are under way now to reclaim the military barracks in front of the rebuilt temple. These will be torn down and something like the "original" design of the temple will emerge. Then there will be even more space for the reception of incense-bearing groups from throughout the Three in One network. Despite efforts on the part of the leadership committee to stagger the visits of delegations, many simply come on their own accord when they choose.

FROZEN SPACE/TIME

A final spatial and temporal issue relates to the transformation of some temples into museums. Indeed, most outside observers of China see "popular religion" only in its museumified form, in temples transformed into tourist attractions, or with a small staff of Daoist priests or Buddhist monks under the watchful eye of the Bureau of Religious Affairs. A number of major temples have been transformed in part into museums in Fujian. These sites exhibit a strange relationship with time. A museum can be a place that claims to have stopped time and preserved a moment of the past. In fact, museums are often transparent efforts to construct a past with clear ideological purposes. The displays in the Temple of the Empress of Heaven (Mazu) in Quanzhou, or in the former Eastern Peak Temple in Putian, desperately celebrate a seemingly eternal link with Taiwan based on the spread of the cult of Mazu that is scarcely older than the paint on the walls. One senses that the state has staked a lot on these sites but cannot contain the forces of the renewal of popular culture and local cults.

In the early 1990s Malaysian Overseas Chinese adherents donated funds for the establishment of a Lin Longjiang Jiniantang (Memorial Hall) next to the Honorable Confucius Temple on East Mountain in Putian. Inside the temple a local artist has painted murals depicting the life and legends of Lin Zhao'en. Part museum, part testimonial, the Memorial Hall serves to bridge the historical reality (and legitimacy) of Lin Zhao'en with the powerful god worshiped by the Three in One. Yet it remains an ambiguous monument, with almost nothing on display inside. The Overseas Chinese sponsors have been frustrated in their demand for authentic memorabilia connected in some concrete way to Lin Zhao'en's life. Such objects, in their view, would lend authenticity and legitimacy to the museum and to the cult. Yet regardless of the difficulty of locating any such object, the museum functions differently for the local leadership. A public monument, even an empty monument, is a symbol of potent presence in the context of a constant denial of official government recognition.

One final example of state intervention in centers of popular cult activity may clarify some of the issues at stake. The celebration in the spring of 1994 of the thousandth anniversary of Mazu's ascension to Heaven was conducted at the Temple of the Empress of Heaven on Meizhou Island under the auspices of the Putian Bureau of Tourism. This celebration took place under the shadow of the recent robbery and murder of a group of Taiwanese tourists in China, which had resulted in the cancelation of scores of Taiwanese tours to China, including many to Meizhou. Nevertheless, enough officials from the provincial and central levels of government attended the ceremony to make it a success in the eyes of the local government. The pièce de résistance of the ceremony was the command performance of an elaborately staged "Song dynasty ritual" that had not been performed "in a thousand years." A cast of thousands, including all the children on the island, lined the streets in extraordinary costumes. This was a case in which the very inventedness of the rituals allowed all the participants to accept the fact that no fundamental change was being imposed on the cult.

Nevertheless, some observers feel that the combination of Taiwanese or Overseas Chinese funding, cynical, self-serving, and grudging governmental approval, and the local scrambling for monetary support has led to a distorted form of popular religion in Fujian. There are at least two issues at stake here. First there is the question of the authenticity of the religious expression in the cult centers in Fujian. That question would still deserve serious study, assuming an interest in the phenomenology of religion, but the important thing to note for the purposes of this discussion is that the new circumstances outlined above and their constitutive symbols provide new possibilities, new tools for local appropriation and co-optation. The potential roles for popular religion in Fujian are expanding, rather than being perverted into an empty simulacrum. The range of support for the conferences discussed above indicates that we are dealing with a widespread and deeply rooted phenomenon with important implications not only for Fujian–Taiwan relations, but also for the cultural development of China as a whole.

A second question concerns the role of the Fujian cult centers in relation to Taiwanese and Overseas Chinese circuits of pilgrimage and local cultural self-identification. There are many possibilities here as well. The mainland centers may fade in importance after the novelty wears off, and the complications of dealing with the authorities there take their toll. In terms of the dynamics of the division of incense system, however, access to the Fujian cult centers can certainly expand the range and flexibility of the Taiwanese and Overseas Chinese systems. One can indeed imagine stronger connections being built up over the long term. In the short term, my guess is that the paradoxical situation of semi-open status of the mainland cult centers will lead Taiwanese and Overseas Chinese cults to turn inward focusing upon their own links and organizations. This could take a number of forms, some institutional, some anti-institutional. An example of the former would be the recent formation of a Taiwan-wide Baosheng Dadi temple association, and the publication of an illustrated volume listing all the Baosheng Dadi temples on Taiwan. Another example would be the self-conscious effort on the part of some Taiwanese intellectuals to claim that Mazu belief-spheres (regional networks of temples) represent a peculiarly Taiwanese phenomenon, one that could be said to define the essence of the Taiwanese experience (Lin, 1990). An example of a somewhat anti-institutional formation might include the increasing adoption of wider, more commercialized pilgrimage circuits around several of the main Mazu temples all around the island, rather than just to one. This too has the consequence of identifying religious/ritual spheres with Taiwanese identity (Sangren, 1988). The invitation of Daoist priests, Buddhist monks, and a Mulian theater group to the Jiulidong (Nine Carp Cavern) in Singapore in 1994 is another example of the complex negotiation of the resources and meanings of "tradition" occurring between mainland and overseas groups.

The extraordinary sight of exuberant celebrations of popular cult festivals in Fujian, and the ambivalent involvement of the Communist party and intellectuals, also raises a series of fascinating contrasts with developments on Taiwan. Recall the early Guomindang efforts to limit or suppress Taiwanese popular cults and festivals. These efforts were in part a carryover from the early policies of the Republican period, with their iconoclastic attack on Chinese traditions, especially religious or popular traditions. The would-be architects of the new Chinese nation-state intended to replace such localized structures with a nationwide bureaucracy of schools and police stations, set up within former temples (Duara, 1988). But on Taiwan there was an added gulf between Mandarin elite culture, even if Westernized and Christianized, and Hokkien culture. Despite these deep-seated contradictions, the realm of popular religion has grown and flourished in Taiwan, becoming an important political force in local elections, as well as a center of local power, prestige, and cultural expression. The degree to which popular religion has maintained itself in a rapidly modernizing economy is indeed interesting and may suggest a possible direction for the evolving relationship among local cultural, political, and economic forces in Fujian. A great deal of work is now being done on Taiwan on local customs, what with major annual festivals of local theater, several new museums in the planning stages, massive research projects under way, and Hokkien and Hakka being taught in the schools. One could also argue that this attention reflects a concern that these traditions are threatened as never before by ever-accelerating modernization, or that these efforts are part of a larger project of cultural nationalism (Chun, 1994). Do similar concerns and structural changes underlie the renewal of popular religious activity in Fujian, including the bizarre, ritualistic "conferences of the gods"?

Myron Cohen (1991) has noted the severe gaps that already divide the PRC state, in its own programatic definition, from the cultural identification of the traditional, rural sector. He also has remarked on the revival of traditional practices in the wake of the state's retreat from direct control of society and economy. Cohen senses a growing crisis of cultural representation in China. Another way of looking at the matter would be to say that the reforms have returned an element of flexibility and renewed potentiality to contemporary Chinese culture. This greater flexibility of Chinese culture as a whole, and particularly the growing ability of local cultures to manipulate official codes and symbols of authority, may paradoxically be a result of the loosening up of both the central-command codes and the territorial codes by the spreading of capitalist flows of all kinds. Yet it is precisely those flows that threaten the local cultural forms with new kinds of appropriation and transformation, not to mention imposing grave risks to economic stability. The commercialization of Chinese television, the commodification of culture, the transformation of pilgrimage into cash-crop tourism, and the expanding impact of homogenized, international, postmodern, capitalist culture (best exemplified by the karaoke craze sweeping across China) all serve to confuse the traditional structural interface between the state and the locale, providing new arenas, new opportunities, and new technologies for both sides while transforming the contestants in the process. The overriding impression given by the economy and society (and culture) of southeastern China over the past decade is one of sheer speed—like an accelerating train that everyone is trying desperately to catch a ride on, and which we can only hope will not suddenly derail.

THIS DISCUSSION of the spread of the Three in One has focused on its impact as a vector of local cultural transformation. The unified vision of the Three Religions presented in Lin Zhao'en's philosophic works has given way to the most remarkable diversity. Throughout its transformations, the Three in One has been pulled in contradictory directions by the polar attractors of Confucian sagehood and immediate spiritual power. On one level, this could be seen as a struggle between orthodoxy and heterodoxy, but only if one were to view the entire range of religious and social expression in the Three in One exclusively from the perspective of the state. It is more illuminating to see these contradictory pulls as arising out of an underlying problematic and to follow its operation through all the different phases of the Three in One. Each phase brings into play a unique constellation of social, political, and libidinal forces. Different stategies were advanced in each phase to expand the influence of the Three in One in different areas—at the level of the local scholarly elite, at the level of regional groupings, at the level of village life. The Three in One attempted to actualize its potentialities in a variety of public and semi-public spaces by establishing academies, building networks of temples, developing and performing rituals in market centers and temple courtyards. Depending on the concrete circumstances encountered in different areas, the Three in One was more or less successful in merging with, or overtaking, institutions of local power such as gentry alliances, lineages, or village temple .networks. Yet these efforts to enter into and dominate these spheres (or at least to achieve autonomy within them) were inevitably unstable and thus constantly driven to continue to transform.

Looking back over earlier scholarship, we have seen that although J. J. M. De Groot (1903–1904) presented convincing material based on texts and fieldwork on the "destructive fanaticism of the state" in its persecution of sectarianism, many subsequent studies of sectarianism in China concentrated on the millenarian aspirations and propensity for rebellion of sectarian groups, their "occasional explosive acts of organized violence" (Naquin, 1981: xi; see also Sawada, 1975b; Overmyer, 1976; Naquin, 1976). More recent studies of the modes of transmission and the evolution of the values of religious groups often labeled as "White Lotus sects" (Naquin, 1985; Overmyer, 1985; ter Haar, 1992) reveal a more successful pattern of peaceful integration within local society. Naquin discusses the evolution of both congregational sutra-recitation societies and meditational, martial arts groups in White Lotus Sectarianism. Ter Haar also suggests a distinction between meditational and scripture-recitation groups and suggests that the Three in One might fall into the former category.

Explanations that attempt to define the essence of a particular kind of religious organization or movement, or that attempt to categorize religious movements in a strict typology, sometimes fail to grasp the complexity of the ways in which the movement absorbed and affected changing social forces as it developed, transforming them as it was in turn transformed. The Three in One defies essentialistic classifications because it was a living, transforming collective investment of desire caught between and driven by polar attractors of Confucian utopia and the immediate efficacy of spiritual power. The Three in One, as we have seen, included both a meditative and a ritual dimension. Indeed, these continue to be inseparable. Like many other local religious movements, the Three in One tradition was singularly unmilitant. The central values of the Three in One are "orthodox" and less explicitly millenarian, egalitarian, and utopian than some of those associated with the White Lotus tradition. We have seen how the Three in One carved out a role for itself in the ritual traditions of the area by borrowing and expanding from the ritual complexes of Daoism and Buddhism available in the region, and by entering into relationships with existing power structures from lineage formations to temple networks to other smaller religious movements. It was thus deeply connected to local society.

The Three in One rapidly became a rival ritual tradition to others in the area, open to anyone. A growing sector of displaced, unemployed scholars could obtain a sense of self-respect and public acclaim through their involvement in such meritorious activities. More entrepreneurial ritualists could band together to provide services at a lower cost than Daoist priests or Buddhist monks or Confucian liturgists demanded. The Three in One provided people without powerful bureaucratic or lineage connections a new form of social organization, within a new liturgical framework. In the rapidly commercializing society of Southeast China in the late Imperial period, this kind of social formation provided prospects for moral and social advancement to disadvantaged groups. In a society where flows of money were unseating bureaucratic and hereditary power structures, social hierarchy was in turmoil. The possibility of direct investment by the poor and powerless in an open liturgical framework implies an appropriation and co-optation of traditional symbols and forms of the reproduction of cosmic power. For these initiates, the group practice of inner alchemy, ritual, and scriptural study provided an avenue to immortality with immediate secular rewards.

The Three in One encountered many changing circumstances and social, political, and libidinal forces in the course of its own transformations and efforts to reinvent itself. In the Putian plains during the formative period of the Three in One, a rapidly expanding population began to put impossible demands on the coastal irrigation systems. In response, systemwide nested hierarchies of temples and communities emerged to resolve conflicts that would have torn the various irrigation systems apart and brought down mutual destruction, while at the same time local, village-based ritual took on new comprehensiveness as well. Ever since the late Ming pirate raids and the coastal evacuations, village temples had become increasingly important to sociocultural life, whereas lineage organization and ancestral worship appear to have declined. As we have seen, the Three in One was able to fit itself into these developments in certain communities.

This phase can also be seen as one in which there developed local forms of self-government, financing, and regulation of local infrastructure and cultural activity. The single-whip tax reform of the mid-Ming, the curbing of overseas trade, the rise of piracy in the area, the growth of population, and increasingly unregulatable commercialization all led to the gradual abdication by the central government of concrete support of local infrastructure and social regulation. Into this vacuum arose a midlevel gentry formation, capable of mobilizing major irrigation repair projects not because they were deputized by the government to do so, but because of their networks of contacts within and across the various communities of the different irrigation systems. The local-level literati were generally sympathetic to the Three in One, as we have seen above. The organizational potential of the Three in One provided interesting nonofficial networks of communication during those periods when the government was not actively suspicious.

The Three in One developed and interacted with all these forces. In the irrigated plains, they tended to remain relatively discrete from village or systemwide cultural realms. In the coastal and mountainous areas, they tended to provide local village elders a new avenue for the expression of moral and political authority. After the ban on open activity, the Three in One appears to have continued to spread through the Xinghua area. In some cases, as we have seen above, this meant that the Three in One became the central force in village life. We found evidence in the late Qing and Republican period that groups of marginal or displaced peoples had found in the Three in One an organizational framework for the expression of their values, and a platform for the presentation of their self-worth and sense of morality. Ultimately, we can see that the Three in One, in its multiplicity, contributed to the process of local cultural self-definition, or the concrete practices of individuation, that constituted the changing arenas and discourses of life in the Xinghua area. One crucial mechanism of the expansion of the Three in One has been the process of division of incense, and the reverse flow of presentation of incense. But this process in and of itself cannot explain the range of cultural roles or the variety of social formations the Three in One has actualized in this region. Institutional developments and the development of a local set of practices based on and appropriating the discourse of the founders of the Three in One must be examined in each particular area as well as in a broader historical context.

Vectors and Spirals

Throughout this account of the Three in One we have encountered flows of texts, ritual traditions, music and liturgy, and individuals and groups. Both the starting point and end point of the flows, that is, both the community and the gods, are continually undergoing modification by people remaking their cultural traditions. New social forces transform communities, creating new opportunities for new alliances. The local pantheons of different communities are also constantly evolving, from internal migration, the ceaseless production of new cults, official intrusiveness, and so forth. New ritual traditions develop in response to these new possibilities and connections, and to sustain and enact these changes.

One could trace a circuit between rituals designed to address individual life crises to rituals that involve families, then neighborhoods, and on to entire villages, entire irrigation systems, entire geographic or linguistic formations. Spirit-mediums, Daoists, Buddhist monks, Confucian ritualists, and Three in One masters all produce scriptures and liturgies for the locally defined pantheon. Plays are developed to integrate further the local pantheon and local mythology with rituals for individuals and communities. The circuit moves in a spiral from individual ritual needs to spirit-medium incantations to liturgical texts to ritual theater to testimonials on stone to massive temple fairs to transversal flows of local-level social and cultural power to memorials written by local gentry to temple gazetteers to government titles of investiture, a tremendous circulation of texts, bodies, food, money, music, legends, desire. We are talking about the process of the production and reproduction of local popular culture.

Perhaps we need to reconsider the starting point of the spiral of popular culture. Rather than basing it on individual crises, individual needs, or a fundamental sense of lack, loss, or limitation, we could look instead to the relationships *between* and *beyond* individuals. This goes for the question of agency in cultural production as well. We can extend our search for the authors of popular cultural texts forever and come up with a few over time. Indeed, with Lin Zhao'en and his disciples, we seem to have encountered just such a group. Yet even within this group contradictory tendencies are apparent. The Three in One ritual tradition would develop from its original problematic in more and more paradoxical ways, as it encountered different circumstances. With the Qing bans on the Three in One, we lose sight of the individuals on whom we might attempt to hang a smooth evolutionary narrative of an organic whole. A more productive approach might be to focus on the nature of ritual-events within the Three in One, looking at the in-between of bodies, the flows of language and legend, and the shifting organization in relation to the range of communities it encountered. The transformations of the Three in One then can be analyzed in relation to external forces it encountered, such as the rising tide of commercialization, the militarization of society, the decline of the Buddhist monasteries, the decline of the major lineages, and the rise of the temple networks within the irrigation systems.

Rather than search for specific individuals or agents that can be said to have shaped popular culture, we might look beyond the model of the individual author or intentional ego—and look as well beyond the generalized, reified model of the impact on popular religion of Daoist liturgy or some organic Three in One movement—to the modes and mediums of the communication of culture: the rituals, the plays, the festivals themselves as processes of cultural self-expression.

In this way, one could see new formations of relationships between bodies emerging through ritual as a process of incessant becoming. It is crucial that we do not see ritual as an endpoint or a circle of constant return, a motor of changeless cultural reproduction. Instead, we need to study changes in local culture over time, as revealed in evolving ritual traditions, changing regional theatrical genres, and their ever-changing ritual contexts in relation to other, simultaneous changes in Chinese society.

The process of circle or spiral of textual proliferation from seance to chant to scripture to liturgy to playscript and back to chant and seance involves a joyous and continuous excess, a colossal collective word-play, a process of language speaking itself, of a local culture working itself out. Texts take shape not so much as efforts to impose a hegemonic homology of elite values upon the unsuspecting, illiterate, and powerless masses, but instead as the manifestation of the power of local culture, defining itself, exulting in itself, playing itself out.

Many specialists have stressed the techniques of cultural hegemonism employed by the Chinese empire in late imperial times (Hsiao, 1960; Johnson, 1985; Ellman, 1991). However, growing evidence from concrete studies in Ming and Qing history increasingly reveals a picture of spreading commercialism, weakening government control, and growing local self-government (Rowe, 1985; Zheng, 1993). Indeed, as more and more anthropologists join forces with historians to research the cultural histories of distinct regional or local cultures in China, a vibrant picture of local culture begins to emerge that does not conform to the accepted hegemonic/homologies model (Sangren, 1986; Weller, 1984). Tu Weiming's essay on "Cultural China: The Periphery as Center" (1991) quotes a remark by Yu Yingshi to the effect that "the center is nothing, the periphery is all." Tu uses this idea to discuss the Chinese diaspora and the situation of the contemporary international Chinese intelligentsia. But the notion can be useful in rethinking the process of local cultural self-definition in late Imperial China itself.

One could argue that over the late Imperial period, Confucian classical texts and political philosophy increasingly attained transparently ideological status, while at the same time local cultures came more into themselves through a process of manipulating and co-opting Confucian ideology, bending it to fit the needs and realities of their own local customs, which were continually changing. Lin Zhao'en and the Three in One would certainly seem to fit into this framework. While Cohen (1991) has suggested that unified traditional Chinese culture actually demanded a degree of assimilable marked traits of localization from its localities, there may be scope for a historical inquiry into the meanings of local struggles or transformations of elements of traditional cultural codes that does not give the last word to totalizing co-optation of such local efforts by the national elite.[1]

The scope and nature of the renewal of traditional popular religious practices compels us to reexamine popular religion and ritual and their role in contemporary Fujian. One is faced with an extraordinary situation. So-called traditional forms and feudal superstitions are once again playing a central role in the elaboration of local cultural identity. Chinese Marxists might well be forced to ask themselves if this is an entirely reactionary development, or if it could possibly mean something rather different in a new and changing situation. Marxian analysts may well wonder if these processes will (must?) be based on an alienated notion of power.[2] What are the underlying mechanisms of cultural production and reproduction encountered in Chinese religion and ritual?

Functionalist approaches to Chinese religion were dominant in the 1960s and 1970s. Such approaches fail to account for these rapid changes, nor do they explore the process of individuation and the potential for multiplicity outlined in this account of the historical transformations of the Three in One movement. This does not mean that one should not be interested in how things work, rather, it requires one to be aware of the simultaneity of several competing temporalities and vectors of change in the agonistic relationship between the state and the locale.

In examining popular cult centers and the Three in One in Fujian, I first looked at various *fenxiang* systems not from the perspective of the commu-

---

[1] These comments raise the issue of the long-term historical development of culture, economy, and society in Fujian and the impact of this background on contemporary developments. To demonstrate the creative force of local culture, rather than seeing it as a predetermined set of (epiphenomenal) timeless collective representations, further research into the history of the Fujian–Taiwan connection would be useful. Such research would explore the extraordinary propensity for international trade and coastal transshipping that have from the Song dynasty onward made Fujian something of an anomaly in a Skinnerian model of economic macroregions. The acceleration of commercialization in Fujian in the latter half of the Ming dynasty, leading among other things to the colonization and development of Taiwan, resulted in a fundamental rearrangement of sociocultural forms and forces within Fujian. These included the development of what Zheng Zhenman (1992) has called "contractual lineages," in addition to the more traditional "hereditary" and "power-dependent" forms of lineages. Internal relations within these "contractual lineages" required new avenues for the circulation and translation of force, and the popular cults took on a new significance as a network transcending lineages, or as a symbolic means of translating and channeling the new, commercialized relations within large-scale, complex localized lineages. It is in light of these and other socioeconomic and cultural changes that the contemporary movements for the restoration of temples and regional religious systems must be interpreted.

[2] In his book and in a series of articles, Steven Sangren (1986, 1988, 1989) has analyzed the mechanisms of the alienation of power in Taiwanese pilgrimages, territorial cults, and individual worship. Sangren applies Terrence Turner's notion of the logical structure of alienation or self-mystification within cultural representation to the example of the Mazu pilgrimages on Taiwan. He applies this notion to the process of pilgrimage to a cult center, which he suggests exteriorizes the source and nature of spiritual power, which is in fact a product of the collective cultural production of the pilgrims themselves. He further notes a parallel between the levels of alienation and the nested systems of temple hierarchies culminating in cult centers.

nity on pilgrimage, but from the central point of these systems. At these centers, there is nowhere else to go (no way to leave the home community behind) in search of an alienated representation of spiritual power, nowhere, that is, but up—either up into the Daoist heavens (Boltz, 1986) or to the imperial court in pre-Revolutionary times (Watson, 1985). The history of the major cult centers of Fujian suggests that their local leadership groups were quite capable of manipulating the court, or simply ignoring it and generating their own Daoist or syncretic ranks and titles for their gods (Dean, 1993). These co-optations of hierarchical, imperial codes suggest a more immediate channeling or circulating of forces than a model of alienated spiritual power would allow. This could mean a greater awareness on the part of temple leadership of the cultural media. This in turn could imply a more transparently ideological manipulation of cultural symbols; that is, in the sense of gentry- or contemporary elite-dominated models of the mystification of the collective sources of cultural representations of spiritual power.

In the case of the Three in One, one finds a very complex representation of spiritual power in the cult center. On the one hand, Lin Zhao'en is worshiped and prayed to as a god. His talismans are collected and his oracular poetry is consulted. The temple committee at the Dongshanci Zongkongtang is consciously involved in efforts to coordinate and unify the Three in One to achieve both government recognition and authority within the movement. This authority could translate into control over representations of spiritual power. On the other hand, Lin's writings, his hagiography, and the inner alchemical teachings provide a quasi-materialist theory of spiritual power and point to the possibility of individual effort in recycling the dot of spiritual power instilled at conception into spiritual enlightenment and personal salvation. This opens the way to individual experience and differentiated reception of the Three in One in distinct communities.

A second issue concerns the degree to which the *fenxiang* (division of incense) system is fundamentally hierarchical, thus reflecting and underpinning the social hierarchy in certain functionalist readings of the structure of Chinese popular religion. Sangren (1989) notes that *jinxiang* pilgrimages also serve to heighten local differentiation. There is also the question of the stability of the system over time. I suspect that there is a tendency toward horizontal flows between groups rather than necessarily a strengthening of the vertical chain (Schipper, 1990). This would allow for different levels of temples to manifest a sudden change in fortune by making a particularly magnificent gift to the temple. This is the same mechanism underlying the funding of temple activities—on the one hand, everyone gives an equal amount, but on the other, anyone is allowed to give more. The division of the Three in One movement into several distinct second-order temple division networks (e.g., Mingxia temples originating from the Daxingci, or the branch temples of the Yushanci in Bangtou) demonstrates the propensity for division of incense networks to complexify, frustrating efforts toward hierarchical unification.

The flexibility of the *fenxiang* system, and its ability to accommodate the ceaselessly changing situations of its constituent members, has to be seen in the context of the probable proximity and intermingling of several such systems, active to varying degrees, within any one locale. There is the distinct possibility that different cults in any given community could clash or merge, producing local results in the sphere of the circulation and representation of power. The interrelationships of these local temples may, under certain circumstances, coalesce into a nested hierarchy, but even in these cases, local irruptions of "spiritual power" may be more significant than external, alienated representations. In addition to spirit-mediumism or the formation of new popular cults, one might also point to the role of Daoist, Buddhist, or Three in One rituals as another means of generating and circulating spiritual power within a community. Furthermore, many of the cult temple, including some of the cult centers, are closely linked to local lineages and thus find some expression of their force through those circuits. This multiplicity of local cultural symbolism suggests that we are dealing with an exceptionally rich medium, in which class interests and forces of resistance could all engage. The ability to intervene in the creation of cults, the elaboration of new ritual traditions, the contesting of social power through spirit mediumism, and so forth all imply a wider access to the tools of cultural symbolism than an "ideological victimization" by local gentry would allow.

We are confronted with contradictory findings. On the one hand, the development of local cults from the perspective of the founding temples of successful cults suggests a high level of ideological manipulation of cultural symbols of spiritual power. But a view from the villages, where multiple cults provide a seething site of cultural contestation and competing local interests, suggests a more multivocal understanding of and engagement with the tools of cultural symbolism. We need to recall that even the "successful cult centers" are subject to contestation. Furthermore, the successful cults, although undoubtedly playing a major role in the historical transformations of the local culture of Fujian, represent more of a rhizomatic, transversal network of the distribution of local power than a hierarchical model. Perhaps it is precisely in the efforts of local elites and state officials to hierarchicalize cult centers and *fenxiang* networks that we can see the rise of an alienated representation of spiritual power. By contrast, the volatility and changeability of the representations of spiritual power in particular communities, and the sheer exuberance and excess with which it is celebrated, all open up lines of flight from the status quo. These lines of flight can and do cross and mingle with other forces transversing the community, such as the withering away of the state and the aggressive flows of capital into the area.

What is the nature of the "local elite" involved in supporting ritual-events and temple networks in contemporary Chinese villages and townships? Further research is necessary before we can chart the forces within transforming Chinese rural and township society that have taken the form of renewed traditional popular religious activity. The role of Overseas Chinese relatives and investors cannot be overlooked. Nor can we ignore the power and resilience of the popular forms themselves to engage the desires and interests of members of the local culture. This power of the form of cultural content may explain the willingness of middle-aged entrepreneurs to support the festivals of the gods. The participation of the elder members of the community is more understandable and is of course sanctioned by the form of the cultural expression. The ambivalent participation of party members, and the far more active and open role of retired cadres, adds another element to the calculation of the nature of the "elite" involved in the planning and organization of ritual activities. Local ritual specialists (Daoist priests, Buddhist monks, Three in One masters, spirit-mediums, Confucian ritualists, sectarian groups, etc.) naturally play a key role in the performance of local cultural forms.

Since we are dealing with a collective process, it is important to note the participation of the entire community, excluding only Christian families, sometimes party officials, and disaffected individuals of various kinds. In certain areas youngsters and adolescents are being inducted into the machine of cultural reproduction through collective spirit-medium initiation ceremonies (Dean and Zheng, 1993). In every performance of ritual, the fundamental role of women in preparing the offerings, organizing the family involvement, burning incense, and cooking the feasts is so obvious that it usually goes unremarked. The range of women's involvement in popular religion extends far beyond the domestic sphere to include women's processional troupes, scripture recitation societies, small-scale village nunneries, goddess cults relating to childbirth and childhood diseases, spirit-mediumism, and dream interpretation. And although Christian families reject explicit involvement in communal worships, they are inevitably drawn into sponsorship and participant observation, if only to preserve their network of social relations in their home villages.

James Wilkerson (1994) has critiqued the notion of the inevitability of alienation in *jinxiang* pilgrimage by proposing an alternative model of self-reflexivity in ritual process, based on the work of Victor Turner. Wilkerson provides a sophisticated account of the impact of capitalism upon the political economy of representation. He argues that an awareness of the necessity of kitsch, disjunctive imagery, and co-optive imagery generated by the increasing role of capitalism results in a sharper state of reflexivity within the participants in contemporary pilgrimage. These issues are heightened in the contrastive relationship between sponsored theatrical performances (offered to the gods and enjoyed by the crowd) and voluntary performances of ritual and collective worship. There are, however, difficulties in his account, particularly with regard to the notion of the transparency of meaning in ritual-events (see Tambiah [1979] for an account of the formalist dimensions of ritual that would interfere with all but the most complex critical self-awareness, or Staal [1986] for a more thorough, formalistic analysis that denies any meaning to ritual whatsoever).

To argue exactly how popular religion and ritual have become one of the central modes of local cultural self-definition in contemporary Fujian would entail not only examples of the conscious manipulation of official codes and symbols of spiritual power, but also a detailed account of the concrete circulation of power within communities carrying out ritual activities often in defiance of the authorities. Such an analysis would require an alternative theory of the role of ritual and religious representation to the model of paradoxical alienation employed by Sangren, or the model of self-reflexivity presented by Wilkerson. Both of these models are based on a model of the self as the source and center of meaning. Sangren's account implies the necessity of a process of demystification by means of a conscious articulation of the mechanisms of alienation, but this task appears to require the input of an analyst external to the logical incapacity of individuals within the culture to understand their own processes of alienation. This grants the anthropologist a disturbingly exclusive and objective position vis-à-vis the people or culture under examination. Wilkerson's account of the hyperreflexivity required by the forceful intrusion of capitalism into the ritual process is intriguing, but it appears to rely upon an endless capacity for the transparency of meaning.

An alternative to these powerful models of cultural process would require the elaboration of an abstract theory of force, underlying concrete applications of power—which would be understood to exist only in the moment of its application and resistance. The circulation of forces upon the bodies of the individuals within a local culture takes the form of culturally constructed codes. These codes can be analyzed in various aggregate ritual forms. The coding of the body is paralleled by the shaping of the parameters of the mind, in particular, the categories of space and time within which the individual operates. The body is paralleled by the mind and is the field of the registering of intensity, or affect. Cultural codes embedded in ritual forms induce a range of affects from the body and achieve a parallel channeling of the forms of cogitation on the mind. The material force of desire, the immanence of the potentiality of the body, always exceeds a particular cultural assemblage and allows for particular avenues of flight from any given set of ritual forms, social institutions, and discourses. The task of cultural analysis includes the mapping of the flows of force, the formation of codes, and the channeling of affect and subjectivity in particular cultural contexts (see Gil [1989] for a philosophical analysis of anthropological studies of ritual). A developed theory of ritual would exceed the limits of this book but the following reconsideration of the role of ritual-events in the phases of Xinghua culture may give some indication of the issues involved.

PHASES AND PLANES

Each ritual tradition active in the Xinghua region, whether Confucian, Buddhist, Daoist, Three in One, or popular cult based, developed and differentiated its own multidimensional field of potential. By capturing, channeling, and intensifying all kinds of intercorporeal and infracorporeal forces (social, economic, political, ideational, libidinal, cosmic), each ritual-event folded into itself its entire multidimensional field of potential and redistributed it anew in a differentiated way. These ritual-events opened up spaces along a set of four overlapping yet analytically distinct strata: the space of the Earth, of Territory, of Commodity and Cultural Networks, and of Collective Experimentation (based, with alterations, on Levy, 1994, 1995). These spaces can be provisionally conceived of as geological levels, or strata, within the field of potential opened up by Xinghua local culture. Each space/stratum builds upon rather than overcomes or subsumes the other. The different fields of potential of the different ritual traditions overlapped to different degrees and juxtaposed themselves on these four strata.

Thought of in this way, specific strata can be seen to have achieved a particular degree of consistency in each successive phase of Xinghua culture outlined in chapter 1. But the strata interpenetrate and coexist in each of the phases, and within each ritual-event they are infolded, mixed, and redistributed. To put it another way, each phase of Xinghua local culture is chiefly characterized by the planes of consistency established within it by the disjunctive synthesis of various abstract ritual machines, but the potentialities actualized by these ritual machines return to the pool of potential in a process of the re-virtualization of the potential. These recharged potentials are then drawn upon, phased in and phased out, within each phase, and in each and every ritual-event.

To review, the phases of Xinghua culture outlines in chapter 1 are as follows:

Phase 1, sixth to eleventh centuries: Government-sponsored rites were held at official shrines established in commemoration of officials who had supervised the construction of irrigation systems. Buddhist and Daoist festivals were held around temples built in lineage settlements. Rituals were also held in Buddhist monasteries, which ran immense monastic estates that opened up the area for cultivation.

Phase 2, eleventh to fifteenth centuries: Lineages constructed their own non-canonical ancestral halls, local cults began to contest the prominence of official shrines, and differentiated processions began marking spiritual boundaries of different cults.

Phase 3, sixteenth to eighteenth centuries: a nested hierarchy of rituals and processions involved larger and larger segments of the irrigation system, and lineage structures were transcended by popular cult temple systems marked in some areas by village-based rituals of collective spirit-medium training.

Phase 4, nineteenth to early twentieth centuries: a patchwork of lineage feuds and secret religions and secret societies constituted by discrete ritual forms exploded into peasant rebellions.

Phase 5, early twentieth century onward: Local cultural forms were politicized through the intrusion of the state into village life and decision making; central forms of culture were contested, and local culture was reinvented.

   The early settlements and secluded Buddhist monastic estates of the first phase of Han Xinghua local culture represent an opening up of the space of the Earth. This space is characterized by myths and rites, and a relationship between the Earth and the cosmos. "Identity" is primarily structured in relation to lineage and totem. With the elaboration of state administration and the consolidation of settlements dominated by lineage principles, we see the opening up of the second space, the space of territory. The territorial space is characterized by writing and map-making and is in an intimate relationship with the state. "Identity" on this stratum is primarily a function of territorial inscription, the establishment of boundaries. In this space, lineages compose genealogical records, establish ancestral halls, and organize rituals at the graves of their ancestors. An ideology of the patriline is elaborated in text, territory, and rite. Property becomes subject to a level of collective, lineage control (including the establishment of lineage estates and a principle of priority in land claims), while rules are established for partible inheritance. Writing is also used in this space to transform the chants and ecstatic possession of the space of the Earth into Buddhist or Daoist scripture, as cults begin to emerge from isolated communities and claim wider powers. These cults begin to expand their temples. Some temples begin to divide incense. The state interacts with the territory through taxation and corvée and the performance of graduated homological ritual displays or enactments of authority. This requires the construction of state temples, shrines, and altars.

   The third space is the space of networks—networks of commodity exchanges and cultural interactions. This space is characterized by the elaboration of networks and a relationship to capital. "Identity" on this stratum is primarily a function of one's place within processes of production and consumption. In the third phase of Xinghua local culture, the lineages expanded beyond single settlements into extended, higher-order lineages. They responded to commodification by the establishment of tax shelters and joint-stock corporations. But an even greater transformation in this phase was the rise of networks of temples. These took several forms, most commonly nested hierarchies of temples within geographically defined boundaries such as irrigation systems. A second form was an alliance of temples representing scattered single- and multisurname communities in opposition to extended lineages in the vicinity. Another form was the division of incense from a founding temple, such as the Dongshan Zongkongtang. These temple networks extended beyond geographical, territorial limits. Of course, the most rapidly growing network in this period was that of regional markets, which linked the Xinghua region to coastal, overland, and international trade circuits.

   The fourth space is the space of collective experimentation opened up by groups moving along transversal and transnational flows. Although it is difficult to see anything besides chaos in the fourth and fifth phases of Xinghua local culture outlined above, one can conceive of the last hundred years as a period of intense reexamination and experimentation, brought on by internal pressures as well as external, transversal forces. This space is also the space of the imagination, of technological experimentation, collective transformations, and hybridization.

The renaissance of the Three in One and a multitude of other reinvented ritual traditions and reconstructed communities in the Republican period, as well as over the last decade and a half, represents a collective return to the powers of the earth and a reassertion of the relationship of the individual to the cosmos. This is not to say that these are primitivist or anachronistic movements. On the contrary, they are viable networks working out of newly revitalized communities. Moreover, the energies they are working with include new transversal flows of transnational capital, ideologies, floating populations, tourism, and so forth (Appadurai, 1990).

The spaces of the Earth, territory, commercial and cultural networks, and collective experimentation are strata traversed by the spheres of the economic, the political, and knowledge. Each of these spheres has its specific form on each stratum, but they can also fold upon one another. Thus the transformations of the state fold back on these spaces/strata, as, for example, when the transversal flow of a new conception of the modern nation-state forces a reimagining of the nature of territory and the nature of identity at all levels. Economic forces fold back on the different levels as well, with capital searching out natural resources at the level of the Earth, speculating in real estate at the level of territory, and partitioning collective experimentation into individual work and careers.

One concrete example of the reopening of these spaces over the past fifteen years is the ritual system of the Jiangkou plains, mentioned in chapter 8 above. In the late 1970s isolated, individual villages began reclaiming their local temples and reviving or reinventing rituals that opened a space of the Earth, of individual and cosmic identification, at the level of the immediate physical surroundings, the village. As these underground, illicit ritual-events began to take place sporadically around the area, coalitions of villages began to hold processions to reestablish their territorial alliances. As more and more territories came to life in this manner, the entire network of the area was gradually restored, culminating in the 1993 five-day procession of the Belvedere of the Eastern Peak involving over seventy villages and tens of thousands of participants. Yet this procession was financed in part by capital donated by Overseas Chinese groups from Indonesia, Malaysia, Taiwan, and the Philippines. These groups successfully urged the expansion of the procession beyond its "traditional" limits to include areas of the adjoining county of Fuqing, from which many of them had emigrated. Through collective experimentation with traditional forms, new spaces were opened up for a reconstructed and redefined community.

The Three in One has also opened up spaces of the earth, the territory, the network, and the space of collective experimentation. We have seen how certain Three in One temples became centers of village life. Other filiations, such as local lines of division of incense, or circuits of ritual collaboration between Three in One shrines in particular regions, opened up territorial spaces. The complex interrelationships among the various branches of the Three in One led to the opening of complex transregional networks. The revival of the Three in One in the 1970s and early 1980s has involved many groups, both local and Overseas Chinese, in collective experimentations in which the Three in One tradition has been reinvented and reshaped.

Looking at the Three in One over time in relation to the phases of Xinghua local culture, we can see that the movement arose long after a complex culture had developed composed of different fields of potential interacting with one another on the strata of the Earth, territorial ties, and cultural and commodity networks. The Three in One originated as a collective experiment, an opening up of the fourth kind of space described above. Beginning at the margins of local society, the movement expanded into village life, established regional filiations, and developed regional and transregional networks. From a marginal group the movement gradually transformed into a central feature of Xinghua local culture. This process involved the appropriation and reinvention of a multitude of local cultural forces. In order for the Three in One to achieve a position of leadership in local society, it had to merge with local institutions and classes. In some villages, we see this taking place through a merging of the Three in One with localized lineages. This is most evident in Lindou village, where the head of the lineage is the hereditary master of the Three in One altar. There are many less extreme examples of the merging of the Three in One and the local, lineage-based leadership class. This tendency is most evident in the less commercialized, less culturally sophisticated villages of the Xianyou area. In the complex society of the Putian-Hanjiang corridor, a vast array of nested temple systems, commercial circuits, centers of Confucian study, and tightly knit, higher-order extended lineages made it more difficult for the Three in One to rise to a leading role or to achieve a broad popular base. The inclusion of more and more women in the Three in One in the Republican period is another instance of the employment of new cultural strategies to expand the power and influence of the Three in One. The involvement of Overseas Chinese groups in the post-Mao era is yet another instance of collective experimentation opening up new spaces for the expansion of the Three in One.

The Three in One opened up spaces for itself through its performance of ritual-events. These ritual-events involved the channeling of forces through ritual machines constructed out of parts and elements of Confucian, Daoist, and Buddhist rituals. Some drew as well on popular spirit-writing and, in some cases, spirit-possession. Various kinds of space-time continuums were opened up through the ritual-events of the Three in One: recall the role of visualization, incantation, and liturgical dance. Different spaces were occupied through the transformation of private property into temples, the transformation of the space of the private academy and the public relief organization, and the absorption of popular gods into Three in One temples (thereby involving the temple in processions and circuits). The Three in One gradually established regional ritual groupings and an incense-offering network centered on the founding temple, the Zongkongtang, and other sites.

But in the process of building the ritual machines of the Three in One, the new spaces and arenas into which it entered absorbed and transformed it, disorienting the movement from its early vision of cultural unity. The phase of what appears in the historical record as an almost entropic devolution (mid to late Qing) led to the formation of self-organizing assemblages that actively reinvented and reorganized the Three in One in the Republican period. A similar process has occurred in the past decade and a half. The ritual machines of the Three in One do not produce the Same (the unity of culture). Ritual-events produce difference, that is, self-differentiating variations to the nth degree.

We can see the Three in One as an invented ritual tradition, a vector of communal ritual and inner alchemical practice that was developed collectively first by the founder and early disciples of the Three in One, and then by the many different groups in separate locations throughout the Xinghua area who fused the Three in One with local cults and practices. Participation in the Three in One gathers individuals into flows of ritual events and intensities, whether as children attending a festival; as worshipers preparing food offerings, burning incense, and consulting divination poems; as mediums relaying the words of the gods; as initiates practicing mediation; or as ritualists combining inner alchemy, liturgical practice, and scriptural study. The ritual-events of the Three in One actualize some of the virtual planes of Xinghua local culture, traversing the spaces of the Earth, the territory, networks of culture and commodities, and collective experimentation, to reconnect the individual with the cosmos. In the context of the transversal flows of force between these levels, and the folding of these spaces upon one another, the individual is inscribed within a zone of subjectivation created by a folding inward of the outside, an outside that is composed of constantly changing lines of force operating along multiple levels.[3]

[3] This definition of the individual is based on Gilles Deleuze's comments on the fold in his study of Foucault (1988: 94–123). Contrary to many postmodern theorists, Deleuze and Foucault provide a poststructuralist, constructivist theory and an ethics of subject formation. The subject that emerges from their reflections is quite unlike the static self-conscious self that is often assumed in social-scientific discussions of ritual (see Boundas, 1994). The discussion of contested and expanding spaces occupied by rhythmic repetitions of ritual can be extended to the realm of discursive practice, drawing on the work of Laclau and Mouffe (1985). Different discursive positions contended against the hegemonic status of imperial ritual discourse, imposing their own hegemony on local cultural formations. For example, the epigraphical records of the Xinghua area are replete with debates on the "true meaning" of the classical rites of ancestral worship, which were in fact being radically transformed in the process of the expansion of the corporate lineages in the area (Dean and Zheng, 1995). The Three in One epigraphy translated above can also be analyzed in this way. It is important to note that the opening up of multiple public spaces involves not only communal ritual events and institutional transformations, *but also* the elaboration of hegemonic discursive formations. These processes continue today, in new discursive and communal practices.

Disjunctive Syntheses of Transversal Flows in Ritual-Events

Brian Massumi, in a comment on the research that has led to this book, made the following remarks:

> What should or could be the place of tradition and ritual in social movements and cultural studies? Imported Western theoretical tools for the analysis of cultural change tend to focus attention on the one hand on the movement of investment capital into special economic zones and the often blatantly exploitative effects of unregulated capitalist production, and on the other hand, they focus on the consumption of imported, commodified cultural forms in those urbanized zones and in the media (Gold, 1993). On this consumption side, the emphasis is often on creative appropriations of imported cultural forms that introduce a measure of self-definition and self-determination into an otherwise bleak picture (Chow, 1990–91).
>
> In both cases, the rural majority all but disappears from the picture. When the focus is on investment and production, the rural majority figures only negatively, as a reserve labor force drawn to the urban centers. On the consumption side, they do not figure at all, lacking the disposable income to "appropriate" imported cultural forms. There is one Western theoretical approach in which the rural population does figure prominently, that is the ethnographic approach. All too often, ethnography depicts rural culture as frozen in time, an archaic holdover completely unadapted to the modern, let alone post-modern world. The rural world either disappears, or is frozen in time.
>
> One can attempt to maneuver around this shortcoming by combining cultural studies and ethnography in such a way that they critique and compensate for each other's weaknesses. For there is no viable option of simply going native, and somehow miraculously stepping outside of the Western systems of knowledge in which one was formed. But there is an option of combining Western theoretical approaches in a way that makes them interrogate each other, and rooting that interrogation in a sustained participation and affective involvement in the cultural phenomenon under study.
>
> The most striking thing about rural popular culture is its dynamic nature. Far from being changeless and sheltered from the transformations of the larger world, it is in intimate connection with them and continuously reinvents itself in response to them. Popular religion in South China has been actively responding to capital since the Song dynasty.
>
> The form of response is noteworthy. Money is transformed from a means of payment into a means for accumulating spiritual capital. The way this is done is by sacrificing it, burning a simulacrum of it. This is achieved within the framework of massive ritual expenditure of energy and resources. It is achieved through ornate social technologies of *excess*. These technologies of excess and expenditure form a realm of anti-capital and anti-production, and by doing that create a kind of safe zone in which traditional cultural forms can continue, in spite of changes in the larger world. They continue, however, only at the price of changing in response to these wider changes (the addition of ritual forms). The relation of rit-

ual forms to capital is not only negative, as an analysis of the contemporary situation shows. Ritual revival is now a key magnet for attracting overseas investment capital into the *rural* regions of China. Ritual at the same time *interrupts* capital in a way that safeguards local cultural forms, and *reconnects* with capital in a way that begins to integrate the rural areas into the very system its rituals interrupt. And the way it does this to some extent runs counter to State control. Because the eagerness of the State to attract overseas capital forces it to compromise on its social agenda. So through one side of its mouth, the state bureaucracy finds itself nurturing popular cultural forms that it condemns through the other side of its mouth, through anti-superstition campaigns. The State also finds itself compromising on its economic control, as what are seemingly the most archaic segments of society start to determine where international capital flows.

That brings up another realm where ritual interrupts and reconnects with larger systems: the State. Popular religion is the pivot for a complex network of forms of local social organization that counterbalance state interventions from above: family, lineages, village, regional alliances of villages. This relative autonomy of local organization is also safeguarded by sacrifice. Initiates undergo long years of training in the production of gibberish—incomprehensible talismanic texts that are simulacra of state decrees. These texts are sacrificed, producing in the spirit world, an accumulation of excess signification paralleling the accumulation of spiritual capital achieved through the sacrifice of money.

The sacrifice of texts interrupts the downward flow of state signification aimed at reforming the individual in the image of the Emperor (or the Helmsman [see Apter and Saich, 1994]). This homological technology of individuation is not limited to the old Empire or to Mao, but in one form or another is a characteristic of any centralized state. Every state in one way or another attempts to model the individual as a microcosmic expression of itself—to create a homology between the basic unit of society and society as a whole. The sacrifice of texts to produce an excess-signification interrupts the homology, much as the sacrifice of money interrupts the flow of capital. And once again it interrupts in order to reconnect: the anti-State element of ritual strengthens local organization *within* the State— it integrates the local and the national, modifying both.[4]

TRANSVERSAL FLOWS

This interruption of the normal flows of capital and ideology and their subsequent reconnection into different directions that traverse the local community takes place in an arena already riddled with transversal flows among communities, cult centers, and local lineages of knowledge and power. Consider the following by no means exhaustive list:

[4] Massumi's comments were delivered in response to my paper on "Despotic Empire/Nation-State: Local Responses to Chinese Nationalism in an Age of Global Capitalism" at the Trajectories II Conference, Taipei, January 10–17, 1995, organized by Chen Kuan-Hsing. See also Massumi (1992).

1. A multitude of transversal flows within and between different cults and incense division networks

2. A considerable number of parallel, sometimes rival ritual traditions available at the communal level

3. Multiple vertical lineages of literacy/cultural knowledge (symbolic capital or intellectual property) handed down within households or through apprenticeships and reaching into village life (Chinese medicine, geomancy, divination, literate scribes, Confucian masters of ceremony, etc.)

4. Multiple principles of interbelonging or co-ownership criss-crossing the community such as lineage or kinship group, state-based systems related to taxation and mutual self-defense and policing, temple-based circuits involving shares in the collective community—all of these distinguished by different regimes of offerings, prestations, and ritual performance (Wilkerson, 1994)

5. Complex interlarding of representatives of official culture—retired officials, failed literati, and local gentry—in village life

6. A profusion of associational forms that could take shape within many of the other social groupings already mentioned (lineage, temple, etc.), and which often are used to pool capital or mitigate against capital fluctuations (Sangren, 1984). Perhaps most intriguing of all is the structural principle of transformation of household, based on the effects of partible inheritance, which theoretically impel a movement from small families to extended families, to hereditary lineages, to class-dominated to contractual lineages, and then back again into smaller and smaller units (Zheng, 1992). In other words, many of these different elements of discrete multiplicities are constantly in movement.

7. The ever-present potential for revelation, the eruption of a representation of spiritual power into the community, the formation of a new cult, which can cause a rearrangement of the flow of power between all the social groupings mentioned above. Revelation through spirit-writing means that the history of the community can constantly be renarrated. The codification of these contested histories is part of the role of ritual specialists in bringing local culture into the sphere of national culture.

8. The supersaturation of the senses, particularly the role of sound, in rituals and processions. These events, because they are periodic, are also deeply rhythmic and cut through with lines of innovation and improvisation. Alinguistic elements (sensation, music and rhythm, movements and gestures) traverse levels and create resonant alignments between hitherto distinct registers within ritual-events.

9. The rejection of contradiction and the positive experience of multiplicity. Despite understandings of the god that are contradictory (Daoist astral deity to the Daoist or Three in One ritual specialists, powerful but dangerous force to the temple committee, beneficent source of protection to the villagers, immediate possessing force to the spirit medium), the contradictions are not allowed to erupt openly. Instead, a positive experience of the multiplicity of supernatural force is enjoined. Such positive experience of mutability and transformation, encompassing contradiction, help explain the extraordinary vitality and richness of rural Chi-

nese culture. We should bear in mind that many of these different elements of dis-crete multiplicities are constantly in movement. To this list we must also add those transnational flows of capital, floating populations, ideology, tourism, and so forth that permeate Xinghua local culture.

The image that arises from all of this is of rural Chinese popular culture as highly complex, and always evolving—as dynamic and utterly contemporary, while remaining traditional. It also offers a view of cultural forms as always polyvalent. A multifunctional cultural form such as ritual is seen as simulta-neously interrupting and reconnecting, as destructuring and restructuring. It then becomes very difficult to characterize it according to the usual binary schema: national or transnational, state or antistate, even capitalist or anti-capitalist. A cultural form is all of these things, differently in every case. So it becomes meaningless to try to pigeon-hole it, or designate it once and for all as this *or* that. It also becomes counterproductive to focus on one level at the expense of the others, as if one level, whether capital, nation, or local, held the interpretive key to all the rest. The approach that this work suggests is to see each cultural form as a node in a complex, self-organizing network in which there is no last organizing instance and no preset progression. Each form or stage or level interrupts and reconnects with all the others and in the process modifies them and is modified by them. A cultural form appears as a transformer, a transformative social technology that receives, modifies, and retransmits flows. Thus, culture can be understood in terms of flow, or economies of movement, rather than in terms of structure or characteristic properties. The challenge for cultural theory would be to find ways of ana-lyzing, specifically and in detail, the particular economy of movement of the cultural form in question, and to do this in a way that places in the foreground the contemporaneousness and dynamism, its transformative potential.[5]

ALTERNATIVE COMMUNITIES

Recently in the West, in the wake of the rise of vicious ethnic and nationalis-tic strife in former Yugoslavia and elsewhere, a number of questions have been asked about underlying assumptions of modernization theory and the recidi-vism of nationalism (Zizec, 1990). The revival of ethnic nationalism in the West, in Québec as well as at the fringes of the Soviet empire, also raises com-plex problems for those theorists of postmodernism and late capitalism who had announced the imminent end of the nation-state, the withering away of civil society, and the rise of all kinds of transnational flows of ethnic groups, information, capital, and communications (Harvey, 1989; Jameson, 1991; Appadurai, 1990). The relentless rise of the right wing in American politics, particularly under the Reagan administration, and more recently with the Contract with America, reveals the continuing role of archaic processes in the

[5] See note 4 above.

U.S. body-politic that will very likely have extremely unfortunate consequences, involving the reassertion of nationalist themes (Dean and Massumi,
1992).

Certain observers have remarked on the fact that many theories of the end
of the nation come out of a series of reflections upon the most developed
sectors of the developed world and may fail to comprehend the continuing
importance of nationalistic or nationally based socialist movements in other
contexts (Ahmad, 1992). The nature of this support is marked by the ever-
increasing hybridization of the center of the empire by the peoples of its periphery, which has been widely remarked (Bhahba 1994; Chow, 1994). At the
very least, we will have to continue to respond to, and seek alternatives to, nationalist pressures well into the next century. One way to do this, I would suggest, lies in the examination of the resources of local cultural formations such
as the Three in One, in the context of local Xinghua popular culture.

Partha Chatterjee (1993) provides a series of interesting perspectives on
colonial and nationalist narratives of the nation. He suggests that *community*
may be the disruptive term under the seamless surface of the interlocked discourse of reason and capital, and he further suggests that there is a great deal
to be learned from the study of marginalized, subaltern communities, as well
as the contradiction between community and nation in postcolonial states. He
argues that, in the West, capitalist relations and capitalist forces have increasingly invested in the public sphere, which was conceived as a bridge between
civil society and the state. With the investment by capital in the public sphere,
state and society become linked in the form of the nation. At this point, the
only community imaginable is the nation, which extends its disciplinary mechanisms throughout society in an effort to extend cultural hegemony, homogenizing social forms and preventing any independent development of alternative community. In his analysis of Gandhi's political movement, he suggests
that nationalist thought in its anticolonial mode moves through a communi-
tarian rejection of the pseudo-community constructed by capital (Chatterjee,
1986). He argues that this is a necessary moment in nationalist logic, but that
with the successful establishment of the independent nationalist nation-state,
the drive toward development, whether socialist or capitalist, falls back into
the narrative of the march of capital, which demands the homogenization of
cultural forms, and their subsumption under the aegis of a nation-state.

Anthropologists such as Marilyn Strathern (1992) have examined ways in
which alternative modes of exchange build up alternative modes of community and personhood. The narrative of the endless expansion of capital would
appear to threaten to subsume all such alternative forms. The "subject" (in
both senses of the word) of this narrative is the "individual," defined as the
isolated, self-contained, rational decision-making unit. Nationalism then appears as a particular moment in this all-consuming trajectory. The power of
the local community to disrupt the nation and its narration(s) was, however,
already suggested by Maurice Godelier (1978) in his cautious effort to revive
a refurbished version of the Asiatic Mode of Production and to raise questions

about historical necessity in a Marxist context. Godelier was raising the possibility of a series of alternative rearrangements of the developmental phases of orthodox Marxist teleology. Perhaps the analysis of multiplicity in community will enable us to think beyond determinate developmental schemes and find resources to respond to the rush of capital into the postmodern.

If we consider the forms of community and subject positions provided by movements such as the Three in One in these terms, we discover a mode of production of alternative temporalities, different forms of "worlding," arising out of participation in a ritual tradition that works within complex communities to create new collectivities. For the individual adherent, liturgy and inner alchemy merge with everyday practice, transforming time and the realm of experience.

Can one reach any conclusions about the relationship among the forces of individual construction, local cultural self-organization, and the nationalistic desires of the state, or the visions of a Greater Chinese Economic Cooperative sphere of the future? Increasingly, the urge toward unification that was manifest in early discussions of Greater China have given way to a vision of informal ties, or ties that bypass explicit political form (Harding, 1994). This is not to say that tremendous nationalistic pressures do not threaten to erupt into open conflict within China and in different sectors in Taiwan, or between China and Taiwan. But what I have been outlining above is the potentiality on the part of local Chinese culture to achieve maximum flexibility by reinventing itself at a level of individuation both below that of the homogeneity demanded by a modernized nation and yet at the same time suppler and more vibrant than the rigid consistency of a cog in a state machine.

Observers of China are now familiar with the circulation of talismanic images of Chairman Mao displayed in taxicabs, buses, and trucks as commodified cult objects.[6] Some of these fetishized fragments have since been gathered up in the formation of a broader spiral, the process of reinvention of local cultural forms. During the Chinese New Year's festivities in Xianyou in 1995 I saw a portrait of the young Mao on a placard decorated with Christmas tree lights leading a procession of lanterns and gods in sedan chairs around the backstreets of a city in Xianyou. The procession featured floats adorned with laser lights and technological fetish objects. A hundred brand-new red Japanese motorcycles led the procession. A few days later a similarly decorated portrait of Mao, Deng Xiaoping, Marshal Zhu De, and Premier Zhou Enlai led a ritual procession of several thousand people representing a coalition of thirty-six villages. The spiral of local culture(s) is in part a response to the hegemonic, totalizing project of nationalist modernity, in its particularly convoluted Chinese expression. Some may feel that by opposing local culture and community to nationalistic modernization I am resurrecting a utopian vision with which to flail the evils of capitalism. The point is rather that "the 'uni-

---

[6] *Taoist Ritual and Popular Cults of Southeast Asia* (Dean, 1993) concludes with a reference to the role of these fetishistic images in popular cultural circulation.

versalist'" claims of "modern Western social philosophy are themselves limited by the contingencies of global power" (Chatterjee, 1993). As Naoki Sakai (1989) pointed out, this kind of universalism is dependent on particularism. I am more interested in pointing to evidence of widespread, fragmented resistances to the normalizing project of nationalism, and suggesting that it is in the study and performance of these forces of resistance, these "insurrections of subjugated knowledge . . . whose validity is not dependent on the approval of the established regimes of thought" (Foucault, 1980: 79–82), that we may find the resources for creative local responses to global capitalism and nationalistic cultural hegemony.

This book has sought to explore some of the changing strategies of resistance to state desire within Chinese culture and to analyze the shifting boundaries of local formations of desire that escape the totalizing pressure of the capitalist-invested "social ensemble," as much as they avoid the individualizing, homogenizing pressures of the modernizing nation-state. However, no one should deceive themselves into thinking that local Chinese communities will renounce their patrilocal nature, with its attendant patriarchal domination of women. The potential for human abuse is enormous under these conditions. It is precisely in its ability to achieve and activate a separate sphere of domination from the totalizing and individualizing powers of the state that the community manifests its powers of resistance. Part of the task of analysis is to uncover the assemblages of desire operating at the communal level simultaneously to resist the state and to inscribe the all too human.[7]

For participants in these local movements, the Three in One is an expression of the unity of "Chinese culture." Indeed, they imply that the Three in One expresses "Chinese culture" more completely than the contemporary modern nation-state. Yet their sense of the unity of "Chinese culture" rests on their active involvement in a fundamental, and potentially divisive, heterogeneity. The Three in One embodies this paradox, both in the range of its concrete actualizations within the Xinghua area (from orthodox Confucian scholastic sect to center of communal village cult activity) and in its ambiguous relation to both constantly changing Xinghua local culture and constantly contested understandings of "Chinese culture." The Three in One has expanded both the distinctness of local Xinghua culture and the richness and multiplicity of "Chinese culture" as a whole, transforming both in the process. This process involves a constant struggle, a never-ending agonistic effort to

[7] A darker view of the Three in One might see in its combination of microcosmic inner alchemical methods and Confucian moral injunctions the construction of a miniaturized machine of despotic desire. The rise of microcosmic thinking in China is clearly related to the emergence of Empire (see Sivin, 1996). Confucian ritual in imperial contexts can be seen to reinscribe the participant in encompassing forms of hierarchical power relations. Daoist ritual mimicry of court hierarchy could be interpreted as an effort to bring this hierarchical vision down to the village level. It is important to recall, however, that the Three in One's ritual machines deterritorialized the elements from which they were drawn and reterritorialized them in an evolving space of shifting power relations. In this sense, the disciplined powers of inner alchemy and ritual practice could lead to unexpected openings.

Plate 20. A young man surrounded by elders performs as head scriptural master in Mingxia rites in Xianyou

achieve autonomy and self-definition. From the perspective of local leaders bent on the unification of the Three in One, such appeals can be seen as a call for official recognition and legitimation, an affirmation of their own positions within the movement, and a general claim for the validity and significance of local religious movements. From the state's viewpoint, even this degree of "multiplicity within unity" is difficult to accept. This study has attempted to question these reifications of "Chinese culture," pointing to the diversity and complexity of local movements, and suggesting that "culture" itself is a category of thought that must be questioned. Perhaps in this realm of difference we have already entered into the unrepresentable.

Is it conceivable that the "vanguard of Chinese culture" in the twenty-first century may be made up of local spirit-mediums, Three in One ritualists, or other local movements, rather than Confucian cadres in business suits? That what has been termed the "ecstatic substratum of Chinese culture" has the power to resist and *transform* alongside transnational forces to prevent the formation of rigid statist forms? If so, then we can expect autonomous communal organizations and movements within localities and regions of China to continue to respond creatively to the problems and potentials of the coming millennium.

Editions of Lin Zhao'en's Writings

LIN ZHAO'EN wrote voluminously, composing over 130 works ranging from short essays to full-length studies. Many of these works were printed shortly after having been written. For example, the National Palace Museum in Taipei has a version of his *Linzi Daode shilue* (Master Lin's brief interpretation of the Way and its power) in 6 juan. The *Linzi xingshi, Linzi nianpu,* and *True Record* note the printing of many individual volumes, and the collections of several different editions of Lin's collected works. Collections were compiled in 1567, 1584, 1589, and 1593. Prefaces and colophons to certain collections provide further information on additional editions. About 73 of Lin Zhao'en's titles can be dated quite precisely. These are listed in order of composition, followed by the undated texts, in Lin (1992: 22–28). Eventually Lin and his followers began to gather these writings into various collected editions. According to Ma and Han (1992: 852), an early collection of Lin's writings in 2 juan entitled *Sanjiao zhengzong* (Correct principles of the Three Teachings), said to date from the Jiajing period (1522–1566), is in the Polinsi Buddhist monastic library in Beijing. There are currently several different editions of various collections of Lin's writings in libraries in China, Taiwan, Japan, and the United States. These are as follows:

1. *Sanjiao huipian yaolue,* 8 volumes, 9 *juan,* printed in 1563, in the Beijing University Rare Books Collection. Prefaces by Lin Zhao'en (*Shu Sanjiaohuipian juanduan* (Written at the head of the collected works on the Three Teachings) and Mu Zishou, "Minor Preface."

2. *Linzi shengxue tongzong sanjiaoguiru ji* (Collection of Master Lin's doctrine of the sages uniting the schools of the Three Teachings under true Confucianism), compiled in 1567. Prefaces dated 1569 and 1570. Tadao Sakai (1960) states that the collection was printed after 1575. 4 juan, 17 titles and several prefaces. (See table of contents in Berling: [1980: 246–247]. Sonkeikaku Bunko collection.

3. *Linzi fenneiji Sanjiao fenzhe bianlan* (Selected readings from Master Lin's "the world as my family" collection), compiled by Chen Dadao at Lin Zhao'en's request in 1588, preface by Lin Zhao'en, 1588. Originally bound in 10 volumes with 62 juan. Beijing University Library Rare Books collection has 36 juan in 5 volumes (Ma and Han, 1992: 852–853). Mano Senryu has a 9-volume set in his personal collection (Mano, 1979). The Institute of History and Philology of the Academia Sinica in Nankang, Taiwan, has a copy of a related text, the 12-juan edition of the *Linzi fenneiji cuanyao* from the Tianqi period (1621–1627).

4. *Sanjiao zhengzong tonglun* (Discussions on the combination of correct principles of the Three Teachings), 1597 edition, Library of Congress Peking Library Rare Book Microfilm Series, reels 1038–39. Preface by Lin Zhao'en, 1595. (Table

of contents in Berling [1980: 254–257]). This may be the same edition as that mentioned in Ma and Han (1992: 852), as having been printed by the Xiaxintang in Hanjiang and dating from 1600, divided into 6 volumes, with 20 juan, now in the collection of the Bolinsi Buddhist monastic library in Beijing. Prefaces by Lin Zhao'en, Luwenhui, and Mu Zishou. The Taipei National Central Library has an edition of this collection from the Tianqi period (1621–1627) in 119 juan.

5. *Linzi quanji* (Collected works of Master Lin), 20 volumes, 40 juan. Printed in 1606. Prefaces by Lin Jiaoke and Jiang Yifang, 1606. Naikaku Bunko collection. (See table of contents in Berling [1980: 248–253].)

6. *Linzi quanji* (Collected works of Master Lin), 41 volumes, in 4 cases (entitled *yuan, heng, li, zhen*), 1631, Beijing Library collection. (Table of contents in Ma and Han [1992: 854–857].)

7. *Linzi quanji* (Collected works of Master Lin), 48 volumes, colophon 1631, Princeton University Gest Library. (Table of contents in Berling [1980: 258–259].)

8. *Linzi quanji* (Collected works of Master Lin). Several differently bound versions of this title have been preserved in various libraries, but these have not yet been systematically compared. These sets include (1) 32 volumes, 112 chapters, 4 cases (entitled *yuan, heng, li, zhen*); (2) *Naikaku bunko*, 40-volume set; (3) *Naikaku bunko*, 39-volume set; (4) Kyoto University Jinbun library, 119-juan edition; (5) Kyoto Fuli University set; (6) Harvard-Yenching set; (7) Zhejiang Provincial library, 40-juan set, with a 1631 colophon by Xu Wenping.

9. *Linzi Sanjiao zhengzong tonglun* (Master Lin's discussions on the combination of correct principles of the Three Teachings), 1644 edition. The "Explanation of the Table of Contents," in juan 1, mentions that Lu Wenhui passed the task of carving blocks on to Chen Shuyu in 1618. Colophons dated 1644 suggest that the collection was not printed until that time. The collection includes a number of short works by Lu Wenhui and Guo Zengzhao. This set has been reprinted in Putian in 1925 and in 1982 and again in the 1990s. This edition of the writings of Lin Zhao'en is considered as scripture by the Three in One in Xinghua. Another set was printed in Malaysia in the 1960s.

10. *Linzi huipian* (Comprehensive edition of [the works of] Master Lin), 30 volumes, 118 juan, prefaces by Lin Zhaoke and Jiang Lianfang (1588). A colophon by Fang Junshi dated 1873 states that the edition is missing some 10 juan. Beijing Library and Nanjing University Library collections.

In addition to the works included in these collections, Lin Zhao'en is also credited with writing the *Jiuxu zheyan neijingtu,* edited by Lu Wenhui, 1583 (1986 reprint), and the *Sishu zhengyi* (Correct meaning of the Four Books), edited by Zhang Hongdu. The first is dated 1595; the second includes a new preface dated 1597. The latter date corresponds to that of the edition in the Peking Library Rare Book Room Microfilm Series, reels 1038–39, available in the Library of Congress (Berling 1980: Appendix D, 254–257). For detailed discussions of certain of these editions, and the date of composition of works included in them, see Sakai (1960); Mano (1979); Berling (1980); Zheng (1988); Ma and Han (1992); and Lin (1992).

The *Chart of the Inner Landscape of the Nine Stages*

THE FOLLOWING is a summary of the first part of the text, followed by a translation of the nine stages, which gives first the commentary drawn from Lin Zhao'en's *Jiuxu zheyan* (Nine stages) essay, followed by the heart method (*xinfa*) visualizations appropriate to each stage. I have also translated passages from other Three in One texts that comment directly on the nine stages.

The *Chart of the Inner Landscape of the Selected Sayings on the Nine Stages* has a preface dated Wanli 11 (1583), "reverently recorded by Initiate Lu Wenhui." The general description of the body found on pages 2 and 3 of the texts is translated in chapter 4 above. Page 3 gives further instances of alchemical transformation, with phases like "The single spark of light between the two kidneys, when forced to move in a regressive direction, is the mother of the inner elixir. When it moves in the usual direction, it results in human [birth]." "The single dot of the Niwan expands(?) into the Heavenly Palace of Pure Yang. This Way is called the Way of the flying golden lights at the back of the elbows, and it cannot be casually transmitted to bad people." "The technique of the Three Islands of Penglai is sometimes called the aperture of the coccyx; it is also called the Palace of Yama (the Underworld). The Daoists state: the external nine apertures are also called the Valley Way. The Buddhists state: Shoot arrows at the nine-storied iron drum." The following pages provide diagrams to illustrate certain alchemical concepts. Thus on page 4 we find a diamond-shaped diagram, with the character *ding* (head) in a circle at the top, the heart in the middle, and the coccyx at the bottom. On either side of the head circle are the "jade pillows." Further down the sides of the diamond we find labeled the left and right spinal column. At the bottom of either side of the diamond are the words "eight ounces of dark cord." On either side of the heart circle are the words "After the *Qian* and the *Kun* have been matchmade, a single point [of light] descends into the Yellow Chamber." There are also the words: "Sun—*Xu,* and Moon—*Yi.*" Along the sides of the diagram "the entranceway of the Dark Female is the root of Heaven and Earth—the home of the husband and wife is of itself within its midst." (*Left*) "The entirety of fundamental Nothingness, at the height of tranquility, gives birth to the Yang. The Primal Yang and the True Qi rise up from down below." Page 5 is entitled "The chart of the rising and falling of water and fire: this is the chart of the inner medicine." On the right side of the chart are the nodes of the spinal column. On the left are the circles on a string of the storied chamber of the esophagus. Below are two circles indicating the kidneys. That on the left is marked "Send it in reverse motion upward and it forms the elixir." That on the right is marked "the bubbling fountain." In the center at the top, the words read "The Central Palace is the Niwan." Below the words read "The Sea of Qi is the Elixir Field." The text reads: "The oral instructions for putting into practice: From the Bubbling Fountain to the lower elixir field, from the coccyx through the spine, the jade pass, and the jade pillow, let it ascend to the Niwan and descend into the Flowery pond. Then over the pigeon bridge let it descend the twelve-storied tower, penetrate the scarlet palace, and enter the Dark Pass. This is called The Void. There are oral instructions for its implementation." Page 6 provides "The inner medicine chart; there are oral instructions." The chart is a rectangle, with hexagrams above and below. Around the exterior of the rectangle we read, "Shapeless and traceless," "Flowing radiance shines back," "Doing nothing yet leaving nothing undone." There are also the words written reversed for heart, spirit, and nature. Below the rectangle we read, "When Qian and Kun are mated, a single spark drops into the Yellow Chamber." Inside we find the words, "The Yellow Old Women, the old slave, has made a match." At the very center of the diagram we see the phrase "Yellow Old Woman." Page 7 shows an image of the insides of a human body. Page 8 gives a diagram of the refinement of Breath and Seminal Essence: On the right we read, "Refine the seminal essence into Breath which rises on high." On the left, "Refine the Breath into Spirit and let it descend below." Inside the diagram there are three circles identified as the Upper, Middle, and Lower Elixir Fields. The top circle contains the Primal Breath. The middle circle contains the Primal Spirit. The lower circle contains the Primal seminal Essence. Page 9 is a diagrammatic side view of the human body, identifying certain features. Three Gates are identified in the head: the Gates of Heaven, the Main Gate, and the Cranial Gate. Two openings are identified in the throat. These are the esophagus, which transmits food, and the bronchial tubes, which transmit breath. On the torso, the position of the left and right lung are indicated. The position of the left kidney is shown. The spleen is said to be above the elixir field. The point beneath the bladder is identified as the point where the urine is emitted. The anus is indicated. Page 10 shows the right side view of the body. Page 11 provides a frontal view of the body, indicating the position of the Heavenly Court, the cheeks, the shoulders, the armpits, the forearms, the elbows, the throat, the lungs and the heart, the liver, the spleen, and the stomach, the lower arms, the smaller and larger intestine, the bladder, the spleen, the inner thighs, the "frontal yin," the lower leg, the outer knees, the tendons of the legs, the ankle, the foot, and the bubbling spring at the bottom of the feet. Page 12 provides a back view of the body, showing the proper position of the *Gen* hexagram in the back. Below it is written "the Breath in the middle part becomes the Dark Female." Below this the position of the bladder is shown. Beneath that the position of the *weizhi* (coccygeal channel) and the *weilutai* (enchymoma?) are indicated. Page 13 provides an inner view of the left side of the body showing the position of the internal organs and their relationship with the joints of the spinal column. Page 14 gives the inner view of the right side of the body showing the positions of various spiritual forces within the body. Pages 15 and 16 are a narrative description of the internal organs and their various functions entitled "That unto which the five internal organs belong." Page 17 is entitled "An explanation of the placement of certain areas pointed out" and contains an explication of terms used in the alchemical understanding of the body. Pages 18 and 19 provide "Introductory pointers on self-cultivation." Page 20 provides an illustration of the interior of the alchemical body, identical to that used in the *Shilin guangji* and reproduced in Needham (1983: p. 112). Pages 21 to 30 are a detailed exposition of the Heart Method:

STAGE 1: THE FIRST IS "[STILL THE MIND BY MEANS OF THE] GEN [HEXAGRAM] IN THE BACK"

The *Book of Changes* says, "Stilling [lit. *Gen* Hexagram in] the back." The character for "back" is composed of the [characters for] north and flesh. North is the direction of water, but the mind is connected with fire. If one can take the fire of the south and cultivate it in the water of the north, this is what the *Book of Changes* said: "Wash the mind, move it back, and hide it in a secret place." When it says "stop the thoughts with thought," it means to stop the depravity of outer-[directed] thoughts by means of the correctness of inner thought. However, prize the state of no thought. Even if the inward thought is correct, it is still thought. How could this be what Chengzi called "forgetting both inner and outer"? This is to use error to leave error behind, to use an illusion to extinguish an illusion. This is the method of mind-cultivation handed down by sages of old. Therefore the sequence of study is first to forget the outer; then one can forget the inner. [Text of *Nine Stages* passages are drawn from J. Berling (1980).]

The mind is [originally] connected with water, for when one is first born, one emits a single cry, and the spirit is within the navel. At seven or eight years, the spirit moves to a point between heaven and earth. At twelve or thirteen, the spirit has not yet left the back. If one can hold it (*nian*) inside the navel within the abdomen, this is the beginning of the process of the storing up of life. At fifteen or sixteen, the spirit has already risen up from the back, and at this point one can begin to study techniques of control (*gongfu*). The teaching has one utilize the middle finger to count out the right position, and then to penetrate the *kunlun* cranium with an opening, and to visualize with all one's might the method of restoring the spirit. When you have reached the [correct] point in the back, imagine a cavity there. A radiance will flow downward into the cavity from the head. Practice this diligently.

The *Jiuxu yaojue xuzhi* (Necessary information on the essential secrets of the nine stages), an undated manuscript by one Zheng Erqing, claims that the point where one should concentrate in the back (the *genbei* position) is "behind the heart, within the back . . . the empty place in the back, slightly lower than the level of the heart, [this] is the so-called opening of the void." (This and subsequent passages are quoted in Lin [1992: 89–105]).

Stage 2: The Second is the Revolution of the Heavens; Imitate Qian and Kun in order to Establish the Ultimate

The mind forms the Great Ultimate and the revolutions of the *qian* and *kun* revolve around it; this is the meaning of the "four seasons following their course." Then my body is a microcosm of the universe. [Text of *Nine Stages,* stage 2]

[Master Lin] said: The four seasons, these are spring, summer, fall, and winter; these are the phases of birth, growth, reaping, and hiding away. The mind is connected to fire. Now from heaven to earth the distance is 84,000 li, and the 42,000-li point is the midpoint. My mind is a microcosm of the universe, thus from the heart to the navel (*qi*) the distance is 8.4 Chinese inches, and [the center of this distance] is the place of the *gen* hexagram in the back. A single divine light the size of a star penetrates through the central 4.2 inch point and thereby establishes the Ultimate. Visualize the divine light like a mirror, 1.2 inches large, revolving to the right like the wheels of a cart. In spring it is born, in summer it grows, in fall it is gathered, in winter it hides away, thereby returning to the Ultimate. Again it begins to revolve, rising from the Ultimate [point]. Practice this in accordance with the four seasons.

The *Necessary Information* expands on this passage as follows:

To carry this out, recite aloud and concentrate on the four words "Sanjiao Xiansheng" (Master of the Three Teachings). After a long time, bring your concentration to rest between the heart and the navel. Four finger-breadths above the (midpoint) of the heart to the navel should be the standard, not in front or behind, nor left nor right, but right there establish the ultimate (point). At this ultimate point visualize a golden needle standing upright. From the golden needle suspend a magnetic pointer. Revolve (the light) downwards to one inch beneath the navel, then turn left and raise it upwards to behind the heart. Then revolve it to the right and downward to a point again below the navel. This is like the shining of a sundial. In this way, water is above while fire is below. Therefore follow these revolvings with one's will, and if the revolutions stop then lead them on with the will. Practice this until you are completely familiar with it, and the smoother the [process], the more marvelous it will be. This is the means to congeal the *qi* and harmonize the spirit.

Elsewhere the same text elaborates:

The point four inches above the navel is the central node. Neither before nor behind, to the left or the right. Here we find east-wood, west-metal, south-fire, north-water, and center-earth. Set up the ultimate point upon the earth of the center. Feel a golden needle flow through from behind to the front. Then from the base of the needle to an inch below the navel, revolve to the east past the *Li* Hexagram, then revolve west past the *Kan* Hexagram, and revolve back to the starting point. Start small and then make it larger, then from the large return to the small. Above don't go beyond the *jiuwei,* and below don't extend past the Gate of the Spirit. At first use your will to guide the revolutions. After a long time they will revolve by themselves. During the revolutions, the will is poured into the ultimate point at the yellow center. In accord with its natural way, it harmonizes its certainty. If it does not revolve [by itself], it will be necessary to use the will to guide it [around] several times. This is the marvelous teaching of the upside down *yin* and *yang* for the accumulation of perfection and the refining of the *qi*. If one wishes to cure an illness, then move the perfected *qi* to the afflicted area and turn it round and round there, then release it through all the four directions. Thereupon the blood will flow freely and the *qi* will go through by itself.

STAGE 3: THE THIRD IS PENETRATING THE PASSES; [THE BRIGHTNESS] PENETRATES
THE LIMBS AND APERTURES TO REFINE THE BODY

If one can understand how to penetrate the passes in order to refine the body, then the so-called seven apertures will penetrate each other and every aperture will be bright, rendering both body and spirit wondrous. How could this [method] not lead to union with the perfection of the Dao? [*Nine Stages*]

The heart/mind is connected to fire. At the Ultimate point think of a divine light, then a divine fire will light up and revolve. After nine revolutions it will descend to the navel and then revolve three times. Below the navel, it will proceed separately down both legs, revolving three times. Next it will go beneath the knees and revolve three times before going to the soles of the feet where it again revolves three times. Next it rises directly to the crown of the head and then descends again into the chest. In front it descends to the navel and stops. Then it revolves about the navel three times. Next it rises up and divides at the two breasts and moves to the shoulders, where it revolves three times. Then it descends to the elbows and revolves three times. Next it descends to the palm of the hand and revolves three times. Then it goes up into the middle finger before returning to the palm. Next it rises straight up to the shoulders, revolves three times, and then rises to the two ears. Next it rises to the forehead and then descends down the throat, and on down to the Ultimate point, where it revolves nine times and returns to the ultimate point. Repeat the process. If you do not continue, you must return to the revolutions of the heavens. If you practice it, you can preserve yourself. Each time you do this, do it only twenty-five times. [Followed by an illustration of the Holding onto the Central.]

The *Necessary Information* repeats much of this detailed description of the directed movement of revolving lights through the body, adding a few details to fill in the routing. One passage comments that "[the revolving light] descends just like flowing water, and rises like moving clouds. Practice this day and night, either twenty-one times, or forty-nine times, the more times the more marvelous [the results]. The faster the better. For in this way one refines the form to harmonize the *qi*." Another passage comments that this can be practiced day and night, while walking or lying down. "If one wishes to eradicate an illness, use the ultimate point in the yellow center to circulate the *qi* to get rid of the affliction. One need not worry about such things again. When one has not yet started this practice, one must sit up straight and stroke the navel with the left hand, which commands the spirit and coagulates the *qi*. Then it can be started."

STAGE 4: THE FOURTH IS: REST IT IN EARTH AND SINCERELY CULTIVATE HUMANITY IN ORDER TO FORM THE HIDDEN ELIXIR

One must correct one's faults and turn to the good, just as the humane love mountains, and so the humane live long, for the humane take rest in humanity.

The zenith of heaven is 84,000 li from the nadir of earth. Thus there is a central place between heaven and earth at 42,000 li from each. If we regard the human body as a microcosm, the heart and navel are 8.4 Chinese inches apart, and there is a central place between the heaven and earth of the body 4.2 inches from both. What is it we call the East? East is wood; west is metal; south is fire; north is water; and the center is earth. If we can rest the spark of humanity in our mind in the earth-center and thereby sincerely nurture it, the water and fire will be combined and the hidden elixir will be formed. [*Nine Stages*]

The heart method: When fire and water are equal, from within the Ultimate point set up an earthen crucible of a yellow color, with an open mouth. Visualize: the heart/mind is a lotus, its flower and leaves are one. Within there is a spark of divine light, white as dew, as a star. Move it along until the divine light drops into the mouth of the crucible. If this doesn't work, you will need to [visualize] a young child seated by the crucible to warm it. This is called: Fire and Water are brought together to form the secret elixir. The child is in fact one's own spirit, which enters into the nature within the spirit, thus using one's own materials to seal the mouth of the crucible. The shape is like a lotus flower, with a divine light on the leaves like a star. The star glimmers with complete clarity. When it drops into the crucible, then [the process of] resting it in Earth and sincerely cultivating the [seed of] humanity is completed. With this the mouth of the crucible is sealed. This should be practiced throughout the day from the *hai* to the *zi* hours. It may be practiced sitting or lying down.

Chen Zhida remarked in his *Sanjiao quxue zhinan:* "Take this little dot of a void-bright spirit and settle it in the central palace to sincerely cultivate it. The water and fire are mixed and form the yin elixir. This is what the Lord of the Teachings called the Union of *Kan* and *Li* [hexagrams] in the formation of the embryonic yin."

STAGE 5: THE FIFTH: GATHER FROM HEAVEN AND EARTH TO COLLECT THE DRUGS

The order of the breaths between heaven and earth:

Between *hai* and *zi* points a single yang appearing in heaven and earth brings the hexagram *fu*. The same is true in the body's microcosm. Between the *si* and the *wu* points, a single *yin* appearing in heaven and earth brings the hexagram *kou*. The same is true in the body's microcosm. Thus between *hai* and *zi*, even if we gather the yang from within our body, we thereby also gather the *yang* appearing in heaven and earth. When we have gathered the yang in heaven and earth, will not the yang of heaven and earth all return to our body? Between the *si* and the *wu* hours, even if we gather the *yin* from our body, we thereby also gather the yin appearing in heaven and earth. When we have gathered the yin appearing in heaven and earth, will not the yin of heaven and earth all return to our body? But are not heaven and earth far off? In fact the method of gathering them must be like this. For indeed heaven and earth are not far off; their yin and yang vital forces constantly flow in and out of our body. Our body is not near: its yin and yang vital forces constantly form connections with heaven and earth. Therefore although heaven and earth are extremely broad and vast, one can nevertheless gather them from the body and have something left over. [*Nine Stages*, slightly modified]

This phase has occasioned a great deal of discussion with the Three in One. Lin Zhenming remarked in his *Zhuowu shiyi* (True meaning of the Lord Zhuo) that "the drugs are the ancestral *qi* of the former heavens, that is, the one yin and the one yang . . . picking yin and yang is gathering drugs." He warned that one must be completely quiescent in order to gather these breaths. "The body and heart must be completely still, and one's nature and heaven must be finely attuned, and only then by forgetting that one is gathering, there is nothing that is not gathered." Other commentators also stress the need for quiescence. The *Necessary Information* remarks:

At the time one is gathering drugs, one must be completely empty and still, to the extreme of empty stillness. A tiny grain of pearl drops into the middle of the Yellow Chamber, brightly shining. [It is] not a passing glimmer and yet [it is] a thing within the passing glimmer. At this time there emerge many images, some of them rushing forward, others manifesting from within the body, with strange transformations, causing one to be both frightened and delighted. At this juncture, one must be cautious and follow what comes naturally, so as not to think extraneous thoughts. Constantly gather this treasure within the opening of the *qi*, congealing the spirit and marrying it to the true yang. When yin and yang are conjoined, the elixir of the Dao is complete. One must understand the fire phases. When the fire phases are understood, the saintly embryo is ready.

Another passage in the *Necessary Information* is even more detailed:

Visualize within the heart chamber a pearl of water, shining white and pure. Hold on to [this image] for an instant, then cause it to descend into the navel area. Then visualize it transforming into a fire pearl, gleaming red. Hold on to [this image] for an instant, and then cause it to rise up to the heart palace. Continue in this way; with each gathering it descends, and with each taking it rises again. On the eighth revolution, on the descent do not go as far as the navel, but stop midway between the heart and the navel. In this way nine transformations complete one cycle. Each time you do this do it only three times. Carefully hold it within the central palace, cause the true water and the true fire to mix together to be the drugs of the metallic elixir. But this skilled practice (*gongfu*) can only be done four times in a row. To do it more times will move the [inner] fire and cause overheating. But the elixir belongs to the fire element, so one cannot do without heat.

If [the practitioner] becomes too hot, move [*the visualized pearl*] 1.3 inches below the navel, wait for a moment, and then send it straight back behind the navel to the spine and on up the spine to an empty space outside the *niwan* (in the cranium) to rinse it. Thereupon its heat will decrease. Afterwards, only practice it with the *gongfu* that transcends the *niwan*, and after three months, one can progress to the next stage.

STAGE 6: THE SIXTH: COALESCE THE SPIRIT IN THE CAVITY OF VITAL FORCE

The space between the two kidneys is called the cavity of vital force; it is the aperture within the aperture. It is mysterious and more mysterious. Lao Zi said, "The gate of the mysterious female is called the root of heaven and earth." If one is able to take what is coalesced in the space between the heart and the navel and lower and hide it in the cavity of vital force, then one sends it back to the cauldron of Earth, firmly sealing it there to wait until the true yang elixir comes from outside. But the spirit is the elixir, and moving the elixir into the Earth cauldron is to coalesce the spirit in the cavity of vital force. [*Nine Stages*]

Below, the heart method: Within the position of the Sea of *Qi*, think of a white divine light enclosing a red divine light, like an egg of fire. Continually concentrate your spirit on preserving this, in order to wed the yang elixir.

Lin Zhenming remarked on this phase: "Human life is made up of *qi* and *shen* (spirit) and that is all. When the spirit is coalesced within heaven and earth this is called the yin elixir. Next move it to the exit point between the two kidneys (*sheng*), which is called the *qi* cavity. This is what is known as moving the sun (*taiyang*) into the midst of the bright moon. Coalescing the spirit in the cavity of vital force is like the descent to earth of the heavenly *qi*. The mixing together of spirit and *qi* is like the Way of Earth taking on the heavens. Heaven and Earth by this give birth to [all] beings. People in this way conjoin the elixir (*Zhuowu shiyi*)."

The *Necessary Information* states: "I can coalesce the yin elixir in the space between the heart and the navel and then conceal it below in the cavity of vital force. The earthen crucible is tightly sealed; it does not move nor leak. Thus the external elixir of perfected yang comes to mate with none other then the yin elixir of my [immortal] embryo. This can be called the study of perfection. Otherwise, a disciple understands only the conjoining of the yin elixir, and not the mating with it by the yang elixir. This is like a chicken scratching itself; it's rooster is missing. How could this be anything but the mere cultivation of life (*ming*), rather than the true cultivation of one's nature (*xing*)."

STAGE 7: FREE YOURSELF FROM BIRTH AND DEATH BY EMBODYING HEAVEN AND EARTH

Now heaven and earth are very vast. If we say "embody heaven and earth," how could it be other than to take the vastness of heaven and earth to be my own body? My vital force is the vital force of heaven and earth. Therefore I can first use my own vital force and then use the vital force of heaven and earth as my vital force.

When I use the vital force of heaven and earth as my vital force, then my vital force can permeate the vital force of heaven and earth and circulate with it. In this case, in the center of the vastness of heaven and earth something will naturally coalesce which conjoins with my elixir. Only after that can it be called the yang elixir. (*Nine Stages*)

Below, the heart method: Within the Sea of *Qi* think of a white pearl and a red pearl, which emerge from the waist and rise up to the forehead, where they enter, and then descend straight down to the Sea of *Qi*. Repeat this eight or nine times, concentrating your spirit on this.

Lin Zhenming stressed that this stage could not be forced: "It is an error to assume that one can depend entirely upon one's own effort to bring about the coming of the [yang elixir]. This is something that happens spontaneously (*ziran er ran ye*)." Chen Zhida notes: "As for the yin elixir, this is the product of one's inner effort (*gongfu*). It can be attained. If only one is willing to cultivate it and refine oneself, one may definitely attain results. As for the yang elixir, it depends on nonaction. Even should one rely entirely on their personal effort, it is still beyond human strength to achieve it. In general, one must cultivate oneself to the utmost, practice to the best of one's abilities, and when one's merit is complete, one spontaneously completes the Dao" (*Sanjiao chuxue zhinan*).

STAGE 8: THE EIGHTH SAYS: TRANSCEND HEAVEN AND EARTH TO EMBODY THE GREAT VOID

Now the Great Void is perfect empty vastness. When we say "embody the Great Void," how could it be other than to take the empty vastness of the Great Void as my body? Now my void is the same as the void of the Great Void. Therefore I can first take my own void as the void, and then later I can take the void of the Great Void as my void, then I unite my void with the void of the Great Void, forming one substance. When I have accomplished this, then in the Center of the empty vastness of the Great Void something will naturally coalesce which conjoins with my elixir. Only after that can I name it the sha-li ray. [*Nine Stages*]

Below, the heart method: Within the Sea of *Qi* visualize a black pearl. Also visualize a white and a red pearl. These exit from the back door, flow into the forehead, and descend straight down, eighty-nine times. Concentrate your spirit on this.

Lin Zhao'en noted that the śarīra ray is "neither yin nor yang, chaotic and confused, it comes from the center of the great void" (*Destroying Illusions*). Chen Biao is recorded in the *Necessary Information* as having said: "As for embodying heaven and earth, although this can be said to be broad and vast, yet still it is contained within [the extent of] heaven and earth. Therefore not only the combining [with] heaven and earth but also the forgetting of both [of them] begins with the shapeless, *qi*-less Great Void, where there is neither heaven nor earth. One is not only no longer constricted within the three realms, one has already gone beyond the three realms. Flowing and mixing, the self-so and the Great Void form one body. Thus it is said, "Embody the Great Void."

Chen Zhida commented, "The practice of this eighth stage is greatly different from that of the preceding stages. Here one reverses the crucible and overturns the cauldron, taking away the lead and reserving the gold. It is the most fitting to block the lead and let fall the cinnabar. One must use the returning light's reversed illumination, then the Primal Spirit will rise up into the Great Void, and the Great Void will merge with the Primal Spirit. When Spirit and Void respond together, one has conjoined the divine pearl (*Sanjiao chuxue zhinan*).

STAGE 9: THE NINTH SAYS: BREAK UP THE VOID IN ORDER TO REALIZE THE ULTIMATE PRINCIPLES

This is the perfection [of the nine stages], nothing more can be added. What thought or contemplation is there? There is no will or action. How can there be a "principle"? Why then do we insist on saying "principle"? How can there be "realization"? Why then do we insist on saying "realization"? We cannot even speak the single word "ultimate." We depend on the words "principle" and "realization" in order to clarify it. Therefore simply by taking the broadness of heaven and earth as my body, embodying their body, I have not yet done it. By taking the empty vastness of the Great Void as my body, embodying heaven and earth, I have not yet reached the perfection [of the nine stages]. Thus I must arrive at emptiness and break it up; then it is empty and moreover forgotten. How much more would I forget heaven and earth. How much more would I forget the body? When one arrives at this place, if you seek the three masters, not even they are there.

Below, the heart method: Cleanse the heart and sit correctly, then think of controlling the mind so that the former karma of ten thousand deeds ceases. Think, my body is the golden body of the Lord of the Teachings. In the Sea of *Qi* hold onto a black elixir pill. Think of a white elixir pill, that rises up behind to the forehead and becomes ever larger until it illumines eternity.

Summary of the *Xiawunijing* (Lord Xia Scriptures)

1. Xiazongchijing (Scripture of the general [principles] upheld within the Xia [Teachings]): The Way of the Three Teachings are but one Way (Dao). The differences between them were the work of disciples, not the founders of the Teachings. Each of the Teachings has its stages of establishing a foundation, initiation, and ultimate principles. Confucianism should be used to establish the foundation as this accords with practical, everyday requirements. Daoism should be used as an initiation, and Buddhism as the ultimate principle. Thus each finds its place, and the order is as it should be, for without morality there would not be grounds for training in inner alchemy, and inner alchemy is a prerequisite for attainment of the ultimate principles. Confucianism is a *shi-jianfa* (this-worldly method); Daoism and Buddhism are *chushijianfa* (other-worldly methods). Next several terms in the Three Teachings are equated, and several earlier efforts to combine the teachings are mentioned. The term Xia is linked to the central concepts and ultimate ends of the Three Teachings. The second juan discusses the importance of maintaining human relations and family ties, condemning Buddhism and Daoism for turning their backs on the Three Bonds and the Five Constancies. Even Laozi and Śākyamuni had children and descendants, and in fact, there is considerable talk of morality in the teachings of these schools. The third juan discusses inner alchemy, using hexagrams and diagrams, and mentions the role of the heart, the breath, and the seminal essence in the inner work. *Ren* (humanity) is equated with the elixir. The text links *xing* (underlying nature) with the development of *shen* (spirit), and *ming* (human destiny) with the channeling of the *qi* (breath). Several passages then denounce the contemporary hypocrisy of the Three Teachings. There follows a discussion of the relationship between the microcosm and the void. Lin states that he is the void, and that heaven and earth are a small vessel (*xiao qi*) within his heart. He claims that he both is and is not Confucian, Buddhist, and Daoist. "I am all that is called by the name 'Daoist' [including a long list of Daoist deities] . . . and all that is called by the name of Buddha."

2. Xia xunshijing (Scripture of the Xia interpretation): *Ren* (humanity) is identified as the Tathāgata nature. He who can shoulder the heavy responsibility of *ren* is a Great Man. The Great Body of Confucius consisted of the *haoranzhiqi* (great, billowing breath) that filled the cosmos. This is what the Confucians call forming one body with the Great Void. The empty original substance is discussed, using Confucian quotes, Daoist alchemical poetry, and Buddhist verses. A section follows on the constancy of the Dao, and on actionless action. Desirelessness is advocated as a means of polishing the mirror of the mind and realizing the empty, original substance. The second juan discusses the original substance, which is described as beyond form or time, and empty. Confucius is quoted on the dimensionlessness of the Dao. A Daoist alchemical poem is explicated. The joining of male and female is related to the striking of a flint, which emits a spark of goodness into the womb. The inner work requires the transformation of the yin elixir into the yang elixir: this is said to be the work of those who save themselves (*zi du zhe*). Inner alchemy is related to the work of the seasons and the way of the kings. All men have the heart of Confucius, Laozi, and Buddha. Finding one's way home is discovering the dharma within the heart. The third juan urges the true study of the heart, which requires a true understanding of the nature of consciousness, and perseverance in sagely conduct. One need only act on the basis of the goodness of the heart. The heart is a mirror and a still pond. The heart is a mirror of the Great Void, the mirror of all things and all times. Everyone has this heart, but each covers it in their own dust. The sage and the common man have the same heart, but they understand the impact of sensations differently. The sage accords with the heavenly impulse, which arises spontaneously within the heart. Unification with the heavenly impulse requires forgetting distinctions between the self and the heavenly impulse. Just so the true transmission forgets itself.

3. *Rulaixing jing* (Scripture of the Tathāgata nature): In contrast to the first two scriptures, this is an extended, continuous discussion of the Tathāgata nature, which is identified as the real self within the silent emptiness. This Buddha nature can realize itself. However, the Tathāgata nature is inexpressible. The Way that cannot be spoken, the void, the that-I-am, and the nonself, all are based in the Tathāgata nature. Emptiness arises from the not-empty, which is the self-so of the real self, from which arises the empty void, from which arises the Great Void, from which arise heaven and earth, from which are born the ten thousand things. The (real) self establishes its own destiny. The (real) self gives rise to it own nature. One begins with spirit and breath and one creates and transforms them to return to one's (original) nature and destiny. Starting with the Tathāgata nature within the sensory body's nature and destiny given by one's parents, one can recover one's original nature and destiny, and then, by "emptying" them, discover one's dharma body. The original, inherent, true nature is eternal, formless, and without a body or an image. The Tathāgata is the Buddha Mother, underlying all dharma bodies, transformation bodies, causation bodies, the supreme ultimate, yin and yang, the five elements, the numbers, and the myriad beings. Attaining to this state is nirvana and bliss. The second juan discusses the empty void as the Tathāgata nature. This void of the (true) self underlies the cosmos. Without it there would be neither time nor space. Yet it is contradictory to speak of its qualities, or knowledge of it, as it is beyond qualities or consciousness. This underlying, eternal Buddha nature is within us all. The myriad Buddhas are but one Bud-

dha. The true self is the one Buddha. Juan three discusses the process of self-realization. The spiritual power within the *qi* (breath) circulating through the world is divine. That by which spirit is divine is the original nature, which is the empty void of the Tathāgata nature. This underlying nature inspires, protects, and instructs me. The very possibility of enlightenment proves the existence of this underlying nature. Several pages follow on the contradictory status of the Buddha-nature. They conclude by saying that it is necessary to begin with the minor dharma of creating one's own nature and returning it to the void, but that such understandings and minor methods must ultimately be forgotten in the realization of Buddha-nature.

4. *Zhongmiaoxuanjing* (Scripture of the multitude of miraculous mysteries). The Way is unknowable and cannot be obtained by effort. The sage is spontaneous, beyond knowledge or striving. An overview of inner alchemy follows, noting its roots in the original breath, original seminal essence, and the original spirit of the void. At conception, the mingling of the seminal essence of the man and woman produces a drop which enters the womb, then at the cutting of the umbilical cord, this enters the "true exit point" of the child, located between the kidneys. This is the place where women raise children in their wombs; it is also the place where sages raise Buddhas in their wombs. This is the center of the Yellow Center, which is the void. The remainder of the juan covers the basic stages of alchemical progress and comments on the need to merge with the void and then to shatter the void. This is a state of responsiveness that transcends time, space, the void, and consciousness. A chant on the Great Void follows. The second juan discusses the interpenetration of the Way and objects in the world. The heart is the master of the myriad images, and the heart is based on the Great Void. Being one with the Great Void, I am beyond life and death, one with all things in the Void. This union requires the emptying of the heart. Within the empty heart there stirs the elixir of *ren* (humanity). There are four elixirs: the purple gold yin elixir called the human elixir, the black metal yang elixir called the heavenly elixir, the yellow gold embryo that mixes yin and yang, and the śarīra ray that emerges from the Great Void, a chaotic mix that is neither yin nor yang. The void transforms into spirit, spirit into *qi* (breath), breath into shapes, and shapes into the ten thousand things. Thus all things are one thing, and all spirits are one spirit. A chain of negative reasoning leads to a sentence in which the word "wu" (nonbeing? nonpresence? not-so?) is used six times: "There is nothing that is not not nothing and nothing that is not nothing." This is followed by a hymn. The third juan discusses the selflessness of heaven, earth, and the sage. Heaven and earth are composed of forms and breath, yet what surpasses them, subtends them, and produces them is the Great Void. Things are in fact nothingness. The breath that congeals into things is actually the nonbreath. The text goes on to introduce the figure of the Master of the Chaotic Void as a further instance of the Great Void.

5. *Dachengshijing* (Scripture of the time of great completion): Virtue is manifest in conduct. It must harmonize with the Way. Confucian teachings encompass the other teachings. The Confucian heart method imparts true understanding. Virtue seeks no reward on its investment (*siren zhicai*). The sage understands due to his (spark) of spiritual power from the void within his heart. And everyone has the heart of Confucius. Inborn knowledge of good and evil proves the universality of this heart in all people. The cosmic understanding arising from practice of the heart method is based on the empty, spiritual consciousness within the heart. The islands of immortality and the Pure Land should be sought within the body. Confucian teachings are timely teachings which are easy to understand and easy to follow. All Three Teachings must be combined in One. The second juan notes that the Three Teachings can be organized into three stages of study, but they are ultimately but one Way. One must begin simply, step by step, nourishing the spirit and nourishing the *qi*. This will lead ultimately to inspiration by the *ji* (cosmic mechanism, cosmic key or trigger). The *qi* of heaven, the forms of earth, and the heart and body of people all decline over time and are surpassed by the deathless, timeless Way. This is similar to the *Yuanjie jing*'s Tathāgata total enlightenment and is identical to the reestablishing of the *xingming* in Lin's own *Yuanshen shiyi*. One should congeal one's inborn spirit and cause it to enter the cavity of the breath to congeal one's fate. The *qi* within my body flows throughout the cosmos. The *ren* (humanity) within my heart is the same *ren* power of generation that fills the cosmos. My (*ming*) force is the force of the cosmos. The ability of the sage to complete his nature and fulfill his (*ming*) destiny is the ability to *liao* (finish) one's nature and destined force. This ability to finish off one's nature and destined force is due to my being and not being the void. The single speck of light in the void is the Great Beginning, which expands to create the One, which transforms to fill the world. A hymn ends this section. The third juan discusses the concept of the Center in Confucian, Buddhist, and Daoist classics. The center is the constantly changing center of correct action. It is the as yet inactive original substance. This virtuality is compared to the fire inside flint, which only activates when struck. In this center the *ren* within the heart is forever born. "Grasping the center" means restoring the inborn unity of *jing* and *shen* within the original substance. The scripture concludes with a hymn.

6. *Fanshenchengjing* (Scripture of the turning over of the person to complete sincerity): Starting with two lines of Mencius, this section begins with a discussion of the concept of *yong* (function, actualization). Mencius stated that "The myriad things are all complete in me." This me is the true self (the nonself). Mencius also stated, "Turn the body around and become sincere." This refers to the true, great body (the nonbody). By voiding the heart the void becomes spiritually responsive and communicates with all things. The void becomes illumined and thereby contacts and shines upon all things. One must begin by concentrating the heart (*cunxin*) in order to void the heart. Yet the

heart is the Great Void and can never really be "concentrated." "Preserving" the heart is really a matter of forgetting the heart, for the true heart of the void is in all things, eternal, and unknowable. Similarly, the original substance can not be "returned" to, since it is beyond distinctions. There is no distinction between the inner and the outer. A hymn summarizes these themes. The second juan discusses inherent Buddha nature, which is bequeathed by one's parents and which one must use to create one's own nature. This is not a matter of instant enlightenment, but of understanding one's nature. Several Buddhist scriptures are quoted on the confusion caused by the senses.

7. *Dushizhengyijing* (Scripture of the salvation of the world by the orthodox unification): The scripture begins with a discussion of the affairs of the world and the service of the sage. Since the heart encompasses heaven and earth and all forms (*xing*), all the affairs of the world are the affairs of the sage. The sage serves by saving the world within himself. The greater leaders of antiquity and Confucius were deeply involved in worldly affairs, yet they served to save (*du*, deliver) the world. Their attainment is forever and extends everywhere. Lin quotes Cheng Mingdao on how realized humanity makes heaven and earth into one body. The embodiment of the cosmos through the completion of humanity is analogized to a medical treatment of the body. Forms are not separate (pre-existing) forms. Only by harmonizing with heaven and earth (within the humanity inside the human heart) do they achieve their individualization. All men are brothers. The people and I are born of the same womb (as stated in the *Ximing*). Even Buddhists and Daoists should realize this and take up their filial responsibility to have offspring. The rejection of human relations and the pursuit of purity and solitude arise from misplaced curiosity. If one accepts the cosmic role of the heart, then all should love the heart, the body, and offspring. It is necessary to reform Buddhists and Daoists who reject human relations because they have become an obstruction in the internal workings of the cosmic body. Moreover, they have no proper occupation. Thus they must be corrected and brought into unanimity with the proper workings of the cosmic body and society. The second juan discusses the constant Way and the constant occupations. Anyone who recognizes constancy and commonality will agree with my presentation of the constant Way and the constant occupations. A child's body is of the greatest importance. From sons there come grandsons. Grandsons produce sons. This goes on to eternity. At the opening up of heaven and earth the ancestral *jingshen* (seminal essence and spirit) gathered, and it descends down past the end of time, the (constant) resting point of the veins of vital force of the sons and grandsons (of the line). Lack of progeny will interfere with attainment of the Way. Buddhists and Daoists should marry young, have children, and then pursue the Way. Several Buddhist sutras are quoted on the importance of progeny and filiality, and human relations. Similar opinions are quoted from Daoist texts. Having settled this issue, Lin turns to the issue of being immersed in worldly affairs. The sage remains a sage in the midst of all activity, whether it be government, war-

fare, education, or Confucian worship. The third juan discusses the salvific role of the Confucian sage. Lin comments on bodhisattva salvation versus individual salvation, citing the selfless work of the ancient culture heroes. Shun was also a savior. Yet the sage's worries are never-ending. He first illumines the Way within his body, then within his times, and finally for all time. Confucius, though not a king, illumined the kingly Way through his words and deeds. He could accommodate any criticism because all human affairs were his concern. Since my *jing, shen,* and *qi* flow through and connect with the heaven and earth, spirits and ghosts, there is nothing I am not in contact with. This is the underlying meaning of the *wuzhe dahui* (the great meeting with no boundaries). This notion is present in Confucian, Buddhist, and Daoist texts. The objective of all teachings is to bring everyone back to the midst of the ever-transforming Way. Luo Hongxian raised several important points about the *wuzhe dahui.* Because heaven and earth are within my body, the circulation of my *qi* has an impact on the cosmos. Thus I can meet with and speak to all within and beyond the four seas. Thus nothing can be a body beyond my body or *qi* beyond my *qi* or emptiness beyond my emptiness. I drum and dance it, move it, change it, transform it. This is beyond knowing. Yet only at this point can one speak of the true meaning of the great meeting beyond all borders.

8. *Zhongheweiyujing* (Scripture of the nurture achieved by positioning oneself in the central harmony): Heaven and earth have neither heart/mind nor consciousness, yet their *xingming* (nature and force) is pure and correct. People have heart/minds and consciousness, and fulfill their *xingming* by drilling through to their true (selves). The sage models himself on heaven and earth, and the later rely on the sage to give them a locus and to nurture the myriad things. The sage is thus the heart/mind of heaven and earth. Only the sage can fulfill the potential of heaven and earth, because both share the same *xingming.* It is the nonself (the real self) that completes *xingming,* transforming and nurturing the myriad things. The *zhen chu chu* (point of the emergence of the true) created by centering, harmonizing, and localizing heaven and earth is the same process at all levels. Centering allows one to guide one's nature, which allows one to complete one's nature, which allows one to complete one's destiny. One should spend at least ten years on a Confucian, "this-worldly" approach to the cultivation of *xinshen xingming,* combining it with the Three Bonds and the Five Constancies, and then continue with "otherworldly" Buddhist or Daoist approaches, as both approaches are necessary. To maintain the other-worldy within the this-worldly is what Confucius managed to do. There follows a discussion of Buddhist mercy and the "Confucian" system of punishments, including capital punishment. Lin argues that this system is in fact merciful. The Yellow Emperor, Yao, and Shun of antiquity are given as examples. Next there is a discussion of the *jingtian* (well-field) system of land distribution. Lin suggests that the system should be revived, noting, however, that the per capita landholdings had fallen to 20 mu (three and

a third acres) from the classical ideal of 100 mu per farmer. Distribution of lands along the well-field system would protect the destitute and allow for ecological replenishment of the soil. Wealth and privilege have eroded the system, but the blame for altering the classical model is placed on Shang Yang (Legalist adviser of the king of Qin). The second juan is in the form of a dialogue between Lin and one Zong Nianjiu on the subject of irrigation. After politely stating his lack of expertise in irrigation, Lin embarks on an extended analogy of the irrigation of the body through the cultivation of *xin, shen, xing-ming*. The basic principle is to preserve the natural flow, and not the struggle to guide or even worse, to reverse the flow of *qi* in the body. The sage is likened to a doctor, as are early heroes of irrigation, such as the Divine Yu, who worked on the body of the land. The sage first regulates his internal flows, and then the rivers and oceans follow in his path. The sage does this by unifying his will and moving his *qi*. His virtue moves the heavens and his complete sincerity causes spirits to react. When asked about the phrase "no waves rise on the sea," Lin comments that the nature of water is like the nature of the true self within. One should follow its natural flow. Water is the first of the five elements. Within human beings, this refers to the combining of semen and blood in the conception of a new person. Conception commences the entire chain of human relations and Confucian values. Lin next discusses Yu, who had the Grand Pattern of the Nine Continents of China inborn within his heart. This inborn pattern also includes the august ultimate, which establishes heaven and earth, the sun, moon, and constellations, the mountains, rivers, and seas, as well as the insects and the vegetation. The human body, like the heavens, has 360 degrees/joints. By finding the center, one finds the center of microcosm/macrocosm. This center is the empty void, and this emptiness can unblock the seven openings of the body. For the sage completes the potential of heaven and earth by working within his own body. When the openings of the center of the earth element have been unblocked, above they connect with Kunlun Mountain, and below they connect with the four seas. Then inhaling and exhaling are like the tides of the ocean. The breathing of the sage joins heaven and earth. The ancient kings used music and rites to harmonize the cosmos. When I illumine the mechanism of advance and reversal within my heart, then music and rites can flourish. Preserving the purity and tranquility of my heart localizes heaven and earth. The *Luoshu* and the *Hetu* are within the heart of the sage, which is modeled on the model of heaven and earth. Thus the heart/mind of the sage is the heart of heaven and earth. By unifying his substance with the Great Void, and enabling the marvels of the heaven and earth, the sage engages in a bodiless (substanceless) ritual and creates soundless music. The third juan first compares the definitions of *xin-xing* (heart/mind and nature) in the Three Teachings. The three "centerings"—*zhizhong, shouzhong,* and *kongzhong* (grasp the center, guard the center, and empty the center)—all refer to the underlying emptiness of the original substance. Yet this is hard to know and hard to believe. So too with the three "unifications": *deyi, guiyi,* and *yi guan zhi* (attain the one, return to the one, and connect them with the one) all refer to the oneness of the original substance. Yet it is difficult to know what makes them the same or different. It is the heart that is the immortal and the Buddha; the heart that is the Master and the Lord of Heaven, the Spirit Terrace and Residence of the Spirit. There is no need to struggle to reverse the breath or sit in meditation. The eternity of the ever-gleaming point of spirit, the mysterious, the elixir, the seed of Buddha consciousness, are all to be found in the Confucian Classics, yet this is hard to know and believe. Centering and harmonizing the cosmos is possible, but hard to know or believe. The world is lost in confusion and considers this normal. My immortality is the immortality of the spark of spiritual light within me. My deathless longevity comes from my having illumined the Three Teachings for all time, so that they shine together with heaven and earth. For although my body is in the world, my heart/mind is in another, empty realm. There is no such thing as rebirth in Amitahba's Western Paradise, rather, one realizes one's inner Buddha nature. Paradise is within. My way is simple, everyday, and based on the greatness of the heart and the underlying nature. Later elaborations of the Three Teachings have all departed from the Way. Only a few central writings of the Three Teachings contain the essential way. The commentaries all descend into bickering. But the truth is available and waiting for a divine connection. My true scripture of self-nature is based on this truth. My self-nature is a mirror. A mirror of mirrors shows only external shadows, but my self-nature reveals itself in this mirror. The self-nature of the true self is beyond time and space. The true self is indestructible, beyond life and death.

9. *Mingguang puzhaojing* (Scripture of the universal radiance of the bright luminence): The Way revolves beyond the void, yet it illumines the sun and the moon and gives the sage his divine power. It is beyond all values. The sage is the illumination of the Way, like the sun in the center of the sky. This sun is the elixir. The brilliant radiance of the Buddha that shines through the ten worlds is equated with the sage rulers of antiquity. Confucius is a sun that has shown for over two thousand years. His only worry was that in later ages there would be someone whom he did not shine upon. Amitabha Buddha is explicated word for word as meaning "there is nowhere it does not fill, and nowhere its radiance does not shine upon." This was a quality Confucius had already achieved. The Buddha is the heart, and "washing the Buddha" means cleansing the dust that has settled on the heart and revealing its original purity. A dialogue on the contradictory nature of the Buddha/heart/mind follows: it is within and without; unlocalizable, unattainable, and unknowable. To find it look for your inner nature and then your inner nature will manifest. There is no Chan, no Buddha, no nature, no emptiness—all these things leave a word behind. Prajnaparamita is a form of consciousness without content and observation without object. It is a way of dwelling in a place of no dwelling. This dwelling is hard to speak of. The heart does not dwell in me, nor in heaven and earth, nor in the void, nor in the dharma body. If it had any of

these things to dwell in, it would not be the true heart. The śarīra ray is explicated as the heart's ever-moving spirit, which is the source of illumination. The Lamplighter Buddha is described in an anecdote as one who uses his body for kindling and his actions for inflammable oil. The "Transmission of the Lamp" shows that *shen* (spirit) belongs to the fire element. The *Heart Sutra* maintains correctly that the original substance is radiant. All one's efforts to achieve illumination boil down to recovering the radiance of the original substance. This is similar to the elixir in Daoist texts, for the sun is the elixir of the heavens, while the heart is the elixir of man. *Ren* (humanity) is the elixir, the tiny drop of spiritual light that separates humans from birds and beasts. The substance of humanity and the elixir is the Great Void, and their function is the Way of life, constantly giving birth, developing the fruit from the seed. The formation of the elixir involves first regathering the *jixi xingming* (most rare original nature) that had fallen into the *zhenchuchu* (point of emergence of the true) at the cutting of the umbilical cord and then spread through the body. The *xingming* is next regathered in the carnal heart, and then it is returned to heaven and earth, leading to the formation of the yin elixir. This is then returned once again to the *zhenchuchu* to form the yang elixir. This elixir comes from the Great Void beyond. With it secure, one next returns from the *zhenchuchu* to the original substance of the void. Next smash the void and confirm the fruit of the Buddha. The second juan begins with a reflection on Lin's own avid pursuit of the Way, first studying with Confucian teachers, then with Daoist masters, then with Buddhist monks, all the while recalling the seventy-two instructors of the Yellow Emperor. How hard is the Way! He first found that the imperative to *gewu* (examine the principle inherent in each and every external thing) following Zhu Xi's method was an impossible task given the innumerable things of the world. Therefore he turned to Daoism. He wished to inquire into the time before heaven and earth, and the mysterious female, the root of heaven and earth. But the Daoist Master insisted that he first internalize lead and mercury, dragon and tiger (inner alchemy), divination, numerology, and calendrical sciences. Lin felt these would only weigh down his heart. He further argued that guiding or reversing the breath would only damage the natural flow of the breath, and efforts to regulate breathing only got in the way. So he went on to study with Chan monks, but they were only capable of repeating platitudes. He then attended lectures at an academy, which were filled with paradoxes but no answers to his questions. Finally he met an enlightened master who transmitted the heart method and gave him practical advice on using it to interest people in his teachings. People nowadays are sick from academic study. One must depend on drilling through to (true) self-knowledge. Lin counters Zhu Xi by advocating *gequ* (examine [the heart by means of] expelling [external things]). He also counters facile Buddhist and Daoist notions. All talk of immortality or even prolonging life should be denied. Moreover, Daoists had children from Zhang Daoling onward, and only stopped when Song Yizu refused to allow Daoist belvederes and temples to keep dependents in order to get them off the tax rolls. All talk of giving up grains and renouncing the common realm should also be denied. Talk of "harmonizing and plucking" easily descends into sexual license, and talk of "setting up the alchemical crucible" easily degenerates into covetousness and selfishness. All these must be denied. Chan sitting easily rigidifies into a meaningless routine, instead of the inner manifestation of self-nature. And the Buddhist denial of filial piety shown in their renouncing progeny and abandoning parents must also be denied. When one does good, then people respect and admire you, ghosts and spirits esteem you. Isn't it said that the halls of heaven are only what we have before our eyes? If you behave badly, then people despise you, scholars and teachers punish you, and ghosts and spirits torment you. Isn't it said that the underworld is only what we have before our eyes? Such people have the form of humans but the hearts of beasts. This is the way of the animal. People who have no standard occupation (such as monks and wandering Daoists) have no means to support themselves. This is the way of the hungry ghost. Isn't it said that reincarnation is only what we have before our eyes? If only people could all become *junzi* (superior men, gentlemen), then they would truly not have to worry about (rebirth) as an animal, hungry ghosts, or the underworld. Lin then denies that his unification of the Three Teachings resembles the grafting of three trees into one which bears three different kinds of flowers. Rather, he has planted three trees in his garden, but because the garden is small, and the trees are crowding it, he selects the most beautiful and preserves it. The most beautiful is the *ren* (humanity) of Confucius. Buddhism and Daoism must return to Confucianism. Lin seeks to lift the clouds obscuring the Three Teachings to reveal the eternal luminance cast by Confucius. The third juan begins by discussing the proper course of study of the Way. All three teachings state that the ultimate truths surpass speech. They all begin with authoritativeness, and it is only later that their method is borne out. Confucius spoke in both elegant and rare phrases. The former could be comprehended by even the most ignorant man and woman, while the latter can never be exhausted by the profoundest sage. The Classics present a graduated form of instruction. The three stages of the Lin's teachings must be followed in order. They are establishing the basis in the Three Bonds and the Five Constancies, entering the door by concentrating the heart and cultivating the inner nature, and (attaining) the ultimate principle, by constantly transforming and flowing everywhere through the six voids. Cultivation must begin with the seemingly useless back, by placing the *gen* hexagram in the back. The back is like winter among the seasons. Only those who understand its uses use it. The word back is composed of "north" and "flesh." The heart is the fire of the south that dwells in front, while the north is the water of yin that dwells behind. Wash the fire of the heart in the waters of the back. These are spirit waters and spirit fires. In normal people, the spirit is in the eye, and it only rests at night, when it is concealed within the kidneys, where it is washed and refreshed. At the beginning of study, one must constantly recite "Masters of the Three Teachings," shifting one's concentration from the mouth to the back, and fixing it there. In this way, one forgets the external realm. Next one must forget the internal realm as well. One forgets everything besides the back, even forgetting one's own body. The center of the heart is where one "moves within the chamber." It is the center of heaven and earth and can be likened to the yolk of an egg. The moving in the court means a circling around the central point of the supreme ultimate, the still point or the Pole Star within the body. The point of the supreme ultimate is the point of spiritual light bequeathed (*ming*) as one's nature (*xing*) by heaven at one's birth. After birth, this supreme ultimate divides into yin and yang, and so the *xing* and *ming* divide, the former residing in the heart as the spirit, the later residing in the navel and the spleen as the *qi* and the *jing*. But the spirit is of fire and burns on contact with external things. Only by holding the spirit in the back (by concentrating on the *gen* hexagram) can one begin to restore *shen, jing,* and *qi* to the original *xingming,* and reunite yin and yang in the supreme ultimate, and return to the single point of spiritual light. This is the drop of goodness inborn within all people that Mencius called "most rare." People act as if they do not have it, but one must make it still within the earth/center of the body and cultivate it. Complete sincerity is perfect stillness, within which a point of spiritual light spontaneously manifests. This is the ever-luminous spirit that suffuses the original substance. The supreme ultimate is a point of spiritual light. So too is complete sincerity. This light sometimes flares up and sometimes returns to the empty original substance. Like the light of the sun and the moon, the luminence of sincerity is without end. The Great Void forms into heaven, into earth, into the sun. And the Great Void of the sage breathes the breath of heaven and shapes the shapes of earth. And the point of spiritual light (within the sage) is also the sun. Its light reaches everywhere. The breath of heaven is the *haoranzhiqi* (billowing *qi*) of the sage, which circulates everywhere. Yet the Great Void of the Great Void was originally both within and beyond heaven and earth, for nothing was not the Great Void, and so it is with my own empty and cavernous Great Void.

10. *Zuishangyichengjing* (Scripture of the most high single [Mahāyāna] path): Lin begins with a discussion of the Buddhist notion of *weiyin wang,* which he equates with the Great Void of the Confucians. As Pangu divided heaven from earth, so there is a Pangu within the body. Heaven and earth are not divided prior to birth, but only after birth. Lin keeps two mirrors, one round and one square, and yet the mirror of the heart is beyond shape and reflects all. This mirror can be traced back to Pangu, who got it from the self-so. Mirrors can mirror other mirrors within themselves, and the mirror of the heart can mirror the heart of the sages of antiquity. Thus the Six Classics are within me, and my mirror heart mirrors the sages of all time. There is only one *jing,* one *qi,* and one *shen* within me and within the world. For my body is a microcosm wherein I bring about creation and transformation. A Buddhist monk asks Lin if his notion of the *yuanshen* (primal, original spirit) is not in fact the *shishen* (spirit of consciousness). Lin argues instead that the primal spirit must over-

come the spirit of consciousness, which is produced only at the time of birth. The monk is enlightened by his words, which he describes as the Most High Single Vehicle. Lin goes on to discourse on the true void, the true *xingming,* and the true primal spirit. He points out that the *xingming is* the process of creation and transformation itself. The second juan discusses how true *xing* is beyond life or death. Having forgotten thought itself, one attains Buddha consciousness. One must establish teachings on the basis of the true nature. The single point of spiritual light is likened to a seed that can grow into the fruit of the Buddha. Lin opposes theories of instant enlightenment, however, arguing for a gradual process. Mencius said those who extend to the utmost their heart/mind know their natures. Lin interprets "extend to the utmost" as meaning to rid oneself of one's thought and worry-filled mind to obtain the empty, spiritual original substance. A hymn follows on the understanding of the original nature. Yet true enlightenment and salvation surpasses self-realization itself. Terms such as nature, emotion, substance, function, empty, not-empty are all distinctions that cannot be used to express true enlightenment. There is no before or after between heaven, earth, and I. The Great Void penetrates all things and preceded heaven and earth and man. A hymn on the Great Void follows. The third juan compares the Buddhist idea of the completion of the myriad dharmas with Confucius's idea of extending the *xing* to the fulfill *ming* (one's destiny). This is the Most High Single Vehicle. Next lower is the cultivation of the dharma, then comes the understanding of the meaning of dharma, and last but not least, the reading and recitation of sutras. All are necessary, as the Way is gradual. Buddhist renunciation and vows must arise from oneself for all time. The self-nature is what Lin calls the true heart's real ground. It is beyond the sensory realm, and beyond distinctions. Thus can one can manifest one's own dharma body and become the Buddha in your heart. A poetic passage on the original substance follows, and then all formulations of the original substance are denied. The original substance is void and empty, yet these are not fixed qualities. The void emptiness was originally shattered, but this does not result in a shattered heart. Only when one does not know that there is an empty void can one begin to talk of the original substance of the Great Void and heaven and earth. Only when one does not know that there is a shattering (of the void) can one talk of the emptiness of the Great Void and heaven and earth. A long hymn on nonbirth and samadhi follows.

11. Tongxuanjizejing (Scripture of the cavernous mystery of the ultimate principle): There is a single breath that arises from the void emptiness prior to the separation of heaven and earth. This is the one that becomes the two (heaven and earth, sun and moon) and then the three (heaven, earth, man). Man, if he grasps the principles of the former heavens, can form a universe within his own body, with the forces of creation and transformation in his hands. My breath (the one breath) is the movement of the seasons. With it, I move with the Way, beyond all limits. A poem on the illumination of the one breath follows. The one that arises before heaven and earth gives purity to heaven and tranquility to earth. The sageliness of Confucius, the mysteriousness of Laozi, and the Zen of the Buddha all preceded the division of the one. They acted without awareness of their qualities, and one will never understand them if one searches merely in words and records. The River Chart uses eight points, leaving the center empty to show that the spirit has no fixed location. The Luo Writ uses nine points to show the fullness of the spirit at the center, yet it circulates constantly through the eight other points. These charts are modeled on the heart of heaven, the Great Void, which is a substanceless substance. They are not metaphors. My heart gives them their images, as it gives purity to heaven, tranquility to earth, and a knowledge that can not be forced. The lines of the hexagrams of the *Book of Changes:* The word *gua* (hexagrams) is formed from two earth characters. Zhu Xi said that the earth was the divine element within the other four elements. The hexagrams are the movements of the heart. The *qian* hexagram is the force of *qi* penetrating the blockage marked by the *kun* hexagram. The *Book of Changes* says, "Changing and moving without cease, it circulates everywhere through the six voids." These and related descriptions in the Confucian Classics are what the Buddhists call the ultimate principles. Confucians, Buddhists, and Daoists all have methods for establishing the basis, entering the door, and (attaining the) ultimate principles. Dao Pu stated the ultimate principles of Daoism thus: "Beyond the body there is another body. Don't think this strange. The void is shattered, and then emerges the total body." Other instances are cited, including the *Huashu* (*Book of Transformations*). The second juan begins by commenting that all things emerge out of nothingness, and that nothingness is never born. The supreme ultimate, Yin and Yang, and the Eight Trigrams and sixty-four hexagrams described in the *Book of Changes* are all within my body. The changes of the sage unify heaven; thus spring and autumn, hot and cold, brightness and dark, day and night are within me. The greatest study is the study of one's nature (*xing*). Although one can see spirit (*shen*) and qi (*breath*), *xing* and *ming* cannot be seen. Moreover, *xing* and *ming* are neither present nor absent (*you* or *wu*). The seed of nature that is planted by one's parents can be re-created and retransformed by the sage by his "husband and wife within the belly, in order to grow an Immortal or a Buddha in the womb." The physical form dies off, but that which outlasts time is neither nature, breath, spirit, nor life-force. It is like the gold extracted from an alchemical experiment. Knowledge of the (true) nature is required to enter the gateway. One moves the *gen* hexagram into the back in order that the water will rise and the fire descend; harmoniously flowing in this way one "moves in the courtyard" (also called "circling the heavens"). This process collects pure *qi* inside the body to protect the spirit, while expelling stale *qi* to refine the body. The "opening of the passes" allows the conduits of the body to be free of any obstructing *qi*. Thereupon the spirit is illumined in the void. Next one "rests it in Earth and sincerely cultivates humanity in order to form the hidden elixir." The drop of spiritual light left by one's parents in the womb is the greatest treasure and the true elixir. This drop is so powerful it transforms into the five viscera, the six receptacles, the four limbs, the hundred bones. It allows one to hear, to hold, to walk. In it all good things are complete. And still it grows, and changes, and becomes a sage, and surpasses understanding. At birth one emits a cry and the point of light falls to a point one *cun*, three *fen*, below the navel. Later it moves to a point between the heart and the navel called the center of heaven and earth, eight cun, four fen, away. Then it moves into the heart/mind of five elements and from there it dissipates in whatever the ears hear, eyes see, mouth tastes, etc. So one must concentrate this point of spiritual light in the heart and move it back to the point of heaven and earth, which is neither within nor without. And at this point between the kidneys the true water naturally wells up and joins with it. Since the elixir is on fire and often hot, move it to the point one *cun*, three *fen*, below the navel when it heats up. Wait for a moment, then move it backward from the navel and up the spine to the *niwan* in the head, then down through the nose and mouth to a point one *cun* below the navel. This is the so-called gateway of the mysterious female. The text here shifts from a description of alchemical processes to attacks on Daoists who have confused themselves by searching for external elixirs, and Buddhists who have lost themselves in their own profundity. Lin emphasizes that the heart/mind he speaks of is the true nature, not the carnal organ. The scripture concludes with three pages devoted to a rhapsodic description of the attainment of the ultimate principle. This allows one to mingle with heaven and earth and transform and nurture all things. Effortless, faultless, at peace, beyond the self, beyond knowing, doing nothing yet leaving nothing undone, one sees one original heart, and one becomes a Buddha. This Buddha is the original non-Buddha—that is the true Buddha. That which comes from nowhere to come from is the Future Buddha (*rulai*, lit., as if come). A brief hymn follows. The third juan is dedicated to an exposition of the concept of *yan* (primordial expansion, flow, and transformation), using charts and diagrams to show how heaven and earth, the sun and the moon expand and transform into one another from noncommencement onward in distinct vectors, up and down, horizontally, in circles, and in squares. All this expansion and transformation takes place within the heart. The human at the center of these changes does not shift but arrays all the transformations in their places. These positions are also the basis for numerological transformations. Knowledge of these transformations provides insight into the Great Void and noncommencement. One realizes that one is prior to all things. Since the Great Void and I are one and the same, heaven and earth, the sun and the moon arise from me/the Void. This is demonstrated through an analysis of the hexagrams of the *Book of Changes*. The priorness of the Void is demonstrated, and my role in birthing heaven, earth, sun, and moon is proclaimed.

12. *Daotongzhongyijing* (Scripture of the unity of the Dao in the one in the center): Each of the three juan of this scripture explicates a diagram. The first

is the Diagram of the Great Void and Former Heaven and the Diagram of the Supreme Ultimate and Later (Created) Heaven. The Void is represented by a circle and is based on the River Chart within my body, with its vacant center. The Supreme Ultimate is a dot inside a circle and is based on the Luo Writ within my body, which fills up heaven and earth. Using a mix of characters and geometrical designs, Lin argues that circles and squares originate in their central point. The vertical line in a square symbolizes the one line connecting the heart to the kidneys. The point in the circle symbolizes the establishment of the ultimate, which comes from the outside. Yet these two (line and point) are the same. A square represents the Great Void as well as the center, which is the void and empty original substance. These diagrams are said to represent all the Confucian, Daoist, and Buddhist phrases describing the Way or enlightenment. A diamond-shaped cross-hatch pattern represents my embodying heaven and earth and the principles of the *Book of Changes*. A dot within the cross-hatching shows the sprouting of the heart and the transformation of the nonultimate into the supreme ultimate. The dot also represents the manifestation of my heart out of the Great Void. By studying the void within the empty square, one can first comprehend the spontaneous responsiveness of emptiness. The dot in the circle is also the point of spiritual light given me by the joining of my parents. This circle can encompass heaven and earth and circulate the void emptiness. And heaven and earth are born from it. The empty square is also the substance, and the line within is the spirit. Lin uses these figures in his typical paradoxical constructions—is it X? Is it not X? Is it not X and yet X? Don't think of the body as small. Instead, forget the heart and the body and do not be restricted by form and breath. Then how could your void emptiness not fill heaven and earth, and form one body with them? Then forget heaven and earth, don't be bound by their forms and breath. Then your void emptiness will circulate beyond heaven and earth and form one body with the Great Void. The empty square representing heaven, earth, and humankind is the same square. The openings (within the body, within heaven and earth) are opened by the void. The void is attained by opening the openings. The one opening is what Laozi called the gateway of the mysterious female. There are openings within the opening. Yet my body also has (within it) heaven and earth and the Great Void. The Great Void within my body uses heaven and earth as an opening. Heaven and earth within my body use my body as an opening. Pushing this to its origins, what could be beyond the opening of my body's opening? Thus embody this opening and it becomes one person's entire body. Expand it and embody heaven and earth. Then is not the vastness of heaven and earth my own body? It fills both dimensions and merges with the process of creation and nurture. Again expand it to embody the Great Void. Then is not the vastness of the Great Void my own body, encompassing the limitless? The gate of the mysterious female is like a lotus seed. Within the heart of the lotus the Way of Life lies still, when it sprouts, it brings forth meaning without end. The second juan explicates three diagrams of the heart of humankind (diamond cross-hatch), heaven (circle

crossed by four lines), and earth (square crossed by four lines). The text begins with classic reference to the Three Talents (Heaven, Earth, Humankind)
of the appendices of the *Book of Changes*. The Three Teachings approach this
realization of human potential with different expressions. The use of the term
Xia to unify them has just begun (with Lin's teachings). The true self and the
true heart are hard to know, so I have set up the Xia teachings to repudiate
the false self and false heart. The empty square and the line/point are related
to Confucian tenets. Lin points out that *ming* precedes *xing*. To complete
one's *ming*, one must exhaust one's *xing*, and to do that one must make manifest one's *xing*. Since *xing* is the empty square, one need only get hold of the
not-yet-active empty square. Since *xing* is also the line/point, it can manifest
itself within the square. By attaining the empty square, the *xing* and *ming* of
heaven and earth are within me. The empty square is my original substance
and my Great Void. The empty square and the line are the one within all things
which is within me as well. Attaining perfect goodness and stopping there can
be done while farming or fishing, for by itself perfect goodness will make all
the world good. It will solidify virtue within me and find the right locus for
heaven and earth, while assuring the equitable distribution of goods to all people and nurturing all things. The single dot of humanity within the empty circle is a doubling of the one. It is the action of spirit. The dot is already within
the Former Heaven. The cultivating of the dot of spiritual power (humanity)
within the earth of the empty circle is the establishing of the supreme ultimate
within my body. This is the "entrance of the gateway" of self-cultivation. The
establishing of the ultimate operates at the three levels of human ultimate, august ultimate (of governance), and the heavenly ultimate, regulating the body,
the state, and the heavens. The empty circle is the original void of Yao and
Shun where the single point of humanity was born. One must study and practice this ceaselessly. Yet this learning is not the accumulation of knowledge in
investigation of things championed by Zhu Xi. When Lin first studied Confucian studies, he thought he had learned alot. But later he realized he had
just attained the dregs of the teachings. So he renounced his studies and
sought to personally embody the teachings, obtain them in his heart, and
manifest them in his conduct. He sought to be a first class person in the world.
Such study has nothing to do with wealth or poverty. To obtain the *zhen
xiaoxi* (truth) you must have tremendous strength, tremendous confidence,
and great courage, and push forward as though ahead of you there will no
longer be your body, your family, nor heaven above nor earth below, nor
enemy before nor lord behind. It will be like dying. Only then can you do it!
Don't let a single thought or a single matter distract you. Empty and unify
any momentary distractions, even distractions of an abstract kind, all must be
emptied and unified in order to attain the truth! The third juan begins with
a Chart of the Round Heavens and the Square Earth designed to show that
my heart is the heart of heaven and earth, the source of salvation, and the
point of access to knowledge of reality and the powers of self-creation and
self-transformation. The empty square and the one line/point that can be

grasped or attained are not the empty square and point of noncommencement, but rather that which Laozi called the mother of all things. This is the elixir/humanity that can be grasped. Return it to its beginnings. This is the essence of the Three Teachings, and the movement from the entrance to the gateway to the ultimate principles. Lin compares the pupil of the cavity of the eye, which allows the myriad images to appear and be unified by vision, to the point of spiritual power in the heart. The sage has only the empty circle; the heart, body, shapes and *qi* are all false. My nonbody Great Body fills heaven and earth, and they are all me. My nonbody Great Body fills the Great Void, and it is me. My original substance is the Great Void and the Great Emptiness; thus it can revolve in the empty void. My original substance is prior to heaven and earth; thus it can give birth to them. My original substance is Xia and Great, because it allows for the sage and the nonsage and contains within it the "place of the emergence of the true." The heart has openings. When they are all open one can penetrate radiantly throughout the body. The body has 9 large openings and 84,000 small openings. When they are all open one can penetrate radiantly throughout heaven and earth. Heaven and earth have countless openings, and when they are all open and radiant, one can penetrate beyond heaven and earth and form one body with the Great Void. First void your heart, then your body, then heaven and earth. Void and yet not void. Not void and yet void. Not knowing whether it is void or not. This is the ultimate principle of the Three Teachings. Why do I say that my heart is inside my body and also within heaven and earth? Why do I say it is within heaven and earth, and also beyond heaven and earth? And as for heaven and earth, why do I say they are within the void emptiness, and also beyond the void emptiness? This is my illumination of the common return of the Three Teachings to the one point of Xia. Shao Kangjie said, "Heaven and earth sleep deeply within Xia (the great expanse)." Thereupon I knew that there is no heart and no body, no heaven and no earth, no inside and no outside. They are all this one void emptiness.

Scriptures to Popular Deities: The God of Theater

THE PRECIOUS SCRIPTURE OF SAINTLY MARSHAL TIAN OF THE
[BUREAU] OF WIND AND FIRE OF THE NINE HEAVENS WHO SAVES
FROM COSMIC DISASTER

1. Gatha for Commencing the Scripture
2. Sacred Spell for Purification
3. Sacred Spell for Purifying Water and Land
4. Sacred Spell for Purifying *Qian* and *Kun* [Hexagrams]

In the midst of the Palace of the *Xun* and *Li* Hexagrams of the Mystic Garden of the Seven Treasures, a melancholy free spirit spreads verdant spring through ten thousand ages. Utterly talented in literary and martial arts, he seized the ultimate rank of Autumn Bodyguard [of the Emperor]. Two flower maidens of the palace and three cups of imperial wine made him deeply drunk at the rosegem banquet. How unusual his countenance, and how accomplished his merit. His followers, White-tooth and Wind and Fire, escort him, one in front and two behind. An imperial edict summoned him to the Jade Emperor. He ascended in broad daylight. No one outdoes him in serving the Jade Sovereign. He was commanded to descend to the common realm to dispense spells and talismans. The hundred diseases all are cured. His awesome spiritual powers broadly shown forth. With one cast of ritual water spring comes to the ten thousand things. Brightly manifesting mercy, intelligence and wisdom, [this is] Marshall Tian of the [Bureau] of Wind and Fire of the Golden Gate of the Nine Heavens, retainer of the Three Halls of the Jade Sovereign.

With resolute hearts we reverently invoke: The Eight Marshals and the Eight Generals from within the Bureau of Wind and Fire. Generalissimo White Tooth and Commandant Oriole Flower, the Two Lads of the Wind and Fire [Bureau]. All the awesome spiritual powers and divine generals attached to the talismans descend as commanded and protect the scripture.

THE PRECIOUS SCRIPTURE OF SAINTLY MARSHAL TIAN FOR DELIVERANCE
FROM DISASTER, SALVATION FROM DIFFICULTY, [PROVIDING]
LIBERATION AND EXPIATION

At that time, the Venerable Emperor, the Jade Sovereign, in his fully arrayed heavenly court, each year on the 24th [of the 12th month] commanded the masses of saints of the Three Offices [of Heaven, Earth and Water], the Nine Bureaus, the Four Departments, and the Two Dippers to array themselves by rank at his side without fail. The emperor permits spirits of the lower realms, city gods, village superintendents, and household gods of destiny to investigate good and evil deeds and to memorialize on the merits and transgressions. On the 25th day [of the 12th month] he personally descends to examine and summarize the lightness or severity [of the offenses]. He instructs the Northern and Southern Dippers to compile registers of good and evil deeds. As for those listed as good, the heavenly officials give them a place in the Blessed Lands, the terrestrial officials pardon their sins, and the aquatic officials liberate them from any difficulties. As for evil people, [their cases] are handed down to the Pestilence Bureau, which commands the masses of the Five Plague Gods to go on a procession on the 22d of the 2d [lunar] month. They seize people on their lists, who cannot escape misfortune.

Should there be, in the lower realm, good men and faithful women, whether old or young, who do not know how to avoid the prohibitions of Yin and Yang, and so contract difficulties, their tears will be of no use. Before they have completed their heaven-sent lifespan, they will have been reported on, and tragically die. Their darkened souls, feeble and tangled, rush to the Bureau of Hell. The Merciful Emperor administers [their cases], how deeply sorrowful they are!

In the 9th year of the Yuan Tian [Primal Heaven] reign period, on the 5th day of the 5th month, at the time of the Great Meeting of the Dragon Flower, the Great Emperor, the Officer of Heaven, brought up the issue in a missive before the Perfected Venerable.

In the mortal realm, good men and faithful women of the world do not know about the Tribunals of Hell. The case books are filled with their transgressions. All of them, due to their not having completed their heaven-sent lifespan, descend to the Bureau of Hell. By what means can they be pardoned and avoid this?

The Heavenly Venerable felt pity and released an edict to the lower realm so that they could avoid encounters with demons and death. The Jade Emperor announced:

Saintly Marshall Tian of the Mystic Garden of the Seven Treasures was born at the same time as the Buddha on the 8th day of the 4th month. At eighteen years of age, he surpassed all others in literary attainments. His martial abilities were difficult to surpass. He had mastered play writing. The key phrases of [his] Offering vows contain lines praying for liberation and expiation. His merciful nature is benevolent and harmonious. He will comfort mankind. He has a great general whose body is like white jade. His hair is like drill bits, his eyes like striking lightning. His teeth are like spear points. He has control over the great affairs of the vault of Heaven. He commands the awesome power of the Bureau of Pestilence. He has the assistance of all the marshals who together work to accomplish mysterious merit. You may return to your position. I shall command him to immediately present himself before my desk.

[I, Your] Marshal, have been honored with a summons and I have hastened to the Jade Steps. What is your command?

The Heavenly Venerable said:

Today, at the Great Assembly, the Officer of Heaven urgently memorialized that people in the common realm do not understand Yin and Yang. Their crimes fill the case books. They are just like untutored children, blind and ignorant. You may descend to the common realm. Illuminate the principles of Yin and Yang. Open forth and propagate my edict.

The marshal carefully received the Jade Writing and issued orders for soldiers, talismans, and seals. He faithfully led Generalissimo White Tooth down to the common realm. Descending as a spirit into the human realm, he faithfully transmitted the Great Dao. He enlightened the masses so that they too understood the prohibitions. As for those who had transgressed against the statutes in the mandate of the Bureau and Tribunals of Pestilence, he substituted just measures, delivering and absolving them. He protected them from difficulty and supported them when in danger. He ordered that they be left at peace. He preserved the rising peace of the nation and protected the health of people throughout their life span. The Great Dao of the book of the Precious Appellation of the Jade Sovereign was carried out and spread throughout the world.

[With] one [recitation of this] scripture and one [accompanying] talisman, all [dangerous] transitions [of childhood] and killer specters withdraw. A child can [live to] enjoy his destiny.

If anyone, with a sincere heart, in the course of a [ritual] assembly seeking liberation and deliverance from adversity, the prolongation of life or the salvation of the dead, should recite this scripture once through, I personally shall descend to protect the altar, carrying sacred orders and jade scriptures. Evil spirits and filthy goblins have no hope. I will take care of striking them so that they sink or fly beyond the seas. I will bestow limitless good fortune.

If anyone should write this scripture or carve blocks for its publication, and circulate it, then all the generals worshipped in the scripture will together come to protect you. The entire family will avoid adversity, and years of good fortune will be extended to them.

Should one carry this scripture on their body, then malign demons and heterodox beings will all melt away.

Should one sincerely uphold and recite this scripture, then one's father and mother and the last three generations will all be reborn in heaven.

If a family worships this scripture, their gate and courtyard will be pure and auspicious, and plague and fire will not encroach upon them.

If someone wishes for descendants and recites this scripture thrice every 2d and 8th day (i.e., 2, 8, 12, 18, 22, 28), then this will give rise to blessed virtue, and they will soon have sons and male youngsters.

If a person's [astrological] destiny transgresses against an orphan constellation or widow lodge, resulting in the misfortune of the reduction of years and the confinement of destiny, then they should quickly recite this scripture ten times. Then the Great Emperor Who Records Life will raise up the auspicious ledger of Life and add an increased figure to the sum of longevity.

The merit of this scripture is immense. You should try it out. Then you will take the Precious Appellation of the Jade Emperor and the Mystical Writings of the High Saint as your personal treasure. Revere and always keep it in your thoughts. If nonbelievers receive and slander or destroy the True Writings, then this sort of person will be inspected by the Bureau of Fire and the Bureau of Pestilence and the Bureau of Thunder. I reverently advise you all to definitely not be careless.

(Recite) The Precious Appellation of the Jade Sovereign

At this time, the Heavenly Venerable had finished speaking the scripture. The mass of saints before the emperor praised the Marshal in song (gathas):

Saintly Marshal Tian, from within the Bureau of Wind and Fire of the Golden Gate of the Nine Heavens,

> A free spirit, brave and melancholy
> His great deeds stand out above the ages.
> In literature, etiquette, and music,
> He towered above his times.
> With his red face and mustache
> He was the flower of them all.
> The spiritual [White] Tooth stood in attendance
> [As did they of] the awesome name of Wind and Fire
> When his humaneness and integrity had shown forth
> He came to assist the Jade Emperor
> Bringing solace to the masses
> If you have prayers about your record in the case books
> Depend on him to lightly delete [bad marks]
> His marvelous principles are difficult to describe
> Plague and disease ruled the world
> And he was ordered to descend to the common realm
> On behalf of heaven he carried out transformations
> Revealing his comprehensive conduct
> He gathered in the eight generals
> His power shook the *qian* and *kun* hexagrams
> Prayers and requests to him bring results
> Brilliant without fading
> He distributes talismans and circulates his commands
> Ghosts and goblins sink and hide
> [As for] fear over the (dangerous) barriers children face
> He carries them through smoothly
>
> Respond to the Cavern Stanzas

With all your heart worship and revere
The Great Dao in the center of heaven
The scripture has been written

Guide our worship and carry it out
With sincere hearts truly precious
Plant jade in fine fields
False words and slanders
Will be punished by the Three Bureaus
The virtuous sounds and Advisory Edict
Should each be propagated and carefully preserved
I carry out the Heavenly Venerable Method of Commanding Thunder
    Swiftly, swiftly, as the ordinances do command!

At that time the ranked saints finished singing this chant of praise. The Marshal bowed his head and bowed to express his thanks.

The Heavenly Venerable before his desk again commanded him to vouchsafe forever the lower quarter. Then all said their farewells and withdrew.

CONCLUSION OF THE PRECIOUS SCRIPTURE OF SAINTLY
MARSHAL TIAN FOR DELIVERANCE FROM DISASTER, SALVATION
FROM DIFFICULTY, LIBERATION AND EXPIATION

The Marshal's Scripture is a precious scripture famed for its myriad virtues. Read it line by line, word by word, with truly careful examination. Sentence by sentence it diminishes sins. It has been transmitted through the ages. Bringing spring to harmonious households.

Refrain

His free spirit and melancholy airs
have been transmitted throughout the ages

Completely talented in literature and martial arts,
he became drunk at the Rosegem Banquet.

For the masses who resolutely worship him
he increases good fortune and longevity.

Desiring to increase good fortune and longevity forever.

September, 1981. Naisheng Academy. Reverently copied by Member Li.

Ritual Documents in the Wubentang *Guitiao*

1. *Churujiao* (First initiation)
2. *Shang daqi* (Forwarding of the Great Declaration) (a document burnt during the second stage of initiation)
3. *Jian chanxiu* (Setting up of a requiem service)
4. *Li zhangjiao* (Confirmation ritual for a controller of the Teachings)
5. *Li zongchi* (Confirmation ritual for a general controller)
6. *Qingcan huidao* (Notes on celebratory ritual)
7. *Kai qinggong* (Notes on rites of pure offering)
8. *Kai chanxiu* (Notes on requiem services)
9. *Sikai chanxiu* (Notes on privately established requiem services)
10. *Kai Xiawuni jingcuan* (Notes on the abstract of the Xiawuni Scripture rite)
11. *Ki jingxun* (Notes on the performance of the Essence of the Xiawuni Scripture rites)
12. *Kai sini* (Notes on the performance of the Scriptures of the Four [Masters of the different Teachings] rites)
13. *Kai jingcuan* (Notes on the performance of the abstract of the Xiawuni Scripture rites)
14. *Kai xiawujing* (Three days and nights) (notes on the performance of the Xiawuni Scripture rites)
15. *Kai Xiawujing* (Five days and nights) (Notes on the performance of the Xiawuni Scripture rites)
16. *Kai Xiawujing* (Seven days and nights) (notes on the performance of the Xiawuni Scripture rites)
17. *Nanren churujiao qi* (Testimonial given by males upon first entering the Teachings)
18. *Nuren churujiao qi* (Testimonial given by females upon first entering the Teachings)
19. *Nanren daqi* (Great testimonial for males)
20. *Nuren daqi* (Great testimonial for females)
21. *Huijiao chanxiu dushu shi* (Form for the general memorial for use in requiem services of members or families of a Three in One association)
22. *Chanxiu jiedie shi* (Forms for the composition of the certificate of prohibitions for use in requiems)
23. *Wubenyu chanxiu yongshi* (Form of the instructions of the Wuben Hall for use in requiems)
24. *Li zongcchi dushushi* (Forms for use in the confirmation ritual for a general controller)

25. *Zhutang li zhangjiao shushi* (Forms for the memorial in a confirmation service by all the [Three in One] temples of a director of the [Three in One] Teachings)

26. *Zhushen qingcan shushi* (Forms for the memorial to be used in celebratory rites dedicated to the various gods)

27. *Anqing dushushi* (Form for the general memorial [used in] rites for the settling in and consecration [of a temple or home])

28. *Xingcuan xu* (Preface to the Distillation of the [Xiawuni] Scriptures, used during *baoben* and *jiexie* [expiatory] rituals)

29. *Wubenyu* (Instructions for the Enlightened Basis Hall, used in Kaican rites)

30. *Hongban Xiawu dazhaitan* (Red proclamation for a Xiawu major altar of fasting) (with formularies for rites of building, consecration, animation of the god statues, and announcement of the completion of the ceremonies)

31. *Baibang Wushi dahuizhang* (White proclamation for a Mount Wu Major Assembly) (with formularies for animation of god statues and announcement of the completion of ceremonies)

32. *Hanlinfu* (Rhymeprose rhapsodies of the Hanlin Academy) (multiple versions)

33. *Jiaozhu benxing xushi* (Formulary based on the preface to the Lord of the Teaching's Scripture of Original Substance)

34. *Wubenyu* (Instructions of the Enlightened Basis Hall)

35. *Hongban Xiawu dazhaitan; chanxiu yong* (Red proclamation for a Xiawu major altar of fasting for use in requiems)

36. *Baibang Wushi dahuizhang; chanxiu yong* (White proclamation for a Mount Wu Major Assembly for use in requiems)

37. *Hongban Xiawu dazhaitan; jiexie yong* (Red proclamation for a Xiawu major altar of fasting for use in rites of expatiation)

38. *Baibang Wushi dahuizhang; jiexie yong* (White proclamation for a Mount Wu Major Assembly for use in rites of expatiation)

39. *Zhongyong tonglun* (General discussion of the *Doctrine of the Mean*)

40. *Daode tonglun* (General discussion of the *Way and Its Power*)

41. *Jingang tonglun* (General discussion of the *Diamond Sutra*)

42. *Xiawujingxu* (Preface to the *Xiawu Scriptures*)

43. *Zhongyi tonglun* (General discussion of the One in the Center)

44. *Wubenyu* (Instructions of the Enlightened Basis Hall)

45. *Baibang Xiawu dahuizhang; jiexie yong* (White proclamation for a Xiawu Major Assembly) (for use in rites of expatiation)

46. *Baibang Xiawu dahuizhang; jiexie yong* (White proclamation for a Xiawu Major Assembly) (for use in rites of expatiation)

47. *Hongbang Linshan dafa zhi, baoben yong* (Red proclamation for a Unicorn Mountain Great Rite (for use in ritual repayment of one's basic obligations)

48. *Jingxun shushi, jiexie yong, sini yike* (Forms for memorials for use in the *Essence of the Scriptures of Lord Xia* rites (for use in expiatory rites, and also permissible in *Sini* rites)

49. *Kaijing xuan jiexie shushi* (Forms for memorials for use in expiatory versions of the *Abstract of the Scriptures of Lord Xia* rites)

50. *Kai Xiawujing jiexie shushi* (Forms for memorials for use in expiatory versions of the [full-length] *Scriptures of Lord Xia* rites)

51. *Qian qishi* (Forms for the overture document for a ritual of prayer for peace)

52. *Qinggong shushi* (Forms for the memorial use in the pure offerings rite)

53. *Changong jiexie shushi* (Forms for the memorial for use in requiem offerings and expiatory rites)

54. *Sikai chanxiu shushi* (Forms for memorials for use in privately established requiem services)

55. *Xiubin dieshi* (Documentary form for encoffining rites)

56. *Xiubin shushi* (Form for memorials for use in encoffining rites)

57. *Jingxun baoben shushi* (Forms for memorials for use in *baoben* versions of the *Essence of the Scriptures of Lord Xia* rites)

58. *Kai xuanyao baoben shushi* (Forms for memorials for use in *baoben* versions of the *Abstract of the Scriptures of Lord Xia* rites)

59. *Kai Xiawujing jiexie shushi* (Forms for memorials for use in *baoben* versions of the [full-length] *Scriptures of Lord Xia* rites)

60. *Lanpen xiaoshi shushi* (Forms for memorials for use in the Minor Distribution [to the Hungry Ghosts] in the Ullambana rites)

61. *Lanpen fuxie dushushi* (Forms for the principal memorials appended to the Ullambana rites

62. *You Lanpen fuxie dushushi* (Additional forms for the principal memorials appended to the Ullambana rites)

63. *Mujian Lanpen shushi* (Form for a memorial listing contributors to a Ullambana rite)

64. *Jingxun lie shushi* (Listed forms for memorials for the *Essence of the Scriptures of Lord Xia* rites)

65. *Sini lie shushi* (Listed forms for memorials for the *Sini* rites)

66. *Cuanyao, Lanpen li shushi* (Listed forms for *Abstract of the Xiawuni Scriptures* and Ullambana rites)

67. *Pushi shushi* (Forms for memorials for the Universal Distribution [to Hungry Ghosts] rites)

68. *Hongbang Lanpen fu xie yongshi* (Models for the Red Proclamation used in Ullambana rites, with attached expiatory forms)

69. *Baibang Lanpen yongshi* (Model for the white proclamation used in Ullambana rites)

70. *Chenghun gaotian shushi* (Forms for memorials for use in rites of marriage and the announcement to Heaven)

71. *Zhaohun dieshi* (Form for a passport summoning the soul)

72. *Dieshi* (Forms for passports)

73. *Wenbiao shushi* (Forms for memorials for use in Wenbiao [announcement rites])

74. *Zuo wugong shushi* (Forms for the memorials for use in the Noon Offering rites)

75. *Zaogong shushi qiju* (Opening sentences for models of memorials for use in the Morning Offering)
76. *Wangong qiju shi* (Opening phrases for models [of memorials] for use in the Evening Offering)
77. *Jiexie qiju duiju shu shidui* (Collection of antithetical couplets and opening phrases for expiatory rites)
78. *Badu qiju shiyu ju* (A score of opening phrases for use in rites of deliverance)
79. *Chong tian fan, chantongfan, pengjiaofan shi* (Models for the Banner that Pierces the Sky, the Requiem Lad Banner, and the Banner that Stands at the Edge of the Stage/Altar)
80. *Wufang lei bing shi fu* (Ten Good fortunes simultaneously for the creatures of the five directions)
81. *Du qi shushi qiju shuzhong* (Multiple opening phrases for memorials for sevenfold deliverance)
82. *Lingshan shuofa yinyuan* (The Lingshan Explication of the dharma [of] karma)
83. *Wuben Sanyitang wei fanyu shuilu guizi shi* (The Wuben Three in One Hall forms for Instructions to Demons of the Land and the Waters)
84. *Anqing dushu qiju shi* (Models for opening phrases for use in general memorials in consecration rites)
85. *Anqing gaojun shushi* (Forms for memorials announcing the completion of a consecration rite)

Ritual Calendars

THE SEVEN STAR SHRINE OF FENGTING'S
"SCHEDULE OF THE ANNUALLY CELEBRATED GODS' BIRTHDAYS ARRANGED
BY MONTH AND DAY OF THE LUNAR CALENDAR"

1/1　Milefo (Maitreya Buddha)
1/4　Zhenming Lin Xiansheng (Master Lin Zhenming, second attendant of Lin Zhao'en and founder of the Mingxia branch)
1/8　Yanluo Tianzun (God of the Underworld)
1/9　Yuhuang Shangdi (The Jade Emperor)
1/14　Sanyi Jiaozhu (The Lord of the Three in One [Lin Zhao'en])
1/15　Tianguan Dadi (The Great Emperor of the Celestial Officials)
1/25　Fadu Dadi (The Great Emperor of the Dharma Capital)
2/2　Fude Zhengshen (the Earth God)
2/3　Wenchang Dijun (God of Literature)
2/5　Ji Kong (Sacrifice to Confucius)
2/15　Taishang Laojun (The Most High Lord Lao[zi])
2/15　Guanyin Dashi (Buddhist Goddess of Mercy)
2/19　Shezhu Mingwang (Earth God of the Village, the Brilliant King)
3/3　Xuantian Shangdi (Emperor of the Dark Heavens)
3/15　Baosheng Dadi (Great Emperor Who Protects Life)
3/17　Wudao Weng Xiansheng (Master Weng Wudao [Second Transmitter of the Mingxia branch])
3/19　Taiyang Xingjun (Astral Lord of the Sun)
3/23　Taishang Shengmu (The Most High Divine Mother [Mazu])
3/28　Cang Jie Xianshi (Immortal Master Cang Jie [inventor of writing])
4/4　Yushu Xingjun (Astral Lord of the Jade Pivot [identified in the Mingxia tradition with Lin Zhenming])
4/6　Zhenming Lin Xiansheng (Master Lin Zhenming [second attendant of Lin Zhao'en, and founder of the Mingxia tradition])
4/8　Śākyamuni Buddha
4/8　Rigong Yuanshuai (Marshal of the Sun)
4/12　Kongshi Zhenren (The Realized Being, Confucius)
4/14　Luzu Xianshi (Immortal Master, Patriarch Lu [Dongbin])
4/15　Zhongli Laozu (Ancient Patriarch Zhongli)
4/16　Huixu Zhu Xiansheng (Master Zhu Huixu [fourth attendant of Lin Zhao'en])
4/18　Ziwei Dadi (Great Emperor of Purple Tenebrity)
4/26　Yang Gong Taishi (Commander in Chief Yang)

5/13	Xietian Dadi (Great Emperor Who Assists Heaven)
5/16	Tiandi Zhizun (The Revered Spirits of Heaven and Earth)
5/18	Jinyan Xianshi (The Immortal Master of the Golden Cliff)
5/23	Mulian Zunzhe (The Reverent [Filial Buddhist Monk] Mulian)
6/2	Weituo Zunzhe (The Reverent Weituo, Protector of the Buddhist Faith)
6/6	Jialan Zhenzai (True Chancellor Jialan, Guarantor of the Buddhist Faith)
6/12	Zhuoshi Xianshi (The Prior Master, [Daoist priest] Zhuo [Wanchun])
6/16	Zhoushi Xianshi (The Prior Master, Zhou)
6/18	Longshou Dawang (The Great King Dragonhead)
6/19	Guanyin Dashi (Buddhist Goddess of Mercy)
6/24	Xietian Dadi (The Great Emperor Who Assists the Heavens)
7/7	Kuidou Xinjun (Astral Lord Kuidou, God of Literature)
7/12	Wuxin Xiansheng (Master [Weng] Wuxin)
7/15	Diguan Dadi (The Great Emperor of the Terrestial Officials)
7/18	Zhuoshi Zhenren (Realized Being [Daoist Priest] Zhuo [Wanchun])
7/23	Zhang Gong Shengjun (Saint Zhang)
7/28	Hongdu Zhang Xiansheng (Master Zhang Hongdu [The Third Attendant of Lin Zhao'en)
7/30	Dizang Wang Pusa (Buddhist God of the Underworld, Ksitigarbha)
8/3	Siming Zaojun (The Stove God, Inspector of Destiny)
8/9	Ji Kong (Sacrifice to Confucius)
8/15	Sanfeng Zhang Zhenren (Realized Being [Daoist Saint] Zhang Sanfeng)
8/15	Taiyang Xingjun (Astral Lord of the Extreme Yang [Sun])
8/22	Guangze Zunwang (Reverent King of the Broad Compassion)
8/23	Hufa Jiangjun (The General Who Protects the [Buddhist] Law)
8/27	Ji Kong (Sacrifices to Confucius)
9/1–9	Beidou Xingjun (Astral Lords of the Northern Dipper)
9/15	Xianxian Zhuzi (Former Sage Zhu [Xi])
9/19	Guanyin Dashi (Buddhist Goddess of Mercy)
9/20	Xinyin He Xiansheng (Master He Xinyin [a scholar literati associate of Lin Zhao'en])
9/27	Lingguan Dadi (The Great Emperor of the Divine Officials)
10/15	Shuiguan Dadi (The Great Emperor of the Underwater Officials)
10/27	Zhian Dong Xiansheng (Master Dong Zhi'an [Dong Shi, the Third Transmitter])
10/27	Ziwei Dadi (Great Emperor of Purple Tenebrity)
11/2	Yiyang Weng Xiansheng (Master Weng Yiyang)
11/3	Xingru Lu Xiansheng (Master Lu Xingru [Lu Wenhui, the First Transmitter])
11/19	Jiulian Fozu (The Buddhist Patriarch of the Nine Lotuses)
11/19	Hu Dao Jiangjun (The General Who Protects the Dao)
11/21	Zhisheng Xianshi (Former Masters who have become Saints)

12/15   Huodu Dadi (Great Emperor of the Fire Capital)
12/23   Zhuhua Chen Xiansheng (Master Chen Zhuhua [Zhongyu] Second Transmitter])

THE JADE POOL ACADEMY OF HANJIANG'S
"POSTED LIST OF THE GODS' BIRTHDAYS OF THE XIA ORDER"

1/1   Mile Zunfo (Maitreya, the Future Buddha)
1/7   Beidou Jiuhuang Sifu Xingjun (Astral Lords of the Northern Dipper, the Nine Emperors who bequeath good fortune)
1/9   Jinque Yuhuang zhizun (The Revered Jade Emperor of the Golden Portal)
1/14   Sanyi Jiaozhu (The Lord of the Three in One, Lin Zhao'en)
1/15   Sifu Tianguan Dadi (The Great Emperor of the Celestial Heavens who bequeaths good fortune)
1/25   Hongdu Zhang Xiansheng (Master Zhang Hongdu, third attendant of Lin Zhao'en)
2/13   Zhida Chen Xiansheng (Master Chen Zhida, late Qing reviver of the Three in One)
2/15   Daode Tianzun (The Heavenly Venerable of the Way and Its Power)
3/3   Xuantian Shangdi (The Supreme Emperor of the Dark Heavens)
3/16   Xuantan Yuanshuai (The Marshal of the Mystic Altar)
4/4   Zhenming Lin Xiansheng (Master Lin Zhenming, second attendant of Lin Zhao'en)
4/8   Shijiarulai (The Rulai Buddha)
4/15   Huoguan Dadi (The Great Emperor of the Office of Fire)
4/16   Huixu Zhu Xiansheng (Master Zhu Huixu, fourth attendant of Lin Zhao'en)
5/5   Ruiyang Shengling (The Victorious Commander of Auspicious Yang)
6/2   Hufa Longtian (The Protector of the Dharma of the Dragon Heavens)
6/12   Wanchun Zhuo Zhenren (The Realized Being Zhuo Wanchun)
6/15   Guanyin Dashi (The Buddhist Goddess of Mercy)
6/24   Puhua Tianzun (The Heavenly Venerable of Broad Transformation)
7/15   Diguan Dadi (The Great Emperor of the Terrestial Officials)
7/16   Sanyijiao Zhu (The Lord of the Three in One)
7/18   Puyao Liang Xiansheng (Master Liang Puyao, early Republican Leader of the Three in One)
8/8   Sanfeng Zhang Zhenren (Realized Being Zhang Sanfeng)
8/18   Tian Gong Yuanshuai (Marshal Tian Gong)
8/23   Puyao Liang Xiansheng (Master Liang Puyao, early Republican leader of the Three in One)

9/2   Hufa Longtian (Protector of the Dharma of the Dragon Heavens)

9/14   Daode Tianzun (The Heavenly Venerables of the Way and Its Power)

10/15   Shuiguan Dadi (The Great Emperor of the Underwater Officials)

10/15   Zhida Chen Xiansheng (Master Chen Zhida, late Qing reviver of the Three in One)

10/27   Zhi'an Dong Xiansheng (Master Dong Zhi'an, third transmitter of the Three in One)

11/3   Xingru Liang Xiansheng (Master Liang Xingru, first attendant of Lin Zhao'en)

11/21   Zhisheng Xianshi (The former Masters who have attained sainthood)

12/23   Zhuhua Chen Xiansheng (Master Chen Zhuhua, second transmitter of the Three in One)

12/30   Di Nian (end of the year)

Liturgies: The Purification of a Stage

THE FOLLOWING is a translation of a typical short liturgical text. The ritual corresponding to this liturgy is performed at the beginning of a pudu (Feast for the Universal Deliverance [of the Hungry Ghosts]). During this elaborate set of rites, the masters of the Three in One Religion sit on a stage and recite certain scriptures in imitation of Buddhist monks. This platform is, in fact, also the stage that will subsequently be utilized for the theatrical performances. The liturgy below is a double consecration. First the stage is described as a *daochang* (sacred altar). Then it is referred to as a *yanchang* (performance space). The same sequence of recitations (and presumably perambulations, censing, and sprinkling with purificatory waters) is repeated for the front of the stage in its aspect as sacred altar, and for both the front and the backstage, in their aspect as auspicious performance space. Tian Gong Yuanshuai is invoked immediately after the gods of the Three in One Religion. This text also introduces the important figure of Generalissimo White Tooth, a ferocious dog spirit associated with Tian's exorcistic side.

LITURGY TO CONSECRATE THE STAGE FOR A THREE RELIGIONS PROLONGATION OF LIFE RITUAL PERFORMED ON A LARGE STAGE PLATFORM

Opening Hymn

> The Central Heaven opens a Day of Xia
> The Great Earth turns into lapis
> The 503 Dragon Flower Assembly
> Man and heaven bless this happy hour

Invocation

Reverently we have heard that the Assembly of the Dragon Flower [Tree] illumines the mystic mechanism of Confucianism, Daoism and Buddhism. The doors of the Xiawu tradition opened, continuing the unification of the Sagely, the Mystical, and the Channist. Venerable was this originary merit. His virtuous conduct matched the *qian* and *kun* hexagrams. The correct Way was greatly illumined. The mercy of the teachings penetrates both antiquity and modern times. Carrying onward the transmitted [teachings] of the Three Sages. Delivering heaven and earth. Penetrating the command to be consistent to one principle. Penetrating antiquity and modern times. The dead and the living all look up to it for its mercy. Its merit equally waters the [spirits of] the water and of the land. At this first ascending onto the stage let us first present the marvelous hymn:

Preamble of the Original Master

The original Master was the Maitreya Buddha who came from the East. Heavenly Ruler of Heaven and People of the Three Realms. Kind father of the four beings. He wrote and collected the Orthodox Teachings in several tens of thousands of sentences. He opened the way for followers. His originary merit [resulted] in his completing the Nine Phases [of the heart method]. His essence was the One lofty, subtle Dao. The Three Lineages all joined in [one]. Most profound, subtle, and marvelous. This it is that Master Xia Guzi created. Most deep and profound. With a determined heart return to the Great Dao.

> The Great Void has just revealed the Golden Image.
> People and Heaven all look up. Limitless is his Dao
> and virtue. Subduing dragons and prostrating tigers,
> his orientation is within the Kan Hexagram. Above the
> earthen mound a point of spiritual light shines.

Invocation

Carefully present the marvelous hymn. Reverently invoke the Sacred Space of the Dao. Sprinkle and purify, recite the True Words. Carefully we should recite:

> A spoonful of water, the clear void is seen to be empty,
> The Thousand Sages and ten thousand Saints move with divine penetration.
> Cleansing and instructing, returning the filthy to a purified state.
> Transformations are numinous and endless. A purified ground [for]
> Bodhisattva Mahasattvas [and the] Mahaprajnaparamita.

Sacred Spell to Purify Heaven and Earth

> The Mysterious Spiritual powers in the center of the Cavern
> The Shining Light of the Ultimate Origin
> The Protector Spirits of the Eight Directions
> All cause me to be as I am
> The Talismanic orders of the Numinous Treasure
> Are announced everywhere throughout the Nine Heavens ha.ratna.
> The Ultimate Mystery of the Cavern Mainstays
> Beheads malevolent beings and binds evil ones
> Kills ghosts by the hundreds of thousands
> The Central Mountain Sacred Spell I recite once through

[And it] removes ghosts and prolongs my years
Using it I can walk the Five Sacred Mountains
The eight Seas have heard it
The King of the Demons is tied at the neck
And made to serve at the side of my cart
Vicious loathesome beings are exterminated
The breath of the Dao lasts long
Swiftly, swiftly, as the ordinances do so command.
Om. . . .

Read the Memorial

We have finished the ascending [of the stage] and the purification. Now we must reverently recite the words of the Gatha of Hope expressed through Incense.

The true incense of Discipline and Meditation illumines Reality. Plum, sandalwood, and aloeswood burn in the golden censor. Fragrant smoke, rich and fine, transforms the empty Void. We use it to express that now our character is completely sincere.

> Incense burns: discipline and meditation
> Spontaneously, without action
> Five colors flourished
> Spiritual winds gathered up the smoke
> All returned to the Realm of the Dharma
> The vapors entered the Mysterious Mystery
> Today, [I, your] servant, open my announcement
> It is heard on high in the Nine Heavens

Sacred Spell Mantra to Offer Incense

Nama. . . .

Read Memorial

> The incense smoke has just [risen]
> Sages and Saints approach
> We worship and gaze on the golden countenance
> and with all our hearts we invite:

Reverent Invocation

Kowtowing we take refuge in Master Xiawu
And [Masters] Zhang, Zhuo, and Chu from the Assembly of the Three
 Teachings
The Three Successive Transmitters of the Three Teachings

342 · *APPENDIX 7* ·

The Great Generals who Protect the Way and the Dharma
All the Perfected Ministers of City God temples, neighborhoods and villages.
Marshal Tian, Imperial Son of the Nine Heavens
The Two Lads of Wind and Fire, and General Numinous Tooth.
The Two Messengers who sweep away filth and remove [evil] vapors
All of you we bow to and invite with resolve in our hearts
Together overlook the Sacred Altar and act as warrantors.

Mantra to Universally Summon: Nama. . . .
Mantra of Sweet Dew (Amithaba): Nama. . . .
Offering Mantra: Om. . . .
Invitation of the Memorial.

We have come up and completed the offering. Now we should read the Memorial through.

Proclamation of the Memorial

We have come up and completed the proclaiming of the Memorial. Please burn it in front and below the altar to send it up.

Recitation

The Ritual Water has just splashed, purifying the performance space.
The singing and dancing of the Li Yuan (theater troupe) will bring auspiciousness.
Songs and melodies of burgeoning spring will coalesce eternal good fortune.
Happy to be lustrated by the Moisture of the Three Teachings forever.

Enter the backstage and settle the seats of the gods. To left and right recite the Precious Appellations and present incense.

Sacred Mantra Spell of Purification
Sacred Mantra Spell to Transform Food
Sacred Mantra Spell to Universally Summon
Sacred Mantra Spell of Sweet Dew (Amitahba)
Sacred Mantra Spell of Offering

Go out in front of the Stage Platform. The presentation of flowers and incense is concluded. The coming up to do an offering is concluded. Everyone sincerely and with resolution recall [that:].

Refrain

The original appearance was that of the true
Recognizable in Sariputra's radiance.
The mountains and rivers of the great earth conceal an opening
That opening is capable of taking in the Ultimate Void.

SHUOWANG GONG CHASHUI JING (SCRIPTURE OF THE OFFERING OF TEA EACH NEW AND FULL MOON)

The *Shuowang gong chashui jing* (Scripture of the offering of tea each new and full moon) is probably the most frequently recited of liturgical texts in the Wuben tradition. The text begins with a hymn, a song, and a set of chanted verses to cleanse the six roots, to pacify the locality, and to call for the enlightenment, propriety and purification of all living beings. These hymns are followed by the *True Words to Illumine the Spirit* (translated above), and another hymn. Next the following deities and sages are invoked: Confucius, Laozi, Sākyamuni Buddha, Xiawuni (Lin Longjiang), Zhang Sanfeng, Zhuo Wanchun, Lu Wenhui, Chen Juhua, Dong Shi, Chen Zhida, Liang Puyao, and all former and present saints, sages, gods, and Buddhas. The names of the initiates and their hall are then filled in, and tea is presented. The *Scripture of Fundamental Substance* is recited. Next the *Xingling* (Human nature's spiritual power) stanzas are recited, followed by the *Xinda* (Greatness of the heart) stanzas, and the *Daoyi* (Unity of the Way) stanzas. Finally, a *Vow* is made, and a *Text of Return* is recited, and a final hymn concludes the scripture.

· A P P E N D I X   8 ·

Ritual Spells and Visualizations

THE FOLLOWING spells and visualizations are also provided in the text discussed in chapter 6.

The Heart Method for the Harrowing of Hell has the chief officiant take on the role of the Buddhist monk Mulian, who shattered the gates of the underworld in search of his mother. Like Mulian, the officiant carries a staff with six metal rings and holds a "bright pearl" in his hand.

Chants and visualizations for the Lord of the Teachings, the Humane Teacher, Guanyin, Pumen, the Three Officials, and the gods of the Five Directions.

Heart method for the destruction of the Gates of the Underworld

Heart method for the invitation of the Great Master, King of the Demons

Heart method for the invitation of the Twelve Classes of Beings, from the Five Directions, and the Ten Coordinates above and below

Heart method for summoning from the Five Directions

Heart method for summoning Lonely Souls into their Spirit Tablets.

Heart method for the opening of the Throats [of the Hungry Ghosts]

Heart method for the involvement in the rites of the Lonely Souls

Heart method for the transformation of foodstuffs

QITAN QIJIAN YIWEN: LITURGY FOR THE OVERTURE OF THE ALTAR

Heart method for the [summoning of] Sweet Dew

Heart method for the revolving of the Three Radiances

Heart method for the transformation of Underworld Clothing

Sacred spells for strengthening the heart method

Heart method for the setting out of Fragrant Offerings

Heart method for the taking of refuge in the Dharma, the Commandments, and the True Words

Heart method for the purification of the Heart

Heart method for the purification of the Mouth

Heart method for the Three Professions

Heart method for the invitation of the Tutelary Deity

Heart method for the invitation of the Gods and Elders who Protect the Dharma

Heart method for the recitation of the *Heart Sutra*

Secret recitation of the Sacred Spell for the transformation of soul money

Heart method for [sending] the deceased to the Pure Land

DASHI YANKOU WUFANGJIEJIE: XIAN HUAMI XINFA: THE GREAT DISPENSATION OF
THE FLAMING MOUTH OF THE UNDERWORLD FOR THE RESOLUTION OF THE
ENTANGLEMENTS OF THE FIVE DIRECTIONS

Heart method for the presentation of flowers and rice
Heart method for the Great Dispensation of the Flaming Mouth of the Under-
world
First Talismans for the safeguarding of the Lands

PRAYER LAMP LITURGY AND FIVEFOLD SACRIFICE NINE HEAVENS MYSTIC
SYMBOL LITURGY

Heart method for the securing of the Eight Hexagrams
Heart method for the Placating of the Earth of the Five Emperors of the Five Di-
rections
Heart method for the Roseate Heavens and the Cavern Headquarters
Heart method for the protection of the various infant (messengers)
Heart method for the Ten Professions within the Underworld
Heart method for the resolution of Plaints and the explication of entanglements
Heart method for the presentation of an Offering to Conclude the Liturgy
Heart method for the reverent sending off of sincere prayers through the raising
up of incense and flowers
Heart method for the sending off of incense and flowers
Heart method for the secret prayer spell for the raising up of incense and flowers
Secret Words for the prayers to send off of incense and flowers

GUOGUAN KEYI: LITURGY FOR THE TRAVERSING OF PASSES [OF ADVERSITY] AND
QINGZAN KEYI: LITURGY FOR THE CONSECRATION OF A STOVE [REQUIEM
RITUALS]

Heart method for the raising of the banner, the setting forth of incense and flow-
ers, and the invitation of the saints for all major liturgies (including the raising
of the banner in requiem services)
Heart method for the invitation of a saint into its emplacement
Heart method for the putting in order of the offerings
Golden Radiance Spell
Heart method for the resting the [gods] in their seats
Heart method for the universal summons to take up the divine seats
Heart method for the lifting up of the sacrificial offerings
Heart method for the purification and lustration of the altar
Heart method for the summoning of the talismanic messengers at the conclusion
of the rite of presentation of the memorial for a requiem service
Heart method for the raising of the Banner
Heart method for the Twelve Radiances
Heart method for the invitation of the Buddhas
Heart method for the offering of Flowers and Rice

Heart method for the raising of a Tower [of the Underworld]
Heart method for the transformation of the Tower
Heart method for the Commanding Summons
Burning and transforming of the Immortal Garments
Settling of a Soul into a Tablet
Heart method for the Universal Summons of the Soul
Heart method for the opening of the Throat
Heart method for the presentation of offerings to the Soul
Heart method for the resolution of plaints and the explication of entanglements of the Ten Courts of Ksitigarbha
Heart method of the Nine Lotuses
Heart method for the sacrifice to heaven
Heart method for the Water Lamp Liturgy

WENBU JIAO QIAN XINFA: HEART METHOD FOR A PESTILENCE BUREAU JIAO SACRIFICE TO PRAY FOR PEACE

Heart method for the dotting [animation] of the Great Man
Heart method for the dotting of the Boat and the eyes of the Boat [with talismans]

HUOJIAO LAIJIAO QIYUJIAO XINFA: HEART METHOD FOR FIRE SACRIFICES, THUNDER SACRIFICES, AND SACRIFICES PRAYING FOR RAIN

Heart method for the transformation of Pearls
Heart method for the Harmonization
Reception of the Golden Radiance Spell

SECRET INSTRUCTIONS FOR THE ANIMATION OF THE [STATUES] OF THE GODS

Talismans for the dotting of the eyes, ears, mouth, nose, inner organs, feet, and hands of the gods

The Evolution of the Dragon Mountain Hall
(1986 Stele Inscription in the Longshantang, Taipei)

THE ORIGINS of the Dragon Mountain Hall are in the Honorable Confucius
Hall on East Mountain in Putian City, Fujian Province. The Lord of the Three
in One is worshiped [therein]. At the end of the Qing, there was a Dragon
Mountain Hall in Ditou village in Huian County in Fujian Province. This
temple was a branch temple [through division of incense] of the Honorable
Confucius Temple. The incense was abundant, and the worshipers numerous.
In 1914 a worshiper from Ditou village, Chen Zhaoxing, brought some of
the incense from the temple to Taiwan. The [Lord] was worshiped in four
different locations, in Jiancheng Road, Desheng Road, Yixing Road, and in
Mucha Dingqianhou. In 1955 the number of worshipers had dwindled, and
there was scripture recitation and worship conducted only on the days of the
Upper, Middle, and Lower Prime festivals. In the spring of 1958 the adherents Chen Zhaoxing, Chen Jiaocai, Chen Tianfu, etc., determined to move
the temple into the home of Chen Jiaocai at Number 1, Alley 81, Lane 5, Division 1, Zhongshan Road. The main room of the house was devoted to worship, and at the same time it was decided to carve an image of the Lord of the
Teaching's Golden Body, to add luster to the sacred space. This took from the
winter of 1959 to the 5th day of the 10th month of 1960. [Officiants from]
the Xingyang tang, Number 7, Lane 1, Division 2, Zhongshan North Road,
performed the ceremony of the animation of the god by the dotting of the
eyes. The next year, on lunar 1/14, the statue was settled in place [through
a ritual] in Chen Jiaocai's home and was worshiped in the main room. From
this time onward, the incense accumulated, and the worshipers increased daily.
Because of this, Chen Jincai, Chen Jiaocai, Chen Zhaoxing, Chen Tianfu, etc.
all observed the inclinations of people's hearts. Deciding that the time had
come to build a new temple to propagate the doctrine, they invited senior
worshipers and warm-hearted fellow native-place compatriots to hold a temporary meeting. They encouraged the assembled friends in the Way to col-
laborate in building a structure that would last forever. Due to the support of
all the initiates and members of the [Xinghua] native-place association, they
selected a spot on Number 75-1, Lane 5, Division 1, Zhongshan North Road,
and built the Dragon Mountain Temple. As for finances, the majority came
from the public account established at the Mucha location, and the remainder was made of voluntary contributions by initiates and warm-hearted sages
from the [Xinghua native-place] association. Thereupon cinnabar sands
formed into a stupa, and the temple was built in no time. It was magnificent

in appearance, and overbrimming with the breath of the Dao. Construction began in the spring of 1961 and a ceremony to mark completion was held on lunar 1/14 of 1962. The Lord of the Teachings was worshiped. Inside the temple a Sacred Space [ritual] was conducted while outside plays were performed. A great many people attended, and it was very festive and bustling. As for the organization [of the temple], in accordance with the regulations of the Three Teachings back in the home country, divining blocks were cast before the altar of the Lord of the Teachings, with three positive casts determining the selection. A great assembly was held in 1960 on 2/1, and the results of the divination held in front of the Lord's altar before the entire group of friends in the Way was that Chen Jincai would serve as the first founding manager, Chen Fulai was the chief ritual master (*Daozhang*), and Chen Xunyou would be *zhangjiao*. Other matters were then handled by election. The result of the casting of ballots was that Lin Dekun would be chairman of the Board, Chen Zhaoxing, Cheng Tianfu, Chen Lishui, Chen Jiaocai, Chen Qinxun, and Chen Xian would be appointed members of the Board. Lin Fengmei and Xu Maofa were made assistants. At this the human resources were complete. The doctrines were clarified and the image of the Lord was clear and lofty, and worshipped all around. On lunar 7/13, 1969, Lin Dekun asked his relative, Lin Zhilong, to go to the Zongshengtang (Hall of the Ancestral Sage) in Malaysia to borrow a copy of the *Correct Principles of the Three Teachings*, originally in 36 juan, and to print this text in Taiwan. Thereupon the doctrine was greatly expanded, and the activities of the hall became more abundant by the day. In the spring of 1986 the initiates noticed that the temple had not been repaired for a long time, and its appearance was no longer elegant. Thereupon, Chen Longshui, Chen Bingxie, Chen Tianfu, etc. suggested the establishment of a "Dragon Mountain Hall Restoration Committee" to discuss the matter of repairing the temple. Due to the strong support of the initiates and [Xinghua] association members, contributions were rapidly gathered, and the temple was swiftly repaired. It stood tall and magnificent, sparkling new, and the Three Teachings grew by the day. Believers increased gradually day by day. An account of this evolution was carefully composed and carved in stone, to last forever, on an auspicious date, lunar 7/16, 1986.

Chinese Text of the *Bentijing*
(Scripture of the Original Body [Fundamental Substance])

三一教主夏午尼本體經

我是開天都統行法大師無始以來一人而已釋迦與我比肩諸極在我下方我今現補釋迦佛處龍華三會普度人天天地之內天地之外何處不是我何處不是神何處不是氣何處不是我三一教主夏午尼之金身曾畫八卦易之始曾為證涅槃了生曾為九天大宗王曾為九地大法王珠在庫里諸佛議舉帳飛月輪倡明三氏豈其三氏必歸于儒惟世間法為世所需能無深淺道固不殊入孝出悌非近非迂鑿崑崙以為竅立太極以為基參兩儀以為材列四象以為紀金鐵混合陰陽相符炯炯二珠照耀六虛即儕二尊玉封而賓法與權俱得百千億三金神移居太極前復位無始先百萬人一人能動百萬神天曰天神地曰地祇七十九萬神兵赫赫其威濯濯其靈常擁護圍繞我三一教主夏午尼之金身天地效順日月效明四時效序鬼神效能一發號令若雷若霆如有天妖地妖人妖物妖山妖水妖禽妖獸妖及諸依草附木一切之妖孰不悚懼孰不戰兢破膽裂形碎為灰塵金身金身三妙法金身百千億三金身無氣之氣不神之神常充滿乎法界何處不是我三一教主夏午尼之本體何處不是我三一教主夏午尼之金身唵金嚂嚂玉嚂嚂吽吾奉開天混虛無始至尊敕令

List of Three in One Books and Manuscripts

THREE IN ONE BOOKS AND MANUSCRIPTS

東山集草　　　　　三一教主說彌勒尊佛寶經

金陵中一堂行實　　三一教主夏午尼本體經

九序摘言內景圖　　詩談

居家通俗俚語　　　四書正義

林龍江先生年譜　　孝經

林子本體經釋略　　夏午尼經

林子本行實錄　　　夏午尼經訓

林子分內集纂要　　夏午尼經纂

林子會集　　　　　夏午尼三才普度真經

林子門賢實錄　　　心海經

林子年譜　　　　　養真集

林子全集　　　　　宇合編

林子三教正宗統論　正宗易知錄

龍華別傳　　　　　鎮家寶正義

明夏集　　　　　　鎮家寶補義

三會懺文　　　　　卓午實義

三教初學指南　　　卓午真人志

LITURGICAL MANUSCRIPTS

北極玄天上帝寶經　　慈悲三昧九懺文

畢婚儀文　　　　　　慈濟真君聖誕儀文

彩旌英盛儀文　　　　大乘心經

懺拔參神揚旛儀文　　道德經全本

傳缽詳文解號儀文　　大聖北斗星君延生儀文

出旛接駕諸駕雜記　　大午供儀文

大興書院演革記　　　　　進表儀文
大藏正經血盆　　　　　　金剛般若波羅密經
點眼科儀　　　　　　　　淨牲儀文
地藏菩薩本原經卷　　　　九天田聖元帥救劫寶經
地藏仁師十業儀文　　　　九序要訣須知
地藏十業真言寶經　　　　傳赦儀文
東廚司命灶經元文　　　　開光點眼儀文
東嶽寶經　　　　　　　　犒賞儀文
東嶽天濟經文寶典　　　　蘭盆請赦儀文
佛說大乘阿彌陀寶經　　　老師諸神點眼儀文
佛說觀音消災寶經　　　　雷尊普化玉樞寶經
佛說護諸童子陀羅尼經　　龍華三會懺文
佛說壽生轉生寶經　　　　龍江張卓真人經史
佛說土地黃妙寶經　　　　妙法蓮華經
高上玉皇本行集經　　　　觀識音菩薩普門品
高上玉皇天尊赦罪寶懺　　明夏關聖夫子寶經
高王觀識音經　　　　　　明夏經訓寶經
艮背法　　　　　　　　　明夏禳關過限儀文
供庫儀文　　　　　　　　目連淨棚儀文
供神儀文　　　　　　　　南斗延生真經
供祖供爺儀文　　　　　　內科行囊
觀音消災寶經　　　　　　普門真經
規條　　　　　　　　　　普施儀文
花冊　　　　　　　　　　莆仙惠各村宮社譜
建壇請聖安位儀文　　　　啓建通唱儀文
建壇濩灑淨元宵報安儀文　啓建儀文
荐修啓建　　　　　　　　清供儀文
教主祝壽儀文　　　　　　請門友儀文
解冤儀文　　　　　　　　慶土啓建五帝鎮庫科
祭夫儀文　　　　　　　　慶土起五帝鎮庫儀文

齊天大聖聖誕儀文

禳關過限儀文

禳關儀文

儒道釋聖誕

儒道釋夏四尼經略

儒教致聖先師儒經

儒經寶經

三乘九品蓮台拔度儀文

三官寶經

三教彩慶淨壇儀文

三教發關晚朝儀文

三教發奏儀文

三教醮告九天玄象儀文

三教供神儀文

三教關限儀文

三教規條

三教會神儀文

三教薦修攝招儀文

三教薦修資度啓建

三教淨牲儀文

三教金丹發揮訣

三教九蓮儀文

三教開光度旬啓建

三教蘭盆大會儀文

三教蘭盆祝語儀文

三教龍華建壇

三教龍華建壇進表用

三教龍華薦修普度儀文

三教龍華醮禱八掛五方儀文

三教龍華醮禱道場儀文

三教龍華醮禱進貢儀文

三教懺悔解怨儀文

三教上中下元疏式

三教十王還報經

三教小施儀文

三教謝請祖儀文

三教心法

三教延生大棚淨臺儀文

三教延生發奏進表儀文

三教延生建壇寶經

三教延生普濟儀文

三教延生儀文

三教中施儀文

三教轉輪寶藏儀文

三教祝壽儀文

三教資度發使儀文

三教資度赦儀文

三經度旬啓建

　度旬進貢儀文

三昧水懺法

三一教主靈籤

三一教主夏午尼本體經

三元三品三官大帝寶經

薩師琉璃光如來本原功德

　經

向陽書院錄儒道釋聖誕

上元天官賜福寶懺

聖教孔門孝經正文

聖母誕辰儀文

十二公懺

十二光燈招魂儀文　　　夏教薦修建靈儀文
十二光佛儀文　　　　　夏教進陳十供儀文
十二光王品偈靈文　　　夏教進貢送聖儀文
師說彌勒尊佛寶經　　　夏教進貢晚科儀文
十王還報經　　　　　　夏教龍華三會懺文
十獻儀文　　　　　　　夏教蒙山施食儀文
水燈儀文　　　　　　　夏教普放水燈儀文
水官下元解厄玄寶懺　　夏教慶篆儀文
朔望早晚供茶水經　　　夏教慶天地全卷冊
司馬聖王聖誕儀文　　　夏教慶祖安神儀文
四尼寶旌　　　　　　　夏教啟壇早朝發啟儀文
素供儀文　　　　　　　夏教初表申詳儀文
太上靈寶補謝灶王妙經　夏教禳關度限分花儀文
太上老君道德寶經　　　夏教三元起建請聖儀文
太上玄靈北斗延生寶經　夏教三元疏式
太上玄靈北斗真經　　　夏教上中下元疏式
太上玄天謝罪寶懺　　　夏教聖誕啟請儀文
太上灶經儀文　　　　　夏教五富祝燈儀文
田公元帥聖誕儀文　　　夏教謝祖儀文
田聖寶經　　　　　　　夏教喜文供祖請祖送祖儀文
瘟部下馬儀文　　　　　夏教血湖法懺
文昌帝君陰騭寶經　　　夏教延生彩宴疏稿
午供進貢儀文　　　　　夏教延生醮謝懺修蒙山儀文
五雷寶懺　　　　　　　夏教延生填庫儀文
五顯靈官本行元文　　　夏教延生小進貢三獻儀文
夏教拜表早朝儀文　　　夏教中下元攝招儀文
夏教彩舟花舟儀文　　　夏教追修資度解接儀文
夏教初表申詳儀文　　　夏教資度修殯儀文
夏教度旬儀文　　　　　小道場進貢壽生經
夏教護兒子陀羅尼經　　孝經

孝經正文
小施儀文
消災吉祥咒
霞天洞府
夏午宗師點眼諸神通用
夏午尼經訓
夏午尼經纂
夏午尼師三一教主普度法
　門謹書設科傳道開經說
　法規條
下元水官解厄寶懺
協天夫子關聖寶經
攝召儀文
喜事請祖儀文
修殯建壇懺文
玄壇元帥寶經
玄天上帝懺
玄天上帝救劫法懺
血湖法懺
血盆寶經
血盆胎骨經
揚旛寶懺
楊公太師聖誕儀文
楊公太師英烈護世消災解
　厄經
延生符使點眼儀文
延生醮禱送聖儀文

延生醮謝延生儀文
藥師琉璃光如來本原功德經
迎旌淨牲揚幡十二光九蓮
　大集
迎旌儀文
元宵參與收兵儀文
玉皇懺
玉皇懺全本
玉山書院演革記
玉樞寶經
張公聖君寶經
張公聖誕儀文
招魂儀文
至真五顯靈君經
中施儀文
中元地官赦罪寶懺
轉藏天宮儀文
轉藏儀文
卓祖寶經
諸神聖誕儀文
諸聖真寶經進表請神頌
祝壽儀文
諸尊列聖慶讚
資度供齋解接儀文
資度祭天彩舟給諜謝師
資度啓建請魂儀文
總集科儀曲

· G L O S S A R Y ·

Anqing — 安慶
Anwei — 安位
Anxi — 安溪
Aofeng shuyuan — 鰲峰書院

bagua — 八卦
baidou qifu — 拜斗祈福
Bailianjiao — 白蓮教
Bangtou Pumingci — 榜頭普明祠
Bangtou Pumingcun — 榜頭普明村
bangwen — 榜文
Baoben — 報本
Baosheng Dadi — 保生大帝
Baosongci — 寶松祠
Baxiacun Zhuguang Shuyuan — 壩下村珠光書院
Beidou qixingwang — 北斗七星王
Beidou zhifu — 北斗致福
Beidouxi — 北斗戲
Beigang Chaotiangong — 北港朝天宮
benti — 本體
Bentijing — 本體經
Benyuantang — 本源堂
bingjiaoshi — 秉教師
Budai — 布袋
bushi — 布施

Caigong chushi — 蔡公出世
Caijing yingsheng yiwen — 彩旌迎神儀文
Cai Xiang — 蔡襄
Cai Wenju — 蔡文舉
Cang Jie Xianshi — 蒼頡仙師
Cantongji — 參同契
Changqingjingjing — 常清靜經
changsheng — 長生
chanhui — 懺悔
chanxiu shoujie — 懺修受戒
chanzui — 懺罪
Chen Baisha — 陳白沙
Chen Biao, hao Daquan — 陳標號道泉

Chen Chiyang — 陳池洋
Chen Dadao — 陳大道
Chen Daoqing — 陳道清
Chen Gong Shenghou — 陳公聖侯
Chen Hongmou — 陳宏謀
Chen Jinggu — 陳靖姑
Chen Longshui — 陳龍水
Chen Maoshan — 陳茂山
Chen Rui — 陳瑞
Chen Wenbing — 陳文炳
Chen Wenzhang — 陳文章
Chen Zhaojing — 陳兆鏡
Chen Zhenren — 陳真人
Chen Zhida — 陳智達
Chen Zhongyu, zi Rujing, hao Juhua — 陳衷瑜字汝經號聚華
Cheng Hao — 程顥
Cheng Mingdao — 程明道
Chengsan Shuyuan — 承三書院
Cheng Xingben — 程性本
Cheng Wenjian, Yi Lao tongyan, — 程文簡, 易老通言
Cheng Yi — 程頤
Cheng Zhu, Laozi lun — 程俱, 老子論
Chengzi — 程子
Chenshi Dashi — 陳氏大師
Ch'iu Te-tsai, Taiwan miaoshen chuan — 邱德栽, 台灣廟神傳
Chongjian libei — 重建立碑
chushifa — 出世法
citian — 祠田
Cunsheng guitiao — 存生規條
cunxin — 寸心
cuozhu — 厝主

Dachengjiao — 大乘教
Dafutang — 大福堂
Da Huizong Mou Chanshi, Dahui yulu — 大慧宗杲禪師大慧語錄
Dajia — 大甲
dan — 丹

dang — 黨

dantian — 丹田

danwei — 單位

danzhong — 丹中

Dao — 道

Daochang — 道場

Daode zixiu yexueguan — 道德自
修夜學館

Dao Pu — 道璞

Daoqi yuehui — 道期樂會

daota — 倒塔

Daoyi — 道一

Daoyou — 道友

Daozhang — 道長

Dashi — 大士

Dashi Yankou wufangjiejie — 大士
焰口五方解接

Datongzhong yijing — 大同中一經

Daxingci — 大興祠

Daxing shuyuan yange ji — 大興書
院演革記

Deshan'an — 德善庵

Dexing shuyuan — 德興書院

deyi, guiyi, yi guan zhi — 得一歸一
一貫之

Deyuantang — 德源堂

dian — 殿

dian (crazy) — 顛

dianhu shima — 點戶食馬

Dianyan keyice — 點眼科儀冊

die — 謀

Ding Hesheng — 丁荷生

Dingmen — 頂門

Dizang zunwang — 地藏尊王

dizhu — 地主

dizici — 弟子祠

Donglaisi — 東來寺

Dongshanci — 東山祠

Dong Shi, hao Zhi'an — 董史號直
庵

Dongshihui — 董事會

Dongshizhang — 董事長

Dong Xizi — 董希子

Dongyue Dadi — 東岳大帝

du — 度

duilian — 對聯

Dushizhengyijing — 度世正一經

Du Wenhuan — 杜文煥

faming — 法名

Fan Qianyi — 凡千一

Fang Junshi — 方浚師

fangnei — 方內

fangwai — 方外

Fanshen chengjing — 反身誠經

fashu — 法術

fazou jinbiao — 發奏進表

Feishantang — 蜚山堂

Fendeng — 分燈

Fengshansi — 鳳山寺

Fengting — 楓亭

fenxiang — 分香

Foshuo huzhudongzi duoluoni
jing — 佛説護助童子哆羅尼經

Fu Yiling, Yang Guozhen, Ming Qing
Fujian shehui yu xiangcun jingji —
傅一凌, 楊國楨, 明清福建與鄉
村經濟

Fujian — 福建

Fupuxian Huiguan — 福莆仙會館

Fuqing — 福清

Fusi jiaoshi — 副司教師

Futanshi — 副壇師

Fuzhou — 福州

fuzhou — 符咒

ganbu — 干部

Gaotian shugao — 告天疏稿

gechu — 格去

Gen — 艮

genbei — 艮背

Geng Dingxiang, zi Zailun, hao
Qutong — 耿定向字再倫號楚侗

gewu — 格物

gong — 宮

gongde — 功德

gongfu — 功夫

gongguoge — 功過格

gongtoutian — 宮頭田

gua — 卦

guan — 關
Guan Foxin, Putian shihua — 關佛
　心, 莆田史話
Guan Shengwang — 關聖王
Guan Zhidao — 管志道
Guanghuasi — 廣化寺
Guanghuatang — 廣化堂
Guangze zunwang — 廣澤尊王
Guanmenjiao — 關門教
Guanyin — 觀音
Guanyinge — 觀音閣
Guanyinjiao — 觀音教
Gufo zongpai — 古佛宗派
Guijiao jingli lueji — 歸教經歷略
　記
guiziwu — 鬼子舞
Guo Sizhou — 郭嗣周
guoguan — 過關
Guoguan keyi — 過關科儀
Gutian — 古田

han — 函
Han Wudi — 漢武帝
Hanjiang — 涵江
Hansantang — 函三堂
Hanshan Deqing — 憨山德清
Hanyitang — 函一堂
haoranzhiqi — 浩然之氣
He Qiaoyuan — 何喬遠
　Mingshan zang — 名山集
　Minshu — 閩書
He Xinyin — 何心隱
Heimian Jiangjun — 黑面將軍
Hepingcun Delinci — 和平村德麟
　祠
Hetu — 河圖
Hongdupai — 洪都派
Hsing-hua (see Xinghua) — 興化
Hu Tinglan — 胡庭蘭
Hu Zhenren — 胡真人
Hu Zhi — 胡直
Hua To neizhaotu — 華陀內昭圖
Huang Chengyi — 黃承一
Huang Daben — 黃大本
Huang Debiao — 黃德標

Huang Dehui — 黃德惠
Huang Fang — 黃芳
Huang Hongxian — 黃洪憲
Huang Longqing — 黃龍卿
Huang Qingyi — 黃清儀
Huang Wenjing — 黃文景
Huang Zhou — 黃州
Huangshi — 黃石
Huangtingjing — 黃庭經
Huangzhong — 黃中
Huang Zongxi, Nanlei wen'an, Lin
　sanjiao zhuan — 黃宗羲, 南雷文
　案, 林三教傳
Huashu — 化書
Huating — 華亭
Hugong — 壺公
hujiao — 護教
Hui'an — 惠安
Hui Neng — 慧能
Huixing — 慧性
huizu — 回族
hun — 魂
Hunxu shi — 混虛氏
Huodu Dadi — 火都大帝
Huoguan Dadi — 火官大帝
Huojiao, leijiao, qiyujiao xinfa — 火
　醮雷醮祈雨醮心法
Hushi — 笏石
Huwei jiangjun — 護圍將軍

ji (encased) — 寄
ji (cosmic mechanism) — 機
Jiang Yifang — 蔣奕芳
Jiangdongci — 江東祠
Jiangjing — 講經
Jiangkou — 江口
Jiang Yifang — 蔣奕芳
Jiantan — 建壇
Jianyang — 建陽
Jianzu — 荐族
jiao — 醮
jiao — 教
Jiao Hong — 焦竑
jiaogui — 教規
jiaoyi — 教議

jiaoyin yishi — 交印儀式
jiaozhu dizi — 教主弟子
Ji jiaofu — 祭驕夫
jie'er tian — 節日田
Jiejie Shi — 戒戒室
Jin Daren — 金大人
jinbiao — 進表
jindan — 金丹
Jinfengci — 金峰祠
jing (spiritual precincts) — 境
jing (classics) — 經
Jingangjing — 金剛經
jingong — 進供
Jingshantang — 金山堂
jingshen — 精神
jingshen qimai — 精神氣脈
Jingshi — 經師
jingtian — 井田
Jinguang shenzhou — 金光神咒
jingxin — 靜心
jingxue — 精血
jingzuo — 靜坐
Jinjiang — 晉江
Jinling Zhongyitang — 金陵中一堂
Jinshan shuyuan — 金山書院
Jinshanci — 金山祠
Jinshancun — 金山村
Jinshangong — 金山宮
jinshi — 進士
Jintongjiao (Jintang) — 金童教 (金堂)
jinxiang — 進香
Jinyan xianshi — 金眼仙師
Jiulian — 九蓮
Jiulian Fozu — 九蓮佛祖
Jiulidong — 九鯉洞
Jiulidong jingce — 九鯉洞經冊
Jiulihu — 九鯉湖
Jiuliyang — 九里洋
Jiumu Lin — 九牧林
Jiutian Tiansheng yuanshuai jiujie baojing — 九天田聖元帥救劫寶經
Jiuxu yaojue xuzhi — 九序要訣須知
Jiuxu zheyan — 九序摘言

Jiuxu zheyan neijingtu — 九序摘言內景圖
Jixiang Dajiang — 吉享大將軍
jixi xingming — 極希性命
jize — 極則
jun — 郡
junzi — 君子
juren — 舉人

Kai Jingxun — 開經訓
Kai Jintangjiaoshu — 開金堂教敘
Kai Sinijing — 開四尼經
Kai Xiawunijing — 開夏午尼經
kaiguang dianyan — 開光點眼
Kaiyuanci — 開元寺
Kaizhang Shengwang: Chen Yuanguang — 開漳聖王陳元光
kan — 坎
kaojun — 犒軍
ke — 科
Kennaicun Beishangong — 墾奈村北山宮
Kongmen xinfa — 孔門心法
Kongshi zhenren — 孔氏真人
Kongzhongni — 孔仲尼
Kuidou — 魁斗
Kuishengci — 魁聖祠
kun — 坤
Kunlun — 崑崙

Laidian — 賴店
lanpen pudu — 蘭盆普度
Laoguan zhaijiao — 老關齋教
Laozi — 老子
Lei Haiqing — 雷海青
Lei Yinglong — 雷應龍
Leisheng Tianzun — 雷聲天尊
Lengyanjing — 楞嚴經
Leshanci — 樂善祠
Li (rites, protocol) — 禮
li (hexagram) — 離
li (subcanton) — 里
Li Daosheng — 李道生
Li Mingdeng — 李明燈
Li Tieguai — 李鐵拐

Li Xianjiang, Boso shinko no kenkyu — 李獻璋, 媽祖信仰の研究

Li Zhi — 李贄

Lian Lichang, Fujian mimishehui — 連立昌, 福建秘密社會

Liang Puyao zi Junlong — 梁普耀字君龍

Lianghuang can — 梁皇讚

liangzhi — 良知

liao — 了

Libao: Tati (Dadi) — 立寶大地

liben — 立本

Lichan Dahui — 禮懺大會

Licu Zongyutang — 李厝宗玉堂

lijia — 里甲

Lin Ah-be — 林阿媚

Lin Fan — 林蕃

Lin Fu — 林富

Lin Guoping Lin Zhao'en yu Sanyijiao — 林國平, 林兆恩與三一教 Sanyijiao xianzhuang gaikuang — 三一教現狀概況

Lin Hengshan — 林恆山

Lin Jingmian — 林敬冕

Lin Jun — 林浚

Lin Longjiang — 林龍江

Lin Meirong — 林美容

Lin Pi — 林披

Lin Sanjiao juan — 林三教傳

Lin Shaoyun, zi Zhaokai — 林少云字肇開

Lin Wanchao — 林萬潮字養晦號石樓

Lin Wanren — 林萬仞

Lin Wei — 林葦

Lin Wengui — 林文桂

Lin Wenhao, Haineiwai xueren lun Mazu — 林文豪, 海內外學人論媽祖

Lin Xiangje, Ouliziji — 林向哲, 甌離子集

Lin Yuntong, zi Ruiyu, hao Tuizhai, yi Duanjian — 林云同字汝雨號退齋

Lin Zhao'en, zi Maoxun, hao Long-jiang, Daohao Ziguzi — 林兆恩字懋勛號龍江道號自谷子

Lin Zhao'en juan — 林兆恩傳

Lin Zhaogao — 林兆誥字懋楊號曉江

Lin Zhaojing — 林兆金

Lin Zhaoju — 林兆居

Lin Zhaoke, zi Xueming, hao Rong-men — 林兆珂號孟鳴

Lin Zhenming (see Lin Zhijing) — 林貞明

Lin Zhijing, hao Danle, you hao Zhen-ming — 林至敬號坦樂又號貞明

Lindoucun Jingshan Shuyuan — 嶙兜村鏡山書院

ling — 靈

Lingguan Dadi — 靈官大帝

Lingshujing — 靈樞經

Lingyundian — 凌雲殿

Linshanci — 嶙山祠

Linshangong — 嶙山宮

Linshui furen — 臨水夫人

Linzi — 林子

Linzi bentijing shilue — 林子本體經釋略

Linzi benxing shilu — 林子本行實錄

Linzi Daode shilue — 林子道德釋略

Linzi fenneiji cuanyao — 林子分內集纂要

Linzi fenneiji Sanjiao fenzhe bian-lan — 林子分內集三教分摘編覽

Linzi Huibian — 林子會編

Linzimenxian shilu — 林子門賢實錄

Linzi nianpu — 林子年譜

Linziquanji — 林子全集

Linzi sanjiaozhengzong tonglun — 林子三教正宗通論

Linzi shengxue tongzong sanjiao gui-ru ji — 林子聖學統宗三教歸儒集

Linzi xingshi — 林子行實

Liu Huisun — 劉蕙孫

Liu Jin — 劉謹

Liu Shirui — 劉仕銳

Liu Siwen, zi Ruzhi — 劉思問字汝制

Liu Xia — 劉霞
Liu Xun — 劉勳
Lixue — 理學
liyiyiqi — 禮以義起
Liyuanxi — 梨園戲
Longhua — 龍華
Longhua biezhuan — 龍華別傳
Longhuatang — 龍華堂
Longhushan — 龍虎山
Longjinggong — 龍井宮
Longquansi — 龍泉寺
Longshanci — 龍山祠
Longshantang — 龍山堂
Longshengci — 龍聖祠
Lu Dongbing — 呂洞賓
Lu Jiuyuan (Xiangshan) — 陸九淵
　象山
Lu Shiyuan — 盧士元
Lu Wenhui, zi Yanzheng, hao
　Xingru — 盧文輝字延征號性如
Lu Xubai, Laozitongyan — 呂虛白,
　老子講義
Lu Yijing — 呂一靜
Lufuxi — 瘟府戲
Lugang — 鹿港
lunhui — 輪回
Lunyu zhengyi zheyao — 論語正義
　摘要
Luo Daye — 羅大爺
Luo Hongxian — 羅洪先字達夫
Luojiao — 羅教
Luo Rufang — 羅汝芳
Luoshu — 洛書
Luo Zongyan — 羅從彥
Lushan — 盧山, 閭山
Lushan Dafayuan dudie — (閭) 盧
　山大法院度諜
Luzu xianshi — 呂祖仙師

Ma Xixia and Han Bingfang, Zhong-
　guo minjian zongjiaoshi — 馬西
　沙, 韓秉芳, 中國民間宗教史
Mano Senryu, Mindai bunkashi ken-
　kyu — 間野潛龍, 明代文化史研
　究

Mazu — 媽祖
Meifengsi — 梅峰寺
Meiqigong — 梅啓宮
Meizhou — 湄洲
Meizhou Tianhougong — 湄洲天后
　宮
Mengzhongren pian — 夢中人篇
Mengzi zhengyi zheyao — 孟子正
　議摘要
menren — 門人
mentu — 門徒
miao — 廟
mijue — 密訣
Mile zunfo — 彌勒尊佛
Minbeihua — 閩北話
ming — 命
Ming Taizu — 明太祖
Ming Taizu yuzhu Daode zhenjing —
　明太祖御注道德真經
Mingfeng — 明豐
Mingguang puzhaojing — 明光普
　照經
Minghemiao — 鳴鶴廟
Mingxia — 明夏
Mingxiaci — 明夏祠
Mingxiapai — 明夏派
Minnan — 閩南
Minqing — 閩清
Minshu — 閩書
Minsu quyi congshu (Min-su ch'u-i
　ts'ung-shu) — 民俗曲藝叢書
minxiao — 民校
Mituojing — 彌陀經
miyu — 密語
Mulan — 木蘭
Mulian — 目連
Mu Zishou — 木子壽

Naisheng Shuyuan (tang) — 耐聖
　書院 - 耐聖堂
Nananbi — 南安坡
Nanchanci — 南禪寺
Nanglitang — 囊理堂
Nanshansi (Guanghuasi) — 南山寺
　廣化寺

Nanyang — 南洋
nian — 念
niqi — 逆氣
niwan — 泥丸

Ofuchi Ninji, Chugokujin no shukyo girei — 大淵忍爾, 中國人の
  宗教儀禮

Pan Huang — 潘潢字荐叔號朴溪
Pan Jingruo, Sanjiao kaimi guizheng
  yanyi — 潘鏡若, 三教開迷歸正
  演義
Pangu — 磐古
Penglai — 蓬萊
po — 魄
Pomipian — 破迷篇
pu — 鋪
pudu — 普度
Puguangci — 普光祠
Pulinci — 普麟祠
Pumenfo — 普門佛
Pumingci — 普明祠
Pushengci — 普聖祠
pushi — 普施
Pushi yiwen — 普施儀文
Putian — 莆田
Putian Huiguan — 莆田會館
Putianxian minsu xuehui — 莆田縣
  民俗學會
Putianxian shouju Lin Longjiang
  Minsuwenhua xueshu yantaohui
  lunwenchi — 莆田縣首舉林龍江
  民俗文化學術研討會論文集
Putian xianzong jiaozhi (chugao) —
  莆田縣宗教志初稿
Putian zhengxie — 莆田政協
Puxi — 莆僖
Puxianhua — 莆仙話
Puyang — 莆陽

qi — 氣
Qi — 祁
qian — 乾
qiangban tian — 槍班田

Qianlong — 乾隆
Qianshi furen — 錢氏夫人
Qianta — 牽塔
qianwang — 牽亡
qigong — 氣功
Qigu — 起鼓
Qijian — 啓建
Qijian yiwen — 啓建儀文
Qi Jiguang — 戚繼光
qili — 氣力
Qingcan keyi — 慶贊科儀
Qingcanhui — 慶贊會
Qingjiang — 清江
Qingni — 青尼
qingshen — 請神
qingxiang — 請香
Qingyuntang — 慶雲堂
Qiongyao dafayuan — 瓊瑤大法院
Qiongyaotang — 瓊瑤堂
Qiongyao xiandao — 瓊瑤仙道
Qiongyao zhengjing — 瓊瑤真經
Qitan qijian yiwen — 啓壇啓建儀文
Qitian Dasheng — 齊天大聖
Qi wufu — 祈五福
Qixingci — 七星祠
Qixingci juantianbei — 七星祠捐田
  碑
Quan'an zhuang — 泉安壯
Quanzhen — 全真
Quanzhou — 泉州

ranghua — 禳花
rangqing — 禳請
raojing — 繞境
ren — 仁
Rensheng Dadi — 仁聖大帝
ren, yi, li, zhi, xin — 仁義禮智信
Rigong yuanshuai — 日公元帥
Ruifengci — 瑞風祠
Ruiyun Shuyuan — 瑞雲書院
rujiao — 儒教
Rulaixingjing — 如來性經
rumen — 入門
Rusongan — 入松庵
ruyi — 如意

Sakai Tadao, Chugoku zensho no kenkyu — 酒井忠夫, 中國善書の研究
Sangang wuchang — 三綱五常
Sangshi chanyan — 喪事懺言
Sanguan baojing — 三官寶經
Sanguan Dadi — 三官大帝
Sanjiao — 三教
Sanjiao genyuan xingjiao shiji ji — 三教根源行腳事迹集
Sanjiao huiguan — 三教會館
Sanjiao huipian yaolue — 三教會編要略
Sanjiao huizong — 三教會宗
Sanjiao jiulian yiwen — 三教九蓮儀文
Sanjiaotang — 三教堂
Sanjiaoxiansheng — 三教先生
Sanjiao zhenzong — 三教正宗
Sanjiao zhenzong tonglun — 三教正宗通論
Sanjiao zhushou yiwen — 三教祝壽儀文
Sannai — 三奶
Sanqi pudu — 三期普度
Sanyi jiaozhu — 三一教主
Sanyi jiaozhu shuo Milejing jing — 三一教主説彌勒佛經
Sanyijiao — 三一教
Sanyipai — 三一派
Sawada Mizuho — 澤田瑞澤穗, Bukkyo to Chugoku bungaku — 佛教と中國文學 Zoho Hokan no kenkyu — 增修寶卷の研究
shaliguang — 舍利光
Shandetang — 善德堂
Shang Yang — 商鞅
Shangdi — 上帝
shangyuan — 上元
Shangyuan tianguan sifu baochan — 上元天官賜福寶懺
shanshu — 善書
shanxin zongjiaozhe — 善心宗教者
Shaowu — 邵武

Shao Yong (Kangjie) — 邵雍 (康節)
she — 社
Shegong — 社公
shehui — 社會
Shema — 社媽
shen — 神
shengchandui — 生產隊
shengci — 生祠
shengdan — 聖誕
shengminghui — 神明會
Shengmu danchen yiwen — 聖母誕辰儀文
Shengmu Keshi niangniang — 聖母柯氏娘娘
shengtian chaodu — 升天超度
shengxing yiwen — 升牲儀文
Shengxinggong — 盛興宮
shengyuan — 生員
shentong — 神通
shexi — 社戲
shezhang — 社長
Shezhu Mingwang — 社祖明王
shichu shifa — 世出世法
shidafu — 士大夫
Shijiamouni — 釋迦牟尼
shijianfa — 世間法
Shijie qizhang — 誓戒啓章
Shiling — 時令
Shilin guangji — 事林廣記
Shimenci — 石門祠
shishen — 識神
Shiting — 石亭
Shizuo — 師佐
shou — 壽
shoujiao — 受教
shoujing — 收警
Shuiguan Dadi — 水官大帝
Shun — 舜
Shunjidian — 順濟殿
Shunzhongtang — 順中堂
Shuowang gongcha shuijing — 朔望供茶水經
shuwen — 疏文
si — 司
Siku quanshu — 四庫全書

Siku quanshu zongmu tiyao — 四庫
　全書綜目提要
Sima Guang, Qianxu — 司馬光, 潛虛
Sima Shengwang — 司馬聖王
sipei sanchuan — 四配三傳
siren zhi cai — 私人之財
Sishu daquan — 四書大全
siyuan — 寺院
sona — 嗩吶
Song Gaozong — 宋高宗
Song Huiyao jigao — 宋會要輯稿
Song Huizong — 宋徽宗
Song Lizong — 宋禮宗
Song Yizu — 宋懿祖
songshen — 送神
Su Shi, Laozijie — 蘇轍, 老子解
Sun Jiyou — 孫繼有
Sun Wukong — 孫悟空
Suqi xuan tanke — 宿啓玄壇科

Taihuci — 太湖祠
taiji — 太極
Taiqing — 太清
Taishan — 泰山
Taishang Shengmu — 太上聖母
Taisui — 太歲
taiyang — 太陽
Taiyang xingjun — 太陽星君
Taizhou — 泰州
Tan Qian, Zaolin Zacu — 談遷, 棗
　林雜俎
Tanaka Issei, Chugoku saishi engaki
　kenkyu — 田仲一成, 中國祭祀
　演劇研究
　　Chugoku zonzo to engaki kenkyu
　　—中國宗族と演劇研究
　　Chugoku fukei engaki kenkyu —
　　中國巫系演劇研究
tanban — 壇班
Tangan — 塘岸
Tanjing — 檀經
tanyuezhu — 檀越主
Tao Wangling — 陶望齡
Tian Gong Yuanshuai — 田公元帥
Tian Hou — 天后

Tian Rucheng, zi Shuhe — 田汝成
　字叔禾
Tianbao jinjing lingshu shenjing nei-
　jing — 天寶金鏡靈樞神景内經
tiantang diyu — 天堂地獄
Tianxinlou — 天心樓
Tingzhou — 汀州
Tongde shuyuan — 通德書院
Tongxuan jizejing — 通玄極則經
tu — 圖
Tu Long — 屠隆
Tudigong — 土地公

waijing — 外景
Wang Bi — 王弼
Wang Dao, Laoziyi — 王道, 老子億
Wang Keshou — 汪可受
Wang Shimao, zi Jingmwi, hao Lin-
　zhou — 王世懋字敬美號麟洲
Wang Tu — 王圖
Wang Xing — 王興
Wang Yangming — 王陽明
Wangyejiao — 王爺教
Wang Zhaolong — 王兆龍
Wang Zuotang — 王佐塘
wanjian jianzu — 晚間荐族
weilutai — 尾閭胎
Weimojiejing — 維摩詰經
Weito — 韋馱
weizhi — 尾胝
Wenbujiao — 瘟部醮
Wencao Wuban — 文曹武班
Wenchang — 文昌
Wenchang Dijun — 文昌帝君
Wendao — 文道
Weng Wenfeng — 翁文峰
Weng Wudao — 翁吾道
Weng Yao — 翁曜
Weng Yiyang — 翁一陽
Wengpai — 翁派
wu — 無
Wu — 吳
Wu Yingbin — 吳應賓號觀我
Wu Zheng, Daode zhenjingzhu —
　吳澄, 道德真經注

Wu Zhenren yanjiu — 吳真人研究
Wubenpai — 悟本派
Wubentang — 悟本堂
Wubentang guitiao — 悟本堂規條
Wudao — 舞蹈
Wugong — 午供
Wuhuangxi — 五皇戲
Wujing daquan — 五經大全
Wushishi — 無始師
Wuweijiao — 無為教
Wuxian lingguan — 五顯靈官
Wuyan lu — 無言錄
Wuyi Chongyuanguan — 武夷重元觀
Wuzhe dahui — 無遮大會

Xia — 夏
xian — 仙
xiang — 鄉
xiangxian — 鄉賢
Xiangyang Shuyuan — 向陽書院
Xianhua baochan fajuan — 慈悲懸華寶懺法卷
Xianshengtang — 先聖堂
Xiantianjiao — 先天教
Xianyou — 仙游
xiao — 孝
Xiao Heyi — 蕭合一
Xiao Pingxie — 蕭平諧
Xiao Yiping, Mazu yanjiu ziliao huibian — 蕭一平,媽祖研究資料匯編
Xiao Yunju — 蕭雲舉
Xiaodaochang qijian yiwen, jingong yiwen — 小道場啓建儀文
xiaoqi — 小器
Xiaoshi yiwen — 小施儀文
Xiashantang — 霞山堂
Xiawu jingcuan — 夏午經纂
Xiawu jingxun — 夏午經訓
Xiawuni — 夏午尼
Xiawunishi sanjiaodushi dazongshi — 夏午尼師三教度師大宗師
Xiaxintang — 夏心堂
xiayuan — 下元

Xie Hui, Laozijicheng — 薛蕙,老子集成
Xie Liangzuo (Shangcai) — 謝良佐,上蔡
Xie Zhaozhe, Wu zacu — 謝肇淛,五雜俎
Xie tiandi — 謝天地
Xietian Dadi — 協天大帝
Xihong — 西洪
Ximing — 西銘
xin — 心
xinbing — 心病
Xinda — 心大
xinfa — 心法
xing — 性
xing (form) — 形
Xingan Huiguan — 興安會館
Xinghua — 興化
Xingli daquan — 性理大全
Xingling — 性靈
xingming — 性命
xingnuo — 行儺
xingtian — 行天
Xinhaijing — 心海經
Xinjing — 心經
xin, shen, xingming — 心神性命
Xinsheng zhizhi — 心聖直指
xinxing — 心性
Xinxingci — 心性祠
Xishengjing — 西昇經
xiucai — 秀才
Xiwangmu — 西王母
Xuange — 玄歌
Xuanhuaci — 玄化祠
Xuanmiaoguan — 玄妙觀
Xuantan — 玄談
Xuantan yuanshuai — 玄壇元帥
Xuantian shangdi — 玄天上帝
Xue Dachun — 薛大純
Xuefengsi — 雪峰寺
Xuehu fachan — 血湖法懺
Xueshengci — 學聖祠
xunqi — 順氣
Xu Shiyang — 許仕揚
Xu Wanren — 徐萬仞

Xu Wenpu, zi Zuoheng — 徐文浦 字左恆

yan — 衍
Yan Jiunie — 閻九臬
Yan Junping, Daode zhiguilun — 嚴君平, 道德指歸論
yanchang — 演場
yang — 陽
Yang Jiajiang — 楊家將
Yang Qiyuan — 楊起元
Yang Shi (Guishan) — 楊時, 龜山
Yang Sizhi, zi Yuanshu — 楊四知字元述
Yang Taishi — 楊太師
Yang Zhizhai — 楊質齋
Yangfan — 揚幡
Yanggong taishi shengdan yiwen — 楊公太師聖誕儀文
Yangxinci — 養心祠
Yangxing Yaofang — 養性藥房
Yanluo Wang — 閻羅王
Yanping — 延平
Yao (people) — 瑤族
Yao (hero) — 堯
Yaochi shuyuan — 瑤池書院
Yaochidao — 瑤池道
Yaodaoci — 瑤島祠
yaoren — 妖人
Yaoshiwang — 藥師王
yaoyan — 謠言
Yi Daotan — 易道譚
yigui (return) — 以歸
Yijie liyu — 易解俚語
yin — 陰
Yin Zhenren, Xingming xuangxiu wanshen guizhi — 尹真人, 性命雙修萬神圭旨
Yinfujing — 陰符經
yingguo — 應果
Yingling bozhu — 英靈伯主
yinshen saihui — 迎神賽會
yinsi — 淫祠
Yintai — 印台
Yishengci — 義聖祠

yixing — 義行
Yiyuantang — 一源堂
Yizimen — 義子門
yong — 用
Yongzheng — 雍正
you — 有
Yu — 禹
Yu Shizhang — 俞士章
yuan, heng, li, zhen — 元亨利貞
Yuan Hongdao — 袁宏道
Yuan Huang — 袁黃
Yuanjiejing — 圓解經
yuanshen — 元神
Yuanshen shiyi — 元神釋義
Yuanshi Tianzun — 元始天尊
Yuanxi — 願戲
yuanzhai — 怨債
Yuan Zongdao — 袁宗道
Yue — 越
Yue Zheng — 岳正
Yuexiuci — 岳秀祠
Yuhuang Shangdi — 玉皇上帝
Yuhuici — 玉慧祠
Yulanpen hui — 盂蘭盆會
Yulinci — 玉麟祠
Yumingci — 玉明祠
Yunqi Zhuhong — 云棲袾宏
Yushanci — 玉山祠
Yushu xingjun — 玉樞星君
Yuxici — 玉溪祠
Yuzhang — 豫章

zai zao qiankun — 再造乾坤
zaochao — 早朝
Zaojun jingchan — 灶君經懺
zao qiankun — 造乾坤
Zhaijiao — 齋教
Zhandouci — 瞻斗祠
Zhang Qin, Kaoli zhengsu baocun shenshe shuodie — 張琴, 考禮正俗保存神社說諜
Zhang Daoling — 張道陵
Zhang Daoxue — 張道學
Zhang Diye — 張帝爺
Zhang Gong — 張公

Zhang Hongdu, zi Shengzi, hao Yilin — 張洪都字升子號翼林
Zhang Juzheng — 張居正
Zhang Qin — 張琴
Zhang Sanfeng — 張三丰
Zhang Tianyi — 章天乙
Zhang Zai — 張載
Zhanggong shengjun baojing — 張公聖君寶經
Zhangjiao — 掌教
Zhangjiao — 張教
Zhangjiaoshi — 掌教師
Zhangzhou — 漳州
Zhangzhou Wuzhenren yanjiuhui, Wuzhenren xueshu yanjiu wenji — 漳州吳真人研究會, 吳真人學術研究文集
Zhao Gongming, Xuantan — 趙公明, 玄壇
Zhaohun — 招魂
zhen chu chu — 真出處
Zhen Dexiu — 真德修
Zhen Lai, hao Liaoxuan — 真賴號了玄
Zheng Erqing — 鄭而清
Zheng Xuegui — 鄭學規
Zheng Zhenman — 鄭振滿
　Ming Qing Fujian jiazu zuzhi yu shehui bianqian — 明清福建家族組織與社會變遷
Zheng Zhiming, — 鄭志明
　Minjiande sanjiao xinfa — 民間的三教心法
　Mingdai Sanyijiaozhu yanjiu — 明代三一教主研究
　Zhongguo shanshu yu zongjiao — 中國善書與宗教
zheng qi — 正氣
Zhengshun Shenghou — 正順聖候
zhengxie — 政協
Zhengyipai — 正乙派
Zhengzong tonglun — 正宗統論
zhenxiaoxi — 真消息
Zhenwu — 真武
zhi — 治

Zhizhongci — 執中祠
Zhizhong shuyuan — 執中書院
zhong — 忠
Zhongheweiyujing — 中和位育經
Zhongmenzhen — 忠門鎮
Zhongmiaoxuanjing — 眾妙玄經
Zhongshantang — 中善堂
Zhongyong zhengyi zheyao — 中庸正義摘要
zhongyuan — 中元
Zhou Dashi — 周大師
Zhou Dunyi — 周敦頤
zhoutian — 周天
Zhu Bajie — 豬八戒
Zhu Fengshi, hao Xuhui — 朱逢時號虛惠
Zhu Guangyu, zi Deming, hao Wen-lu — 朱光宇字德明號文麓
Zhu Heng, zi Shinan, zi Weiping, hao Zhenshan — 朱衡字士南又字惟平號鎮山
Zhu Hong — 袾宏
Zhu Kun — 朱昆
Zhu Weiguan, Fujian shigao — 朱維杆, 福建史稿
Zhu Xi — 朱熹
Zhu Yizun, Jingzhiju shihua — 朱一尊, 靜志居詩話
Zhu Youkai — 朱有開
Zhu Zhihe — 祝致和
zhuang — 狀
Zhuangyanjing — 庄嚴經
zhudeng — 祝燈
Zhuguangci — 珠光祠
Zhuguang Shuyuan — 珠光書院
Zhuo Wanchun — 卓晚春
Zhuo Xiaoxian — 卓小仙
Zhusheng zhenbaojing, Jinbiao qing-shen song — 諸神真寶經進表請神頌
Zhushen shengdan yiwen — 諸神聖誕儀文
Zhushi Laoye xiangfan jiapu — 住世老爺降凡家譜
Zhushou yiwen — 祝壽儀文

Zhutanshi — 主壇師
ziduzhe — 自度者
Ziguzi — 自谷子
Zimao shan — 紫帽山
ziran erran ye — 自然而然也
Zitong huashu — 梓桐化書
Ziwei Dadi — 紫微大帝
Ziyangtang — 紫陽堂
zizao xingming — 自造性命
zongchi — 總持
zongjiao — 宗教
Zongkongtang — 宗孔堂

zongli — 總理
Zong Nianjiu — 宗念九
Zongshanci — 宗山祠
Zongshengtang — 宗聖堂
Zongxingtang — 宗興堂
Zou Yuanbiao — 鄒元標字爾瞻別
　號南白
Zucipai — 祖祠派
zucuo — 祖厝
Zuishangyi chengjing — 最上一乘經
Zunshengci — 尊聖祠

· B I B L I O G R A P H Y ·

PRIMARY SOURCES ON THE THREE IN ONE

Printed Texts

Dongshan jicao (Collected drafts from East Mountain), Dong Shi, collophon, 1677.

Jinling zhongyitang xingshi (True activities of the One in the Center Temple of Jinling [Nanjing]), Zhen Lai, included in an early edition of the *Linzi chuanji* (Complete collected works of Master Lin), preserved in the Beijing Library and at the Gest Library, Princeton University, editions of the *Linzi quanji,* in the second half of the final juan (36) of the collection.

Jiuxu zheyan neijingtu, Lin Longjiang, ed. Lu Wenhui, 1583; 1920s reprint; 1986 reprint.

Jujia tongsu liyu (Common sayings on dwelling at home), Lin Huaiyu, printed in 1994.

Lin Longjiang Xiansheng nianpu (Chronological biography of Master Lin Dragon River) (including the *Puguang xiaoshi* [Brief history of Puguang Academy]), lithographic edition, no date (circa 1989).

Linzi bentijing shilue (Interpretation of the Scripture of Original Substance of Master Lin), Liang Puyao, Guangxu 14 (1888); 1986 reprint.

Linzi benxing shilu (True record of the actions of Master Lin), comp. Lu Wenhui, Chen Zhongyu, and Dong Shi, 1655; 1940 reprint; 1969 Taipei reprint.

Linzi menxian shilu (True record of the sagely disciples of Master Lin), Dong Shi, 1672; 1910 reprint.

Linzi nianpu (Chronological biography of Master Lin), Lin Zhaoke, 1610; 1983 reprint.

Linzi quanji ("Complete collected Works of Master Lin), preserved in the Beijing Library and at the Gest Library, Princeton University.

Linzi sanjiao zhengzong tonglun, 36 juan, Lin Zhao'en; 1986 reprint, Putian, in lithographic form. For a detailed table of contents, see Berling (1980).

Longhua biezhuan (Alternative account of the Dragon Flower [Assembly]), Lin Zhenming, preface, 1610.

Mingxiaji (Collection on illumining Xia), 4 juan, Lin Zhenming, 1598 preface. 1980's reprint.

Sanhui chanwen (Litany of the Three Assemblies), Lu Wenhui. N.d.

Sanjiao chuxue zhinan (Pointers for the beginning study of the Three Teachings), collated by Chen Zhida (d. 1872); 1986 mimeograph reprint, Putian.

Sanyijiaozhu shuo Mile zunfo baojing (The Precious Scripture of the Revered Maitreya Buddha as spoken by the Lord of the Three in One), Lin Longjiang, ed. Lu Wenhui. N.d.

Sanyijiaozhu Xiawuni bentijing, Lin Longjiang, ed. Lu Wenhui. N.d.

Shitan (Poetic discussions), Liang Puyao, printed from a manuscript in 1984, ed. Xu Shiyang.

Sishu zhengyi (Correct meaning of the Four Books), ed. Zhang Hongdu. N.d.

Xiaojing, Classic of Filial Piety. N.d.

Xiawunijing (The scriptures of Xiawuni), 12 vol., ed. Lu Wenhui; 1920 reprint; 1989 reprint (4 vol.).

Xiawunijingxun (Essence of the scriptures of Lord Xia), ed. Lu Wenhui. 1980s reprint.

Xiawunijing cuan (Abstract of the scriptures of Lord Xia), ed. Lu Wenhui. 1980s reprint.

Xiawuni sancai pudu zhengjing (True scripture for the Universal Salvation of the Hungry Ghosts by the Three Talents of Lord Xiawuni). Taipei: Yucheng wenju yishuachang, 1984.

Xinhaijing (Scripture of the Sea of the Heart), Zhu Xuhui, 1590; 1977 manuscript; 1989 reprint.

Yangzhenji (Collection on cultivating perfection), 2 vols., preface Qianlong *dingmao* (1747 or 1807), postscript to [re]printing dated Daoguang 15 (1835); 1989 lithographic reprint.

Yuhebian (Collection on the harmony of the universe), Lin Zhaoke. N.d.

Zhengzong yizhilu (Record of easily comprehended aspects of the comprehensive teachings), ed. Hansantang (Shrine of the Embodiment of the Three [Teachings]), 1921.

Zhenjiabao buyi (Supplement to the treasures that vouchsafe the home), 2 vols., 1935.

Zhenjiabao zhengyi (True collection of the treasures that vouchsafe the home), 3 vols., preface 1917.

Zhuowu shiyi (True meaning of [Master] Zhuo [Wanchun]), Lin Zhenming. N.d.

Zhuozu zhenren zhi (Record of the Perfected Being, the Ancestor Zhuo [Wanchun], contemporary mimeographed and stapled text added to the 1986 edition of the *Sanjiao chuxue zhinan* (see above).

Three in One Liturgical Manuscripts (Including Alchemical Manuscripts and Scriptures)

KEY

DXC Collection of a liturgist attached to the Chengsan shuyuan, a branch temple of the Daxingci

LGP Collection of Lin Guoping, Shifan University, Fuzhou, Fujian

NST Collection of the Naishengtang, Hall of the Arrived Sage, Laidian, Xianyo

SDT Collection of the Shandetang, Halll of Excellent Virtue, in Hanjiang

ZDC Collection of the Zhandouci: Shrine for Staring at the Dipper, in Fengting, Xianyou

Beiji xuantianshangdi baojing (Precious scripture of the High Emperor of the Dark Heavens of the Northern Polestar), NST

Bihun yiwen (Liturgy for the completion of marriage), SDT

Caiqing yingjing yiwen (Liturgy for the raising of the banner of color and good fortune), ZDC

Chanba canshen yangfan yiwen (Liturgy for the litany of deliverance for the summoning of the soul by the raising of the banner), NST

Chuanbo xiangwen jiehao yiwen (Liturgy for the bestowal of the bowl [ordination] and the explication of the text and interpretation of the [ritual] name), NST

Chuyou jiejia zhujia zaji (Miscellaneous collection for the processions of the gods, the receptions of the palanquins, and the settling on the altar of the gods), NST

Cibei sanmei jiuchanwen (Ninefold litany of merciful samadhi), LGP

Cijizhenjun shengdan yiwen (Liturgy for the celebration of the birthday of the True Lord of Merciful Salvation), ZDC

Dacheng xinjing (The Heart Sutra of the Great Vehicle), NST

Daodejing quanben (Complete text of the Way and its power), ZDC

Dasheng Beidouxingjun yansheng baojing (Precious scripture of the Great Saints, the astral lords of the Northern Dipper, for the prolongation of life), ZDC

Dawu gong yiwen (Great [Xia]wu liturgy of offering), ZDC

Daxingshuyuan yangeji (Record of the development of the Great Flourishing Academy), ed. Huang Chengyi et al., manuscript, ca. 1945, DXC

Dazang zhengjing xuepen (Correct scripture from the Tripitaka for the Blood Pool ritual), ZDC

Dianyan keyice (Set of liturgies for the dotting of the eyes [i.e., the consecration of a statue of a god]), LGP

Dizang pusa benyuan jingjuan (3 juan) (Scripture on fundamental causes by Ksitigarbha), ZDC; LGP

Dizang renshi shiye yiwen (Liturgy of the ten deeds of benevolent teacher Ksitigarbha, Lord of the Underworld), ZDC; LGP

Dizang shiye zhenyan baojing (Precious sutra of the True Words and Ten Deeds of Ksitigarbha), NST

Dongqu Siming zaojing yuanwen (Primal scripture of the Stove God, master of fate of the Eastern Kitchen), NST

Dongyue baojing (Precious scripture of the [Emperor] of the Eastern Peak), LGP

Dongyue tianji jingwen baodian (Precious scripture of the Heavenly Savior, the [Emperor] of the Eastern Peak), NST

Foshuo dacheng Amito baojing (Precious Amitabha Sutra of the Great Vehicle, as spoken by the Buddha), NST

Foshuo Guanyin xiaozai baojing (Precious sutra of the Elimination of Disaster by Guanyin, as spoken by the Buddha), NST

Foshuo huzhudongzi duoluoni jing (Dharani scripture for the protection of all youths, spoken by the Buddha), ZDC

Foshuo Shousheng juansheng baojing (Precious sutra of the invincible success of longevity, spoken by the Buddha), NST

Foshuo tudi huangmiao baojing (Precious scripture of the Yellow Marvel of the Earth God, spoken by the Buddha), ZDC

Gaoshang yuhuang benxing jijing (Collected scripture on deeds of the High Jade Emperor), LGP (*zhenjing*); NST (*shang zhong xia*)

Gaoshang Yuhuang tianzun shezui baochan (shang, zhong, xia) (Precious litany of the forgiveness of sins by the Heavenly Perfected High Jade Emperor), NST

Gaowang Guanshiyin jing (Scripture of the High King Guanshiyin), ZDC

Genbeifa (Method of [fixing the mind upon the] Gen [hexagram] in the back)

Gongku yiwen (Liturgy for the offering to [replenish] the Treasury), ZDC; LGP

Gongshen yiwen (Offering liturgy), ZDC

Gongzu gongye yiwen (Liturgy for making offerings to ancestors and patrons), LGP

Guanyin xiaozai baojing (Precious scripture for the elimination of disaster by [Bodhisattva] Guanyin)

Guitiao (Regulations), SDT

Huace (Flowery [choreographic] manual), ZDC

Jiantan qingsheng yiwen (Liturgy for the establishment of an altar and the invitation of the gods); followed by a *Wugong qiwanjian yiwen* (Liturgy for the midday and evening offerings to the ancestors); followed by a *Ji gao yiwen* (Liturgy for the sacrifice to the [soul summoning] banner), SDT

Jiantan sajing yuanxiao/baoan yiwen (Liturgy for the establishment and purification of an altar for Upper Prime/Preservation of Peace rites), NST

Jianxiu qijian (Commencement and establishment of an altar for the refinement of the ancestors), ZDC

Jianxiu qing shenganwei yiwen (Liturgy for inviting the ancestors into their spirit tablets during a requiem service), ZDC

Jiaozhu zhushou yiwen (Liturgy to congratulate the Lord of the Teachings on his longevity), LGP

Jieyuan yiwen (Liturgy for the repayment of vows), ZDC

Jifu yiwen (Liturgy for the sacrifice of the goddess [of childbirth]), ZDC

Jinbiao yiwen (Liturgy for the presentation of the memorial), ZDC

Jinggang panruo puoluomijing (Puoluomiduojing), NST

Jingsheng yiwen (Liturgy for the purification of sacrificial offerings), LGP

Jiutian Tian Sheng Yuanshuai jiujie baojing (Precious scripture of the salvation from the kalpa by the Saintly Marshal Tian of the Nine Heavens [Tian Gong Yuanshuai]) LGP

Jiuxu yaojue xuzhi (Essential information on the nine phases) manuscript, LGP

Juanshe yiwen (Liturgy for the transmission of a pardons)

Kaiguang dianyan yiwen (Liturgy for the opening to the light [consecration of a statue] by the dotting of eyes), NST

Kaoshang yiwen (Liturgy for the feasting [of spirit soldiers])

Lanpen qingshen yiwen (Liturgy for the requesting of pardon at a Ullambana rite), LGP

Laoshi zhushen dianyan yiwen (Liturgy for the dotting the eyes [i.e., consecration of statues] of the masters and various gods), ZDC

Leizun puhua yushu baojing (Precious Scripture of the Thunder Lord of Universal Transformation of the Jade Pivot) NST

Longhua biezhuan (Alternate account of the Dragon Flower [Assembly], written by Lin Zhenming), NST

Longhua sanhui chanwen (Third Assembly of the Dragon Flower Litany), written by Lu Wenhui

Longjiang, Zhang, Zhuo Zhenren jingshi (Scriptural history of the Realized Beings [Lin] Longjiang, Zhang [Sanfeng], and Zhuo [Wanchun]

Miaofa lianhuajing, Guanshiyin pusa pumenpin (Most marvelous Lotus Flower Scripture), NST

Mingxia Guanshengfuzi baojing (Mingxia precious scripture of the Saintly Master Guan [Gong]), DXC

Mingxia jingxun baojing (Mingxia precious scripture of the Essentials of the Scripture [of Xiawuni]), DXC

Mingxia Rangguan guoxian yiwen (Mingxia liturgy for the deliverance from the passes of adversity and the safe passage through danger), DXC

Mulian jingpeng yiwen (Liturgy for the purification of the stage by Mulian), LGP

Nandou yanshou zhenjing (True scripture of the Southern Dipper for the prolongation of life), ZDC

Neike xingnan (Satchel for carrying out inner liturgy), (LGP)

Pumen zhenjing (True scripture of Pumen Guanyin), ZDC; LGP (*Miaofa pumen zhenjing*)

Pushi yiwen (Liturgy for the distribution [of blessed food to hungry ghosts]), LGP

Pu(tian), Xian(you), Hui(an) gecun gongshepu (Register of the village shrines and temples of Hui'an, Xianyou, and Putian), ZDC

Qijian tongchang yiwen (Liturgical songs for establishment of the altar rites)

Qijian yiwen (Liturgy for the establishment of an altar), ZDC

Qinggong yiwen (Liturgy for a pure offering), SDT

Qingmenyou yiwen (Liturgy for the invitation of the [Three in One] initiates), ZDC

Qingtu qijian wudi zhenku ke (Liturgy for the replenishing of the treasury, the consecration of ground turned for construction belonging to the Five Emperors), ZDC

Qingtu qiwudi zhenku ke (Liturgy for the consecration of earth, the summoning forth of the five emperors, and the replenishment of the treasury), ZDC

Qitian dasheng shengdan yiwen (Liturgy for the celebration of the birthday of the Great Sage Equal to Heaven), ZDC

Rangguan guoxian yiwen (Liturgy for the deliverance from the passes of adversity and the safe passage through danger), ZDC

Rangguan yiwen (Liturgy for the deliverance from the passes [of adversity]), LGP

Ru, Dao, Shi Shengdan (Sacred birthdates of Confucian [sages], Daoist [immortals], and Buddhas)

Ru, Dao, Shi, Xia Sinijinglue (Extracted scriptures of the Four Ni: Confucian, Daoist, Buddist, and Xia), NST

Rujiao zhisheng xianshi Rujing (Confucian scripture of the Most Saintly Former Masters of Confucianism), NST

Rujing baojing (Precious scriptures of the Confucian Classics), ZDC

Sancheng jiupin liantai badu yiwen (Liturgy for the salvation of [the deceased] by means of the Three Vehicles Nine Grades Lotus Platform), NST

Sanguan baojing (Precious scripture of the Three Officials [of Heaven, Earth, and Water], ZDC; LGP

Sanjiao caiqing jingtan yiwen (Three Teachings liturgy for the brilliant blessing and purification of the altar), LGP

Sanjiao chanhui jieyuan yiwen (Three Teachings liturgy for the elimination of grievances and the confessions of wrongdoings), LGP

Sanjiao faguan wanchao yiwen (Three Teachings liturgy for the sending off of documents for the Evening Audience), LGP

Sanjiao fazou yiwen (Three Teachings liturgy for the presentation of a memorial), LGP

Sanjiao gao jiutian xuanxiang yiwen (Three Teachings liturgy for a communal sacrifice for the announcement of the mystic symbols of the Nine Heavens), ZDC

Sanjiao gongshen yiwen (Three Teachings liturgy for the offering to the gods), ZDC

Sanjiao guanxian yiwen (Liturgy for the crossing of dangerous passes), LGP

Sanjiao guitiao (Regulations of the Three Teachings), LGP

Sanjiao huishen yiwen (Three Teachings liturgy for the assembling of the gods), LGP

Sanjiao jianxiu shezhao yiwen (Three Teachings liturgy for the summoning of souls and the cultivating of ancestors), LGP

Sanjiao jianxiu zidu qijian (Three Teachings [liturgy] for the establishment of an altar for the ritual salvation [of the decreased] through a requiem service), ZDC

Sanjiao jindan fahui jue (Secret instructions on the flowering of the golden elixir of the Three Teachings), by Dong Xizu, 1722, manuscript copy dated 1917

Sanjiao jingsheng yiwen (Three Teachings liturgy for the purification of [meat] offerings), NST

Sanjiao jiulian yiwen (Three Teachings liturgy for a Three Teaching's Nine Lotus [rite]), LGP

Sanjiao kaiguang duxun qijian (Three Teachings [liturgy for the] commencement of the ritual of the week of mourning and dotting of the spirit tablet [of the ancestor]), ZDC

Sanjiao lanpen dahui yiwen (Three Teachings liturgy for the Great Ullambana Assembly)

Sanjiao lanpen zhuyu yiwen (Three Teachings Ullambana liturgy for the sending of prayers to the underworld), ZDC

Sanjiao longhua jiantan (Three Teaching's [liturgy] for the construction of an altar for a Dragon Flower Assembly [rite])

Sanjiao longhua jiantan jinbiao yong (For use in Three Teaching's Dragon Flower Assembly [rites] of constructing an altar and presenting a memorial), ZDC

Sanjiao longhua jianxiu pudu yiwen (Three Teaching's liturgy for a Dragon Flower Assembly universal deliverance sacrifice)

Sanjiao longhua jiaodao bagua wufang yiwen (Liturgy for the communal sacrifice of the Eight Trigrams and the Five Directions of the Dragon Flower Assembly of the Three Teachings), ZDC; LGP

Sanjiao longhua jiaodao daochang yiwen (Three Teachings liturgy for a Dragon Flower Assembly communal sacrifice Land of the Way rite), ZDC

Sanjiao longhua jiaodao jingong yiwen (Three Teachings liturgy for a Dragon Flower Assembly communal sacrifice presentation of offerings), ZDC

Sanjiao shang, zhong, xiayuan shushi (Three Teachings documentary forms for Upper, Middle, and Lower Prime [rites])

Sanjiao shiwang huanbao jing (Three Teachings scripture of the karmic retribution of the Ten Kings [of the underworld]), NST

Sanjiao xiaoshi yiwen (Three Teachings liturgy for the minor distribution [food to the hungry ghosts]), ZDC

Sanjiao xie/qing zu yiwen (Three Teachings liturgy for thanksgiving/congratulations to the ancestors)

Sanjiao xinfa (Three Teachings heart method), manuscript copied in the Huibai Fuyang Zongzhengci, now in the collection of the Jingshanci in Kennai village, Fengting, Xianyou

Sanjiao yansheng dapeng jingtai yiwen (Three Teachings prolongation of life liturgy for the purification of the great stage platform), ZDC

Sanjiao yansheng fazou jinbiao yiwen (Three Teachings prolongation of life [liturgy] for the announcement and presentation of the memorial) NST

Sanjiao yansheng jiantan baojing (Three Teachings prolongation of life scripture for the establishment of an altar), NST

Sanjiao yansheng puji yiwen (Three Teachings prolongation of life liturgy for universal salvation), NST

Sanjiao yanshen yiwen (Three Teachings liturgy for the feasting of the gods), ZDC; LGP

Sanjiao yinjing yiwen (Three Teachings liturgy for the summoning banner), NST; LGP

Sanjiao zhongshi yiwen (Three Teachings liturgy for the Middle Prime feedings of the [hungry ghosts])

Sanjiao zhuanlun baozang yiwen (Three Teachings liturgy for the revolving of the cylinders of the precious canon), NST

Sanjiao zhushou yiwen (Three Teachings liturgy for the wishing of longevity [upon a birthday]), ZDC

Sanjiao zidu fashi yiwen (Three Teachings liturgy for the assistance and deliverance of the deceased, and the sending forth of messengers), NST

Sanjiao zidushe yiwen (Three Teachings liturgy for the assistance, deliverance and raising up [of the deceased])

Sanjingduxun qijian; duxun jingong yiwen (Three Scriptures liturgy for the establishment of the altar and the presentation of offerings during the week of mourning), ZDC

Sanmei shuichanfa (shang, zhong, xia) (The Samadhi water litany rites), NST

Sanyijiaozhu lingqian (lu yu Dongshan zuci cungao) (Numinous divinatory poetry of the Lord of the Three in One, recorded at the Ancestral Shrine on East Mountain)

Sanyijiaozhu Xiawuni bentijing (Scripture of the Fundamental Substance of Xiawuni, the Lord of the Three in One), SDT; NST; ZDC

Sanyuan, sanpin, sanguan dadi baojing (Precious scripture of the Great Emperors of the Three Origins, the Three Classes, and the Three Offices [of Heaven, Earth, and Water], NST

Sashi liuliguang rulai benyuan gongdejing (Scripture of the great good merit of the original vow of the Buddha of the Future), ZDC

Shangyang shuyuan lu Ru, Dao, Shi shengdan (Xiangyang Academy list of the sacred birthdates of Confucian (sages), Daoist (immortals), and Buddhas)

Shangyuan tianguan sifu baochan (Precious litany of the Celestial Officials of the Upper Prime who bequeath good fortune), ZDC; NST; LGP

Shengjiao Kongmen xiaojing zhengwen (Orthodox text of the Scripture of filial piety of the saintly teachings of Confucianism), NST

Shengmu danchen yiwen (Liturgy for the birthday of the Saintly Mother [Mazu]), ZDC

Shezhao yiwen (Liturgy for commanding [spirit-soldiers]), ZDC

Shi'er gong chan (Litany of the twelve officials), LPG

Shi'er guangdeng zhaohun yiwen (Liturgy for the summoning of the soul [by means of] the Twelve Shining Lamps), LGP

Shi'er guangfo yiwen (Liturgy of the Twelve Radiant Buddhas), ZDC

Shi'er guangwang pinjie lingwen (Divine text of the gathas of the Twelve Radiant Kings), NST

Shishuo Mile zunfo baojing (Precious sutra of the Maitreya Buddha, as spoken by the Master), NST

Shiwang huanbaojing (Scripture on the repayment of debts to the Ten Kings), ZDC; LGP

Shixian yiwen (Liturgy for the Tenfold Offering), LGP

Shuideng yiwen (Liturgy for the Water Lamp Ritual), ZDC; LGP

Shuiguan xiayuan jie'e xuanbaochan (Mystic precious litany for the deliverance from adversity by the Water Officials of the Lower Prime [10/15]), ZDC

Shuowang, zao, wan gong chashui jing (Scripture [for recitation at] morning and evening bimonthly offerings of tea), SDT

Simashengwang shengdan yiwen (Liturgy for the celebration of the birthday of the saintly King Sima), ZDC

Sinibaojing (Precious scripture of the Four Lords [Confucius, Laozi, Śākyamuni Buddha, and Lin Zhao'en (Xiawuni)]), ZDC

Sugong yiwen (Liturgy for the presentation of vegetarian offerings), NST

Taishang lingbao buxie zaowang miaojing (Marvelous scripture of thanksgiving to the Most High Spiritual Treasure King of the Stove)

Taishang Laojun Daode baojing (Precious scripture of the Way and its power of the Most High Lord Lao), NST

Taishang xuanling beidou yansheng baojing (Precious scripture for the prolongation of life of the mystic spiritual powers of the Most High Northern Dipper), NST

Taishang xuanling beidou zhenjing (True scripture of the Most High Mystical Power of the Northern Dipper)

Taishang xuantian xiezui baochan (Precious litany for the excusing of wrongdoing by the Most High [Emperor] of the Dark Heavens), LGP

Taishang zaojing yiwen (Liturgy for the Most High Scripture of the Stove), NST

Tiangong yuanshuai shengdan yiwen (Liturgy for the celebration of the birthday of Commander Tian), ZDC

Tiansheng baojing (Precious scripture of the Saint Tian), ZDC

Wenbu xiama yiwen (Liturgy for the dismounting of the [officials] of the Bureau of Pestilence), LGP

Wenchang dijun yinzhi baojing (Precious scripture on the secret good deeds performed by Emperor Wenchang), ZDC; NST; LGP

Wugong jinggong yiwen (Liturgy for the presentation of offerings at the Noon Offering), LGP

Wulei baochan (Precious litany for the Five Thunder [Gods]), ZDC

Wuxian lingguang benxing yuanwen (Prime text of the deeds of the Precious Officials of the Five Manifestations), NST

Xiajiao baibiao zaochao yiwen (Xia teaching liturgy for the worshipful presentation of the memorial during the morning audience), NST

Xiajiao caizhou huazhou yiwen (Xia teaching liturgy for the [sending off] of a painted or flower boat)

Xiajiao chubiao shenxiang yiwen (Xia teaching liturgy for detailing of [the contents of the] initial memorial), NST

Xiajiao duxun yiwen (Xia teaching liturgy for the week of mourning), NST

Xiajiao hu'erzi duolouni jing (Xia teaching dharani scripture for the protection of children), DXC

Xiajiao jianxiu jianling yiwen (Xia teaching liturgy for worshiping and establishing of a spirit tablet [for the deceased]), NST

Xiajiao jinchen shigong yiwen (Xia teaching liturgy for the presentation of the ten offerings), NST

Xiajiao jingong songsheng yiwen (Xia teaching liturgy for the presentation of offerings and the sending off of the saints), NST

Xiajiao jingong wanke yiwen (Xia teaching liturgy for the presentation of offerings in the evening service), NST

Xiajiao longhua sanhui chanwen (Xi teaching litany for the Third Dragon Flower Assembly), NST

Xiajiao mengshan shishi yiwen (Xia teaching liturgy for the Mengshan dispensation of food), NST

Xiajiao pufang shuideng yiwen (Xia teaching liturgy for the widespread dispersal of water lamps), NST

Xiajiao qingzhuan yiwen (Xia teaching liturgy for the celebration of seal-script [writs]), NST

Xiajiao qing tiandi quanjuance (Complete handbook for the Xia teaching blessing of heaven and earth), NST

Xiajiao qingzu anshen yiwen (Xia teaching liturgy for the invitation of an ancestral spirit to take their place in their spirit tablet), NST

Xiajiao qitan zaochao faqi yiwen (Xia teaching liturgy for the establishing and open-ing of the altar and the morning audience vespers)

Xiajiao rangguan duxian fenhua yiwen (Xia teaching liturgy for the deliverance from the passes of adversity, the safe passage through danger, and the distribution of flow-ers [for newborn children])

Xiajiao sanyuan qijian fazou jinbiao yiwen (Xia teaching Three Origins liturgy for the establishment of an altar, the announcement of a memorial, and the presentation of the memorial), NST

Xiajiao sanyuan qijian qingsheng yiwen (Xia teaching Three Origins liturgy for the extablishment of an altar and the invitation of the saints), NST

Xiajiao sanyuan shushi (Xia teaching Three Origins documentary formularies), NST

Xiajiao Shang, Zhong, Xiayuan shushi (Xia teaching documentary formularies for the Upper, Middle, and Lower Prime festivals), NST

Xiajiao shengdan qiqing yiwen (Xia teaching liturgy for invitations on the birthdays of the gods), NST

Xiajiao wufu zhudeng yiwen (Xia teaching liturgy for the blessing lamps of the five good fortunes), NST

Xiajiao xiezu yiwen (Xia teaching liturgy for offering thanksgiving to the ancestors), NST

Xiajiao xiwen, gongzu, qingzu, songzu yiwen (Xia teaching liturgy for auspicious affairs, for offering to the ancestors, for celebrating the ancestors, and for sending off the ancestors), NST

Xiajiao xuehu fachan (shang, zhong, xia) (Xia Teaching litany of the Lake of Blood: three volumes), NST

Xiajiao yansheng caiyan shugao (Xia teaching documentary forms for the feasting of the gods and the spreading forth of the colorful banquet), NST

Xiajiao yansheng Jiaoxie chanxiu mengshan yiwen (Xia teaching Mengshan liturgy for the prolongation of life for sacrifice and thanksgiving, penitence and self-cultivation)

Xiajiao yansheng tianku yiwen (Xia teaching prolongation of life liturgy for the re-plenishing of the treasury), NST

Xiajiao yansheng xiaojingong sanxian yiwen (Xia teaching prolongation of life liturgy for the minor threefold presentation of the offerings), NST

Xiajiao zhong, xia yuan niezhao yiwen (Xia teaching liturgy for the commanding [of the spirits] on the Upper, Middle, and Lower Prime festival), NST

Xiajiao zhuixiu zidu jiejie yiwen (Xia teaching liturgy for the carrying out of the giv-ing of assistance to the deceased in order to eliminate entanglements), NST

Xiajiao zidu xiubin yiwen (Xia teaching liturgy for the giving of assistance to the de-ceased and attending by the side of the coffin), NST

Xiaodaochang qijian yiwen, jingong yiwen (Liturgies for the establishment of an altar for a small-scale ritual, and for the offering ritual), ZDC

Xiaodaochang jingong shousheng jing (Scripture for prolonging life and presenting offerings for use in a small-scale ritual), ZDC

Xiaojing (Classic of filial piety), ZDC

Xiaojing zhengwen (Correct text of the classic of filial piety), ZDC

Xiaoshi yiwen (Liturgy for the minor distribution [of blessed food to the hungry ghosts], NST; LGP

Xiaozai jixiang zhou (Spells for the elimination of disaster and for good fortune)

Xiatian dongfu (The Cavern Headquarters of the Misty Heavens), ZDC

Xiawu zongshi dianyan (zhushen tongyong) (Dotting of the eyes [animation] of the Patriarch of the Xiawu [Teachings]—to be used for all other gods as well) (copied in 1990 in the Tongde shuyuan, now in the collection of the Jingshanci)

Xiawuni jingcuan, 4 juan (Compilation of Xiawuni scriptures), ZDC

Xiawunijingxun (Essentials of the scripture of Xiawuni), ZDC; NST

Xiawunishi Sanyijiaozhu pudu famen jinshu skeke chuandao kaijing shuofa guitiao (Carefully recorded regulations of the Ritual Gate for Universal Deliverance of the Lord of the Three in One, Master Xiawunishi, for the establishment of the liturgies, the transmission of the Way, the reciting of scriptures, and the Preaching of the Law) (preface, Guangxu 9 [1883], undated manuscript copy from the Shandetang in the collection of Mr. Chen Zhaojing) SDT

Xiayuan shuiguan jie'e baochan (Precious litany for the deliverance from adversity by the Lower Prime Water Official), NST; LGP

Xietian fuzi Guansheng baojing (Precious scripture of the Master who assists heaven, Saint Guan [Gong], NST

Xishi qingzu yiwen (Liturgy for the invitation of patriarchs to attend auspicious rites), NST

Xiubin jiantan chanwen (Litany for the establishment of an altar for a requiem), SDT

Xuantan Yuanshuai baojing (Precious scripture of the Marshal of the Dark Altar), NST

Xuantian shangdi chan (Litany of the High Emperor of the Dark Heavens)

Xuantian shangdi jiujie fachan (Ritual litany for the salvation from kalpas of the Supreme Emperor of the Dark Heavens), ZDC; LGP (*baochan*); *jing*

Xuehu fachan (Ritual litany for [deliverance from the] Lake of Blood) LGP

Xuepen baojing (Precious scripture of the Lake of Blood), LGP

Xuepen taigu jing (Scripture of the foetal bones within the Lake of Blood), NST

Yangfan baochan (Precious litany for the raising of the spirit banner), ZDC

Yanggong taishi shengdan yiwen (Liturgy for the celebration of the birthday of Marshal Yang), ZDC

Yanggong taishi yinglie hushi xiaozai jie'e jing (Scripture of the overcoming of adversities, the elimination of disaster, and the heroic protection of the times by Marshal Yang), LGP

Yansheng fushi dianyan yiwen (Prolongation of life liturgy for the dotting of the eyes of the Talismanic Messengers), NST

Yansheng jiaodao songsheng yiwen (Prolongation of life liturgy for sacrificial prayers to and sending off of the saints), NST

Yansheng jiaoxie yansheng yiwen (Prolongation of life liturgy for sacrifice and thanksgiving), NST

Yaoshi Liuliguang rulai benyuan gongdejing (Merit sutra of the Medical Master, the Buddha of the future of the lapus light), ZDC; LGP

Yingjing jingxing yangfan shierguang jiulian daji (Great collection of the welcoming banner, the purifying of the sacrificial victims, and the raising of the flag for the twelvefold radiant rite of the nine lotuses), ZDC

Yingjing yiwen (Liturgy for the [raising of the] welcoming banner)

Yuanxiao canyu shoubing yiwen (Liturgy for the gathering of spirit soldiers of participating households at the Upper Prime festival), LGP

Yuhuang chan (Jade Emperor litany), ZDC; LGP

Yuhuang chan quanben (Complete text of the litany of the Jade Emperor), ZDC

Yushan shuyuan yangeji (Record of the development of the Jade Mountain Academy of Bangtou Township), included in a handbook of spells and visualizations in the possession of the chief priest of the Yushanci

Yushu baojing (Precious scripture of the Jade Pivot), ZDC; LGP

Zaojun jingchan (Scripture and litany of the Stove God), ZDC

Zhanggong shengjun baojing (Precious scripture of the saintly Lord Zhang)

Zhanggong shengdan yiwen (Liturgy for the celebration of the birthday of Lord Zhang), ZDC

Zhaohun yiwen (Liturgy for the summoning of the soul), SDT

Zhizhen wuxian lingjun (Taihui jingci miaole tianzun shuo lingjun miaojing) ([Scripture] of the Perfected Beings, the marvelous lords of the Five Manifestations) (Mingxiatang), DXC

Zhongshi yiwen (Liturgy for the middle distribution [of food to the hungry ghosts]), ZDC; LGP

Zhongyuan diguan chizui baochan (Precious litany for the pardoning of wrongdoing by the Terrestrial Officials of the Central Prime), ZDC; LGP (*miezui xuanyuan baochan*), NST

Zhuanzang tiangong yiwen (Liturgy for the revolution of the cylinders for delivery to the heavenly palaces), LGP

Zhuanzang yiwen (Liturgy for the revolution of the cylinders), ZDC

Zhuozu baojing (Precious scripture of the Patriarch Zhuo) [from the Baiyundong— White Cloud Cavern]

Zhushen shengdan yiwen (Liturgy for the birthdays of the various gods), ZDC

Zhusheng zhenbaojing, jinbiao qingshen song (True precious scriptures of all the saints; chants for the presentation of the memorial and the invitation of the gods), ZDC

Zhushou yiwen (Liturgy for congratulation on longevity on a birthday)

Zhuzun liesheng qingcan shushi (Documentary forms for the praising of the various reverent saints)

Zidu gongzhai jiejie yiwen (Liturgy for the giving of assistance to save the deceased by offering vegetarian offerings to undo entanglements), NST

Zidu jitian caizhou geidie xieshi ([Liturgy for] the giving of passports and the thanking of masters in the rite of salvation by means of sacrificing to heaven with a painted boat), NST

Zidu qijian qinghun yiwen (Liturgy for the giving of assistance to save the deceased by establishing an altar and inviting the souls), NST

Zongji keyi qu (Collected song tunes for different rites), ZDC

Regional Gazetteers

[Hongzhi] *Da Ming Xinghua fuzhi* 54 juan (1503). Edited by Chen Xiao; composed by Zhou Ying and Huang Zhongzhao *tsuan*.

[Hongzhi] *Xianxi zhi*, 16 juan (1491). Chen Qian.

[Jiaqing] *Xianyou xianzhi*, 8 juan (1538). Lin Younian.

[Kangxi] *Xianyou xianzhi*. 40 juan (1678). Edited by Lu Xuechun *hsiu;* composed by Guo Yanchun.

[Kangxi] *Xinghuafu Putian xianzhi*, 36 juan, shou 1 juan (1705). Edited by Qin Gaoxie; composed by Lin Linchang.

[Minguo] *Putian xianzhi*, 40 juan (1945). Edited by Shi Youji; written by Zhang Qin.

[Qianlong] *Xianyou xianzhi*, 53 juan (1770). Edited by Hu Jizhi, Wang Chun; composed by Ye Hegan et al.

[Qianlong] *Xinghuafu Putian xianzhi,* 36 juan, shou 1 juan (1758). Edited by Wang Daqing, Wang Heng et al.; composed by Liao Biji and Lin Hong.

[Wanli] *Xinghua fuzhi,* 26 juan (1575). Edited by Lu Yijing; composed by Gang Tahe.

[Wanli] *Xinghua fuzhi,* 59 juan (1613). Edited by Ma Mengjie and Xu Mu; composed by Lin Yaoyou.

Xianxi zhi, 4 juan (1257). Edited by Zhao Youmi; composed by Huang Yansun; revised in the Yuan by Huang Zhenchong.

[Zhengtong] *Fujian Xinghua xianzhi,* 8 juan (1844). Composed and edited by Zhou Hua.

Other Primary Sources

Guan Foxin, *Putian shihua* (1966), draft manuscript, Fuzhou Shifan University Library.

He Qiaoyuan, *Minshu* (preface 1612, printed 1629) (Fujian Provincial Library). Reprinted in 5 volumes by the Fujian renmin chubanshe, 1995–96.

_____. *Mingshan zang* (Storehouse of the mountain of names), written 1586, printed in 1640.

Huang Zongxi, "Lin sanjiao juan" (Biography of Lin of the Three Teachings), in *Nanlei wen'an* (Critical comments on literature by Huang Nanlei).

Jiulidong jingce (Handbook of scriptures from the Nine Carp Cavern), undated, Singapore.

Lin Xiangje, *Ouliziji,* 1947 manuscript (Fujian Provincial Library).

Pan Jingruo, *Sanjiao kaimi guizheng yanyi* (Romance of the Three Teachings exposing delusions and returning to the truth), 100 juan, written about 1615, preserved in Tenri University Library.

Putianxian shouju Lin Longjiang Minsuwenhua xueshu yantaohui lunwenchi (Collected essays for the First Putian County Academic Conference on the Folklore and Culture of Lin Longjiang), edited by the Putianxian Minsu xuehui (Putian County Folklore Association) and the Houjiao Shimenshan Zongkongci dongshihui (Temple Committee of the Honorable Confucius Shrine of Shimen Mountain in Houjiao), 1995.

Putianxian zongjiao shiwuju, Putianxian zongjiaoshi (chugao), (Preliminary draft of the Putian County State of Religious Affairs Report), Putian, 1991.

Qiongyao zhengjing (Yuanshi tianzn shuo Qiongyao zhenxian dushi xiaozai jiuqie zhifu zhenjing) (True Scripture of the Rosegem Jasper), undated, Singapore.

Siku quanshu zongmutiyao.

Xie Zhaozhe, *Wu zacu* (Five miscellanous sacrifical plates), 16 juan, 1616; reprinted in 1789 in Japan.

Yin Zhenren, *Xingming xuangxiu wanshen guizhi* (Revealed doctrine of the dual cultivation of nature and life store taught by the myriad spirits), 4 juan, preface 1615.

Zhang Qin, *Kaoli zhengsu baocun shenshe shuodie,* undated blockprint.

Zhu Yizun, *Jingzhiju shihua.*

SECONDARY SOURCES

Ahern, Emily (1975). "The Power and Pollution of Chinese Women," in Margery Wolf and Roxanne Witke, eds., *Women in Chinese Society.* Stanford: Stanford University Press: 193–214.

_____ (1981a). *Chinese Ritual and Politics.* London: Cambridge University Press.

_____ (1981b). "The Tai Ti Kong Festival," in E. M. Ahern and Hill Gates, eds., *The Anthropology of Taiwanese Society*. Stanford: Stanford University Press: 397–426.

Ahmad, Aijaz (1992). *In Theory: Classes, Nations, Literatures*. London New York: Verso.

Anagnost, Ann S. (1987). "Politics and Magic in Contemporary China," *Modern China* 13, 1: 40–61.

_____ (1994). "The Politics of Ritual Displacement," in Charles F. Keyes, Laurel Kendall, and Helen Hardacre, eds., *Asian Visions of Authority: Religion and the Modern States of East and Southeast Asia*. Honolulu: University of Hawaii Press: 221–254.

Anderson, Benedict (1983). *Imagined Communities, Reflections on the Origin and Spread of Nationalism*. London: Verso and New Left Books.

Anderson, Samantha (1996). "Gender Performativity and Ritual Performance in South-east China." M.A. thesis, McGill University.

Appadurai, Arjun (1990). "Disjuncture and Difference in the Global Cultural Economy," *Public Culture* 2, 2 (Spring): 1–11, 15–45.

Apter, David, and Tony Saich (1994). *Revolutionary Discourse in Mao's Republic*. Cambridge: Harvard University Press.

Asad, Talal (1993). *Genealogies of Religion: Discipline and Reasons of Power in Christianity and Islam*. Baltimore: The Johns Hopkins University Press.

Bakhtin, Michael M. (1981). *The Dialogic Imagination: Four Essays*, trans. C. Emerson and M. Holquist. Austin: University of Texas Press.

_____ (1990). "The Problem of Content, Material, and Form in Verbal Art," trans. K. Brostrom, in M. Holmquist and V. Laipanov, eds., *Art and Answerability: Early Philosophical Essays*. Austin: University of Texas Press: 257–327.

Baldrain-Hussein F. (1984). *Procédés secrets du joyau magique, traité d'alchimie du XIe siècle*. Paris: Les Deux Océans.

Barlow, Tani (1993). "Theorizing Women: Funu, Guojia, Jiating," in Angela Zito and Tani Barlow, eds., *Body, Power, and Subject in China*. Chicago: University of Chicago Press: 253–290.

Bell, Catherine (1989). "Religion and Chinese Culture: Towards an Assessment of 'Popular Religion,'" *History of Religions* 29: 35–57.

_____ (1992). *Ritual Theory, Ritual Practice*. Oxford: Oxford University Press.

Bergson, Henri (1983). *Creative Evolution*, trans. Arthur Mitchell. New York, UPA, originally published by Henry Holt, 1911.

Berling, Judith (1980). *The Syncretic Religion of Lin Chao-en*. IASWR Series. New York: Columbia University Press.

_____ (1985). "Religion and Popular Culture: The Management of Moral Capital in *The Romance of the Three Teachings*," in David Johnson, A. J. Nathan, and E. S. Rawski, eds., *Popular Culture in Late Imperial China*. Berkeley, University of California Press, 1985: 188–219.

Berthier, Brigitte (1988). *La Dame au Bord de l'Eau*. Nanterre: Societé d'Ethnologie.

Bhabha, Homi (1994). "DissemiNation and Introduction," in H. Bhabha, ed., *Nation and Narration*. London: Routledge.

Bielenstein, Hans (1959). "The Chinese Colonization of Fujian until the End of T'ang," in *Studia-Serica Bernhard Karlgren Dedicata*. Copenhagen: Ejnar Munksgaard: 98–122.

Bodde, Derk (1975). *Festivals in Classical China: New Year and Other Annual Observances during the Han Dynasty, 2206 B.C.–A.D. 220*. Princeton: Princeton University Press.

Boltz, Judith (1983). "Opening the Gates of Purgatory: A Twelfth Century Taoist Meditation Technique for the Salvation of Souls," in M. Strickmann, ed., *Tantric and Taoist Studies in Honour of R. A. Stein,* vol. 2. Melange Chinois et Bouddhiques, vol. 21. Bruxelles: 487–511.

―――― (1986). "In Homage to Tian-fei," *Journal of the American Oriental Society* 106, 1: 211–232.

―――― (1987). *A Survey of Taoist Literature: Tenth to Seventeenth Century.* Berkeley: Institute of East Asian Studies China Research Monographs.

Boundas, Constatine V. (1994). "Deleuze: Serialization and Subject-Formation," in C. V. Boundas and D. Olkowski, eds., *Gilles Deleuze and the Theater of Philosophy.* New York: Routledge 99–119.

Bourdieu, Pierre (1977). *Outline of a Theory of Practice,* trans. Richard Nice. Cambridge: Cambridge University Press.

Brim, John A. (1974). "Village Alliance Temples in Hong Kong," In A. Wolf, ed., *Religion and Ritual in Chinese Society.* Stanford: Stanford University Press: 93–104.

Brokaw, Cynthia (1991). *The Ledgers of Merit and Demerit: Social Change and Moral Order in Late Imperial China.* Princeton: Princeton University Press.

Brook, Timothy (1985). "The Spatial Structure of Ming Local Administration." *Late Imperial China* 6, 1: 1–55.

―――― (1989). "Funerary Ritual and the Building of Lineages in Late Imperial China," *Harvard Journal of Asiatic Studies* 49, 2: 465–499.

―――― (1992). "Rethinking Syncretism: The Unity of the Three Teachings and Their Joint Worship in Late-Imperial China," *Journal of Chinese Religions* 13–43.

―――― (1993). *Praying for Power: Buddhism and the Formation of Gentry Society in Late-Ming China.* Cambridge: Harvard University Press.

Brown, Peter (1981). *The Cult of the Saints: Its Rise and Function in Latin Christianity.* Chicago: University of Chicago Press.

―――― (1988). *The Body and Society: Men, Women, and Sexual Renunciation in Early Christianity.* New York: Columbia University Press.

Butler, Judith (1990). *Gender Trouble: Feminism and the Subversion of Identity.* London: Routledge.

―――― (1992). *Bodies That Matter.* London: Routledge.

Bynum, Caroline W. (1991). *Fragmentation and Redemption: Essays on Gender and the Human Body in Medieval Religion.* New York: Zone Books.

Cedzich, Ursuala-Angelika (1995). "The Cult of the Wu-t'ung/Wu-hsien in History and Fiction: The Religious Roots of the *Journey to the South*," in David Johnson, ed., *Ritual and Scripture in Chinese Popular Religion, Five Studies.* Berkeley: Chinese Popular Culture Project 3: 137–218.

Chan, Wing-tsit, trans. (1963). *Instructions for Practical Living and Other Neo-Confucian Writings by Wang Yangming.* New York: Columbia University Press.

―――― (1967). *Reflection of Things at Hand: The Neo-Confucian Anthology* (by Chu Hsi and Lu Tsu-chien). New York: Columbia University Press.

Chatterjee, P. (1986). *Nationalist Thought and the Colonial World: A Derivative Discourse.* London: Zed.

―――― (1993). *The Nation and Its Fragments: Colonial and Postcolonial Histories,* Princeton: Princeton University Press.

Ch'ien, Edward (1986). *Chiao Hung and the Restructuring of Neo-Confucianism in the Late Ming,* New York: Columbia University Press.

Ch'iu Te-tsai (1981). *Taiwan miaoshen chuan* (Accounts of the temple gods of Taiwan). 4 vols. Taichung: Taiwan chih ssu miao yu shenming, Taiwansheng wenhsien weiyuan hui.

Chow, Kaiwang (1994). *The Rise of Confucian Ritualism in Late Imperial China: Ethics, Classics and Lineage Discourse*. Stanford: Stanford University Press.

Chow, Rey (1990–91). "Listening Otherwise, Music Miniaturized: A Different Type of Question about Revolution," *Discourse* 13, 1 (Winter): 129–148.

—— (1991). *Woman and Chinese Modernity: The Politics of Reading between East and West*. Minnesota: University of Minnesota Press.

Chun, Allen (1994). "From Nationalism to Nationalizing: Cultural Imagination and State Formation in Postwar Taiwan," *Australian Journal of Chinese Affairs*, no. 31 (January): 49–69.

Clark, Hugh (1991). *Community, Trade, and Networks: Southern Fujian Province from the Third to the Thirteenth Century*. Cambridge: Cambridge University Press.

—— (1995). "The Fu of Minnan: A Local Clan in the Late Tang and Song China (9th–13th Centuries)," *Journal of the Economic and Social History of the Orient* 38, 1: 1–74.

Cohen, Myron (1988). "Souls and Salvation: Conflicting Themes in Chinese Popular Religion," in James L. Watson and Evelyn S. Rawski, eds., *Death Ritual in Late Imperial China*. Berkeley: University of California Press, 180–202.

—— (1990). "Lineage Organization in North China," *Journal of Asian Studies* 49, 3: 509–534.

—— (1991). "Being Chinese: The Peripheralization of Traditional Identity," *Daedalus* 120, 2: 113–134.

Comaroff, J. (1985). *Body of Power, Spirit of Resistance: The Culture and History of a South African People*. Chicago: University of Chicago Press.

Curley, Edwin, ed. and trans. (1994). *A Spinoza Reader:* The Ethics *and Other Works*. Princeton: Princeton University Press.

Dean, Kenneth (1986). "Field Notes on Two Taoist Jiao Observed in Zhangzhou in December, 1985," *Cahiers d'Extrême-Asie* 2: 191–209.

—— (1988a). "Funerals in Fujian," *Cahiers d'Extrême-Asie* 4: 191–209.

—— (1988b). "Manuscripts from Fujian," *Cahiers d'Extrême-Asie* 4: 217–226.

—— (1990). "Mulien and Lei Yü-sheng ('Thunder Is Noisy') in the Theatrical and Funerary Traditions of Fukien," in D. Johnson, ed., *Ritual Opera/Operatic Ritual: "Mulien Rescues His Mother" in Chinese Popular Culture*. Berkeley: Institute of East Asian Studies, University of California: 46–104.

—— (1993). *Taoist Ritual and Popular Religion in Southeastern China*. Princeton: Princeton University Press.

—— (1994a). "Comic Inversion and Cosmic Renewal in the Ritual Theater of Putian: The God of Theater in Southeast China," in Wang Ch'iu-kui, ed., *Proceedings of the International Conference on Popular Beliefs and Chinese Culture*. Taipei: Center for Chinese Studies: 683–732.

—— (1994b). "Irrigation and Individuation: Cults of Water Deities along the Putian Plains," in *Proceedings of the Conference on Chinese Ritual and Ritual Theater, Min-su ch'u-yi (Folklore and Theater)* 91: 567–640.

—— (1995). "The Development of the Three-In-One Religion in Southeast China," in *Proceedings of the International Conference on Temple Fairs and Chinese Culture*. Taipei: Center for Chinese Studies: 601–670.

—— (1998). "Transformations of the She (Altars of the Soil) in Fujian," in F. Verellen, ed., *Cults of Saints/Cults of Sites, Cahier d'Extreme-Asie* 9.

Dean, Kenneth, and Brian Massumi (1992). *First and Last Emperors: The Absolute State and the Body of the Despot*. New York: Autonomedia.

Dean, Kenneth (Ding Hesheng), and Lin Guoping (1989). "'Sanyijiao' zai Fujian lishi yijide chubu kaocha" (A preliminary investigation of the historical remains of the Three in One religion in Fujian), *Fujian wenbo* (Fujian cultural journal) 13, 14: 114–119. Reprinted in expanded form in *Putianshi wenshiziliao* 8 (1993): 129–143.

Dean, Kenneth (Ding Hesheng), and Zheng Zhenman (1993). "Min-Tai Daojiao yu minjian zhushen chungbai chukao" (A preliminary investigation of Daoism and popular cult worship in Minnan and Taiwan), *Bulletin of the Institute of Ethnology, Academia Sinica* 73: 33–52.

Dean, Kenneth, and Zheng Zhenman (1993). "Group Initiation and Exorcistic Dance in the Xinghua Region," in Wang Ch'iu-kui, ed., *Minsu quyi 85: Zhongguo Nuoxi, Nuo wenhua guojiyantaohui lunwenji* (Folklore and theater: Proceedings of the International Conference on Nuo Theater and Nuo Culture), 2: 105–95.

———— (1995). *Epigraphical Materials on the History of Religion in Fujian*. Volume 1: *The Xinghua Region*. Fuzhou: Fujian People's Press.

DeBary, Wm. Theodore (1970). "Individualism and Humanitarianism in Late Ming Thought," in Wm. T. deBary, ed., *Self and Society in Ming Thought*. New York: Columbia University Press: 291–330.

———— (1975). "Neo-Confucian Cultivation and Seventeenth Century Enlightenment," in Wm. T. deBary, ed., *The Unfolding of NeoConfucianism*. New York: Columbia University Press: 141–216.

De Certeau, Michel (1984). *The Practice of Everyday Life*, trans. Steven F. Rendall, Berkeley: University of California Press.

deGroot, J. J. M. (1903–1904). *Sectarianism and Persecution in China*. Amsterdam. Reprint edition, Taipei: Ch'eng-wen, 1971.

DeLanda, Manual (1992). "Nonorganic Life," in J. Crary and S. Kwinter, eds., *Incorporations*. New York: Zone 6: 129–167.

Delehaye, Hippolyte, S. J. (1961). *The Legends of the Saints: An Introduction to Hagiography*, trans. V. M. Crawford. London: University of Notre Dame Press.

Deleuze, Gilles (1988). *Foucault*, trans. Sean Hand. Minneapolis: University of Minnesota Press.

———— (1994a). *Difference and Repetition*, trans. Paul Patton. New York: Columbia University Press.

———— (1994b). *Negotiations*, trans. Martin Joughin. New York: Columbia University Press.

Deleuze, Gilles, and Felix Guattari (1989). *Thousand Plateaus*, trans. Brian Massumi. Minnesota: University of Minnesota Press.

Duara, Prasenjit (1988a). *Culture, Power, and the State: Rural North China: 1900–1942*. Stanford: Stanford University Press.

———— (1988b). "Superscribing Symbols: The Myth of Guandi, Chinese God of War," *Journal of Asian Studies* 47, 4 (November): 778–795.

———— (1991). "Knowledge and Power in the Discourse of Modernity: The Campaigns against Popular Religion in the Early Twentieth Century," *Journal of Asian Studies* 50, 1: 67–83.

———— (1993). "De-constructing the Chinese Nation," *Australian Journal of Chinese Affairs*, no. 30 (July): 1–26.

_____ (1995). *Rescuing History from the Nation: Questioning Narratives of Modern China*. Chicago: University of Chicago Press.

Dutton, Michael R. (1992). *Policing and Punishment in China: From Patriarchy to "the People."* Cambridge: Cambridge University Press.

Ebrey, Patricia (1991a). *Chu Hsi's Family Rituals: A Twelfth Century Chinese Manual for the Performance of Cappings, Weddings, Funerals, and Ancestral Rites*. Princeton: Princeton University Press.

_____ (1991b). *Confucianism and Family Rituals in Imperial China: A Social History of Writing about Rites*. Princeton: Princeton University Press.

Ebrey, Patricia, and Peter Gregory (1993). "The Religious and Historical Landscape," in P. Ebrey and P. Gregory, eds., *Religion and Society in Tang and Sung China*. Honolulu: University of Hawaii Press: 1–44.

Elman, Benjamin A. (1984). *From Philosophy to Philology: Intellectual and Social Aspects of Change in Late Imperial China*. Cambridge: Council on East Asian Studies, Harvard University Press.

_____ (1991). "Political, Social, and Cultural Reproduction via Civil Service Examinations in Late Imperial China," *Journal of Asian Studies* 50.1: 7–28.

Elwood, Robert S. (1973). *Religious and Spiritual Groups in Modern America*. Englewood Cliffs, NJ: Prentice Hall.

Fabian, Johannes (1983). *Time and the Other*. New York: Columbia University Press.

Fang, Lienche Tu (1976). "Lin Chao-en," in L. Carrington Goodrich and Chaoying Fang, eds., *Dictionary of Ming Biography, 1368–1644*. 2 vols. New York: Columbia University Press: 1: 912–915.

Farquhar, Judith, and James Hevia (1993). "Culture and Postwar American Historiography of China," *Positions 1.2* (Fall): 486–525.

Faure, Bernard (1991). *The Rhetoric of Immediacy: A Cultural Critique of Ch'an/Zen Buddhism*. Princeton: Princeton University Press.

Faure, David (1986). *The Structure of Chinese Rural Society: Lineage and Village in the Eastern New Territories, Hong Kong*. Oxford: Oxford University Press.

Feuchtwang, Stephen (1975). "Investigating Religion," in M. Bloch, ed., *Marxist Analyses and Social Anthropology*. London: Malaby: 61–84.

_____ (1977). "School-Temple and City God," in G. W. Skinner, ed., *The City in Late Imperial China*. Stanford: Stanford University Press: 581–608.

_____ (1992). *The Imperial Metaphor: Popular Religion in China*. London: Routledge.

Finagrette, Herbert (1972). *Confucius: The Secular as Sacred*. New York: Harper and Row.

Foucault, Michel (1970). *The Order of Things (Les Mots et les Choses: une archelogoie des sciences humaines)*. New York: Pantheon.

_____ (1972). "The Subject and Power," afterword to *Michel Foucault: Beyond Structuralism and Hermeneutics,* by Herbert L. Dreyfus and Paul Rabinow. Chicago: University of Chicago Press: 208–228.

_____ (1980). "Truth and Power" [Intervista a Michel Foucault, 1977], trans. Colin Gordon, in C. Gordon, ed., *Power/Knowledge: Selected Interviews and Other Writing 1972–1977 by Michel Foucault*. Brighton, Sussex: Harvester Press: 109–133.

_____ (1988). "Technologies of the Self," in L. H. Martin, H. Gutman, and P. H. Hutton, eds., *Technologies of the Self: A Seminar with Michel Foucault*. Amherst: University of Massachusetts: 16–49.

Franke, Wolfgang (1968). *An Introduction to the Sources of Ming History*. Kuala Lumpur and Singapore: University of Malaya Press.

—— (1972). "Some Remarks on the 'Three in One Doctrine' and Its Manifestations in Singapore and Malaysia," *Oriens Extremus* 19: 121–130.

—— (1973). "Some Remarks on Lin Chao-en (1517–1598)," *Oriens Extremus* 20: 161–174.

—— (1975). "Notes on Chinese Temples and Deities in Northwestern Borneo," *Religion und Philosophie in Ostasien: Festschift fur Hans Steiniger zun 65*. Geburtstag: Wurzburg: 267–289.

—— (1980). "Some Remarks on the "Three in One Doctrine" and Its Manifestations in Singapore and Malaysia, part 2." *Oriens Extremus* 27: 267–289.

—— (1988). "Chinese Religion in Southeast Asia, with Particular Consideration of Medan, North Sumatra," *Journal of the South Seas Society* 43: 23–42.

—— (1989). *Sino-Malaysiana: Selected Papers on Ming and Qing History and on the Overseas Chinese in Southeast Asia: 1942–1988*. Singapore: South Seas Society.

Franke, Wolfgang, and Chen Tieh Fan (1983, 1985, 1987). *Chinese Epigraphic Materials in Malaysia*. 3 vols. Kuala Lumpur: University of Malaysia Press.

Franke, Wolfgang, Claudine Salmon, and Anthony K. C. Siu (1988). *Chinese Epigraphic Materials in Indonesia*, vol. 1. Singapore: South Seas Society.

Freedman, Maurice (1958). *Lineage Organization in Southeast China*. London: London School of Economics Monographs on Social Anthropology 18.

—— (1966). *Chinese Lineage and Society: Fukien and Kwangtung*. London: London School of Economics Monographs on Social Anthropology 33.

—— (1974). "On the Sociological Study of Chinese Religion," in A. P. Wolf, ed., *Religion and Ritual in Chinese Society*. Stanford: Stanford University Press: 19–42.

—— (1978). "Ritual Aspects of Chinese Kinship and Marriage," in M. Freedman, ed., *Family and Kinship in Chinese Society*. Stanford: Stanford University Press: 163–188.

Fu Yiling and Yang Guozhen, eds. (1987). *Ming Qing Fujian shehui yu xiang cun jingji* (Fujian society and village economy in Ming and Qing times). Xiamen: Xiamen University Press.

Gates, Hill (1987). "Money for the Gods: The Commoditization of the Spirit," *Modern China* 13, 3: 259–277.

Geary, Patrick (1978). *Furta Sacra: Theft of Relics in the Central Middle Ages,* Princeton: Princeton University Press.

Geertz, Clifford (1980). *Negara: The Theatre State in 19th Century Bali*. Princeton: Princeton University Press.

Gernet, Jacques (1995). *Buddhism in Chinese Society: An Economic History from the Fifth to the Tenth Centuries,* trans. Franciscus Verellen. New York: Columbia University Press (first published 1956).

Gil, Jose (1989). *Metamophoses du corp*. Paris: La Difference.

Godelier, Maurice (1978). "The Concept of the 'Asiatic Mode of Production' and Marxist Models of Social Evolution," in D. Seddon, ed., *Relations of Production*. London: 209–258.

Gold, Thomas (1993). "Go with Your Feelings: Hong Kong and Taiwan Popular Culture in Greater China," *China Quarterly* 136: 907–925.

Goodrich, L. Carrington, and Chaoyang Fang, eds. (1976). *Dictionary of Ming Biography, 1368–1644*. 2 vols. New York: Columbia University Press.

Granet, Marcel (1930). *Chinese Civilization,* trans. K. Innes and M. Brailsford. London: Keegan Paul, 1930.

Gregory, Peter (1987). *Sudden and Gradual: Approaches to Enlightenment in Chinese Thought*. Honolulu: University of Hawaii Press.

Guattari, Felix (1995). *Chaosmosis: An Ethico-Aesthetic Paradigm,* translated by Paul Bains and Julian Pefanis. Sydney: Power Publications.

Hall, David L., and Roger T. Ames (1987). *Thinking through Confucius*. Albany: State University of New York Press.

Hall, Michael (1987). "Sects," in M. Eliade et al., eds., *The Encyclopedia of Religion,* 13 vols. New York: Macmillan.

Hardacre, Helen (1989). *Shinto and the State, 1868–1988*. Princeton: Princeton University Press.

Harding, Harry (1994). "The Concept of 'Greater China': Themes, Variations, and Reservations," *China Quarterly* 136: 660–686.

Harper, Donald (1995). "Chinese Religions: The State of the Field, Part I: Warring States, Chin and Han Periods," *Journal of Asian Studies* 54.1: 152–160.

Harvey, David (1989). *The Condition of Postmodernity*. Oxford: Basil Blackwell.

Hevia, James L. (1994). "Sovereignty and Subject: Constituting Relations of Power in Qing Guest Ritual," in A. Zito and Tani Barlow, eds., *Body, Subject & Power in China*. Chicago: University at Chicago Press: 181–200.

_____ (1995) *Cherishing Men from Afar: Qing Guest Ritual and the Macartney Embassy of 1793*. Durham: Duke University Press.

Hou Ching-lang (1975). *Monnaies d'offrande et la notion de tresorerie dans la religion chinoises*. Memoires de l'Institut des Hautes Etudes Chinoises, vol. 1. Paris: College de France.

Hsia, C. T. (1974). "The Military Romance: A Genre of Chinese Fiction," in Cyril Birch, ed., *Studies in Chinese Literary Genres*. Berkeley: University of California Press: 339–390.

Hsiao, Kung-chuan (1960). *Rural China: Imperial Control in the Nineteenth Century*. Seattle: University of Washington Press.

Huang Meiying (1994). *Taiwan matsu ti hsianghuo yu ishih* (The incense and ritual of Taiwan's Matsu). Taipei: Taiwan tzuli wanpao chupanshe.

Huang, Ray (1981). *1587, A Year of No Significance: The Ming Dynasty in Decline*. New Haven: Yale University Press.

Huang Ts'ung-hsi (1987). *The Record of Ming Scholars,* trans. Julia Ching, with Chaoying Fang. Honolulu: University of Hawaii Press.

Hucker, Charles O., ed., (1969). *Chinese Government in Ming Times: Seven Studies*. New York: Columbia University Press.

_____ (1985). *A Dictionary of Official Titles in Imperial China*. Stanford: Stanford University Press.

Hummel, Arthur W., ed. (1943). *Eminent Chinese of the Ch'ing Period (1644–1912)*. 2 vols. Washington, DC: United States Government Printing Office.

Jameson, Frederic (1991). *Postmodernism, or The Cultural Logic of Late Capitalism*. Durham: Duke University Press.

Jiang Weitan, ed. (1992). *Mazu wenxian ziliao* (Documentary materials on Mazu). Fuzhou: Fujian People's Publishing House.

Johnson, David (1985). "Communication, Class and Consciousness in Late Imperial China," in David Johnson, Andrew J. Nathan, and Evelyn S. Rawski, eds., *Popular Culture in Late Imperial China*. Berkeley: University of California Press: 34–72.

Jordan, David K., and Daniel L. Overmyer (1986). *The Flying Phoenix: Aspects of Chinese Sectarianism in Taiwan*. Princeton: Princeton University Press.

Kamata, Shigeo (1986). *China's Buddhist Ceremonies*. Tokyo: Daizo.

Kendall, Laurel (1985). *Shaman, Housewives, and Other Restless Spirits: Women in Korean Ritual Life*. Honolulu: University of Hawaii Press.

Kleeman, Terry F. (1994). *A God's Own Tale: The Book of Transformations of Wenchang, the Divine Lord of Zitong*. Albany: State University of New York Press.

Kohn, Livia (1995). *Laughing at the Tao: Debates among Buddhists and Taoists in Medieval China*. Princeton: Princeton University Press.

Kuhn, Philip (1970). *Rebellion and Its Enemies in Late Imperial China: Militarization and Social Structure, 1796–1864*. Cambridge: Harvard University Press.

———— (1990). *Soulstealers: The Chinese Sorcery Scare of 1768*. Cambridge: Harvard University Press.

Laclau, Ernesto, and Chantal Mouffe (1985). *Hegemony and Socialist Strategy: Towards a Radical Democratic Politics*. London: Verso.

Lagerwey, John (1987a). *Taoist Ritual in Chinese Society and History*. New York: Macmillan.

———— (1987b). "Les têtes les démons tombent par les milliers: Le fachang, rituel exorciste du nord de Taiwan," *L'Homme* 27, 101 (January & March): 101–116.

LaMarre, Thomas (1994). "Writing Doubled Over, Broken," *positions*.

———— (1998). *The Order of the Senses: Poetry, Calligraphy, and Cosmology in Heian Japan*. Durham: Duke University Press.

Leach, Edmund (1970). *Claude Levi-Strauss*, New York: Viking.

Lefevre, Henri (1991). *The Production of Space*, trans. D. Nicholson-Smith. Oxford: Blackwell.

Le Goff, Jacques (1980). *Time, Work, and Culture in the Middle Ages*, trans. A. Goldhammer. Chicago: University of Chicago Press.

Levi, Jean (1986). "Les fonctionnaires et le divin—Luttes de pouvoir entre divinités et administrateurs dans les contes des Six Dynasties et des Tang," *Cahiers d'Extrême-Asie* 2: 81–110.

Levy, Pierre (1994). *L'intelligence collective: pour une anthropologie du cyberspace*. Paris: Éditions la découverte.

———— (1995). *Qu'est-ce que le virtuel?* Paris: Éditions la découverte.

Li Xianjiang (1979). *Boso shinko no kenkyu* (Studies in belief in Mazu). Tokyo: Bumbutsusha.

Lian Lichang (1988). *Fujian mishe* (Secret societies of Fujian). Fujian: Lujiang chubanshe.

Lin Chengbin (1995). "Luelun Puxian yinyue zai 'Sanjiao' zhong de yicun" (Brief discussion of the survival of Puxian music in the Three Teachings), in *Putianxian shouju Lin Longjiang Minsuwenhua xueshu yantaohui lunwenji* (Collected essays for the First Putian County Academic Conference on the Folklore and Culture of Lin Longjiang), ed. Putianxian Minsu Xuehui (Putian County Folklore Association) and Houjiao Shimenshan Zongkongci Dongshihui (Temple Committee of the Honorable Confucius Shrine of Shimen Mountain in Houjiao): 41–44.

Lin Guoping (1985). "Shishi Lin Zhao'en de 'Jiuxu' qigong lilun" (Initial discussion of theory of Qigong in Lin Zhao'en's nine stages), *Zongjiao xue yanjiu*, no. 1.

———— (1986a). "Sanyijiao zhuoshu kaoshi" (Interpretive study of the writings of the Three in One religion), *Fujian luntan*, no. 6.

———— (1986b). "Shilun Lin Zhao'en de Sanjiaoheyi sixiang he sanyijiao" (Initial discussion of Lin Zhao'en's philosophy of unifying the Three and One religion), *Fujian Shifan Daxue xuebao*, no. 2.

_____ (1992). *Lin Zhao'en yu Sanyijiao* (Lin Zhao'en and the Three in One). Fuzhou: Fujian renmin chubanshe.

_____ (1993). "Sanyijiao xianzhuang gaikuang" (The general situation of the Three in One religion today), paper presented at the Conference on Secret Religions and Secret Societies, Nanjing, 1990. Published in Japanese as "Sanichikyo no sensetsu ni tsuite no kocha," in *Chugoku no hibishakai no kenlkyn*. Tokyo: Tokyo Daigaku, 1994: 15–30.

Lin Meirong (1990). "Zhanghua Mazu de xinyangquan" (The Zhanghua Mazu belief circle), *Bulletin of the Institute of Ethnology*, Academia Sinica, no. 68: 41–104.

Lin Wenhao (1992). *Haineiwai xueren lun Mazu* (Foreign and domestic scholars discuss Mazu). Putian: Zhongguo shehui kexue chubanshe.

Lin Chih-wan (Lin Zhiwan). (1974). *Chungguo minchien hsinyang lunwenchi* (Essays on Chinese popular beliefs). Monograph no. 22. Taipei: Institute for Ethnology, Academia Sinica.

_____ (1984). *Taiwan minchien hsinyang lunwenchi* (Essays on Taiwanese popular beliefs). Taipei: Lienching.

Liu Ts'ung-yuan (1966). "Lu Hsi-hsing: A Confucian Scholar, Taoist Priest and Buddhist Devotee of the Sixteenth Century," Asiatische Studien, SVIII/XIX, 1966; reprinted in *Selected Papers from the Hall of Harmonious Winds*, Leiden, Brill 1976: 175–202.

_____ (1968). "Lin Chao-en (1517–1598), the Master of the Three Teachings," *T'oung-pao* 53:4–5; reprinted in *Selected Papers from the Hall of Harmonious Winds*. Leiden: Brill, 1976: 149–174.

_____ (1970a). "The Penetration of Taoism into the Ming Neo-Confucianist Elite," *T'oung Pao* 57: 1–4; reprinted in *Selected Papers from the Hall of Harmonious Winds*. Leiden: Brill, 1976: 76–148.

_____ (1970b). "Taoist Self-Cultivation in Ming Thought," in Wm. T. deBary, ed., *Self and Society in Ming Thought*. New York: Columbia University Press: 291–330.

_____ (1984a). "Ming Thought: The Static and the Dynamic," in *New Excursions from the Hall of Harmonious Winds*. Leiden: E. J. Brill, 96–116.

_____ (1984b). "The Syncretism of the Three Teachings in Sung-Yuan China," in *New Excursions from the Hall of Harmonious Winds*. Leiden: E. J. Brill: 3–95.

Liu Ts'ung-yuan and Judith Berling (1982). "The 'Three Teachings' in the Mongol-Yuan Period," in Wm. T. deBary and Hok-lam Chan, eds., *Yuan Thought: Chinese Thought and Religion under the Mongols*. New York: Columbia University Press: 479–512.

van der Loon, Piet (1977). "Les origines rituelles du theatre chinois," *Journal Asiatique* 265: 141–168.

Ma Xixia and Han Bingfang (1984). "Lin Zhao'en de sanyi sixiang yu sanyijiao" (Lin Zhao-en's Three in One philosophy and the Three in One Religion), *Shijie zongjiao yanjiu*, no. 3.

_____ (1992). "Lin Zhao'en yu Sanyijiao" (Lin Zhao'en and the Three in One religion), in *Zhongguo minjian zongjiaoshi* (A history of Chinese popular religion). Shanghai: Shanghai renmin chubanshe: 719–858.

Mano Senryu (1952). "Mindai ni okeru sankyo shiso; toku ni Rin Choon o chushin toshite" (Three Teachings thought in the Ming dynasty, with special reference to Lin Zhao'en), *Toyoshi kenkyu* 12: 18–34.

_____ (1962). "Rin Choin to sono chosaku ni tsuite" (On Lin Zhao'en and his writings), in *Shimisu hakushi tsuitō kinen Mindaishi ronsō*. Tokyo: Daian.

_____ (1979). *Mindai bunkashi kenkyu* (Studies in Ming cultural history). Kyoto: Dohosha.

_____ (1980). "Rin Choin tsugiko" (Supplemental study of Lin Zhao'en), *Toho shukyo* 52.

Maspero, Henri (1981). *Taoism and Chinese Religion,* trans. Frank A. Kierman, Jr. Amherst: University of Massachusetts Press.

Massumi, Brian (1992). *User's Guide to Capitalism and Schizophrenia: Deviations from Deleuze and Guattari.* Boston: Swerve Editions, MIT Press.

Mauss, Marcel (1979). "A Category of the Human Mind: The Notion of Person, the Notion of Self" and "Body Techniques," in *Sociology and Psychology: Essays,* trans. Ben Brewster. London: Routledge and Kegan Paul. 57–124.

Mote, Frederick W., and Dennis Twitchett (1988). *The Cambridge History of China.* Vol. 7: *The Ming Dynasty, 1368–1644.* Cambridge: Cambridge University Press.

Naquin, Susan (1976). *Millenarian Rebellion in China: The Eight Trigrams of 1813.* New Haven: Yale University Press.

_____ (1981). *Shantung Rebellion: The Wang Lun Uprising of 1774.* New Haven: Yale University Press.

_____ (1985). "The Transmission of White Lotus Sectarianism in Late Imperial China," in David Johnson, Andrew J. Nathan, and Evelyn S. Rawski, eds., *Popular Culture in Late Imperial China.* Berkeley: University of California Press: 255–291.

Naquin, Susan, and Evelyn Rawski (1987). *Chinese Society in the Eighteenth Century.* New Haven: Yale University Press.

Naquin, Susan, and Yü Chün-fang (1992). *Pilgrims and Sacred Sites in China.* Berkeley: University of California Press.

Needham, Joseph, and Lu Gwei-Djen (1974). *Science and Civilization in China.* Vol. 5: *Chemistry and Chemical Technology: Spagyrical Discovery and Invention, Part II: Magisteries of Gold and Immortality.* Cambridge: Cambridge University Press.

_____ (1983). *Science and Civilization in China.* Cambridge: Cambridge University Press, vol. 5.5.

Ofuchi Ninji (1983). *Chugokujin no shukyo girei* (Chinese religious ritual). Okayama: Fukutaka shuten.

Overmyer, Daniel (1976). *Folk Buddhist Religion: Dissenting Sects in Late Traditional China.* Cambridge: Harvard University Press.

_____ (1985). "Values in Chinese Sectarian Literature: Ming and Ch'ing Pao-chuan," in David Johnson, Andrew J. Nathan, and Evelyn S. Rawski, eds., *Popular Culture in Late Imperial China.* Berkeley: University of California Press: 219–254.

_____ (1987). "Chinese Religion: An Overview," in M. Eliade et al., *The Encyclopedia of Religion,* 13 vol. New York: Macmillan: 3: 257–289.

Pang, Duane (1977). "The Pudu Ritual: A Celebration of the Chinese Community of Honolulu," in M. Saso and D. W. Chappell, eds., *Buddhist and Taoist Studies I.* Honolulu: University of Hawaii Press: 95–112.

Parsons, James B. (1969). "The Ming Dynasty Bureaucracy," in Charles Hucker, ed., *Chinese Government in Ming Times: Seven Studies.* New York: Columbia University Press: 175–232.

Potter, Jack M. (1974). "Cantonese Shamanism," in Arthur Wolf, ed., *Religion and Ritual in Chinese Society.* Stanford: Stanford University Press: 207–234.

Rawski, Evelyn S. (1972). *Agricultural Change and the Peasant Economy of South China.* Cambridge: Harvard University Press.

_____ (1979). *Education and Popular Literacy in Ch'ing China*. Ann Arbor: University of Michigan Press.

Reynolds, Frank E., and Donald Capps. (1976). *The Biographical Process: Studies in the History and Psychology of Religion*. The Hague: Mouton.

Robinet, Isabelle (1989). "Original Contributions of Neidan to Taoism and Chinese Thought," in L. Kohn, ed., *Taoist Meditation and Longevity Techniques*. Ann Arbor: Center for Chinese Studies Publication, University of Michigan: 297–330.

_____ (1989–1990). "Recherche sur la alchimie intérieure (neidan): L'école Zhenyuan," *Cahiers d'Extrême-Asie* 5: 141–162.

_____ (1993). *Taoist Meditation*, trans. J. Pas and N. Giradot. Albany: State University of New York Press.

Rowe, William T. (1984). *Hankow: Commerce and Society in a Chinese City, 1796–1889*. Stanford: Stanford University Press.

_____ (1985). "Approaches to Modern Chinese History," in O. Zinz, ed., *Reliving the Past: The Worlds of Social History*. Chapel Hill: University of North Carolina: 236–296.

_____ (1989). *Hankow: Conflict and Community in a Chinese City, 1796–1889*. Stanford: Stanford University Press.

Sahlins, Marshall (1985). *Islands of History*. Chicago: University of Chicago Press.

Sakai Tadao (1960). *Chugoku zensho no kenkyu* (Researches on Chinese morality books). Tokyo: Kokusho kankokai.

Sangren, P. Steven (1984). "Traditional Chinese Corporations: Beyond Kinship," *Journal of Asian Studies* 43, 3: 391–415.

_____ (1986). *History and Magical Power in a Chinese Town*. Stanford: Stanford University Press.

_____ (1988). "History and the Rhetoric of Legitimacy: The Ma Tsu Cult of Taiwan," *Comparative Studies in Society and History* 30, 4: 674–697.

_____ (1993). "Power and Transcendance in the Ma Tsu Pilgrimages of Taiwan. *American Ethnologist* 20, 3: 564–582.

Saso, Michael (1975). *Chuang Lin hsu Tao-tsang* (The appended Taoist canon of Chuang-Lin), Taipei: Cheng-wen.

_____ (1978a). *The Teachings of Taoist Master Chuang*. New Haven: Yale University Press.

_____ (1978b). *Dokyo hiketsu shusei* (Collection of Daoist secret instructions). Tokyo: Ryukei shosha.

Sawada Mizuho (1960). "Sankyo shiso to heiwa shosetsu" (Colloquial novels and Three Teachings thought), *Biburia* 16: 37–39.

_____ (1975a). *Bukkyo to Chugoku bungaku* (Buddhism and Chinese literature). Tokyo: Kokusho kankokai.

_____ (1975b). *Zoho Hokan no kenkyu* (Expanded researches on Baojuan). Tokyo: Kokusho kankokai.

Schafer, Edward (1954). *The Empire of Min*. Rutland, Vermont: Charles E. Tuttle.

Schipper, Kristofer M. (1973). *Concordance du Tao-tsang, titres des ouvrages*. Publications de l'Ecole Francaise d'Extreme-Orient, vol. 102. Paris.

_____ (1975). *Le Fen-teng: Rituel taoiste*. Publications de l'Ecole Francaise d'Extreme-Orient, vol. 104. Paris.

_____ (1977). "Neighborhood Cult Associations in Traditional Tainan," in G. W. Skinner, ed., *The City in Late Imperial China*. Stanford: Stanford University Press: 651–676.

_____ (1985a). "Vernacular and Classical Ritual in Taiwan," in *Journal of Asian Studies* 45: 21–57.

_____ (1985b). "Seigneurs Royaux, Dieux des Epidemies," *Archives de Sciences Sociales des Religions,* no. 59, 1: 31–40.

_____ (1989). "Taoist Ritual and Local Cults of the T'ang Dynasty," in M. Strickmann, ed., *Tantric and Taoist Studies in Honor of R. A. Stein.* Brussels: Institut Belge des Hautes Etudes Chinois, Melanges chinois et bouddhiques, vol. 22; 3: 812–834.

_____ (1990). "The Cult of Baosheng Dadi and Its Spread to Taiwan—A Case of Fenxiang," in E. Vermeer, ed., *Development and Decline of Fukien Province in the 17th and 18th Centuries.* Leiden: E. J. Brill: 397–416.

_____ (1993). *The Taoist Body,* Berkeley: University of California Press.

Schipper, Kristofer M., and Wang Hsiu-hui (1986). "Progressive and Regressive Time Cycles in Daoist Ritual," in J. T. Fraser, N. Lawrence, and F. C. Haber, eds., *Time, Science, and Society in China and the West (The Study of Time V).* Amherst: University of Massachusetts: 185–205.

Seaman, Gary (1978). *Temple Organization in a Chinese Town.* Taipei: The Orient Cultural Service.

_____ (1981). "The Sexual Politics of Karmic Retribution," in *The Anthropology of Taiwanese Society,* ed. E. M. Ahern and Hill Gates. Stanford: Stanford University Press: 381–396.

Seidel, Anna (1970). "A Taoist Immortal of the Ming Dynasty: Chang Sanfeng," in Wm. T. deBary, ed., *Self and Society in Ming Thought.* New York: Columbia University Press: 483–531.

_____ (1989–1990). "Chronicle of Taoist Studies," *Cahier d'Extreme-Asie* 5: 223–347.

Simendon, Gilbert (1989). *L'individuation psychique et collective.* Paris: Aubier.

_____ (1992). "The Genesis of the Individual," *Zone 6: Incorporations* (1992): 297–319.

Siu, Helen (1990). "Recycling Ritual," in P. Link, R. Madsen, and P. Pickowicz, ed., *Unofficial China: Popular Culture and Thought in the People's Republic.* Boulder: Westview: 121–137.

Sivin, Nathan (1966). "Chinese Concepts of Time." *Earlham Review,* no. 1.

_____ (1980). "The Theoretical Background of Elixir Alchemy," in J. Needham et al., *Science and Civilization in China.* Cambridge: Cambridge University Press: 5.4: 210–323.

_____ (1996). "State, Cosmos, and Body in China," *Harvard Journal of Asiatic Studies* 55, 2: 5–36.

Skinner, G. William (1985). "The Structure of Chinese History," *Journal of Asian Studies* 44: 271–292.

Staal, Fritz, ed. (1983). *Agni: The Vedic Ritual of the Fire Altar.* Berkeley: Asian Humanities Press.

_____ (1985). "Subsitutions de paradigms et religions de Asie," *Cahiers d'Extrême-Asie* 1: 21–57.

_____ (1986). "The Sound of Religion," *Numen,* vol. 33, fasc. 1: 33–64 and 2: 185–224.

Stein, Rolf (1963). "Remarques sur les mouvements du taoisme politico-religieux au IIe siecle apres J.-C.," *T'oung Pao* 50: 1–78.

_____ (1979). "Religious Taoism and Popular Religion from the Second to the Seventh Centuries." In H. Welch and A. Seidel, eds., *Facets of Taoism*. New Haven: Yale University Press: 53–81.

Stewart, Charles, and Rosalind Shaw (1994). *Syncretism/Anti-Syncretism: The Politics of Religious Synthesis*. London: Routledge.

Strathern, Marilyn (1992). "Qualified Value: the Perspective of Gift Exchange," in *Barter, Exchange and Value: An Anthropological Approach,* ed. C. Humphrey and S. Hugh-Jones. Cambridge: Cambridge University Press: 169–191.

Strickmann, Michel (1980). "History, Anthropology and Chinese Religion." *Harvard Journal of Asiatic Studies* 40: 201–248. Review of Saso, 1978.

Tambiah, Stanley (1979). "A Performative Approach to Ritual," *Proceedings of the British Academy* 65: 113–169.

Tanaka Issei (1981). *Chugoku saishi engaki kenkyu* (Research on Chinese ritual drama). Tokyo: Toyo bunka kenkyujo.

_____ (1983). *Chugoku zonzo to engaki kenkyu* (Research on Chinese lineages and theater). Tokyo: Toyo bunka kenkyujo.

_____ (1993). (Research on Chinese shamanistic dance). Tokyo: Toyo bunka kenkyujo.

Taussig, Michael (1980). *The Devil and Commodity Fetishism in South America*. Chapel Hill: University of North Carolina Press.

Taylor, Rodney (1990). *The Religious Dimensions of Confucianism*. Albany: State University of New York Press.

Teiser, Stephen F. (1988). *The Ghost Festival in Medieval China*. Princeton: Princeton University Press.

_____ (1995). "Popular Religion," in D. L. Overmyer et al., eds., "Chinese Religion: The State of the Field," *Journal of Asian Studies* 54, 1 and 2 (February and May): 314–395.

ter Haar, B. J. (1990). "The Genesis and Spread of Temple Cults in Fukien," in *Development and Decline of Fukien Provice in the 17th and 18th Centuries,* ed. E. B. Vermeer. Leiden: E. J. Brill: 83–100.

_____ (1992). *The White Lotus Teachings in Chinese Religious History*. Leiden: E. J. Brill.

Tian Rukang (1990). "The Decadence of Buddhist Temples in Fukien in Late Ming and Early Ch'ing," in *Development and Decline of Fukien Province in the 17th and 18th Centuries*. Leiden: E. J. Brill: 83–100.

Topley, Marjorie (1963). "The Great Way of Former Heaven: A Group of Chinese Secret Religious Sects," *Bulletin of the School of Oriental and African Studies* 26: 362–392.

Troetsch, Ernst (1981). *The Social Teaching of the Christian Churches*. 2 vols. Chicago: University of Chicago Press.

Tu Weiming, "Cultural China: The Periphery as Center," *Daedelus* 120, 2.

Turner, Victor (1969). *The Ritual Process: Structure and Anti-Structure*. Ithaca: Cornell University Press, 1969.

Turner, Victor, and Edith Turner (1978). *Image and Pilgrimage in Christian Culture: Anthropological Perspectives*. New York: Columbia University Press.

_____ (1986). "Anti-Temporality," in V. T. Turner and E. Bruner, eds., *The Anthropology of Experience*. Urbana: University of Illinois Press: 227–246.

Van Dam, Richard (1993). *Saints and Their Miracles in Ancient Gaul*. Princeton: Princeton University Press.

Vermeer, Eduard B. (1990). "Introduction" and "The Decline of Hsing-hua Prefecture in the Early Ch'ing," in *Development and Decline of Fukien Province in the 17th and 18th Centuries*. Leiden: E. J. Brill: 5–34, 101–162.

Wach, Joachim (1962). Master and disciples," *Journal of Religion* 42: 1–21.

Wakeman, Frederic E. (1985). *The Great Enterprise: The Manchu Reconstruction of Imperial Order in Seventeenth-Century China.* Berkeley: University of California Press.

Wallis, Roy, ed. (1975). *Sectarianism: Analyses of Religious and Non-religious Sects.* London: Peter Owen.

_____ (1977). *The Road to Total Freedom: A Sociological Analysis of Scientology.* New York: Columbia University Press. London: Heinemann, 1976.

Wang Jianchuan (1994). "Cong Fujian Putian Xiancun shiliao kan Taiwan Jintongjiao de lishi" (Viewing the history of the Taiwanese Jintong religion from the perspective of historical materials from Putian, Fujian), in *Taiwan shiliao yanjiu* 4.

Wang Mingming (1992). "Flowers of the State, Grasses of the People: Yearly Rites and Aesthetics of Power in Quanzhou in the Southeast Coastal Macro-region of China." Ph.D. thesis, Dept. of Sociology and Anthropology, SOAS, University of London.

_____ (1995). "Place, Administration, and Territorial Cults in Late Imperial China: A Case Study from South Fujian," *Late Imperial China* 16, 1 (June): 33–78.

Watson, James (1985). "Standardizing the Gods: The Promotion of Tian Hou ("Empress of Heaven") Along the South China Coast, 960–1960," in David Johnson, Andrew J. Nathan, and Evelyn S. Rawski, eds., *Popular Culture in Late Imperial China.* Berkeley: University of California Press: 292–324.

Weber, Max (1951). *The Religion of China,* trans. H. Gerth. New York: Free Press.

_____ (1958). *The Protestant Ethic and the Spirit of Capitalism,* trans. Talcott Parsons. New York: Charles Scribner's Sons.

Welch, Holmes (1967). *The Practice of Chinese Buddhism, 1900–1950.* Cambridge: Harvard University Press.

_____ (1968). *The Buddhist Revival in China.* Cambridge: Harvard University Press.

_____ (1972). *Buddhism under Mao.* Cambridge: Harvard University Press.

Weller, Robert (1987). *Unities and Diversities in Chinese Religion.* Seattle: University of Washington Press.

_____ (1994). *Resistance, Chaos, and Control in China.* Seattle: University of Washington Press.

Wilkerson, James (1994a). "The 'Ritual Master' and His 'Temple Corporation' Rituals," *Proceedings of the International Conference on Popular Beliefs and Chinese Culture.* Taipei: Center for Chinese Studies: 2: 471–521.

_____ (1994b). "Self-Referential Performances: Victor Turner and Theoretical Issues in Chinese Performative Genre," *Minsu quyi (Min-su ch'ü-yi)* 90 (July): 99–146.

_____ (1995). "Rural Village Temples in the P'enghu Islands and Their Late Imperial Corporate Organization," in *Proceedings of the Conference on Temples and Popular Culture.* Taipei: Center for Chinese Studies, 1: 67–95.

Wilson, Brian (1973). *Magic and the Millennium: A Sociological Study of Religious Movements of Protest among Tribal and Third-World Peoples,* London: Heinemann.

_____ (1990). *The Social Dimension of Sectarianism: Sects and New Religious Movements in Contemporary Society.* Oxford: Clarendon Press.

Wilson, Stephen, ed. (1984). *Saints and Their Cults: Studies in Religious Sociology, Folklore, and History.* Cambridge: Cambridge University Press.

Wittfogel, Karl (1957). *Oriental Despotism: A Comparative Study of Total Power.* New Haven: Yale University Press.

Wolf, Arthur P. (1974). "Gods, Ghosts and Ancestors," in A. Wolf, ed., *Religion and Ritual in Chinese Society.* Stanford: Stanford University Press: 131–182.

Wolf, Margery (1992). *A Thrice Told Tale: Feminism, Postmodernism, and Ethnographic Responsibility.* Stanford: Stanford University Press.

Xiamen Wuzhenren yanjiuhui and the Qingjiao Ciji donggong dongshihui, ed. (1992). *Wu Zhenren yanjiu* (Research on the Perfected Wu). Xiamen: Lujiang chubanshe.

Xiao Yiping, Lin Yunsen, and Yang Dejin, eds. (1987). *Mazu yanjiu ziliao huibian* (Comprehensive collection of research materials on Mazu). Fuzhou: Fujian People's Publishing House.

Yang, Ch'ing-k'un (1961). *Religion in Chinese Society.* Berkeley: University of California Press.

Yang, Mayfair Mei-hui (1994). *Gifts, Favors, and Banquets: The Art of Social Relationships in China.* Ithaca: Cornell University Press.

Yinger, J. Milton (1957). *Religion, Society, and the Individual: An Introduction to the Sociology of Religion.* New York: Macmillan.

Young, Robert J. C. (1995). *Colonial Desire: Hybridity in Theory, Culture, and Race.* London: Routledge.

Yu Chun-fang (1980). *The Renewal of Buddhism in China: Chu-hung and the Late Ming Synthesis.* New York: Columbia University Press.

Yuan Jiahua, *Hanyu fangyan gaiyao,* Beijing, 1960.

Zhangzhou Wuzhenren Yanjiuhui, ed. (1989). *Wuzhenren xueshu yanjiu wenji* (Collected academic essays on the Perfected Wu). Xiamen: Xiamen University Press.

Zheng Zhiming (1988a). *Mingdai Sanyijiaozhu yanjiu* (Research on the Ming dynasty founder of the Three in One religion). Taipei: Xuesheng shuju.

——— (1988b). *Zhongguo shanshu yu zongjiao* (Chinese morality books and religion) Taibei: Xuesheng shuju.

——— (1990a). "Xiajiaode zongjiao tixijiqi shanshu sixiang" (The religious system of the Xia religion and its morality book philosophy), in the author's *Minjiande sanjiao xinfa* (The heart method of the Three Teachings in popular [religion]). Banqiao: Zheng yishanshu chubanshe.

——— (1990b). "Lin Zhao'en yu wan Ming Wangxue" (Lin Zhao'en and late Ming Wang [Yangming] studies), in the author's *Minjiande sanjiao xinfa* (The heart method of the Three Teachings in popular [religion]). Banqiao: Zheng yishanshu chubanshe.

Zheng Zhenman (1987). "The System of Irrigation of Agricultural Lands in the Fujianese Coastal Areas in the Ming and Qing and (Its Relationship to) Local and Lineage Organization," *Studies in Chinese Socioeconomic History* 3.

——— (1992). *Ming Qing Fujian jiazu zuzhi yu shehui bianqian* (Family-lineage organization and social change in Fujian during the Ming and Qing). Hunan: Hunan Educational Press, Ph.D Dissertation Series.

Zhu Weiguan (1986). *Fujian shigao* (Draft history of Fujian). Fuzhou: Fujian jiaoyu chubanshe.

Zito, Angela (1984). "Re-presenting Sacrifice: Cosmology and the Editing of Texts," *Ch'ing-shih wen-t'i* 5, 2: 47–78.

——— (1987). "City Gods, Filiality, and Hegemony in Late Imperial China," *Modern China* 13, 3 (July): 333–371.

——— (1993). "Ritualizing *Li:* Implications for Studying Power and Gender," *Positions* 1, 2: 321–348.

_____ (1994). "Skin and Silk: Significant Boundaries," in A. Zito and Tani Barlow, eds., *Body, Subject & Power in China*. Chicago: University of Chicago Press: 103–130.

Zizec, Slavoj (1990). "Eastern Europe's Republics of Gilead," *New Left Review* 183: 50–62.

Zurcher, Erik (1983). "Prince Moonlight: Messianism and Eschatology in Early Medieval Chinese Buddhism," *T'oung-pao* 68, 1–3: 1–75.

398

398

Manichaeism, 97n.2
Mano Senryu, 5n.3, 6, 297–98
mantras, 209, 210
Mao Zedong, 193, 286, 289, 293
marionettes, 57, 158
marriage, 226
Massumi, Brian, 27n.30, 288–89, 289n.4
Maudgalyayana, 218. *See also* Mulian
Mazu (Tianhou), 51, 63, 114, 118n.18, 156,
    157n.16, 177, 181, 236–40, 255, 261,
    262, 262n.3, 264–65, 268, 270, 278n.2,
    335
medical recipes, 122
mediums, 13n.11, 62, 78. *See* shamanism;
    spirit-mediums
Mencius, 72, 76, 81, 129, 312
microcosm, 210, 289, 294n.7, 315. *See also*
    body: microcosmic
mijue (secret instructions), 210
millenarianism, 8, 12, 23, 23n.25, 273, 274
Mingxia (Mingxiapai, Mingxia branch), 137,
    154, 160, 163n.18, 166, 168, 186, 187nn.
    4 and 5, 190–94, 198, 201, 203, 209n.12,
    215, 227–30, 238, 245, 335
Mingxiaji, 119, 119n.22, 123
modernity, 4, 293; and modernization, 20;
    modernization theory, 291; and nation-
    state, 20, 294
modes of temporality, 194
mudra, 3, 30, 417
Mulian, 62, 181, 218, 271, 336, 344; Mu-
    lian plays, 159n.17

Naishengtang, 194
Naquin, Susan, 273
narrative devices, 67
Neeham, Joseph, 138, 301
Niebhur, Rudolph, 12
Nine Stages, 120, 141, 142, 146. *See also*
    Heart Method
Niwan (palace in cranium), 119n.22, 141,
    212, 299–300, 306, 322
Nuo exorcism, 160n.16, 217n.16

official cult, 50; and official recognition, 257
Orthodox Breath talisman, 88, 92–93
Ouyang Deyuan, 164n.4
Overmyer, Daniel, 12
Overseas Chinese, 184, 223, 224, 254, 266,
    269, 270, 271, 285–86

Pan Huang, 106
Pan Jingruo, 128
Pangu, 319

patriarchy, 13n.11, 25, 225, 241, 294
People's Consultative Congress, 266
Philippines, 285
Platform Sutra, 110n.13
polar attractors, 27, 40, 58, 241, 244, 273,
    274
Political Consultative Congress (zhengxie),
    4, 262, 265
popular religion, 4, 11, 16, 26n.29, 56, 105,
    119, 169, 181, 228, 268–69, 271–72,
    277–79, 281–82, 288–89; as "common re-
    ligion," 11; C. K. Yang's theory of diffused
    structure of, 10. *See also* religion
popular temples, 16, 45, 50, 53; incense-divi-
    sion networks (fenxiang), 53, 208; incense-
    presentation processions (jinxiang), 18, 67,
    205, 275; multiple village alliances of, 55;
    networks of, 274, 276; and social organiza-
    tion, 54; temple committees, 209
positive unconscious, 34–36, 36n.1
potentiality, 224, 241, 268, 272–73, 282–83,
    286. *See also* actualization; virtuality
Pratyeka-buddha, 87, 93
Prefect Lei Yinglong, 48
Prefect Yue Zheng, 48
Primal Breath, Primal Spirit, 65n.2, 138,
    147–48, 149n.10, 300, 308, 317, 320
Pudu. *See* Lanpen rites
Puxian opera (drama, theater), 3n.1,
    159n.17, 215, 217n.15

qi (breath), 19, 36, 73, 84, 119n.22, 139,
    142, 148, 162, 299–308, 311–12,
    314–15, 319–25. *See also* zhengqifu
Qi Jiguang, 77
Qiongyao, 182; Qiongyao Dafayuan,
    183n.17; Qiongyao xiandao, 181
Qixingci (Seven Star Shrine), 205, 239; man-
    uscripts of, 194

religion, 8, 9, 10n.8, 12, 264; and feudal su-
    perstition, 10n.8, 56; Marxist-Leninist def-
    inition of, 10; religious organization and,
    28. *See also* popular religion
ren (humanity), 25, 80n.12, 107, 197, 309,
    311–12, 318; as seed of life/spark of
    goodness/elixir), 107, 318; as Tatāgatha
    nature, 309
ritual, 4n.2, 9, 10n.7, 30; calendars for, 28,
    62; and cultural difference, 60–63; eco-
    nomics of, 221–25; and performance of
    gender, 225–26; ritual complexes, 27
ritual-events, 9, 28, 30, 34, 38–41, 46, 58,
    60, 185n.1, 194, 217, 224–25, 276, 282,

About the Author

KENNETH DEAN is Associate Professor of East Asian Studies
at McGill University. His books include
Taoist Ritual and Popular Cults in Southeast China (Princeton)
and, with Brian Massumi, *First and Last Emperor:
The Absolute State and the Body of the Despot.*